T

Postcolonialisms

An Anthology of Cultural Theory and Criticism

EDITED BY

GAURAV DESAI AND SUPRIYA NAIR

BERG

Oxford

First published outside North and South America and the Philippines by Berg
Editorial Office:
1st Floor, Angel Court
81 St Clements Street
Oxford OX4 1AW
UK

Berg is the imprint of Oxford International Publishers Ltd.

A catalogue record for this book is available from the British Library.

ISBN - 13 978 184520 331 3 (Cloth)
ISBN - 10 1 84520 331 3   (Cloth)
ISBN - 13 978 184520 332 0 (Paper)
ISBN - 10 1 84520 332 1   (Paper)

Printed in the United States of America

www.bergpublishers.com

For Sameer

Contents

Acknowledgments

Several years ago, when we were both teaching courses in literary theory, gender, and feminism, we independently came upon *Feminisms: An Anthology of Literary Theory and Criticism,* edited by Robyn R. Warhol and Diane Price Herndl and published by Rutgers University Press. That anthology, with its expansive coverage of feminist theory and criticism, its reprinting (for the most part) of full-length texts, and its judicious balance between the canonical and the innovative, inspired us with a desire to see a similar undertaking in the field of postcolonial studies. In our original correspondence with Leslie Mitchner, our editor at Rutgers, we invoked this anthology and proposed a companion volume in postcolonial theory. Changes in the economics of publishing since the early nineties have meant that we have not been able to produce an equally capacious volume with over fifty essays. But we hope this project stimulates the kind of heated debates that its model has provoked through the years in our classes.

We would like to thank all the authors who intervened on our behalf with publishers in an attempt to reduce the permissions fees associated with reprinting their scholarship. Oftentimes this has meant that the authors have forgone their own share of the proceeds. In the case of authors who have held their own rights, we have been particularly grateful to receive their permission gratis or for a very small token fee. We have made every attempt to locate all the living authors included in this anthology. We hope that the few authors whom we have not been able to contact personally will be pleased to find their work in this volume.

This anthology has been a collaboration not only between the two of us as editors but also with our students and colleagues. Our students challenged us to make the connections outside the classroom and kept the issues from losing their edge. The number of colleagues across the country and even internationally who have advised us on the inclusions and exclusions herein are far too many to cite here. We do want to acknowledge, however, the work of our research assistants, Elizabeth Brubaker and Michael Griffith, who spent hours at the photocopying machine and the computer scanner, and Paige Bailey, who prepared the index. We cannot thank them enough for sparing us the steep learning curve that this entire process would otherwise have entailed. It has been a personal and professional pleasure to work with Leslie Mitchner and the rest of the editorial and production team at Rutgers University Press.

We thank all our friends in the English Department, the Program in African and African Diaspora Studies, and the Women's Studies Program at Tulane. We are very grateful to Molly Travis, chair of the English Department, Cynthia Lowenthal, the dean of Newcomb College, and Teresa Soufas, dean of Liberal Arts and Sciences, for their support. Our thanks to Michael Kuczynski and Dennis Kehoe for help with some translations from the Latin.

We dedicate this book to Sameer, who was particularly understanding on those long weekends when one or the other of us spent time away working on this anthology.

Postcolonialisms

Introduction

Over the past few decades there has been an exponential growth in the study and teaching of postcolonial literatures and cultures in the U.S. academy. Originally taught under a variety of rubrics such as "Commonwealth literatures," "nonwestern literatures," "emergent literatures," and "world literatures," the field of postcolonial studies has emerged as a more comprehensive undertaking than any one of its earlier guises. The central questions of coloniality, power, and knowledge have, in this domain, been increasingly cast in a comparative framework, raising, in turn, more questions about the historical parameters of colonialisms, the relevance of regionalisms in an increasingly interconnected world, and the possibility of a postcolonial politics that speaks at once to local goals as well as to universal human rights.

The large conceptual grasp of the field of postcolonial studies has meant that even scholars who define themselves as specialists in a region—say, Anglophone West Africa—have nevertheless often thought of their projects in comparative terms. Likewise, despite the primarily literary origins of much postcolonial criticism, scholars in fields as varied as international relations and anthropology regularly draw upon this scholarship in their research as well as in their teaching. As the field has come to maturity, the most pressing issues that postcolonial theorists have engaged in have in fact been as much the result of the critical demands of corollary disciplines as of literary studies. Thus, for example, discussions of subaltern history and consciousness have been driven as much by the critical projects of historians as by those of scholars of literary and cultural studies.

Postcolonialisms: An Anthology of Cultural Theory and Criticism presents a broad view of this interdisciplinary terrain. With the book's inclusion of texts by historians, sociologists, and anthropologists, along with documents penned by colonial administrators and the U.S. Congress, we note that the designation "Cultural Theory and Criticism" in our subtitle is to be read in a decisively open manner. Likewise, we refer to "Postcolonialisms" in the plural not only because of the differences between the actual histories of colonialism in various world contexts but also because our aim is to foreground the variety of work that is carried on under this name. One of the ongoing debates in postcolonial studies, for instance, is the question of whether one can talk of the contemporary condition as universally "postcolonial"—some have suggested that it may be more appropriate to focus instead on "actually existing colonialisms"; others have noted the neocolonial aspects of global relations not only in the cold war era but also in the post–cold war expansion of neoliberal capitalism; yet others, in the more recent context of the second U.S.-led war in Iraq, have chosen to revive the discourse of "empire" and its association with American notions of exceptionalism and manifest destiny.

If the sheer multitude of historical experiences means that it makes sense to talk about "postcolonialisms" or even perhaps of "(post)colonialisms"—to invoke that once-popular bracketing gesture—then it is also the case that the plural form is appropriate to an enterprise that by now has moved in several different directions, and one that has always had multiple legacies. And yet, while insisting on multiple, even competing "postcolonialisms," as well as on postcolonial theories that have significant, irreconcilable differences with one another, we can still usefully map out the field in terms of recognizable patterns, shared family resemblances, and common genealogies.

Edward Said's *Orientalism*, published in 1978, gave a newfound legitimacy to a form of critique that gradually began to be labeled "postcolonial," but the impetus of this critique shared much in common with predecessors as varied as Mohandas Gandhi, Lala Lajpat Rai, Sardar Patel, Frantz Fanon, C.L.R. James, Amilcar Cabral, and Chinua Achebe.[1] In this regard, "postcolonial studies," referring as it often does to the rapid growth in the eighties of scholarly interest in colonial relations and nationalisms, is best understood as a belated project. It is based on a long history of debate about issues such as the struggle for independence, the appropriability of the colonial languages, the role of regional cultures in nationalist traditions, the marginalization of gender and women's issues in many newly independent nations, and the role of indigenous traditions in shaping a postcolonial modernity. These discussions that took place among creative writers and critics, theater workers and teachers, revolutionary thinkers and nationalist leaders at various moments and sites of the colonial and newly independent world continue to be echoed in contemporary postcolonial scholarship. A history of the continuities of such debates is yet to be written, but the "rediscovery" of earlier activists (such as Frantz Fanon) battling colonialism has become an important dimension of postcolonial scholarship around the globe (Gordon, Sharpley-Whiting, and White 1996; for a critique see Gates 1991).

At the same time, however, postcolonial scholarship in its contemporary guise is no longer just connected to the struggles that defined the early period. It is also enabled by the institutional rise of literary theory in the Western world. The (post)structuralist shift from questions of literariness to questions of textuality associated with thinkers such as Roland Barthes, Jacques Derrida, and Michel Foucault; the increasing attention to issues of ideology, subalternity, and hegemony as in the work of Louis Althusser and Antonio Gramsci; the efforts of feminists such as Susan Gubar and Sandra Gilbert to articulate the parameters of the emergence of a women's literary tradition—these are just some of the more visible markers of the kind of cultural criticism that has informed postcolonial theory. And likewise, as postcolonial scholarship benefited from these early efforts, it too has had a critical role to play in the rethinking of these and other related fields. Marxism, feminism, and the New Historicism, as well as the less clearly demarcated field of "cultural studies," all carry the traces of postcolonial studies today.

To survey the institutional rise of postcolonial theory in the Anglo-American academy, it may help to think of it as participating in two simultaneous projects. One aspect of postcolonial scholarship has been to reread the canonical texts of Euro-American literature and to place them in a critical relation to the larger project of imperialism and colonialism. Works that come to mind in this context are George Lamming's critical essay on Shakespeare's *The Tempest*, provocatively titled "A Monster, a Child, a Slave"; Chinua Achebe's early essay on Conrad entitled "An Image of Africa: Racism in Conrad's *Heart of Darkness*"; Gayatri Spivak's focus on the rise of white, middle-class women's individualism amid the background of empire in "Three Women's Texts and a Critique of Imperialism" (see chapter 24); Abdul Jan-Mohamed's *Manichean Aesthetics*, which, by juxtaposing English colonial literature with African literary texts, already carries over into the project of the second mode of postcolonial criticism we describe below; and Patrick Brantlinger's pathbreaking study *Rule of Darkness: British Literature and Imperialism, 1830–1914*, which moved Victorian studies in the direction of self-critique. These early works have been followed by a whole coterie of studies in the nineties and include works such as Sara Mill's *Discourses of Difference*, which analyzes the relationship between women's travel writing and colonialism; Sara Suleri's *The Rhetoric of English India*, which, like JanMohamed's work (though to radically different ends), also includes readings of postcolonial writers; Jenny Sharpe's *Allegories of Empire*, focusing, as its subtitle suggests, on the "Figure of Woman in the Colonial Text"; Firdous Azim's important intervention on Charlotte Brontë in *The Colonial Rise of the Novel*; Edward Said's survey *Culture and Imperialism* (1993); the work of critics such as David Lloyd, Enda Duffy, and Vincent Cheng, who have worked to include Ireland and canonical Irish writers such as Joyce within the intellectual context framed by postcolonial theory; and, finally, Simon Gikandi's *Maps of Englishness: Writing Identity in the*

Culture of Colonialism, which invites us to rethink colonial "Englishness" as always-already constituted by the experience and subjectivities of the colonized.

Closely related to this form of postcolonial critique and often overlapping with it is the legacy of what is labeled "colonial discourse studies," an interdisciplinary investigation not only of literary works but also of letters, memoranda, diaries, political speeches, legal rulings, and so on written by imperial agents and colonial observers. This study of what V. Y. Mudimbe has called the "colonial library" is interested, much like Said's *Orientalism,* in the intersections of colonial knowledge and power and its "inventions" of colonized spaces and other exotic lands. Although many of the books just cited also exhibit these tendencies, of particular note in this context are works such as Mudimbe's *The Invention of Africa* and *The Idea of Africa,* Timothy Mitchell's *Colonising Egypt,* David Spurr's *The Rhetoric of Empire,* Nicholas Thomas's *Colonialism's Culture,* and the edited collections *Colonialism and Culture, Orientalism and the Postcolonial Predicament,* and *After Colonialism.*

If the study of colonialism and its culture is a major preoccupation of the postcolonial project, a second aspect of this scholarship is no less important. This other project is more concerned with the literary and cultural production of the *colonized subjects* and their postcolonial inheritors. At one level, this is the study of what was once called, in the context of the Anglophone world, "Commonwealth Literature," but it also takes quite seriously, as Commonwealth literary studies often did not, the interface between English and the native languages, the negotiations between nationalist and minoritarian representations, the tensions with the metropolis, and masculinist biases and womanist concerns. Examples of this range of scholarship include, among others, Abiola Irele's *The African Experience in Literature and Ideology;* Barbara Harlow's *Resistance Literature;* Timothy Brennan's *Salman Rushdie and the Third World; Out of the Kumbla,* a volume of essays on Caribbean women and literature edited by Carole Boyce Davies and Elaine Savory Fido; Neil Lazarus's study of Ayi Kwei Armah, *Resistance in Postcolonial African Fiction;* Rob Nixon's critical study of V. S. Naipaul, *London Calling;* Chikwenye Ogunyemi's *Africa Wo/Man Palava* on Nigerian women novelists; and innumerable articles in journals such as *Ariel, Callaloo, Small Axe, Research in African Literatures, Wasafiri, Kunapipi,* and *World Literature Written in English,* to mention only a few.

Because the literary and cultural production of colonized subjects is often part of their broader experience of colonialism, literary scholars find that their interests overlap with the work of cultural historians, sociologists, and anthropologists. In this way, this second mode of postcolonial scholarship too finds recourse in materials not conventionally thought of as "literature" and includes in its analysis social analysis, performance, film, and even the circulation of food such as *chapatis* (see, for instance, Guha 1983, 239–246; Bhabha 1994). Much of what gets labeled postcolonial cultural theory today is the result of such cross-fertilization between disciplines, but it is arguably not entirely disconnected from the emphasis on literature and culture that is the primary interest of the scholars concerned. Despite the differences in their enunciative intent, texts as varied as Kwame Anthony Appiah's *In My Father's House*, Homi Bhabha's *The Location of Culture*, Dipesh Chakrabarty's *Provincializing Europe*, Rey Chow's *The Protestant Ethnic and the Spirit of Capitalism*, Paul Gilroy's *Against Race*, Edouard Glissant's *Caribbean Discourse*, and Antonio Benítez-Rojo's *The Repeating Island* all share in common a desire to make sense of the discrepant ways in which literatures and cultures—both high and low—inform postcolonial subjectivities.

Postcolonial studies, then, comes in several guises. Rereadings of the Euro-American canon, investigations of the production of colonial stereotypes and the "inventions" of the other, materialist analyses of social conditions, critical analyses of postcolonial literatures and cultures, theorizations of categories such as subalternity, ambivalence, mimicry, and hybridity—all these are part of the vast territory of the "postcolonial," primarily in the Anglo-American academy. Although this scholarship is included in this anthology, we also note that it represents only some of the faces of the "postcolonial," since other emphases and concerns often shape the study of postcoloniality in locations as varied as Kenya, South Africa, Australia, and the Caribbean. If any truly comprehensive anthology of postcolonial studies seems impossible, it is due to the plurality afforded by the various local articulations of the "postcolonial" in different global contexts.

Nevertheless, despite such limitations—which not coincidentally also reflect limitations of language (the majority of our texts being oriented toward the Anglophone world)—we have sought to bring together some of the seminal articles in the field in some form of conversation with one another. What we attempt here is a functional breadth that is attuned primarily to the pedagogical needs of the advanced undergraduate and graduate classroom. Our location in the U.S. academy has for better or for worse shaped our decisions, and this, we imagine, will be particularly felt by readers elsewhere. But rather than claim any strict representativeness, which would be impossibly ambitious in a single volume given the shape of the field today, we see this anthology as one articulation of central debates that have influenced contemporary postcolonial theory.

Our decision to include a particular text has rested on our estimation of the balance between the canonical status of the text and its pedagogical value. For, as any teacher knows, not all canonical texts are easy to teach in the classroom, and likewise, a text that may not generally be recognized as canonical may well have the virtue of providing students with a clear sense of a particular position in the field. Oftentimes the less commonly cited texts may be those that are simply later arrivals on the critical scene or those that strive to move the field in different directions but are not yet recognized. In our choices, we have therefore sought to balance the canonical texts in the field with those that we feel shift the debates toward new ground.

Our aim has been to ensure that the collection presents teachers with some of the (particularly teachable) canonical pieces on each topic, but at the same time to allow different essays to stimulate classroom debate. Our organizational scheme has been dictated foremost by a pedagogical impulse—the sequence of articles within a section is oftentimes chronological, but not always so. We would caution against any impression that the final essay in any section is necessarily a position that we ourselves favor as the "last word." Indeed, one of the most productive aspects of working on this anthology together has been to learn as much about our own intellectual disagreements and disparate tastes. There are positions articulated in this anthology with which we both concur, some of which we both reject, and yet others with which one of us agrees and the other disagrees.

Planning the sections with an eye to such concerns, we have been eager to include the great majority of texts in unexcerpted forms. In the case of long texts this has not always been possible, but even in those few instances where we have had to make cuts, we have attempted to reprint selections that do justice to the larger project of the author or to the position that the selection has occupied in critical discourse. We have also been mindful of the importance of diversity of voices and regional concerns. Thus the essays collected here are cautious in not replicating the overwhelming focus on India in much postcolonial discourse. Certainly the balance between representing canonicity in the field and expanding its horizons has meant that India continues to occupy an important role as a frame of reference. But as scholars, one of whom works primarily on the Caribbean and the other on Africa, we are interested in asserting the centrality of other world contexts in the discourse of postcolonial studies. A quick look at the table of contents will indicate essays on the discovery of the New World; on indigenous identities in Central America and the Pacific; on settler colonies in the United States, Africa, and Australia; on the post-Soviet world as postcolonial; on the American Colonization Society; on language politics and nationalist consciousness in Africa and the Caribbean; on the colonial construction of gender in Nigeria and Egypt; on diasporic and indigenous figurations of the "Chinese woman"; on English colonialism in Ireland; and even an official apology by the U.S. Congress to the indigenous peoples of Hawai'i for the illegal overthrow of their sovereign queen.

A charge often made in critiques of postcolonial studies is that it has become a self-referential enterprise disconnected from the original postcolonies or from the world outside the academy. Our primary emphasis in this collection on the academic location of much of what gets studied as "postcolonial discourse," however, is not to belittle the actual experience of colonization elsewhere or to silence the revolutionary voices of subsequent postcolonial struggles in former European colonies and in much of the so-called Third World. Indeed, though our focus has been the work of academics, we have also included seminal contributions by intellectuals such as Aimé Césaire, Léopold Sédar Senghor, and Frantz Fanon, who all operated outside the Anglo-American academy and challenged the traditional divide between the theorist and the activist. Nevertheless, as the Samoan writer Albert Wendt remarked in a keynote address in Honolulu to a 2003 NEH Summer Institute on "Rethinking Indigenous Cultures in the Pacific," putting together an anthology is an inherently political act and is bound to be read as such.[2] Our exclusions and inclusions are open to critique, but we hope that our selections will ultimately withstand the test of the pedagogical contexts for which they are intended.

Coda

On June 19, 2003, only a few months before Edward Said's death, a U.S. Congressional Subcommittee on Select Education met to discuss "International Programs in Higher Education and Questions of Bias."[3] Ostensibly a routine evaluation conducted before the reauthorization of the next cycle of funding of Title VI in the Higher Education Act, the proceedings were marked by the testimony of Stanley Kurtz, a research fellow at the Hoover Institution and contributing editor of the *National Review Online*.[4] Kurtz, whose Conradian overtones Said would have ironically noted, alleged that area studies programs funded by Title VI monies were fundamentally anti-American in orientation and critical of American foreign policy. This was, he asserted, in no small part a result of the dominance of postcolonial scholarship in the academy. "The ruling intellectual paradigm in academic area studies," Kurtz testified, "is called 'post-colonial theory.' Post-colonial theory was founded by Edward Said. Said is famous for equating professors who support American foreign policy with the 19th-century European intellectuals who propped up racist colonial empires. The core premise of post-colonial theory is that it is immoral for a scholar to put his knowledge of foreign languages and cultures at the service of American power" (CH, 9).

In addition to what he considered to be the antipatriotic stance of postcolonialist and area studies scholars, Kurtz complained that various area studies organizations and Title VI centers had agreed to boycott military and defense funding, particularly from the NSEP (National Security Education Program). The NSEP program, which provides funding for foreign language study, requires students to work for national security–related agencies for a defined period of time after the funded period of study.

The two testimonies that followed Kurtz's are remarkable in the radically different approaches they took to counter his accusations. As such, they are symptomatic of the inherent contradictions of an enterprise that is at once alert to the importance of advocating its own relevance without at the same time being corrupted by an unsavory complicity. The first came from Gilbert Merkx, vice provost for international affairs at Duke University and co-chair of the Council of Directors of all Title VI programs. Merkx testified that there is "no boycott whatsoever of NSEP by Title VI centers," and that, as a matter of fact, not only have Title VI centers repaid the patronage of their federal sponsors, but they have done so with remarkable consistency. "Let me give you some direct examples of how Title VI centers that I have directed at New Mexico and Duke serve the national interest," said Merkx. "In my 20 years as director of New Mexico, we trained 44 active duty U.S. Army foreign area officers who received the M.A. degree, and four Air Force officers. During the period of the Central American conflict, my center in New Mexico hosted four workshops for the Defense Intelligence Agency in which academic specialists from around the country, whom I selected, met with intelligence officers from the DIA, the CIA, and the State Department. In 1997, my center organized and hosted a conference, in collaboration with the U.S. Army war college, the United States Southern Command, the National Guard Bureau, and the Inter-American Defense Board, on the subject of civil military issues in the Americas. It was attended by 150 military, civilian, and academic personnel" (CH, 12).

If Merkx's rebuttal of Kurtz is marked by a certain overzealousness in asserting the relevance of Title VI programs to state interests, the testimony of Terry Hartle, senior vice president of the American Council of Education, sought to unearth the latent motivations of Kurtz's project. Hartle argued that despite Kurtz's overarching claims about the problems with Title VI programs, his real concern was with programs that deal with the Middle East, and "to be even more specific, he's concerned about the teaching of history and political science at these centers" (CH, 14). It is for this reason that Edward Said becomes the primary exhibit in Kurtz's accusatory lineup. Though implicitly accepting Kurtz's ascription of a critical view to Edward Said, Hartle denied the monolithic status of the latter: "I believe Dr. Kurtz errs in the importance he ascribes to Edward Said's viewpoint. Few Middle Eastern scholars subscribe to this view, and none that I have spoken to in preparation for this hearing, all of whom are at Title VI centers, agree with Mr. Kurtz that Mr. Said's work is the ruling intellectual paradigm in their field" (CH, 15).[5]

What is noteworthy in these testimonies is the valence that the different speakers give to "postcolonial studies" in general and to the influence of Edward Said in particular. For Kurtz, postcolonial studies is the defining paradigm of all academic work in area studies today and is characterized by an unpardonable distrust of and disengagement with American foreign policy and security interests. For this, Kurtz argues, Said is mainly to blame. But the blame, Kurtz suggests, may be extended further to a loss of cultural confidence during the 1960s and the accompanying postmodern malaise in general. On being questioned by Congressman Timothy Ryan as to why "post-colonial theory has drawn such interest" (CH, 25), Kurtz responds: "I think there has been a cultural shift in this country since the 1960s, and it has become increasingly difficult in certain circles of our country to criticize anything other than the United States. . . . People who take a post-modern perspective, like Professor Said, followed Michele [*sic*] Foucault. Michele Foucault doesn't take very seriously the traditional democratic guarantees" (CH, 25–26). Those familiar with Foucault's work are likely to be baffled by the revelation of his antidemocratic tendencies, but Kurtz explains his position a little later. He says that postmodernists are suspicious of "notions of liberal balance" as no more than the deception of powerful people, and this results in the academic hiring of like-minded scholars (CH, 26). Postcolonial scholarship, by implication, is supposedly a field characterized by very little internal dissent and tension.

Merkx and Hartle, in contrast, have a different view of the status of postcolonial studies in the world of area studies. Indeed, it is no small irony that in his testimony against Kurtz, Merkx comes across as a textbook case exemplifying the critique that Said's *Orientalism* made about the complicities of area studies scholars with Western policy interests.[6] But it is Hartle's choice to present Said as only one factor in area studies that most irks Kurtz, since it risks suggesting that area studies, and by implication postcolonial studies, is in the main intellectually diverse and not politically monolithic.

The scholars testifying in this hearing saw their task as debating the degree of influence that postcolonial studies, read through the metonymical figure of Said, has had on area studies. Reading through these testimonies from the standpoint of a scholar of postcolonial studies, however, one is left with the feeling that none of the testimonies really attempts to present a fair and coherent description of "postcolonial studies" as such. This is the case not only with Kurtz but also with his detractors. Although they dispute Kurtz's allegations that postcolonial studies has corrupted area studies, Kurtz's critics allow his one-sided impression of postcolonial studies to remain unchallenged. At the end of the day, one gets the sense that the debate remained unresolved and that it left the congressmen still hazy about the nature of the scholarship. The concluding sentiment of Congressman Ryan is both dismissive and self-congratulatory: "I think that the fact that our federal money is going to teach, whether it's to the extent that Dr. Kurtz thinks or Dr. Hartle thinks, post-colonial theory, I think, speaks volumes about what kind of country we live in and what we stand for, that that would even be an option" (CH, 28–29). The rather muddled formulation rests on the by now numbingly familiar apotheosis of democratic debate in this country but perhaps more complacently depends on the arguable irrelevance of critiques to state dominance. And yet the gnat must have some sting to warrant even momentary congressional energy.

What would have been appropriate testimony on the part of a postcolonial theorist at such a hearing? Perhaps something discreetly reticent. Perhaps in the calculating world of legislative politics the less said the better, the fuzzier the representations the more maneuverable and subversive the desired result. We hope, nevertheless, that this anthology helps provide a more accurate sense of the work that is carried on under the rubric of postcolonial studies. We hope it shows that postcolonial studies has multiple legacies that go beyond and indeed before the critique of Orientalism; that postcolonialism as a critical enterprise is attentive not only to the imperial abuses of state power in the United States but to those it finds anywhere and everywhere in the world; that the postcolonial ethic is an auto-critical one which in its most useful moments is suspicious of any political orthodoxy;[7] that such critique has also taken into account the failures of the postcolonial state and has not been satisfied with an easy Manichean (West/non-West) politics of blame; that it has also been attentive to minoritarian positions such as those inhabited by subaltern subjects within postcolonial nations; that oftentimes the (much criticized) scholarly bent of postcolonial literary criticism has been to read, teach, and write about the literary and cultural production of the ex-colonies with only an incidental interest in its specific postcoloniality; that rather than being embraced by the left, mainstream postcolonial criticism, with its increasing emphasis on diasporas, hybrid identities, and global fluidities, has in fact been accused by more orthodox scholars on the left as being complicitous with the larger project of neoliberal capitalism; and finally that postcolonial insights have given new life to questions of American identity and, contra Kurtz, have done so in ways crucial to self-critique precisely because they challenge blind patriotism. And while postcolonial studies has many mansions, the following selections demonstrate its continuing relevance to some of the most enduring questions of culture, politics, and identity.

NOTES

1   The following seven paragraphs are drawn from Desai (2000).

2   Albert Wendt's comments were made in a keynote lecture at Honolulu on July 18, 2003. The talk was also the occasion of a release of a newly edited anthology of contemporary Polynesian poems to which Wendt referred. See Wendt, Sullivan, and Whaitiri (2003).

3   See U.S. Government Printing Office (2003). This document is also accessible at *http://edworkforce.house.gov/hearings/108th/sed/sedhearings.htm* (hereafter CH). Portions of the coda will appear simultaneously as Desai, "Edward Said, Area Studies and Postcoloniality," in the *Journal of Contemporary Thought* (Baroda, India).

4   Accuracy demands that we note that before Kurtz presented his testimony, two other speakers, Dr. Peyton Roden (director of the Center for NAFTA Studies at the University of North Texas) and Vivien Stewart (vice president of education of the Asia Society), testified on the importance of Title VI funding to international studies. But neither of their presen-

tations was centrally related to the debates that ensued on the issue of bias in international education.

5 Michael Kennedy, vice provost for international affairs at the University of Michigan, echoes this sentiment in his written testimony added to the congressional record. "As a case in point, to assert Edward Said's centrality is simply wrong. Professor Said has visited our campus, and he drew a great crowd. But that crowd or the frequency that Said is cited in books and articles certainly does not do justice to the totality of the academy's work in area and international studies. For example, I cannot recall a single reference to Said, much less dominance, in a substantial multi-year public event series developed in response to the September 11, 2001 attacks. Entitled 'Religion, Security, and Violence in Global Contexts,' and organized by the U-M International Institute with heavy involvement of our Middle Eastern and South Asian area centers, this series reflected both the diversity and value of area studies and its centrality to the university's mission in international affairs. I can only imagine that those who make such claims about Said's general influence travel in very limited circles, perhaps living the very problem they seek to identify elsewhere" (CH, 179).

6 See Said (1978), 284–328.

7 So that, for instance, even a thinker like Frantz Fanon, hailed as a revolutionary voice of the colonized, and a proponent of national liberation from colonialism, was at the same time cautious of the "pitfalls" of nationalism. See Fanon (1963).

REFERENCES

Achebe, Chinua. 1977/1989. "An Image of Africa: Racism in Conrad's *Heart of Darkness.*" In Achebe, *Hopes and Impediments,* 1–20. New York: Bantam Doubleday.

Appiah, Kwame Anthony. 1992. *In My Father's House: Africa in the Philosophy of Culture.* New York: Oxford University Press.

Azim, Firdous. 1993. *The Colonial Rise of the Novel.* New York: Routledge.

Benítez-Rojo, Antonio. 1992. *The Repeating Island: The Caribbean and the Postmodern Perspective.* Trans. James Maraniss. Durham, N.C.: Duke University Press.

Bhabha, Homi 1994. "By Bread Alone: Signs of Violence in the Mid-Nineteenth Century." In Bhabha, *The Location of Culture.* New York: Routledge.

Brantlinger, Patrick. 1988. *Rule of Darkness: British Literature and Imperialism, 1830–1914.* Ithaca, NY: Cornell University Press.

Breckenridge, Carol, and Peter van der Veer, eds. 1991. *Orientalism and the Postcolonial Predicament.* Philadelphia: University of Pennsylvania Press.

Brennan, Timothy. 1989. *Salman Rushdie and the Third World.* New York: St. Martin's Press.

Chakrabarty, Dipesh. 2000. *Provincializing Europe: Postcolonial Thought and Historical Difference.* Princeton: Princeton University Press.

Cheng, Vincent. 1995. *Joyce, Race, and Empire.* New York: Cambridge University Press.

Chow, Rey. 2002. *The Protestant Ethnic and the Spirit of Capitalism.* New York: Columbia University Press.

Davies, Carole Boyce, and Elaine Savory Fido, eds. 1990. *Out of the Kumbla: Caribbean Women and Literature.* Trenton, NJ: Africa World Press.

Desai, Gaurav. 2000. "Rethinking English: Postcolonial English Studies." In *A Companion to Postcolonial Studies,* ed. Henry Schwartz and Sangeeta Ray, 523–539. Malden, Mass.: Blackwell Publishers.

Dirks, Nicholas, ed. 1992. *Colonialism and Culture.* Ann Arbor: University of Michigan Press.

Duffy, Enda. 1994. *The Subaltern Ulysses.* Minneapolis: University of Minnesota Press.

Fanon, Frantz. 1963. *The Wretched of the Earth.* Trans. Constance Farrington. New York: Grove Press.

Gates, Henry Louis, Jr. 1991. "Critical Fanonism." *Critical Inquiry* 17, 457–470.

Gikandi, Simon. 1996. *Maps of Englishness: Writing Identity in the Culture of Colonialism*. New York: Columbia University Press.

Gilroy, Paul. 2000. *Against Race: Imagining Political Culture beyond the Color Line*. Cambridge, Mass.: Harvard University Press.

Glissant, Edouard. 1989. *Caribbean Discourse: Selected Essays*. Trans. J. Michael Dash. Charlottesville: University Press of Virginia.

Gordon, Lewis R., T. Denean Sharpley-Whiting, and Renee T. White, eds. 1996. *Fanon: A Critical Reader*. Cambridge, MA: Blackwell.

Guha, Ranajit. 1983. *Elementary Aspects of Peasant Insurgency*. Delhi: Oxford University Press.

Harlow, Barbara. 1987. *Resistance Literature*. New York: Routledge.

Irele, Abiola. 1981/1990. *The African Experience in Literature and Ideology*. Reprint. Bloomington: Indiana University Press.

JanMohamed, Abdul. 1983. *Manichean Aesthetics*. Amherst: University of Massachusetts Press.

Lamming, George. 1960/1992. "A Monster, a Child, a Slave." In Lamming, *The Pleasures of Exile*, 95–117. Ann Arbor: University of Michigan Press.

Lazarus, Neil. 1990. *Resistance in Postcolonial African Fiction*. New Haven: Yale University Press.

Lloyd, David. 1993. *Anomalous States: Irish Writing and the Post-Colonial Moment*. Durham, NC: Duke University Press.

Mills, Sara. 1991. *Discourses of Difference*. New York: Routledge.

Mitchell, Timothy. 1988. *Colonising Egypt*. New York: Cambridge University Press.

Mudimbe, V. Y. 1988. *The Invention of Africa*. Bloomington: Indiana University Press.

———. 1994. *The Idea of Africa*. Bloomington: Indiana University Press.

Nixon, Rob. 1992. *London Calling*. New York: Oxford University Press.

Ogunyemi, Chikwenye O. 1996. *Africa Wo/Man Palava: The Nigerian Novel by Women*. Chicago: University of Chicago Press.

Prakash, Gyan, ed. 1995. *After Colonialism: Imperial Histories and Postcolonial Displacements*. Princeton, NJ: Princeton University Press.

Said, Edward. 1978. *Orientalism*. New York: Random House.

———. 1993. *Culture and Imperialism*. New York: Alfred Knopf.

Sharpe, Jenny. 1993. *Allegories of Empire: The Figure of Woman in the Colonial Text*. Minneapolis: University of Minnesota Press.

Spivak, Gayatri Chakravorty. 1986. "Three Women's Texts and a Critique of Imperialism." In *"Race," Writing, and Difference,* ed. Henry Louis Gates, Jr., 262–280. Chicago: University of Chicago Press. (Rprinted in this volume.)

Spurr, David. 1993. *The Rhetoric of Empire*. Durham, NC: Duke University Press.

Suleri, Sara. 1992. *The Rhetoric of English India*. Chicago: University of Chicago Press.

Thomas, Nicholas. 1994. *Colonialism's Culture: Anthropology, Travel, and Government*. Princeton, NJ: Princeton University Press.

U.S. Congress. House of Representatives. 2003. *International Programs in Higher Education and Questions of Bias*. Hearing before the Subcommittee on Select Education of the Committee on Education and the Workforce, House of Representatives, 108th Congress, 1st session. Serial no. 108-21. Washington, DC: U.S. Government Printing Office.

Wendt, Albert, Robert Sullivan, and Reina Whaitiri, eds. 2003. *Whetu Moana: Contemporary Polynesian Poems in English*. Auckland: Auckland University Press.

1

Ideologies of Imperialism

Although most of us acknowledge that periodizing history is more complex than assigning tidy dates to bracket an era, marking the beginning and end of imperialism in time and space is a particularly difficult enterprise. Scholars pin down dates depending on how they define imperialism, and when definitions differ, the epochal spans and geographical terrain tend to vary with them. In some accounts of imperialism, its origins are emblematized by the iconic figures of Christopher Columbus and Amerigo Vespucci, whose forays into the Americas in the fifteenth century radically altered more than the cosmography of the modern map. The "discovery" of the New World portends the emerging dominance of western Europe on the world stage, but it is not just this singular arrival that inscribes a "new" history and geography over that which is discovered; other events, such as the final defeat of the Moors in Spain, reinforce the coming shift in global power. In a fanciful revolution of the compass, the sun begins to set on the East and rise on the West.

Other accounts enact the imperial drama of modern history in a later period and with a different stage description. Eric Hobsbawm (1989), for instance, identifies the "Age of Empire," in the title of the third volume in his magisterial survey of the "long nineteenth century," as the period between 1875 and 1914. Although he admits that emperors and empires have existed for centuries before the time and focus of his volume, the imperialism he analyzes is closely related not to the ancient or medieval world, or even to the early modern "preindustrial" empires of Spain and Portugal that inaugurated the historic transformation of the Americas, but to the relatively recent colonial acquisition of vast areas of the earth's surface by a small number of European states: Britain, France, Germany, Belgium, and Italy among them. Although the United States, Russia, and Japan were also eager to follow the "international fashion" of gaining an imperial aura by collecting colonial territories, the western European states were at this point the main agents in formalizing the process of control and carving up different parts of the earth between them. The reason "imperialism" became a keyword in the late nineteenth century, according to Hobsbawm, is its intimate coupling with another key phrase, "monopoly capital," which, in its need for a world market, kindled the territorial expansion, the more formal state control of foreign regions, and the annexations of colonialism proper.

Some scholars reject a primarily economist explanation for this period in history. Still others would be skeptical of any claims for the end of imperialism with the implosion of Europe in the world wars. The precise distinction between imperialism and colonialism, and between neo- and postcolonialism, may seem fuzzy to those who experience the former's continuing effects in a period of late capitalism and supposed decolonization. The 2003 invasion of Iraq might mean the displacement of European imperialism as primary agent (and the demotion of a once dominant Britain to a mere ally), but the confused, oscillating rhetoric of impending threat from and promised liberation for the same region bears chilling similarities to the schizophrenic discourse of imperialism. Certainly the resurgence of terms such as "empire" and "imperialism" in contemporary North American public culture and in academia suggests that whatever the interpretation, "democracy and freedom" or "foreign occupation," and however debatable the cause-effect analysis—who started it first and who exactly are the real victims, the real heroes, and the real villains of this scenario—the cultural baggage of imperialism and its explosive consequences continue to resonate among those who still feel their impact.

Part I provides examples of the discourses of imperialism that were ultimately to generate and, in turn, be reconstituted by specific colonial practices. Although imperialism and colonialism have, as the selections reflect, different definitions and time frames, the texts in this section suggest certain recurring tropes and gestures in their ideologies of empire, even as they range across a plurality of contexts and periods. Although Part IX raises the possibility of a separation between writing and political practice, here we stress the relationship between the disciplinary acts of writing and other forms of representation—literature, history, art, ethnography, travel logs, legal statutes, political minutes, religious edicts—and the practice of dominance.

Part I opens with a founding text of imperialism, a letter by Columbus, the Genoese explorer who inadvertently journeyed into the Americas and whose account of his voyages was eventually published. The official correspondence between adventuring subject and incipient empire and Columbus's inauguration of Americana demonstrate how the pervasive themes of imperial discourse functioned as the driving motor of the putative colonial enterprise. The thrilling revelation of exotic landscape, the conflicting presence of savage and timorous natives, the not always reliable "eyewitness" accounts, the promise of infinite, almost fortuitous wealth, the possession and renaming of apparently unclaimed territories and inhabitants through royal and religious decrees commonly appear in texts of discovery written on the occasion of such audacious voyages.

Columbus, with the *Santa Maria*, the *Pinta*, and the *Niña*, reached one of the islands of the Bahamas in early October 1492. In his initial detour into the cluster of islands we now know as the Caribbean, Columbus erroneously believed that he was somewhere in Asia, and misidentified the Taino-speaking peoples he saw as Indians. The letter he addressed in 1493 rather appropriately to Don Gabriel Sanchez, treasurer of King Ferdinand of Spain, who financed the expedition, expresses some anticipation of seeing a "city or large residences," but the curious absence of such signs of Asian civilization does not really seem to register here. The expected monsters and men "born with tails" also fail to make themselves evident, but despite his various (mis)apprehensions, Columbus discovers, it seems, other self-evident truths. Ultimately it is not Asia that operates as visible sign, but Spain itself, as Columbus announces ownership and renames the islands, "for our most fortunate king, with proclaiming heralds and flying standards, no one objecting." The fatal incomprehension of the natives, who do not "object" to a ceremony they do not fully understand, already signifies that their consent is a matter of indifference. As V. Y. Mudimbe will show in part II (chapter 4), the enduring collusion between individual profiteers, evangelical traders, royal patronage, and religious sanction is tellingly revealed in the letter's conclusion: "Let us be glad also, as well on account of the exaltation of our faith, as on account of the increase of our temporal affairs, of which not only Spain, but universal Christendom will be partaker."

The excerpt from a speech of Edmund Burke, the British statesman and temporary nemesis of Warren Hastings, first governor-general of British Bengal, embodies the moral crisis of the adventurer implicit in Columbus's triumphant narrative. If Columbus comes to stand, in many accounts, for the heady promise of empire building, the figure of Hastings, who began his Indian career as a clerk in the East India Company in the mid-eighteenth century, assumes, in Burke's rhetoric, the nightmarish potential of that promise. Upon his return to England after resigning his post, Hastings was charged in 1786 with high crimes and misdemeanors, and Burke was given the task of presenting the various articles of alleged criminal activity to the House of Commons. Burke's moralizing reminders of the duty of the imperialist state to its subjects in conjunction with his account of Hastings's alleged abuses show how precarious the ethical claims of colonial ideology really are. Contrary to the frequent Columbian assertion of uncivilized and potentially colonizable regions, Burke's sentimental, crisis-ridden rhetoric locates the heart of darkness in the very center of empire.

Despite its complexity, Burke's opening speech in February 1788 nevertheless cracks under the weight of its contradictions. The outrage that Burke expresses over the abuses of the East India Company and Hastings's official sanction of an "unbounded license to plunder" the tempting wealth of the Indian colony is based upon his conviction that the economies of empire can indeed be executed with ethical propriety. "British delinquency" in a relatively early period of colonial trade and governance, the adolescent lawlessness of the administrative cadre under the reprehensible patronage of Hastings, can be leashed, Burke hopes, by the mature intervention of the British state. Despite the weighty implication that it is not Hastings but Britain itself on trial, Burke tries to distinguish the imperial state from the East India Company, which "began in commerce and ended in empire." The shameful misadventures of the latter, therefore, are not part of an inevitable process but merely the corruption of its essentially benevolent intent. The House of Lords was unable to implicate Hastings without tarring the entire colonial apparatus, and the vote to impeach by the House of Commons was followed by his acquittal in the former body in 1795.

As in Columbus's conflicting observations about the disposition of the natives, Burke is unable to preserve his initial martyred presentation of India as suffering and patient supplicant, pathetically awaiting justice from overseas. In a stunning reversal, he declares that "it is not the Englishman, it is the black banian, that is the master." The rapacious colonizers, who initially embody the loathsome excesses of Hastings and are misled by a façade of power, are "nothing but the inferior, miserable instruments of the tyranny which the lowest part of the natives of India exercise." Hastings, however, is not vindicated by the exposure of the vaunted authority held ironically not by the indigenous higher-caste and upper-class elites but by the despised native intermediaries in trade. He is guilty of the crime of encouraging intimacy between the master and the servant and blurring their separate identities. Or as Burke puts it, Hastings has supported "the system of banianism, and of concealment," and worse, "enlarged [it] by converting even Europeans into that dark and insidious character."

Although Burke emphasizes the ultimately principled role of the British state that ought to eschew the potential of filthy colonial lucre, the colonial administrator (British East Africa Company) and later governor of Nigeria (1912–1919) Frederick Lugard, writing in 1922, is unapologetic about the "dual mandate" of British territories in tropical Africa. Three decades after England assumed formal control, Lugard demands: "How has her task as trustee, on the one hand, for the advancement of the subject races, and on the other hand, for the development of its material resources for the benefit of mankind, been fulfilled?" Rebuking those critics who have wearied of "the white man's burden" and would prefer to shirk their "Imperial responsibility" to the "subject races," Lugard goes on, without any apparent sense of irony, to echo Sir C. Lucas that Empire "has infected the whole world with liberty and democracy." The philanthropic motive is immediately followed by the utilitarian one, again without any appearance of contradiction. Apart from the monetary value to England, its citizens stand to gain an increased standard of living, additional comforts, raw materials (including "material for munitions in time of war"), and the critical military and naval bases necessary to win wars. Accepting that imperialist practice, despite the paternalist rhetoric, was not always about improving the conditions of the natives, Lugard pragmatically recognizes the necessity of tropical possessions as a stimulus for what some might call the capitalist motives of "independent initiative and individual enterprise and ambition." The instability of contradictory imperialist motives, swinging between personal gain and philanthropic interventions, is smoothed over in Lugard's public acknowledgment of a "dual mandate."

Although Burke is shaken by the possibility of the corruption of English agents of empire by their deceptively hapless "banians," Lugard's faith in the essential scrupulousness of the English character knows no such doubt. Refusing to "digress" into the occasionally sordid economic enterprises of "Macaulay's 'Nabobs'" and others, Lugard chooses to point out that the end of slavery and the commencement of missionary activities were stimulated by the real benevolence of the colonizers. If the exercise of these "nobler motives" proved to be a windfall for England, then, by Lugard's account, one can only assume that the "great gain" of the colonizing process was not just a fringe benefit but also a meritorius bonus. Because Africans, not knowing their "use and value," had "wasted" their "surplus products," their more appropriate use by Europe was beneficial not just to European living standards but in "the substitution of [British] law and order for the [African] methods of barbarism." Africans not sufficiently gratified by this expropriation of their products could take comfort in Lugard's promise of "endeavouring to teach the native races to conduct their own affairs with justice and humanity, and to educate them alike in letters and in industry." When Lugard's conviction of increasing peace and prosperity within the colonies is disrupted by the turmoil in India and Egypt, in a brilliant stroke, he turns their "discontent" into "a measure of their progress," since they had after all been taught the principles of liberty and freedom by the British. In an unnerving prophecy which signals that the ideology of conquest and domination "in the cause of liberty and civilisation" will have a long shelf life, Lugard locates the British as only the temporary custodians of the ideals that they hold "in trust for those who shall come after" them.

REFERENCES

Hobsbawm, Eric. 1989. *The Age of Empire, 1875–1914*. New York: Vintage.

1

The Letter of Christopher Columbus on the Discovery of America

Because my undertakings have attained success, I know that it will be pleasing to you: these I have determined to relate, so that you may be made acquainted with everything done and discovered in this our voyage. On the thirty-third day after I departed from Cadiz,[1] I came to the Indian sea, where I found many islands inhabited by men without number, of all which I took possession for our most fortunate king, with proclaiming heralds and flying standards, no one objecting. To the first of these I gave the name of the blessed Saviour,[2] on whose aid relying I had reached this as well as the other islands. But the Indians call it Guanahany. I also called each one of the others by a new name. For I ordered one island to be called Santa Maria of the Conception,[3] another Fernandina,[4] another Isabella,[5] another Juana,[6] and so on with the rest. As soon as we had arrived at that island which I have just now said was called Juana, I proceeded along its coast towards the west for some distance; I found it so large and without perceptible end, that I believed it to be not an island, but the continental country of Cathay;[7] seeing, however, no towns, or cities situated on the sea-coast, but only some villages and rude farms, with whose inhabitants I was unable to converse, because as soon as they saw us they took flight. I proceeded farther, thinking that I would discover some city or large residences. At length, perceiving that we had gone far enough, that nothing new appeared, and that this way was leading us to the north, which I wished to avoid, because it was winter on the land, and it was my intention to go to the south, moreover the winds were becoming violent, I therefore determined that no other plans were practicable, and so, going back, I returned to a certain bay that I had noticed, from which I sent two of our men to the land, that they might find out whether there was a king in this country, or any cities. These men traveled for three days, and they found people and houses without number, but they were small and without any government, therefore they returned. Now in the meantime I had learned from certain Indians, whom I had seized there, that this country was indeed an island, and therefore I proceeded towards the east, keeping all the time near the coast, for 322 miles, to the extreme ends of this island. From this place I saw another island to the east, distant from this Juana 54 miles, which I called forthwith Hispana;[8] and I sailed to it; and I steered along the northern coast, as at Juana, towards the east, 564 miles. And the said Juana and the other islands there appear very fertile. This island is surrounded by many very safe and wide harbors, not excelled by any others that I have ever seen. Many great and salubrious rivers flow through it. There are also many very high mountains there. All these islands are very beautiful, and distinguished by various qualities; they are accessible, and full of a great variety of trees stretching up to the stars; the leaves of which I believe are never shed, for I saw them as green and flourishing as they are usually in Spain in the month of May; some of them were blossoming, some were bearing fruit, some were in other conditions; each one was thriving in its own way. The nightingale and various other birds without number were singing, in the month of November, when I was exploring them. There are besides in the said island Juana seven or eight kinds of palm trees, which far excel ours in height and beauty, just as all the other trees, herbs, and fruits do. There are also excellent pine trees, vast plains and meadows, a variety of birds, a variety of honey, and a variety of metals, excepting iron. In the one which was called Hispana, as we said above, there are great and beautiful mountains, vast fields, groves, fertile plains, very suitable for planting and cultivating, and for the building of houses. The convenience of the harbors in this island, and the remarkable number of rivers contributing to the healthfulness of man, exceed belief, unless one has seen them. The trees, pasturage, and fruits of this island differ greatly from those of Juana. This Hispana, moreover, abounds in different kinds of spices, in gold, and in metals. On this island, indeed, and on all the others which I have seen, and of which I have knowledge, the inhabitants of both sexes go always naked, just as they came into the world, except some of the women, who use a covering of a leaf or some foliage, or a cotton cloth, which they make themselves for that purpose. All these people lack, as I said above, every kind of iron; they are also without weapons, which indeed are unknown; nor are they competent to use them, not on account of deformity of body, for they are well formed, but because they are timid and full of fear. They carry for weapons, however, reeds baked in the sun, on the lower ends of which they fasten some shafts of dried wood rubbed down to a point; and indeed they do not venture to use these always; for it frequently happened when I sent two or three of my men to some of the villages, that they might speak with the natives, a compact troop of the Indians would march out, and as soon as they saw our men approaching, they would quickly take flight, children being pushed aside by their fathers, and fathers by their children. And this was not because any hurt or injury had been inflicted on any one of them, for to every one whom I visited and with whom I was able to converse, I distributed whatever I had, cloth and many other things, no return being made to me; but they are by nature fearful and timid. Yet when they perceive that they are safe, putting aside all fear, they are of simple manners and trustworthy, and very liberal with everything they have, refusing no one who asks for anything they may possess, and even themselves inviting us to ask for things. They show greater love for all others than for themselves; they give valuable things for trifles, being satisfied even with a very small return, or with nothing; however, I forbade that things so small and of no value should be given to them, such as pieces of plates, dishes and glass, likewise keys and shoe-straps; although if they were able to obtain these, it seemed to them like getting the most beautiful jewels in the world. It happened, indeed, that a certain sailor obtained in exchange for a shoe-strap as much worth of gold as would equal three golden coins; and likewise other things for articles of very little value, especially for new silver coins, and for some gold coins, to obtain which they gave whatever the seller desired, as for instance an ounce and a half and two ounces of gold, or thirty and forty pounds of cotton, with which they were already acquainted. They also traded cotton and gold for pieces of bows, bottles, jugs, and jars, like persons without reason, which I forbade because it was very wrong; and I gave to them many beautiful and pleasing things that I had brought with me, no value being taken in exchange, in order that I might the more easily make them friendly to me, that they might be made worshippers of Christ, and that they might be made full of love towards our king, queen, and prince, and the whole Spanish nation; also that they might be zealous to search out and collect, and deliver to us those things of which they had plenty, and which we greatly needed. These people practice no kind of idolatry; on the contrary they firmly believe that all strength and power, and in fact all good things are in heaven, and that I had come down from thence with these ships and sailors; and in this belief I was received there after they had put aside fear. Nor are they slow or unskilled, but of excellent and acute understanding; and the men who have navigated that sea give an account of everything in an admirable manner; but they never saw people clothed, nor these kind of ships. As soon as I reached that sea, I seized by force several Indians on the first island, in order that they might learn from us, and in like manner tell us about those things in these lands of which they themselves had knowledge; and the plan succeeded, for in a short time we understood them and they us, sometimes by gestures and signs, sometimes by words; and it was a great advantage to us. They are coming with me now, yet always believing that I descended from heaven, although they have been living with us for a long time, and are living with us to-day. And these men were the first who announced it wherever we landed, continually proclaiming to the others in a loud voice, "Come, come, and you will see the celestial people." Whereupon both women and men, both children and adults, both young men and old men, laying beside the fear caused a little before, visited us eagerly, filling the road with a great crowd, some bringing food, and some drink, with great love and extraordinary good-will. On every island there are many canoes of a single piece of wood; and though narrow, yet in length and shape similar to our row-boats, but swifter in movement. They steer only by oars. Some of these boats are large, some small, some of medium size. Yet they row many of the larger row-boats with eighteen cross-benches, with which they cross to all those islands, which are innumerable, and with these boats they perform their trading, and carry on commerce among them. I saw some of these row-boats or canoes which were carrying seventy and eighty rowers. In all these islands there is no difference in the appearance of the people, nor in the manners and language, but all understand each other mutually; a fact that is very important for the end which I suppose to be earnestly desired by our most illustrious king, that is, their conversion to the holy religion of Christ, to which in truth, as far as I can perceive, they are very ready and favorably inclined. I said before how I proceeded along the island Juana in a straight line from west to east 322 miles, according to which course and the length of the way, I am able to say that this Juana is larger than England and Scotland together; for besides the said 322 thousand paces, there are two more provinces in that part which lies towards the west, which I did not visit; one of these the Indians call Anan, whose inhabitants are born with tails. They extend to 180 miles in length, as I have learned from those Indians I have with me, who are all acquainted with these islands. But the circumference of Hispana is greater than all Spain from Colonia to Font-arabia.[9] This is easily proved, because its fourth side, which I myself passed along in a straight line from west to east, extends 540 miles. This island is to be desired and is very desirable, and not to be despised; in which, although as I have said, I solemnly took possession of all the others for our most invincible king, and their government is entirely committed to the said king, yet I especially took possession of a certain large town, in a very convenient location, and adapted to all kinds of gain and commerce, to which we give the name of our Lord of the Nativity. And I commanded a fort to be built there forthwith, which must be completed by this time; in which I left as many men as seemed necessary, with all kinds of arms, and plenty of food for more than a year. Likewise one caravel, and for the construction of others men skilled in this trade and in other professions; and also the extraordinary good will and friendship of the king of this island toward us. For those people are very amiable and kind, to such a degree that the said king gloried in calling me his brother. And if they should change their minds, and should wish to hurt those who remained in the fort, they would not be able, because they lack weapons, they go naked, and are too cowardly. For that reason those who hold the said fort are at least able to resist easily this whole island, without any imminent danger to themselves, so long as they do not transgress the regulations and command which we gave. In all these islands, as I have understood, each man is content with only one wife, except the princes or kings, who are permitted to have twenty. The women appear to work more

than the men. I was not able to find out surely whether they have individual property, for I saw that one man had the duty of distributing to the others, especially
refreshments, food, and things of that kind. I found no monstrosities among them, as
very many supposed, but men of great reverence, and friendly. Nor are they black
like the Ethiopians. They have straight hair, hanging down. They do not remain where
the solar rays send out the heat, for the strength of the sun is very great here,
because it is distant from the equinoctial line, as it seems, only twenty-six degrees.
On the tops of the mountains too the cold is severe, but the Indians, however, moderate it, partly by being accustomed to the place, and partly by the help of very hot
victuals, of which they eat frequently and immoderately. And so I did not see any
monstrosity, nor did I have knowledge of them any where, excepting a certain island
named Charis,[10] which is the second in passing from Hispana to India. This island is
inhabited by a certain people who are considered very warlike by their neighbors.
These eat human flesh. The said people have many kinds of row-boats, in which they
cross over to all the other Indian islands, and seize and carry away every thing that
they can. They differ in no way from the others, only that they wear long hair like the
women. They use bows and darts made of reeds, with sharpened shafts fastened to
the larger end, as we have described. On this account they are considered warlike,
wherefore the other Indians are afflicted with continual fear, but I regard them as of
no more account than the others. These are the people who visit certain women, who
alone inhabit the island Mateunin,[11] which is the first in passing from Hispana to
India. These women, moreover, perform no kind of work of their sex, for they use
bows and darts, like those I have described of their husbands; they protect themselves with sheets of copper, of which there is great abundance among them. They
tell me of another island greater than the aforesaid Hispana, whose inhabitants are
without hair, and which abounds in gold above all the others. I am bringing with me
men of this island and of the others that I have seen, who give proof of the things
that I have described. Finally, that I may compress in few words the brief account of
our departure and quick return, and the gain, I promise this, that if I am supported
by our most invincible sovereigns with a little of their help, as much gold can be
supplied as they will need, indeed as much of spices, of cotton, of chewing gum
(which is only found in Chios), also as much of aloes wood, and as many slaves for
the navy, as their majesties will wish to demand. Likewise rhubarb and other kinds
of spices, which I suppose these men whom I left in the said fort have already found,
and will continue to find; since I remained in no place longer than the winds forced
me, except in the town of the Nativity, while I provided for the building of the fort,
and for the safety of all. Which things, although they are very great and remarkable,
yet they would have been much greater, if I had been aided by as many ships as the
occasion required. Truly great and wonderful is this, and not corresponding to our
merits, but to the holy Christian religion, and to the piety and religion of our sover-

eigns, because what the human understanding could not attain, that the divine will has granted to human efforts. For God is wont to listen to his servants who love his precepts, even in impossibilities, as has happened to us on the present occasion, who have attained that which hitherto mortal men have never reached. For if anyone has written or said any thing about these islands, it was all with obscurities and conjectures; no one claims that he had seen them; from which they seemed like fables. Therefore let the king and queen, the princes and their most fortunate kingdoms, and all other countries of Christendom give thanks to our Lord and Saviour Jesus Christ, who has bestowed upon us so great a victory and gift. Let religious processions be solemnized; let sacred festivals be given; let the churches be covered with festive garlands. Let Christ rejoice on earth, as he rejoices in heaven, when he foresees coming to salvation so many souls of people hitherto lost. Let us be glad also, as well on account of the exaltation of our faith, as on account of the increase of our temporal affairs, of which not only Spain, but universal Christendom will be partaker. These things that have been done are thus briefly related. Farewell. Lisbon, the day before the ides of March.[12]

Christopher Columbus, admiral of the Ocean fleet.

Epigram of R. L. de Corbaria, bishop of Monte Peloso.
To the most invincible King of Spain.

No region now can add to Spain's great deeds:
To such men all the world is yet too small.
An Orient land, found far beyond the waves,
Will add, great Betica, to thy renown.
Then to Columbus, the true finder, give
Due thanks; but greater still to God on high;
Who makes new kingdoms for himself and thee:
Both firm and pious let thy conduct be.

NOTES

1 A mistake of the Latin translator. Columbus sailed from Palos on the 3d of August, 1492; on the 8th of September he left the Canaries, and on the 8th of October, or thirty-three days later, he reached the Bahamas.

2 In Spanish, San Salvador, one of the Bahama islands. It has been variously identified with Grand Turk, Cat, Watling, Mariguana, Samana, and Acklin islands. Watling's Island seems to have much in its favor.

3 Perhaps Crooked Island, or, according to others, North Caico.

4 Identified by some with Long Island; by others with Little Inagua.

5 Identified variously with Fortune Island and Great Inagua.

6 The island of Cuba.

7 China.

8 Hispaniola, or Hayti.

9 From Catalonia by the sea-coast to Fontarabia in Biscay.

10 Identified with Dominica.

11 Supposed to be Martinique.

12 March 14th, 1493.

2

EDMUND BURKE

Speech in the Impeachment of Warren Hastings

You will therefore recollect, that the East India Company had its origin about the latter end of the reign of Elizabeth, a period of projects, when all sorts of commercial adventures, companies, and monopolies were in fashion. At that time the Company was constituted with extensive powers for increasing the commerce and the honor of this country; because increasing its commerce, without increasing its honor and reputation, would have been thought at that time, and will be thought now, a bad bargain for the country. The powers of the Company were, under that charter, merely commercial. By degrees, as the theatre of operation was distant, as its intercourse was with many great, some barbarous, and all of them armed nations, nations in which not only the sovereign, but the subjects, were armed, it was found necessary to enlarge their powers. The first power they obtained was a power of naval discipline in their ships,—a power which has been since dropped; the next was a power of law martial; the next was a power of civil, and, to a degree, of criminal jurisdiction, within their own factories, upon their own people and their own servants; the next was (and here was a stride indeed) the power of peace and war. Those high and almost incommunicable prerogatives of sovereignty, which were hardly ever known before to be parted with to any subjects, and which in several states were not wholly intrusted to the prince or head of the commonwealth himself, were given to the East India Company. That Company acquired these powers about the end of the reign of Charles the Second; and they were afterwards more fully, as well as more legally, given by Parliament after the Revolution. From this time, the East India Company was no longer merely a mercantile company, formed for the extension of the British commerce: it more nearly resembled a delegation of the whole power and sovereignty of this kingdom sent into the East. From that time the Company ought to be considered as a subordinate sovereign power: that is, sovereign with regard to the objects which it touched; subordinate with regard to the power from whence its great trust was derived.

Under these successive arrangements things took a course very different from their usual order. A new disposition took place, not dreamt of in the theories of speculative politicians, and of which few examples in the least resembling it have been seen in the modern world, none at all in the ancient. In other instances, a political body that acts as a commonwealth was first settled, and trade followed as a consequence of the protection obtained by political power; but here the course of affairs was reversed. The constitution of the Company began in commerce and ended in empire. Indeed, wherever the sovereign powers of peace and war are given, there wants but time and circumstance to make these powers supersede every other. The affairs of commerce will fall at last into their proper rank and situation. However primary in their original intention, they will become secondary. The possession, therefore, and the power of assertion of these great authorities coinciding with the improved state of Europe, with the improved state of arts in Europe, with the improved state of laws, and, what is much more material, the improved state of military discipline, more and more perfected every day with us,—universal improvement in Europe coinciding with the general decay of Asia, (for the proud day of Asia is passed,) this improvement coinciding with the relaxation and dissolution of the Mogul government, with the decline of its warlike spirit, with the total disuse of the ancient strictness of the military discipline established by Tamerlane, the India Company came to be what it is, a great empire, carrying on, subordinately, a great commerce; it became that thing which was supposed by the Roman law irreconcilable to reason and propriety,—*eundem negotiatorem et dominum:* the same power became the general trader, the same power became the supreme lord.

In this exalted situation, the India Company, however, still preserves traces of its original mercantile character. The whole exterior order of its political service is carried on upon a mercantile plan and mercantile principles. In fact, the East India Company in Asia is a state in the disguise of a merchant. Its whole service is a system of public offices in the disguise of a counting-house. Accordingly, the whole external order and series of the service, as I observed, is commercial; the principal, the inward, the real, is almost entirely political.

This system of the Company's service, its order and discipline, is necessary to be explained to your Lordships, that you may see in what manner the abuses have affected it. In the first place, all the persons who go abroad in the Company's civil service enter as clerics in the counting-house, and are called by a name to correspond to it,—*writers*. In that condition they are obliged to serve five years. The second step is that of a *factor*, in which they are obliged to serve three years. The third step they take is that of a *junior merchant,* in which they are obliged to serve three years more. At that period they become *senior merchants,* which is the highest stage of advance in the Company's service,—a rank by which they had pretensions, before the year 1774, to the Council, to the succession of the Presidency, and to whatever other honors the Company has to bestow.

The Company had, in its early times, established factories in certain places; which factories by degrees grew to the name of Presidencies and Council, in proportion as the power and influence of the Company increased, and as the political began first to struggle with, and at length to predominate over, the mercantile. In this form it continued till the year 1773, when the legislature broke in, for proper reasons urging them to it, upon that order of the service, and appointed to the superior department persons who had no title to that place under the ordinary usage of the service. Mr. Hastings and Mr. Barwell, whatever other titles they might have had, held solely under the act of Parliament nominating them to that authority; but in all other respects, except where the act and other subsequent acts have not broken in upon it, the whole course of the service remains upon the ancient footing, that is, the commercial footing, as to the gradation and order of service.

Your Lordships see here a regular series of gradation, which requires eleven years before any persons can arrive at the highest trusts and situations. You will therefore be astonished, when so long a probationary service was required, that effects very different from those to be expected from long probation have happened, and that in a much shorter time than those eleven years you have seen persons returning into this kingdom with affluent, with overbearing fortunes. It will be a great part of your inquiry, when we come before your Lordships to substantiate evidence against Mr. Hastings, to discover how that order came to be so completely broken down and erased that scarce a trace of it for any good purpose remains. Though I will not deny that that order, or that any order in a state, may be superseded by the ruling power, when great talents, upon pressing exigencies, are to be called forth, yet I must say the order itself was formed upon wise principles. It furnished the persons who were put in that course of probation with an opportunity (if circumstances enabled them) of acquiring experience in business of revenue, trade, and policy. It gave to those who watched them a constant inspection of their conduct through all their progress. On the expectants of office it imposed the necessity of acquiring a character in proportion to their standing, in order that all which they had gained by the good behavior of years should not be lost by the misconduct of an hour. It was a great substantial regulation. But scarce a trace of the true spirit of it remains to be discovered in Mr. Hastings's government; for Mr. Hastings established offices, nay, whole systems of offices, and especially a system of offices in 1781, which being altogether new, none of the rules of gradation applied to them; and he filled those offices in such a manner as suited best, not the constitution nor the spirit of the service, but his own particular views and purposes. The consequence has been, that persons in the most immature stages of life have been appointed to conduct affairs which required the greatest maturity of judgment, the greatest possible temper and moderation. Effects naturally consequent have followed upon it.—I shall not trouble your Lordships with any further observations on this system of gradation.

I must, however, remark, before I go further, that there is something in the representation of the East India Company in their Oriental territory different from that, perhaps, of any other nation that has ever transported any part of its power from one country to another. The East India Company in India is not properly a branch of the British nation: it is only a deputation of individuals. When the Tartars entered into China, when the Arabs and Tartars successively entered into Hindostan, when the Goths and Vandals penetrated into Europe, when the Normans forced their way into England, indeed, in all conquests, migrations, settlements, and colonizations, the new people came as the offset of a nation. The Company in India does not exist as a national colony. In effect and substance nobody can go thither that does not go in its service. The English in India are nothing but a seminary for the succession of officers. They are a nation of placemen; they are a commonwealth without a people; they are a state made up wholly of magistrates. There is nothing to be in propriety called people, to watch, to inspect, to balance against the power of office. The power of office, so far as the English nation is concerned, is the sole power in the country: the consequence of which is, that, being a kingdom of magistrates, what is commonly called the *esprit du corps* is strong in it. This spirit of the body predominates equally in all its parts; by which the members must consider themselves as having a common interest, and that common interest separated both from that of the country which sent them out and from that of the country in which they act. No control upon them exists,—none, I mean, in persons who understand their language, who understand their manners, or can apply their conduct to the laws. Therefore, in a body so constituted, confederacy is easy, and has been general. Your Lordships are not to expect that that should happen in such a body which never happened in any body or corporation,—that is, that they should, in any instance, be a proper check and control upon themselves. It is not in the nature of things. The fundamental principle of the whole of the East India Company's system is monopoly, in some sense or other. The same principle predominates in the service abroad and the service at home; and both systems are united into one, animated with the same spirit, that is, with the corporate spirit. The whole, taken together, is such as has not been seen in the examples of the Moors, the Portuguese, the Spaniards, the Romans,—in no old, in no recent examples. The Dutch may resemble it, but they have not an empire properly so denominated. By means of this peculiar circumstance it has not been difficult for Mr. Hastings to embody abuse, and to put himself at the head of a regular system of corruption.

Another circumstance in that service is deserving of notice. Except in the highest parts of all, the emoluments of office do not in any degree correspond with the trust, nor the nature of the office with its name. In other official systems, the style, in general, is above the function; here it is the reverse. Under the name of junior merchant, senior merchant, writer, and other petty appellations of the counting-house, you have magistrates of high dignity, you have administrators of revenues truly royal, you have judges, civil, and in some respects criminal, who pass judgment upon the greatest properties of a great country. The legal public emoluments that belong to them are very often so inadequate to the real dignity of the character, that it is impossible, almost absolutely impossible, for the subordinate parts of it, which, though subordinate, are stations of power, to exist, as Englishmen, who look at a fortune to be enjoyed at home as their ultimate object, and to exist in a state of perfect incorruption in that service.

In some parts of Europe, it is true that the greatest situations are often attended with but little emolument; yet still they are filled. Why? Because reputation, glory, fame, the esteem, the love, the tears of joy which flow from happy sensibility, the honest applauses of a grateful country, sometimes pay the cares, anxieties, and toils which wait on great situations in the commonwealth; and in these they pay in money what cannot be paid in fame and reputation. It is the reverse in the service of the India Company. Glory is not the lot of subordinated merit,—and all the subordinate parts of the gradation are officers who, in comparison with the offices and duties intrusted to them, are miserably provided for; whereas the chief of each great Presidency has emoluments securing him against every mode of temptation. But if this has not secured the head, we may easily judge how the members are to be coerced. Mr. Hastings, at the head of the service, with high legal emoluments, has fouled his hands and sullied his government with bribes. He has substituted oppression and tyranny in the place of legal government. With all that unbounded, licentious power which he has assumed over the public revenues, instead of endeavoring to find a series of gradual, progressive, honorable, and adequate rewards for the persons who serve the public in the subordinate, but powerful situations, he has left them to prey upon the people without the smallest degree of control. In default of honest emolument, there is the unbounded license of power; and, as one of the honestest and ablest servants of the Company said to me in conversation, the civil service of the Company resembled the military service of the Mahrattas,—little pay, but unbounded license to plunder. I do not say that some of the salaries given in India would not sound well here; but when you consider the nature of the trusts, the dignity of the situation, whatever the name of them may be, the powers that are granted, the hopes that every man has of establishing himself at home, I repeat, it is a source of infinite grievance, of infinite abuse: of which source of corrupt power we charge Mr. Hastings with having availed himself, in filling up the void of direct pay by finding out and countenancing every kind of oblique and unjust emolument; though it must be confessed that he is far from being solely guilty of this offence.

Another circumstance which distinguishes the East India Company is the youth of the persons who are employed in the system of that service. The servants have almost universally been sent out to begin their progress and career in active occupation, and in the exercise of high authority, at that period of life which, in all other places, has been employed in the course of a rigid education. To put the matter in a few words,—they are transferred from slippery youth to perilous independence, from perilous independence to inordinate expectations, from inordinate expectations to boundless power. School-boys without tutors, minors without guardians, the world is let loose upon them with all its temptations, and they are let loose upon the world with all the powers that despotism involves.

It is further remarkable, these servants exercise what your Lordships are now exercising, high judicial powers, and they exercise them without the smallest study of any law, either general or municipal. It is made a sort of rule in the service, a rule confirmed even by the attempts that were made to correct it, (I mean confirmed by Sir Elijah Impey, when, under the auspices of Mr. Hastings, he undertook to be legislator for India,) that the judicial character, the last in the order of legal progress, that to which all professional men look up as the crown of their labors, that ultimate hope of men grown gray in professional practice, is among the first experimental situations of a Company's servant. It is expressly said in that body of regulations to which I allude, that the office and situation of a judge of the Dewanny Courts of Adawlut is to be filled by the *junior* servants of the Company; and as the judicial emolument is not substantially equal to that of other situations, the office of a judge is to be taken, as it were, *in transitu,* as a passage to other offices not of a judicial nature. As soon, therefore, as a young man has supplied the defects of his education by the advantage of some experience, he is immediately translated to a totally different office; and another young man is substituted, to learn, at the expense of the property of India, to fill a situation which, when he may be qualified to fill, he is no longer to hold.

It is in a great measure the same with regard to the other situations. They are the situations of great statesmen, which, according to the practice of the world, require, to fill properly, rather a large converse with men and much intercourse in life than deep study of books,—though that, too, has its eminent service. We know that in the habits of civilized life, in cultivated society, there is imbibed by men a good deal of the solid practice of government, of the true maxims of state, and everything that enables a man to serve his country. But these men are sent over to exercise functions at which a statesman here would tremble, without any theoretical study, and without any of that sort of experience which, in mixed societies of business and converse, form men gradually and insensibly to great affairs. Low cunning, intrigue, and stratagem are soon acquired; but manly, durable policy, which never sacrifices the general interest to a partial or momentary advantage, is not so cheaply formed in the human understanding.

Mr. Hastings, in his defence before the House of Commons, and in the defences he has made before your Lordships, has lamented his own situation in this particular. It was much to be lamented, indeed. How far it will furnish justification, extenuation, or palliation of his conduct, when we come to examine that conduct, will be seen.

These circumstances in the system have in a great degree vitiated and perverted what is in reality (and many things are in reality) excellent in it. They have rendered the application of all correctives and remedies to abuse, at best, precarious in their operation. The laws that we have made, the covenants which the Company has obliged its servants to enter into, the occasional orders that have been given, at least ostensibly good, all have proved noxious to the country, instead of beneficial.

To illustrate this point, I beg leave to observe to your Lordships, that the servants of the Company are obliged to enter into that service not only with an impression of the general duty which attaches upon all servants, but are obliged to engage in a specific covenant with their masters to perform all the duties described in that covenant (which are all the duties of their relation) under heavy penalties. They are bound to a repetition of these covenants at every step of their progress, from writer to factor, from factor to junior merchant, and from junior merchant to senior merchant. They ought, according to the rule, to renew these covenants at these times by something (I speak without offence) which may be said to resemble confirmation in the Church. They are obliged to renew their obligation in particular to receive no gifts, gratuities, or presents whatsoever.

This scheme of covenants would have been wise and proper, if it had belonged to a judicious order, and rational, consistent scheme of discipline. The orders of the Company have forbidden their servants to take any extraneous emoluments. The act of Parliament has fulminated against them. Clear, positive laws, and clear, positive private engagements, have no exception of circumstances in them, no difference *quoad majus et minus;* but every one who offends against the law is liable to the law. The consequence is this: he who has deviated but an inch from the straight line, he who has taken but one penny of unlawful emolument, (and all have taken many pennies of unlawful emolument,) does not dare to complain of the most abandoned extortion and cruel oppression in any of his fellow-servants. He who has taken a trifle, perhaps as the reward of a good action, is obliged to be silent, when he sees whole nations desolated around him. The great criminal at the head of the service has the laws in his hand; he is always able to prove the small offence, and crush the person who has committed it. This is one grand source of Mr. Hastings's power. After he had got the better of the Parliamentary commission, no complaint from any part of the service has appeared against Mr. Hastings. He is bold enough to state it as one presumption of his merit, that there has been no such complaint. No such complaint, indeed, can exist. The spirit of the corps would of itself almost forbid it,—to which spirit an informer is the most odious and detestable of all characters, and is hunted down, and has always been hunted down, as a common enemy. But here is a new security. Who can complain, or dares to accuse? The whole service is irregular: nobody is free from small offences; and, as I have said, the great offender can always crush the small one.

If you examine the correspondence of Mr. Hastings, you would imagine, from many expressions very deliberately used by him, that the Company's service was made out of the very filth and dregs of human corruption; but if you examine his conduct towards the corrupt body he describes, you would imagine he had lived in the speculative schemes of visionary perfection. He was fourteen years at the head of that service; and there is not an instance, no, not one single instance, in which he endeavored to detect corruption, or that he ever, in any one single instance, attempted to punish it; but the whole service, with that whole mass of enormity which he attributes to it, slept, as it were, at once under his terror and his protection: under his protection, if they did not dare to move against him; under terror, from his power to pluck out individuals and make a public example of them, whenever he thought fit. And therefore that service, under his guidance and influence, was, beyond even what its own nature disposed it to, a service of confederacy, a service of connivance, a service composed of various systems of guilt, of which Mr. Hastings was the head and the protector. But this general connivance he did not think sufficient to secure to him the general support of the Indian interest. He went further. We shall prove to your Lordships, that, when the Company were driven by shame, not by inclination, to order several prosecutions against delinquents in their service, Mr. Hastings, directly contrary to the duty of his office, directly contrary to the express and positive law of the Court of Directors, which law Parliament had bound upon him as his rule of action, not satisfied with his long tacit connivance, ventured, before he left his government, and among his last acts, to pass a general act of pardon and indemnity, and at once ordered the whole body of the prosecutions directed by his masters, the Company, to be discharged.

Having had fourteen years' lease of connivance to bestow, and giving at the end a general release of all suits and actions, he now puts himself at the head of a vast body enriched by his bounties, connivances, and indemnities, and expects the support of those whom he had thus fully rewarded and discharged from the pursuit of the laws. You will find, in the course of this business, that, when charges have been brought against him of any bribery, corruption, or other malversation, his course has been to answer little or nothing to that specific bribery, corruption, or malversation: his way has been to call on the Court of Directors to inquire of every servant who comes to Europe, and to say whether there was any one man in it that will give him an ill word. He has put himself into a situation in which he may always safely call to his character, and will always find himself utterly incapable of justifying his conduct.

So far I have troubled your Lordships with the system of confederacy and con-nivance, which, under his auspices, was the vital principle of almost the whole serv-ice. There is one member of the service which I have omitted: but whether I ought to have put it first, or, as I do now, last, I must confess I am at some loss; because, though it appears to be the lowest (if any regular) part of the service, it is by far the most considerable and the most efficient, without a full consideration and explana-tion of which hardly any part of the conduct of Mr. Hastings, and of many others that may be in his situation, can be fully understood.

I have given your Lordships an account of writers, factors, merchants, who exer-cise the office of judges, lord chancellors, chancellors of the exchequer, ministers of state, and managers of great revenues. But there is another description of men, of more importance than them all, a description you have often heard of, but which has not been sufficiently explained: I mean the *banian*. When the Company's service was no more than mercantile, and the servants were generally unacquainted with the country, they used the intervention of certain factors among the natives, which were called *banians:* we called them so, because they were of the tribe or caste of the banians or merchants,—the Indians being generally distributed into trades accord-ing to their tribes. The name still continues, when the functions of the banians are totally altered. The banian is known by other appellations. He is called *dewan,* or steward; and, indeed, this is a term with more propriety applied to him in several of his functions. He is, by his name of office, the steward of the household of the Euro-pean gentleman: he has the management of his affairs, and the ordering of his ser-vants. He is himself a domestic servant, and generally chosen out of that class of natives who, by being habituated to misery and subjection, can submit to any orders, and are fit for any of the basest services. Trained under oppression, (it is the true education,) they are fit to oppress others. They serve an apprenticeship of servitude to qualify them for the trade of tyranny. They know all the devices, all the little frauds, all the artifices and contrivances, the whole panoply of the defensive armor by which ingenious slavery secures itself against the violence of power. They know all the lurking-holes, all the winding recesses, of the unfortunate; and they hunt out distress and misery even to their last retreats. They have suffered themselves; but, far from being taught by those sufferings to abstain from rigor, they have only learned the methods of afflicting their fellow-slaves. They have the best intelligence of what is done in England. The moment a Company's servant arrives in India, and his English connections are known to be powerful, some of that class of people immediately take possession of him, as if he were their inheritance. They have knowledge of the country and its affairs; they have money; they have the arts of making money. The gentleman who comes from England has none of these; he enters into that world, as he enters into the world at large, naked. His portion is great simplicity, great indi-gence, and a strong disposition to relieve himself. The banian, once in possession, employs his tyranny, not only over the native people of his country, but often over the master himself, who has little other share in the proceedings of his servant but in giving him the ticket of his name to mark that he is connected with and supported by an European who is himself well connected and supported at home. This is a commission which nothing can resist. From that moment forward it is not the Englishman, it is the black banian, that is the master. The nominal master often lives from his hand. We know how young men are sent out of this country; we know how happy we are to hear soon that they are no longer a burden to their friends and parents. The banian knows it, too. He supplies the young servant with money. He has him under his power: first, from the necessity of employing such a man; and next, (and this is the more important of the two,) he has that dreadful power over his master which every creditor has over his debtor. Actions the most abhorrent to his nature he must see done before his face, and thousands and thousands worse are done in his absence, and he dare not complain. The banian extorts, robs, plunders, and then gives him just what proportion of the spoil he pleases. If the master should murmur, the very power that was sent over to protect the people of India from these very abuses, (the best things being perverted, when applied to unknown objects and put into unsuitable situations,) the very laws of England, by making the recovery of debts more easy, infinitely increase the power of the banian over his master. Thus the Supreme Court of Justice, the destined corrector of all abuses, becomes a collateral security for that abominable tyranny exercised by the moneyed banians over Europeans as well as the natives. So that, while we are here boasting of the British power in the East, we are in perhaps more than half our service nothing but the inferior, miserable instruments of the tyranny which the lowest part of the natives of India exercise, to the disgrace of the British authority, and to the ruin of all that is respectable among their own countrymen. They have subverted the first houses, totally ruined and undone the country, cheated and defrauded the revenue,—the master a silent, sometimes a melancholy spectator, until some office of high emolument has emancipated him. This has often been the true reason that the Company's servants in India, in order to free themselves from this horrid and atrocious servitude, are obliged to become instruments of another tyranny, and must prostitute themselves to men in power, in order to obtain some office that may enable them to escape the servitudes below, and enable them to pay their debts. And thus many have become the instruments of Mr. Hastings.

3

FREDERICK LUGARD

The Value of British Rule in the Tropics to British Democracy and the Native Races

Three decades have passed since England assumed effective occupation and administration of those portions of the interior of tropical Africa for which she had accepted responsibility when the nations of Europe partitioned the continent between them. How has her task as trustee, on the one hand, for the advancement of the subject races, and on the other hand, for the development of its material resources for the benefit of mankind, been fulfilled? There is no one, I think, who has been privileged to bear a share in the task, with its immeasurable opportunities, who, looking back, would not echo Mr. Rhodes' dying words, "So much to do—so little done!"

In the foregoing chapters I have endeavoured to describe some of the problems which confront the administrator, and with diffidence to indicate the path by which, as it seems to me, the best solution may in the course of time be found.

Viceroys and Governors of the older dependencies, of Colonies and of Dominions, occupy posts of greater titular importance than those who are entrusted with the charge of these tropical dependencies in Africa, but their own personal initiative is circumscribed and controlled by Ministers, by effective assemblies and councils, by a local press which reflects public opinion and criticism, and to a greater or less extent by the Parliament and press of England. The Governors in Africa are to-day gradually being brought under the same guiding and controlling influences, but in the earlier beginnings of our rule these influences hardly existed. Neither the Foreign Office nor the Colonial Office had any experience of Central African conditions and administration, when, at the close of the nineteenth century, the summons for effective Occupation compelled this country to administer the hinterlands of the West African colonies, and to assume control of vast areas on the Nile, the Niger, the Zambesi, and the great lakes in the heart of Africa.

The self-governing Dominions grew by slow stages from small municipalities to the status of United Nations. In India and the Eastern colonies, territorial expansion was the slow increment of many decades. But in Africa it was not a matter of expansion from existing nuclei of administration, but of sudden creation and improvisation. Perhaps it was well that Great Britain, following the tradition of the Empire, did not (as she might have been expected to do) select from her most experienced servants, trained in the school of Indian administration, those who should grapple with this sudden emergency, but trusted to the men on the spot. The pioneers of African administration came to their task with minds unbiassed by traditions unsuited to the races and conditions of Africa, and more ready to attempt to make bricks without straw. The perspective of history will perhaps show more clearly the magnitude of that task, and the opportunity it gave for initiative, almost unprecedented in the annals of the Empire.

It was for these pioneers to cope with the internal slave-trade, the very existence of which was hardly known in England, to devise their own laws, to set up their courts of justice, to deal with foreign aggression, to create an administration, and bring order out of chaos. The funds at their disposal were wholly inadequate, the staff poorly paid, painfully insufficient, and recruited somewhat at haphazard, whether for chartered companies or for Crown dependencies. The areas to be controlled were most of them many times the size of England, with populations numbered in millions, seething with internal strife, and wholly without roads or means of communication.

The nation is justified in demanding how, in such circumstances, the administrative officers and their colleagues in the judicial and educational departments on the one hand, and the engineers, the medical, agricultural, and forestry officers, and the rest of the technical staff on the other hand, have acquitted themselves in their respective responsibilities towards the native races, and the material progress of these countries.

We are all familiar with the creed of the "Little Englander." At each fresh access of responsibility and expansion of the Empire he has warned us that "the white man's burden" was already growing too heavy for this country to bear, that the British taxpayer was being called on to support the ambitions of chauvinists, and that the native races were misgoverned and robbed of their lands and their proper profits by the greed of exploiters.

Of late, since the war, it would almost seem as if an organized attempt was being made to promulgate these doctrines among the Labour Party, and to persuade them that the existence of the Empire is antagonistic alike to their own interests and to those of the subject races. That Party has not as yet had experience of overseas problems. Its "Research Department" for the investigation of these subjects appears to have fallen under the influence of those who hold these narrow views. They would persuade the British democracy that it is better to shirk Imperial responsibility, and relegate it to international committees; that material development benefits only the capitalist profiteer; and that British rule over subject races stands for spoliation and self-interest. Guided by these advisers—some of the more prominent of whom are apparently not of British race—the Labour Party has not hesitated to put forward its own thesis of Government of tropical dependencies under the Mandates. To these views I hope that I have already in some measure offered a reply, and I will endeavour briefly to summarise in these concluding pages.

"Nothing," says Sir C. Lucas, "should appeal so strongly as the Empire to democracy, for it is the greatest engine of democracy the world has ever known. . . . It has infected the whole world with liberty and democracy."[1] There is no doubt that the control of the tropics, so far from being a charge on the British taxpayer, is to him a source of very great gain. I have in a previous chapter shown how the products of the tropics have raised the standard of comfort of the working man, added to the amenities of his life, and provided alike the raw materials on which the industry and wealth of the community depend, and the market for manufactures which ensure employment.

So keenly do other nations value the assured possession of these sources of supply and these markets, that they have been willing to expend enormous sums for their acquisition and development,[2] and (unlike Great Britain) have built tariff walls around them to exclude other nations from participation. "Never in the world's history was there an Empire which in proportion to its size encroached so little upon the public time and the public cost."[3]

The temporary subsidies which have been paid to some of these tropical possessions in their earlier years, as "grants-in-aid," have decreased yearly until the countries became self-supporting, since which time they have not cost the taxpayer a penny, and the temporary grants have been indirectly much more than repaid.

Prior to the war Nigeria was the latest addition to the Empire, and if against the original payment to the Chartered Company and all subsequent grants, be set the profit derived by the British Exchequer on the import of silver coin, and the contributions offered by Nigeria to the war, it will be found that the debit is on the other side, and the country, with all its potentialities and expanding markets, has cost the British taxpayer nothing. Its trade—already £42,000,000—the greater part of which is with the United Kingdom, is of the kind which is the most valuable possible to the workers of this country—raw materials and foodstuffs in exchange for textiles and hardware.

Democracy has learnt by the war how absolutely dependent it is on the supply of these vital necessities from overseas, and even for the material for munitions in time of war. We have realised that the import can only be maintained by command of the seas. Some of these tropical dependencies are essential as naval bases, as cable and wireless stations, and as aerodromes, for that command of sea and air and of world communications upon which these islands depend for their existence.

Without them we could only survive on such terms as the powerful nations might choose to dictate.

Before the war the Little Englander was wont to argue that these world-wide outposts were a source of weakness, and in time of war their defence would be a burden which we could not sustain. But when Armageddon came, we required no additional garrisons to hold these vast territories in check; on the contrary, thousands of volunteers were ready to fight the Empire's battles. The West African colonies (relying, of course, on British supremacy at sea) were able, with the French, to capture the German Cameruns and Togoland, and to send thousands to fight or serve as transport units in German East Africa, and if need be in Palestine. These colonies asked for no financial assistance to help them through the crisis; indeed, they subscribed largely to the cost of the war and to war charities.

But let us return to the more normal conditions of peace and commerce. It is alleged that we could do an equally lucrative trade in the possessions of other Powers, instead of incurring the cost and responsibility of maintaining possessions of our own. But I have shown that foreign colonies are increasingly exclusive, and do not welcome British competition; that the cost of maintenance is borne by the revenues of the colonies themselves, and not by the British taxpayer; and, finally, it were easy to demonstrate that the largest proportion of their trade is done with the United Kingdom and not with foreign nations.

The fallacies put forward by these critics have long since been disproved, though the Labour Party may not be familiar with the statistics. It suffices here to point out that the trade of the single dependency of Nigeria for 1920 stood at over £42,200,000 in value, which, however, was probably abnormal and due to the "boom" of that year. Of this 96.74 per cent of the imports and 97.35 per cent of the exports were carried in British vessels—mainly, of course, to British ports.[4] For East Africa and Uganda the latest figures (1918–1919) show 84.3 per cent of imports and 91.1 per cent of exports from and to the Empire (United Kingdom 61 percent and 53.5 per cent).[5] How rapidly the trade of these colonies is expanding may be judged from the fact that the trade of Nigeria in 1913 (pre-war) was under 13.5 million.

As to the assertion that we do just as good trade with countries in tropical Africa which are not under the British flag, I find in the 'Statistical Abstract for the British Empire'[6] that the trade of the United Kingdom with all French possessions (including those in India and the Far East) was, in 1913, £6,730,244, while our trade with the single dependency of Nigeria for the same year stood at £8,278,813, in spite of the fact that in that year Germany had monopolised nearly half the Nigerian trade, which has since reverted to the United Kingdom.[7]

The critics quote statistics showing the proportion that the trade of this or that tropical dependency bears to the whole volume of our foreign trade, as though any comparison could be instituted between our commerce with wealthy, populous, and highly industrialised countries like the United States, Germany, or France, and that of new and undeveloped markets in the tropics, whose present output or demands are no measure whatever of their future potentialities.

And though our markets are free to all the world, British merchants have no small advantage in the first-hand and early knowledge of the conditions and resources of each country, available in their own language. They can and do bring their influence to bear in order to secure as far as possible that the conditions of trade shall be made to suit their own convenience. The home market, provided it can hold its own as to quality, price, and rapidity of delivery, has the first opportunity of supplying colonial demands.

These are indeed matters of such common knowledge that I refrain from dilating further upon them, and will content myself with referring to one or two other aspects which have perhaps received less recognition. The abounding progress of our tropical dependencies calls not only for millions of pounds worth of railway and other construction material, but for men to construct and to maintain the railways and other works. The expansion of administration equally demands officers for every branch—administrative, medical, educational, &c. The development of commerce requires local agents. The opening of mine-fields calls for expert workers.

In all these fields of activity openings are afforded for every class of the youth of England, whether from the universities, the technical schools, or the workshop. It is difficult to realise how severe would be the blow to the life of the nation if these thousands of avenues to independent initiative and individual enterprise and ambition were closed, as Germany has largely closed them to her people by her crime against the world.

I have already pointed out that this large field of opportunity and of responsibility must undoubtedly have contributed very greatly to the formation of the national character, which the late Lord Salisbury described in memorable words: "Our people, when they go into the possession of a new territory, carry with them such a power of initiative, such an extraordinary courage and resource in the solving of new problems and the facing of new difficulties, that if they are pitted against an equal number—I care not what race it is, or what the part of the world is—and if you keep politics and negotiations off them, it will be our people that will be masters, it will be our commerce that will prevail, it will be our capital that will rule, though not a sword has been unsheathed, and though not a blow has been struck in their defence."[8] He did but echo the words of Adam Smith, which I have quoted elsewhere, that the debt of the colonies to the motherland consists in the fact that "it bred and formed the men who were capable of achieving such great actions, and of laying the foundations of so great an Empire."

The British working man is told that the exploitation of Africa was undertaken by groups of financiers and capitalists, who desired to profiteer at the expense of the nation and of the native races alike. "Common greed," says the reviewer of the Labour Research Committee's report, summing up the gist of the argument, "came to be avowed openly as the most respectable of reasons for establishing colonies or protectorates anywhere and everywhere,"[9] in contrast with the nobler motives which prompted the bold adventurers of the spacious Elizabethan days.

I will not digress to discuss those motives here, or the navigation laws which treated the colonies merely as sources of profit, or the fortunes which Macaulay's "Nabobs" brought from India, or the quest for an "El Dorado." The partition of Africa was, as we all recognise, due primarily to the economic necessity of increasing the supplies of raw materials and food to meet the needs of the industrialised nations of Europe. It is a cheap form of rhetoric which stigmatises as "common greed" the honourable work by which men and nations earn their bread and improve their standard of life.[10]

But while admitting this we must not lose sight of the fact that several of our West African colonies had been acquired solely as depots to assist in the suppression of the overseas slave-trade, others in support of missionary endeavours which were certainly not prompted by greed for profit. Others again, as I have shown, were necessary for the maintenance of our sea-power. In all these cases a higher civilisation was brought into contact with barbarism, with the inevitable result, as history teaches, that boundaries were enlarged in the effort to protect the weak from the tyranny of the strong, to extend the rule of justice and liberty, to protect traders, settlers, and missions, and to check anarchy and bloodshed on our frontiers, even though territorial expansion was not desired.[11] Nor must we ignore the very real desire of the people of this country to assist in the suppression of slavery and barbarous practices. These are matters in which I am convinced that the British democracy has a deep interest, deeper perhaps than its political leaders credit it with. They cannot be disposed of with a sneer. But I return to the economic question, since this argument of "capitalist exploitation" appears to be a favourite one with which to capture the ear of Labour.

In the introductory chapter I cited statistics to show that, at the time of the first impulse of Imperial expansion in the reign of Queen Elizabeth, the small and chiefly agricultural population of these islands was able to supply its own essential needs in food and materials; that when the second impulse came 240 years later, after the Napoleonic wars, the population had quadrupled, while in the next seventy-five years of the nineteenth century, 1816–1891 (when the partition of Africa began in earnest), it again nearly doubled itself. The congestion of the population, assisted by the discovery of the application of steam to industrial uses, led to the replacement of agriculture by manufacturing industry, with the consequent necessity for new markets for the product of the factory, and the importation of raw materials for industry, and of food to supplement the decreased home production, and feed the increased population. The same phenomenon was to be seen in Germany and elsewhere in Europe.[12] I recapitulate these figures because their importance in this connection can hardly be over-estimated.

But mere increase in population alone, prodigious though it was, does not represent the full measure of the pressure on the Governments of the industrial nations of Europe. The standard of comfort, and what had come to be regarded as the absolute necessities of life by the mass of the population, had, during the nineteenth century, advanced in an even greater ratio. I cannot here attempt to depict the contrast. It is enough to recall the fact that 100 years ago a labourer's wage was 4s. to 6s. a week. He rarely tasted white bread, for the quartern loaf stood at 11d., and had been double that price a few years before. Still less could he afford to eat beef or mutton. Towards the close of the nineteenth century, tea, coffee, and cocoa, previously unknown luxuries, were his daily beverages and white bread his daily food. Sugar was cheap, and rice, sago, and other tropical products were in daily use. If my reader will turn to the pages of Miss Martineau's history,[13] or to those of Carlyle, and contrast the condition of squalor and misery in which the bulk of the people of these islands lived in 1816 with the conditions prevailing in 1891, he will realise how insistent had become the demand alike for the food-supplies and for the raw materials which were the product of the tropics.

These products lay wasted and ungarnered in Africa because the natives did not know their use and value. Millions of tons of oil-nuts, for instance, grew wild without the labour of man, and lay rotting in the forests. Who can deny the right of the hungry people of Europe to utilise the wasted bounties of nature, or that the task of developing these resources was, as Mr. Chamberlain expressed it, a "trust for civilisation" and for the benefit of mankind? Europe benefited by the wonderful increase in the amenities of life for the mass of her people which followed the opening up of Africa at the end of the nineteenth century. Africa benefited by the influx of manufactured goods, and the substitution of law and order for the methods of barbarism.

Thus Europe was impelled to the development of Africa primarily by the necessities of her people, and not by the greed of the capitalist. Keen competition assured the maximum prices to the producer. It is only where monopolies are granted that it can be argued that profits are restricted to the few, and British policy has long been averse to monopolies in every form. The brains, the research, the capital, and the enterprise of the merchant, the miner, and the planter have discovered and utilised the surplus products of Africa. The profits have been divided among the shareholders representing all classes of the people,[14] and no small share of them has gone to the native African merchant and the middleman as well as to the producer. It is true to say that "a vast area of activity has been opened up to the British workman, in which he shares with the capitalist the profits of the development of tropical resources."[15]

In accepting responsibility for the control of these new lands, England obeyed the tradition of her race. British Africa was acquired not by groups of financiers, nor yet (as I have related in chapter i) by the efforts of her statesmen, but in spite of them. It was the instinct of the British democracy which compelled us to take our share. When Mr. Gladstone's Cabinet in 1893 had decided to evacuate Uganda, he was told by his Scottish agent that if he did so he would have to evacuate Downing Street too. Even were it true—and I have shown that it is not—that we could do as lucrative a trade in the tropical possessions of other nations, there can be no doubt that the verdict of the British people has been emphatic that we will not ask the foreigner to open markets for our use, or leave to him the responsibility and its reward. Nor will tariff walls, like those of Jericho, fall flat at the sound of the trumpet of the new Labour leaders.

"The general effects of European policy in Africa have been almost wholly evil," says the Labour reporter, yet he admits that "experience and temperament have made the rule of the British over non-adult races an example of everything that is best in modern imperialism." The verdict of another of the prophets of Labour is to the same effect. The fundamental character of British official policy in West Africa, he says, has primarily been influenced by a desire to promote the welfare and advancement of the native races. England, he points out, led the way in the suppression of the overseas slave-trade, paying enormous sums in compensation to slaveowners in the West Indies, and at the Cape, and to Spain and Portugal, and in patrolling the seas. She espoused the cause of Congo reform, and of the indentured labour in Portuguese West Africa. The extension of British control in the Gold Coast hinterland was (he adds) to secure protection of the natives, and in Southern Nigeria to suppress war and human sacrifice.

The indictment against European misrule in Africa appears therefore to lack consistency, and to be directed chiefly against foreign Powers, though bitter charges, as we have seen, are made against some of the Eastern British dependencies in Africa, which have been fully discussed in these pages. In so far as they concern the territories of other Powers, this attitude of what Mr Rhodes called " unctuous righteousness," which has the appearance of assuming that others are actuated by less generous motives than our own, is more likely to promote resentment than reform. That the aims of these critics are good will not be denied, but they write without actual experience, and they create prejudice where sympathy and appreciation would be more promising of results.

Let it be admitted at the outset that European brains, capital, and energy have not been, and never will be, expended in developing the resources of Africa from motives of pure philanthropy; that Europe is in Africa for the mutual benefit of her own industrial classes, and of the native races in their progress to a higher plane; that the benefit can be made reciprocal, and that it is the aim and desire of civilised administration to fulfil this dual mandate.

By railways and roads, by reclamation of swamps and irrigation of deserts, and by a system of fair trade and competition, we have added to the prosperity and wealth of these lands, and checked famine and disease. We have put an end to the awful misery of the slave-trade and inter-tribal war, to human sacrifice and the ordeals of the witch-doctor. Where these things survive they are severely suppressed. We are endeavouring to teach the native races to conduct their own affairs with justice and humanity, and to educate them alike in letters and in industry.

When I recall the state of Uganda at the time I made the treaty in 1890 which brought it under British control, or the state of Nigeria ten years later, and contrast them with the conditions of to-day, I feel that British effort—apart from benefits to British trade—has not been in vain. In Uganda a triangular civil war was raging— Protestants, Roman Catholics, and Moslems, representing the rival political factions of British, French, and Arabs, were murdering each other. Only a short time previously triumphant paganism had burnt Christians at the stake and revelled in holocausts of victims. To-day there is an ordered Government with its own native parliament. Liberty and justice have replaced chaos, bloodshed, and war. The wealth of the country steadily increases.[16] The slave-raids and tyranny of the neighbouring kingdom of Unyoro have given place to similar progress and peace.

In Nigeria in 1902 slave-raiding armies of 10,000 or 15,000 men laid waste the country, and wiped out its population annually in the quest for slaves. Hundreds of square miles of rich well-watered land were depopulated. Barth bore witness to a similar condition of things fifty years ago. Men were impaled in the market-place of Kano. I have described its dungeon. Nowhere was there security for life and property. To-day the native Emirs vie with each other in the progress of their schools; the native courts administer justice, and themselves have liberated over 50,000 slaves. The Sultan of Sokoto and the other Emirs are keenly interested in such questions as afforestation, artesian well-boring, and vaccination. The native prisons have been pronounced by the medical authority to be a model for Government to imitate; the leper settlement in Bornu under purely native control is the most successful I know of.

I refer to these two countries because I happen to have personally witnessed their condition prior to the advent of British control, but similar results may be seen in every other British dependency in tropical Africa.

As Roman imperialism laid the foundations of modern civilisation, and led the wild barbarians of these islands along the path of progress, so in Africa to-day we are repaying the debt, and bringing to the dark places of the earth, the abode of barbarism and cruelty, the torch of culture and progress, while ministering to the material needs of our own civilisation. In this task the nations of Europe have pledged themselves to co-operation by a solemn covenant. Towards the common goal each will advance by the methods most consonant with its national genius. British methods have not perhaps in all cases produced ideal results, but I am profoundly convinced that there can be no question but that British rule has promoted the happiness and welfare of the primitive races. Let those who question it examine the results impartially. If there is unrest, and a desire for independence, as in India and Egypt, it is because we have taught the value of liberty and freedom, which for centuries these peoples had not known. Their very discontent is a measure of their progress.

We hold these countries because it is the genius of our race to colonise, to trade, and to govern. The task in which England is engaged in the tropics—alike in Africa and in the East—has become part of her tradition, and she has ever given of her best in the cause of liberty and civilisation.[17] There will always be those who cry aloud that the task is being badly done, that it does not need doing, that we can get more profit by leaving others to do it, that it brings evil to subject races and breeds profiteers at home. These were not the principles which prompted our forefathers, and secured for us the place we hold in the world to-day in trust for those who shall come after us.

NOTES

1 'United Empire,' March 1919.

2 Herr Dernburg stated that Algeria had cost France £343,720,000 up to 1906.—'Times' 23rd November 1906.

3 Lucas, "The British Empire."

4 Governor's address to Nigerian Council, December 1920. The destinatin is not stated, but in 1918 92.4 per cent of exports, and 87 per cent of imports, were to and from the Empire.— Cmd 508114 of 1919.

5 East African Report, 1918–19, No. 1073 of 1919.

6 Cd. 7827 of 1915. It is to be regretted that no later edition has yet appeared.

7 The war has, of course, exercised a great influence on the origin of imports and the destination of exports of the African dependencies. In Nigeria prior to the war Germany by importing trade spirits had, as we have seen, been able to monopolize the export of palm-kernels, and so to secure 44 per cent of the exports. This has been almost completely absorbed by British merchants. In other West African colonies, however, the place of Germany has been largely taken by the United States. The pre-war proportion of the East African trade with the Empire is given by the Economic Commission (p. 11) as 62.5 per cent of imports and 54.5 per cent of exports.

8 Debate, House of Lords, 14th February, 1895.

9 'The New Statesman,' 19th June 1920.

10 Carlyle, describing all that work has done for England, and what it has made England, says: "The English are a dumb people. They can do great acts but not describe them. . . . Their epic is written on the earth's surface: England her mark."—'Past and Present,' p. 135.

11 As Bacon says: "It was not the Romans who spread themselves upon the world, but the world which spread itself upon the Romans."—'Essays,' p. 44.

12 The population of the United Kingdom in 1816 was about 19,890,000 and in 1891 it had increased to 38,104,000. That of Germany was respectively 24,831,000 and about 50,000,000, and of France about 29,000,000 and 38,342,000. The pressure of population was thus not so great a factor in France, who was foremost in the scramble for Africa. Her Motives, as I have said, were chiefly due to the belief that it was by expansion in Africa alone that she could hope to find means to recover from the effects of the war with Germany in 1870.

13 'The Thirty Years' Peace,' vol. i, chapters 4, 7, &c.

14 Lord Leverhulme lately stated that in his Company alone—which is largely concerned in the development of the African tropics—there were no less than 127,000 shareholders.

15 Bruce, 'Broad Stone of Empire,' p. 4. In view of all these facts I read with amazement the verdict of the Labour Research Committee, that "it is doubtful whether the acquisition of territory in Africa has added to the power of the European States who have assumed it. It is certain that it has not added to their wealth."—'Empire and Commerce,' p. 317.

16 The last report, 1918–19, shows an export of cotton alone valued at close on a million sterling.—Cmd. 508/37, 1920.

17 "I believe," says Sir C. Lucas, "that to our people has been given the work of carrying justice and freedom throughout the world. I do not claim for them any immunity from wrong-doing. Like other people, they have sought and found gain. But I find the weak peoples of the world looking to and trusting England. I find British justice a proverb among nations. . . . I believe the world to be a better world for the fact that the British have peopled some lands with their own race, and taken the rule of others into their own hands."

"We of West Africa ought from our heart of hearts to thank Almighty God that we have been born into the British Empire," says a Lagos paper on Empire Day 1920; while a Gold Coast journal observed that "to us of West Africa Empire means a relation of goodwill between the Imperial unit and its links, harmonizing all interests irrespective of race and colour." West Africa, it adds, looks to Imperial Britain to lead the nations to a just recognition of Africa's claims.

Beaulieu pays a very generous tribute to England's success. "La nation qui tient le premier rang dans la colonisation, celle qui donne à tous l'exemples de vastes empire fondés en dela des mers, c'est l'Angleterre. . . . Mais le temps le grand maître et ce juge impartial, qui met enfin de compte chaque peuple à la place que ses qualités ou ses défauts lui assignent sédormé à l'Angleterre pour ne plus le lui reprendre le premier rang parmi les nations colonisatrices."—*Historie de la Colonisation chez les peuples Moderne,* vol. ii, p. 246. See also vol. i, p. 92.

II

The Critique of Colonial Discourse

As a curtain raiser for emerging European dominance on the global stage, Columbus's erratic entry into the Americas was a spectacularly successful, even theatrical, proto-type of the more directed imperial voyages that followed. Valentin Mudimbe's account of official papal letters in 1493 historically dates the early modern germination of sym-bols and ritualized ceremonies, the "invented traditions" that gradually lent weight and speed to the later expansion of Europe. The aggrandized encroachment of Spain and Portugal into "newly discovered countries" fundamentally relied on the salvational doc-trines of Christianity, although the papal bulls also reveal the alliance between the Catholic church and European royalty. The forcible appropriation of lands and the enslavement of natives on the basis of the doctrine of *terra nullius* (literally, empty land), Mudimbe explains, were apparently vindicated by the grace of conversion to Christian-ity. In a religious and aristocratic monopoly over international law, proprietary rights and issues of sovereignty were rewritten on the basis of both Christian identity and royal charter. In most cases, the religious and aristocratic cooperation abrogated the rights of the natives to their lands and even their bodies, since non-Christians were automatically disenfranchised. The codified language and rites of initiation and pos-session on each of the voyages make up what Linda Tuhiwai Smith calls the "deep structure which regulates and legitimates imperial practices." Running through much of this "grammar" and performative authorization of imperialism was the almost invariable assumption of native inferiority and barbarism that presumably made the often violent annexation to higher civilization through colonialism as salutary as the native's coerced induction to Christianity (see part I).

The chronological leap between parts I and II is considerable, but this is not to imply that there were no challenges to imperialist discourse or to colonial conquest until the twentieth century. The following selections, however, speak eloquently to the discourses in part I. Just as one can identify a "deep structure" to imperial discourses, anti-imperialist discourses, despite their equally complex range and contexts, also share certain fundamental similarities, including what Frantz Fanon would call a "complete calling in question" of the truths of colonial narratives. The writers in this part forcefully challenge the most persistent and seemingly incontestable belief in the superiority of European civilization, which, as colonial administrators such as Lugard would insist, ultimately justified colonialism as a benevolent, even compulsory enterprise. Although these authors all ascribe the ascendance, or what Mudimbe calls the expansion, of Europe to its colonial adventures, none of them is willing to concede uncritically its presumed higher state of civilization.

Aimé Césaire, the black Martinican poet and playwright, one of the progenitors of negritude and paradoxically also an admirer of French high culture, is one of the most vocal opponents of unreserved faith in the noble motives of colonialism. In his long essay *Discours sur le colonialisme*, translated into English in 1972, he announces that the colonized now incontrovertibly realize that the various atrocities carried out on the pretext of higher civilization were, like Europe itself, "indefensible." He reverses the charges of savagery and brutishness onto the Europeans, and rejects the various exculpatory and often contradictory claims for the benefits of colonialism such as improved living conditions, the introduction of democratic principles, conversion to Christianity, and the abolition of indigenous injustice. In an almost direct refutation of Lugard's text (see chapter 3), he refuses to accept the one-sided and sometimes disingenuous "evidence" of progress and reform and chooses, instead, to enumerate the devastating consequences of colonial rule.

Similarly, Roberto Fernández Retamar, the Cuban poet, essayist, and scholar, fires his own "ideological arsenal" in response to Eurocentrist dismissals of even the possibility of a Latin American culture. His controversial essay "Sobre cultura y revolución en la América Latina," which first appeared in *Casa de las Américas* in 1971, has seen different incarnations, including the English translation in *Massachusetts Review* in 1974. So certain seems to be the belief in Europe as cultural exemplar that Latin Americans are perceived as "rough drafts or dull copies" of Europeans, the mixed racial and geographic heritage of the former, their *mestizaje*, apparently a corruption of originary nation and race. Retamar (re)claims for Latin Americans the non-European aspect of their cultural constitution through the figure of Caliban, the "savage and deformed slave" in Shakespeare's drama *The Tempest*, published in 1623 (there were earlier stage productions). Appropriating Caliban for revolutionary purposes is part of a long cross-cultural tradition in postcolonial writing, which now has its critics among those wanting to preserve Shakespeare's canonical aura and others less interested in Shakespeare's heritage and more troubled, for example, by the sexist legacy of Caliban's resistance. Like Césaire, Retamar inverts the charges of superstition leveled against the Amerindian tribes, from whom, some claim, the unendearing portrait of Caliban, with all the suggestive, anagrammatic echoes of cannibalism, was drawn.

Retamar satirically refers to the irrational beliefs that Columbus and his caravel held in one-eyed men or men with tails. "It is a question of the typically degraded vision offered by the colonizer of the man he is colonizing. That we ourselves may have at one time believed in this version only proves to what extent we are infected with the ideology of the enemy," he warns. As an antidote to the diseased prose of canonical representations of the future colonies, of demonized and dehumanized characterizations of the indigenous peoples by European voyagers, Retamar restores Caliban to another line of American descent: "Caliban is our Carib." Against the elevated origins of European Creoles who traced their roots back to the Old World, Retamar resuscitates the debased aboriginal of the Americas.

Edward Said and Linda Tuhiwai Smith, both of whom explicitly identify what Said calls a "personal dimension" in their scholarly work, address questions of indigeneity and agency. Said's early education in Palestine and Egypt and his later professional success in the United States have never been free, he implies, of the enduring myths of the Orient which were to formulate and sustain European and later U.S. policies in the Middle East. Rather than use the image of infection, as Retamar does in his indictment of imperial ideologies, Said turns to the trope of legal trials, and challenges the idea that "literature and culture" can be "politically, even historically innocent." Along with the other writers in this section, Said identifies the humanities as a field rife not just with politics but with strong influence in matters of state policy. However ideal the desire for impartiality in academic work, Said is convinced that just like religion, the humanities have colluded with the violence of colonialism, a violence Gayatri Spivak calls "epistemic." The abiding influence of Said's *Orientalism*, its canonical and controversial status in the field, its ability to reach even the Olympian height of the U.S. Congress (see the Introduction), is a testament to the power of the humanities. It is therefore as a humanist and as a scholar that Said engages with a critique of Orientalism and challenges the "positional superiority" of Europe. Europe and the Orient are inventions of each other, he suggests provocatively, the superior force of the first enabling the material and ideological occupation of the region that enriched the treasuries of Europe in no small measure. He directly implicates the academic institution in the massive apparatus of Orientalist construction. The link between ideology and practice, between theory and policy, is inextricable, according to Said, since the discourse of Orientalism literally enabled and supported the production and management of "disparate realms" that were homogenized. The sense of relentless inevitability in the construction of a formidable system has laid Said open to charges of depriving both the European Orientalists and the Orient itself of critical agency. If the "hegemony of European ideas" mutes the skepticism of the Orientalists who may find it impossible to break through the inherited ideological screen, the force of "European-Atlantic power" wills the Orient to submission. Indeed, Said would paradoxically see a continuing history of willful misunderstanding in the "willed human work" of Orientalism.

Ultimately, however, Said, invoking Michel Foucault, sees the learned labor as productive and not simply as a unilateral process of defamation. After all, scholars and Orientalized subjects such as Said were capable of launching decisive critiques and even inspiring the field of U.S. colonial discourse studies that came to be associated, however problematically, with his founding text. Equally significant is that the same scholarly fields—literary, anthropological, historical—that promoted the abuses of Orientalism also enabled Said's own "hybrid perspective" and "willed human work" in the course of excavating or constructing other perspectives of the region and its peoples.

The Maori scholar Linda Tuhiwai Smith also believes that "indigenous voices have been overwhelmingly silenced" in her context in Aotearoa/New Zealand, but she notes that the struggle to clear a space for them continues. She sees this struggle as more than metaphoric, reminding us, as Said does in his own personal narrative, that "contested accounts" of histories often imply not simply "struggles over 'facts' and 'truth'" but also ongoing indigenous campaigns to win back lost lands. Smith's advocacy of the rights of indigenous peoples leads her to be critical not just of her embattled place in the Western(ized) academy or in European histories, but in postcolonial formulations as well. In the different conceptualization of the world map after colonialism, Smith often finds that her own geography and genealogy fit neither the colonial nor the postcolonial scheme. She takes issue not just with the temporal closure that the "post" of postcolonial presumes, as other critics of the term have discussed, but also with the fact that postcolonial studies "can still leave out indigenous peoples, our ways of knowing and our current concerns." Like Said, Smith does not complacently locate the legacy of colonial systems somewhere in the distant past.

In reversing the charges of ethnocide and savagery, the writers in this section may seem to run the risk of idealizing precolonial histories, as Césaire, for instance, seems to in his lyrical invocation of such societies. But Césaire anticipates a critique of a romanticized "ante-European past" as well as of a fruitless anti-European stance and insists that he is guilty of neither. His point, he declares, is to denounce the idealized versions of imperialist discourse that, in presenting themselves as the superior alternative, tended to distort precolonial pasts. The politics of returning to a past before colonialism will be considered in subsequent parts, but Smith, in particular, discusses how the process of decolonization need not imply an unreflective hostility to Western knowledge. She is nevertheless not sanguine about the possibility of legitimizing other forms and contexts of knowledge, predicting instead "a new wave of exploration, discovery, exploitation, and appropriation" by academics pillaging "traditional" cultures. She is also acutely aware of the delegitimization of indigenous critiques and concerns through a continued hierarchy in which Western academic models are read as more theoretically sophisticated, as in the antifoundational critiques of racial/ethnic identities or nationalist/nativist ideologies.

4

VALENTIN Y. MUDIMBE

Romanus Pontifex (1454) and the Expansion of Europe

In his 1493 *Inter Coetera* bull, Pope Alexander VI states:

> Among other works well pleasing to the divine majesty and cherished of our heart,
> this assuredly ranks highest, that in our times especially the Catholic faith and the
> Christian religion be exalted and everywhere increased and spread, that the health
> of souls be cared for and that barbarous nations be overthrown and brought to the
> faith itself.

This statement, as well as the general meaning of the bull, has two important implications. First, it signifies that as the successor of Saint Peter, the pope is a visible
representative of God himself, and thus above kings, and can, as he does in *Inter
Coetera*, "give, grant, and assign forever [to European kings] countries and islands
[newly] discovered." Second, non-Christians have no rights to possess or negotiate
any dominion in the then-existing international context, and thus their land is objectively a *terra nullius* (no-man's-land) that may be occupied and seized by Christians
in order to exploit the richness meant by God to be shared by all humankind. In doing
so, they will be helping the inferior "brethren" to insert themselves in the real and
true history of salvation.

Inter Coetera is just one of the official papal letters giving these rights to the
newly joined Houses of Aragon and Castille. It was signed on May 3, 1493. More followed: a sequel, *Inter Coetera (II)*, dated June 28, 1493; and another, also by
Alexander VI, *Eximiae devotionis*, July 1493 (which for political reasons was dated
as if issued on May 3); *Dudum siquidem* of September 25, 1493; *Aeterni Regis* of
June 21, 1497; and *Eximiae devotionis (II)* of November 16, 1501. To these bulls of
the Spanish pope to his king, one should add Julius II's *Universalis Ecclesiae* of July
28, 1508. Apart from giving the king of Spain absolute power over newly discovered
lands, these documents gave him power over ecclesiastical structures in the New

World. The king was to pay for the processes of evangelization, the building of churches, and organization of the new Christianity. And he had a say in the designation of bishops. *Inter Coetera II* of June 28, 1493, confirmed that all lands discovered or to be discovered beyond 100 leagues west and south of the Azores belonged to Spain. The Tordesillas Treaty (June 7, 1493) pushed the line of demarcation further, 270 leagues west of the original. It made Brazil "Portuguese" instead of "Spanish" and divided the world between Portugal and Spain.

Alexander VI gave to the "Kings of Castile and Leon, all singular the aforesaid countries and islands . . . hitherto discovered and to be discovered." Note that *Inter Coetera* I and II, as well as the other documents mentioned, were prepared by a lesser-known bull of Nicolas V, pope from 1447 to 1455 and the founder of the Vatican library. It has been said that, with him, the Renaissance "occupied the papacy," although usually the expression is meant to designate the pontificate of Leo X (1513–21, a Medici).

Romanus Pontifex of 1454 is one of a number of papal bulls that document the Portuguese *ius patronatus,* which include *Dum Diversas* of June 18, 1452; *Ineffabilis et summi* (June 1, 1497) of Alexander VI; *Dudum pro parte* (March 31, 1516), of Leo X; and *Aequum reputamus* of Paul III (November 3, 1534), which codified the dispositions and rights defined in *Dum Diversas, Ineffabilis et summi* and *Dudum pro parte*. They stipulate rights, privileges, and obligations of the House of Portugal in the colonization of newly discovered countries.

Romanus Pontifex (1454) is a five-page letter in the 1730 version of *Magnum Bullarium Romanum seu ejusdem Continuatio* that I consulted. The beginning is interesting for it mentions recent history, but in its overtones alludes to ancient times:

> Alfonso Lusitaniae Regi cujus Filius Henricus studio iter in Indiam Orientalem aperiendi usque ad Guineam ad Nigrum Fluvium penetraverat, et insulas varias detexerat.

> [Alfonso the King of Lusitania, whose son Henry in his zeal to open a route to East India penetrated up to Guinea to the Black River and detected various islands.]

The address to Alfonso pertains to historical events: the discoveries made by the *Infante* Henry the Navigator (1395–1460) in his explorations. *Inter Coetera* of Calixte III (March 13, 1456) gave the *Infante* of Portugal, who was also the grand master of the Military Order of Christ, the *ius patronatus* over all the countries discovered and to be discovered in Africa en route to South Asia. Henry, or more specifically, his executant—the grand prior of the Military Order of Christ residing in the convent of Tomar, Portugal—had absolute civil and religious power over these countries. In 1514, the jurisdictional power passed to the bishop of Funchal and the *ius patronatus* was given back to the king. The second part of the quotation praises Henry for opening up the route to "Oriental India"—Henry had penetrated Guinea up to the Black River *(ad Guineam ad Nigrum Fluvium penetraverat)*. This geographical reference also has Classical overtones. In the first century, Pliny *(Natural History* V, 8, 44) spoke of the *Nigri fluvio eadem natura quae Nilo,* the Black River, which had the same features as the Nile.

The second paragraph of *Romanus Pontifex* establishes the political and theological authority of the letter. Its author states his official title: "Romanus Pontifex Regni coelestis clavigeri successor; et Vicarius Jesus Christi" (Roman Pontiff, successor of the holder of the key to the celestial kingdom, the Vicar of Jesus Christ). It is in this capacity that Nicolas writes to Alfonso V, backed by both a religious and a political history of the papacy, invoked in the controverted bull *Unam Sanctam* (July 11, 1302) of Boniface VIII, in which was affirmed the primacy of the spiritual power (of the pope) over the temporal one (of kings): "It belongs to the spiritual power to institute the temporal one and judge it if it is not good. . . . We say, declare, and define that to be submitted to the Roman pontiff is for any creature a necessity for salvation."

In the second paragraph of the bull, Nicolas specifies the mission of the colonization: to expand Christianity. And he invites the king to follow the tradition exemplified by the royal House of Portugal: a commitment to spread the name of Jesus to the most remote territories of the world.

> Catholicus et versus omnes Creatoris Christimiles, ipsiusque fidei acerrimus ac fortissimus defensor, et intrepidus pugil.

> [A Catholic and soldier of Christ the Creator against all, the keenest and strongest defender of the very faith, and an intrepid fighter.]

The mission is detailed in the third paragraph, and directly linked to Portuguese explorations. An explicit reference, another one, is made to the achievements of the *Infante* Henry, who brought the name of Christ to India and to Guinea: "usque ad *Indos, qui Christi* nomen *colere dicuntur* navigabile fieret . . . *ad Ghineam provinciam tandem parvenirent.*" The Guinea referred to is unclear, but might be the Ethiopia of ancient geographers, since the navigators had reached the source of the Nile *(ad ostium cujusdam magni fluminis Nilis communiter pervenirent).*

Paragraph four of the bull is terrifying. In the name of God, it gives the King of Portugal and his successors the right not only to colonize, but also to convert forcibly to Christianity and enslave *"Saracenos ac paganos"* (Saracens and pagans) in perpetuity. Here is the central statement:

> Nos praemissa omnia et singula debita meditatione pensantes, et attendentes, quod cum olim praefato Alfonso Regi quoscumque Saracenos ac Paganos aliosque Dominia, possessiones, et mobilia et immobilia bona quaecumque per eos detenta

ac possessa invadendi, conquirendi, expugnandi, debellandi et subjugandi, *illo-rumque personas in perpetuam servitute,* ac Regna, Ducatus, Comitatus, Principatus, Dominia, possessiones et bona sibi et successoribus suis applicandi, appropriandi, ac in suos successorumque usus et utilitatem convertendi, *aliis nostris literis* plenam et liberam inter caetera concessimus facultatem.

[We, after weighing with due care the matters put before us altogether and individually, and considering that we have conceded in other letters of ours to the aforementioned King Alfonso among other things the full and free capacity to invade, conquer, take by storm, defeat, and subjugate any Saracens and other Pagans as well as whatever dominions, possessions, movable and immovable property are detained or possessed by them; and to seize and appropriate for himself and for his successors their own persons in perpetual servitude, as well as their kingdoms, dukedoms, counties, principalities, dominions, possessions, and property, and to converty these to his own use and utility and to that of his successors.]

The concept of *terra nullius* resides in the right to dispossess all Saracens and other non-Christians of all their goods (mobile and immobile), the right to invade and conquer these peoples' lands, expel them from it and, when necessary, to fight them and subjugate them in a perpetual servitude *(debellandi et subjugandi, illorumque personas in perpetuam servitute),* and expropriate their possessions.

In the last two paragraphs, Nicolas reinscribes his letter in the tradition of his Church's politics.

The *Romanus Pontifex* makes several points. First, non-Christian peoples have no ownership rights to the land on which they are living. Second, when Christian Europeans—namely, Spanish and Portuguese people—met natives, they would invite the local king or chief and his advisers to a meeting. They would present them with a Christian interpretation of history that closely followed the Old and New Testaments. At the end of the meeting, the natives were invited to pledge submission and to convert. If they failed to accept the "truth" and, politically, to become "colonized," it was not only legal but also an act of faith and a religious duty for the colonizers to kill the natives. The philosophical system underlying the *Romanus Pontifex* and its explanation of how to deal with non-Westerners was Aristotelian, which, as we know, also justifies slavery. Whereas for the "liberal" Father Las Casas (1951), the two *Inter Coetera* bulls signified that Spain had the right to expand Christianity in America, but without taking the Indians' lands, for Father Sepúlveda, a rigorous Aristotelian philosopher, "all natives were meant to be subjugated." According to Sepúlveda, God created natives for a purpose, and it was morally wrong to oppose the enslavement and exploitation of natives because such opposition thwarted that purpose.

A comprehensive study of the *"terra nullius"* politics (by Keller, Lissitzyn, and Mann 1938) indicates that between 1400 and 1800 not one non-European nation was considered to have the right "to possess or to transfer any dominion in the international law sense." Keller, Lissitzyn, and Mann provide concrete illustrations of the ways in which Europeans established their sovereignty rights in newly discovered lands. Following are some of their examples of the Portuguese practice.

In 1419, Joâo Gonzalves Zarco discovered Madeira. In accordance with the instructions he had received from Prince Henry, he took official possession of the island through three symbolic acts: first, he erected a cross; secondly, a mass was celebrated; thirdly, clods of earth from the island were taken and brought back to Portugal, given to Prince Henry. The island was colonized after and became part of Portugal.

In 1494, Diego Caon discovered the mouth of the Congo River on the west coast of Africa. Diego Caon erected "a pillar of stone with the royal arms and letters of Portugal" on it. In the same manner, on his trip to India, Vasco da Gama stopped in the Kingdom of Melinde, on the East Coast of Africa.

In the Kingdom of Melinde, on the east coast of Africa, Da Gama and his company struck up a very cordial friendship with the King. The Portuguese mentioned to the King a certain "mark," the name of the King of Portugal written upon a stone, their King's sign, placed in the countries of all his friends in commemoration of his sincerity. The King of Melinde was highly pleased at this intelligence, and wanted to have the pillar placed at the gates of his palace, but the Portuguese replied ingenuously that it would not be very easily seen by those entering the port, and that it should be displayed in a more prominent location. The King agreeing to this, a tall column of white marble, bearing the two escutcheons mentioned above, with the name of King Manoel I engraved on the base, was set up on a high hill overlooking the harbor, visible far out to sea. Correa adds that Da Gama had six of these pillars, already suitably engraved, with him, ordered made by his King, who commanded that they be set up in countries where friendship was established, so that the remembrance of it might last forever, "and that they might be seen by all nations that might come later." (Keller et al. 1938:25)

A more elaborate ceremony occurred in 1481, when Don Diego took formal possession of the Guinea Coast in West Africa.

There the cavalcade proceeded . . . to a large tree at no great distance from the village Aldea, as the most desirable situation for their intended fortress; the royal arms were immediately displayed upon the tree and an altar raised beneath; the whole company proceeded to join in the first mass that was celebrated in Guinea.

The Spaniards were even less informal. Their usual practice generally included a formal declaration of taking possession of the "terra nullius," a physical sign symbolizing the act and, finally, a symbolic acting out of the new sovereignty. A 1514 royal instruction to the explorer De Solis specifies the steps:

> The manner that you must have in the taking of possession of the lands and parts which you shall have discovered is to be that, being in the land or part that you shall have discovered, you shall make before notary public and the greatest possible number of witnesses, and the best-known ones, an act of possession in our name, cutting trees and boughs, and digging or making, if there be an opportunity, some small building *(edificio)*, which should be in a part where there is some marked hill or a large tree, and you shall say how many leagues it is from the sea, a little more or less, and in which part, and what signs it has, and you shall make a gallows there and have somebody bring a complaint before you.

Indeed, the formal statement stipulates that the new country is taken in "the name of the king of Spain." Thus, for example, Columbus, during his first trip in 1492, took possession of islands in the West Indies "in the name of the Spanish monarchs by public proclamation and unfurled banners." And Spanish explorers usually put up crosses, as did Columbus on his third and fourth voyages, and Vincente Yanéz Pinzon and Diego de Lepe in 1500 in South America at the sites where the ceremonies of taking possession took place. Sometimes, the physical ceremony amounted to simply erecting a pile of stones, as Balboa did in 1513 on the Pacific Coast. Finally, the new jurisdiction and control over the land was symbolized in various acts, such as cutting trees and drinking water, as Pinzon did on the northern coast of South America. Diego de Lepe also cut down trees, but in addition marked his name on others. On his second trip, Columbus took possession of new territories by means of a legal ceremony similar to that by which Unamuno took possession of parts of the coast of California, as described in a report of 1587:

> Having left orders aboard ship as to what was to be done, and having elected *alcaldes* and *regidores*, that there might be some one to take possession of the port and whatever else might be discovered, I landed with twelve soldiers. . . .
>
> When we reached this hill, as it seemed to be a suitable place to take possession in His Majesty's name of the port and the country; seeing that I and the rest of the party had landed and traversed the country roundabout and the port quietly and pacifically, as in territory belonging to his domain [*de la demarcacion i Corona del Rey*], I did so in the name of King Philip our master, in due legal form, through Diego Vasquez Mexia (one of the *alcaldes* elected for this purpose) in his capacity of *Justicia*, setting up a cross as a sign of the Christian faith and of the possession taken in His Majesty's name of the port and the country, cutting branches from the trees which grew thereabouts, and performing the other customary ceremonies.
>
> (Keller et al. 1938:40)

The Spanish taking possession of a "terra nullius" and its symbolism often included a recitation known as the *Requirement,* although it was seldom performed to the extent specified in the instructions. Fundamentally, it was a systematic presentation of the Christian philosophy of creation and history to the natives. At the end of the recitation, the natives were invited "to pledge allegiance to the pope and the king of Spain." If the natives refused to make the pledge, it was legal to occupy the natives' land by force, if necessary.

The French practice before the end of the seventeenth century was rather simple, compared with the Spanish or the English ceremonies. It was almost as informal as the Portuguese practice. It then took on a highly structured form in the last quarter of the seventeenth century, as exemplified by the ritual of June 14, 1671, during which Daumont de Saint-Lusson—representative of Jean Talon, intendant of Canada, and personal representative of the king of France—took possession of the Lake Superior region. Leading his men, de Saint-Lusson marched to the top of a hill where Indian chiefs and representatives were already assembled.

All around the great throng of Indians stood or crouched or reclined at length, with eyes and ears intent. A large cross of wood had been made ready. Dablon [one of the Jesuit missionaries in the party], in solemn form pronounced his blessing on it, and then it was reared and planted in the ground, while the French, uncovered, sang the *Vexilla Regis*. Then a post of cedar was planted beside it, with a metal plate attached, engraven with the Royal Arms; while Saint-Lusson's followers sang the *Exaudiat,* and one of the Jesuits uttered a prayer for the King. Saint-Lusson now advanced, and, holding his sword in one hand, and raising with the other a sod of earth, proclaimed in a loud voice:

"In the name of the Most High, Mighty and Redoubted Monarch, Louis, Fourteenth of that name, Most Christian King of France and Navarre, I take possession of this place, Sainte Marie du Saut, as also of Lakes Huron and Superior, the Island of Manitoulin, and all countries, rivers, lakes and streams contiguous thereunto,— both those which have been discovered and those which may be discovered hereafter, in all their length and breadth, bounded on the one side by the seas of the North and the West and on the other by the South Sea: declaring to the nations thereof that from this time forth they are vassals of His Majesty, bound to obey his laws and follow his customs; promising them on his part all succor and protection against the invasions of their enemies; declaring to all other potentates, princes, sovereigns, states and republics,—to them and to their subjects,—that they cannot and are not to seize or settle upon any parts of the aforesaid countries, save only under the good pleasure of His Most Christian Majesty, and of him who will govern in his behalf; and this on pain of incurring his resentment and the effort of his arms. Vive le Roy!"   (Keller et al. 1938:125)

From the sixteenth century on, the British practice was a highly elaborate procedure, which, like the Spanish, included specific steps: the first was to obtain letters of patent. Then various rites were performed in taking possession of a territory in the name of the king or the queen. These included at least the following three: the erection of a symbolic sign, a formal declaration proclaiming that the land was under English sovereignty, and the promulgation of a set of laws. The voyage of Sir Humphrey Gilbert provides a typical example. Letters of patent, a royal grant of exclusive privilege for his discoveries, were given to him on June 11, 1578. The queen gave him "free libertie and licence . . . to discover, find, search out . . . barbarous lands, countries and territories not actually possessed by any Christian prince or people."

In 1583, Gilbert anchored in St. John's Harbour, Newfoundland. The official ceremony of taking possession was organized on August 5, 1583, "in the presence of the entire company and some 'strangers.'" After the ritual, Gilbert in the name of Queen Elizabeth's right of sovereignty and of his own lordship, promulgated a code of three laws that (a) established the Church of England in Newfoundland; (b) made punishable as high treason any acts prejudicial to the Queen's right of possession; (c) made punishable any words of dishonor to the Queen, for which the penalty was to have one's ears removed and one's ship and goods confiscated.

In conclusion, the *Romanus Pontifex* of 1454 shaped all subsequent agreements concerning rights to newly discovered lands. It not only laid the foundation for the succeeding papal bulls, but throughout the ensuing years its basic tenets were faithfully maintained even as its politics were modified and transformed to fit concrete demands in the expansion of European projects. Despite the great number of agreements and contracts that were made in this connection, no European power considered the natives to have any sovereignty or any accepted rights over their lands, except in a few rare instances in territories of Southeast and Eastern Asia, notably China. These agreements were, in their intent and in their form, devices allowing the Europeans to enter the country and build *avant postes*.

The *Romanus Pontifex* philosophy also reflects two fundamental concepts that were to guide colonization. First, it affirmed the primacy of the papacy over the Christian kings, going back in its most explicit and extreme expression to Boniface VIII's bull *Unam Sanctam* of November 1, 1302. In the mid-fifteenth century, the spiritual primacy and rights were, as we have seen, objects of political negotiations. Second, it provided the basis for the *terra nullius* concept—that is, the concept of the European right of sovereignty outside of Europe, and ultimately the right of colonization and the practice of slavery. This philosophical position was said to spring from "Natural Law." Thus, just as in a forest where there are stronger and weaker essences, the latter living and developing under the protection of the former, the human "races" would observe the same rule. It would be the "mission" of the stronger race to help their inferior "brethren" to grow up; and in any case, according to the doctrine, it was up to the most advanced race to make sure that all goods made by God for the whole of humankind should be exploited. In 1526, Francisco de Vitoria justified colonial conquests on the basis of Christian trade rights, explaining that it was God's intent that all nations should trade with each other. His contemporary, Sepúlveda, invoking Aristotle's lesson, maintained that natives were meant by God to be dominated. In sum, from a Christian point of view, to oppose the process of colonization or that of slavery could only be morally wrong.

REFERENCES

Columbus, Christopher. 1960. *The Journal of Christopher Columbus*. Translated by Jane Vigneras, revised by L. A. Vigneras. London.

Hodgen, Margaret T.. 1971. *Early Anthropology in the Sixteenth and Seventeenth Centuries*. Philadelphia: University of Pennsylvania Press.

Hulme, Peter (editor). 1986. *Colonial Encounters: European and the Native Caribbean 1492–1797*. London: Methuen.

Keller, A. S., O. J. Lissitzyn, and J. F. Mann. 1938. *Creation of Rights of Sovereignty through Symbolic Acts 1400–1800*. New York: Columbia University Press.

Las Casas, B. de. 1951. *Historia de las Indias*. 3 vols. Mexico City: Ed. A. Millares Carlo.

Pliny. 1942. *Natural History*. An English translation by H. Rackham. Cambridge, Mass.: Harvard University Press.

Todorov, T.. 1984. *The Conquest of America*. New York: Harper and Row.

5

AIMÉ CÉSAIRE

From *Discourse on Colonialism*

A civilization that proves incapable of solving the problems it creates is a decadent civilization.

A civilization that chooses to close its eyes to its most crucial problems is a stricken civilization.

A civilization that uses its principles for trickery and deceit is a dying civilization.

The fact is that the so-called European civilization—"Western" civilization—as it has been shaped by two centuries of bourgeois rule, is incapable of solving the two major problems to which its existence has given rise: the problem of the proletariat and the colonial problem; that Europe is unable to justify itself either before the bar of "reason" or before the bar of "conscience"; and that, increasingly, it takes refuge in a hypocrisy which is all the more odious because it is less and less likely to deceive.

Europe is indefensible.

Apparently that is what the American strategists are whispering to each other.

That in itself is not serious.

What is serious is that "Europe" is morally, spiritually indefensible.

And today the indictment is brought against it not by the European masses alone, but on a world scale, by tens and tens of millions of men who, from the depths of slavery, set themselves up as judges.

The colonialists may kill in Indochina, torture in Madagascar, imprison in Black Africa, crack down in the West Indies. Henceforth the colonized know that they have an advantage over them. They know that their temporary "masters" are lying.

Therefore that their masters are weak.

And since I have been asked to speak about colonization and civilization, let us go straight to the principal lie which is the source of all the others.

Colonization and civilization?

In dealing with this subject, the commonest curse is to be the dupe in good faith of a collective hypocrisy that cleverly misrepresents problems, the better to legitimize the hateful solutions provided for them.

In other words, the essential thing here is to see clearly, to think clearly—that is, dangerously—and to answer clearly the innocent first question: what, fundamentally, is colonization? To agree on what it is not: neither evangelization, nor a philanthropic enterprise, nor a desire to push back the frontiers of ignorance, disease, and tyranny, nor a project undertaken for the greater glory of God, nor an attempt to extend the rule of law. To admit once for all, without flinching at the consequences, that the decisive actors here are the adventurer and the pirate, the wholesale grocer and the ship owner, the gold digger and the merchant, appetite and force, and behind them, the baleful projected shadow of a form of civilization which, at a certain point in its history, finds itself obliged, for internal reasons, to extend to a world scale the competition of its antagonistic economies.

Pursuing my analysis, I find that hypocrisy is of recent date; that neither Cortez discovering Mexico from the top of the great teocalli, nor Pizzaro before Cuzco (much less Marco Polo before Cambaluc), claims that he is the harbinger of a superior order; that they kill; that they plunder; that they have helmets, lances, cupidities; that the slavering apologists came later; that the chief culprit in this domain is Christian pedantry, which laid down the dishonest equations *Christianity = civilization, paganism = savagery,* from which there could not but ensue abominable colonialist and racist consequences, whose victims were to be the Indians, the yellow peoples, and the Negroes.

That being settled, I admit that it is a good thing to place different civilizations in contact with each other; that it is an excellent thing to blend different worlds; that whatever its own particular genius may be, a civilization that withdraws into itself atrophies; that for civilizations, exchange is oxygen; that the great good fortune of Europe is to have been a crossroads; and that because it was the locus of all ideas, the receptacle of all philosophies, the meeting place of all sentiments, it was the best center for the redistribution of energy.

But then I ask the following question: has colonization really *placed civilizations in contact?* Or, if you prefer, of all the ways of *establishing contact,* was it the best?

I answer no.

And I say that between *colonization* and *civilization* there is an infinite distance; that out of all the colonial expeditions that have been undertaken, out of all the colonial statutes that have been drawn up, out of all the memoranda that have been despatched by all the ministries, there could not come a single human value.

. . .

I see clearly what colonization has destroyed: the wonderful Indian civilizations—and neither Deterding nor Royal Dutch nor Standard Oil will ever console me for the Aztecs and the Incas.

I see clearly the civilizations, condemned to perish at a future date, into which it has introduced a principle of ruin: the South Sea islands, Nigeria, Nyasaland. I see less clearly the contributions it has made.

Security? Culture? The rule of law? In the meantime, I look around and wherever there are colonizers and colonized face to face, I see force, brutality, cruelty, sadism, conflict, and, in a parody of education, the hasty manufacture of a few thousand subordinate functionaries, "boys," artisans, office clerks, and interpreters necessary for the smooth operation of business.

I spoke of contact.

Between colonizer and colonized there is room only for forced labor, intimidation, pressure, the police, taxation, theft, rape, compulsory crops, contempt, mistrust, arrogance, self-complacency, swinishness, brainless elites, degraded masses.

No human contact, but relations of domination and submission which turn the colonizing man into a classroom monitor, an army sergeant, a prison guard, a slave driver, and the indigenous man into an instrument of production.

My turn to state an equation: colonization = "thingification."

I hear the storm. They talk to me about progress, about "achievements," diseases cured, improved standards of living.

I am talking about societies drained of their essence, cultures trampled underfoot, institutions undermined, lands confiscated, religions smashed, magnificent artistic creations destroyed, extraordinary *possibilities* wiped out.

They throw facts at my head, statistics, mileages of roads, canals, and railroad tracks.

I am talking about thousands of men sacrificed to the Congo-Océan.[1] I am talking about those who, as I write this, are digging the harbor of Abidjan by hand. I am talking about millions of men torn from their gods, their land, their habits, their life—from life, from the dance, from wisdom.

I am talking about millions of men in whom fear has been cunningly instilled, who have been taught to have an inferiority complex, to tremble, kneel, despair, and behave like flunkeys.

They dazzle me with the tonnage of cotton or cocoa that has been exported, the acreage that has been planted with olive trees or grapevines.

I am talking about natural *economies* that have been disrupted—harmonious and viable *economies* adapted to the indigenous population—about food crops destroyed, malnutrition permanently introduced, agricultural development oriented solely toward the benefit of the metropolitan countries, about the looting of products, the looting of raw materials.

They pride themselves on abuses eliminated.

I too talk about abuses, but what I say is that on the old ones—very real—they have superimposed others—very detestable. They talk to me about local tyrants brought to reason; but I note that in general the old tyrants get on very well with the new ones, and that there has been established between them, to the detriment of the people, a circuit of mutual services and complicity.

They talk to me about civilization, I talk about proletarianization and mystification.

For my part, I make a systematic defense of the non-European civilizations.

Every day that passes, every denial of justice, every beating by the police, every demand of the workers that is drowned in blood, every scandal that is hushed up, every punitive expedition, every police van, every gendarme, and every militiaman, brings home to us the value of our old societies.

They were communal societies, never societies of the many for the few.

They were societies that were not only ante-capitalist, as has been said, but also *anti-capitalist*.

They were democratic societies, always.

They were cooperative societies, fraternal societies.

I make a systematic defense of the societies destroyed by imperialism.

They were the fact, they did not pretend to be the idea; despite their faults, they were neither to be hated nor condemned. They were content to be. In them, neither the word *failure* nor the word *avatar* had any meaning. They kept hope intact.

Whereas those are the only words that can, in all honesty, be applied to the European enterprises outside Europe. My only consolation is that periods of colonization pass, that nations sleep only for a time, and that peoples remain.

This being said, it seems that in certain circles they pretend to have discovered in me an "enemy of Europe" and a prophet of the return to the ante-European past.

For my part, I search in vain for the place where I could have expressed such views; where I ever underestimated the importance of Europe in the history of human thought; where I ever preached a *return* of any kind; where I ever claimed that there could be a *return*.

The truth is that I have said something very different: to wit, that the great historical tragedy of Africa has been not so much that it was too late in making contact with the rest of the world, as the manner in which that contact was brought about; that Europe began to "propagate" at a time when it had fallen into the hands of the most unscrupulous financiers and captains of industry; that it was our misfortune to encounter that particular Europe on our path; and that Europe is responsible before the human community for the highest heap of corpses in history.

In another connection, in judging colonization, I have added that Europe has gotten on very well indeed with all the local feudal lords who agreed to serve, woven a villainous complicity with them, rendered their tyranny more effective and more efficient, and that it has actually tended to prolong artificially the survival of local pasts in their most pernicious aspects.

I have said—and this is something very different—that colonialist Europe has grafted modern abuse onto ancient injustice, hateful racism onto old inequality.

That if I am attacked on the grounds of intent, I maintain that colonialist Europe is dishonest in trying to justify its colonizing activity *a posteriori* by the obvious material progress that has been achieved in certain fields under the colonial regime—since *sudden change* is always possible, in history as elsewhere; since no one knows at what stage of material development these same countries would have been if Europe had not intervened; since the technical outfitting of Africa and Asia, their administrative reorganization, in a word, their "Europeanization," was (as is proved by the example of Japan) in no way tied to the European *occupation;* since the Europeanization of the non-European continents could have been accomplished otherwise than under the heel of Europe; since this movement of Europeanization *was in progress;* since it was even slowed down; since in any case it was distorted by the European takeover.

The proof is that at present it is the indigenous peoples of Africa and Asia who are demanding schools, and colonialist Europe which refuses them; that it is the African who is asking for ports and roads, and colonialist Europe which is niggardly on this score; that it is the colonized man who wants to move forward, and the colonizer who holds things back.

NOTES

1 A railroad line connecting Brazzaville with the port of Pointe-Noire. (Trans.)

6

ROBERTO FERNÁNDEZ RETAMAR

Caliban

Notes towards a Discussion of Culture in Our America

. . .

Toward the History of Caliban

Caliban is Shakespeare's anagram for "cannibal," an expression which he had already used to mean anthropophagus, in the third part of *Henry IV* and *Othello,* and which comes in turn from the word "carib." Before the arrival of the Europeans, whom they resisted heroically, the Carib Indians were the most valiant and war-like inhabitants of the very lands which we occupy today. Their name lives on in the term Caribbean Sea (referred to genially by some as the American Mediterranean; just as if we were to call the Mediterranean the Caribbean of Europe). But the name *carib* in itself—as well as in its deformation, *cannibal*—has been perpetuated in the eyes of Europeans above all as a defamation. It is the term in this sense which Shakespeare takes up and elaborates into a complex symbol. Because of its exceptional importance to us, it will be useful to trace in some detail its history.

In the *Diario de Navegación* (Navigation Log Books) of Columbus there appear the first European accounts of the men who were to occasion the symbol in question. On Sunday, 4 November 1492, less than a month after Columbus arrived on the continent which was to be called America, one reads the following entry: "He learned also that far from the place there were men with one eye and others with dogs' muzzles, who ate human beings."[1] On 23 November, this entry: ". . . which they said was very large [the island of Haiti] and that on it lived people who had only one eye and others called cannibals, of whom they seemed to be very afraid." On 11 December it is noted ". . . that *caniba* refers in fact to the people of El Gran Can," which explains the deformation undergone by the name *carib*—also used by Columbus. In the very letter of 15 February 1493, "dated on the caravelle off the island of

Canaria" in which Columbus announces to the world his "discovery," he writes: "I have found, then, neither monsters nor news of any, save for one island [Quarives], the second upon entering the Indies, which is populated with people held by every-one on the islands to be very ferocious, and who eat human flesh."[2]

This *carib/cannibal* image contrasts with another one of the American man presented in the writings of Columbus: that of the Arauaco of the Greater Antilles—our Taino Indian primarily—whom he describes as peaceful, meek, and even timorous and cowardly. Both visions of the American aborigine will circulate vertiginously throughout Europe, each coming to know its own particular development: the Taino will be transformed into the paradisical inhabitant of a utopic world; by 1516 Thomas More will publish his *Utopia*, the similarities of which to the island of Cuba have been indicated, almost to the point of rapture, by Ezequiel Martínez Estrada.[3] The Carib, on the other hand, will become a *cannibal*—an anthropophage, a bestial man situated on the margins of civilization, who must be opposed to the very death. But there is less of a contradiction than might appear at first glance between the two visions; they constitute, simply, options in the ideological arsenal of a vigorous emerging bourgeoisie. Francisco de Quevedo translated "utopia" as "There is no such place." With respect to these two visions, one might add: "There is no such man." The notion of an edenic creature comprehends, in more contemporary terms, a working hypothesis for the bourgeois left, and as such offers an ideal model of the perfect society free from the constrictions of that feudal world against which the bourgeoisie is in fact struggling. Generally speaking, the utopic vision throws upon these lands projects for political reforms unrealized in the countries of origin. In this sense its line of development is far from extinguished. Indeed, it meets with certain perpetuators—apart from its radical perpetuators who are the consequential revolutionaries—in the numerous advisors who unflaggingly propose to countries emerging from colonialism magic formulas from the metropolis to solve the grave problems colonialism has left us and which, of course, they have not yet resolved in their own countries. It goes without saying that these proponents of "There is no such place" are irritated by the insolent fact that the place *does* exist and, quite naturally, has all the virtues and defects not of a project but of genuine reality.

As for the vision of the *cannibal*, it corresponds—also in more contemporary terms—to the right-wing of that same bourgeoisie. It belongs to the ideological arsenal of politicians of action, those who perform the dirty work in whose fruits the charming dreamers of utopias will equally share. That the Caribs were as Columbus depicted them (and after him, an unending throng of followers) is about as probable as the existence of one-eyed men, men with dog-muzzles or tails, or even the Amazons mentioned by the explorer in his pages where Greco-Latin mythology, the medieval bestiary, and the novel of chivalry all play their part. It is a question of the typically degraded vision offered by the colonizer of the man he is colonizing. That we ourselves may have at one time believed in this version only proves to what extent we are infected with the ideology of the enemy. It is typical that we have applied the term *cannibal* not to the extinct aborigine of our isles, but, above all, to the African black who appeared in those shameful Tarzan films. For it is the colonizer who brings us together, who reveals the profound similarities existing above and beyond our secondary differences. The colonizer's version explains to us that owing to his irremediable bestiality, there was no alternative to the extermination of the Carib. What it does not explain is why, even before the Carib, the peaceful and kindly Arauaco was also exterminated. Simply speaking the two groups suffered equally one of the greatest ethnocides recorded in history. (Needless to say, this line of action is still more alive than the earlier one.) In relation to this fact, it will always be necessary to point out the case of those men who, being on the fringe both of Utopianism (which has nothing to do with the actual America) and of the shameless ideology of plunder, stood in their midst opposed to the conduct of the colonialists, and passionately, lucidly, and valiantly defended the flesh-and-blood aborigine. In the forefront of such men stands the magnificent figure of Father Bartolomé de Las Casas, whom Bolívar called "the apostle of America," and whom Martí extolled unreservedly. Unfortunately, such men were exceptions.

One of the most widely disseminated European Utopian works is Montaigne's essay "De los caníbales" ("On Cannibals") which appeared in 1580. There we find a presentation of those creatures who "keep their natural properties and virtues, which are the true and useful ones, vigorous and alive."[4]

Giovanni Floro's English translation of the *Essays* was published in 1603. Not only was Floro a personal friend of Shakespeare, but the copy of the translation that Shakespeare owned and annotated is still preserved. This piece of information would be of no further importance, but for the fact that it proves beyond a shadow of doubt that the book was one of the direct sources of Shakespeare's last great work, *The Tempest* (1612). Even one of the characters of the play, Gonzalo, who incarnates the Renaissance humanist, at one point closely glosses entire lines from Floro's Montaigne, originating precisely in the essay "On Cannibals." This fact makes the form in which Shakespeare presents his character *Caliban/cannibal* even stranger. Because if in Montaigne—in this case, an unquestionable literary source for Shakespeare— "there is nothing barbarian or savage in these nations . . . what happens is that everyone calls what is foreign to his own customs *barbarian,*"[5] in Shakespeare, on the other hand, *Caliban/cannibal* is a savage and deformed slave who cannot be degraded enough. What has happened is simply that in depicting Caliban, Shakespeare, an implacable realist, here takes *the other option* of the emerging bourgeois world. Regarding the utopian vision, it does indeed exist in the work but is unrelated to Caliban; as was said before, it is expressed by the harmonious humanist Gonzalo.

Shakespeare thus confirms that both ways of considering the American, far from being in opposition, were perfectly reconcilable. As for the concrete man, present him in the guise of an animal, rob him of his land, enslave him so as to live from his toil, and at the right moment, exterminate him; this latter of course, only as long as there was someone who could be depended on to perform the arduous tasks in his stead. In one revealing passage, Prospero warns his daughter that they could not do without Caliban: "We cannot miss him: he does make our fire, / Fetch in our wood, and serves in offices / that profit us" (I, ii). The Utopian vision can and must do without men of flesh and blood. After all, *there is no such place.*

There is no doubt at this point that *The Tempest* alludes to America, that its island is the mythification of one of our islands. Astrana Marín, who mentions the "clearly Indian (American) ambience of the island," recalls some of the actual voyages along this continent that inspired Shakespeare and even furnished him, with slight variations, with the names of not a few of his characters: Miranda, Fernando, Sebastian, Alonso, Gonzalo, Setebos.[6] More important than this is the knowledge that Caliban is our Carib.

We are not interested in following all the possible readings that have been made of this notable work since its appearance,[7] and shall merely point out some interpretations. The first of these comes from Ernest Renan, who published his drama *Caliban: Suite de La Tempête* in 1878.[8] In his work, Caliban is the incarnation of the people presented in their worst light, except that this time his conspiracy against Prospero is successful and he achieves power—which ineptitude and corruption will surely prevent him from retaining. Prospero lurks in the darkness awaiting his revenge, and Ariel disappears. This reading owes less to Shakespeare than to the Paris Commune which had taken place only seven years before. Naturally, Renan was among the writers of the French bourgeoisie who savagely took part against the prodigious "assault of heaven."[9] Beginning with this event, his anti-democratic feeling stiffened even further. "In his *Philosophical Dialogues,*" Lidsky tells us, "he believes that the solution would lie in the creation of an *elite* of intelligent beings who alone would govern and possess the secrets of science."[10] Characteristically, Renan's aristocratic and pre-Fascist elitism and his hatred of the common people of his country are united with an even greater hatred for the inhabitants of the colonies. It is instructive to hear him express himself along these lines.

> We aspire [he says] not to equality but to domination. The country of a foreign race must again be a country of serfs, of agricultural laborers or industrial workers. It is not a question of eliminating the inequalities among men but of broadening them and making them law.[11]

And on another occasion:

The regeneration of the inferior or bastard races by the superior races is within the providential human order. With us, the common man is nearly always a *declassé* noble man, his heavy hand is better suited to handling the sword than the menial tool. Rather than work he chooses to fight, that is, he returns to his first state. *Regere imperio populos*—that is our vocation. Pour forth this all-consuming activity onto countries which, like China, are crying aloud for foreign conquest. [. . .] Nature has made a race of workers, the Chinese race, with its marvelous manual dexterity and almost no sense of honor; govern them with justice, levying from them, in return for the blessing of such a government, an ample allowance for the conquering race, and they will be satisfied; a race of tillers of the soil, the black [. . .]; a race of masters and soldiers, the European race. [. . .] *Let each do that which he is made for, and all will be well.*[12]

It is unnecessary to gloss these lines, which as Césaire rightly says, came from the pen, not of Hitler, but of the French humanist Ernest Renan.

The initial destiny of the Caliban myth on our own American soil is a surprising one. Twenty years after Renan had published his *Caliban,* in other words, in 1898, the United States intervened in the Cuban war of independence against Spain and subjected Cuba to its tutelage, converting her as of 1902 (and until 1959) into her first *neocolony;* while Puerto Rico and the Philippines became colonies of a traditional nature. The fact—which had been anticipated by Martí years before—moved the Latin American *intelligentsia.* Elsewhere I have recalled that "ninety-eight" is not only a Spanish date that gives its name to a complex group of writers and thinkers of that country, but it is also, and perhaps most importantly, a Latin American date which should serve to designate a no less complex group of writers and thinkers on this side of the Atlantic, generally known by the vague name of *modernistas.*[13] It is "ninety-eight"—the visible presence of North American imperialism in Latin America—already foretold by Martí, which informs the later work of someone like Darío or Rodó.

. . .

NOTES

1 Cited, along with subsequent references to the *Diario,* by Julio C. Salas, *Etnografía americana. Los indios caribes. Estudio sobre el origen del Mito de la antropofagia* (Madrid, 1920). The book exposes "the irrationality of [the] charge that some American tribes devoured human flesh, maintained in the past by those interested in enslaving [the] Indians and repeated by the chroniclers and historians, many of whom were supporters of slavery" (p. 211).

2 *La carta de Colón anunciando el descubrimiento del nuevo mundo. 15 de febrero—14 de marzo, 1493* (Madrid, 1956), p. 20.

3 Ezequiel Martínez Estrada, "El Nuevo Mundo, la Isla de Utopia y la Isla de Cuba," *Casa de las Américas,* 33 (*noviembre-diciembre,* 1965). This issue is entitled *Homenaje a Ezequiel Martínez Estrada.*

4 Miguel de Montaigne, *Ensayos,* trans. C. Roman y Salamero, Vol. 1 (Buenos Aires, 1948), p. 248.

5 *Loc. cit.*

6 William Shakespeare, *Obras completas.* trans. with an introductory study and notes by Luis Astrana Marín (Madrid, 1961), pp. 107–8.

7 Thus, e.g., Jan Kott notes that until the nineteenth century "there were several Shakespearean scholars who attempted to read *The Tempest* as a biography in the literal sense, or as an allegorical political drama." Jan Kott, *Apuntes sobre Shakespeare,* trans. J. Maurizio (Barcelona, 1969), p. 353.

8 Ernest Renan, *Caliban, Suite de La Tempête. Drame Philosophique* (Paris, 1878).

9 V. Arthur Adamov, *La Commune de Paris* (8 *mars*–28 *mars* 1871): *Anthologie* (Paris, 1959); and especially Paul Lidsky, *Les écrivains contre la Commune* (Paris, 1970).

10 Paul Lidsky, *op. cit.,* p. 82.

11 Cited by Aimé Césaire in *Discours sur le colonialisme,* 3rd ed. (Paris, 1955), p. 13. This is a remarkable work, and I have incorporated many of its hypotheses (partially trans. in *Casa de las Américas*, 36–37 [*mayo–agosto*, 1966], an issue dedicated to *Africa en américa*).

12 *Ibid.,* pp. 14–15.

13 *Vid.* R.F.R., "Modernismo, noventiocho, subdesarrollo," read at the 3rd Congress of the International Association of Hispanists, Mexico City, Aug. 1968; collected in *Ensayo de otro mundo,* 2nd ed. (Santiago de Chile, 1969).

7

EDWARD W. SAID

Introduction to *Orientalism*

I

On a visit to Beirut during the terrible civil war of 1975–1976 a French journalist wrote regretfully of the gutted downtown area that "it had once seemed to belong to . . . the Orient of Chateaubriand and Nerval."[1] He was right about the place, of course, especially so far as a European was concerned. The Orient was almost a European invention, and had been since antiquity a place of romance, exotic beings, haunting memories and landscapes, remarkable experiences. Now it was disappearing; in a sense it had happened, its time was over. Perhaps it seemed irrelevant that Orientals themselves had something at stake in the process, that even in the time of Chateaubriand and Nerval Orientals had lived there, and that now it was they who were suffering; the main thing for the European visitor was a European representation of the Orient and its contemporary fate, both of which had a privileged communal significance for the journalist and his French readers.

Americans will not feel quite the same about the Orient, which for them is much more likely to be associated very differently with the Far East (China and Japan, mainly). Unlike the Americans, the French and the British—less so the Germans, Russians, Spanish, Portuguese, Italians, and Swiss—have had a long tradition of what I shall be calling *Orientalism,* a way of coming to terms with the Orient that is based on the Orient's special place in European Western experience. The Orient is not only adjacent to Europe; it is also the place of Europe's greatest and richest and oldest colonies, the source of its civilizations and languages, its cultural contestant, and one of its deepest and most recurring images of the Other. In addition, the Orient has helped to define Europe (or the West) as its contrasting image, idea, personality, experience. Yet none of this Orient is merely imaginative. The Orient is an integral part of European *material* civilization and culture. Orientalism expresses and represents that part culturally and even ideologically as a mode of discourse with supporting institutions, vocabulary, scholarship, imagery, doctrines, even colonial bureaucracies and colonial styles. In contrast, the American understanding of the Orient will seem considerably less dense, although our recent Japanese, Korean, and Indochinese adventures ought now to be creating a more sober, more realistic "Oriental" awareness. Moreover, the vastly expanded American political and economic role in the Near East (the Middle East) makes great claims on our understanding of that Orient.

It will be clear to the reader (and will become clearer still throughout the many pages that follow) that by Orientalism I mean several things, all of them, in my opinion, interdependent. The most readily accepted designation for Orientalism is an academic one, and indeed the label still serves in a number of academic institutions. Anyone who teaches, writes about, or researches the Orient—and this applies whether the person is an anthropologist, sociologist, historian, or philologist—either in its specific or its general aspects, is an Orientalist, and what he or she does is Orientalism. Compared with *Oriental studies* or *area studies,* it is true that the term *Orientalism* is less preferred by specialists today, both because it is too vague and general and because it connotes the high-handed executive attitude of nineteenth-century and early-twentieth-century European colonialism. Nevertheless books are written and congresses held with "the Orient" as their main focus, with the Orientalist in his new or old guise as their main authority. The point is that even if it does not survive as it once did, Orientalism lives on academically through its doctrines and theses about the Orient and the Oriental.

Related to this academic tradition, whose fortunes, transmigrations, specializations, and transmissions are in part the subject of this study, is a more general meaning for Orientalism. Orientalism is a style of thought based upon an ontological and epistemological distinction made between "the Orient" and (most of the time) "the Occident." Thus a very large mass of writers, among whom are poets, novelists, philosophers, political theorists, economists, and imperial administrators, have accepted the basic distinction between East and West as the starting point for elaborate theories, epics, novels, social descriptions, and political accounts concerning the Orient, its people, customs, "mind," destiny, and so on. *This* Orientalism can accommodate Aeschylus, say, and Victor Hugo, Dante, and Karl Marx. A little later in this Introduction I shall deal with the methodological problems one encounters in so broadly construed a "field" as this.

The interchange between the academic and the more or less imaginative meanings of Orientalism is a constant one, and since the late eighteenth century there has been a considerable, quite disciplined—perhaps even regulated—traffic between the two. Here I come to the third meaning of Orientalism, which is something more historically and materially defined than either of the other two. Taking the late eighteenth century as a very roughly defined starting point Orientalism can be discussed and analyzed as the corporate institution for dealing with the Orient— dealing with it by making statements about it, authorizing views of it, describing it, by teaching it, settling it, ruling over it: in short, Orientalism as a Western style for dominating, restructuring, and having authority over the Orient. I have found it useful here to employ Michel Foucault's notion of a discourse, as described by him in *The Archaeology of Knowledge* and in *Discipline and Punish,* to identify Orientalism. My contention is that without examining Orientalism as a discourse one cannot possibly understand the enormously systematic discipline by which European culture was able to manage—and even produce—the Orient politically, sociologically, militarily, ideologically, scientifically, and imaginatively during the post-Enlightenment period. Moreover, so authoritative a position did Orientalism have that I believe no one writing, thinking, or acting on the Orient could do so without taking account of the limitations on thought and action imposed by Orientalism. In brief, because of Orientalism the Orient was not (and is not) a free subject of thought or action. This is not to say that Orientalism unilaterally determines what can be said about the Orient, but that it is the whole network of interests inevitably brought to bear on (and therefore always involved in) any occasion when that peculiar entity "the Orient" is in question. How this happens is what this book tries to demonstrate. It also tries to show that European culture gained in strength and identity by setting itself off against the Orient as a sort of surrogate and even underground self.

Historically and culturally there is a quantitative as well as a qualitative difference between the Franco-British involvement in the Orient and—until the period of American ascendancy after World War II—the involvement of every other European and Atlantic power. To speak of Orientalism therefore is to speak mainly, although not exclusively, of a British and French cultural enterprise, a project whose dimensions take in such disparate realms as the imagination itself, the whole of India and the Levant, the Biblical texts and the Biblical lands, the spice trade, colonial armies and a long tradition of colonial administrators, a formidable scholarly corpus, innumerable Oriental "experts" and "hands," an Oriental professorate, a complex array of "Oriental" ideas (Oriental despotism, Oriental splendor, cruelty, sensuality), many Eastern sects, philosophies, and wisdoms domesticated for local European use— the list can be extended more or less indefinitely. My point is that Orientalism derives from a particular closeness experienced between Britain and France and the Orient, which until the early nineteenth century had really meant only India and the Bible lands. From the beginning of the nineteenth century until the end of World War II France and Britain dominated the Orient and Orientalism; since World War II America has dominated the Orient, and approaches it as France and Britain once did. Out of that closeness, whose dynamic is enormously productive even if it always demonstrates the comparatively greater strength of the Occident (British, French, or American), comes the large body of texts I call Orientalist.

It should be said at once that even with the generous number of books and authors that I examine, there is a much larger number that I simply have had to leave out. My argument, however, depends neither upon an exhaustive catalogue of texts dealing with the Orient nor upon a clearly delimited set of texts, authors, and ideas that together make up the Orientalist canon. I have depended instead upon a different methodological alternative—whose backbone in a sense is the set of historical generalizations I have so far been making in this Introduction—and it is these I want now to discuss in more analytical detail.

II

I have begun with the assumption that the Orient is not an inert fact of nature. It is not merely *there,* just as the Occident itself is not just *there* either. We must take seriously Vico's great observation that men make their own history, that what they can know is what they have made, and extend it to geography: as both geographical and cultural entities—to say nothing of historical entities—such locales, regions, geographical sectors as "Orient" and "Occident" are man-made. Therefore as much as the West itself, the Orient is an idea that has a history and a tradition of thought, imagery, and vocabulary that have given it reality and presence in and for the West. The two geographical entities thus support and to an extent reflect each other.

Having said that, one must go on to state a number of reasonable qualifications. In the first place, it would be wrong to conclude that the Orient was *essentially* an idea, or a creation with no corresponding reality. When Disraeli said in his novel *Tancred* that the East was a career, he meant that to be interested in the East was something bright young Westerners would find to be an all-consuming passion; he should not be interpreted as saying that the East was *only* a career for Westerners. There were—and are—cultures and nations whose location is in the East, and their lives, histories, and customs have a brute reality obviously greater than anything that could be said about them in the West. About that fact this study of Orientalism has very little to contribute, except to acknowledge it tacitly. But the phenomenon of Orientalism as I study it here deals principally, not with a correspondence between Orientalism and Orient, but with the internal consistency of Orientalism and its ideas about the Orient (the East as career) despite or beyond any correspondence, or lack thereof, with a "real" Orient. My point is that Disraeli's statement about the East refers mainly to that created consistency, that regular constellation of ideas as the pre-eminent thing about the Orient, and not to its mere being, as Wallace Stevens's phrase has it.

A second qualification is that ideas, cultures, and histories cannot seriously be understood or studied without their force, or more precisely their configurations of power, also being studied. To believe that the Orient was created—or, as I call it, "Orientalized"—and to believe that such things happen simply as a necessity of the imagination, is to be disingenuous. The relationship between Occident and Orient is a relationship of power, of domination, of varying degrees of a complex hegemony, and is quite accurately indicated in the title of K. M. Panikkar's classic *Asia and Western Dominance*.[2] The Orient was Orientalized not only because it was discovered to be "Oriental" in all those ways considered commonplace by an average nineteenth-century European, but also because it *could be*—that is, submitted to being—*made* Oriental. There is very little consent to be found, for example, in the fact that Flaubert's encounter with an Egyptian courtesan produced a widely influential model of the Oriental woman; she never spoke of herself, she never represented her emotions, presence, or history. *He* spoke for and represented her. He was foreign, comparatively wealthy, male, and these were historical facts of domination that allowed him not only to possess Kuchuk Hanem physically but to speak for her and tell his readers in what way she was "typically Oriental." My argument is that Flaubert's situation of strength in relation to Kuchuk Hanem was not an isolated instance. It fairly stands for the pattern of relative strength between East and West, and the discourse about the Orient that it enabled.

This brings us to a third qualification. One ought never to assume that the structure of Orientalism is nothing more than a structure of lies or of myths which, were the truth about them to be told, would simply blow away. I myself believe that Orientalism is more particularly valuable as a sign of European-Atlantic power over the Orient than it is as a veridic discourse about the Orient (which is what, in its academic or scholarly form, it claims to be). Nevertheless, what we must respect and try to grasp is the sheer knitted-together strength of Orientalist discourse, its very close ties to the enabling socio-economic and political institutions, and its redoubtable durability. After all, any system of ideas that can remain unchanged as teachable wisdom (in academies, books, congresses, universities, foreign-service institutes) from the period of Ernest Renan in the late 1840s until the present in the United States must be something more formidable than a mere collection of lies. Orientalism, therefore, is not an airy European fantasy about the Orient, but a created body of theory and practice in which, for many generations, there has been a considerable material investment. Continued investment made Orientalism, as a system of knowledge about the Orient, an accepted grid for filtering through the Orient into Western consciousness, just as that same investment multiplied—indeed, made truly productive—the statements proliferating out from Orientalism into the general culture.

Gramsci has made the useful analytic distinction between civil and political society in which the former is made up of voluntary (or at least rational and noncoercive) affiliations like schools, families, and unions, the latter of state institutions (the army, the police, the central bureaucracy) whose role in the polity is direct domination. Culture, of course, is to be found operating within civil society, where the influence of ideas, of institutions, and of other persons works not through domination but by what Gramsci calls consent. In any society not totalitarian, then, certain cultural forms predominate over others, just as certain ideas are more influential than others; the form of this cultural leadership is what Gramsci has identified as *hegemony*, an indispensable concept for any understanding of cultural life in the industrial West. It is hegemony, or rather the result of cultural hegemony at work, that gives Orientalism the durability and the strength I have been speaking about so far. Orientalism is never far from what Denys Hay has called the idea of Europe,[3] a collective notion identifying "us" Europeans as against all "those" non-Europeans, and indeed it can be argued that the major component in European culture is precisely what made that culture hegemonic both in and outside Europe: the idea of European identity as a superior one in comparison with all the non-European peoples and cultures. There is in addition the hegemony of European ideas about the Orient, themselves reiterating European superiority over Oriental backwardness, usually overriding the possibility that a more independent, or more skeptical, thinker might have had different views on the matter.

In a quite constant way, Orientalism depends for its strategy on this flexible *positional* superiority, which puts the Westerner in a whole series of possible relationships with the Orient without ever losing him the relative upper hand. And why should it have been, otherwise, especially during the period of extraordinary European ascendancy from the late Renaissance to the present? The scientist, the scholar, the missionary, the trader, or the soldier was in, or thought about, the Orient because he *could be there,* or could think about it, with very little resistance on the Orient's part. Under the general heading of knowledge of the Orient, and within the umbrella of Western hegemony over the Orient during the period from the end of the eighteenth century, there emerged a complex Orient suitable for study in the academy, for display in the museum, for reconstruction in the colonial office, for theoretical illustration in anthropological, biological, linguistic, racial, and historical theses about mankind and the universe, for instances of economic and sociological theories of development, revolution, cultural personality, national or religious character. Additionally, the imaginative examination of things Oriental was based more or less exclusively upon a sovereign Western consciousness out of whose unchallenged centrality an Oriental world emerged, first according to general ideas about who or what was an Oriental, then according to a detailed logic governed not simply by empirical reality but by a battery of desires, repressions, investments, and projections. If we can point to great Orientalist works of genuine scholarship like Silvestre de Sacy's *Chrestomathie arabe* or Edward William Lane's *Account of the Manners and Customs of the Modern Egyptians,* we need also to note that Renan's and Gobineau's racial ideas came out of the same impulse, as did a great many Victorian pornographic novels (see the analysis by Steven Marcus of "The Lustful Turk").[4]

And yet, one must repeatedly ask oneself whether what matters in Orientalism is the general group of ideas overriding the mass of material—about which who could deny that they were shot through with doctrines of European superiority, various kinds of racism, imperialism, and the like, dogmatic views of "the Oriental" as a kind of ideal and unchanging abstraction?—or the much more varied work produced by almost uncountable individual writers, whom one would take up as individual instances of authors dealing with the Orient. In a sense the two alternatives, general and particular, are really two perspectives on the same material: in both instances one would have to deal with pioneers in the field like William Jones, with great artists like Nerval or Flaubert. And why would it not be possible to employ both perspectives together, or one after the other? Isn't there an obvious danger of distortion (of precisely the kind that academic Orientalism has always been prone to) if either too general or too specific a level of description is maintained systematically?

My two fears are distortion and inaccuracy, or rather the kind of inaccuracy produced by too dogmatic a generality and too positivistic a localized focus. In trying to deal with these problems I have tried to deal with three main aspects of my own contemporary reality that seem to me to point the way out of the methodological or perspectival difficulties I have been discussing, difficulties that might force one, in the first instance, into writing a coarse polemic on so unacceptably general a level of description as not to be worth the effort, or in the second instance, into writing so detailed and atomistic a series of analyses as to lose all track of the general lines of force informing the field, giving it its special cogency. How then to recognize individuality and to reconcile it with its intelligent, and by no means passive or merely dictatorial, general and hegemonic context?

III

I mentioned three aspects of my contemporary reality: I must explain and briefly discuss them now, so that it can be seen how I was led to a particular course of research and writing.

1. *The distinction between pure and political knowledge.* It is very easy to argue that knowledge about Shakespeare or Wordsworth is not political whereas knowledge about contemporary China or the Soviet Union is. My own formal and professional designation is that of "humanist," a title which indicates the humanities as my field and therefore the unlikely eventuality that there might be anything political about

what I do in that field. Of course, all these labels and terms are quite unnuanced as I use them here, but the general truth of what I am pointing to is, I think, widely held. One reason for saying that a humanist who writes about Wordsworth, or an editor whose specialty is Keats, is not involved in anything political is that what he does seems to have no direct political effect upon reality in the everyday sense. A scholar whose field is Soviet economics works in a highly charged area where there is much government interest, and what he might produce in the way of studies or proposals will be taken up by policymakers, government officials, institutional economists, intelligence experts. The distinction between "humanists" and persons whose work has policy implications, or political significance, can be broadened further by saying that the former's ideological color is a matter of incidental importance to politics (although possibly of great moment to his colleagues in the field, who may object to his Stalinism or fascism or too easy liberalism), whereas the ideology of the latter is woven directly into his material—indeed, economics, politics, and sociology in the modern academy are ideological sciences—and therefore taken for granted as being "political."

Nevertheless the determining impingement on most knowledge produced in the contemporary West (and here I speak mainly about the United States) is that it be nonpolitical, that is, scholarly, academic, impartial, above partisan or small-minded doctrinal belief. One can have no quarrel with such an ambition in theory, perhaps, but in practice the reality is much more problematic. No one has ever devised a method for detaching the scholar from the circumstances of life, from the fact of his involvement (conscious or unconscious) with a class, a set of beliefs, a social position, or from the mere activity of being a member of a society. These continue to bear on what he does professionally, even though naturally enough his research and its fruits do attempt to reach a level of relative freedom from the inhibitions and the restrictions of brute, everyday reality. For there is such a thing as knowledge that is less, rather than more, partial than the individual (with his entangling and distracting life circumstances) who produces it. Yet this knowledge is not therefore automatically nonpolitical.

Whether discussions of literature or of classical philology are fraught with—or have unmediated—political significance is a very large question that I have tried to treat in some detail elsewhere.[5] What I am interested in doing now is suggesting how the general liberal consensus that "true" knowledge is fundamentally nonpolitical (and conversely, that overtly political knowledge is not "true" knowledge) obscures the highly if obscurely organized political circumstances obtaining when knowledge is produced. No one is helped in understanding this today when the adjective "political" is used as a label to discredit any work for daring to violate the protocol of pretended suprapolitical objectivity. We may say, first, that civil society recognizes a gradation of political importance in the various fields of knowledge. To some extent

the political importance given a field comes from the possibility of its direct translation into economic terms; but to a greater extent political importance comes from the
closeness of a field to ascertainable sources of power in political society. Thus an
economic study of long-term Soviet energy potential and its effect on military capa-
bility is likely to be commissioned by the Defense Department, and thereafter to
acquire a kind of political status impossible for a study of Tolstoi's early fiction
financed in part by a foundation. Yet both works belong in what civil society acknowledges to be a similar field, Russian studies, even though one work may be done by a
very conservative economist, the other by a radical literary historian. My point here
is that "Russia" as a general subject matter has political priority over nicer distinctions such as "economics" and "literary history," because political society in Gramsci's sense reaches into such realms of civil society as the academy and saturates
them with significance of direct concern to it.

I do not want to press all this any further on general theoretical grounds: it
seems to me that the value and credibility of my case can be demonstrated by being
much more specific, in the way, for example, Noam Chomsky has studied the instrumental connection between the Vietnam War and the notion of objective scholarship
as it was applied to cover state-sponsored military research.[6] Now because Britain,
France, and recently the United States are imperial powers, their political societies
impart to their civil societies a sense of urgency, a direct political infusion as it were,
where and whenever matters pertaining to their imperial interests abroad are concerned. I doubt that it is controversial, for example, to say that an Englishman in
India or Egypt in the later nineteenth century took an interest in those countries that
was never far from their status in his mind as British colonies. To say this may seem
quite different from saying that all academic knowledge about India and Egypt is
somehow tinged and impressed with, violated by, the gross political fact—and yet
that is what I am saying in this study of Orientalism. For if it is true that no production of knowledge in the human sciences can ever ignore or disclaim its author's
involvement as a human subject in his own circumstances, then it must also be true
that for a European or American studying the Orient there can be no disclaiming the
main circumstances of *his* actuality: that he comes up against the Orient as a European or American first, as an individual second. And to be a European or an American in such a situation is by no means an inert fact. It meant and means being aware,
however dimly, that one belongs to a power with definite interests in the Orient, and
more important, that one belongs to a part of the earth with a definite history of
involvement in the Orient almost since the time of Homer.

Put in this way, these political actualities are still too undefined and general to
be really interesting. Anyone would agree to them without necessarily agreeing also
that they mattered very much, for instance, to Flaubert as he wrote *Salammbô*, or
to H.A.R. Gibb as he wrote *Modern Trends in Islam*. The trouble is that there is too

great a distance between the big dominating fact, as I have described it, and the details of everyday life that govern the minute discipline of a novel or a scholarly text as each is being written. Yet if we eliminate from the start any notion that "big" facts like imperial domination can be applied mechanically and deterministically to such complex matters as culture and ideas, then we will begin to approach an interesting kind of study. My idea is that European and then American interest in the Orient was political according to some of the obvious historical accounts of it that I have given here, but that it was the culture that created that interest, that acted dynamically along with brute political, economic, and military rationales to make the Orient the varied and complicated place that it obviously was in the field I call Orientalism.

Therefore, Orientalism is not a mere political subject matter or field that is reflected passively by culture, scholarship, or institutions; nor is it a large and diffuse collection of texts about the Orient; nor is it representative and expressive of some nefarious "Western" imperialist plot to hold down the "Oriental" world. It is rather a *distribution* of geopolitical awareness into aesthetic, scholarly, economic, sociological, historical, and philological texts; it is an *elaboration* not only of a basic geographical distinction (the world is made up of two unequal halves, Orient and Occident) but also of a whole series of "interests" which, by such means as scholarly discovery, philological reconstruction, psychological analysis, landscape and sociological description, it not only creates but also maintains; it *is*, rather than expresses, a certain *will* or *intention* to understand, in some cases to control, manipulate, even to incorporate, what is a manifestly different (or alternative and novel) world; it is, above all, a discourse that is by no means in direct, corresponding relationship with political power in the raw, but rather is produced and exists in an uneven exchange with various kinds of power, shaped to a degree by the exchange with power political (as with a colonial or imperial establishment), power intellectual (as with reigning sciences like comparative linguistics or anatomy, or any of the modern policy sciences), power cultural (as with orthodoxies and canons of taste, texts, values), power moral (as with ideas about what "we" do and what "they" cannot do or understand as "we" do). Indeed, my real argument is that Orientalism is—and does not simply represent—a considerable dimension of modern political-intellectual culture, and as such has less to do with the Orient than it does with "our" world.

Because Orientalism is a cultural and a political fact, then, it does not exist in some archival vacuum; quite the contrary, I think it can be shown that what is thought, said, or even done about the Orient follows (perhaps occurs within) certain distinct and intellectually knowable lines. Here too a considerable degree of nuance and elaboration can be seen working as between the broad superstructural pressures and the details of composition, the facts of textuality. Most humanistic scholars are, I think, perfectly happy with the notion that texts exist in contexts, that there is such a thing as intertextuality, that the pressures of conventions, predecessors, and rhetorical styles limit what Walter Benjamin once called the "overtaxing of the productive person in the name of . . . the principle of 'creativity,'" in which the poet is believed on his own, and out of his pure mind, to have brought forth his work.[7] Yet there is a reluctance to allow that political, institutional, and ideological constraints act in the same manner on the individual author. A humanist will believe it to be an interesting fact to any interpreter of Balzac that he was influenced in the *Comédie humaine* by the conflict between Geoffroy Saint-Hilaire and Cuvier, but the same sort of pressure on Balzac of deeply reactionary monarchism is felt in some vague way to demean his literary "genius" and therefore to be less worth serious study. Similarly—as Harry Bracken has been tirelessly showing—philosophers will conduct their discussions of Locke, Hume, and empiricism without ever taking into account that there is an explicit connection in these classic writers between their "philosophic" doctrines and racial theory, justifications of slavery, or arguments for colonial exploitation.[8] These are common enough ways by which contemporary scholarship keeps itself pure.

Perhaps it is true that most attempts to rub culture's nose in the mud of politics have been crudely iconoclastic; perhaps also the social interpretation of literature in my own field has simply not kept up with the enormous technical advances in detailed textual analysis. But there is no getting away from the fact that literary studies in general, and American Marxist theorists in particular, have avoided the effort of seriously bridging the gap between the superstructural and the base levels in textual, historical scholarship; on another occasion I have gone so far as to say that the literary-cultural establishment as a whole has declared the serious study of imperialism and culture off limits.[9] For Orientalism brings one up directly against that question—that is, to realizing that political imperialism governs an entire field of study, imagination, and scholarly institutions—in such a way as to make its avoidance an intellectual and historical impossibility. Yet there will always remain the perennial escape mechanism of saying that a literary scholar and a philosopher, for example, are trained in literature and philosophy respectively, not in politics or ideological analysis. In other words, the specialist argument can work quite effectively to block the larger and, in my opinion, the more intellectually serious perspective.

Here it seems to me there is a simple two-part answer to be given, at least so far as the study of imperialism and culture (or Orientalism) is concerned. In the first place, nearly every nineteenth-century writer (and the same is true enough of writers in earlier periods) was extraordinarily well aware of the fact of empire: this is a subject not very well studied, but it will not take a modern Victorian specialist long to admit that liberal cultural heroes like John Stuart Mill, Arnold, Carlyle, Newman, Macaulay, Ruskin, George Eliot, and even Dickens had definite views on race and imperialism, which are quite easily to be found at work in their writing. So even a specialist must deal with the knowledge that Mill, for example, made it clear in *On*

Liberty and *Representative Government* that his views there could not be applied to India (he was an India Office functionary for a good deal of his life, after all) because the Indians were civilizationally, if not racially, inferior. The same kind of paradox is to be found in Marx, as I try to show in this book. In the second place, to believe that politics in the form of imperialism bears upon the production of literature, scholarship, social theory, and history writing is by no means equivalent to saying that culture is therefore a demeaned or denigrated thing. Quite the contrary: my whole point is to say that we can better understand the persistence and the durability of saturating hegemonic systems like culture when we realize that their internal constraints upon writers and thinkers were *productive,* not unilaterally inhibiting. It is this idea that Gramsci, certainly, and Foucault and Raymond Williams in their very different ways have been trying to illustrate. Even one or two pages by Williams on "the uses of the Empire" in *The Long Revolution* tell us more about nineteenth-century cultural richness than many volumes of hermetic textual analyses.[10]

Therefore I study Orientalism as a dynamic exchange between individual authors and the large political concerns shaped by the three great empires—British, French, American—in whose intellectual and imaginative territory the writing was produced. What interests me most as a scholar is not the gross political verity but the detail, as indeed what interests us in someone like Lane or Flaubert or Renan is not the (to him) indisputable truth that Occidentals are superior to Orientals, but the profoundly worked over and modulated evidence of his detailed work within the very wide space opened up by that truth. One need only remember that Lane's *Manners and Customs of the Modern Egyptians* is a classic of historical and anthropological observation because of its style, its enormously intelligent and brilliant details, not because of its simple reflection of racial superiority, to understand what I am saying here.

The kind of political questions raised by Orientalism, then, are as follows: What other sorts of intellectual, aesthetic, scholarly, and cultural energies went into the making of an imperialist tradition like the Orientalist one? How did philology, lexicography, history, biology, political and economic theory, novel-writing, and lyric poetry come to the service of Orientalism's broadly imperialist view of the world? What changes, modulations, refinements, even revolutions take place within Orientalism? What is the meaning of originality, of continuity, of individuality, in this context? How does Orientalism transmit or reproduce itself from one epoch to another? In fine, how can we treat the cultural, historical phenomenon of Orientalism as a kind of *willed human work*—not of mere unconditioned ratiocination—in all its historical complexity, detail, and worth without at the same time losing sight of the alliance between cultural work, political tendencies, the state, and the specific realities of domination? Governed by such concerns a humanistic study can responsibly address itself to politics *and* culture. But this is not to say that such a study establishes a

hard-and-fast rule about the relationship between knowledge and politics. My argument is that each humanistic investigation must formulate the nature of that connection in the specific context of the study, the subject matter, and its historical
circumstances.

2. *The methodological question.* In a previous book I gave a good deal of thought and
analysis to the methodological importance for work in the human sciences of finding
and formulating a first step, a point of departure, a beginning principle.[11] A major
lesson I learned and tried to present was that there is no such thing as a merely
given, or simply available, starting point: beginnings have to be made for each project in such a way as to *enable* what follows from them. Nowhere in my experience
has the difficulty of this lesson been more consciously lived (with what success—or
failure—I cannot really say) than in this study of Orientalism. The idea of beginning,
indeed, the act of beginning, necessarily involves an act of delimitation by which
something is cut out of a great mass of material, separated from the mass, and made
to stand for, as well as be, a starting point, a beginning; for the student of texts one
such notion of inaugural delimitation is Louis Althusser's idea of the *problematic,* a
specific determinate unity of a text, or group of texts, which is something given rise
to by analysis.[12] Yet in the case of Orientalism (as opposed to the case of Marx's
texts, which is what Althusser studies) there is not simply the problem of finding a
point of departure, or problematic, but also the question of designating which texts,
authors, and periods are the ones best suited for study.

It has seemed to me foolish to attempt an encyclopedic narrative history of Orientalism, first of all because if my guiding principle was to be "the European idea of
the Orient" there would be virtually no limit to the material I would have had to deal
with; second, because the narrative model itself did not suit my descriptive and
political interests; third, because in such books as Raymond Schwab's *La Renaissance orientale,* Johann Fück's *Die Arabischen Studien in Europa bis in den Anfang
des 20. Jahrhunderts,* and more recently, Dorothee Metlitzki's *The Matter of Araby
in Medieval England*[13] there already exist encyclopedic works on certain aspects of
the European-Oriental encounter such as make the critic's job, in the general political and intellectual context I sketched above, a different one.

There still remained the problem of cutting down a very fat archive to manage-
able dimensions, and more important, outlining something in the nature of an intellectual order within that group of texts without at the same time following a
mindlessly chronological order. My starting point therefore has been the British,
French, and American experience of the Orient taken as a unit, what made that
experience possible by way of historical and intellectual background, what the quality and character of the experience has been. For reasons I shall discuss presently I
limited that already limited (but still inordinately large) set of questions to the

Anglo-French-American experience of the Arabs and Islam, which for almost a thousand years together stood for the Orient. Immediately upon doing that, a large part of the Orient seemed to have been eliminated—India, Japan, China, and other sections of the Far East—not because these regions were not important (they obviously have been) but because one could discuss Europe's experience of the Near Orient, or of Islam, apart from its experience of the Far Orient. Yet at certain moments of that general European history of interest in the East, particular parts of the Orient like Egypt, Syria, and Arabia cannot be discussed without also studying Europe's involvement in the more distant parts, of which Persia and India are the most important; a notable case in point is the connection between Egypt and India so far as eighteenth- and nineteenth-century Britain was concerned. Similarly the French role in deciphering the Zend-Avesta, the pre-eminence of Paris as a center of Sanskrit studies during the first decade of the nineteenth century, the fact that Napoleon's interest in the Orient was contingent upon his sense of the British role in India: all these Far Eastern interests directly influenced French interest in the Near East, Islam, and the Arabs.

Britain and France dominated the Eastern Mediterranean from about the end of the seventeenth century on. Yet my discussion of that domination and systematic interest does not do justice to (a) the important contributions to Orientalism of Germany, Italy, Russia, Spain, and Portugal and (b) the fact that one of the important impulses toward the study of the Orient in the eighteenth century was the revolution in Biblical studies stimulated by such variously interesting pioneers as Bishop Lowth, Eichhorn, Herder, and Michaelis. In the first place, I had to focus rigorously upon the British-French and later the American material because it seemed inescapably true not only that Britain and France were the pioneer nations in the Orient and in Oriental studies, but that these vanguard positions were held by virtue of the two greatest colonial networks in pre-twentieth-century history; the American Oriental position since World War II has fit—I think, quite self-consciously—in the places excavated by the two earlier European powers. Then too, I believe that the sheer quality, consistency, and mass of British, French, and American writing on the Orient lifts it above the doubtless crucial work done in Germany, Italy, Russia, and elsewhere. But I think it is also true that the major steps in Oriental scholarship were first taken in either Britain or France, then elaborated upon by Germans. Silvestre de Sacy, for example, was not only the first modern and institutional European Orientalist, who worked on Islam, Arabic literature, the Druze religion, and Sassanid Persia; he was also the teacher of Champollion and of Franz Bopp, the founder of German comparative linguistics. A similar claim of priority and subsequent pre-eminence can be made for William Jones and Edward William Lane.

In the second place—and here the failings of my study of Orientalism are amply made up for—there has been some important recent work on the background in Biblical scholarship to the rise of what I have called modern Orientalism. The best and the most illuminatingly relevant is E. S. Shaffer's impressive *"Kubla Khan" and The Fall of Jerusalem,*[14] an indispensable study of the origins of Romanticism, and of the intellectual activity underpinning a great deal of what goes on in Coleridge, Browning, and George Eliot. To some degree Shaffer's work refines upon the outlines provided in Schwab, by articulating the material of relevance to be found in the German Biblical scholars and using that material to read, in an intelligent and always interesting way, the work of three major British writers. Yet what is missing in the book is some sense of the political as well as ideological edge given the Oriental material by the British and French writers I am principally concerned with; in addition, unlike Shaffer I attempt to elucidate subsequent developments in academic as well as literary Orientalism that bear on the connection between British and French Orientalism on the one hand and the rise of an explicitly colonial-minded imperialism on the other. Then too, I wish to show how all these earlier matters are reproduced more or less in American Orientalism after the Second World War.

Nevertheless there is a possibly misleading aspect to my study, where, aside from an occasional reference, I do not exhaustively discuss the German developments after the inaugural period dominated by Sacy. Any work that seeks to provide an understanding of academic Orientalism and pays little attention to scholars like Steinthal, Müller, Becker, Goldziher, Brockelmann, Nöldeke—to mention only a handful—needs to be reproached, and I freely reproach myself. I particularly regret not taking more account of the great scientific prestige that accrued to German scholarship by the middle of the nineteenth century, whose neglect was made into a denunciation of insular British scholars by George Eliot. I have in mind Eliot's unforgettable portrait of Mr. Casaubon in *Middlemarch*. One reason Casaubon cannot finish his Key to All Mythologies is, according to his young cousin Will Ladislaw, that he is unacquainted with German scholarship. For not only has Casaubon chosen a subject "as changing as chemistry: new discoveries are constantly making new points of view": he is undertaking a job similar to a refutation of Paracelsus because "he is not an Orientalist, you know."[15]

Eliot was not wrong in implying that by about 1830, which is when *Middlemarch* is set, German scholarship had fully attained its European pre-eminence. Yet at no time in German scholarship during the first two-thirds of the nineteenth century could a close partnership have developed between Orientalists and a protracted, sustained *national* interest in the Orient. There was nothing in Germany to correspond to the Anglo-French presence in India, the Levant, North Africa. Moreover, the German Orient was almost exclusively a scholarly, or at least a classical, Orient: it was made the subject of lyrics, fantasies, and even novels, but it was never actual, the way Egypt and Syria were actual for Chateaubriand, Lane, Lamartine, Burton, Disraeli, or Nerval. There is some significance in the fact that the two most renowned

German works on the Orient, Goethe's *Westöstlicher Diwan* and Friedrich Schlegel's *Über die Sprache und Weisheit der Indier,* were based respectively on a Rhine journey and on hours spent in Paris libraries. What German Oriental scholarship did was to refine and elaborate techniques whose application was to texts, myths, ideas, and languages almost literally gathered from the Orient by imperial Britain and France.

Yet what German Orientalism had in common with Anglo-French and later American Orientalism was a kind of intellectual *authority* over the Orient within Western culture. This authority must in large part be the subject of any description of Orientalism, and it is so in this study. Even the name *Orientalism* suggests a serious, perhaps ponderous style of expertise; when I apply it to modern American social scientists (since they do not call themselves Orientalists, my use of the word is anomalous), it is to draw attention to the way Middle East experts can still draw on the vestiges of Orientalism's intellectual position in nineteenth-century Europe.

There is nothing mysterious or natural about authority. It is formed, irradiated, disseminated; it is instrumental, it is persuasive; it has status, it establishes canons of taste and value; it is virtually indistinguishable from certain ideas it dignifies as true, and from traditions, perceptions, and judgments it forms, transmits, reproduces. Above all, authority can, indeed must, be analyzed. All these attributes of authority apply to Orientalism, and much of what I do in this study is to describe both the historical authority in and the personal authorities of Orientalism.

My principal methodological devices for studying authority here are what can be called *strategic location,* which is a way of describing the author's position in a text with regard to the Oriental material he writes about, and *strategic formation,* which is a way of analyzing the relationship between texts and the way in which groups of texts, types of texts, even textual genres, acquire mass, density, and referential power among themselves and thereafter in the culture at large. I use the notion of strategy simply to identify the problem every writer on the Orient has faced: how to get hold of it, how to approach it, how not to be defeated or overwhelmed by its sublimity, its scope, its awful dimensions. Everyone who writes about the Orient must locate himself vis-à-vis the Orient; translated into his text, this location includes the kind of narrative voice he adopts, the type of structure he builds, the kinds of images, themes, motifs that circulate in his text—all of which add up to deliberate ways of addressing the reader, containing the Orient, and finally, representing it or speaking in its behalf. None of this takes place in the abstract, however. Every writer on the Orient (and this is true even of Homer) assumes some Oriental precedent, some previous knowledge of the Orient, to which he refers and on which he relies. Additionally, each work on the Orient affiliates itself with other works, with audiences, with institutions, with the Orient itself. The ensemble of relationships between works, audiences, and some particular aspects of the Orient therefore constitutes an analyzable formation—for example, that of philological studies, of anthologies of extracts from Oriental literature, of travel books, of Oriental fantasies—whose presence in time, in discourse, in institutions (schools, libraries, foreign services) gives it strength and authority.

It is clear, I hope, that my concern with authority does not entail analysis of what lies hidden in the Orientalist text, but analysis rather of the text's surface, its exteriority to what it describes. I do not think that this idea can be overemphasized. Orientalism is premised upon exteriority, that is, on the fact that the Orientalist, poet or scholar, makes the Orient speak, describes the Orient, renders its mysteries plain for and to the West. He is never concerned with the Orient except as the first cause of what he says. What he says and writes, by virtue of the fact that it is said or written, is meant to indicate that the Orientalist is outside the Orient, both as an existential and as a moral fact. The principal product of this exteriority is of course representation: as early as Aeschylus's play *The Persians* the Orient is transformed from a very far distant and often threatening Otherness into figures that are relatively familiar (in Aeschylus's case, grieving Asiatic women). The dramatic immediacy of representation in *The Persians* obscures the fact that the audience is watching a highly artificial enactment of what a non-Oriental has made into a symbol for the whole Orient. My analysis of the Orientalist text therefore places emphasis on the evidence, which is by no means invisible, for such representations *as representations,* not as "natural" depictions of the Orient. This evidence is found just as prominently in the so-called truthful text (histories, philological analyses, political treatises) as in the avowedly artistic (i.e., openly imaginative) text. The things to look at are style, figures of speech, setting, narrative devices, historical and social circumstances, *not* the correctness of the representation nor its fidelity to some great original. The exteriority of the representation is always governed by some version of the truism that if the Orient could represent itself, it would; since it cannot, the representation does the job, for the West, and *faute de mieux,* for the poor Orient. "Sie können sich nicht vertreten, sie müssen vertreten werden [they cannot represent themselves, they must be represented]," as Marx wrote in *The Eighteenth Brumaire of Louis Bonaparte.*

Another reason for insisting upon exteriority is that I believe it needs to be made clear about cultural discourse and exchange within a culture that what is commonly circulated by it is not "truth" but representations. It hardly needs to be demonstrated again that language itself is a highly organized and encoded system, which employs many devices to express, indicate, exchange messages and information, represent, and so forth. In any instance of at least written language, there is no such thing as a delivered presence, but a *re-presence,* or a representation. The value, efficacy, strength, apparent veracity of a written statement about the Orient therefore relies very little, and cannot instrumentally depend, on the Orient as such. On the contrary, the written statement is a presence to the reader by virtue of its having excluded, displaced, made supererogatory any such *real thing* as "the Orient." Thus all of Orientalism stands forth and away from the Orient: that Orientalism makes sense at all depends more on the West than on the Orient, and this sense is directly indebted to various Western techniques of representation that make the Orient visible, clear, "there" in discourse about it. And these representations rely upon institutions, traditions, conventions, agreed-upon codes of understanding for their effects, not upon a distant and amorphous Orient.

The difference between representations of the Orient before the last third of the eighteenth century and those after it (that is, those belonging to what I call modern Orientalism) is that the range of representation expanded enormously in the later period. It is true that after William Jones and Anquetil-Duperron, and after Napoleon's Egyptian expedition, Europe came to know the Orient more scientifically, to live in it with greater authority and discipline than ever before. But what mattered to Europe was the expanded scope and the much greater refinement given its techniques for receiving the Orient. When around the turn of the eighteenth century the Orient definitively revealed the age of its languages—thus outdating Hebrew's divine pedigree—it was a group of Europeans who made the discovery, passed it on to other scholars, and preserved the discovery in the new science of Indo-European philology. A new powerful science for viewing the linguistic Orient was born, and with it, as Foucault has shown in *The Order of Things,* a whole web of related scientific interests. Similarly William Beckford, Byron, Goethe, and Hugo restructured the Orient by their art and made its colors, lights, and people visible through their images, rhythms, and motifs. At most, the "real" Orient provoked a writer to his vision; it very rarely guided it.

Orientalism responded more to the culture that produced it than to its putative object, which was also produced by the West. Thus the history of Orientalism has both an internal consistency and a highly articulated set of relationships to the dominant culture surrounding it. My analyses consequently try to show the field's shape and internal organization, its pioneers, patriarchal authorities, canonical texts, doxological ideas, exemplary figures, its followers, elaborators, and new authorities; I try also to explain how Orientalism borrowed and was frequently informed by "strong" ideas, doctrines, and trends ruling the culture. Thus there was (and is) a linguistic Orient, a Freudian Orient, a Spenglerian Orient, a Darwinian Orient, a racist Orient—and so on. Yet never has there been such a thing as a pure, or unconditional, Orient; similarly, never has there been a nonmaterial form of Orientalism, much less something so innocent as an "idea" of the Orient. In this underlying conviction and in its ensuing methodological consequences do I differ from scholars who study the history of ideas. For the emphases and the executive form, above all the material effectiveness of statements made by Orientalist discourse are possible in ways that any hermetic history of ideas tends completely to scant. Without those emphases and that material effectiveness Orientalism would be just another idea, whereas it is and was much more than that. Therefore I set out to examine not only scholarly works but also works of literature, political tracts, journalistic texts, travel books, religious and philological studies. In other words, my hybrid perspective is broadly historical and "anthropological," given that I believe all texts to be worldly and circumstantial in (of course) ways that vary from genre to genre, and from historical period to historical period.

Yet unlike Michel Foucault, to whose work I am greatly indebted, I do believe in the determining imprint of individual writers upon the otherwise anonymous collective body of texts constituting a discursive formation like Orientalism. The unity of the large ensemble of texts I analyze is due in part to the fact that they frequently refer to each other: Orientalism is after all a system for citing works and authors. Edward William Lane's *Manners and Customs of the Modern Egyptians* was read and cited by such diverse figures as Nerval, Flaubert, and Richard Burton. He was an authority whose use was an imperative for anyone writing or thinking about the Orient, not just about Egypt: when Nerval borrows passages verbatim from *Modern Egyptians* it is to use Lane's authority to assist him in describing village scenes in Syria, not Egypt. Lane's authority and the opportunities provided for citing him discriminately as well as indiscriminately were there because Orientalism could give his text the kind of distributive currency that he acquired. There is no way, however, of understanding Lane's currency without also understanding the peculiar features of *his* text; this is equally true of Renan, Sacy, Lamartine, Schlegel, and a group of other influential writers. Foucault believes that in general the individual text or author counts for very little; empirically, in the case of Orientalism (and perhaps nowhere else) I find this not to be so. Accordingly my analyses employ close textual readings whose goal is to reveal the dialectic between individual text or writer and the complex collective formation to which his work is a contribution.

Yet even though it includes an ample selection of writers, this book is still far from a complete history or general account of Orientalism. Of this failing I am very conscious. The fabric of as thick a discourse as Orientalism has survived and functioned in Western society because of its richness: all I have done is to describe parts of that fabric at certain moments, and merely to suggest the existence of a larger whole, detailed, interesting, dotted with fascinating figures, texts, and events. I have consoled myself with believing that this book is one installment of several, and hope there are scholars and critics who might want to write others. There is still a general essay to be written on imperialism and culture; other studies would go more deeply into the connection between Orientalism and pedagogy, or into Italian, Dutch, German, and Swiss Orientalism, or into the dynamic between scholarship and imaginative writing, or into the relationship between administrative ideas and intellectual discipline. Perhaps the most important task of all would be to undertake studies in contemporary alternatives to Orientalism, to ask how one can study other cultures and peoples from a libertarian, or a nonrepressive and nonmanipulative, perspective. But then one would have to rethink the whole complex problem of knowledge and power. These are all tasks left embarrassingly incomplete in this study.

The last, perhaps self-flattering, observation on method that I want to make here is that I have written this study with several audiences in mind. For students of literature and criticism, Orientalism offers a marvelous instance of the interrelations between society, history, and textuality; moreover, the cultural role played by the Orient in the West connects Orientalism with ideology, politics, and the logic of power, matters of relevance, I think, to the literary community. For contemporary students of the Orient, from university scholars to policymakers, I have written with two ends in mind: one, to present their intellectual genealogy to them in a way that has not been done; two, to criticize—with the hope of stirring discussion—the often unquestioned assumptions on which their work for the most part depends. For the general reader, this study deals with matters that always compel attention, all of them connected not only with Western conceptions and treatments of the Other but also with the singularly important role played by Western culture in what Vico called the world of nations. Lastly, for readers in the so-called Third World, this study proposes itself as a step towards an understanding not so much of Western politics and of the non-Western world in those politics as of the *strength* of Western cultural discourse, a strength too often mistaken as merely decorative or "superstructural." My hope is to illustrate the formidable structure of cultural domination and, specifically for formerly colonized peoples, the dangers and temptations of employing this structure upon themselves or upon others.

The three long chapters and twelve shorter units into which this book is divided are intended to facilitate exposition as much as possible. Chapter One, "The Scope of Orientalism," draws a large circle around all the dimensions of the subject, both in terms of historical time and experiences and in terms of philosophical and political themes. Chapter Two, "Orientalist Structures and Restructures," attempts to trace the development of modern Orientalism by a broadly chronological description, and also by the description of a set of devices common to the work of important poets, artists, and scholars. Chapter Three, "Orientalism Now," begins where its predecessor left off, at around 1870. This is the period of great colonial expansion into the Orient, and it culminates in World War II. The very last section of Chapter Three characterizes the shift from British and French to American hegemony; I attempt there finally to sketch the present intellectual and social realities of Orientalism in the United States.

3. *The personal dimension.* In the *Prison Notebooks* Gramsci says: "The starting-point of critical elaboration is the consciousness of what one really is, and is 'know-

ing thyself' as a product of the historical process to date, which has deposited in you an infinity of traces, without leaving an inventory." The only available English translation inexplicably leaves Gramsci's comment at that, whereas in fact Gramsci's Italian text concludes by adding, "therefore it is imperative at the outset to compile such an inventory."[16]

Much of the personal investment in this study derives from my awareness of being an "Oriental" as a child growing up in two British colonies. All of my education, in those colonies (Palestine and Egypt) and in the United States, has been Western, and yet that deep early awareness has persisted. In many ways my study of Orientalism has been an attempt to inventory the traces upon me, the Oriental subject, of the culture whose domination has been so powerful a factor in the life of all Orientals. This is why for me the Islamic Orient has had to be the center of attention. Whether what I have achieved is the inventory prescribed by Gramsci is not for me to judge, although I have felt it important to be conscious of trying to produce one. Along the way, as severely and as rationally as I have been able, I have tried to maintain a critical consciousness, as well as employing those instruments of historical, humanistic, and cultural research of which my education has made me the fortunate beneficiary. In none of that, however, have I ever lost hold of the cultural reality of, the personal involvement in having been constituted as, "an Oriental."

The historical circumstances making such a study possible are fairly complex, and I can only list them schematically here. Anyone resident in the West since the 1950s, particularly in the United States, will have lived through an era of extraordinary turbulence in the relations of East and West. No one will have failed to note how "East" has always signified danger and threat during this period, even as it has meant the traditional Orient as well as Russia. In the universities a growing establishment of area-studies programs and institutes has made the scholarly study of the Orient a branch of national policy. Public affairs in this country include a healthy interest in the Orient, as much for its strategic and economic importance as for its traditional exoticism. If the world has become immediately accessible to a Western citizen living in the electronic age, the Orient too has drawn nearer to him, and is now less a myth perhaps than a place crisscrossed by Western, especially American, interests.

One aspect of the electronic, postmodern world is that there has been a reinforcement of the stereotypes by which the Orient is viewed. Television, the films, and all the media's resources have forced information into more and more standardized molds. So far as the Orient is concerned, standardization and cultural stereotyping have intensified the hold of the nineteenth-century academic and imaginative demonology of "the mysterious Orient." This is nowhere more true than in the ways by which the Near East is grasped. Three things have contributed to making even the simplest perception of the Arabs and Islam into a highly politicized, almost raucous matter: one, the history of popular anti-Arab and anti-Islamic prejudice in the West, which is immediately reflected in the history of Orientalism; two, the struggle between the Arabs and Israeli Zionism, and its effects upon American Jews as well as upon both the liberal culture and the population at large; three, the almost total absence of any cultural position making it possible either to identify with or dispassionately to discuss the Arabs or Islam. Furthermore, it hardly needs saying that because the Middle East is now so identified with Great Power politics, oil economics, and the simple-minded dichotomy of freedom-loving, democratic Israel and evil, totalitarian, and terroristic Arabs, the chances of anything like a clear view of what one talks about in talking about the Near East are depressingly small.

My own experiences of these matters are in part what made me write this book. The life of an Arab Palestinian in the West, particularly in America, is disheartening. There exists here an almost unanimous consensus that politically he does not exist, and when it is allowed that he does, it is either as a nuisance or as an Oriental. The web of racism, cultural stereotypes, political imperialism, dehumanizing ideology holding in the Arab or the Muslim is very strong indeed, and it is this web which every Palestinian has come to feel as his uniquely punishing destiny. It has made matters worse for him to remark that no person academically involved with the Near East—no Orientalist, that is—has ever in the United States culturally and politically identified himself wholeheartedly with the Arabs; certainly there have been identifications on some level, but they have never taken an "acceptable" form as has liberal American identification with Zionism, and all too frequently they have been radically flawed by their association either with discredited political and economic interests (oil company and State Department Arabists, for example) or with religion.

The nexus of knowledge and power creating "the Oriental" and, in a sense obliterating him as a human being is therefore not for me an exclusively academic matter. Yet it is an *intellectual* matter of some very obvious importance. I have been able to put to use my humanistic and political concerns for the analysis and description of a very worldly matter, the rise, development, and consolidation of Orientalism. Too often literature and culture are presumed to be politically, even historically innocent; it has regularly seemed otherwise to me, and certainly my study of Orientalism has convinced me (and I hope will convince my literary colleagues) that society and literary culture can only be understood and studied together. In addition, and by an almost inescapable logic, I have found myself writing the history of a strange, secret, sharer of Western anti-Semitism. That anti-Semitism and, as I have discussed it in its Islamic branch, Orientalism resemble each other very closely is a historical, cultural, and political truth that needs only to be mentioned to an Arab Palestinian for its irony to be perfectly understood. But what I should like also to have contributed here is a better understanding of the way cultural domination has operated. If this stimulates a new kind of dealing with the Orient, indeed if it eliminates the "Orient" and "Occident" altogether, then we shall have advanced a little in the process of what Raymond Williams has called the "unlearning" of "the inherent dominative mode."[17]

NOTES

1 Thierry Desjardins, *Le Martyre du Liban* (Paris: Plon, 1976), p. 14.

2 K. M. Panikkar, *Asia and Western Dominance* (London: George Allen & Unwin, 1959).

3 Denys Hay, *Europe: The Emergence of an Idea*, 2nd ed. (Edinburgh: Edinburgh University Press, 1968).

4 Steven Marcus, *The Other Victorians: A Study of Sexuality and Pornography in Mid-Nineteenth Century England* (1966; reprinted., New York: Bantam Books, 1967), pp. 200–19.

5 See my *Criticism between Culture and System* (Cambridge, Mass.: Harvard University Press, forthcoming).

6 Principally in his *American Power and the New Mandarins: Historical and Political Essays* (New York: Pantheon Books, 1969) and *For Reasons of State* (New York: Pantheon Books, 1973).

7 Walter Benjamin, *Charles Baudelaire: A Lyric Poet in the Era of High Capitalism,* trans. Harry Zohn (London: New Left Books, 1973), p. 71.

8 Harry Bracken, "Essence, Accident, and Race," *Hermathena* 116 (Winter 1973): 81–96.

9 In an interview published in *Diacritics* 6, no. 3 (Fall 1976): 38.

10 Raymond Williams, *The Long Revolution* (London: Chatto & Windus, 1961), pp. 66–7.

11 In my *Beginnings: Intention and Method* (New York: Basic Books, 1975).

12 Louis Althusser, *For Marx*, trans. Ben Brewster (New York: Pantheon Books, 1969), pp. 65–7.

13 Raymond Schwab, *La Renaissance orientale* (Paris: Payot, 1950); Johann W. Fück, *Die Arabischen Studien in Europa bis in den Anfang des 20. Jahrhunderts* (Leipzig: Otto Harrassowitz, 1955); Dorothee Metlitzki, *The Matter of Araby in Medieval England* (New Haven, Conn.: Yale University Press, 1977).

14 E. S. Shaffer, *"Kubla Khan" and The Fall of Jerusalem: The Mythological School in Biblical Criticism and Secular Literature, 1770–1880* (Cambridge: Cambridge University Press, 1975).

15 George Eliot, *Middlemarch: A Study of Provincial Life* (1872; reprint ed., Boston: Houghton Mifflin Co., 1956), p. 164.

16 Antonio Gramsci, *The Prison Notebooks: Selections*, trans. and ed. Quintin Hoare and Geoffrey Nowell Smith (New York: International Publishers, 1971), p. 324. The full passage, unavailable in the Hoare and Smith translation, is to be found in Gramsci, *Quaderni del Carcere,* ed. Valentino Gerratana (Turin: Einaudi Editore, 1975), 2: 1363.

17 Raymond Williams, *Culture and Society, 1780–1950* (London: Chatto & Windus, 1958), p. 376.

8

LINDA TUHIWAI SMITH

Imperialism, History, Writing, and Theory

The master's tools will never dismantle the master's house. —Audre Lorde[1]

Imperialism frames the indigenous experience. It is part of our story, our version of modernity. Writing about our experiences under imperialism and its more specific expression of colonialism has become a significant project of the indigenous world. In a literary sense this has been defined by writers like Salman Rushdie, Ngũgĩ wa Thiong'o and many others whose literary origins are grounded in the landscapes, languages, cultures, and imaginative worlds of peoples and nations whose own histories were interrupted and radically reformulated by European imperialism. While the project of creating this literature is important, what indigenous activists would argue is that imperialism cannot be struggled over only at the level of text and literature. Imperialism still hurts, still destroys and is reforming itself constantly. Indigenous peoples as an international group have had to challenge, understand and have a shared language for talking about the history, the sociology, the psychology and the politics of imperialism and colonialism as an epic story telling of huge devastation, painful struggle and persistent survival. We have become quite good at talking that kind of talk, most often amongst ourselves, for ourselves and to ourselves. 'The talk' about the colonial past is embedded in our political discourses, our humour, poetry, music, story telling and other commonsense ways of passing on both a narrative of history and an attitude about history. The lived experiences of imperialism and colonialism contribute another dimension to the ways in which terms like 'imperialism' can be understood. This is a dimension that indigenous peoples know and understand well.

In this chapter the intention is to discuss and contextualise four concepts which are often present (though not necessarily clearly visible) in the ways in which the ideas of indigenous peoples are articulated; imperialism, history, writing and theory.

These terms may seem to make up a strange selection, particularly as there are more obvious concepts such as self-determination or sovereignty which are used commonly in indigenous discourses. I have selected these words because from an indigenous perspective they are problematic. They are words which tend to provoke a whole array of feelings, attitudes and values. They are words of emotion which draw attention to the thousands of ways in which indigenous languages, knowledges and cultures have been silenced or misrepresented, ridiculed or condemned in academic and popular discourses. They are also words which are used in particular sorts of ways or avoided altogether. In thinking about knowledge and research, however, these are important terms which underpin the practices and styles of research with indigenous peoples. Decolonization is a process which engages with imperialism and colonialism at multiple levels. For researchers, one of those levels is concerned with having a more critical understanding of the underlying assumptions, motivations and values which inform research practices.

Imperialism

There is one particular figure whose name looms large, and whose spectre lingers, in indigenous discussions of encounters with the West: Christopher Columbus. It is not simply that Columbus is identified as the one who started it all, but rather that he has come to represent a huge legacy of suffering and destruction. Columbus 'names' that legacy more than any other individual.[2] He sets its modern time frame (500 years) and defines the outer limits of that legacy, that is, total destruction.[3] But there are other significant figures who symbolize and frame indigenous experiences in other places. In the imperial literature these are the 'heroes,' the discoverers and adventurers, the 'fathers' of colonialism. In the indigenous literature these figures are not so admired; their deeds are definitely not the deeds of wonderful discoverers and conquering heroes. In the South Pacific, for example, it is the British explorer James Cook, whose expeditions had a very clear scientific purpose and whose first encounters with indigenous peoples were fastidiously recorded. Hawai'ian academic Haunani Kay Trask's list of what Cook brought to the Pacific includes: 'capitalism, Western political ideas (such as predatory individualism) and Christianity. Most destructive of all he brought diseases that ravaged my people until we were but a remnant of what we had been on contact with his pestilent crew.'[4] The French are remembered by Tasmanian Aborigine Greg Lehman, 'not [for] the intellectual hubbub of an emerging anthropologie or even with the swish of their travel-weary frocks. It is with an arrogant death that they presaged their appearance. . . .'[5] For many communities there were waves of different sorts of Europeans; Dutch, Portuguese, British, French, whoever had political ascendancy over a region. And, in each place, after figures such as Columbus and Cook had long departed, there came a vast array of military personnel, imperial administrators, priests, explorers, missionaries, colonial officials, artists, entrepreneurs and settlers, who cut a devastating swathe, and left a permanent wound, on the societies and communities who occupied the lands named and claimed under imperialism.

The concepts of imperialism and colonialism are crucial ones which are used across a range of disciplines, often with meanings which are taken for granted. The two terms are interconnected and what is generally agreed upon is that colonialism is but one expression of imperialism. Imperialism tends to be used in at least four different ways when describing the form of European imperialism which 'started' in the fifteenth century: (1) imperialism as economic expansion; (2) imperialism as the subjugation of 'others'; (3) imperialism as an idea or spirit with many forms of realization; and (4) imperialism as a discursive field of knowledge. These usages do not necessarily contradict each other; rather, they need to be seen as analyses which focus on different layers of imperialism. Initially the term was used by historians to explain a series of developments leading to the economic expansion of Europe. Imperialism in this sense could be tied to a chronology of events related to 'discovery,' conquest, exploitation, distribution and appropriation.

Economic explanations of imperialism were first advanced by English historian J. A. Hobson in 1902 and by Lenin in 1917.[6] Hobson saw imperialism as being an integral part of Europe's economic expansion. He attributed the later stages of nineteenth-century imperialism to the inability of Europeans to purchase what was being produced and the need for Europe's industrialists to shift their capital to new markets which were secure. Imperialism was the system of control which secured the markets and capital investments. Colonialism facilitated this expansion by ensuring that there was European control, which necessarily meant securing and subjugating the indigenous populations. Like Hobson, Lenin was concerned with the ways in which economic expansion was linked to imperialism, although he argued that the export of capital to new markets was an attempt to rescue capitalism because Europe's workers could not afford what was being produced.

A second use of the concept of imperialism focuses more upon the exploitation and subjugation of indigenous peoples. Although economic explanations might account for why people like Columbus were funded to explore and discover new sources of wealth, they do not account for the devastating impact on the indigenous peoples whose lands were invaded. By the time contact was made in the South Pacific, Europeans, and more particularly the British, had learned from their previous encounters with indigenous peoples and had developed much more sophisticated 'rules of practice.'[7] While these practices ultimately lead to forms of subjugation, they also lead to subtle nuances which give an unevenness to the story of imperialism, even within the story of one indigenous society. While in New Zealand all Maori tribes, for example, lost the majority of their lands, not all tribes had their lands confiscated, were invaded militarily or were declared to be in rebellion. Similarly, while many indigenous nations signed treaties, other indigenous communities have no treaties. Furthermore, legislated identities which regulated who was an Indian and who was not, who was a *metis,* who had lost all status as an indigenous person, who had the correct fraction of blood quantum, who lived in the regulated spaces of reserves and communities, were all worked out arbitrarily (but systematically), to serve the interests of the colonizing society. The specificities of imperialism help to explain the different ways in which indigenous peoples have struggled to recover histories, lands, languages and basic human dignity. The way arguments are framed, the way dissent is controlled, the way settlements are made, while certainly drawing from international precedents, are also situated within a more localized discursive field.

A third major use of the term is much broader. It links imperialism to the spirit which characterized Europe's global activities. Mackenzie defines imperialism as being 'more than a set of economic, political and military phenomena. It is also a complex ideology which had widespread cultural, intellectual and technical expressions.'[8] This view of imperialism locates it within the Enlightenment spirit which signalled the transformation of economic, political and cultural life in Europe. In this wider Enlightenment context, imperialism becomes an integral part of the development of the modern state, of science, of ideas and of the 'modern' human person. In complex ways imperialism was also a mode through which the new states of Europe could expand their economies, through which new ideas and discoveries could be made and harnessed, and through which Europeans could develop their sense of Europeanness. The imperial imagination enabled European nations to imagine the possibility that new worlds, new wealth and new possessions existed that could be discovered and controlled. This imagination was realized through the promotion of science, economic expansion and political practice.

These three interpretations of imperialism have reflected a view from the imperial centre of Europe. In contrast, a fourth use of the term has been generated by writers whose understanding of imperialism and colonialism have been based either on their membership of and experience within colonized societies, or on their interest in understanding imperialism from the perspective of local contexts. Although these views of imperialism take into account the other forms of analysis, there are some important distinctions. There is, for example, a greater and more immediate need to understand the complex ways in which people were brought within the imperial system, because its impact is still being felt, despite the apparent independence gained by former colonial territories. The reach of imperialism into 'our heads' challenges those who belong to colonized communities to understand how this occurred, partly because we perceive a need to decolonize our minds, to recover ourselves, to claim a space in which to develop a sense of authentic humanity. This analysis of imperialism has been referred to more recently in terms such as 'post-colonial discourse,' the 'empire writes back' and/or 'writing from the margins.' There is a more political body of writing, however, which extends to the revolutionary, anti-colonial work of various activists (only some of whom, such as Frantz Fanon, actually wrote their ideas down) that draws also upon the work of black and African American writers and other minority writers whose work may have emerged out of a concern for human and civil rights, the rights of women and other forms of oppression.

Colonialism became imperialism's outpost, the fort and the port of imperial outreach. Whilst colonies may have started as a means to secure ports, access to raw materials and efficient transfer of commodities from point of origin to imperial centre, they also served other functions. It was not just indigenous populations who had to be subjugated. Europeans also needed to be kept under control, in service to the greater imperial enterprise. Colonial outposts were also cultural sites which preserved an image or represented an image of what the West or 'civilization' stood for. Colonies were not exact replicas of the imperial centre, culturally, economically or politically. Europeans resident in the colonies were not culturally homogeneous, so there were struggles within the colonizing community about its own identity. Wealth and class status created very powerful settler interests which came to dominate the politics of a colony. Colonialism was, in part, an image of imperialism, a particular realization of the imperial imagination. It was also, in part, an image of the future nation it would become. In this image lie images of the Other, stark contrasts and subtle nuances, of the ways in which the indigenous communities were perceived and dealt with, which makes the stories of colonialism part of a grander narrative and yet part also of a very local, very specific experience.

A constant reworking of our understandings of the impact of imperialism and colonialism is an important aspect of indigenous cultural politics and forms the basis of an indigenous language of critique. Within this critique there have been two major strands. One draws upon a notion of authenticity, of a time before colonization in which we were intact as indigenous peoples. We had absolute authority over our lives; we were born into and lived in a universe which was entirely of our making. We did not ask, need or want to be 'discovered' by Europe. The second strand of the language of critique demands that we have an analysis of how we were colonized, of what that has meant in terms of our immediate past and what it means for our present and future. The two strands intersect but what is particularly significant in indigenous discourses is that solutions are posed from a combination of the time before, *colonized time,* and the time before that, *pre-colonized time*. Decolonization encapsulates both sets of ideas.

There are, however, new challenges to the way indigenous peoples think and talk about imperialism. When the word globalization is substituted for the word imperialism, or when the prefix 'post' is attached to colonial, we are no longer talking simply about historical formations which are still lingering in our consciousness. Globalization and conceptions of a new world order represent different sorts of challenges for indigenous peoples. While being on the margins of the world has had dire consequences, being incorporated within the world's marketplace has different implications and in turn requires the mounting of new forms of resistance. Similarly, post-colonial discussions have also stirred some indigenous resistance, not so much to the literary reimagining of culture as being centred in what were once conceived of as the colonial margins, but to the idea that colonialism is over, finished business. This is best articulated by Aborigine activist Bobbi Sykes, who asked at an academic conference on post-colonialism, 'What? Post-colonialism? Have they left?' There is also, amongst indigenous academics, the sneaking suspicion that the fashion of post-colonialism has become a strategy for reinscribing or reauthorizing the privileges of non-indigenous academics because the field of 'post-colonial' discourse has been defined in ways which can still leave out indigenous peoples, our ways of knowing and our current concerns.

Research within late-modern and late-colonial conditions continues relentlessly and brings with it a new wave of exploration, discovery, exploitation and appropriation. Researchers enter communities armed with goodwill in their front pockets and patents in their back pockets, they bring medicine into villages and extract blood for genetic analysis. No matter how appalling their behaviours, how insensitive and offensive their personal actions may be, their acts and intentions are always justified as being for the 'good of mankind.' Research of this nature on indigenous peoples is still justified by the ends rather than the means, particularly if the indigenous peoples concerned can still be positioned as ignorant and undeveloped (savages). Other researchers gather traditional herbal and medicinal remedies and remove them for analysis in laboratories around the world. Still others collect the intangibles: the belief systems and ideas about healing, about the universe, about relationships and ways of organizing, and the practices and rituals which go alongside such beliefs, such as sweat lodges, massage techniques, chanting, hanging crystals and wearing certain colours. The global hunt for new knowledges, new materials, new cures, supported by international agreements such as the General Agreement on Tariffs and Trade (GATT), brings new threats to indigenous communities. The ethics of research, the ways in which indigenous communities can protect themselves and their knowledges, the understandings required not just of state legislation but of international agreements—these are the topics now on the agenda of many indigenous meetings.

On Being Human

> The faculty of imagination is not strongly developed among them, although they permitted it to run wild in believing absurd superstitions. —A. S. Thompson, 1859[9]

One of the supposed characteristics of primitive peoples was that we could not use our minds or intellects. We could not invent things, we could not create institutions or history, we could not imagine, we could not produce anything of value, we did not know how to use land and other resources from the natural world, we did not practice the 'arts' of civilization. By lacking such virtues we disqualified ourselves, not just from civilization but from humanity itself. In other words we were not 'fully human'; some of us were not even considered partially human. Ideas about what counted as human in association with the power to define people as human or not human were already encoded in imperial and colonial discourses prior to the period of imperialism covered here.[10] Imperialism provided the means through which concepts of what counts as human could be applied systematically as forms of classification, for example through hierarchies of race and typologies of different societies. In conjunction with imperial power and with 'science,' these classification systems came to shape relations between imperial powers and indigenous societies.

Said has argued that the 'oriental' was partially a creation of the West, based on a combination of images formed through scholarly and imaginative works. Fanon argued earlier that the colonized were brought into existence by the settler and the two, settler and colonized, are mutual constructions of colonialism. In Fanon's words 'we know each other well.'[11] The European powers had by the nineteenth century already established systems of rule and forms of social relations which governed interaction with the indigenous peoples being colonized. These relations were gendered, hierarchical and supported by rules, some explicit and others masked or hidden. The principle of 'humanity' was one way in which the implicit or hidden rules could be shaped. To consider indigenous peoples as not fully human, or not human at all, enabled distance to be maintained and justified various policies of either extermination or domestication. Some indigenous peoples ('not human') were hunted and killed like vermin, others ('partially human') were rounded up and put in reserves like creatures to be broken in, branded and put to work.

The struggle to assert and claim humanity has been a consistent thread of anti-colonial discourses on colonialism and oppression. This struggle for humanity has generally been framed within the wider discourse of humanism, the appeal to human 'rights,' the notion of a universal human subject, and the connections between being human and being capable of creating history, knowledge and society. The focus on asserting humanity has to be seen within the anti-colonial analysis of imperialism and what were seen as imperialism's dehumanizing imperatives which were structured into language, the economy, social relations and the cultural life of colonial societies. From the nineteenth century onwards the processes of dehumanization were often hidden behind justifications for imperialism and colonialism which were clothed within an ideology of humanism and liberalism and the assertion of moral claims which related to a concept of civilized 'man.' The moral justifications did not necessarily stop the continued hunting of Aborigines in the early nineteenth century nor the continued ill-treatment of different indigenous peoples even today.

Problems have arisen, however, within efforts to struggle for humanity by overthrowing the ideologies relating to our supposed lack of humanity. The arguments of Fanon, and many writers since Fanon, have been criticized for essentializing our 'nature,' for taking for granted the binary categories of Western thought, for accepting arguments supporting cultural relativity, for claiming an authenticity which is overly idealistic and romantic, and for simply engaging in an inversion of the colonizer/colonized relationship which does not address the complex problems of power relations. Colonized peoples have been compelled to define what it means to be human because there is a deep understanding of what it has meant to be considered not fully human, to be *savage*. The difficulties of such a process, however, have been bound inextricably to constructions of colonial relations around the binary of colonizer and colonized. These two categories are not just a simple opposition but consist of several relations, some more clearly oppositional than others. Unlocking one set of relations most often requires unlocking and unsettling the different constituent parts of other relations. The binary of colonizer/colonized does not take into account, for example, the development of different layerings which have occurred within each group and across the two groups. Millions of indigenous peoples were ripped from their lands over several generations and shipped into slavery. The lands they went to as slaves were lands already taken from another group of indigenous peoples. Slavery was as much a system of imperialism as was the claiming of other peoples' territories. Other indigenous peoples were transported to various outposts in the same way as interesting plants and animals were reclimatized, in order to fulfil labour requirements. Hence there are large populations in some places of non-indigenous groups, also victims of colonialism, whose primary relationship and allegiance is often to the imperial power rather than to the colonized people of the place to which they themselves have been brought. To put it simply, indigenous peoples as commodities were transported to and fro across the empire. There were also sexual relations between colonizers and colonized which led to communities who were referred to as 'half-castes' or 'half-breeds,' or stigmatized by some other specific term which often excluded them from belonging to either settler or indigenous societies. Sometimes children from 'mixed' sexual relationships were considered at least half-way civilized; at other times they were considered worse than civilized. Legislation was frequently used to regulate both the categories to which people were entitled to belong and the sorts of relations which one category of people could have with another.

Since the Second World War wars of independence and struggles for decolonization by former parts of European empires have shown us that attempts to break free can involve enormous violence: physical, social, economic, cultural and psychological. The struggle for freedom has been viewed by writers such as Fanon as a necessarily, inevitably violent process between 'two forces opposed to each other by their very nature.'[12] Fanon argues further that 'Decolonization which sets out to change the order of the world is, obviously, a programme of complete disorder.'[13] This introduces another important principle embedded in imperialism, that of order. The principle of order provides the underlying connection between such things as: the nature of imperial social relations; the activities of Western science; the establishment of trade; the appropriation of sovereignty; the establishment of law. No great conspiracy had to occur for the simultaneous developments and activities which took place under imperialism, because imperial activity was driven by fundamentally similar underlying principles. Nandy refers to these principles as the 'code' or 'grammar' of imperialism.[14] The idea of code suggests that there is a deep structure which regulates and legitimates imperial practices.

The fact that indigenous societies had their own systems of order was dismissed through what Albert Memmi referred to as a series of negations: they were not fully human, they were not civilized enough to have systems, they were not literate, their languages and modes of thought were inadequate.[15] As Fanon and later writers such as Nandy have claimed, imperialism and colonialism brought complete disorder to colonized peoples, disconnecting them from their histories, their landscapes, their languages, their social relations and their own ways of thinking, feeling and interacting with the world. It was a process of systematic fragmentation which can still be seen in the disciplinary carve-up of the indigenous world: bones, mummies and skulls to the museums, artwork to private collectors, languages to linguistics, 'customs' to anthropologists, beliefs and behaviours to psychologists. To discover how fragmented this process was one needs only to stand in a museum, a library, a bookshop, and ask where indigenous peoples are located. Fragmentation is not a phenomenon of postmodernism as many might claim. For indigenous peoples fragmentation has been the consequence of imperialism.

Writing, History, and Theory

A critical aspect of the struggle for self-determination has involved questions relating to our history as indigenous peoples and a critique of how we, as the Other, have been represented or excluded from various accounts. Every issue has been approached by indigenous peoples with a view to *re*writing and *re*righting our position in history. Indigenous peoples want to tell our own stories, write our own versions, in our own ways, for our own purposes. It is not simply about giving an oral account or a genealogical naming of the land and the events which raged over it, but a very powerful need to give testimony to and restore a spirit, to bring back into existence a world fragmented and dying. The sense of history conveyed by these approaches is not the same thing as the discipline of history, and so our accounts collide, crash into each other.

Writing or literacy, in a very traditional sense of the word, has been used to determine the breaks between the past and the present, the beginning of history and the development of theory.[16] Writing has been viewed as the mark of a superior civilization and other societies have been judged, by this view, to be incapable of thinking critically and objectively, or having distance from ideas and emotions. Writing is part of theorizing and writing is part of history. Writing, history and theory, then, are key sites in which Western research of the indigenous world has come together. As we saw at the beginning of this chapter, however, from another perspective writing and especially writing theory are very intimidating ideas for many indigenous students. Having been immersed in the Western academy which claims theory as thoroughly Western, which has constructed all the rules by which the indigenous world has been theorized, indigenous voices have been overwhelmingly silenced. The act, let alone the art and science, of theorizing our own existence and realities is not something which many indigenous people assume is possible. Frantz Fanon's call for the indigenous intellectual and artist to create a new literature, to work in the cause of constructing a national culture after liberation still stands as a challenge. While this has been taken up by writers of fiction, many indigenous scholars who work in the social and other sciences struggle to write, theorize and research as indigenous scholars.

Is History Important for Indigenous Peoples?

This may appear to be a trivial question as the answer most colonized people would give, I think, is that 'yes, history is important.' But I doubt if what they would be responding to is the notion of history which is understood by the Western academy. Poststructuralist critiques of history which draw heavily on French poststructural thought have focused on the characteristics and understandings of history as an Enlightenment or modernist project. Their critique is of both liberal and Marxist concepts of history. Feminists have argued similarly (but not necessarily from a poststructuralist position) that history is the story of a specific form of domination, namely of patriarchy, literally 'his-story.'

While acknowledging the critical approaches of poststructuralist theory and cultural studies the arguments which are debated at this level are not new to indigenous peoples. There are numerous oral stories which tell of what it means, what it feels like, to be present while your history is erased before your eyes, dismissed as irrelevant, ignored or rendered as the lunatic ravings of drunken old people. The negation of indigenous views of history was a critical part of asserting colonial ideology, partly because such views were regarded as clearly 'primitive' and 'incorrect' and mostly because they challenged and resisted the mission of colonization.

Indigenous peoples have also mounted a critique of the way history is told from the perspective of the colonizers. At the same time, however, indigenous groups have argued that history is important for understanding the present and that reclaiming history is a critical and essential aspect of decolonization. The critique of Western history argues that history is a modernist project which has developed alongside imperial beliefs about the Other. History is assembled around a set of interconnected ideas which I will summarize briefly here. I have drawn on a wide range of discussions by indigenous people and by writers such as Robert Young, J. Abu-Lughod, Keith Jenkins, C. Steadman.[17]

1. THE IDEA THAT HISTORY IS A TOTALIZING DISCOURSE

The concept of totality assumes the possibility and the desirability of being able to include absolutely all known knowledge into a coherent whole. In order for this to happen, classification systems, rules of practice and methods had to be developed to allow for knowledge to be selected and included in what counts as history.

2. THE IDEA THAT THERE IS A UNIVERSAL HISTORY

Although linked to the notion of totality, the concept of universal assumes that there are fundamental characteristics and values which all human subjects and societies share. It is the development of these universal characteristics which are of historical interest.

3. THE IDEA THAT HISTORY IS ONE LARGE CHRONOLOGY

History is regarded as being about developments over time. It charts the progress of human endeavour through time. Chronology is important as a method because it allows events to be located at a point in time. The actual time events take place also makes them 'real' or factual. In order to begin the chronology a time of 'discovery' has to be established. Chronology is also important for attempting to go backwards and explain how and why things happened in the past.

4. THE IDEA THAT HISTORY IS ABOUT DEVELOPMENT

Implicit in the notion of development is the notion of progress. This assumes that societies move forward in stages of development much as an infant grows into a fully developed adult human being. The earliest phase of human development is regarded as primitive, simple and emotional. As societies develop they become less primitive, more civilized, more rational, and their social structures become more complex and bureaucratic.

5. THE IDEA THAT HISTORY IS ABOUT A SELF-ACTUALIZING HUMAN SUBJECT

In this view humans have the potential to reach a stage in their development where they can be in total control of their faculties. There is an order of human development which moves, in stages, through the fulfilment of basic needs, the development of emotions, the development of the intellect and the development of morality. Just as the individual moves through these stages, so do societies.

6. THE IDEA THAT THE STORY OF HISTORY CAN BE TOLD IN ONE COHERENT NARRATIVE

This idea suggests that we can assemble all the facts in an ordered way so that they tell us the truth or give us a very good idea of what really did happen in the past. In theory it means that historians can write a true history of the world.

7. THE IDEA THAT HISTORY AS A DISCIPLINE IS INNOCENT

This idea says that 'facts' speak for themselves and that the historian simply researches the facts and puts them together. Once all the known facts are assembled they tell their own story, without any need of a theoretical explanation or interpretation by the historian. This idea also conveys the sense that history is pure as a discipline, that is, it is not implicated with other disciplines.

8. THE IDEA THAT HISTORY IS CONSTRUCTED AROUND BINARY CATEGORIES

This idea is linked to the historical method of chronology. In order for history to begin there has to be a period of beginning and some criteria for determining when something begins. In terms of history this was often attached to concepts of 'discovery,' the development of literacy, or the development of a specific social formation. Everything before that time is designated as prehistorical, belonging to the realm of myths and traditions, 'outside' the domain.

9. THE IDEA THAT HISTORY IS PATRIARCHAL

This idea is linked to the notions of self-actualization and development, as women were regarded as being incapable of attaining the higher orders of development. Furthermore they were not significant in terms of the ways societies developed because they were not present in the bureaucracies or hierarchies where changes in social or political life were being determined.

OTHER KEY IDEAS

Intersecting this set of ideas are some other important concepts. Literacy, as one example, was used as a criterion for assessing the development of a society and its progress to a stage where history can be said to begin. Even places such as India, China and Japan, however, which were very literate cultures prior to their 'discovery' by the West, were invoked through other categories which defined them as uncivilized. Their literacy, in other words, did not count as a record of legitimate knowledge.

The German philosopher Hegel is usually regarded as the 'founding father' of history in the sense outlined here. This applies to both liberal and Marxist views.[18] Hegel conceived of the fully human subject as someone capable of 'creating (his) own history.' However, Hegel did not simply invent the rules of history. As Robert Young argues, 'the entire Hegelian machinery simply lays down the operation of a system already in place, already operating in everyday life.'[19] It should also be self-evident that many of these ideas are predicated on a sense of Otherness. They are views which invite a comparison with 'something/someone else' which exists *on the outside,* such as the oriental, the 'Negro,' the 'Jew,' the 'Indian,' the 'Aborigine.' Views about the Other had already existed for centuries in Europe, but during the Enlightenment these views became more formalized through science, philosophy and imperialism, into explicit systems of classification and 'regimes of truth.' The racialization of the human subject and the social order enabled comparisons to be made between the 'us' of the West and the 'them' of the Other. History was the story of people who were regarded as *fully human*. Others who were not regarded as human (that is, capable of self-actualization) were prehistoric. This notion is linked also to Hegel's master-slave construct which has been applied as a psychological category (by Freud) and as a system of social ordering.

A further set of important ideas embedded in the modernist view of history relates to the origins (causes) and nature of social change. The Enlightenment project involved new conceptions of society and of the individual based around the precepts of rationalism, individualism and capitalism. There was a general belief that not only could individuals remake themselves but so could societies. The modern industrial state became the point of contrast between the premodern and the modern. History in this view began with the emergence of the rational individual and the modern industrialized society. However, there is something more to this idea in terms of how history came to be conceptualized as a method. The connection to the industrial state is significant because it highlights what was regarded as being worthy of history. The people and groups who 'made' history were the people who developed the underpinnings of the state—the economists, scientists, bureaucrats and philosophers. That they were all men of a certain class and race was 'natural' because they were regarded (naturally) as fully rational, self-actualizing human beings capable, therefore, of creating social change, that is history. The day-to-day lives of 'ordinary' people, and of women, did not become a concern of history until much more recently.

Contested Histories

For indigenous peoples, the critique of history is not unfamiliar, although it has now been claimed by postmodern theories. The idea of contested stories and multiple discourses about the past, by different communities, is closely linked to the politics of everyday contemporary indigenous life. It is very much a part of the fabric of communities that value oral ways of knowing. These contested accounts are stored within genealogies, within the landscape, within weavings and carvings, even within the personal names that many people carried. The means by which these histories were stored was through their systems of knowledge. Many of these systems have since been reclassified as oral *traditions* rather than histories.

Under colonialism indigenous peoples have struggled against a Western view of history and yet been complicit with that view. We have often allowed our 'histories' to be told and have then become outsiders as we heard them being retold. Schooling is directly implicated in this process. Through the curriculum and its underlying theory of knowledge, early schools redefined the world and where indigenous peoples were positioned within the world. From being direct descendants of sky and earth parents, Christianity positioned some of us as higher-order savages who deserved salvation in order that we could become children of God. Maps of the world reinforced our place on the periphery of the world, although we were still considered part of the Empire. This included having to learn new names for our own lands. Other symbols of our loyalty, such as the flag, were also an integral part of the imperial curriculum.[20] Our orientation to the world was already being redefined as we were being excluded systematically from the writing of the history of our own lands.

This on its own may not have worked were it not for the actual material redefinition of our world which was occurring simultaneously through such things as the renaming and 'breaking in' of the land, the alienation and fragmentation of lands through legislation, the forced movement of people off their lands, and the social consequences which resulted in high sickness and mortality rates.

Indigenous attempts to reclaim land, language, knowledge and sovereignty have usually involved contested accounts of the past by colonizers and colonized. These have occurred in the courts, before various commissions, tribunals and official enquiries, in the media, in Parliament, in bars and on talkback radio. In these situations contested histories do not exist in the same cultural framework as they do when tribal or clan histories, for example, are being debated within the indigenous community itself. They are not simply struggles over 'facts' and 'truth'; the rules by which these struggles take place are never clear (other than that we as the indigenous community know they are going to be stacked against us); and we are not the final arbiters of what really counts as the truth.

It is because of these issues that I ask the question, 'Is history in its modernist construction important or not important for indigenous peoples?' For many people who are presently engaged in research on indigenous land claims the answer would appear to be self-evident. We assume that when 'the truth comes out' it will prove that what happened was wrong or illegal and that therefore the system (tribunals, the courts, the government) will set things right. We believe that history is also about justice, that understanding history will enlighten our decisions about the future. *Wrong*. History is also about power. In fact history is mostly about power. It is the story of the powerful and how they became powerful, and then how they use their power to keep them in positions in which they can continue to dominate others. It is because of this relationship with power that we have been excluded, marginalized and 'Othered.' In this sense history is not important for indigenous peoples because a thousand accounts of the 'truth' will not alter the 'fact' that indigenous peoples are still marginal and do not possess the power to transform history into justice.

This leads then to several other questions. The one which is most relevant to this book is the one which asks, 'Why then has revisiting history been a significant part of decolonization?' The answer, I suggest, lies in the intersection of indigenous approaches to the past, of the modernist history project itself and of the resistance strategies which have been employed. Our colonial experience traps us in the project of modernity. There can be no 'postmodern' for us until we have settled some business of the modern. This does not mean that we do not understand or employ multiple discourses, or act in incredibly contradictory ways, or exercise power ourselves in multiple ways. It means that there is unfinished business, that we are still being colonized (and know it), and that we are still searching for justice.

Coming to know the past has been part of the critical pedagogy of decolonization. To hold alternative histories is to hold alternative knowledges. The pedagogical implication of this access to alternative knowledges is that they can form the basis of alternative ways of doing things. Transforming our colonized views of our own history (as written by the West), however, requires us to revisit, site by site, our history under Western eyes. This in turn requires a theory or approach which helps us to engage with, understand and then act upon history. It is in this sense that the sites visited in this book begin with a critique of a Western view of history. Telling our stories from the past, reclaiming the past, giving testimony to the injustices of the past are all strategies which are commonly employed by indigenous peoples struggling for justice. On the international scene it is extremely rare and unusual when indigenous accounts are accepted and acknowledged as valid interpretations of what has taken place. And yet, the need to tell our stories remains the powerful imperative of a powerful form of resistance.

Is Writing Important for Indigenous Peoples?

As I am arguing, every aspect of the act of producing knowledge has influenced the ways in which indigenous ways of knowing have been represented. Reading, writing, talking, these are as fundamental to academic discourse as science, theories, methods, paradigms. To begin with reading, one might cite the talk in which Maori writer Patricia Grace undertook to show that 'Books Are Dangerous.'[21] She argues that there are four things that make many books dangerous to indigenous readers: (1) they do not reinforce our values, actions, customs, culture and identity; (2) when they tell us only about others they are saying that we do not exist; (3) they may be writing about us but are writing things which are untrue; and (4) they are writing about us but saying negative and insensitive things which tell us that we are not good. Although Grace is talking about school texts and journals, her comments apply also to academic writing. Much of what I have read has said that we do not exist, that if we do exist it is in terms which I cannot recognize, that we are no good and that what we think is not valid.

Leonie Pihama makes a similar point about film. In a review of *The Piano* she says: 'Maori people struggle to gain a voice, struggle to be heard from the margins, to have our stories heard, to have our descriptions of ourselves validated, to have access to the domain within which we can control and define those images which are held up as reflections of our realities.'[22] Representation is important as a concept because it gives the impression of 'the truth.' When I read texts, for example, I frequently have to orientate myself to a text world in which the centre of academic knowledge is either in Britain, the United States, or Western Europe; in which words such as 'we,' 'us,' 'our,' 'I' actually exclude me. It is a text world in which (if what I am interested in rates a mention) I have learned that I belong *partly* in the Third World, *partly* in the 'Women of Colour' world, *partly* in the black or African world. I read myself into these labels *partly* because I have also learned that, although there may be commonalities, they still do not entirely account for the experiences of indigenous peoples.

So, reading and interpretation present problems when we do not see ourselves in the text. There are problems, too, when we do see ourselves but can barely recognize ourselves through the representation. One problem of being trained to read this way, or, more correctly, of learning to read this way over many years of academic study, is that we can adopt uncritically similar patterns of writing. We begin to write about ourselves as indigenous peoples as if we really were 'out there,' the 'Other,' with all the baggage that this entails. Another problem is that academic writing is a form of selecting, arranging and presenting knowledge. It privileges sets of texts, views about the history of an idea, what issues count as significant; and, by engaging in the same process uncritically, we too can render indigenous writers invisible or unimportant while reinforcing the validity of other writers. If we write without thinking critically about our writing, it can be dangerous. Writing can also be dangerous because we reinforce and maintain a style of discourse which is never innocent. Writing can be dangerous because sometimes we reveal ourselves in ways which get misappropriated and used against us. Writing can be dangerous because, by building on previous texts written about indigenous peoples, we continue to legitimate views about ourselves which are hostile to us. This is particularly true of academic writing, although journalistic and imaginative writing reinforces these 'myths.'

These attitudes inform what is sometimes referred to as either the 'Empire writes back' discourse or post-colonial literature. This kind of writing assumes that the centre does not necessarily have to be located at the imperial centre.[23] It is argued that the centre can be shifted ideologically through imagination and that this shifting can re-create history. Another perspective relates to the ability of 'native' writers to appropriate the language of the colonizer as the language of the colonized and to write so that it captures the ways in which the colonized actually use the language, their dialects and inflections, and in the way they make sense of their lives. Its other importance is that it speaks to an audience of people who have also been colonized. This is one of the ironies of many indigenous peoples' conferences where issues of indigenous language have to be debated in the language of the colonizers. Another variation of the debate relates to the use of literature to write about the terrible things which happened under colonialism or as a consequence of colonialism. These topics inevitably implicate the colonizers *and their literature* in the processes of cultural domination.

Yet another position, espoused in African literature by Ngũgĩ wa Thiong'o, was to write in the languages of Africa. For Ngũgĩ wa Thiong'o, to write in the language of the colonizers was to pay homage to them, while to write in the languages of Africa was to engage in an anti-imperialist struggle. He argued that language carries culture and the language of the colonizer became the means by which the 'mental universe of the colonized' was dominated.[24] This applied, in Ngũgĩ wa Thiong'o's view, particularly to the language of writing. Whereas oral languages were frequently still heard at home, the use of literature in association with schooling resulted in the alienation of a child from the child's history, geography, music and other aspects of culture.[25]

In discussing the politics of academic writing, in which research writing is a subset, Cherryl Smith argues that 'colonialism, racism and cultural imperialism do not occur only in society, outside of the gates of universities.'[26] 'Academic writing,' she continues, 'is a way of "writing back" whilst at the same time writing to ourselves.'[27] The act of 'writing back' and simultaneously writing to ourselves is not simply an inversion of how we have learned to write academically.[28] The different audiences to whom we speak makes the task somewhat difficult. The scope of the literature which we use in our work contributes to a different framing of the issues. The oral arts and other forms of expression set our landscape in a different frame of reference. Our understandings of the academic disciplines within which we have been trained also frame our approaches. Even the use of pronouns such as 'I' and 'we' can cause difficulties when writing for several audiences, because while it may be acceptable now in academic writing, it is not always acceptable to indigenous audiences.[29]

Edward Said also asks the following questions: 'Who writes? For whom is the writing being done? In what circumstances? These it seems to me are the questions whose answers provide us with the ingredients making a politics of interpretation.'[30] These questions are important ones which are being asked in a variety of ways within our communities. They are asked, for example, about research, policy making and curriculum development. Said's comments, however, point to the problems of interpretation, in this case of academic writing. 'Who' is doing the writing is important in the politics of the Third World and African America, and indeed for indigenous peoples; it is even more important in the politics of how these worlds are being represented 'back to' the West. Although in the literary sense the imagination is crucial to writing, the use of language is not highly regarded in academic discourses which claim to be scientific. The concept of imagination, when employed as a sociological tool, is often reduced to a way of seeing and understanding the world, or a way of understanding how people either construct the world or are constructed by the world. As Toni Morrison argues, however, the imagination can be a way of sharing the world.[31] This means, according to Morrison, struggling to find the language to do this and then struggling to interpret and perform within that shared imagination.

Writing Theory

Research is linked in all disciplines to theory. Research adds to, is generated from, creates or broadens our theoretical understandings. Indigenous peoples have been, in many ways, oppressed by theory. Any consideration of the ways our origins have been examined, our histories recounted, our arts analysed, our cultures dissected, measured, torn apart and distorted back to us will suggest that theories have not looked sympathetically or ethically at us. Writing research is often considered marginally more important than writing theory, providing it results in tangible benefits for farmers, economists, industries and sick people. For indigenous peoples, most of the theorizing has been driven by anthropological approaches. These approaches have shown enormous concern for our origins as peoples and for aspects of our linguistic and material culture.

The development of theories by indigenous scholars which attempt to explain our existence in contemporary society (as opposed to the 'traditional' society constructed under modernism) has only just begun. Not all these theories claim to be derived from some 'pure' sense of what it means to be indigenous, nor do they claim to be theories which have been developed in a vacuum separated from any association with civil and human rights movements, other nationalist struggles or other theoretical approaches. What is claimed, however, is that new ways of theorizing by indigenous scholars are grounded in a real sense of, and sensitivity towards, what it means to be an indigenous person. As Kathie Irwin urges, 'We don't need anyone else developing the tools which will help us to come to terms with who we are. We can and will do this work. Real power lies with those who design the tools—it always has. This power is ours.'[32] Contained within this imperative is a sense of being able to determine priorities, to bring to the centre those issues of our own choosing, and to discuss them amongst ourselves.

I am arguing that theory at its most simple level is important for indigenous peoples. At the very least it helps make sense of reality. It enables us to make assumptions and predictions about the world in which we live. It contains within it a method or methods for selecting and arranging, for prioritising and legitimating what we see and do. Theory enables us to deal with contradictions and uncertainties. Perhaps more significantly, it gives us space to plan, to strategize, to take greater control over our resistances. The language of a theory can also be used as a way of organising and determining action. It helps us to interpret what is being told to us, and to predict the consequences of what is being promised. Theory can also protect us because it contains within it a way of putting reality into perspective. If it is a good theory it also allows for new ideas and ways of looking at things to be incorporated constantly without the need to search constantly for new theories.

A dilemma posed by such a thorough critical approach to history, writing and theory is that whilst we may reject or dismiss them, this does not make them go away, nor does the critique necessarily offer the alternatives. We live simultaneously within such views while needing to pose, contest and struggle for the legitimacy of oppositional or alternative histories, theories and ways of writing. At some points there is, there has to be, dialogue across the boundaries of oppositions. This has to be because we constantly collide with dominant views while we are attempting to transform our lives on a larger scale than our own localized circumstances. This means struggling to make sense of our own world while also attempting to transform what counts as important in the world of the powerful.

Part of the exercise is about recovering our own stories of the past. This is inextricably bound to a recovery of our language and epistemological foundations. It is also about reconciling and reprioritizing what is really important about the past with what is important about the present. These issues raise significant questions for indigenous communities who are not only beginning to fight back against the invasion of their communities by academic, corporate, and populist researchers, but to think about, and carry out research, on their own concerns. One of the problems discussed in this first section of this book is that the methodologies and methods of research, the theories that inform them, the questions which they generate and the writing styles they employ, all become significant acts which need to be considered carefully and critically before being applied. In other words, they need to be 'decolonized.' Decolonization, however, does not mean and has not meant a total rejection of all theory or research or Western knowledge. Rather, it is about centering our concerns and world views and then coming to know and understand theory and research from our own perspectives and for our own purposes.

As a site of struggle research has a significance for indigenous peoples that is embedded in our history under the gaze of Western imperialism and Western science. It is framed by our attempts to escape the penetration and surveillance of that gaze whilst simultaneously reordering and reconstituting ourselves as indigenous human beings in a state of ongoing crisis. Research has not been neutral in its objectification of the Other. Objectification is a process of dehumanization. In its clear links to Western knowledge research has generated a particular relationship to indigenous peoples which continues to be problematic. At the same time, however, new pressures which have resulted from our own politics of self-determination, of wanting greater participation in, or control over, what happens to us, and from changes in the global environment, have meant that there is a much more active and knowing engagement in the activity of research by indigenous peoples. Many indigenous groups, communities and organisations are thinking about, talking about and carrying out research activities of various kinds. In this chapter I have suggested that it is important to have a critical understanding of some of the tools of research—not just the obvious technical tools but the conceptual tools, the ones which make us feel uncomfortable, which we avoid, for which we have no easy response.

> I lack imagination you say
> No. I lack language.
> The language to clarify
> my resistance to the literate . . .
> —Cherrie Moraga[33]

NOTES

1 Audre Lorde (1979), 'The Master's Tools Will Never Dismantle the Master's House,' comments at 'The Personal and the Political' panel, Second Sex Conference, reproduced in C. Moraga and G. Anzaldua (1981), *This Bridge Called My Back*, New York: Kitchen Table Women of Color Press, New York, pp. 98–101.

2 See K. Sale (1990), *The Conquest of Paradise, Christopher and the Colombian Legacy*, New York: Alfred Knopf.

3 See W. Churchill (1994), *Indians Are Us? Culture and Genocide in North America*, Monroe, ME: Common Courage Press.

4 H. K. Trask (1993), *From a Native Daughter*, Monroe, ME: Common Courage Press, p. 7.

5 G. Lehman (1996), 'Life's Quiet Companion,' paper, Riawunna Centre for Aboriginal Studies, University of Tasmania, Hobart, Australia.

6 A. Giddens (1989), *Sociology*, Cambridge: Polity Press, pp. 530–3.

7 The term 'rules of practice' comes from Foucault. See, for this encounter, A. Salmond (1991), *Two Worlds, First Meetings between Maori and Europeans 1642–1772*, Auckland: Viking.

8 J. K. Mackenzie (1990), *Imperialism and the Natural World*, Manchester University Press, England.

9 A. S. Thompson (1859), *The Story of New Zealand—Past and Present, Savage and Civilized*, London: John Murray, p. 82.

10 D. T. Goldberg (1993), *Racist Culture, Philosophy and the Politics of Meaning*, Oxford: Blackwell. See also Z. Sardar, A. Nandy and W. Davies (1993), *Barbaric Others, A Manifesto of Western Racism*, London: Pluto Press.

11 Frantz Fanon (1990), *The Wretched of the Earth*, London: Penguin.

12 Ibid., pp. 27–8.

13 Ibid., p. 27.

14 A. Nandy (1989), *The Intimate Enemy: Loss and Recovery of Self under Colonialism*, Delhi: Oxford University Press.

15 A. Memmi (1991), *The Colonizer and the Colonized*, Boston: Beacon Press, p. 83.

16 For a critique of these views refer to B. V. Street (1984), *Literacy in Theory and Practice*, New York: Cambridge University Press.

17 I have drawn on a wide range of discussions both by indigenous people and by various writers such as Robert Young, J. Abu-Lughod, Keith Jenkins and C. Steadman. See, for example, R. Young (1990), *White Mythologies, Writing, History and the West*, London: Routledge; J. Abu-Lughod (1989), 'On the Remaking of History. How to Reinvent the Past,' in *Remaking History*, Dia Art Foundation, Seattle: Bay Press, pp. 111–29; C. Steadman (1992), 'Culture,

Cultural Studies and the Historians,' in *Cultural Studies,* ed. G. Nelson, P. A. Treicher and L. Grossberg, New York: Routledge, pp. 613–20; Trask, *From a Native Daughter.*

18 Young, *White Mythologies.*

19 Ibid., p. 3.

20 J. Mangan (1993), *The Imperial Curriculum—Racial Images and Education in the British Colonial Experience,* London: Routledge.

21 P. Grace (1985), 'Books Are Dangerous,' paper presented at the Fourth Early Childhood Convention, Wellington, New Zealand.

22 L. Pihama (1994), 'Are Films Dangerous? A Maori Woman's Perspective on *The Piano,'* *Hecate,* Vol. 20, No. 2, p. 241.

23 B. Ashcroft, G. Griffiths and H. Tiffin (1989), *The Empire Writes Back, Theory and Practice in Post-colonial Literatures,* London: Routledge.

24 Ngũgĩ wa Thiong'o (1986), *Decolonizing the Mind. The Politics of Language in African Literature,* London: James Currey.

25 Ibid.

26 C. W. Smith (1994), 'Kimihia Te Matauranga: Colonization and Iwi Development,' MA thesis, University of Auckland, New Zealand, p. 13.

27 Ibid., p. 13.

28 T. A. van Dijk (1989), *Elite Discourses and Racism,* Newbury Park, CA: Sage Publications.

29 L. T. Smith (1994), 'In Search of a Language and a Shareable Imaginative World: E Kore Taku Moe, E Riro i a Koe', *Hecate,* Vol. 20, No. 2, pp. 162–74.

30 E. W. Said (1983), 'Opponents, Audiences, Constituencies, and Community,' in *The Politics of Interpretation,* ed. W.J.T. Mitchell, Chicago: University of Chicago Press, p.7.

31 T. Morrison (1993), *Playing in the Dark. Whiteness and the Literary Imagination,* New York: Vintage Books.

32 K. Irwin (1992), 'Towards Theories of Maori Feminisms,' in *Feminist Voices: Women's Studies Texts for Aotearoa/New Zealand,* ed. R. du Plessis, Auckland: Oxford University Press, p. 5.

33 Cherrie Moraga (1983), quoted by G. Anzaldúa in 'Speaking Tongues: a Letter to 3rd World Women Writers,' in *This Bridge Called My Back,* p. 166.

III

The Politics of Language and Literary Studies

Although Edmund Burke's attempt to impeach Warren Hastings ultimately failed, neither his dire warnings about the rampant corruption of East India Company officials nor his plea for more direct supervision by the British Parliament in the affairs of its distant Indian empire fell on deaf ears (see chapter 2). Earlier unsuccessful attempts to check the power of the controversial company were followed by the increasing intervention of the British Crown in Indian political and social matters and the gradual diminishment of company influence. The Charter Act of Parliament in 1813, in particular, was to have a tremendous impact on Indian schooling that resonates even today, since it conferred on British officials decisive authority over the education of the natives of India.

However cavalier Hastings was accused of being in his performance as administrator, while he was governor-general between 1773 and 1784, he did at least encourage members of the British minority in India to familiarize themselves with Indian culture and customs, in order to ease their daily transactions with the majority they ruled. His relative flexibility was not in itself revolutionary given the prominence of British Orientalists such as William Jones, who approached the East with some respect for its antiquity and its civilizations, albeit imbued with a heavily exotic flavor. Somewhat different in tenor from the virulent Orientalism Edward Said discusses in relation to the Middle East (see chapter 7), the Orientalist school of thought in India stressed continued and systematized native education in the local traditions and histories. By the middle of the eighteenth century, however, the Orientalist inability to concede cultural equality between the conquerors and the conquered found its logical sequel in the Anglicist school, which explicitly favored English-language education and European cultural heritage over Indian vernaculars and traditions. Thomas Babington Macaulay, the English historian and author, belonged to the Anglicist party, and his 1835 Minute on Indian education is an impassioned plea for the institutionalization of English studies in India.

The Charter Act of 1813, with its official consent to missionary activity in India, also opened up another important venue of British control over Indian social affairs. Despite the appearance of concern for the well-being of Indians, the various trade, educational, and religious imperatives of this period ultimately reveal the increasing consolidation of British authority in India. Macaulay's comprehensive contempt for anything Indian is deliberately complacent in contrast to Burke's manifest anxiety about the Indianization of the English rather than the Anglicization of the Indians. Macaulay demolishes Burke's reverse-power binary of master and servant by insisting on the irrevocable inferiority of Indian systems of thought: "absurd history, absurd metaphysics, absurd physics, absurd theology." Macaulay here relies on repetitive proclamation over reasoned argument, and apparently considers logical rhetorical procedures irrelevant in establishing the all-too-obvious outmodedness of Indian culture. He admits that he has "no knowledge of either Sanscrit or Arabic," but nevertheless confidently estimates their worth(lessness). A nineteenth-century English reader might understand that Milton's Leviathan-like Satan is mythical, while the gullible Indian native, whose history "abound[s] with kings thirty feet high," is incapable of such rational discrimination. Indeed, Christian myths themselves seem self-evidently judicious, but the various "superstitions" of Hinduism and Islam seriously impede the scientific consciousness. Macaulay, however, is careful not to explicitly support Christian proselytism in India, given the official leaning toward more secular trends in the production and dissemination of knowledge. His famous objective of creating "a class of persons, Indian in blood and colour, but English in taste, in opinions, in morals, and in intellect," despite its dubious dependence on culture as a transparent and benevolent agent of national transformation, was to be prophetic after English was made the official language in India in 1835.

The second essay in part III, by Alexander Crummell, exemplifies not just the resounding success of Macaulay's edict in India for other colonial spaces but Ngũgĩ wa Thiong'o's warning, more than a hundred years later, that "the final triumph of a system of domination [comes] when the dominated start singing its virtues." Alexander Crummell delivered his address "The English Language in Liberia" in 1860 to commemorate the thirteenth anniversary of the nation's independence from the American Colonization Society. Crummell was one among many thousands of African Americans who had migrated to the colony, and he remained there for almost two decades. Although perceived as one of the primary figures of pan-Africanism, the Reverend Crummell privileges his North American, English, and Christian backgrounds as the worthy foundation of his contributions to the future of Liberia. The trauma of black diasporic "return" from the New World, while indelibly scarred by the experiences of slavery and exile, is redeemed for Crummell by Africans' formative and improving sojourn in the West. The violence of the initial encounter does not deter Crummell from acknowledging what he considers his providential debt to a "higher and nobler civilization," just as Macaulay briefly acknowledges his indebtedness to the Roman colonization of England. In his address, Crummell makes it clear that his access to superior culture has largely been enabled by his acquisition of the English language. Virtually all of Macaulay's sentiments about native languages as evidence of the barbarism of native thought are shared by Crummell, who uncannily echoes Macaulay's hope that cultural assimilation would atone for the inherent flaws of racial imperfections.

Ngũgĩ wa Thiong'o's essay "The Language of African Literature," from his significantly titled collection of essays *Decolonising the Mind: The Politics of Language in African Literature*, examines the enduring legacy of "europhone" literary politics, now uncritically and passively accepted, he argues, by some of Africa's canonical writers. What was revolutionary in Macaulay's time seems, more than a century later, an accepted given of African literary studies in European languages. Unlike Macaulay, though, who couches his claims for English-language education in the rhetoric of disinterested philanthropy, immutable reason, and a pragmatic study of the "state of the market," Ngũgĩ exposes the muted complicity of colonial force and colonial ideology, the cannon and the canon. A system of reward and punishment in school was magnified in the economic sphere, leaving most colonized subjects with few gainful options but to choose languages that were imposed on them. Absorbing European worldviews through Europe's languages and literatures, African subjects, according to Ngũgĩ, inherited and internalized the damaging stereotypes of their native cultures and traditions. Ngũgĩ's temporary renunciation of English for Gĩkũyũ as his primary language of communication was an attempt to protest the marginalization of the language debate in African literary studies. Ironically, where Crummell sees educational failure in the persistence of African dialects and Creoles or in the survival of African folktales, Ngũgĩ, like Carolyn Cooper, reads resistance.

Unlike Ngũgĩ's powerful argument for a reorientation toward native languages, which gives perhaps too much agency, intentionality, and uniformity to the destructive potential of colonial education, Cooper, writing from a black Jamaican context, retrieves in women's popular and folk culture the oral traditions that evade or survive disciplinary measures. Ngũgĩ and Cooper legitimately challenge the traditional subordination of peasant and lower-class peoples to middle-class ambitions in the colonies, and they both seem to agree that a middle-class accommodation to colonial education implies a less authentic nationalism. Indeed, Cooper's book title is derived from a phrase in Jamaican novelist Victor Reid's *Nanny Town*, which says that "knowledge comes . . . like an echo in the bone or a noise in the blood," suggesting a biological retention of African languages in Cooper's adaptation. (Both Kamau Brathwaite and Edouard Glissant, Caribbean theorists of creolization, have also used the concept of linguistic "noise," though not in the same way.) Cooper also genders resistance to standard European languages as in the "Jamaican mother-tongue," which is articulated against "the imperial authority of the English father-tongue," whereas Ngũgĩ locates a truly nationalist spirit in what he considers more rooted peasant cultures. When Macaulay triumphantly notes the readiness of colonial subjects to learn English, he assumes that their preference signifies a gratifying acceptance of the validity of his arguments, rather than a pragmatic, if calculating, estimate of what lies in their immediate best interests. However shortsighted, even occasionally self-defeating, such a calculation was, colonized peoples, regardless of class and region, were perhaps not as radically deprived of their indigenous cultures and traditions as Macaulay anticipated. And even for those who did seem passive objects of Macaulay's cultural assimilation project, critics such as Homi Bhabha would insist that the unstable, incomplete process of such mimicry would eventually prove subversive (see part V).

9

THOMAS BABINGTON MACAULAY

Minute on Indian Education, February 2, 1835

As it seems to be the opinion of some of the gentlemen who compose the Committee of Public Instruction, that the course which they have hitherto pursued was strictly prescribed by the British Parliament in 1813, and as, if that opinion be correct, a legislative Act will be necessary to warrant a change, I have thought it right to refrain from taking any part in the preparation of the adverse statements which are now before us, and to reserve what I had to say on the subject till it should come before me as a member of the Council of India.

It does not appear to me that the Act of Parliament can, by any art of construction, be made to bear the meaning which has been assigned to it. It contains nothing about the particular languages or sciences which are to be studied. A sum is set apart "for the revival and promotion of literature and the encouragement of the learned natives of India, and for the introduction and promotion of a knowledge of the sciences among the inhabitants of the British territories." It is argued, or rather taken for granted, that by literature the Parliament can have only meant Arabic and Sanscrit literature, that they never would have given the honourable appellation of a "learned native" to a native who was familiar with the poetry of Milton, the metaphysics of Locke, and the physics of Newton; but that they meant to designate by that name only such persons as might have studied in the sacred books of the Hindoos all the usages of cusa-grass, and all the mysteries of absorption into the Deity. This does not appear to be a very satisfactory interpretation. To take a parallel case; suppose that the Pacha of Egypt, a country once superior in knowledge to the nations of Europe, but now sunk far below them, were to appropriate a sum for the purpose of "reviving and promoting literature, and encouraging learned natives of Egypt," would anybody infer that he meant the youth of his pachalic to give years to the study of hieroglyphics, to search into all the doctrines disguised under the fable of Osiris, and to ascertain with all possible accuracy the ritual with which cats and onions were anciently adored? Would he be justly charged with inconsistency, if, instead of employing his young subjects in deciphering obelisks, he were to order them to be instructed in the English and French languages, and in all the sciences to which those languages are the chief keys?

The words on which the supporters of the old system rely do not bear them out, and other words follow which seem to be quite decisive on the other side. This lac of rupees is set apart, not only for "reviving literature in India," the phrase on which their whole interpretation is founded, but also for "the introduction and promotion of a knowledge of the sciences among the inhabitants of the British territories,"— words which are alone sufficient to authorize all the changes for which I contend.

If the Council agree in my construction, no legislative Act will be necessary. If they differ from me, I will prepare a short Act rescinding that clause of the Charter of 1813, from which the difficulty arises.

The argument which I have been considering affects only the form of proceeding. But the admirers of the Oriental system of education have used another argument, which, if we admit it to be valid, is decisive against all change. They conceive that the public faith is pledged to the present system, and that to alter the appropriation of any of the funds which have hitherto been spent in encouraging the study of Arabic and Sanscrit would be downright spoliation. It is not easy to understand by what process of reasoning they can have arrived at this conclusion. The grants which are made from the public purse for the encouragement of literature differed in no respect from the grants which are made from the same purse for other objects of real or supposed utility. We found a sanatarium on a spot which we suppose to be healthy. Do we thereby pledge ourselves to keep a sanatarium there, if the result should not answer our expectation? We commence the erection of a pier. Is it a violation of the public faith to stop the works, if we afterwards see reason to believe that the building will be useless? The rights of property are undoubtedly sacred. But nothing endangers those rights so much as the practice, now unhappily too common, of attributing them to things to which they do not belong. Those who would impart to abuses the sanctity of property are in truth imparting to the institution of property the unpopularity and fragility of abuses. If the Government has given to any person a formal assurance; nay, if the Government has excited in any person's mind a reasonable expectation that he shall receive a certain income as a teacher or a learner of Sanscrit or Arabic, I would respect that person's pecuniary interests—I would rather err on the side of liberality to individuals than suffer the public faith to be called in question. But to talk of a Government pledging itself to teach certain languages and certain sciences, though those languages may become useless, though those sciences may be exploded, seems to me quite unmeaning. There is not a single word in any public instructions from which it can be inferred that the Indian Government ever intended to give any pledge on this subject, or ever considered the destination of these funds as unalterably fixed. But, had it been otherwise, I should have denied the competence of our predecessors to bind us by any pledge on such a subject. Suppose that a Government had in the last century enacted in the most solemn manner that all its subjects should, to the end of time, be inoculated for the small-pox: would that Government be bound to persist in the practice after Jenner's discovery? These promises, of which nobody claims the performance, and from which nobody can grant a release; these vested rights, which vest in nobody; this property without proprietors; this robbery, which makes nobody poorer, may be comprehended by persons of higher faculties than mine—I consider this plea merely as a set form of words, regularly used both in England and India, in defence of every abuse for which no other plea can be set up.

I hold this lac of rupees to be quite at the disposal of the Governor-General in Council, for the purpose of promoting learning in India, in any way which may be thought most advisable. I hold his Lordship to be quite as free to direct that it shall no longer be employed in encouraging Arabic and Sanscrit, as he is to direct that the reward for killing tigers in Mysore shall be diminished, or that no more public money shall be expended on the chanting at the cathedral.

We now come to the gist of the matter. We have a fund to be employed as Government shall direct for the intellectual improvement of the people of this country. The simple question is, what is the most useful way of employing it?

All parties seem to be agreed on one point, that the dialects commonly spoken among the natives of this part of India contain neither Literary nor scientific information, and are, moreover so poor and rude that, until they are enriched from some other quarter, it will not be easy to translate any valuable work into them. It seems to be admitted on all sides that the intellectual improvement of those classes of the people who have the means of pursuing higher studies can at present be effected only by means of some language not vernacular amongst them.

What, then, shall that language be? One half of the Committee maintain that it should be the English. The other half strongly recommend the Arabic and Sanscrit. The whole question seems to me to be, which language is the best worth knowing?

I have no knowledge of either Sanscrit or Arabic.—But I have done what I could to form a correct estimate of their value. I have read translations of the most celebrated Arabic and Sanscrit works. I have conversed both here and at home with men distinguished by their proficiency in the Eastern tongues. I am quite ready to take the Oriental learning at the valuation of the Orientalists themselves. I have never found one among them who could deny that a single shelf of a good European library was worth the whole native literature of India and Arabia. The intrinsic superiority of the Western literature is, indeed, fully admitted by those members of the Committee who support the Oriental plan of education.

It will hardly be disputed, I suppose, that the department of literature in which the Eastern writers stand highest is poetry. And I certainly never met with any Orientalist who ventured to maintain that the Arabic and Sanscrit poetry could be compared to that of the great European nations. But, when we pass from works of imagination to works in which facts are recorded and general principles investigated, the superiority of the Europeans becomes absolutely immeasurable. It is, I believe, no exaggeration to say, that all the historical information which has been collected from all the books written in the Sanscrit language is less valuable than what may be found in the most paltry abridgments used at preparatory schools in England. In every branch of physical or moral philosophy the relative position of the two nations is nearly the same.

How, then, stands the case? We have to educate a people who cannot at present be educated by means of their mother-tongue. We must teach them some foreign language. The claims of our own language it is hardly necessary to recapitulate. It stands preeminent even among the languages of the West. It abounds with works of imagination not inferior to the noblest which Greece has bequeathed to us; with models of every species of eloquence; with historical compositions, which, considered merely as narratives, have seldom been surpassed, and which, considered as vehicles of ethical and political instruction, have never been equalled; with just and lively representations of human life and human nature; with the most profound speculations on metaphysics, morals, government, jurisprudence, and trade; with full and correct information respecting every experimental science which tends to preserve the health, to increase the comfort, or to expand the intellect of man. Whoever knows that language, has ready access to all the vast intellectual wealth, which all the wisest nations of the earth have created and hoarded in the course of ninety generations. It may safely be said that the literature now extant in that language is of far greater value than all the literature which three hundred years ago was extant in all the languages of the world together. Nor is this all. In India, English is the language spoken by the ruling class. It is spoken by the higher class of natives at the seats of Government. It is likely to become the language of commerce throughout the seas of the East. It is the language of two great European communities which are rising, the one in the south of Africa, the other in Australasia; communities which are every year becoming more important, and more closely connected with our Indian empire. Whether we look at the intrinsic value of our literature, or at the particular situation of this country, we shall see the strongest reason to think that, of all foreign tongues, the English tongue is that which would be the most useful to our native subjects.

The question now before us is simply whether, when it is in our power to teach this language, we shall teach languages in which, by universal confession, there are no books on any subject which deserve to be compared to our own; whether, when we can teach European science, we shall teach systems which, by universal confession, whenever they differ from those of Europe, differ for the worse; and whether, when we can patronise sound Philosophy and true History, we shall countenance, at the public expense, medical doctrines which would disgrace an English Farrier—Astronomy, which would move laughter in girls at an English boarding school—History, abounding with kings thirty feet high, and reigns thirty thousand years long—and Geography, made up of seas of treacle and seas of butter.

We are not without experience to guide us. History furnishes several analogous cases, and they all teach the same lesson. There are in modern times, to go no further, two memorable instances of a great impulse given to the mind of a whole society—of prejudices overthrown—of knowledge diffused—of taste purified—of arts and sciences planted in countries which had recently been ignorant and barbarous.

The first instance to which I refer is the great revival of letters among the Western nations at the close of the fifteenth and the beginning of the sixteenth century. At that time almost everything that was worth reading was contained in the writings of the ancient Greeks and Romans. Had our ancestors acted as the Committee of Public Instruction has hitherto acted; had they neglected the language of Cicero and Tacitus; had they confined their attention to the old dialects of our own island; had they printed nothing and taught nothing at the universities but Chronicles in Anglo-Saxon and Romances in Norman-French, would England have been what she now is? What the Greek and Latin were to the contemporaries of More and Ascham, our tongue is to the people of India. The literature of England is now more valuable than that of classical antiquity. I doubt whether the Sanscrit literature be as valuable as that of our Saxon and Norman progenitors. In some departments—in History, for example—I am certain that it is much less so.

Another instance may be said to be still before our eyes. Within the last hundred and twenty years, a nation which had previously been in a state as barbarous as that in which our ancestors were before the Crusades, has gradually emerged from the ignorance in which it was sunk, and has taken its place among civilised communities—I speak of Russia. There is now in that country a large educated class, abounding with persons fit to serve the state in the highest functions, and in nowise inferior to the most accomplished men who adorn the best circles of Paris and London. There is reason to hope that this vast empire, which in the time of our grandfathers was probably behind the Punjab, may, in the time of our grandchildren, be pressing close on France and Britain in the career of improvement. And how was this change effected? Not by flattering national prejudices; not by feeding the mind of the young Muscovite with the old woman's stories which his rude fathers had believed: not by filling his head with lying legends about St. Nicholas: not by encouraging him to study the great question, whether the world was or was not created on the 13th of September: not by calling him "a learned native," when he has mastered all these points of knowledge: but by teaching him those foreign languages in which the greatest mass of information had been laid up, and thus putting all that information within his reach. The languages of Western Europe civilized Russia. I cannot doubt that they will do for the Hindoo what they have done for the Tartar.

And what are the arguments against that course which seems to be alike recommended by theory and by experience? It is said that we ought to secure the co-operation of the native public, and that we can do this only by teaching Sanscrit and Arabic.

I can by no means admit that, when a nation of high intellectual attainments undertakes to superintend the education of a nation comparatively ignorant, the learners are absolutely to prescribe the course which is to be taken by the teachers. It is not necessary, however, to say anything on this subject. For it is proved by unanswerable evidence that we are not at present securing the co-operation of the natives. It would be bad enough to consult their intellectual taste at the expense of their intellectual health. But we are consulting neither—we are withholding from them the learning for which they are craving; we are forcing on them the mock-learning which they nauseate.

This is proved by the fact that we are forced to pay our Arabic and Sanscrit students, while those who learn English are willing to pay us. All the declamations in the world about the love and reverence of the natives for their sacred dialects will never, in the mind of any impartial person, outweigh the undisputed fact, that we cannot find, in all our vast empire, a single student who will let us teach him those dialects unless we will pay him.

I have now before me the accounts of the Madrassa for one month—the month of December, 1833. The Arabic students appear to have been seventy-seven in number. All receive stipends from the public. The whole amount paid to them is above 500 rupees a month. On the other side of the account stands the following item: Deduct amount realised from the out-students of English for the months of May, June, and July last, 103 rupees.

I have been told that it is merely from want of local experience that I am surprised at these phenomena, and that it is not the fashion for students in India to study at their own charges. This only confirms me in my opinion. Nothing is more certain than that it never can in any part of the world be necessary to pay men for doing what they think pleasant and profitable. India is no exception to this rule. The people of India do not require to be paid for eating rice when they are hungry, or for wearing woollen cloth in the cold season. To come nearer to the case before us, the children who learn their letters and a little elementary Arithmetic from the village schoolmaster are not paid by him. He is paid for teaching them. Why, then, is it necessary to pay people to learn Sanscrit and Arabic? Evidently because it is universally felt that the Sanscrit and Arabic are languages the knowledge of which does not compensate for the trouble of acquiring them. On all such subjects the state of the market is the decisive test.

Other evidence is not wanting, if other evidence were required. A petition was presented last year to the Committee by several ex-students of the Sanscrit College. The petitioners stated they had studied in the college ten or twelve years; that they had made themselves acquainted with Hindoo literature and science; that they had received certificates of proficiency: and what is the fruit of all this? "Notwithstanding such testimonials," they say, "we have but little prospect of bettering our condition without the kind assistance of your Honourable Committee, the indifference with which we are generally looked upon by our countrymen leaving no hope of encouragement and assistance from them." They therefore beg that they may be recommended to the Governor-General for places under the Government, not places of high dignity or emolument, but such as may just enable them to exist. "We want means," they say, "for a decent living, and for our progressive improvement, which, however, we cannot obtain without the assistance of Government, by whom we have been educated and maintained from childhood." They conclude by representing, very pathetically, that they are sure that it was never the intention of Government, after behaving so liberally to them during their education, to abandon them to destitution and neglect.

I have been used to see petitions to Government for compensation. All these petitions, even the most unreasonable of them, proceeded on the supposition that some loss had been sustained—that some wrong had been inflicted. These are surely the first petitioners who ever demanded compensation for having been educated gratis—for having been supported by the public during twelve years, and then sent forth into the world well-furnished with literature and science. They represent their education as an injury which gives them a claim on the Government for redress, as an injury for which the stipends paid to them during the infliction were a very inadequate compensation. And I doubt not that they are in the right. They have wasted the best years of life in learning what procures for them neither bread nor respect. Surely we might, with advantage, have saved the cost of making these persons useless and miserable; surely, men may be brought up to be burdens to the public and objects of contempt to their neighbours at a somewhat smaller charge to the state. But such is our policy. We do not even stand neuter in the contest between truth and falsehood. We are not content to leave the natives to the influence of their own hereditary prejudices. To the natural difficulties which obstruct the progress of sound science in the East we add fresh difficulties of our own making. Bounties and premiums, such as ought not to be given even for the propagation of truth, we lavish on false taste and false philosophy.

By acting thus we create the very evil which we fear. We are making that opposition which we do not find. What we spend on the Arabic and Sanscrit colleges is not merely a dead loss to the cause of truth: it is the bounty-money paid to raise up champions of error. It goes to form a nest, not merely of helpless place-hunters, but of bigots prompted alike by passion and by interest to raise a cry against every useful scheme of education. If there should be any opposition among the natives to the change which I recommend, that opposition will be the effect of our own system. It will be headed by persons supported by our stipends and trained in our colleges. The longer we persevere in our present course, the more formidable will that opposition be. It will be every year re-inforced by recruits whom we are paying. From the native society left to itself we have no difficulties to apprehend; all the murmuring will come from that Oriental interest which we have, by artificial means, called into being and nursed into strength.

There is yet another fact, which is alone sufficient to prove that the feeling of the native public, when left to itself, is not such as the supporters of the old system represent it to be. The Committee have thought fit to lay out above a lac of rupees in printing Arabic and Sanscrit books. Those books find no purchasers. It is very rarely that a single copy is disposed of. Twenty-three thousand volumes, most of them folios and quartos, fill the libraries, or rather the lumber-rooms, of this body. The Committee contrive to get rid of some portion of their vast stock of Oriental literature by giving books away. But they cannot give so fast as they print. About twenty thousand rupees a year are spent in adding fresh masses of waste paper to a hoard which, I should think, is already sufficiently ample. During the last three years, about sixty thousand rupees have been expended in this manner. The sale of Arabic and Sanscrit books, during those three years, has not yielded quite one thousand rupees. In the meantime the Schoolbook Society is selling seven or eight thousand English volumes every year, and not only pays the expenses of printing, but realizes a profit of 20 per cent on its outlay.

The fact that the Hindoo law is to be learned chiefly from Sanscrit books, and the Mahomedan law from Arabic books, has been much insisted on, but seems not to bear at all on the question. We are commanded by Parliament to ascertain and digest the laws of India. The assistance of a law commission has been given to us for that purpose. As soon as the code is promulgated, the Shasters and the Hedeya will be useless to a Moonsiff or Sudder Ameen. I hope and trust that, before the boys who are now entering at the Madrassa and the Sanscrit college have completed their studies, this great work will be finished. It would be manifestly absurd to educate the rising generation with a view to a state of things which we mean to alter before they reach manhood.

But there is yet another argument which seems even more untenable. It is said that the Sanscrit and Arabic are the languages in which the sacred books of a hundred millions of people are written, and that they are, on that account, entitled to peculiar encouragement. Assuredly it is the duty of the British Government in India to be not only tolerant, but neutral on all religious questions. But to encourage the study of a literature admitted to be of small intrinsic value only because that literature inculcates the most serious errors on the most important subjects, is a course hardly reconcilable with reason, with morality, or even with that very neutrality which ought, as we all agree, to be sacredly preserved. It is confessed that a language is barren of useful knowledge. We are told to teach it because it is fruitful of monstrous superstitions. We are to teach false history, false astronomy, false medicine, because we find them in company with a false religion. We abstain, and I trust shall always abstain, from giving any public encouragement to those who are engaged in the work of converting natives to Christianity. And, while we act thus, can we reasonably and decently bribe men out of the revenues of the state to waste their youth in learning how they are to purify themselves after touching an ass, or what text of the Vedas they are to repeat to expiate the crime of killing a goat?

It is taken for granted by the advocates of Oriental learning that no native of this country can possibly attain more than a mere smattering of English. They do not attempt to prove this; but they perpetually insinuate it. They designate the education which their opponents recommend as a mere spelling-book education. They assume it as undeniable, that the question is between a profound knowledge of Hindoo and Arabian literature and science on the one side, and a superficial knowledge of the rudiments of English on the other. This is not merely an assumption, but an assumption contrary to all reason and experience. We know that foreigners of all nations do learn our language sufficiently to have access to all the most abstruse knowledge which it contains, sufficiently to relish even the more delicate graces of our most idiomatic writers. There are in this very town natives who are quite competent to discuss political or scientific questions with fluency and precision in the English language. I have heard the very question on which I am now writing discussed by native gentlemen with a liberality and an intelligence which would do credit to any member of the Committee of Public Instruction. Indeed, it is unusual to find, even in the literary circles of the continent, any foreigner who can express himself in English with so much facility and correctness as we find in many Hindoos. Nobody, I suppose, will contend that English is so difficult to a Hindoo as Greek to an Englishman. Yet an intelligent English youth, in a much smaller number of years than our unfortunate pupils pass at the Sanscrit college, becomes able to read, to enjoy, and even to imitate, not unhappily, the composition of the best Greek authors. Less than half the time which enables an English youth to read Herodotus and Sophocles ought to enable a Hindoo to read Hume and Milton.

To sum up what I have said: I think it clear that we are not fettered by the Act of Parliament of 1813; that we are not fettered by any pledge expressed or implied; that we are free to employ our funds as we choose; that we ought to employ them in teaching what is best worth knowing; that English is better worth knowing than

Sanscrit or Arabic; that the natives are desirous to be taught English, and are not desirous to be taught Sanscrit or Arabic; that neither as the languages of law, nor as the languages of religion, have the Sanscrit and Arabic any peculiar claim to our encouragement; that it is possible to make natives of this country thoroughly good English scholars, and that to this end our efforts ought to be directed.

In one point I fully agree with the gentlemen to whose general views I am opposed. I feel, with them, that it is impossible for us, with our limited means, to attempt to educate the body of the people. We must at present do our best to form a class who may be interpreters between us and the millions whom we govern; a class of persons, Indian in blood and colour, but English in taste, in opinions, in morals, and in intellect. To that class we may leave it to refine the vernacular dialects of the country, to enrich those dialects with terms of science borrowed from the Western nomenclature, and to render them by degrees fit vehicles for conveying knowledge to the great mass of the population.

I would strictly respect all existing interests. I would deal even generously with all individuals who have had fair reason to expect a pecuniary provision. But I would strike at the root of the bad system which has hitherto been fostered by us. I would at once stop the printing of Arabic and Sanscrit books; I would abolish the Madrassa and the Sanscrit college at Calcutta. Benares is the great seat of Brahmanical learning; Delhi, of Arabic learning. If we retain the Sanscrit college at Benares and the Mahomedan college at Delhi, we do enough, and much more than enough in my opinion, for the Eastern languages. If the Benares and Delhi colleges should be retained, I would at least recommend that no stipend shall be given to any students who may hereafter repair thither, but that the people shall be left to make their own choice between the rival systems of education without being bribed by us to learn what they have no desire to know. The funds which would thus be placed at our disposal would enable us to give larger encouragement to the Hindoo college at Calcutta, and to establish in the principal cities throughout the Presidencies of Fort William and Agra schools in which the English language might be well and thoroughly taught.

If the decision of his Lordship in Council should be such as I anticipate, I shall enter on the performance of my duties with the greatest zeal and alacrity. If, on the other hand, it be the opinion of the Government that the present system ought to remain unchanged, I beg that I may be permitted to retire from the chair of the Committee. I feel that I could not be of the smallest use there—I feel, also, that I should be lending my countenance to what I firmly believe to be a mere delusion. I believe that the present system tends, not to accelerate the progress of truth, but to delay the natural death of expiring errors. I conceive that we have at present no right to the respectable name of a Board of Public Instruction. We are a Board for wasting public money, for printing books which are of less value than the paper on which they are printed was while it was blank; for giving artificial encouragement to absurd history, absurd metaphysics, absurd physics, absurd theology; for raising up a breed of scholars who find their scholarship an encumbrance and a blemish, who live on the public while they are receiving their education, and whose education is so utterly useless to them that, when they have received it, they must either starve or live on the public all the rest of their lives. Entertaining these opinions, I am naturally desirous to decline all share in the responsibility of a body which, unless it alters its whole mode of proceeding, I must consider not merely as useless, but as positively noxious.

10

ALEXANDER CRUMMELL

The English Language in Liberia

Two years ago to-day, when we were assembled together here, as now, to celebrate our National Anniversary, I was called up, after the Orator of the day, to make a few remarks. And perhaps, some who are here, may remember that, in setting forth a few of the advantages we pilgrims to these shores possess for a noble national growth and for future superiority, I pointed out among other providential events the fact, that the exile of our fathers from their African homes to America, had given us, their children, at least this one item of compensation, namely, the possession of the Anglo-Saxon tongue; that this language put us in a position which none other on the globe could give us: and that it was impossible to estimate too highly the pre-rogatives and the elevation the Almighty has bestowed upon us, in our having as our own, the speech of Chaucer and Shakespeare, of Milton and Wordsworth, of Bacon and Burke, of Franklin and Webster. My remarks were unpremeditated, and they passed from my thoughts as the meeting was dismissed, and we went forth to the festivities of the day. But it happened that, shortly afterwards, I had occasion to seek health by a journey up the Cavalla. There, on the banks of that noble river, fully 80 miles from the ocean, I met with hospitality from a native trader, a man who presented all the signs of civilization, and who spoke with remarkable clearness and precision, the English language. The incident struck me with surprise, and started a crowd of thoughts and suggestions concerning the future; among these came back the lost and forgotten words of our Anniversary of 1858. More than once since, in conversations, speeches, and sermons, have I expressed the ripened convictions which that occurrence created in my mind; and the other day, after I received the invitation to speak before you on this occasion, I concluded to take this for the subject of remark:

"The English Language in Liberia"

I shall have to ask your patience this day, for, owing to that fatality of tardiness which seems to govern some of our public movements, I have had but a fortnight to prepare for this duty, and hence I cannot be as brief as is desirable. I shall have to ask your attention also, for I can promise you nothing more than a dry detail of facts.

I trust, however, that I may be able to suggest a few thoughts which may be fitted to illustrate the responsibilities of our lot in this land, and to show forth the nature and the seriousness of the duties which arise out of it.

1. Now, in considering this subject, what first arrests attention is the bare simple fact that here, on this coast, that is, between Gallinas and Cape Pedro, is an organized negro community, republican in form and name; a people possessed of Christian institutions and civilized habits, with this one marked peculiarity, that is, that in color, race, and origin, they are identical with the masses of rude natives around them; and yet speak the refined and cultivated English language—a language alien alike from the speech of their sires and the soil from whence they sprung, and knowing no other. It is hardly possible for *us* fully to realize these facts. Familiarity with scenes, events, and even truths, tends to lessen the vividness of their impression. But without doubt no thoughtful traveler could contemplate the sight, humble as at present, it really is, without marvel and surprise. If a stranger who had never heard of this Republic, but who had sailed forth from his country to visit the homes of West African Pagans, should arrive on our coast, he could not but be struck with the Anglican aspect of our habits and manners, and the distinctness, with indeed undoubted mistakes and blunders, of our English names and utterance. There could be no mistaking the history of this people. The earliest contact with them vouches English antecedents and associations. The harbor master who comes on board is perhaps a Watts or a Lynch; names which have neither a French, a Spanish, nor a German origin. He steps up into the town, asks the names of storekeepers, learns who are the merchants and officials, calls on the President or Superintendent or Judge; and although sable are all the faces he meets with, the *names* are the old familiar ones which he has been accustomed to in the social circles of his home, or on the signs along the streets of New York or London, viz.: the *Smiths,* (a large family in Liberia as everywhere else in Anglo-Saxondom,) and their broods of cousins, the Johnsons, Thompsons, Robinsons, and Jacksons, then the Browns, the Greens, the [paradoxical] Whites, and the [real] Blacks; the Williams', James', Paynes, Draytons, Gibsons, Roberts', Yates', Warners, Wilsons, Moores, and that of his Excellency President Benson.

Not only names, but titles also are equally significant, and show a like origin. The streets are Broad, and Ashmun, and as here, Griswold. The public buildings are a Church, a Seminary, a Senate House, and a Court House.

If our visitor enters the residence of a thriving, thoughtful citizen, the same peculiarity strikes him. Everything, however humble, is of the same Anglo-Saxon type and stamp. On the book-shelves or tables, are Bibles, Prayer or Hymn Books, Harvey's *Meditations* or Bunyan's *Pilgrim's Progress,* Young's *Night Thoughts* or Cowper's *Poems,* Walter Scott's *Tales,* or *Uncle Tom's Cabin.* In many places he will find well-used copies of Shakespeare and Milton. Not a few have enriched themselves with the works of Spenser and Wordsworth, Coleridge and Campbell, Longfellow and Bryant, Whittier and Willis, and of that loftiest of all the bards of the day, Alfred Tennyson. Should it happen to be a mail-day, or the "Stevens" has just glided into our waters, he would find at the Post Office, papers from America and England: "The Times," "Illustrated London News," "Daily Advertiser," "The Star," "The Guardian," "The New York Tribune," and "Commercial Advertiser," the "Protestant Churchman," and the "Church Journal." In one heap, "Littell's Living Age;" in another, "Chambers' Journal." Here, "Harpers Monthly;" there, "The Eclectic." Amid the mass of printed matter he would see, ever and anon, more ambitious works: Medical and Scientific Journals, Quarterly Reviews, the "Bibliotheca Sacra," "Blackwood's" and other Magazines.

Such facts as these, however, do not fully represent the power of the English tongue in our territory. For, while repressing all tendencies to childish vanity and idle exaggeration we are to consider other telling facts which spring from our character and influence, and which are necessary to a just estimate of the peculiar agency we are now contemplating. And here a number of facts present themselves to our notice. Within a period of thirty years, thousands of heathen children have been placed under the guardianship of our settlers. Many of these have forgotten their native tongue, and know now the English language as *their* language. As a consequence, there has sprung up, in one generation, within our borders, a mighty army of English-speaking natives, who, as manhood approached, have settled around us in their homes from one end of the land to the other. Many of these take up the dialect of the other tribes in whose neighborhood their masters lived, but even then English is their speech. Thus it is that everywhere in the Republic, from Gallinas to Cape Palmas, one meets with a multitude of natives who have been servants in our Liberian families, and are daily in the utterance of English. A considerable number of these have enjoyed the opportunity of school instruction, and have carried back to the country the ability to read and to write English. In many cases, it is, in truth impossible to say whether their attainments should be suggestive of sorrow or of joy. I have had naked boys working for me on the St. Paul, who, when they wanted any thing, would write a note with as much exactness as I could. We all here know *one* native man, over the river, who is a leader in Devil-dances, and yet can read and write like a scholar. A friend of mine, traveling in the bush, nigh 200 miles from Monrovia, stopt one night, exhausted, at the hut of a native man, who brought him his own Bible to read, but alas! it was accompanied by a decanter of rum! The moral of such facts I shall not enter upon; but here is the simple fact, that by our presence, though in small numbers, we have already spread abroad, for scores of miles, the English language, written as well as spoken, among this large population of heathen.

The trading schemes of merchants and settlers is another powerful auxiliary in disseminating this language. At every important point on the coast, Liberian, English, and American merchants have, for years, established their factories between Cape Palmas and Monrovia, there cannot be less than 30 factories. In each of these depots, some three or four English-speaking persons—Liberians—are living; in a few cases families have made them their permanent abodes; and thus, what with the native servants, the natives in neighboring towns, the more remote natives who flock hitherward for trade, and the few happy cases where pious young men devote a portion of their time to teaching, there is, and has been, a powerful, a widespread system in operation for the teaching and extension of English.

Another process has been for some time at work to spread our language. The interior natives have found out that a home in our vicinity is equivalent to an act of emancipation; and as a consequence, remnants of tribes who for centuries have been the prey of their stronger neighbors, for the slave trade; and boys and men, upwards of 100 miles inland, who have been held in slavery, crowd in upon our neighborhood for freedom. Behind our settlements, on the St. Paul, there is the most heterogeneous mixture conceivable, of divers tribes and families, who have thus sought the protection of our commonwealth. Numbers of the Bassas, Veys, Deys, Golahs, and especially the Pessas, the hereditary slaves of the interior, have thus come to our immediate neighborhoods. Although I am doubtful of the *moral* effect of this movement upon *ourselves,* yet I feel no little pride in the fact that this young nation should become, so early, a land of refuge, an asylum for the oppressed! And I regard it as a singular providence, that at the very time our government was trumpeted abroad as implicated in the slave trade, our magistrates, in the upper counties, were adjudicating cases of runaway slaves, and declaring to interior slave holders that, *on our soil,* they could not reclaim their fugitives!

Just here another important item claims attention, that is the *Missionary* agency in propagating this language. The reference here will be, chiefly, to the two uppermost counties of Liberia. Their younger sister, Sinou, I am sorry to say, has not, as yet, made any marked impression upon her surrounding heathen; more we believe through youth and weakness, and suffering, than through indifference or neglect. Missionary operations, though participated in by others, have been chiefly carried on, in Bassa, by the Baptists. The means which have been employed have been preaching and schools. On the St. John's they have had for years a Manual Labor School, instructed by white Missionaries. This school has passed into the hands of a *native* Teacher, educated at Sierra Leone—a man who is the son of a prominent chieftain, and who possesses unbounded influence, as far as the Bassa tongue reaches. He has, moreover, these three prominent qualities, that is, he is a well-trained English scholar, a thoroughly civilized man, and a decided and well-tried disciple of the Lord Jesus Christ. His earnestness is evidenced in the fact that his work is unaided and self-supporting, and numbers of his tribe are glad to send him their children. Besides this means of influence, ministers have been accustomed to visit numerous towns and villages, preaching the Gospel. And thus, by preaching and schools, a multitude of the Bassas have gained the English tongue, with many of its ideas and teachings.

The same Anglicising influence has been carried on, but on a larger scale, in Montserrada County, but mainly through the Methodists; and they have spread our language widely abroad through that county, by the means of native schools, native children in their American schools, and Missionaries residing in country towns, teaching and preaching as far back as the Golah tribe, and now among the Veys: native preachers too, men converted to the faith, and moved by the Spirit to proclaim the glad tidings to their needy parents, brothers, and kin. I must not fail to mention the fact, that during the last two years one of their ministers has carried the English tongue some 200 miles in the interior,[1] and has spread it abroad amid the homes of the mild Pessas; thus preparing the way for legitimate trade, for civilization, for the Gospel of Jesus Christ, by the means of the spoken Word and the English Bible.

Thus, fellow-citizens, by these varied means the English language has been pushing its way among the numerous tribes of our territory. And thus, in a region of not less than 50,000 square miles, there are few places but where an English-speaking traveller can find some person who can talk with him in his own language.

And now I beg you to notice one point: this English, which we are speaking, and likewise teaching the heathen to speak, is not our native tongue. This Anglo-Saxon language, which is the only language ninety-nine hundredths of us emigrants have ever known, is not the speech of our ancestors. We are here a motley group, composed, without doubt, of persons of almost every tribe in West Africa, from Goree to the Congo. Here are descendants of Jalofs, Fulahs, Mandingoes, Sussus, Timmanees, Veys, Congos, with a large intermixture every where of Anglo-Saxon Dutch, Irish, French, and Spanish blood—a slight mingling of the Malayan, and a dash, every now and then, of American Indian. And perhaps I would not exaggerate much, if I ended the enumeration of our heterogeneous elements in the words of St. Luke—"Jews and Proselytes, Cretes and Arabians."

And yet they all speak in a foreign tongue, in accents alien from the utterance of their fathers. Our very speech is indicative of sorrowful history; the language we use tells of subjection and of conquest. No people lose entirely their native tongue without the bitter trial of hopeless struggles, bloody strife, heart-breaking despair, agony and death! Even so we. But this, be it remembered, is a common incident in history, pertaining to almost every nation on earth. Examine all the old histories of men—the histories of Egypt, China, Greece, Rome, and England—and in every case, as in ours, their language reveals the fact of conquest and subjection. But this fact of humiliation seems to have been one of those ordinances of Providence, designed as a means for the introduction of new ideas into the language of a people; or to serve, as the transitional step from low degradation to a higher and nobler civilization.

2. And this remark suggests, in the 2d place, the query—"What is the nature, and if any, the advantage of the exchange, we have thus, in God's providence, been led to make?

The only way in which in a fit manner I can answer this question is, by inquiring into the respective values of our native and our acquired tongue. Such a contrast will set before us the problem of "Loss and Gain" which is involved therein. The worth of our fathers' language will in this way stand out in distinct comparison with the Anglo-Saxon, our acquired speech. And *first*, let us speak of the African dialects. I refer now to that particular group of African aboriginies who dwell in West Africa, from the Senegal to the Niger, and who have received the distinctive title of "Negro."

Within this wide extent of territory are grouped a multitude of tribes and nations with various tongues and dialects, which doubtless had a common origin, but whose point of affiliation it would be difficult now to discover. But how great soever may be their differences, there are, nevertheless, definite marks of inferiority connected with them all, which place them at the widest distance from civilized languages. Of this whole class of languages, it may be said, in the aggregate that (a) "They are," to use the words of Dr. Leighton Wilson, "harsh abrupt, energetic, indistinct in enunciation, meagre in point of words, abound with inarticulate nasal and guttural sounds, possess but few inflections and grammatical forms, and are withal exceedingly difficult of acquisition."[2] This is his description of the Grebo, but it may be taken, I think, as on the whole, a correct description of the whole class of dialects which are entitled "Negro." (b) These languages, moreover, are characterised by lowness of ideas. As the speech of rude barbarians, they are marked by brutal and vindictive sentiments, and those principles which show a predominance of the animal propensities. (c) Again, they lack those ideas of virtue, of moral truth, and those distinctions of right and wrong with which we, all our life long, have been familiar. (d) Another marked feature of these languages is the absence of clear ideas of Justice, Law, Human Rights, and Govermental Order, which are so prominent and manifest in civilized countries; and (e) lastly—These supernal truths of a personal present Deity, of the moral Government of God, of man's Immortality, of the Judgment, and of Everlasting Blessedness, which regulate the lives of Christians, are either entirely absent, or else exist, and are expressed in an obscure and distorted manner.

Now, instead of a language characterized by such rude and inferior features as these, we have been brought to the heritage of the English language. Negro as we are by blood and constitution, we have been, as a people, for generations, in the habitual utterance of Anglo-Saxon speech. This fact is now historical. The space of time it covers runs over 200 years. There are emigrants in this country from the Carolinas and Georgia, who, in some cases, come closer to the Fatherland; but more than a moiety of the people of this country have come from Maryland and Virginia, and I have no doubt that there are scores, not to say hundreds of them, who are unable to trace back their sires to Africa. I know that, in my own case, my *maternal* ancestors have trod American soil, and therefore have used the English language well nigh as long as any descendants of the early settlers of the Empire State.[3] And, doubtless, this is true of multitudes of the sons of Africa who are settled abroad in the divers homes of the white man, on the American continent.

At the present day, be it remembered, there are 10,000,000 of the sons of Africa alien from this continent. They live on the main land, and on the islands of North and South America. Most of them are subjects of European and American Governments. One growing prominent section of them is an independent Republic.[4] They speak Danish, Portuguese, Spanish, French, and English; the English-speaking portion of them, however, is about equal to all the rest together. The sons of Africa under the Americans, added to those protected by the British Flag, number 5,000,000.

Now what is the peculiar advantage which Anglo-Africans have gained by the loss of their mother tongue? In order to answer this query, we must present those direct and collateral lingual elements in which reside the worth and value of the English language, especially in contrast with the defective elements of the African dialects.

I shall not, of course venture to any extent, upon the etymological peculiarities of the English language, for even if I had time, I lack the learning and ability for such disquisition.

Moreover the thoughts presented on such a day as this, should have a force and significance pertaining to national growth and a people's improvement. I shall therefore point out some of those peculiarities of the English language which seem to me specially deserving notice, in this country, and which call for the peculiar attention of thoughtful patriotic minds among us.

The English language then, I apprehend, is marked by these prominent peculiarities;—(a) *It is a language of unusual force and power.* This I know is an elemental excellence which does not pertain, immediately, to this day's discussion; but I venture to present it, inasmuch, as you will see presently, it has much to do with the genius and spirit of a language. English is composed chiefly of simple, terse, and forcible, one and two-syllabled words; which make it incomparable for simplicity and intelligibleness. The bulk of these words are the rich remains of the old Saxon tongue, which is the main stream, whence has flowed over to us the affluence of the English language. It is this element which gives it force, precision, directness, and boldness; making it a fit channel for the decided thoughts of men of common sense, of honest minds, and downright character. Let any one take up the Bible, the Prayer-Book, a volume of Hymns of any class of Christians, the common proverbs, the popular sayings:—which strike deep into the hearts of men and flow over in their common spontaneous utterances; and he will see everywhere these features of force, perspicuity, and directness. Nor is it wanting in beauty, elegance, and majesty; for, to a considerable extent, this same Saxon element furnishes these qualities; but the English, being a composite language, these attractions and commanding elements are bestowed upon it, in fullness, by those other affluent streams which contribute to its wealth, and which go to make up its "well of English undefiled." (b) Again, the *English language is characteristically the language of freedom.* I know that there is a sense in which this love of liberty is inwrought in the very fibre and substance of the body and blood of all people: but the flame burns dimly in some races; it is a fitful fire in some others; and in many inferior people it is the flickering light of a dying candle. But in the English races it is an ardent, healthy, vital, irrepressible flame; and withal normal and orderly in its development. Go back to the early periods of this people's history, to the times when the whole of Europe seemed lost in the night of ignorance and dead to the faintest pulses of liberty—trace the stream of their descent from the days of Alfred to the present time, and mark how they have ever, in law, legislation and religion, in poetry and oratory, in philosophy and literature, assumed that oppression was an abnormal and a monstrous thing! How when borne down by tyranous restraint, or lawless arbitrary rule, discontent and resistance have—

"Moved in the chambers of their soul"

How when misrule became organic and seated, tyranny unreasoning and obstinate, they have demonstrated to all the world, how trifling a thing is the tenure of tyrants, how resistless and invincible is the free spirit of a nation!

And now look at this people—scattered, in our own day, all over the globe, in the Great Republic, in numerous settlements and great colonies, themselves the germs of mighty empires; see how they have carried with them every where, on earth, the same high, masterful, majestic spirit of freedom, which gave their ancestors, for long generations, in their island home—

—"the thews of Anakim,
The pulses of a Titan's heart;"

and which makes *them* giants among whatever people they settle, whether in America, India, or Africa, distancing all other rivalries and competitors.

And notice here how this spirit, like the freshets of some mighty Oregon, rises above and flows over their own crude and distorted obliquities. Some of these obliquities are prominent. Of all races of men, none I ween, are so domineering, none have a stronger, more exclusive spirit of caste, none have a more contemptuous dislike of inferiority: and yet in this race, the ancient spirit of freedom, rises higher than their repugnances. It impels them to conquer even their prejudices: and hence, when chastened and subdued by Christianity, it makes them philanthropic and brotherly. Thus it is that in England this national sentiment would not tolerate the existence of slavery, although it was Negro slavery. Thus in New Zealand and at the Cape of Good Hope, Statesmen, Prelates, Scholars, demand that a low and miserable aboriginal population shall be raised to their own level; and accept, without agonies and convulsions, the providence and destiny which point plainly to amalgamation.[5] Thus in Canada it bursts forth with zeal and energy for the preservation and enlightenment of the decaying Indian. And thus in the United States, rising above the mastery of a cherished and deep-rooted spirit of caste; outrunning the calculations of cold prudence and prospective result; repressing the unwrought personal feeling of prejudice, it starts into being a mighty religious feeling which demands the destruction of slavery and the emancipation of the Negro! (c) *Once more I remark, that the English language is the enshrinement of those great charters of liberty which are essential elements of free governments, and the main guarantees of personal liberty.* I refer now to the right of Trial by Jury, the people's right to a participation in Government, Freedom of Speech, and of the Press, the Right of Petition, Freedom of Religion. And these are special characteristics of the English language. They are rights, which in their full form and rigid features, do not exist among any other people. It is true that they have had historical development: but their seminal principles seem inherent in the constitution of this race. We see in this people, even in their rude condition, the roots from which have sprung so fair and so beautiful a tree. And these conserving elements, carefully guarded, deepened and strengthened in their foundations from age to age, as wisdom and sagacity seemed to dictate, illustrated and eulogized by the highest genius, and the most consumate legal ability; have carried these states, the old country, the Republic of America, and the constitutional colonies of Britian, through many a convulsive political crisis; the ship of state, rocked and tossed by the wild waves of passion, and the agitations of faction; but in the end leaving her to return again to the repose of calm and quiet waters!

. . .

You and I have been accustomed to the utterance of the noblest theories of liberty, the grandest ideas of humanity all our life time; and so were our fathers. And although we have been shorn of our manhood, and have, as yet, attained only a shriveled humanity; still there is some satisfaction in the remembrance, that ideas conserve men, and keep alive the vitality of nations. These ideas, alas! for the consistency of men! though often but abstractions *there,* have been made realities *here.* We have brought them with us to this continent; and in this young nation are striving to give them form, shape, and constant expression. With the noble tongue which

Providence has given us, it will be difficult for us to be divorced from the spirit, which, for centuries, has been speaking through it. For a language acts, in divers ways, upon the spirit of a people; even as the spirit of a people acts with a creative and spiritualizing force upon a language. But difficult though it be, such a separation is a possibility. And hence arises the duty of doing all we can to keep alive these grand ideas and noble principles. May we be equal to this duty—may we strive to answer to this responsibility! Let us endeavor to live up to the sentiments breathed forth in all the legal charters, the noble literature, the religious learning of this tongue. Let us guard, even here, the right of Free Speech. Let us esteem it one of the proudest boasts of this land, and to appropriate the happy language of a heathen— esteem it "the rare felicity of our times that, in this country, one can think what he pleases, and speak what he thinks."[6] Let us prize the principle of Personal Liberty, as one of the richest jewels of our constitutional diadem. Let us not shrink from the severest test to which a heathen and degraded population around us, may at times strain it. Let us, amid all the extravagances of their crude state, guarantee, even them, the full advantage of it. Conscious of the nobleness of this great constitutional principle, may we allow it full force and unrestricted expression. Let us rejoice that our Republic, diminutive as it is in the group of nations, is already a refuge for the fugitives; and congratulate one another on the fact that we can already apply to our state and position, the proud lines of Whittier:—

"No slave-hunt in our borders, no pirate on the strand,
No fetters in Liberia! no slave upon our land."

Let us endeavor, by the reading of their Journals, by close observation of that venturesome enterprize of theirs, which carries them from "beneath the Arctic circle, to the opposite region of Polar cold;"—by a careful inspection of their representations, who visit these shores, and by a judicious imitation of their daring and activity; let us strive to catch and gain to ourselves somewhat the SPIRIT OF ENTERPRIZE AND PROGRESS which characterizes them, in all their world-wide homes. Moreover, let us cultivate the principle of Independence, both as a nation and as individuals, and in our children; as, in itself a needed element of character, as the great antidote to the deep slavishness of a three centuries' servitude, and as a correction to the inactivity, the slothfulness, and the helplessness, which are gendered by a tropical clime. I am well aware of the exaggeration to which all men are liable to carry this sentiment; but this, indeed is the case with all the other noble principles which I have alluded to. This possibility of excess is one of the conditions of freedom. You cannot leave it in, nor any of its accessories, within the line of strict propriety, to the rigid margin of cold exactitude. And the spirit of independence, the disposition to modest self-reliance, the feeling of one's being sufficient for one's own needs, and temporal requirements; is just one of those golden elements of character, which needs to be cultivated everywhere among our population. It is conservative, too, as well as democratic; and if it does overflow, at times, its banks; it will not be long ere it will delight to come back to, and run in, its proper channel. An antidote to its extravagancies, will, moreover, be found, in the cultivation of another prime characteristic of the English language, that is, ITS HIGH MORAL AND SPIRITUAL CHARACTER. Remembering that "righteousness exalteth a nation, but that sin is a reproach to any people;" let us aim at the cultivation among us, of all that sensitive honor, those habits of honesty, that purity of manners and morals, those domestic virtues, and that evangelical piety, which are peculiarly the attributes of Anglo-Saxon society, States, and homes.

So, by God's blessing, shall we prove ourselves not undeserving of the peculiar providence God has bestowed upon us; and somewhat worthy of the inheritance of the great and ennobling English Language.

NOTES

1 The lamented Rev. George L. Seymour, Missionary and Traveler.

2 "Western Africa, &c." 457, By Rev. J. L. Wilson, D.D.

3 New York.

4 Hayti.

5 "See Church in the Colonies, No. xxii. A Journal of the visitation of the Bishop of Capetown. Also, letters of the Bishop of New Zealand, etc. etc."

6 "Rara temporum felicitate, ube sentire quse velis, et quse sentias dicere licet." Tacitus, Hist. Lib. 1 Cap. 2.

11

NGŨGĨ WA THIONG'O

The Language
of African Literature

I

The language of African literature cannot be discussed meaningfully outside the context of those social forces which have made it both an issue demanding our attention and a problem calling for a resolution.

On the one hand is imperialism in its colonial and neo-colonial phases continuously press-ganging the African hand to the plough to turn the soil over, and putting
blinkers on him to make him view the path ahead only as determined for him by the
master armed with the bible and the sword. In other words, imperialism continues
to control the economy, politics, and cultures of Africa. But on the other, and pitted
against it, are the ceaseless struggles of African people to liberate their economy,
politics, and culture from that Euro-American–based stranglehold to usher a new
era of true communal self-regulation and self-determination. It is an ever-continuing
struggle to seize back their creative initiative in history through a real control of all
the means of communal self-definition in time and space. The choice of language and
the use to which language is put is central to a people's definition of themselves in
relation to their natural and social environment, indeed in relation to the entire universe. Hence language has always been at the heart of the two contending social
forces in the Africa of the twentieth century.

The contention started a hundred years ago when in 1884 the capitalist powers
of Europe sat in Berlin and carved an entire continent with a multiplicity of peoples,
cultures, and languages into different colonies. It seems it is the fate of Africa to have
her destiny always decided around conference tables in the metropolises of the western world: her submergence from self-governing communities into colonies was
decided in Berlin; her more recent transition into neo-colonies along the same
boundaries was negotiated around the same tables in London, Paris, Brussels, and

Lisbon. The Berlin-drawn division under which Africa is still living was obviously economic and political, despite the claims of bible-wielding diplomats, but it was also cultural. Berlin in 1884 saw the division of Africa into the different languages of the European powers. African countries, as colonies and even today as neo-colonies, came to be defined and to define themselves in terms of the languages of Europe: English-speaking, French-speaking, or Portuguese-speaking African countries.[1]

Unfortunately writers who should have been mapping paths out of that linguistic encirclement of their continent also came to be defined and to define themselves in terms of the languages of imperialist imposition. Even at their most radical and pro-African position in their sentiments and articulation of problems they still took it as axiomatic that the renaissance of African cultures lay in the languages of Europe.

I should know!

II

In 1962 I was invited to that historic meeting of African writers at Makerere University College, Kampala, Uganda. The list of participants contained most of the names which have now become the subject of scholarly dissertations in universities all over the world. The title? 'A Conference of *African Writers of English Expression.*'[2]

I was then a student of *English* at Makerere, an overseas college of the University of London. The main attraction for me was the certain possibility of meeting Chinua Achebe. I had with me a rough typescript of a novel in progress, *Weep Not, Child,* and I wanted him to read it. In the previous year, 1961, I had completed *The River Between,* my first-ever attempt at a novel, and entered it for a writing competition organised by the East African Literature Bureau. I was keeping in step with the tradition of Peter Abrahams with his output of novels and autobiographies from *Path of Thunder* to *Tell Freedom* and followed by Chinua Achebe with his publication of *Things Fall Apart* in 1959. Or there were their counterparts in French colonies, the generation of Sédar Senghor and David Diop included in the 1947/48 Paris edition of *Anthologie de la nouvelle poésie nègre et malgache de langue française.* They all wrote in European languages as was the case with all the participants in that momentous encounter on Makerere hill in Kampala in 1962.

The title, 'A Conference of African Writers of English Expression,' automatically excluded those who wrote in African languages. Now on looking back from the self-questioning heights of 1986, I can see this contained absurd anomalies. I, a student, could qualify for the meeting on the basis of only two published short stories, 'The Fig Tree (Mūgumo)' in a student journal, *Penpoint,* and 'The Return' in a new journal, *Transition.* But neither Shabaan Robert, then the greatest living East African poet with several works of poetry and prose to his credit in Kiswahili, nor Chief Fagunwa, the great Nigerian writer with several published titles in Yoruba, could possibly qualify.

The discussions on the novel, the short story, poetry, and drama were based on extracts from works in English and hence they excluded the main body of work in Swahili, Zulu, Yoruba, Arabic, Amharic, and other African languages. Yet, despite this exclusion of writers and literature in African languages, no sooner were the introductory preliminaries over than this Conference of 'African Writers of English Expression' sat down to the first item on the agenda: 'What is African Literature?'

The debate which followed was animated: Was it literature about Africa or about the African experience? Was it literature written by Africans? What about a non-African who wrote about Africa: did his work qualify as African literature? What if an African set his work in Greenland: did that qualify as African literature? Or were African languages the criteria? OK: what about Arabic, was it not foreign to Africa? What about French and English, which had become African languages? What if an European wrote about Europe in an African language? If . . . if . . . if . . . this or that, except the issue: the domination of our languages and cultures by those of imperialist Europe: in any case there was no Fagunwa or Shabaan Robert or any writer in African languages to bring the conference down from the realms of evasive abstractions. The question was never seriously asked: did what we wrote qualify as African literature? The whole area of literature and audience, and hence of language as a determinant of both the national and class audience, did not really figure: the debate was more about the subject matter and the racial origins and geographical habitation of the writer.

English, like French and Portuguese, was assumed to be the natural language of literary and even political mediation between African people in the same nation and between nations in Africa and other continents. In some instances these European languages were seen as having a capacity to unite African peoples against divisive tendencies inherent in the multiplicity of African languages within the same geographic state. Thus Ezekiel Mphahlele later could write, in a letter to *Transition* number 11, that English and French have become the common language with which to present a nationalist front against white oppressors, and even 'where the white-man has already retreated, as in the independent states, these two languages are still a unifying force.'[3] In the literary sphere they were often seen as coming to save African languages against themselves. Writing a foreword to Birago Diop's book *Contes d'Amadou Koumba* Sédar Senghor commends him for using French to rescue the spirit and style of old African fables and tales. 'However while rendering them into French he renews them with an art which, while it respects the genius of the French language, that language of gentleness and honesty, preserves at the same time all the virtues of the negro-african languages.'[4] English, French, and Portuguese had come to our rescue and we accepted the unsolicited gift with gratitude. Thus in 1964, Chinua Achebe, in a speech entitled 'The African Writer and the English Language,' said:

> Is it right that a man should abandon his mother tongue for someone else's? It looks like a dreadful betrayal and produces a guilty feeling. But for me there is no other choice. I have been given the language and I intend to use it.[5]

See the paradox: the possibility of using mother-tongues provokes a tone of levity in phrases like 'a dreadful betrayal' and 'a guilty feeling'; but that of foreign languages produces a categorical positive embrace, what Achebe himself, ten years later, was to describe as this 'fatalistic logic of the unassailable position of English in our literature.'[6]

The fact is that all of us who opted for European languages—the conference participants and the generation that followed them—accepted that fatalistic logic to a greater or lesser degree. We were guided by it and the only question which preoccupied us was how best to make the borrowed tongues carry the weight of our African experience by, for instance, making them 'prey' on African proverbs and other peculiarities of African speech and folklore. For this task, Achebe *(Things Fall Apart; Arrow of God)*, Amos Tutuola *(The Palm-wine Drinkard; My Life in the Bush of Ghosts)*, and Gabriel Okara *(The Voice)* were often held as providing the three alternative models. The lengths to which we were prepared to go in our mission of enriching foreign languages by injecting Senghorian 'black blood' into their rusty joints, is best exemplified by Gabriel Okara in an article reprinted in *Transition*:

> As a writer who believes in the utilization of African ideas, African philosophy and African folklore and imagery to the fullest extent possible, I am of the opinion the only way to use them effectively is to translate them almost literally from the African language native to the writer into whatever European language he is using as medium of expression. I have endeavoured in my words to keep as close as possible to the vernacular expressions. For, from a word, a group of words, a sentence and even a name in any African language, one can glean the social norms, attitudes and values of a people.
>
> In order to capture the vivid images of African speech, I had to eschew the habit of expressing my thoughts first in English. It was difficult at first, but I had to learn. I had to study each Ijaw expression I used and to discover the probable situation in which it was used in order to bring out the nearest meaning in English. I found it a fascinating exercise.[7]

Why, we may ask, should an African writer, or any writer, become so obsessed by taking from his mother tongue to enrich other tongues? Why should he see it as his particular mission? We never asked ourselves: how can we enrich our languages? How can we 'prey' on the rich humanist and democratic heritage in the struggles of other peoples in other times and other places to enrich our own? Why not have Balzac, Tolstoy, Sholokov, Brecht, Lu Hsun, Pablo Neruda, H. C. Anderson, Kim Chi Ha, Marx, Lenin, Albert Einstein, Galileo, Aeschylus, Aristotle, and Plato in African languages? And why not create literary monuments in our own languages? Why in other words should Okara not sweat it out to create in Ijaw, which he acknowledges to have depths of philosophy and a wide range of ideas and experiences? What was our responsibility to the struggles of African peoples? No, these questions were not asked. What seemed to worry us more was this: after all the literary gymnastics of preying on our languages to add life and vigour to English and other foreign languages, would the result be accepted as good English or good French? Will the owner of the language criticise our usage? Here we were more assertive of our rights! Chinua Achebe wrote:

> I feel that the English language will be able to carry the weight of my African experience. But it will have to be a new English, still in full communion with its ancestral home but altered to suit new African surroundings.[8]

Gabriel Okara's position on this was representative of our generation:

> Some may regard this way of writing English as a desecration of the language. This is of course not true. Living languages grow like living things, and English is far from a dead language. There are American, West Indian, Australian, Canadian and New Zealand versions of English. All of them add life and vigour to the language while reflecting their own respective cultures. Why shouldn't there be a Nigerian or West African English which we can use to express our own ideas, thinking and philosophy in our own way?[9]

How did we arrive at this acceptance of 'the fatalistic logic of the unassailable position of English in our literature,' in our culture and in our politics? What was the route from the Berlin of 1884 via the Makerere of 1962 to what is still the prevailing and dominant logic a hundred years later? How did we, as African writers, come to be so feeble towards the claims of our languages on us and so aggressive in our claims on other languages, particularly the languages of our colonization?

Berlin of 1884 was effected through the sword and the bullet. But the night of the sword and the bullet was followed by the morning of the chalk and the blackboard. The physical violence of the battlefield was followed by the psychological violence of the classroom. But where the former was visibly brutal, the latter was visibly gentle, a process best described in Cheikh Hamidou Kane's novel *Ambiguous Adventure* where he talks of the methods of the colonial phase of imperialism as consisting of knowing how to kill with efficiency and to heal with the same art.

On the Black Continent, one began to understand that their real power resided not at all in the cannons of the first morning but in what followed the cannons. Therefore behind the cannons was the new school. The new school had the nature of both the cannon and the magnet. From the cannon it took the efficiency of a fighting weapon. But better than the cannon it made the conquest permanent. The cannon forces the body and the school fascinates the soul.[10]

In my view language was the most important vehicle through which that power fascinated and held the soul prisoner. The bullet was the means of the physical subjugation. Language was the means of the spiritual subjugation. Let me illustrate this by drawing upon experiences in my own education, particularly in language and literature.

III

I was born into a large peasant family: father, four wives, and about twenty-eight children. I also belonged, as we all did in those days, to a wider extended family and to the community as a whole.

We spoke Gĩkũyũ as we worked in the fields. We spoke Gĩkũyũ in and outside the home. I can vividly recall those evenings of story-telling around the fireside. It was mostly the grown-ups telling the children but everybody was interested and involved. We children would re-tell the stories the following day to other children who worked in the fields picking the pyrethrum flowers, tea-leaves, or coffee beans of our European and African landlords.

The stories, with mostly animals as the main characters, were all told in Gĩkũyũ. Hare, being small, weak but full of innovative wit and cunning, was our hero. We identified with him as he struggled against the brutes of prey like lion, leopard, hyena. His victories were our victories and we learnt that the apparently weak can outwit the strong. We followed the animals in their struggle against hostile nature drought, rain, sun, wind—a confrontation often forcing them to search for forms of co-operation. But we were also interested in their struggles amongst themselves, and particularly between the beasts and the victims of prey. These twin struggles, against nature and other animals, reflected real-life struggles in the human world.

Not that we neglected stories with human beings as the main characters. There were two types of characters in such human-centred narratives: the species of truly human beings with qualities of courage, kindness, mercy, hatred of evil, concern for others; and a man-eat-man two-mouthed species with qualities of greed, selfishness, individualism, and hatred of what was good for the larger co-operative community. Co-operation as the ultimate good in a community was a constant theme. It could unite human beings with animals against ogres and beasts of prey, as in the story of how dove, after being fed with castor-oil seeds, was sent to fetch a smith working far away from home and whose pregnant wife was being threatened by these man-eating two-mouthed ogres.

There were good and bad story-tellers. A good one could tell the same story over and over again, and it would always be fresh to us, the listeners. He or she could tell a story told by someone else and make it more alive and dramatic. The differences really were in the use of words and images and the inflexion of voices to effect different tones.

We therefore learnt to value words for their meaning and nuances. Language was not a mere string of words. It had a suggestive power well beyond the immediate and lexical meaning. Our appreciation of the suggestive magical power of language was reinforced by the games we played with words through riddles, proverbs, transpositions of syllables, or through nonsensical but musically arranged words.[11] So we learnt the music of our language on top of the content. The language, through images and symbols, gave us a view of the world, but it had a beauty of its own. The home and the field were then our pre-primary school but what is important, for this discussion, is that the language of our evening teach-ins, and the language of our immediate and wider community, and the language of our work in the fields were one.

And then I went to school, a colonial school, and this harmony was broken. The language of my education was no longer the language of my culture. I first went to Kamaandura, missionary run, and then to another called Maanguuū run by nationalists grouped around the Gĩkũyũ Independent and Karinga Schools Association. Our language of education was still Gĩkũyũ. The very first time I was ever given an ovation for my writing was over a composition in Gĩkũyũ. So for my first four years there was still harmony between the language of my formal education and that of the Limuru peasant community.

It was after the declaration of a state of emergency over Kenya in 1952 that all the schools run by patriotic nationalists were taken over by the colonial regime and were placed under District Education Boards chaired by Englishmen. English became the language of my formal education. In Kenya, English became more than a language: it was *the* language, and all the others had to bow before it in deference.

Thus one of the most humiliating experiences was to be caught speaking Gĩkũyũ in the vicinity of the school. The culprit was given corporal punishment—three to five strokes of the cane on bare buttocks—or was made to carry a metal plate around the neck with inscriptions such as I AM STUPID or I AM A DONKEY. Sometimes the culprits were fined money they could hardly afford. And how did the teachers catch the culprits? A button was initially given to one pupil who was supposed to hand it over to whoever was caught speaking his mother tongue. Whoever had the button at the end of the day would sing who had given it to him and the ensuing process would bring out all the culprits of the day. Thus children were turned into witch-hunters and in the process were being taught the lucrative value of being a traitor to one's immediate community.

The attitude to English was the exact opposite: any achievement in spoken or written English was highly rewarded; prizes, prestige, applause; the ticket to higher realms. English became the measure of intelligence and ability in the arts, the sciences, and all the other branches of learning. English became *the* main determinant of a child's progress up the ladder of formal education.

As you may know, the colonial system of education in addition to its apartheid racial demarcation had the structure of a pyramid: a broad primary base, a narrowing secondary middle, and an even narrower university apex. Selections from primary into secondary were through an examination, in my time called Kenya African Preliminary Examination, in which one had to pass six subjects ranging from Maths to Nature Study and Kiswahili. All the papers were written in English. Nobody could pass the exam who failed the English-language paper no matter how brilliantly he had done in the other subjects. I remember one boy in my class of 1954 who had distinctions in all subjects except English, which he had failed. He was made to fail the entire exam. He went on to become a turn boy in a bus company. I who had only passes but a credit in English got a place at the Alliance High School, one of the most elitist institutions for Africans in colonial Kenya. The requirements for a place at the University, Makerere University College, were broadly the same: nobody could go on to wear the undergraduate red gown, no matter how brilliantly they had performed in all the other subjects unless they had a credit—not even a simple pass!—in English. Thus the most coveted place in the pyramid and in the system was only available to the holder of an English-language credit card. English was the official vehicle and the magic formula to colonial elitedom.

Literary education was now determined by the dominant language while also reinforcing that dominance. Orature (oral literature) in Kenyan languages stopped. In primary school I now read simplified Dickens and Stevenson alongside Rider Haggard. Jim Hawkins, Oliver Twist, Tom Brown—not Hare, Leopard, and Lion—were now my daily companions in the world of imagination. In secondary school, Scott and G. B. Shaw vied with more Rider Haggard, John Buchan, Alan Paton, Captain W. E. Johns. At Makerere I read English: from Chaucer to T. S. Eliot with a touch of Graham Greene.

Thus language and literature were taking us further and further from ourselves to other selves, from our world to other worlds.

What was the colonial system doing to us Kenyan children? What were the consequences of, on the one hand, this systematic suppression of our languages and the literature they carried, and on the other the elevation of English and the literature it carried? To answer those questions, let me first examine the relationship of language to human experience, human culture, and the human perception of reality.

IV

Language, any language, has a dual character: it is both a means of communication and a carrier of culture. Take English. It is spoken in Britain and in Sweden and Denmark. But for Swedish and Danish people English is only a means of communication with non-Scandinavians. It is not a carrier of their culture. For the British, and particularly the English, it is additionally, and inseparably from its use as a tool of communication, a carrier of their culture and history. Or take Swahili in East and Central Africa. It is widely used as a means of communication across many nationalities. But it is not the carrier of a culture and history of many of those nationalities. However in parts of Kenya and Tanzania, and particularly in Zanzibar, Swahili is inseparably both a means of communication and a carrier of the culture of those people to whom it is a mother tongue.

Language as communication has three aspects or elements. There is first what Karl Marx once called the language of real life,[12] the element basic to the whole notion of language, its origins and development: that is, the relations people enter into with one another in the labour process, the links they necessarily establish among themselves in the act of a people, a community of human beings, producing wealth or means of life like food, clothing, houses. A human community really starts its historical being as a community of co-operation in production through the division of labour; the simplest is between man, woman, and child within a household; the more complex divisions are between branches of production such as those who are sole hunters, sole gatherers of fruits, or sole workers in metal. Then there are the most complex divisions such as those in modern factories where a single product, say a shirt or a shoe, is the result of many hands and minds. Production is co-operation, is communication, is language, is expression of a relation between human beings and it is specifically human.

The second aspect of language as communication is speech and it imitates the language of real life, that is communication in production. The verbal signposts both reflect and aid communication or the relations established between human beings in the production of their means of life. Language as a system of verbal signposts makes that production possible. The spoken word is to relations between human beings what the hand is to the relations between human beings and nature. The hand through tools mediates between human beings and nature and forms the language of real life: spoken words mediate between human beings and form the language of speech.

The third aspect is the written signs. The written word imitates the spoken. Where the first two aspects of language as communication through the hand and the spoken word historically evolved more or less simultaneously, the written aspect is a much later historical development. Writing is representation of sounds with visual symbols, from the simplest knot among shepherds to tell the number in a herd or the hieroglyphics among the Agĩkũyũ gicaandi singers and poets of Kenya, to the most complicated and different letter and picture writing systems of the world today.

In most societies the written and the spoken languages are the same, in that they represent each other: what is on paper can be read to another person and be received as that language which the recipient has grown up speaking. In such a society there is broad harmony for a child between the three aspects of language as communication. His interaction with nature and with other men is expressed in written and spoken symbols or signs which are both a result of that double interaction and a reflection of it. The association of the child's sensibility is with the language of his experience of life.

But there is more to it: communication between human beings is also the basis and process of evolving culture. In doing similar kinds of things and actions over and over again under similar circumstances, similar even in their mutability, certain patterns, moves, rhythms, habits, attitudes, experiences, and knowledge emerge. Those experiences are handed over to the next generation and become the inherited basis for their further actions on nature and on themselves. There is a gradual accumulation of values which in time become almost self-evident truths governing their conception of what is right and wrong, good and bad, beautiful and ugly, courageous and cowardly, generous and mean in their internal and external relations. Over a time this becomes a way of life distinguishable from other ways of life. They develop a distinctive culture and history. Culture embodies those moral, ethical, and aesthetic values, the set of spiritual eyeglasses, through which they come to view themselves and their place in the universe. Values are the basis of a people's identity, their sense of particularity as members of the human race. All this is carried by language. Language as culture is the collective memory bank of a people's experience in history. Culture is almost indistinguishable from the language that makes possible its genesis, growth, banking, articulation, and indeed its transmission from one generation to the next.

Language as culture also has three important aspects. Culture is a product of the history which it in turn reflects. Culture in other words is a product and a reflection of human beings communicating with one another in the very struggle to create wealth and to control it. But culture does not merely reflect that history, or rather it does so by actually forming images or pictures of the world of nature and nurture. Thus the second aspect of language as culture is as an image-forming agent in the mind of a child. Our whole conception of ourselves as a people, individually and collectively, is based on those pictures and images which may or may not correctly correspond to the actual reality of the struggles with nature and nurture which produced them in the first place. But our capacity to confront the world creatively is dependent on how those images correspond or not to that reality, how they distort or clarify the reality of our struggles. Language as culture is thus mediating between me and my own self; between my own self and other selves; between me and nature. Language is mediating in my very being. And this brings us to the third aspect of language as culture. Culture transmits or imparts those images of the world and reality through the spoken and the written language, that is through a specific language. In other words, the capacity to speak, the capacity to order sounds in a manner that makes for mutual comprehension between human beings is universal. This is the universality of language, a quality specific to human beings. It corresponds to the universality of the struggle against nature and that between human beings. But the particularity of the sounds, the words, the word order into phrases and sentences, and the specific manner, or laws, of their ordering is what distinguishes one language from another. Thus a specific culture is not transmitted through language in its universality but in its particularity as the language of a specific community with a specific history. Written literature and orature are the main means by which a particular language transmits the images of the world contained in the culture it carries.

Language as communication and as culture are then products of each other. Communication creates culture: culture is a means of communication. Language carries culture, and culture carries, particularly through orature and literature, the entire body of values by which we come to perceive ourselves and our place in the world. How people perceive themselves affects how they look at their culture, at their politics and at the social production of wealth, at their entire relationship to nature and to other beings. Language is thus inseparable from ourselves as a community of human beings with a specific form and character, a specific history, a specific relationship to the world.

V

So what was the colonialist imposition of a foreign language doing to us children?

The real aim of colonialism was to control the people's wealth: what they produced, how they produced it, and how it was distributed; to control, in other words, the entire realm of the language of real life. Colonialism imposed its control of the social production of wealth through military conquest and subsequent political dictatorship. But its most important area of domination was the mental universe of the colonised, the control, through culture, of how people perceived themselves and their relationship to the world. Economic and political control can never be complete or effective without mental control. To control a people's culture is to control their tools of self-definition in relationship to others.

For colonialism this involved two aspects of the same process: the destruction or the deliberate undervaluing of a people's culture, their art, dances, religions, history, geography, education, orature, and literature, and the conscious elevation of the language of the coloniser. The domination of a people's language by the languages of the colonising nations was crucial to the domination of the mental universe of the colonised.

Take language as communication. Imposing a foreign language, and suppressing the native languages as spoken and written, were already breaking the harmony previously existing between the African child and the three aspects of language. Since the new language as a means of communication was a product of and was reflecting the 'real language of life' elsewhere, it could never as spoken or written properly reflect or imitate the real life of that community. This may in part explain why technology always appears to us as slightly external, *their* product and not *ours*. The word 'missile' used to hold an alien far-away sound until I recently learnt its equivalent in Gĩkũyũ, *ngurukuhĩ,* and it made me apprehend it differently. Learning, for a colonial child, became a cerebral activity and not an emotionally felt experience.

But since the new, imposed languages could never completely break the native languages as spoken, their most effective area of domination was the third aspect of language as communication, the written. The language of an African child's formal education was foreign. The language of the books he read was foreign. The language of his conceptualisation was foreign. Thought, in him, took the visible form of a foreign language. So the written language of a child's upbringing in the school (even his spoken language within the school compound) became divorced from his spoken language at home. There was often not the slightest relationship between the child's written world, which was also the language of his schooling, and the world of his immediate environment in the family and the community. For a colonial child, the harmony existing between the three aspects of language as communication was irrevocably broken. This resulted in the disassociation of the sensibility of that child from his natural and social environment, what we might call colonial alienation. The alienation became reinforced in the teaching of history, geography, music, where bourgeois Europe was always the centre of the universe.

This disassociation, divorce, or alienation from the immediate environment becomes clearer when you look at colonial language as a carrier of culture.

Since culture is a product of the history of a people which it in turn reflects, the child was now being exposed exclusively to a culture that was a product of a world external to himself. He was being made to stand outside himself to look at himself. *Catching Them Young* is the title of a book on racism, class, sex, and politics in children's literature by Bob Dixon. 'Catching them young' as an aim was even more true of a colonial child. The images of this world and his place in it implanted in a child take years to eradicate, if they ever can be.

Since culture does not just reflect the world in images but actually, through those very images, conditions a child to see that world in a certain way, the colonial child was made to see the world and where he stands in it as seen and defined by or reflected in the culture of the language of imposition.

And since those images are mostly passed on through orature and literature it meant the child would now only see the world as seen in the literature of his language of adoption. From the point of view of alienation, that is, of seeing oneself from outside oneself as if one was another self, it does not matter that the imported literature carried the great humanist tradition of the best in Shakespeare, Goethe, Balzac, Tolstoy, Gorky, Brecht, Sholokov, Dickens. The location of this great mirror of imagination was necessarily Europe and its history and culture and the rest of the universe was seen from that centre.

But obviously it was worse when the colonial child was exposed to images of his world as mirrored in the written languages of his coloniser. Where his own native languages were associated in his impressionable mind with low status, humiliation, corporal punishment, slow-footed intelligence and ability or downright stupidity, non-intelligibility and barbarism, this was reinforced by the world he met in the works of such geniuses of racism as a Rider Haggard or a Nicholas Monsarrat; not to mention the pronouncement of some of the giants of western intellectual and political establishment, such as Hume ('. . . the negro is naturally inferior to the whites . . .'),[13] Thomas Jefferson ('. . . the blacks . . . are inferior to the whites on the endowments of both body and mind . . .'),[14] or Hegel with his Africa comparable to a land of childhood still enveloped in the dark mantle of the night as far as the development of self-conscious history was concerned. Hegel's statement that there was nothing harmonious with humanity to be found in the African character is representative of the racist images of Africans and Africa such a colonial child was bound to encounter in the literature of the colonial languages.[15] The results could be disastrous.

In her paper read to the conference on the teaching of African literature in schools held in Nairobi in 1973, entitled 'Written Literature and Black Images,'[16] the Kenyan writer and scholar Professor Mĩcere Mũgo related how a reading of the description of Gagool as an old African woman in Rider Haggard's *King Solomon's Mines* had for a long time made her feel mortal terror whenever she encountered old African women. In his autobiography *This Life* Sydney Poitier describes how, as a result of the literature he had read, he had come to associate Africa with snakes. So on arrival in Africa and being put up in a modern hotel in a modern city, he could not sleep because he kept on looking for snakes everywhere, even under the bed. These two have been able to pinpoint the origins of their fears. But for most others the negative image becomes internalised and it affects their cultural and even political choices in ordinary living.

Thus Léopold Sédar Senghor has said very clearly that although the colonial language had been forced upon him, if he had been given the choice he would still have opted for French. He becomes lyrical in his subservience to French:

> We express ourselves in French since French has a universal vocation and since our message is also addressed to French people and others. In our languages [i.e. African languages] the halo that surrounds the words is by nature merely that of sap and blood; French words send out thousands of rays like diamonds.[17]

Senghor has now been rewarded by being anointed to an honoured place in the French Academy—that institution for safe-guarding the purity of the French language.

In Malawi, Banda has erected his own monument by way of an institution, The Kamuzu Academy, designed to aid the brightest pupils of Malawi in their mastery of English.

> It is a grammar school designed to produce boys and girls who will be sent to universities like Harvard, Chicago, Oxford, Cambridge and Edinburgh and be able to compete on equal terms with others elsewhere.
>
> The President has instructed that Latin should occupy a central place in the curriculum. All teachers must have had at least some Latin in their academic background. Dr Banda has often said that no one can fully master English without knowledge of languages such as Latin and French . . .[18]

For good measure no Malawian is allowed to teach at the academy—none is good enough—and all the teaching staff has been recruited from Britain. A Malawian might lower the standards, or rather, the purity of the English language. Can you get a more telling example of hatred of what is national, and a servile worship of what is foreign even though dead?

In history books and popular commentaries on Africa, too much has been made of the supposed differences in the policies of the various colonial powers, the British indirect rule (or the pragmatism of the British in their lack of a cultural programme!) and the French and Portuguese conscious programme of cultural assimilation. These are a matter of detail and emphasis. The final effect was the same: Senghor's embrace of French as this language with a universal vocation is not so different from Chinua Achebe's gratitude in 1964 to English—'those of us who have inherited the English language may not be in a position to appreciate the value of the inheritance.'[19] The assumptions behind the practice of those of us who have abandoned our mother-tongues and adopted European ones as the creative vehicles of our imagination, are not different either.

Thus the 1962 conference of 'African Writers of English Expression' was only recognising, with approval and pride of course, what through all the years of selective education and rigorous tutelage, we had already been led to accept: the 'fatalistic logic of the unassailable position of English in our literature.' The logic was embodied deep in imperialism; and it was imperialism and its effects that we did not examine at Makerere. It is the final triumph of a system of domination when the dominated start singing its virtues.

VI

The twenty years that followed the Makerere conference gave the world a unique literature—novels, stories, poems, plays written by Africans in European languages—which soon consolidated itself into a tradition with companion studies and a scholarly industry.

Right from its conception it was the literature of the petty-bourgeoisie born of the colonial schools and universities. It could not be otherwise, given the linguistic medium of its message. Its rise and development reflected the gradual accession of this class to political and even economic dominance. But the petty-bourgeoisie in Africa was a large class with different strands in it. It ranged from that section which looked forward to a permanent alliance with imperialism in which it played the role of an intermediary between the bourgeoisie of the western metropolis and the people of the colonies—the section which in my book *Detained: A Writer's Prison Diary* I have described as the comprador bourgeoisie—to that section which saw the future in terms of a vigorous independent national economy in African capitalism or in some kind of socialism, what I shall here call the nationalistic or patriotic bourgeoisie. This literature by Africans in European languages was specifically that of the nationalistic bourgeoisie in its creators, its thematic concerns, and its consumption.[20]

Internationally the literature helped this class, which in politics, business, and education, was assuming leadership of the countries newly emergent from colonialism, or of those struggling to so emerge, to explain Africa to the world: Africa had a past and a culture of dignity and human complexity.

Internally the literature gave this class a cohesive tradition and a common literary frame of references, which it otherwise lacked with its uneasy roots in the culture of the peasantry and in the culture of the metropolitan bourgeoisie. The literature added confidence to the class: the petty-bourgeoisie now had a past, a culture, and a literature with which to confront the racist bigotry of Europe. This confidence—manifested in the tone of the writing, its sharp critique of European bourgeois civilisation, its implications, particularly in its negritude mould, that Africa had something new to give to the world—reflects the political ascendancy of the patriotic nationalistic section of the petty-bourgeoisie before and immediately after independence.

So initially this literature—in the post-war world of national democratic revolutionary and anti-colonial liberation in China and India, armed uprisings in Kenya and Algeria, the independence of Ghana and Nigeria with others impending—was part of that great anti-colonial and anti-imperialist upheaval in Asia, Africa, Latin America, and Caribbean islands. It was inspired by the general political awakening; it drew its stamina and even form from the peasantry: their proverbs, fables, stories, riddles, and wise sayings. It was shot through and through with optimism. But later, when the comprador section assumed political ascendancy and strengthened rather than weakened the economic links with imperialism in what was clearly a neo-colonial arrangement, this literature became more and more critical, cynical, disillusioned, bitter, and denunciatory in tone. It was almost unanimous in its portrayal, with varying degrees of detail, emphasis, and clarity of vision, of the post-independence betrayal of hope. But to whom was it directing its list of mistakes made, crimes and wrongs committed, complaints unheeded, or its call for a change of moral direction? The imperialist bourgeoisie? The petty-bourgeoisie in power? The military, itself part and parcel of that class? It sought another audience, principally the peasantry and the working class or what was generally conceived as the people. The search for a new audience and new directions was reflected in the quest for simpler forms, in the adoption of a more direct tone, and often in a direct call for action. It was also reflected in the content. Instead of seeing Africa as one undifferentiated mass of historically wronged blackness, it now attempted some sort of class analysis and evaluation of neo-colonial societies. But this search was still within the confines of the languages of Europe whose use it now defended with less vigour and confidence. So its quest was hampered by the very language choice, and in its movement toward the people, it could only go up to that section of the petty-bourgeoisie—the students, teachers, secretaries for instance still in closest touch with the people. It settled there, marking time, caged within the linguistic fence of its colonial inheritance.

Its greatest weakness still lay where it has always been, in the audience—the petty-bourgeoisie readership automatically assumed by the very choice of language. Because of its indeterminate economic position between the many contending classes, the petty-bourgeoisie develops a vacillating psychological make-up. Like a chameleon it takes on the colour of the main class with which it is in the closest touch and sympathy. It can be swept to activity by the masses at a time of revolutionary tide; or be driven to silence, fear, cynicism, withdrawal into self-contemplation, existential anguish, or to collaboration with the powers-that-be at times of reactionary tides. In Africa this class has always oscillated between the imperialist bourgeoisie and its comprador neo-colonial ruling elements on the one hand, and the peasantry and the working class (the masses) on the other. This very lack of identity in its social and psychological make-up as a class, was reflected in the very literature it produced: the crisis of identity was assumed in that very preoccupation with definition at the Makerere conference. In literature as in politics it spoke as if its identity or the crisis of its own identity was that of society as a whole. The literature it produced in European languages was given the identity of African literature as if there had never been literature in African languages. Yet by avoiding a real confrontation with the language issue, it was clearly wearing false robes of identity: it was a pretender to the throne of the mainstream of African literature. The practitioner of what Janheinz Jahn called neo-African literature tried to get out of the dilemma by over-insisting that European languages were really African languages or by trying to Africanise English or French usage while making sure it was still recognisable as English or French or Portuguese.

In the process this literature created, falsely and even absurdly, an English-speaking (or French or Portuguese) African peasantry and working class, a clear negation or falsification of the historical process and reality. This European-language-speaking peasantry and working class, existing only in novels and dramas, was at times invested with the vacillating mentality, the evasive self-contemplation, the existential anguished human condition, or the man-torn-between-two-worlds-facedness of the petty-bourgeoisie.

In fact, if it had been left entirely to this class, African languages would have ceased to exist—with independence!

VII

But African languages refused to die. They would not simply go the way of Latin to become the fossils for linguistic archaeology to dig up, classify, and argue about at the international conferences.

These languages, these national heritages of Africa, were kept alive by the peasantry. The peasantry saw no contradiction between speaking their own mother tongues and belonging to a larger national or continental geography. They saw no necessary antagonistic contradiction between belonging to their immediate nationality, to their multinational state along the Berlin-drawn boundaries, and to Africa as a whole. These people happily spoke Wolof, Hausa, Yoruba, Ibo, Arabic, Amharic, Kiswahili, Gĩkũyũ, Luo, Luhya, Shona, Ndebele, Kimbundu, Zulu, or Lingala without this fact tearing the multinational states apart. During the anti-colonial struggle they showed an unlimited capacity to unite around whatever leader or party best and most consistently articulated an anti-imperialist position. If anything it was the petty-bourgeoisie, particularly the compradors, with their French and English and Portuguese, with their petty rivalries, their ethnic chauvinism, which encouraged these vertical divisions to the point of war at times. No, the peasantry had no complexes about their languages and the cultures they carried!

In fact when the peasantry and the working class were compelled by necessity or history to adopt the language of the master, they Africanised it without any of the respect for its ancestry shown by Senghor and Achebe, so totally as to have created new African languages, like Krio in Sierra Leone or Pidgin in Nigeria, that owed their identities to the syntax and rhythms of African languages. All these languages were kept alive in the daily speech, in the ceremonies, in political struggles, above all in the rich store of orature—proverbs, stories, poems, and riddles.

The peasantry and the urban working class threw up singers. These sang the old songs or composed new ones incorporating the new experiences in industries and urban life and in working-class struggle and organisations. These singers pushed the languages to new limits, renewing and reinvigorating them by coining new words and new expressions, and in generally expanding their capacity to incorporate new happenings in Africa and the world.

The peasantry and the working class threw up their own writers, or attracted to their ranks and concern intellectuals from among the petty-bourgeoisie, who all wrote in African languages. It is these writers like Heruy Wäldä Sellassie, Germacäw Takla Hawaryat, Shabaan Robert, Abdullatif Abdalla, Ebrahim Hussein, Euphrase Kezilahabi, B. H. Vilakazi, Okot p'Bitek, A. C. Jordan, P. Mboya, D. O. Fagunwa, Mazisi Kunene, and many others rightly celebrated in Albert Gérard's pioneering survey of literature in African languages from the tenth century to the present, called *African Language Literatures* (1981), who have given our languages a written literature. Thus the immortality of our languages in print has been ensured despite the internal and external pressures for their extinction. In Kenya I would like to single out Gakaara wa Wanjaũ, who was jailed by the British for the ten years between 1952 and 1962 because of his writing in Gĩkũyũ. His book, *Mwandĩki wa Mau Mau Ithaamĩrioinĩ,* a diary he secretly kept while in political detention, was published by Heinemann Kenya and won the 1984 Noma Award. It is a powerful work, extending the range of the Gĩkũyũ language prose, and it is a crowning achievement to the work he started in 1946. He has worked in poverty, in the hardships of prison, in post-independence isolation when the English language held sway in Kenya's schools from nursery to University and in every walk of the national printed world, but he never broke his faith in the possibilities of Kenya's national languages. His inspiration came from the mass anti-colonial movement of Kenyan people, particularly the militant wing grouped around Mau Mau or the Kenya Land and Freedom Army, which in 1952 ushered in the era of modern guerrilla warfare in Africa. He is the clearest example of those writers thrown up by the mass political movements of an awakened peasantry and working class.

And finally from among the European-language-speaking African petty-bourgeoisie, there emerged a few who refused to join the chorus of those who had accepted the 'fatalistic logic' of the position of European languages in our literary being. It was one of these, Obi Wali, who pulled the carpet from under the literary feet of those who gathered at Makerere in 1962 by declaring in an article published in *Transition* (10, September 1963), 'that the whole uncritical acceptance of English and French as the inevitable medium for educated African writing is misdirected, and has no chance of advancing African literature and culture,' and that until African writers accepted that any true African literature must be written in African languages, they would merely be pursuing a dead end.

> What we would like future conferences on African literature to devote time to, is the all-important problem of African writing in African languages, and all its implications for the development of a truly African sensibility.

Obi Wali had his predecessors. Indeed people like David Diop of Senegal had put the case against this use of colonial languages even more strongly.

> The African creator, deprived of the use of his language and cut off from his people, might turn out to be only the representative of a literary trend (and that not necessarily the least gratuitous) of the conquering nation. His works, having become a perfect illustration of the assimilationist policy through imagination and style, will doubtless rouse the warm applause of a certain group of critics. In fact, these praises will go mostly to colonialism which, when it can no longer keep its subjects in slavery, transforms them into docile intellectuals patterned after Western literary fashions which besides, is another more subtle form of bastardization.[21]

David Diop quite correctly saw that the use of English and French was a matter of temporary historical necessity.

> Surely in an Africa freed from oppression it will not occur to any writer to express, otherwise than in his rediscovered language, his feelings and the feelings of his people.[22]

The importance of Obi Wali's intervention was in tone and timing: it was published soon after the 1962 Makerere conference of African writers of English expression; it was polemical and aggressive, poured ridicule and scorn on the choice of English and French, while being unapologetic in its call for the use of African languages. Not surprisingly it was met with hostility and then silence. But twenty years of uninterrupted dominance of literature in European languages, the reactionary turn that political and economic events in Africa have taken, and the search for a revolutionary break with the neo-colonial status quo, all compel soul-searching among writers, raising once again the entire question of the language of African literature.

VIII

The question is this: we as African writers have always complained about the neo-colonial economic and political relationship to Euro-America. Right. But by our continuing to write in foreign languages, paying homage to them, are we not on the cultural level continuing that neocolonial slavish and cringing spirit? What is the difference between a politician who says Africa cannot do without imperialism and the writer who says Africa cannot do without European languages?

While we were busy haranguing the ruling circles in a language which automatically excluded the participation of the peasantry and the working class in the debate, imperialist culture and African reactionary forces had a field day: the Christian bible is available in unlimited quantities in even the tiniest African language. The comprador ruling cliques are also quite happy to have the peasantry and the working class all to themselves: distortions, dictatorial directives, decrees, museum-type fossils paraded as African culture, feudalistic ideologies, superstitions, lies, all these backward elements and more are communicated to the African masses in their own languages without any challenges from those with alternative visions of tomorrow who have deliberately cocooned themselves in English, French, and Portuguese. It is ironic that the most reactionary African politician, the one who believes in selling Africa to Europe, is often a master of African languages; that the most zealous of European missionaries who believed in rescuing Africa from itself, even from the paganism of its languages, were nevertheless masters of African languages, which they often reduced to writing. The European missionary believed too much in his mission of conquest not to communicate it in the languages most readily available to the people: the African writer believes too much in 'African literature' to write it in those ethnic, divisive, and underdeveloped languages of the peasantry!

The added irony is that what they have produced, despite any claims to the contrary, is not African literature. The editors of the Pelican Guides to English literature in their latest volume were right to include a discussion of this literature as part of twentieth-century English literature, just as the French Academy was right to honour Senghor for his genuine and talented contribution to French literature and language. What we have created is another hybrid tradition, a tradition in transition, a minority tradition that can only be termed as Afro-European literature; that is, the literature written by Africans in European languages.[23] It has produced many writers and works of genuine talent: Chinua Achebe, Wole Soyinka, Ayi Kwei Armah, Sembene Ousmane, Agostino Neto, Sédar Senghor, and many others. Who can deny their talent? The light in the products of their fertile imaginations has certainly illuminated important aspects of the African being in its continuous struggle against the political and economic consequences of Berlin and after. However we cannot have our cake and eat it! Their work belongs to an Afro-European literary tradition which is likely to last for as long as Africa is under this rule of European capital in a neocolonial set-up. So Afro-European literature can be defined as literature written by Africans in European languages in the era of imperialism.

But some are coming round to the inescapable conclusion articulated by Obi Wali with such polemical vigour twenty years ago: African literature can only be written in African languages, that is, the languages of the African peasantry and working class, the major alliance of classes in each of our nationalities and the agency for the coming inevitable revolutionary break with neo-colonialism.

IX

I started writing in Gĩkũyũ language in 1977 after seventeen years of involvement in Afro-European literature, in my case Afro-English literature. It was then that I collaborated with Ngũgĩ wa Mĩriĩ in the drafting of the playscript *Ngaahika Ndeenda* (the English translation was *I Will Marry When I Want*). I have since published a novel in Gĩkũyũ, *Caitaani Mũtharabainĩ* (English translation: *Devil on the Cross*) and completed a musical drama, *Maitũ Njugĩra* (English translation: *Mother Sing for Me*); three books for children, *Njamba Nene na Mbaathi i Mathagu, Bathitoora ya Njamba Nene, Njamba Nene na Cibũ Kĩng'ang'i;* as well as another novel manuscript: *Matigari Ma Njirũũngi*. Wherever I have gone, particularly in Europe, I have been confronted with the question: why are you now writing in Gĩkũyũ? Why do you now write in an African language? In some academic quarters I have been confronted with the rebuke, 'Why have you abandoned us?' It was almost as if, in choosing to write in Gĩkũyũ, I was doing something abnormal. But Gĩkũyũ is my mother tongue! The very fact that what common sense dictates in the literary practice of other cultures is being questioned in an African writer is a measure of how far imperialism has distorted the view of African realities. It has turned reality upside down: the abnormal is viewed as normal and the normal is viewed as abnormal. Africa actually enriches Europe: but Africa is made to believe that it needs Europe to rescue it from poverty. Africa's natural and human resources continue to develop Europe and America: but Africa is made to feel grateful for aid from the same quarters that still sit on the back of the continent. Africa even produces intellectuals who now rationalise this upside-down way of looking at Africa.

I believe that my writing in Gĩkũyũ language, a Kenyan language, an African language, is part and parcel of the anti-imperialist struggles of Kenyan and African peoples. In schools and universities our Kenyan languages—that is, the languages of the many nationalities which make up Kenya—were associated with negative qualities of backwardness, underdevelopment, humiliation and punishment. We who went through that school system were meant to graduate with a hatred of the people and the culture and the values of the language of our daily humiliation and punishment. I do not want to see Kenyan children growing up in that imperialist-imposed tradition of contempt for the tools of communication developed by their communities and their history. I want them to transcend colonial alienation.

Colonial alienation takes two interlinked forms: an active (or passive) distancing of oneself from the reality around; and an active (or passive) identification with that which is most external to one's environment. It starts with a deliberate disassociation of the language of conceptualisation, of thinking, of formal education, of mental development, from the language of daily interaction in the home and in the community. It is like separating the mind from the body so that they are occupying two unrelated linguistic spheres in the same person. On a larger social scale it is like producing a society of bodiless heads and headless bodies.

So I would like to contribute towards the restoration of the harmony between all the aspects and divisions of language so as to restore the Kenyan child to his environment, understand it fully so as to be in a position to change it for his collective good. I would like to see Kenya peoples' mother tongues (our national languages!) carry a literature reflecting not only the rhythms of a child's spoken expression, but also his struggle with nature and his social nature. With that harmony between himself, his language, and his environment as his starting point, he can learn other languages and even enjoy the positive humanistic, democratic, and revolutionary elements in other people's literatures and cultures without any complexes about his own language, his own self, his environment. The all-Kenya national language (i.e. Kiswahili); the other national languages (i.e. the languages of the nationalities like Luo, Gĩkũyũ, Maasai, Luhya, Kallenjin, Kamba, Mijikenda, Somali, Galla, Turkana, Arabic-speaking people, etc.); other African languages like Hausa, Wolof, Yoruba, Ibo, Zulu, Nyanja, Lingala, Kimbundu; and foreign languages—that is, foreign to Africa—like English, French, German, Russian, Chinese, Japanese, Portuguese, Spanish will fall into their proper perspective in the lives of Kenyan children.

Chinua Achebe once decried the tendency of African intellectuals to escape into abstract universalism in words that apply even more to the issue of the language of African literature:

> Africa has had such a fate in the world that the very adjective *African* can call up hideous fears of rejection. Better then to cut all the links with this homeland, this liability, and become in one giant leap the universal man. Indeed I understand this anxiety. *But running away from oneself seems to me a very inadequate way of dealing with an anxiety* [italics mine]. And if writers should opt for such escapism, who is to meet the challenge?[24]

Who indeed?

We African writers are bound by our calling to do for our languages what Spencer, Milton, and Shakespeare did for English; what Pushkin and Tolstoy did for Russian; indeed what all writers in world history have done for their languages by meeting the challenge of creating a literature in them, which process later opens the languages for philosophy, science, technology, and all the other areas of human creative endeavours.

But writing in our languages per se—although a necessary first step in the correct direction—will not itself bring about the renaissance in African cultures if that literature does not carry the content of our people's anti-imperialist struggles to liberate their productive forces from foreign control; the content of the need for unity among the workers and peasants of all the nationalities in their struggle to control the wealth they produce and to free it from internal and external parasites.

In other words writers in African languages should reconnect themselves to the revolutionary traditions of an organised peasantry and working class in Africa in their struggle to defeat imperialism and create a higher system of democracy and socialism in alliance with all the other peoples of the world. Unity in that struggle would ensure unity in our multi-lingual diversity. It would also reveal the real links that bind the people of Africa to the peoples of Asia, South America, Europe, Australia and New Zealand, Canada, and the U.S.A.

But it is precisely when writers open out African languages to the real links in the struggles of peasants and workers that they will meet their biggest challenge. For to the comprador-ruling regimes, their real enemy is an awakened peasantry and working class. A writer who tries to communicate the message of revolutionary unity and hope in the languages of the people becomes a subversive character. It is then that writing in African languages becomes a subversive or treasonable offence with such a writer facing possibilities of prison, exile, or even death. For him there are no 'national' accolades, no new year honours, only abuse and slander and innumerable lies from the mouths of the armed power of a ruling minority—ruling, that is, on behalf of U.S.-led imperialism—and who see in democracy a real threat. A democratic participation of the people in the shaping of their own lives or in discussing their own lives in languages that allow for mutual comprehension is seen as being dangerous to the good government of a country and its institutions. African languages addressing themselves to the lives of the people become the enemy of a neo-colonial state.

NOTES

1 'European languages became so important to the Africans that they defined their own identities partly by reference to those languages. Africans began to describe each other in terms of being either Francophone or English-speaking Africans. The continent itself was thought of in terms of French-speaking states, English-speaking states and Arabic-speaking states.' Ali A. Mazrui, *Africa's International Relations,* London: 1977, p. 92.

Arabic does not quite fall into that category. Instead of Arabic-speaking states as an example, Mazrui should have put Portuguese-speaking states. Arabic is now an African language unless we want to write off all the indigenous populations of North Africa, Egypt, Sudan as not being Africans.

And as usual with Mazrui his often apt and insightful descriptions, observations, and comparisons of the contemporary African realities as affected by Europe are, unfortunately, often tinged with approval or a sense of irreversible inevitability.

2 The conference was organized by the anti-Communist Paris-based but American-inspired and -financed Society for Cultural Freedom which was later discovered actually to have been financed by CIA. It shows how certain directions in our cultural, political, and economic choices can be masterminded from the metropolitan centres of imperialism.

3 This is an argument often espoused by colonial spokesmen. Compare Mphahlele's comment with that of Geoffrey Moorehouse in *Manchester Guardian Weekly,* 15 July 1964, as quoted by Ali A. Mazrui and Michael Tidy in their work *Nationalism and New States in Africa,* London: 1984.

'On both sides of Africa, moreover, in Ghana and Nigeria, in Uganda and in Kenya, the spread of education has led to an increased demand for English at primary level. *The remarkable thing is that English has not been rejected as a symbol of Colonialism; it has rather been adopted as a politically neutral language beyond the reproaches of tribalism*. It is also a more attractive proposition in Africa than in either India or Malaysia because comparatively few Africans are completely literate in the vernacular tongues and even in the languages of regional communication, Hausa and Swahili, which are spoken by millions, and only read and written by thousands.' (My italics.)

Is Moorehouse telling us that the English language is politically neutral vis-à-vis Africa's confrontation with neo-colonialism? Is he telling us that by 1964 there were more Africans literate in European languages than in African languages? That Africans could not, even if that was the case, be literate in their own national languages or in the regional languages? Really is Mr. Moorehouse tongue-tying the African?

4 The English title is *Tales of Amadou Koumba,* published by Oxford University Press. The translation of this particular passage from the *Présence Africaine,* Paris edition of the book was done for me by Dr. Bachir Diagne in Bayreuth.

5 The paper is now in Achebe's collection of essays *Morning Yet on Creation Day,* London: 1975.

6 In the introduction to *Morning Yet on Creation Day* Achebe obviously takes a slightly more critical stance from his 1964 position. The phrase is apt for a whole generation of us African writers.

7 *Transition* No. 10, September 1963, reprinted from *Dialogue,* Paris.

8 Chinua Achebe, 'The African Writer and the English Language,' in *Morning Yet on Creation Day*.

9 Gabriel Okara, *Transition* No. 10, September 1963.

10 Cheikh Hamidou Kane, *L'aventure Ambiguë* (English translation: *Ambiguous Adventure*.) This passage was translated for me by Bachir Diagne.

11 Example from a tongue twister: 'Kaana ka Nikoora koona koora koora: na ko koora koona kaana ka Nikoora koora koora.' I'm indebted to Wangui wa Goro for this example. 'Nichola's child saw a baby frog and ran away: and when the baby frog saw Nichola's child it also ran away.' A Gĩkũyũ-speaking child has to get the correct tone and length of vowel and pauses to get it right. Otherwise it becomes a jumble of *k*'s and *r*'s and *na*'s.

12 'The production of ideas, of conceptions, of consciousness, is at first directly interwoven with the material activity and the material intercourse of men, the language of real life. Conceiving, thinking, the mental intercourse of men, appear at this stage as the direct efflux of their material behaviour. The same applies to mental production as expressed in the language of politics, laws, morality, religion, metaphysics, etc., of a people. Men are the producers of their conceptions, ideas etc.—real, active men, as they are conditioned by a definite development of their productive forces and of the intercourse corresponding to these, up to its furthest form.' Marx

and Engels, *German Ideology,* the first part published under the title, *Feuerbach: Opposition of the Materialist and Idealist Outlooks,* London: 1973, p. 8.

13 Quoted in Eric Williams *A History of the People of Trinidad and Tobago,* London: 1964, p. 32.

14 Ibid., p. 31.

15 In references to Africa in the introduction to his lectures in *The Philosophy of History,* Hegel gives historical, philosophical, rational expression and legitimacy to every conceivable European racist myth about Africa. Africa is even denied her own geography where it does not correspond to the myth. Thus Egypt is not part of Africa; and North Africa is part of Europe. Africa proper is the especial home of ravenous beasts, snakes of all kinds. The African is not part of humanity. Only slavery to Europe can raise him, possibly, to the lower ranks of humanity. Slavery is good for the African. 'Slavery is in and for itself *injustice,* for the essence of humanity is *freedom*; but for this man must be matured. The gradual abolition of slavery is therefore wiser and more equitable than its sudden removal.' (Hegel, *The Philosophy of History,* Dover edition, New York: 1956, pp. 91–9.) Hegel clearly reveals himself as the nineteenth-century Hitler of the intellect.

16 The paper is now in Akivaga and Gachukiah's *The Teaching of African Literature in Schools,* published by Kenya Literature Bureau.

17 Senghor, Introduction to his poems, 'Éthiopiques, le 24 Septembre 1954,' in answering the question: 'Pourquoi, dès lors, écrivez-vous en français?' Here is the whole passage in French. See how lyrical Senghor becomes as he talks of his encounter with French language and French literature.

Mais on me posera la question: 'Pourquoi, dès lors, écrivez-vous en français?' parce que nous sommes des métis culturels, parce que, si nous sentons en nègres, nous nous exprimons en français, parce que le français est une langue à vocation universelle, que notre message s'adresse *aussi* aux Français de France et aux autres hommes, parce que le français est une langue 'de gentillesse et d'honnêteté.' Qui a dit que c'était une langue grise et atone d'ingénieurs et de diplomates? Bien sûr, moi aussi, je l'ai dit un jour, pour les besoins de ma thèse. On me le pardonnera. Car je sais ses ressources pour l'avoir goûté, mâché, enseigné, et qu'il est la langue des dieux. Écoutez donc Corneille, Lautréamont, Rimbaud, Péguy et Claudel. Écoutez le grand Hugo. Le français, ce sont les grandes orgues qui se prêtent à tous les timbres, à tous les effets, des douceurs les plus suaves aux fulgurances de l'orage. Il est, tour à tour ou en même temps, flûte, hautbois, trompette, tamtam et même canon. Et puis le français nous a fait don de ses mots abstraits— si rares dans nos langues maternelles—, où les larmes se font pierres précieuses. Chez nous, les mots sont naturellement nimbés d'un halo de sève et de sang; les mots du français rayonnent de mille feux, comme des diamants. Des fusées qui éclairent notre nuit.

See also Senghor's reply to a question on language in an interview by Armand Guiber and published in *Présence Africaine* 1962 under the title, "Léopold Sédar Senghor":

Il est vrai que le français n'est pas ma langue maternelle. J'ai commencé de l'apprendre à sept ans, par des mots comme 'confitures' et 'chocolat.' Aujourd'hui, je pense naturellement en Français, et je comprend le Français—faut-il en avoir honte? Mieux qu'aucune autre langue. C'est dire que le Français n'est plus pour moi un 'véhicule étranger' mais la forme d'expression naturelle de ma pensée.

Ce qui m'est étrange dans le français, c'est peut-être son style:

Son architecture classique. Je suis naturellement porté à gonfler d'image son cadre étroit, sans la poussée de la chaleur émotionelle.

18 *Zimbabwe Herald,* August 1981.

19 Chinua Achebe, 'The African Writer and the English Language' in *Morning Yet on Creation Day,* p. 59.

20 Most of the writers were from Universities. The readership was mainly the product of schools and colleges. As for the underlying theme of much of that literature, Achebe's statement in his paper, 'The Novelist as a Teacher,' is instructive:

'If I were God I would regard as the very worst our acceptance—for whatever reason—of racial inferiority. It is too late in the day to get worked up about it or to blame others, much as they may deserve such blame and condemnation. What we need to do is to look back and try and find out where we went wrong, where the rain began to beat us.

'Here then is an adequate revolution for me to espouse—to help my society regain belief in itself and put away the complexes of the years of denigration and self-abasement.' *Morning Yet on Creation Day,* p. 44.

Since the peasant and the worker had never really had any doubts about their African-ness, the reference could only have been to the 'educated' or the petty-bourgeois African. In fact if one substitutes the words 'the petty-bourgeois' for the word 'our' and 'the petty-bourgeois class' for 'my society' the statement is apt, accurate, and describes well the assumed audience. Of course, an ideological revolution in this class would affect the whole society.

21 David Diop, 'Contribution to the Debate on National Poetry,' *Présence Africaine* 6, 1956.

22 Ibid.

23 The term 'Afro-European Literature' may seem to put too much weight on the Europeanness of the literature. Euro-African literature? Probably, the English, French, and Portuguese components would then be 'Anglo-African literature,' 'Franco-African literature' or 'Luso-African literature.' What is important is that this minority literature forms a distinct tradition that needs a different term to distinguish it from *African Literature,* instead of usurping the title *African Literature* as is the current practice in literary scholarship. There have even been arrogant claims by some literary scholars who talk as if the literature written in European languages is necessarily closer to the Africanness of its inspiration than similar works in African languages, the languages of the majority. So thoroughly has the minority 'Afro-European Literature' (Euro-African literature?) usurped the name 'African literature' in the current scholarship that literature by Africans in African languages is the one that needs qualification. Albert Gérard's otherwise timely book is titled *African Language Literatures.*

24 Chinua Achebe, 'Africa and Her Writers,' in *Morning Yet on Creation Day,* p. 27.

12

CAROLYN COOPER

Writing Oral History

Sistren Theatre Collective's *Lionheart Gal*

Lionheart Gal: Lifestories of Jamaican Women is an experiment in narrative form that exemplifies the dialogic nature of oral/scribal and Creole/English discourse in Jamaican literature. For *Lionheart Gal* is dialogic in the old-fashioned, literal sense of that word: the text, with three notable exceptions, is the product of a dialogue in Jamaican and English between each woman of Sistren and Honor Ford Smith, the sister confessor, who herself confesses all in solitary script, immaculate in English.

In the fashionably modern, Bakhtinian sense of the word dialogic, *Lionheart Gal* is impeccably subversive. For it engenders an oral, Jamaican subversion of the authority of the English literary canon. Further, its autobiographical form—the lucid verbal flash—articulates a feminist subversion of the authority of the literary text as fiction, as transformative rewriting of the self in the *persona* of distanced, divine omniscience. *Lionheart Gal,* like much contemporary feminist discourse, does not pretend to be authoritative. Indeed, the preferred narrative mode of many feminist writers is the guise of intimate, understated domestic writing by women: letters, diaries or what Sistren, in an oral/Creole context, simply calls testimony. The simultaneously secular and religious resonances of 'testimony' intimate the potential for ideological development from the purely personal to the political that is the usual consequence of this process of communal disclosure.

It is important to distinguish between actual letters and diaries written by women, and the literary use of this sub-genre as fictional frame. For the artifice of these feminist narrative forms is that they are artless, the author having receded in Joycean detachment to pare, and perhaps paint her fingernails, leaving the tape-recorder or word-processor on automatic. For example, Alice Walker in *The Color Purple* describes herself as 'A.W., author and medium,' and courteously 'thank[s] everybody in this book for coming.'[1] She presumably ghost-writes the text.

With *Lionheart Gal* this feminist illusion of narrative artlessness is complicated by the mediating consciousness of Honor Ford Smith, the editorial *persona* who performs a dual function in the making of the text. As testifier, Honor records her own story in 'Grandma's Estate.' As amanuensis, she transcribes the testimonies of the other Sistren (except for 'Ava's Diary' and 'Red Ibo'), shaping the women's responses to her three leading questions: 'How did you first become aware of the fact that you were oppressed as a woman? How did that experience affect your life? How have you tried to change it?' [2]

The full weight of the unprepossessing editorial 'with' on the title page— 'SISTREN with Honor Ford Smith, editor'—is revealed in the polemical 'Introduction,' particularly in the section 'How This Book Was Made.' The editorial explanation of the collaborative process is an illuminating sub-text, as interesting as the stories themselves. For the 'Introduction' offers an ideological frame for the stories that attempts to define the boundaries of their meaning: the stories assume a sociological authority that the improvisational authorial process cannot readily support. The sociologist Herman McKenzie, in his review of the text, issues an instructive *caveat:*

> There are methodological doubts, however, which make me feel that perhaps it is wiser to view these stories as illustrative of generalisations previously arrived at by other means, rather than as providing an independent basis for such generalisations about women in Jamaica. [3]

Editorial intervention in the making of the text is clearly an important issue in *Lionheart Gal*. In an early review Evelyn O'Callaghan argues that 'the life stories related in *Lionheart Gal* stand somewhere *between* fiction and research data. These stories have been so shaped by selection, editing, rewriting and publication that they have become to a large extent "fictionalised."' [4] As editor, Honor seems to doctor the text—less in the pejorative sense of that word and more in the sense of obstetrician. This metaphor signifies both the active creativity of the labouring woman telling her own story, and the somewhat more passive efficiency of the enabling mid-wife dilating the passage of the text. This distinction between text and story, between ideological necessity and narrative autonomy is central to the problem of authorship and authority in *Lionheart Gal*.

In her 'Introduction' Honor acknowledges a methodological uncertainty in the making of *Lionheart Gal:* a tension between illustration and testimony—what I call text and story:

> This book started life as a documentation of the work of the theatre collective. The first section was to put the work in the context of Jamaican society and focus on the conditions of life of Jamaican women. It was to include testimonies from Sistren as illustrations of pre-determined themes and then discuss how we work on our

plays. Soon it was clear that the testimonies would not sit neatly into an introductory section. They refused to become supporting evidence of predetermined factors. They threatened to take over the entire project and they would not behave. So, in the end we gave up trying to trim them and silence them and we decided to change the nature of the entire project. (pp. xxvi–ii)

Lionheart Gal does not entirely transcend its ambiguous origins in social history; but perhaps it ought not to. For as Herman McKenzie concedes in his lively critique, the hybrid nature of the text is a major source of its appeal:

The collection, therefore, while its mode of presentation (and appeal) places it firmly within the arts, suggests conclusions that challenge social scientists to consider both the problems as well as potential contributions, not to say advantages, of this approach.[5]

Indeed, the ideological frame does not totally circumscribe the range of meanings of the stories. For *Lionheart Gal* is literary less by intent than intuition. Somewhat like *Jane and Louisa Will Soon Come Home* (whose author, Erna Brodber, once artlessly described herself as 'innocent of literature'),[6] *Lionheart Gal* subverts the conventional generic boundaries between literature and social document, between autobiography and fiction, between the oral and the scribal traditions.

As story, *Lionheart Gal* is, for the most part, clearly oral. The language of narration is Jamaican, employing proverb, earthy metaphors and folk-tale structures, particularly repetition and apparent digression. In addition, the rural setting of many of the stories reinforces the sense of a 'folk' perspective. The life-stories illustrate what Derek Walcott calls the 'symmetry' of the folk-tale: 'The true folk tale concealed a structure as universal as the skeleton, the one armature from Br'er Anancy to King Lear. It kept the same digital rhythm of three movements, three acts, three moral revelations.'[7] In the case of *Lionheart Gal,* narrative structure is shaped by Honor's three informing questions which compress female experience into riddle. Decoding the riddle is the key to identity and the moral of the fable.

As text, *Lionheart Gal* somewhat ironically affirms the authority of the written word. Documenting the ideological development of the Sistren Theatre Collective cannot, apparently, be fully accomplished in the medium of theatre. The plays do not adequately speak for themselves: thus the scribal intention of the original project. Further, the search for what Honor calls a 'throughline for each story' (p. xxviii) superimposes on these misbehaving, idiosyncratic oral accounts a decidedly scribal narrative necessity. The looping, circular line of oral narration becomes diametrically opposed to the unidirectional, ideological throughline. The autonomous oral stories revolt against the constricting, scribal narrative intention of the predetermined thematic project.

This oral/scribal contradiction is quintessentially linguistic—Jamaican/English—with clear resonances of social class. For, as Honor observes somewhat evangelically in her 'Introduction':

> Those who speak standard English easily are usually middle-class. They usually write in English, but a few also write in Patwah (usually poetry or drama only). Those who are working-class and speak Patwah, write English too—or at least very few write Patwah (usually poetry or drama). This means that Patwah is written for performance, which is excellent, but what is not excellent is that it is not written for silent reflection or for purposes other than entertainment. Yet we all know that Jamaican people reflect all the time in their heads or in conversations in Patwah, and we also know that reflection is part of the process of gaining control over one's own life. So why are certain kinds of written language still dominated totally by English? (pp. xxviii–ix)

This is the seminal/ovular question. But Honor's own written performance, both in the autobiographical 'Grandma's Estate'[8] and the explicatory 'Introduction,' serves to confirm not the appropriateness of the Jamaican mother-tongue, but the imperial authority of the English father-tongue—more often phallic pen—as the instrument of serious, written reflection. But perhaps it is indelicate to notice: the subversive subverted.

In an unpublished 1986 conference paper, entitled 'Creole and the Jamaican Novelist: Redcam, DeLisser and V. S. Reid,' Victor Chang, more sceptical than Honor, poses a series of challenging questions to our writers, which *Lionheart Gal* as story, if not as text, eloquently answers:

> We have been increasingly told that the resources for expression in Creole are no more limited than in Standard English. If this is so, why then is it not used for internal musing and reflection? Could it be that there is still a persistent belief that Creole just will not serve in certain situations, that certain registers require standard English, or that our writers still have yet to learn to manipulate the Creole with total freedom? Perhaps it could be argued that the very spoken nature of the Creole, its very physicality, militates against its use for inner reflection and introspection.[9]

Perhaps it could be argued; but the compelling counter-argument—of sophisticated performance poets like Louise Bennett, Jean Breeze and Mikey Smith, whose reflective, multitonal words are energised, not broken, by the beat; of Sistren's own commanding theatrical productions that move across a wide emotional range, in Jamaican; of Michael Thelwell's linguistic *tour de force* in the novel *The Harder They Come;* of Bob Marley's musing, introspective lyrics; of the DJs' penetrating noises—seems to decisively lay that backward, dead-end line of argument to final rest.

Recognising the dialogic nature of oral/scribal and Jamaican/English discourse in the story/text *Lionheart Gal;* and seeking to narrow the social distance between the language of the stories and the language of textual analysis, I wish to engage in an experimental Jamaican subversion of the authority of English as our exclusive voice of scholarship. My analysis of the testimonies of the women of Sistren—their verbal acts of introspective self-disclosure—will now proceed in Jamaican. I use the Cassidy orthography which differs markedly from the English-oriented orthography of the *Lionheart Gal* text.[10]

'We come together and talk our life story and put it in a lickle scene.' (p. 72) A so Ava se Sistrin staat aaf: a tel wananada stuori. So yu tel, mi tel, so tel di huol a wi fain out se a di wan stuori wi a tel: Uman stuori. Di siem ting uova an uova. Bot it no iizi fi get op tel piipl yu bizniz ma! It tek plenti haat. So Foxy se iina fi har stuori. Shi se:

> Plenty women used to talk bout di children dat we have and di baby-faada problem. At first me was shy to talk about myself. Di impression women always give me is dat dem is a set of people who always lap dem tail, tek yuh name spread table cloth. Me did feel sort a funny at di time, having children fi two different man, especially since me never like Archie. Me never discuss it wid nobody. When me come meet Didi and hear she talk bout her baby faada and how she hate him after she get pregnant, me say, 'Well if yuh can say your own me can say mine,' for we actually deh pon di same ting. Me and she start talk bout it.   (p. 253)

An a di siem Foxy shii kom fi fain out se dat di tingz dem dat hapn tu wi jos bikaazn wi a uman, dem de tingz supuozn fi kaal 'palitiks,' jos laik eni a di ada big tingz de, we a gwaan iina 'palitriks' az di wan Tosh im se. Den wat a wie dem kil im aaf iin! Mi no nuo if a big Palitiks dat, ar a likl palitiks, bot sinting mos iina sinting. Bot dat iz anada stuori. An di ail dat frai sprat kyaan frai jak, so sumaal frai aal laik mii no supuoz fi bizniz iina dem de tingz.

So hier hou Foxy se shi staat fi fain out bout dis uman palitiks:

> Tings develop so—till we start meet more people and talk bout woman and work and woman and politics. We discuss what is politics and how it affect woman. After we done talk ah get to feel dat di little day-to-day tings dat happen to we as women, is politics too. For instance, if yuh tek yuh pickney to hospital and it die in yuh hand—dat is politics. If yuh do someting to yuh own child dat damage him or her fi di future, dat is politics. If yuh man box yuh down, dat is politics. But plenty politicians don't tink dose things have anything to do wid politics.   (p. 253)

A truu. Far yu kyaan andastan 'di little day-to-day tings dat happen to we as women' if yu no andastan se dat di huol ting set op gens plenti uman fram di die dem baan. Tek far iinstans hou so moch a di uman dem we a tel dem stuori iina *Lionheart Gal* jos fain out se dem prignant. Yes! It kom iin laik wan big sopraiz. Grab bag. A no notn dem plan fa. A no laik hou yu hier dem piipl pan di riedyo an t.v. a tel yu se 'Two is better than two many'—laik se pikni iz somz: ad an moltiplai an divaid an subtrak! Wier yu down tu notn. Naat. Dat a we prignant du plenti uman. Nat iivn uman gud. Yong gyal. Fuors raip an blaitid.

Bot iivn duo laif haad, di uman dem stil a trai. Hier hou Barbara put it: 'Di pregnancy a never someting me plan or choose. It just happen. Nadine born '71. After she born, me did just love her. Me always feel a tenderness inside me dat me no waan do notten fi hurt her. At di same time me no pet her till she spoil.' (p. 138) Bot uman an pikni kyaan liv pan suo-so lov. An a wen di uman dem staat fi trai fi fain likl wok dat stuori kom tu bomp. Far a den di palitiks biit dem down. Uongl sertn kain a piipl fi du sertn kain a wok. An daag nyam yu sopa if *yu* no wan a dem. Aal yu fi du a fit luk afta ada piipl bizniz. Yu no hav no bizniz fi luk afta. Dat a we hapn tu Doreen. Neva iivn get a chaans fi go a die skuul. Pyor iivnin skuul, an naa laan notn:

> Me did waan learn, for me did waan be nurse, or a teacher, but me couldn't grasp notten. Me know definitely seh if me no pass di exam, me nah go get di job me did want. As di months pass by and me see seh me couldn't manage di work in di evening school, me know dere and den seh me nah go noweh in life. After school, ah used to walk past di residential areas and wish it was in deh me live. Sometime me used to pretend seh me live deh and dat me get fi go a school like dem pickney.
>
> (p. 92)

So nou wen pikni prablem jain aan pan no-get-fl-go-a-no-gud-skuul, kyaan get no wok, hafi a sidown wiet pan man fi set yu op, dat a wen di palitiks get hat. Dat a Didi stuori. Hier har:

> Sometime when yuh no have notten and yuh have di pickney dem and dem a look to yuh fi food and fi shelter, yuh haffi do sometings weh yuh no really waan fi do, just fit survive. Sometimes a better yuh cyaan do, mek yuh tek certain man. Sometime yuh really in need. A man might use dat fi ketch yuh. Yuh might know a so it go, but yuh in need. Yuh want it, so yuh haffi tek it. (p. 201)

Bot a no aal di taim yu kyan tek it. Fa 'mait an wel' ton iina livin hel. Far nou man aal waan biit yu if yu no mek op yu main fit du we *him* se. An if yu marid to him, dat no mek no difrans. It kuda aal wos, far nou im dairekli fiil se im uon yu. Dat a di preke Yvonne get harself iin Shi se:

> Ah say ah have me three pickney now and ah married. Dem time deh when yuh married, dem say yuh married fi life. Ah never expect fi me and him separate. Me depress and unhappy. Everyting just get confuse inna me brain. Me feel seh me life

mash up tru me never understand bout sex and man. Me never know what me could a do bout di problem. Me say is everyday problem. It cyaan change. Me grow in it. A so life hard. Me no chat to nobody more dan so. Me no know no odder woman fi talk to. Me never have no consideration. Me, like me unconscious. (p. 151)

Dem de bluo gud fi kil yu. Lik yu down flat. Di uongl ting fi bring yu bak fram grievsaid a fi fain out se a no yu wan. Ada uman iina di ring wid yu a go help yu pen op di bul. So yu taak, ak out yu likl siin, an neks ting—yu iina buk.

So hou dem mek di buk? Askaadin tu di ring-liida, Honor, di huol ting staat aaf wid shi a aks di Sistrin dem kwestyan bout hou dem gro op, an di difran-difran tingz dat hapn tu dem fi mek dem fain out se laif haad. An dem go roun an roun, an taak an taak, laik se dem a plie 'Shuo mi yu muoshan.' Aal dis taim dem a tiep evriting we dem se. Den Honor shii lisn bak tu di tiep, an fiksop fiks-op wat shi tink si Sistrin dem a se, an dem gwaan taak an takk so tel dem en op wid laas vershan. An den dem rait it down.

Plenti a di stuori dem soun laik a so di uman dem taak. Bot some a dem mek mi wanda. Dem no soun so kyasier. Tek, far instans 'Ava's Diary.' It kaina miks-op miks-op. It kom iin laik se hou shi taak a bar yaad iina war wid hou dem did waant har fi taak an rait a skuul; an di skuul nan win! Siit ya nou:

> Since me and the children are alone, if a man come to me other than him, I would have to leave them and go out with him. Therefore I have decided not to have any relationship with another man for the time being.
>
> Bertie know seh me no have no man friend, so him come if him want to come, till me and him start to talk good and him start come intensively. (p. 271)

Den nou, 'Grandma's Estate' an 'Red Ibo.' Mii neva laik hou di tuu a dem jos primz op demself iina suo-so Inglish. An dem no ina no taakin bizniz, mi dier; a pyor rait dem a rait. Skuul definetli win out yaso. An it luk lai se Honor shi did nuo se piipl a go aks har bout it, far shi trai fi klier op harself. Shi se:

> With the two middle-strata members of the group, the oral interviews did not work well. Accustomed to standard English and the conventions of academic expression, their stories sounded stilted when spoken, full of jargon, and hollow. Both 'Red Ibo' and 'Grandma's Estate' were written responses to the interview questions.
>
> (p. xxviii)

An yu nuo, mi tink mi andastan: Paasn krisn dem pikni fos. Bot mi stil se, supuozn dem did gi wi di chaans fi hier wat dem did *se*? Miebi notn neva rang wid it. Den neks ting: It no soun laik se dem a se se dem kyaan *taak* gud, dem kyan uongl *rait* gud? Mi no nuo; mi jos a wanda. Den agen, yu no si se fi dem stuori no persanali diil tu dat wid no man an uman bizniz; no likl ruudnis. Bot mii nan se dem fient-a-haat bikaazn dem nan tel piipl di huol a fi dem persnal an praivit bizniz—laik di ada laiyanhaat gyal dem! Iz jos dat fi dem stuori kom iin laik se yu a trai fi eksplien yuself, yu nuo se piipl a lisn, so yu haft fiks it op. Red Ibo stuori it aal soun laik se shi a pri-ich. Bot no testimoni miitn! Evribadi a testifai iina dem uona wie. Bot mi dier, mek mi lef it. Far pus an daag no hav di siem lok, an mi no waan nobadi se a bad main mi bad main mek mi a aks dem ya likl kwestyan.

An stil far aal, yu hail gi it tu dem. A truu se Ella an Red Ibo stuori soun laik buk. Bot wat iz fiyu kyaan bi on-fi-yu! An muor taim dem stil kech wan nais likl ruuts vaib ina di Inglish. Hier hou Red Ibo shii staat aaf fi har stuori kolcharal: 'When I think of childhood, I think of a village squatting on hillslopes with a river running through it and a bridge and a fording midway along the road which ran by the river.' (p. 221) An a Ella grani nierli spwail op di puor likl pikni. No waant har fi aks no kwestyan bout har piipl dem. Shi fi go riid buk. Nat iivn plie di likl pikni kyaan plie. Puor ting. Shi se:

> I packed leaves of croton and pimento into a basket I found in the kitchen. I twisted a piece of cloth into a cotta and put it on my head. I placed the basket on top of it and practised walking while balancing it on my head. Then I stepped off down the pathway arriving with my produce under Grandma's window. 'Lady, Lady, yuh want anyting to buy, maam?' I readjusted the basket which proved difficult to control.
>
> At first there was no answer, so I repeated, 'Lady, Lady, yuh want anyting to buy, maam?'
>
> My grandmother pushed her head through the window.
>
> 'Ella! Come inside at once and put down that basket!'
>
> I obeyed.
>
> 'What do you think you are doing, Miss?'
>
> 'Playing market woman, Grandma,' I said, not sure what I had done wrong.
>
> 'Never let me see you doing that again.'
>
> 'Why Grandma?' I asked. 'What is wrong with market ladies?'
>
> 'Ladies? They are not ladies. They are women. Go and take a seat in your room.'
>
> (pp. 180–1)

A so it go. *Lionheart Gal* iz a siiryos buk. An unu beta riid it. It maita likl haad fi kech di spelin fi di fers, bot afta yu gwaan gwaan, it no so bad. Den wan ting swiit mi: Yu nuo hou som a fi wi piipl simpl; fram dem si sinting set down iina buk dem tink it impuortant. So nou plenti a dem uu neva go a non a Sistrin plie, dem siem wan a go riid Sistrin buk, bikaazn buk hai. Dem a go get kech. Far a siks a wan, haaf dozn a di ada: uman prablem, man prablem, pikni prablem. Plenti palitiks. An huol hiip a juok! Far yuu nuo, hou wii nuo hou fi tek bad tingz mek juok. Stap yu fram mad, go aaf yu hed. Doreen nuo hou it go. Hier har no: 'All my life, me did haffi act in order to survive. Di fantasies and ginnalship were ways of coping wid di frustration. Now me can put dat pain on stage and mek fun a di people who cause it.' Go de, Sistrin. Laas lik swiit.

NOTES

1 Alice Walker, *The Color Purple* (New York: Washington Square Press, 1983), p. 253; first published 1982.

2 SISTREN with Honor Ford Smith (ed.), *Lionheart Gal: Life Stories of Jamaican Women* (London: The Women's Press, 1986), p. xxvii. Subsequent references cited parenthetically in text.

3 Herman McKenzie, Review of *Lionheart Gal, Jamaica Journal* 20.4 (1988): p. 64.

4 Evelyn O'Callaghan, Review of *Lionheart Gal,* in *Journal of West Indian Literature* 2.1 (1987): p. 93.

5 Herman McKenzie, op cit., p. 63.

6 In an unpublished talk to students in the West Indian Literature class, Department of English, UWI, Mona, 1984.

7 Derek Walcott, 'What the Twilight Says: An Overture,' in *Dream on Monkey Mountain and Other Plays* (New York: Farrar, Straus and Giroux, 1970), p. 24.

8 Ella does use Jamaican when she role-plays as the market lady: ' "Lady, lady, yuh want anyting to buy, maam?" I readjusted the basket, which proved difficult to control.' (p. 180) A Freudian slip?

9 Victor Chang, 'Creole and the Jamaican Novelist: Redcam, DeLisser and V. S. Reid', unpublished paper, Sixth Annual Conference on West Indian Literature, UWI, St. Augustine, 1986, p. 5.

10 I am indebted to Celia Blake for transcribing my text into the Cassidy orthography. For my English-based original, see S. Slemon and H. Tiffin (eds.), *After Europe* (Mundelstrup, Denmark: Dangeroo Press, 1989), pp. 52–6.

Nationalisms and Nativisms

Critiques of colonial discourse and arguments for an institutionalized "return" to indigenous languages did not function in a vacuum. They emerged from and, in turn, shaped modern nationalist movements that gained momentum in various European colonies in the early half of the twentieth century. Although formal independence was achieved earlier in some of the South Asian countries, the focus in part IV is on African and black nationalisms, some of which flamed brightly and then dimmed after independence. Although the shared history of colonization fostered a sense of solidarity—albeit tenuous and not always guaranteed—among colonized subjects, nationalist engagements within and between emergent nations were by no means homogeneous. What is striking about black cultural nationalism is that despite some intellectuals' awareness of individual differences, they mobilized black and African identity as a strategic, if essentialist, response to racism against their communities. The fact that a vast and ethnically diverse continent, as Frantz Fanon noted, was conflated with a national, even biological, identity is perhaps not that surprising, given the centuries of collective racist measures by rival European countries against black Africans. In such a scenario, black Afrocentricity was the volley that returned the assault of white Eurocentrism. Black nationalist ideologies such as negritude were forged in the crucible of colonial encounters with western Europe.

The term *negritude* was coined by Aimé Césaire in the March 1935 issue of *L'Étudiant noir*, a student newspaper. One among several black students studying at the time in prestigious French institutions, Césaire was perhaps the most obvious example of the success of French assimilationist policy. From childhood in Martinique he was formally educated in French belletristic traditions, not oral Creole vernaculars, and with the radical alienation that, according to Ngũgĩ wa Thiong'o, is an inevitable process of colonial education, he traced his cultural genealogy through France, not Africa. But Césaire's years in Paris exposed him to the racially driven inconsistencies of French citizenship and paradoxically drew him closer to the repressed but continuing Martinican legacies of slavery and colonization. At the Lycée Louis-le-Grand he met Léopold Sédar Senghor, future president of Senegal, and along with Léon Damas from French Guiana, he launched negritude as a counter-assimilationist ideology that was elaborated largely in their literary works.

In "Negritude: A Humanism of the Twentieth Century," an essay that is often elliptical and therefore hard to summarize, Senghor provides a philosophical justification for the movement. Although Senghor denies a racialist emphasis, his constant invocation of "African" and "black" presupposes a spiritual if not biological essence emanating from the evolving histories of African nations. This particular paradox of insisting on essential difference that nevertheless participates in universal humanism is familiar to feminist thought, along with the structure of reversals underlying the challenge to inherited binaries. In European patriarchal ideology, women's "nature" was tied to emotion, intuition, nurture, and community, unlike men, whose traits were apparently rational, analytic, independent, and individualistic. In racist ideology, black people were feminized in the above series of dualisms (although the binary is complicated by the hypermasculinity of black men and the masculinization of black "matriarchs," proving that stereotypes shift dynamically). Senghor accepts the racialized characterization but reverses the Eurocentric value system. Responding to centuries of racist behavior toward black Africans, including their supposedly providential rescue through the slavery and colonization that were justified by the presumed superiority of European culture, Senghor insists that the African contribution to humanity is precisely what had been devalued and dehumanized by Eurocentric ideology.

Senghor ostensibly rejects the dualistic and deterministic structures of Enlightenment thought and argues that African philosophy, in contrast, views heart-mind, body-soul, matter-spirit, and masculine-feminine as complementary. "A certain way" that Africans have about them is organically related to mysticism and rhythm, to a cosmos that should properly move in concentric harmony rather than competitive hierarchy, an implicit critique of the antagonistic, avaricious colonial mentality. But despite its attempts to break away from the dominant Western matrix, negritude evolved in the explosive vortex of its intellectual traditions. It absorbed the primitivist tendencies of some of the writers of the Harlem Renaissance, the anti-Enlightenment orientation of Romanticism, the artistic innovations of French surrealists, as well as, ironically, the racial typologies of early white supremacists such as Joseph Arthur Gobineau. It was influenced or supported by European thinkers such as Leo Frobenius, Jean-Paul Sartre, and Jahnheinz Jahn, who may have deplored the inequality of races endorsed by Gobineau but ultimately sustained the assumption of inherent racial difference.

Chinweizu, Onwuchekwa Jemie, and Ihechukwu Madubuike, the self-styled *bolekaja* ("come down, let's fight") Nigerian critics, share the passionate belief in an identifiable Africanity—in the immanent "one drop of black blood" (see their introduction) and indigenous "home soil"—but their project is more radical than that of Césaire, Senghor, and Damas. The Nigerians intend, as they put it bluntly in their introduction to Volume I of *Toward the Decolonization of African Literature,* "to help release African culture from the death-grip of the West." Although their polemical intervention in literary criticism seems similar to Ngūgī's language politics, in that all of them seek to dispel the view of African literatures as merely an appendage of European, specifically English "Great Tradition[s]," the Nigerian critics reject Ngūgī's emphasis on language. They argue instead that "it is not the crucial generator of [cultural] values and cannot *alone* be relied upon to supply linguistic criteria." But their suspicion of "pseudouniversalism," by which European literary standards were applied to African literatures, particularly those written in European languages, leads them to generalize an "African consciousness" as against a "British consciousness."

Fanon suggests that the reactive phase in nationalism, the combative rejection of European hegemony, is a "historical necessity" in the struggle to overthrow colonial rule and disavow colonial ideology. But he accepts the legitimacy of this move only as a passing stage in ongoing national struggles, particularly on the part of those who were most exposed to colonial education. What concerns him is the possibility that the predictably reactive phase in nationalism could freeze into a reactionary and romanticized one as well. "The unconditional affirmation of African culture has succeeded the unconditional affirmation of European culture," he observes. Because the colonizers tended to lump all of Africa into one category, "the reply of colonized peoples will be straight away continental in its breadth." While Fanon's commitment to the political projects of decolonization and nationalism cannot be questioned (he has in fact gained prophetic stature with *The Wretched of the Earth,* now a classic in postcolonial theory), his searing insights into the psychology of nationalism do not blind him to its pitfalls, which he lays out in another chapter of the book. He would agree with Senghor that one may reach the universal through the particular, and that national concerns need not undermine humanist ones, but unlike the negritude writers, he refuses to use the enabling myth of a timeless black cultural imaginary as the instinctive foundation for future directions. He warns that an emphasis on racial identity and the affirmative character of culture will only lead to a "blind alley." Although both Senghor and Fanon share an interest in African socialism, Fanon's Marxist orientation makes him less inclined to substitute any revolution in the cultural sphere for material conditions such as "colonial exploitation, poverty, and endemic famine."

Paul Gilroy, in arguably the most controversial of the essays in this section, writes in the twenty-first century, with an eye to a future not irretrievably tied to the colonial past. But even if he believes that nineteenth-century vulgar imperialism and colonial rule have formally ended, he is nevertheless cautious about too radical a break in historical chronology, as his phrases "possibly postcolonial" and "nominally postcolonial" indicate. Unlike any of the other writers who might accept the uses of "strategic essentialism," however, Gilroy argues for "strategic universalism." His choice of phrase might indicate his awareness that those who question Western "Universalism's" double standards and its not-so-universal vested interests might reject the unqualified relevance of Western humanism. But a strategic return to a concept that carries unwanted baggage might be critical in a period in which nondominant populations, once the victims of racial typologies, now themselves invoke "racializing categories" as a source of resistant identity. Like Fanon, whom he explicitly invokes, Gilroy remains skeptical of a "racial self articulated exclusively through the body and its imaginary power to determine human social destiny." Ethnic genocide, class divisions, sexual preferences, and gender conflicts dispel the belief in anything that could "be credibly called a single racial community." Apart from internal schisms of this sort, the external affiliations with strange allies and the opportunistic articulation with inimical groups suggest that racial identification is not as primary or as pure as it is sometimes made out to be.

Gilroy goes even further than Fanon in his warnings about inherited Western modes of identity, of which race is only one example. In fact, Gilroy suggests that neither racism nor its evil kin, fascism, can be safely restricted to Europe. Black nationalists such as Marcus Garvey, Gilroy argues, have shown an unnerving admiration for fascist leaders, rhetoric, and paraphernalia. It will amaze some, whatever Garvey's performative proclivity may be, to consider the prospect of any consanguinity between Hitler and Garvey, or to make the affiliation between them one of fascism proper as against proto-fascist tendencies (and even this will be unacceptable to those who find much that is admirable in Garvey). But Gilroy's assertion that neither fascism nor proto-fascism, neither white nor black racialism (however unequal their effects), needs to be tied to state power to cause significant damage cannot easily be dismissed.

13

LÉOPOLD SÉDAR SENGHOR

Negritude

A Humanism of the Twentieth Century

During the last thirty or so years that we have been proclaiming negritude, it has become customary, especially among English-speaking critics, to accuse us of *racialism*. This is probably because the word is not of English origin. But, in the language of Shakespeare, is it not in good company with the words humanism and socialism? Mphahleles[1] have been sent about the world saying: "Negritude is an inferiority complex"; but the same word cannot mean both "racialism" and "inferiority complex" without contradiction. The most recent attack comes from Ghana, where the government has commissioned a poem entitled "I Hate Negritude"—as if one could hate oneself, hate one's being, without ceasing to be.

No, negritude is none of these things. It is neither racialism nor self-negation. Yet it is not just affirmation; it is rooting oneself in oneself, and self-confirmation: confirmation of one's *being*. Negritude is nothing more or less than what some English-speaking Africans have called the *African personality*. It is no different from the "black personality" discovered and proclaimed by the American New Negro movement. As the American Negro poet Langston Hughes wrote after the first world war: "We, the creators of the new generation, want to give expression to our *black personality* without shame or fear. . . . We know we are handsome. Ugly as well. The drums weep and the drums laugh." Perhaps our only originality, since it was the West Indian poet Aimé Césaire who coined the word negritude, is to have attempted to define the concept a little more closely; to have developed it as a weapon, as an instrument of liberation and as a contribution to the humanism of the twentieth century.

But, once again, what is negritude? Ethnologists and sociologists today speak of "different civilizations." It is obvious that peoples differ in their ideas and their languages, in their philosophies and their religions, in their customs and their institutions, in their literature and their art. Who would deny that Africans, too, have a certain way of conceiving life and of living it? A certain way of speaking, singing, and dancing; of painting and sculpturing, and even of laughing and crying? Nobody, probably; for otherwise we would not have been talking about "Negro art" for the last sixty years and Africa would be the only continent today without its ethnologists and sociologists. What, then, is negritude? It is—as you can guess from what precedes—*the sum of the cultural values of the black world;* that is, a certain active presence in the world, or better, in the universe. It is, as John Reed and Clive Wake call it, a certain "way of relating oneself to the world and to others."[2] Yes, it is essentially relations with others, an opening out to the world, contact and participation with others. Because of what it is, negritude is necessary in the world today: it is a humanism of the twentieth century.

. . .

The Philosophy of Being

The paradox is only apparent when I say that negritude, by its ontology (that is, its philosophy of being), its moral law, and its aesthetic, is a response to the modern humanism that European philosophers and scientists have been preparing since the end of the nineteenth century, and as Teilhard de Chardin and the writers and artists of the mid-twentieth century present it.

Firstly, African ontology. Far back as one may go into his past, from the northern Sudanese to the southern Bantu, the African has always and everywhere presented a concept of the world which is diametrically opposed to the traditional philosophy of Europe. The latter is essentially *static, objective, dichotomic;* it is, in fact, dualistic, in that it makes an absolute distinction between body and soul, matter and spirit. It is founded on separation and opposition: on analysis and conflict. The African, on the other hand, conceives the world, beyond the diversity of its forms, as a fundamentally mobile, yet unique, reality that seeks synthesis. This needs development.

It is significant that in Wolof, the main language of Senegal, there are at least three words to translate the word "spirit": *xel, sago,* or *degal,* whereas images have to be used for the word "matter": *lef* (thing) or *yaram* (body). The African is, of course, sensitive to the external world, to the material aspect of beings and things. It is precisely because he is more so than the white European, because he is sensitive to the tangible qualities of things—shape, color, smell, weight, etc.—that the African considers these things merely as signs that have to be interpreted and transcended in order to reach the reality of human beings. Like others, more than others, he distinguishes the pebble from the plant, the plant from the animal, the animal from Man; but, once again, the accidents and appearances that differentiate these kingdoms only illustrate different aspects of the same reality. This reality is *being* in the ontological sense of the word, and it is life force. For the African, matter in the sense the Europeans understand it, is only a system of signs which translates the single reality of the universe: being, which is spirit, which is life force. Thus, the whole universe appears as an infinitely small, and at the same time an infinitely large, network of life forces which emanate from God and end in God, who is the source of all life forces. It is He who vitalizes and devitalizes all other beings, all the other life forces.

I have not wandered as far as might be thought from modern ontology. European ethnologists, Africanists, and artists use the same words and the same expressions to designate the ultimate reality of the universe they are trying to know and to express: "spider's web," "network of forces," "communicating vessels," "system of canals," etc. This is not very different, either, from what the scientists and chemists say. As far as African ontology is concerned, too, there is no such thing as dead matter: every being, every thing—be it only a grain of sand—radiates a life force, a sort of wave-particle; and sages, priests, kings, doctors, and artists all use it to help bring the universe to its fulfilment.

For the African, contrary to popular belief, is not passive in face of the order— or disorder—of the world. His attitude is fundamentally ethical. If the moral law of the African has remained unknown for so long, it is because it derives, naturally, from his conception of the world: from his ontology—so naturally, that both have remained unknown, denied even, by Europeans, because they have not been brought to their attention by being re-examined by each new generation of Africans.

So God tired of all the possibilities that remained confined within Him, unexpressed, dormant, and as if dead. And God opened His mouth, and he spoke at length a word that was harmonious and rhythmical. All these possibilities expressed by the mouth of God *existed* and had the vocation *to live:* to express God in their turn, by establishing the link with God and all the forces deriving from Him.

In order to explain this *morality in action* of negritude, I must go back a little. Each of the identifiable life forces of the universe—from the grain of sand to the ancestor[3]—is itself and in its turn, a network of life forces—as modern physical chemistry confirms: a network of elements that are contradictory in appearance but really *complementary*. Thus, for the African, Man is composed, of course, of matter and spirit, of body and soul; but at the same time he is also composed of a virile and a feminine element: indeed of several "souls." Man is therefore a composition of mobile life forces which interlock: a world of solidarities that seek to knit themselves together. Because he exists, he is at once end and beginning: end of the three orders of the mineral, the vegetable, and the animal, but beginning of the human order.

Let us ignore for the moment the first three orders and examine the human order. Above Man and based on him, lies this fourth world of concentric circles, bigger and bigger, higher and higher, until they reach God along with the whole of the universe. Each circle—family, village, province, nation, humanity—is, in the image of Man and by vocation, a close-knit society.

So, for the African, living according to the moral law means living according to his nature, composed as it is of contradictory elements but complementary life forces. Thus he gives stuff to the stuff of the universe and tightens the threads of the tissue of life. Thus he transcends the contradictions of the elements and works toward making the life forces complementary to one another: in himself first of all, as Man, but also in the whole of human society. It is by bringing the complementary life forces together in this way that Man reinforces them in their movement toward God and, in reinforcing them, he reinforces himself; that is, he passes from *existing* to *being*. He cannot reach the highest form of being, for in fact only God has this quality; and He has it all the more fully as creation, and all that exists, fulfil themselves and express themselves in Him.

Dialogue

Ethnologists have often praised the unity, the balance, and the harmony of African civilization, of black society, which was based both on the *community* and on the *person,* and in which, because it was founded on dialogue and reciprocity, the group had priority over the individual without crushing him, but allowing him to blossom as a person. I would like to emphasize at this point how much these characteristics of negritude enable it to find its place in contemporary humanism, thereby permitting black Africa to make its contribution to the "Civilization of the Universal" which is so necessary in our divided but interdependent world of the second half of the twentieth century. A contribution, first of all, to international cooperation, which must be, and which shall be the cornerstone of that civilization. It is through these virtues of negritude that decolonization has been accomplished without too much bloodshed or hatred and that a positive form of cooperation based on "dialogue and reciprocity" has been established between former colonizers and colonized. It is through these virtues that there has been a new spirit at the United Nations, where the "no" and the bang of the fist on the table are no longer signs of strength. It is through these virtues that peace through cooperation could extend to South Africa, Rhodesia, and the Portuguese colonies, if only the dualistic spirit of the whites would open itself to dialogue.

In fact, the contribution of negritude to the "Civilization of the Universal" is not of recent origin. In the fields of literature and art, it is contemporary with the "Revolution of 1889." The French poet Arthur Rimbaud (1854–1891) had already associated himself with negritude. But in this article I want to concentrate on the "Negro revolution"—the expression belongs to Emmanuel Berl—which helped to stir European plastic art at the beginning of this century.

Art, like literature, is always the expression of a certain conception of the world and of life; the expression of a certain philosophy and, above all, of a certain ontology. Corresponding to the philosophical and scientific movement of 1889 there was not only a literary evolution—symbolism then surrealism—but another revolution, or rather revolutions, in art, which were called, taking only the plastic arts, nabism, expressionism, fauvism, and cubism. A world of life forces that have to be *tamed* is substituted for a closed world of permanent and continuous substances that have to be reproduced.

Since the Greek *kouroi* (the term used for the statues of young men in classical Greek sculpture), the art of the European West had always been based on realism; the work of art had always been an imitation of the object: a *physeôs mimêsis*, to use Aristotle's expression: a corrected imitation, "improved," "idealized" by the requirements of rationality, but imitation all the same. The interlude of the Christian Middle Ages is significant insofar as Christianity is itself of Asian origin and strongly influenced by the African, St. Augustine. To what will the artist then give expression? No longer to purely objective matter, but to his spiritual self: that is, to his inner self, his spirituality, and beyond himself to the spirituality of his age and of mankind. No longer by means of perspective, relief, and chiaroscuro, but, as the French painter Bazaine writes, "by the most hidden workings of instinct and the sensibility." Another French painter, André Masson, makes it more explicit when he writes: "By a simple interplay of shapes and colors legibly ordered." This interplay of shapes and colors is that of the life forces and which has been illustrated in particular by a painter like Soulages.

"Interplay of life forces": and so we come back to—negritude. As the French painter Soulages, in fact, once told me, the African aesthetic is "that of contemporary art." I find indirect proof of this in the fact that, while the consecration and spread of the new aesthetic revolution have occurred in France, the majority of its promoters were of Slav and Germanic origin; people who, like the Africans, belong to the mystical civilizations of the senses. Of course, without the discovery of African art, the revolution would still have taken place, but probably without such vigor and assurance and such a deepening of the knowledge of Man. The fact that an art of the subject and of the spirit should have germinated outside Europe, in Africa—to which ethnologists had not yet given its true place in world culture—was proof of the human value of the message of the new European art.

Over and above its aesthetic lesson—to which we shall return later—what Picasso, Braque, and the other artists and early explorers of African art were seeking was, in the first place, just this: its human value. For in black Africa art is not a separate activity, in itself or for itself: it is a social activity, a technique of living, a handicraft in fact. But it is a major activity that brings all other activities to their fulfilment, like prayer in the Christian Middle Ages: birth and education, marriage and death, sport, even war. All human activities down to the least daily act must be integrated into the subtle interplay of life forces—family, tribal, national, world, and universal forces. This harmonious interplay of life forces must be helped by *subordinating* the lower forces—mineral, vegetable, and animal—to their relations with Man, and the forces of human society to its relations with the Divine Being through the intermediary of the Ancestral Beings.

A year or two ago I attended, on the cliffs of Bandiagara in the Mali Republic, an entertainment which was a microcosm of Dogon art.[4] Even though it was but a pale reflection of the splendors of the past, this "play-concert" was an extremely significant expression of the Dogon vision of the universe. It was declaimed, sung, and danced; sculptured and presented in costume. The whole of the Dogon universe was portrayed in this symbiosis of the arts, as is the custom in black Africa. The universe—heaven and earth—was therefore *represented* through the intermediary of Man, whose ideogram is the same as that of the universe. Then the world was *re-presented* by means of masks, each of which portrayed, at one and the same time, a totemic animal, an ancestor, and a spirit. Others portrayed the foreign peoples: nomadic Fulani[5] and white Europeans. The aim of the entertainment was, by means of the symbiosis of the arts—poetry, song, dance, sculpture, and painting, used as techniques of integration—to *re-create* the universe and the contemporary world, but in a more harmonious way by making use of African humor, which corrects distortions at the expense of the foreign Fulani and the white conquerors. But this ontological vision was an entertainment—that is, an artistic demonstration—as well: a joy for the soul because a joy for the eyes and ears.

It was perhaps—indeed it was certainly—this last aspect of the African aesthetic lesson that first attracted Picasso and Braque when, toward 1906, they discovered African art and were inspired by it. For my part, what struck me from the start of the Dogon "play-concert," even before I tried to understand its meaning, was the harmony of form and movement, of color and rhythm, that characterized it. It is this harmony by which, as a spectator, I was moved; which, in the re-creation of reality, acts on the invisible forces whose appearances are only signs, subordinates them in a complementary fashion to one another and establishes the link between them and God through the intermediary of Man. By appearances I mean the attributes of matter that strike our senses: shape and color, timbre and tone, movement and rhythm.

I have said that these appearances are signs. They are more than that: they are meaningful signs, the "lines of force" of the life forces, insofar as they are used in their pure state, with only their characteristics of shape, color, sound, movement, and rhythm. Recently M. Lods, who teaches at the National School of Art of Senegal, was showing me the pictures his students intend exhibiting at the projected Festival of African Arts. I was immediately struck by the noble and elegant interplay of shape and color. When I discovered that the pictures were not completely abstract, that they portrayed ladies, princes, and noble animals, I was almost disappointed. There was no need for me to be: the very interplay of colored shapes perfectly expressed that elegant nobility that characterizes the art of the northern Sudan.

This, then, is Africa's lesson in aesthetics: art does not consist in photographing nature but in taming it, like the hunter when he reproduces the call of the hunted animal, like a separated couple, or two lovers, calling to each other in their desire to be reunited. The call is not the simple reproduction of the cry of the Other; it is a call of complementarity, a *song:* a call of harmony to the harmony of union that enriches by increasing *Being.* We call it pure harmony. Once more, Africa teaches that art is not photography; if there are images they are rhythmical. I can suggest or create anything—a man, a moon, a fruit, a smile, a tear—simply by assembling shapes and colors (painting/sculpture), shapes and movement (dance), timbre and tones (music), provided that this assembling is not an aggregation, but that it is ordered and, in short, rhythmical. For it is rhythm—the main virtue, in fact, of negritude— that gives the work of art its beauty. Rhythm is simply the movement of attraction or repulsion that expresses the life of the cosmic forces; symmetry and asymmetry, repetition or position: in short, the lines of force that link the meaningful signs that shapes and colors, timbre and tones, are.

Before concluding, I should like to pause for a moment on the apparent contradiction that must have been noticed between contemporary European art (which places the emphasis on the subject) and African art (which places it on the object). This is because the "Revolution of 1889" began by reacting, of necessity, against the superstition of the *object*; and the existentialist ontology of the African, while it is based on the being-subject, has God as its pole-object; God who is the fullness of Being. What was noticed, then, was simply a nuance. For the contemporary European, and the African, the work of art, like the act of knowing, expresses the confrontation, the embrace, of subject and object: "That penetration," wrote Bazaine, "that great common structure, that deep resemblance between Man and the world, without which there is no living form."

We have seen what constitutes for the African the "deep resemblance between Man and the world." For him, then, the act of restoring the order of the world by recreating it through art is the reinforcement of the life forces in the universe and, consequently, of God, the source of all life forces—or, in other words, the Being of the universe. In this way, we reinforce ourselves at the same time, both as interdependent forces and as beings whose being consists in revitalizing ourselves in the re-creation of art.

NOTES

1 The South African writer Ezekiel Mphahlele, author, among other books, of *The African Image,* strongly disagrees with the concept of negritude.

2 *Léopold Sédar Senghor: Selected Poems,* introduced and translated by John Reed and Clive Wake. See also: *Léopold Sédar Senghor: Prose and Poetry,* by the same authors.

3 In African religion, the ancestors are the essential link between the living and God. This is why they are surrounded by a complex ritual so as to ensure the maintenance of this link.

4 The Dogon are a West African tribe among whom wood sculpture has achieved a very remarkable degree of excellence.

5 The Fulani are a nomadic pastoral people found throughout West Africa.

14

CHINWEIZU, ONWUCHEKWA JEMIE,
AND IHECHUKWU MADUBUIKE

The African Novel and Its Critics (1950–1975)

Eurocentric Charges against the African Novel

There is a long list of charges usually levelled against the African novel by its Western critics, and authoritatively echoed by their African adherents. Where these charges do not emanate from the importation into the African literary scene of problems and pseudo-problems within the Western tradition, they are either the expression of a literary tourist mentality addicted to a nouveaumania whose easily jaded sensibilities cry out for new supplies of exotica or they are underhanded efforts to defend the Western imperialist, pro-bourgeois status quo in the cultural domain. For instance, with respect to *technique,* some African novels are said to suffer from inadequate description or inadequate characterization, motivation, psychology, and depth, or from unrealistic and awkward dialogue, or from alleged problems in the conception and handling of time and space. Others are faulted for being too short or for having thin plots or no plots at all. With respect to their *themes,* some novels are denounced as "situational," and the critical literature is filled with reprimanding laments that too many African novels are autobiographical or preoccupied with culture conflict or unnecessarily fascinated with the African past. With respect to *ideological* matters, some critics claim that there is too much didacticism or not enough of the right kind. Some cry out for what they consider a "consistent moral attitude," and others denounce what they call "protest literature," "topicality," anthropological or journalistic documentation, and "local color."

In levelling these charges, these critics usually ignore several important facts: (1) The African novel is a hybrid out of the African oral tradition and the imported literary forms of Europe, and it is precisely this hybrid origin which needs most to be considered when determining what technical charges could legitimately be made against African novels. (2) The African novel's primary constituency is different from that of the European or other regional novels, and it would be foolhardy to try to impose upon it expectations from other constituencies. (3) The colonial situation imposes a different set of concerns and constraints upon the African novel than upon novels of the imperialist nations. The African novel therefore has every cause to be concerned with issues antithetical to those which the imperialist countries would prefer to see treated in their literatures.

Eurocentric criticism of African fiction stems from colonialist attitudes whereby these critics see the African as an apprentice European whose literary production has no other canons to adhere to but those of whichever part of the Western tradition the critics happen to subscribe to. These critics do not concede the autonomy of African literature. They do not grant it the elementary right to have its own rules and standards, but insist rather on viewing it as an overseas department of European literature. Adrian Roscoe puts it quite bluntly in his *Mother is Gold: A Study in West African Literature:*

> If an African writes in English his work must be considered as belonging to English letters as a whole, and can be scrutinised accordingly.   (Roscoe 1971: x)

He and his publishers reiterate this position even more categorically on the jacket blurb advertising the book:

> *Mother is Gold* expresses a basic critical viewpoint: if an African writes in English his work must be considered as belonging to English literature as a whole, and it must be judged by the same critical standards as any other work written in English.

John Povey goes even further than Roscoe in supplying grounds for this expropriative claim when he says:

> When one can so readily make cross-comparisons with the work of Achebe and, say, Thomas Hardy or Joseph Conrad, one has the satisfying sense that the African writer can be conveniently set within the context of the much wider field of English language writing: the whole "Great Tradition" of which F. R. Leavis so persuasively writes.
> (Povey 1972: 97)

These statements articulate a basic premise of eurocentric criticism of African literature, i.e., the refusal to draw a distinction between European national literatures and non-European literatures in European languages; between English as a language used in literature by many outside the British nation, and English letters as a body of works of the British nation. It is by ignoring or glossing over this crucial distinction that eurocentric critics are able to perform the imperialist trick of justifying the application of British literary standards to African works written in English. There are therefore various preliminary issues which need to be clarified before the specific charges can be properly examined.

Preliminary Issues: Africa's Literature and Orature

WHAT IS AFRICAN LITERATURE?

The central issue is: (1) by what criteria should African literature be judged? In attempting to answer this question, it is important to investigate two underlying matters: (2) what is African literature?—that is, what works, and for what reasons, fall within the body of African literature? (3) what is the proper relationship between this body of works and the other national or regional literatures in the world?

It is important to begin by declaring the separate and autonomous status of African literature, however defined, from all others. By this we mean that genuinely autonomous criteria would have to be applied in judging African literature. As we indicated earlier, eurocentric critics usually answer question 3 by asserting, as Roscoe and his publishers do, that African literature in English, French, or Portuguese are appendages of British, French or Portuguese national literatures. In essence, they would like to appropriate African literature as part of European national literatures, and as necessarily inferior parts thereof.

Problems about the definition of African literature (question 2), or about the proper criteria for judging it (question 1), which arise out of this imperialist hegemonic intention, should be dismissed out of hand as spurious, and as problems for the imperialists, not for Africans. However, some African critics, partly because they have been nurtured on and have internalized the prejudices of imperialist criticism, display genuine confusion in defining African literature, and in choosing the criteria by which to judge it. To such critics we would like, first, to point out that, no matter what disclaimers are proffered, to insist on judging African literature by European criteria, or by criteria allegedly universal which on closer scrutiny turn out to be European, is indeed to define African literature as an appendage of European literature, and to deny its separateness and autonomy.

Now, in order to bring a more judicious attitude to the business of defining African literature, it is necessary to examine the classificatory criteria and how to apply them. We must take cognizance of the following situation in world literature: There are *regional literatures,* for instance the European regional literature, which includes many *national literatures* in different languages, or the American regional literature which includes the literatures of the United States (in English), Canada (in English and French), the Caribbean and South America (in English, French, Spanish, and Portuguese). There are also *language literatures,* some of which include many national literatures. English language literature, for instance, includes (a) British national literature; (b) the national literatures of those countries where an exported English population is in control, e.g., Canada, the United States, Australia, and New Zealand; (c) the national literatures of those countries where English, though neither indigenous nor the mother-tongue of the politically dominant population or group, has become, as a legacy of colonialism, the official language or one of the official languages, e.g., Nigeria, Kenya, South Africa, India, Jamaica, Trinidad, and Malaysia. A similar classification can be made for literatures in the languages of other imperialist nations.

The hegemonic attempt to annex African literature for European literatures has usually been made for such African works as are written in non-African languages. The main instrument of such annexations has been the fact that the language used in writing them is non-African. Those concerned with shaking off these encroachments and annexations would need to (1) examine how much such language-based claims are worth; (2) come to an understanding of what works indubitably constitute African literature; and (3) find a procedure for deciding the doubtful cases.

It seems to us quite clear that works done for African audiences, by Africans, and in African languages, whether these works are oral or written, constitute the historically indisputable core of African literature. Works done by Africans but in non-African languages, and works done by non-Africans in African languages, would be those for which some legitimate doubt might be raised about their inclusion or exclusion from the canon of works of African literature, and it is for them that some decision procedure would have to be established.

Though cultural imperialists have used the language criterion as a subterfuge for appropriating to their national literatures works done by persons from outside their nation, language is not the crucial factor in determining the national or regional literature to which a particular work belongs. Inclusion within a national literature is something to be determined by shared values and assumptions, world outlook, and other fundamental elements of culture—ethos, in short. Although language does embody and is a vehicle for expressing cultural values, it is not the crucial generator of those values and cannot *alone* be relied upon to supply literary criteria.

Given the fundamental differences in values and experiences which often appear between two nations who use the same language, it should be obvious that the fact that two works are written in the same language is far less than sufficient grounds for judging them by identical criteria. For example, British, United States, Canadian, Australian, and New Zealand national literatures share the English language, and German and Austrian national literatures share the German language. In addition, there are multilingual national literatures, e.g., Swiss national literature in German, French, and Italian; Canadian in English and French; Belgian in French and Flemish. And in both kinds of cases, it is elements of national ethos, not the languages, which supply the decisive criteria used in evaluating them.

Coming to the African situation, then, that Achebe's works may be written in the English language and may therefore be considered part of *English-language literature,* does not mean that they can be criticized with British national values. Indeed, the basic differences between British and Igbo experience and values are what make it necessary for Achebe to have to bend the English language in order to express Igbo experience and values in it.

In brief, then, it is such considerations that make it quite clear that, contrary to the emphatic but confused assertions of Adrian Roscoe and his publishers, it is not the case that if an African writes in English his work must be judged by the same critical standards as any other work in English. In short, attempts at annexation based on language claims are worthless. Language and nation are not the same, and language criteria are not the same as national criteria. The two should never be confused. And in particular, *national criteria* are more important in determining critical standards than mere *language criteria*. While we do not deny that a work written, say, in English, must meet some minimal English-language criteria our point is that it does not have to conform to other non-language criteria derived from the English national experience and values. Confusing English-language criteria with non-language criteria derived from the English national experience and values is what allows Roscoe and his publishers to extend their hegemonic claims over African literature written in English. We should not allow ourselves to be taken in by such subterfuges.

As stated before, works done for African audiences, by Africans, and in African languages, whether these works are oral or written, constitute the historically indisputable core of the canon of African literature. In a pragmatic application of family resemblances in order to decide what other works should be included in this evolving canon, the following are some of the most important considerations: (1) the primary audience for whom the work is done; (2) the cultural and national consciousness expressed in the work, whether through the author's voice or through the characters and their consciousness, habits, comportment, and diction; (3) the nationality of the writer, whether by birth or naturalization—a matter that a passport can decide; and (4) the language in which the work is done.

These considerations are ranked in an order that reflects the relative importance of the primary audience, and the treatment required to make the work conform to the values and taste of that audience, by a writer who is conscious of working within and for the purpose of furthering the traditions of that audience, in any language that the circumstances require. Clearly, in this view of things, the instrumental medium, that is, the language employed to carry out larger and more important cultural functions, is hardly by itself to be considered sufficient, let alone exclusive grounds for assigning a work to one tradition or one body of literature rather than another. That Tutuola, Armah, Efua Sutherland, Ama Ata Aidoo, Flora Nwapa, p'Bitek, Brutus, Peter Abrahams, Nicol, Ngũgĩ, Achebe, Mphahlele, or Menkiti, for example, speak or write in English, however perfectly or imperfectly, does not make them Englanders, and their works belong to them and, through them, to African literature—certainly not to England's literature. And the point is not so much their passports as the consciousness they project in their works, and the primary audience to which their works are directed. The grounds for the place accorded language in our ordering of considerations is perhaps best brought out by an example from the other arts. Just because an African or Afro-American plays a piano—a European invention—does not at all mean that the highlife or jazz he produces on it is European music, which therefore should be judged by the same standards as European music.

Another example of the pragmatic application of the above criteria would be Joyce Cary's *Mister Johnson*. It is set in Africa, and most of its characters, and indeed its central character, are African. While these might incline some to include it among the body of African literature in English, we would reject such a classification on the grounds that the writer is an English-born English national describing African characters in an African setting but with a decidedly British consciousness and with prejudices calculated to appeal to his British audience. Similarly, Joseph Conrad's *Heart of Darkness,* though written by a Pole, in English, and set in Africa, with an "all-European" protagonist in Belgian employ, is nevertheless rightly considered a British novel because Conrad is British by naturalization and by assimilation into British culture and its values, and wrote for a British audience. Furthermore, since the body of his works belongs to the central British tradition, one finds no reason to treat *Heart of Darkness* eccentrically by classifying it as anything but a British novel. It is by such judicious examination, combining principle, precedent, and pragmatic considerations, that we believe such classifications can usefully be made.

In addition to the problem of defining specific works into or out of African literature, there is the other problem of how to classify expatriate African writers, i.e., African writers living abroad and working away from Africa, as well as works set in places outside Africa, Mars and fantasyland not excluded. Perhaps the best way to tackle this problem is to ask a few questions: Do the novels of Ernest Hemingway set in Europe with a mixture of Americans and Europeans as characters cease to be American novels? Does Gertrude Stein cease to be an American writer because she lived a good part of her career in France, or James Baldwin because he has lived a good part of his in France and Turkey? Does Ezra Pound's poetry cease to be American because of his long sojourn in Britain, France, and Italy and the tremendous influence he exerted upon the national literatures of some of those countries? Is it impossible for a writer to belong to two or more national or regional or language literatures? If so, is Samuel Beckett to be read out of English or Irish literature because he has lived much of his life in France, has written some of his works in French, and has been appropriated by the French into their national literature? And what would be said of Pound who was appropriated into British literature (at least by F. R. Leavis in his *New Bearings in English Poetry*) even without his being naturalized? What would be said of American-born Henry James and T. S. Eliot who became naturalized British citizens and who are claimed by both British and United States national literatures? Or of British-born W. H. Auden who became a naturalized U.S. citizen in mid-career? Or, again, of Russian-born Vladimir Nabokov who became a naturalized U.S. citizen in mid-career and thereafter wrote in English? With these perspectives on the matter, questions of classification raised about expatriate African writers can be seen to belong to those borderline situations where a judicious exercise of commonsense is what is mostly called for.

In conclusion, we must remind critics and readers alike, and especially the Adrian Roscoes and John Poveys, that there are none but imperialist grounds for insisting that non-British literatures, whether or not written in English, be judged by technical norms and moral values that are specifically British. Efforts to smuggle these British norms and values into the discourse by disguising them as English language criteria, or as criteria of the so-called Great Tradition, shall not be tolerated. . . .

REFERENCES

Povey, John. 1972. "The Novels of Chinua Achebe." In *Introduction to Nigerian Literature,* ed. Bruce King, 97–112. New York: Africana Publishing Corporation.

Roscoe, Adrian A. 1971. *Mother Is Gold: A Study in West African Literature.* Cambridge: Cambridge University Press.

15

FRANTZ FANON

On National Culture

To take part in the African revolution it is not enough to write a revolutionary song; you must fashion the revolution with the people. And if you fashion it with the people, the songs will come by themselves, and of themselves.

In order to achieve real action, you must yourself be a living part of Africa and of her thought; you must be an element of that popular energy which is entirely called forth for the freeing, the progress, and the happiness of Africa. There is no place outside that fight for the artist or for the intellectual who is not himself concerned with and completely at one with the people in the great battle of Africa and of suffering humanity.

—Sékou Touré[1]

Each generation must out of relative obscurity discover its mission, fulfill it, or betray it. In underdeveloped countries the preceding generations have both resisted the work or erosion carried by colonialism and also helped on the maturing of the struggles of today. We must rid ourselves of the habit, now that we are in the thick of the fight, of minimizing the action of our fathers or of feigning incomprehension when considering their silence and passivity. They fought as well as they could, with the arms that they possessed then; and if the echoes of their struggle have not resounded in the international arena, we must realize that the reason for this silence lies less in their lack of heroism than in the fundamentally different international situation of our time. It needed more than one native to say "We've had enough"; more than one peasant rising crushed, more than one demonstration put down before we could today hold our own, certain in our victory. As for we who have decided to break the back of colonialism, our historic mission is to sanction all revolts, all desperate actions, all those abortive attempts drowned in rivers of blood.

In this chapter we shall analyze the problem, which is felt to be fundamental, of the legitimacy of the claims of a nation. It must be recognized that the political party which mobilizes the people hardly touches on this problem of legitimacy. The political parties start from living reality and it is in the name of this reality, in the name of the stark facts which weigh down the present and the future of men and women, that they fix their line of action. The political party may well speak in moving terms of the nation, but what it is concerned with is that the people who are listening understand the need to take part in the fight if, quite simply, they wish to continue to exist.

Today we know that in the first phase of the national struggle colonialism tries to disarm national demands by putting forward economic doctrines. As soon as the first demands are set out, colonialism pretends to consider them, recognizing with ostentatious humility that the territory is suffering from serious underdevelopment which necessitates a great economic and social effort. And, in fact, it so happens that certain spectacular measures (centers of work for the unemployed which are opened here and there, for example) delay the crystallization of national consciousness for a few years. But, sooner or later, colonialism sees that it is not within its powers to put into practice a project of economic and social reforms which will satisfy the aspirations of the colonized people. Even where food supplies are concerned, colonialism gives proof of its inherent incapability. The colonialist state quickly discovers that if it wishes to disarm the nationalist parties on strictly economic questions then it will have to do in the colonies exactly what it has refused to do in its own country. It is not mere chance that almost everywhere today there flourishes the doctrine of Cartierism.

The disillusioned bitterness we find in Cartier when up against the obstinate determination of France to link to herself peoples which she must feed while so many French people live in want shows up the impossible situation in which colonialism finds itself when the colonial system is called upon to transform itself into an unselfish program of aid and assistance. It is why, once again, there is no use in wasting time repeating that hunger with dignity is preferable to bread eaten in slavery. On the contrary, we must become convinced that colonialism is incapable of procuring for the colonized peoples the material conditions which might make them forget their concern for dignity. Once colonialism has realized where its tactics of social reform are leading, we see it falling back on its old reflexes, reinforcing police effectives, bringing up troops, and setting a reign of terror which is better adapted to its interests and its psychology.

Inside the political parties, and most often in offshoots from these parties, cultured individuals of the colonized race make their appearance. For these individuals, the demand for a national culture and the affirmation of the existence of such a culture represent a special battlefield. While the politicians situate their action in actual present-day events, men of culture take their stand in the field of history. Confronted with the native intellectual who decides to make an aggressive response to the colonialist theory of pre-colonial barbarism, colonialism will react only slightly, and still less because the ideas developed by the young colonized intelligentsia are widely professed by specialists in the mother country. It is in fact a commonplace to state that for several decades large numbers of research workers have, in the main, reha-bilitated the African, Mexican, and Peruvian civilizations. The passion with which native intellectuals defend the existence of their national culture may be a source of amazement; but those who condemn this exaggerated passion are strangely apt to forget that their own psyche and their own selves are conveniently sheltered behind a French or German culture which has given full proof of its existence and which is uncontested.

I am ready to concede that on the plane of factual being the past existence of an Aztec civilization does not change anything very much in the diet of the Mexican peasant of today. I admit that all the proofs of a wonderful Songhai civilization will not change the fact that today the Songhais are underfed and illiterate, thrown between sky and water with empty heads and empty eyes. But it has been remarked several times that this passionate search for a national culture which existed before the colonial era finds its legitimate reason in the anxiety shared by native intellectu-als to shrink away from that Western culture in which they all risk being swamped. Because they realize they are in danger of losing their lives and thus becoming lost to their people, these men, hotheaded and with anger in their hearts, relentlessly determine to renew contact once more with the oldest and most pre-colonial springs of life of their people.

Let us go further. Perhaps this passionate research and this anger are kept up or at least directed by the secret hope of discovering beyond the misery of today, beyond self-contempt, resignation, and abjuration, some very beautiful and splen-did era whose existence rehabilitates us both in regard to ourselves and in regard to others. I have said that I have decided to go further. Perhaps unconsciously, the native intellectuals, since they could not stand wonderstruck before the history of today's barbarity, decided to go back further and to delve deeper down; and, let us make no mistake, it was with the greatest delight that they discovered that there was nothing to be ashamed of in the past, but rather dignity, glory, and solemnity. The claim to a national culture in the past does not only rehabilitate that nation and serve as a justification for the hope of a future national culture. In the sphere of psycho-affective equilibrium it is responsible for an important change in the native. Perhaps we have not sufficiently demonstrated that colonialism is not simply content to impose its rule upon the present and the future of a dominated country. Colonialism is not satisfied merely with holding a people in its grip and emptying the native's brain of all form and content. By a kind of perverted logic, it turns to the past of the oppressed people, and distorts, disfigures, and destroys it. This work of devaluing pre-colonial history takes on a dialectical significance today.

When we consider the efforts made to carry out the cultural estrangement so characteristic of the colonial epoch, we realize that nothing has been left to chance and that the total result looked for by colonial domination was indeed to convince the natives that colonialism came to lighten their darkness. The effect consciously sought by colonialism was to drive into the natives' heads the idea that if the settlers were to leave, they would at once fall back into barbarism, degradation, and bestiality.

On the unconscious plane, colonialism therefore did not seek to be considered by the native as a gentle, loving mother who protects her child from a hostile environment, but rather as a mother who unceasingly restrains her fundamentally perverse offspring from managing to commit suicide and from giving free rein to its evil instincts. The colonial mother protects her child from itself, from its ego, and from its physiology, its biology, and its own unhappiness which is its very essence.

In such a situation the claims of the native intellectual are not a luxury but a necessity in any coherent program. The native intellectual who takes up arms to defend his nation's legitimacy and who wants to bring proofs to bear out that legitimacy, who is willing to strip himself naked to study the history of his body, is obliged to dissect the heart of his people.

Such an examination is not specifically national. The native intellectual who decides to give battle to colonial lies fights on the field of the whole continent. The past is given back its value. Culture, extracted from the past to be displayed in all its splendor, is not necessarily that of his own country. Colonialism, which has not bothered to put too fine a point on its efforts, has never ceased to maintain that the Negro is a savage; and for the colonist, the Negro was neither an Angolan nor a Nigerian, for he simply spoke of "the Negro." For colonialism, this vast continent was the haunt of savages, a country riddled with superstitions and fanaticism, destined for contempt, weighed down by the curse of God, a country of cannibals—in short, the Negro's country. Colonialism's condemnation is continental in its scope. The contention by colonialism that the darkest night of humanity lay over pre-colonial history concerns the whole of the African continent. The efforts of the native to rehabilitate himself and to escape from the claws of colonialism are logically inscribed from the same point of view as that of colonialism. The native intellectual who has gone far beyond the domains of Western culture and who has got it into his head to proclaim the existence of another culture never does so in the name of Angola or of Dahomey. The culture which is affirmed is African culture. The Negro, never so much a Negro as since he has been dominated by the whites, when he decides to prove that he has a culture and to behave like a cultured person, comes to realize that history points out a well-defined path to him: he must demonstrate that a Negro culture exists.

And it is only too true that those who are most responsible for this racialization of thought, or at least for the first movement toward that thought, are and remain those Europeans who have never ceased to set up white culture to fill the gap left by the absence of other cultures. Colonialism did not dream of wasting its time in denying the existence of one national culture after another. Therefore the reply of the colonized peoples will be straight away continental in its breadth. In Africa, the native literature of the last twenty years is not a national literature but a Negro literature. The concept of negritude, for example, was the emotional if not the logical antithesis of that insult which the white man flung at humanity. This rush of negritude against the white man's contempt showed itself in certain spheres to be the one idea capable of lifting interdictions and anathemas. Because the New Guinean or Kenyan intellectuals found themselves above all up against a general ostracism and delivered to the combined contempt of their overlords, their reaction was to sing praises in admiration of each other. The unconditional affirmation of African culture has succeeded the unconditional affirmation of European culture. On the whole, the poets of negritude oppose the idea of an old Europe to a young Africa, tiresome reasoning to lyricism, oppressive logic to high-stepping nature, and on one side stiffness, ceremony, etiquette, and scepticism, while on the other frankness, liveliness, liberty, and—why not?—luxuriance: but also irresponsibility.

The poets of negritude will not stop at the limits of the continent. From America, black voices will take up the hymn with fuller unison. The "black world" will see the light and Busia from Ghana, Birago Diop from Senegal, Hampaté Ba from the Soudan, and Saint-Clair Drake from Chicago will not hesitate to assert the existence of common ties and a motive power that is identical.

The example of the Arab world might equally well be quoted here. We know that the majority of Arab territories have been under colonial domination. Colonialism has made the same effort in these regions to plant deep in the minds of the native population the idea that before the advent of colonialism their history was one which was dominated by barbarism. The struggle for national liberty has been accompanied by a cultural phenomenon known by the name of the awakening of Islam. The passion with which contemporary Arab writers remind their people of the great pages of their history is a reply to the lies told by the occupying power. The great names of Arabic literature and the great past of Arab civilization have been brandished about with the same ardor as those of the African civilizations. The Arab leaders have tried to return to the famous Dar El Islam which shone so brightly from the twelfth to the fourteenth century.

Today, in the political sphere, the Arab League is giving palpable form to this will to take up again the heritage of the past and to bring it to culmination. Today, Arab doctors and Arab poets speak to each other across the frontiers, and strive to create a new Arab culture and a new Arab civilization. It is in the name of Arabism that these men join together, and that they try to think together. Everywhere, however, in the Arab world, national feeling has preserved even under colonial domination a liveliness that we fail to find in Africa. At the same time that spontaneous communion of each with all, present in the African movement, is not to be found in the Arab

League. On the contrary, paradoxically, everyone tries to sing the praises of the achievements of his nation. The cultural process is freed from the indifferentiation which characterized it in the African world, but the Arabs do not always manage to stand aside in order to achieve their aims. The living culture is not national but Arab. The problem is not as yet to secure a national culture, not as yet to lay hold of a movement differentiated by nations, but to assume an African or Arabic culture when confronted by the all-embracing condemnation pronounced by the dominating power. In the African world, as in the Arab, we see that the claims of the man of culture in a colonized country are all-embracing, continental, and in the case of the Arabs, worldwide.

This historical necessity in which the men of African culture find themselves to racialize their claims and to speak more of African culture than of national culture will tend to lead them up a blind alley. Let us take for example the case of the African Cultural Society. This society had been created by African intellectuals who wished to get to know each other and to compare their experiences and the results of their respective research work. The aim of this society was therefore to affirm the existence of an African culture, to evaluate this culture on the plane of distinct nations, and to reveal the internal motive forces of each of their national cultures. But at the same time this society fulfilled another need: the need to exist side by side with the European Cultural Society, which threatened to transform itself into a Universal Cultural Society. There was therefore at the bottom of this decision the anxiety to be present at the universal trysting place fully armed, with a culture springing from the very heart of the African continent. Now, this Society will very quickly show its inability to shoulder these different tasks, and will limit itself to exhibitionist demonstrations, while the habitual behavior of the members of this Society will be confined to showing Europeans that such a thing as African culture exists, and opposing their ideas to those of ostentatious and narcissistic Europeans. We have shown that such an attitude is normal and draws its legitimacy from the lies propagated by men of Western culture, but the degradation of the aims of this Society will become more marked with the elaboration of the concept of negritude. The African Society will become the cultural society of the black world and will come to include the Negro dispersion, that is to say the tens of thousands of black people spread over the American continents.

The Negroes who live in the United States and in Central or Latin America in fact experience the need to attach themselves to a cultural matrix. Their problem is not fundamentally different from that of the Africans. The whites of America did not mete out to them any different treatment from that of the whites who ruled over the Africans. We have seen that the whites were used to putting all Negroes in the same bag. During the first congress of the African Cultural Society which was held in Paris in 1956, the American Negroes of their own accord considered their problems from the same standpoint as those of their African brothers. Cultured Africans, speaking of African civilizations, decreed that there should be a reasonable status within the state for those who had formerly been slaves. But little by little the American Negroes realized that the essential problems confronting them were not the same as those that confronted the African Negroes. The Negroes of Chicago only resemble the Nigerians or the Tanganyikans in so far as they were all defined in relation to the whites. But once the first comparisons had been made and subjective feelings were assuaged, the American Negroes realized that the objective problems were fundamentally heterogeneous. The test cases of civil liberty whereby both whites and blacks in America try to drive back racial discrimination have very little in common in their principles and objectives with the heroic fight of the Angolan people against the detestable Portuguese colonialism. Thus, during the second congress of the African Cultural Society the American Negroes decided to create an American society for people of black cultures.

Negritude therefore finds its first limitation in the phenomena which take account of the formation of the historical character of men. Negro and African-Negro culture broke up into different entities because the men who wished to incarnate these cultures realized that every culture is first and foremost national, and that the problems which kept Richard Wright or Langston Hughes on the alert were fundamentally different from those which might confront Léopold Senghor or Jomo Kenyatta. In the same way certain Arab states, though they had chanted the marvelous hymn of Arab renaissance, had nevertheless to realize that their geographical position and the economic ties of their region were stronger even than the past that they wished to revive. Thus we find today the Arab states organically linked once more with societies which are Mediterranean in their culture. The fact is that these states are submitted to modern pressure and to new channels of trade while the network of trade relations which was dominant during the great period of Arab history has disappeared. But above all there is the fact that the political regimes of certain Arab states are so different, and so far away from each other in their conceptions, that even a cultural meeting between these states is meaningless.

Thus we see that the cultural problem as it sometimes exists in colonized countries runs the risk of giving rise to serious ambiguities. The lack of culture of the Negroes, as proclaimed by colonialism, and the inherent barbarity of the Arabs ought logically to lead to the exaltation of cultural manifestations which are not simply national but continental, and extremely racial. In Africa, the movement of men of culture is a movement toward the Negro-African culture or the Arab-Moslem culture. It is not specifically toward a national culture. Culture is becoming more and more cut off from the events of today. It finds its refuge beside a hearth that glows with passionate emotion, and from there makes its way by realistic paths which are the only means by which it may be made fruitful, homogeneous, and consistent.

If the action of the native intellectual is limited historically, there remains nevertheless the fact that it contributes greatly to upholding and justifying the action of politicians. It is true that the attitude of the native intellectual sometimes takes on the aspect of a cult or of a religion. But if we really wish to analyze this attitude correctly we will come to see that it is symptomatic of the intellectual's realization of the danger that he is running in cutting his last moorings and of breaking adrift from his people. This stated belief in a national culture is in fact an ardent, despairing turning toward anything that will afford him secure anchorage. In order to ensure his salvation and to escape from the supremacy of the white man's culture the native feels the need to turn backward toward his unknown roots and to lose himself at whatever cost in his own barbarous people. Because he feels he is becoming estranged, that is to say because he feels that he is the living haunt of contradictions which run the risk of becoming insurmountable, the native tears himself away from the swamp that may suck him down and accepts everything, decides to take all for granted and confirms everything even though he may lose body and soul. The native finds that he is expected to answer for everything, and to all comers. He not only turns himself into the defender of his people's past; he is willing to be counted as one of them, and henceforward he is even capable of laughing at his past cowardice.

This tearing away, painful and difficult though it may be, is however necessary. If it is not accomplished there will be serious psycho-affective injuries and the result will be individuals without an anchor, without a horizon, colorless, stateless, rootless—a race of angels. It will be also quite normal to hear certain natives declare, "I speak as a Senegalese and as a Frenchman . . ." "I speak as an Algerian and as a Frenchman . . ." The intellectual who is Arab and French, or Nigerian and English, when he comes up against the need to take on two nationalities, chooses, if he wants to remain true to himself, the negation of one of these determinations. But most often, since they cannot or will not make a choice, such intellectuals gather together all the historical determining factors which have conditioned them and take up a fundamentally "universal standpoint."

This is because the native intellectual has thrown himself greedily upon Western culture. Like adopted children who only stop investigating the new family framework at the moment when a minimum nucleus of security crystallizes in their psyche, the native intellectual will try to make European culture his own. He will not be content to get to know Rabelais and Diderot, Shakespeare and Edgar Allan Poe; he will bind them to his intelligence as closely as possible:

La dame n'était pas seule
Elle avait un mari
Un mari très comme il faut

Qui citait Racine et Corneille
Et Voltaire et Rousseau
Et le Père Hugo et le jeune Musset
Et Gide et Valéry
Et tant d'autres encore.[2]

But at the moment when the nationalist parties are mobilizing the people in the name of national independence, the native intellectual sometimes spurns these acquisitions which he suddenly feels make him a stranger in his own land. It is always easier to proclaim rejection than actually to reject. The intellectual who through the medium of culture has filtered into Western civilization, who has managed to become part of the body of European culture—in other words who has exchanged his own culture for another—will come to realize that the cultural matrix, which now he wishes to assume since he is anxious to appear original, can hardly supply any figureheads which will bear comparison with those, so many in number and so great in prestige, of the occupying power's civilization. History, of course, though nevertheless written by the Westerners and to serve their purposes, will be able to evaluate from time to time certain periods of the African past. But, standing face to face with his country at the present time, and observing clearly and objectively the events of today throughout the continent which he wants to make his own, the intellectual is terrified by the void, the degradation, and the savagery he sees there. Now he feels that he must get away from the white culture. He must seek his culture elsewhere, anywhere at all; and if he fails to find the substance of culture of the same grandeur and scope as displayed by the ruling power, the native intellectual will very often fall back upon emotional attitudes and will develop a psychology which is dominated by exceptional sensitivity and susceptibility. This withdrawal, which is due in the first instance to a begging of the question in his internal behavior mechanism and his own character, brings out, above all, a reflex and contradiction which is muscular.

This is sufficient explanation of the style of those native intellectuals who decide to give expression to this phase of consciousness which is in the process of being liberated. It is a harsh style, full of images, for the image is the drawbridge which allows unconscious energies to be scattered on the surrounding meadows. It is a vigorous style, alive with rhythms, struck through and through with bursting life; it is full of color, too, bronzed, sunbaked, and violent. This style, which in its time astonished the peoples of the West, has nothing racial about it, in spite of frequent statements to the contrary; it expresses above all a hand-to-hand struggle and it reveals the need that man has to liberate himself from a part of his being which already contained the seeds of decay. Whether the fight is painful, quick, or inevitable, muscular action must substitute itself for concepts.

If in the world of poetry this movement reaches unaccustomed heights, the fact remains that in the real world the intellectual often follows up a blind alley. When at the height of his intercourse with his people, whatever they were or whatever they are, the intellectual decides to come down into the common paths of real life, he only brings back from his adventuring formulas which are sterile in the extreme. He sets a high value on the customs, traditions, and the appearances of his people; but his inevitable, painful experience only seems to be a banal search for exoticism. The sari becomes sacred, and shoes that come from Paris or Italy are left off in favor of pampooties, while suddenly the language of the ruling power is felt to burn your lips. Finding your fellow countrymen sometimes means in this phase to will to be a nigger, not a nigger like all other niggers but a real nigger, a Negro cur, just the sort of nigger that the white man wants you to be. Going back to your own people means to become a dirty wog, to go native as much as you can, to become unrecognizable, and to cut off those wings that before you had allowed to grow.

The native intellectual decides to make an inventory of the bad habits drawn from the colonial world, and hastens to remind everyone of the good old customs of the people, that people which he has decided contains all truth and goodness. The scandalized attitude with which the settlers who live in the colonial territory greet this new departure only serves to strengthen the native's decision. When the colonialists, who had tasted the sweets of their victory over these assimilated people, realize that these men whom they considered as saved souls are beginning to fall back into the ways of niggers, the whole system totters. Every native won over, every native who had taken the pledge not only marks a failure for the colonial structure when he decides to lose himself and to go back to his own side, but also stands as a symbol for the uselessness and the shallowness of all the work that has been accomplished. Each native who goes back over the line is a radical condemnation of the methods and of the regime; and the native intellectual finds in the scandal he gives rise to a justification and an encouragement to persevere in the path he has chosen.

If we wanted to trace in the works of native writers the different phases which characterize this evolution we would find spread out before us a panorama on three levels. In the first phase, the native intellectual gives proof that he has assimilated the culture of the occupying power. His writings correspond point by point with those of his opposite numbers in the mother country. His inspiration is European and we can easily link up these works with definite trends in the literature of the mother country. This is the period of unqualified assimilation. We find in this literature coming from the colonies the Parnassians, the Symbolists, and the Surrealists.

In the second phase we find the native is disturbed; he decides to remember what he is. This period of creative work approximately corresponds to that immersion which we have just described. But since the native is not a part of his people, since he only has exterior relations with his people, he is content to recall their life only. Past happenings of the byegone days of his childhood will be brought up out of the depths of his memory; old legends will be reinterpreted in the light of a borrowed estheticism and of a conception of the world which was discovered under other skies.

Sometimes this literature of just-before-the-battle is dominated by humor and by allegory; but often too it is symptomatic of a period of distress and difficulty, where death is experienced, and disgust too. We spew ourselves up; but already underneath laughter can be heard.

Finally in the third phase, which is called the fighting phase, the native, after having tried to lose himself in the people and with the people, will on the contrary shake the people. Instead of according the people's lethargy an honored place in his esteem, he turns himself into an awakener of the people; hence comes a fighting literature, a revolutionary literature, and a national literature. During this phase a great many men and women who up till then would never have thought of producing a literary work, now that they find themselves in exceptional circumstances—in prison, with the Maquis, or on the eve of their execution—feel the need to speak to their nation, to compose the sentence which expresses the heart of the people, and to become the mouthpiece of a new reality in action.

The native intellectual nevertheless sooner or later will realize that you do not show proof of your nation from its culture but that you substantiate its existence in the fight which the people wage against the forces of occupation. No colonial system draws its justification from the fact that the territories it dominates are culturally nonexistent. You will never make colonialism blush for shame by spreading out little-known cultural treasures under its eyes. At the very moment when the native intellectual is anxiously trying to create a cultural work he fails to realize that he is utilizing techniques and language which are borrowed from the stranger in his country. He contents himself with stamping these instruments with a hallmark which he wishes to be national, but which is strangely reminiscent of exoticism. The native intellectual who comes back to his people by way of cultural achievements behaves in fact like a foreigner. Sometimes he has no hesitation in using a dialect in order to show his will to be as near as possible to the people; but the ideas that he expresses and the preoccupations he is taken up with have no common yardstick to measure the real situation which the men and the women of his country know. The culture that the intellectual leans toward is often no more than a stock of particularisms. He wishes to attach himself to the people; but instead he only catches hold of their outer garments. And these outer garments are merely the reflection of a hidden life, teeming and perpetually in motion. That extremely obvious objectivity which seems to characterize a people is in fact only the inert, already forsaken result of frequent, and not always very coherent, adaptations of a much more fundamental substance which itself is continually being renewed. The man of culture, instead of setting out to find this substance, will let himself be hypnotized by these mummified fragments which because they are static are in fact symbols of negation and outworn contrivances. Culture has never the translucidity of custom; it abhors all simplification. In its essence it is opposed to custom, for custom is always the deterioration of culture. The desire to attach oneself to tradition or bring abandoned traditions to life again does not only mean going against the current of history but also opposing one's own people. When a people undertakes an armed struggle or even a political struggle against a relentless colonialism, the significance of tradition changes. All that has made up the technique of passive resistance in the past may, during this phase, be radically condemned. In an underdeveloped country during the period of struggle traditions are fundamentally unstable and are shot through by centrifugal tendencies. This is why the intellectual often runs the risk of being out of date. The peoples who have carried on the struggle are more and more impervious to demagogy; and those who wish to follow them reveal themselves as nothing more than common opportunists, in other words, latecomers.

In the sphere of plastic arts, for example, the native artist who wishes at whatever cost to create a national work of art shuts himself up in a stereotyped reproduction of details. These artists who have nevertheless thoroughly studied modern techniques and who have taken part in the main trends of contemporary painting and architecture, turn their backs on foreign culture, deny it, and set out to look for a true national culture, setting great store on what they consider to be the constant principles of national art. But these people forget that the forms of thought and what it feeds on, together with modern techniques of information, language, and dress have dialectically reorganized the people's intelligences and that the constant principles which acted as safeguards during the colonial period are now undergoing extremely radical changes.

The artist who has decided to illustrate the truths of the nation turns paradoxically toward the past and away from actual events. What he ultimately intends to embrace are in fact the castoffs of thought, its shells and corpses, a knowledge which has been stabilized once and for all. But the native intellectual who wishes to create an authentic work of art must realize that the truths of a nation are in the first place its realities. He must go on until he has found the seething pot out of which the learning of the future will emerge.

Before independence, the native painter was insensible to the national scene. He set a high value on non-figurative art, or more often specialized in still lifes. After independence his anxiety to rejoin his people will confine him to the most detailed representation of reality. This is representative art which has no internal rhythms, an art which is serene and immobile, evocative not of life but of death. Enlightened circles are in ecstasies when confronted with this "inner truth" which is so well expressed; but we have the right to ask if this truth is in fact a reality, and if it is not already outworn and denied, called in question by the epoch through which the people are treading out their path toward history.

. . .

The colonized man who writes for his people ought to use the past with the intention of opening the future, as an invitation to action and a basis for hope. But to ensure that hope and to give it form, he must take part in action and throw himself body and soul into the national struggle. You may speak about everything under the sun; but when you decide to speak of that unique thing in man's life that is represented by the fact of opening up new horizons, by bringing light to your own country, and by raising yourself and your people to their feet, then you must collaborate on the physical plane.

The responsibility of the native man of culture is not a responsibility vis-à-vis his national culture, but a global responsibility with regard to the totality of the nation, whose culture merely, after all, represents one aspect of that nation. The cultured native should not concern himself with choosing the level on which he wishes to fight or the sector where he decides to give battle for his nation. To fight for national culture means in the first place to fight for the liberation of the nation, that material keystone which makes the building of a culture possible. There is no other fight for culture which can develop apart from the popular struggle. To take an example: all those men and women who are fighting with their bare hands against French colonialism in Algeria are not by any means strangers to the national culture of Algeria. The national Algerian culture is taking on form and content as the battles are being fought out, in prisons, under the guillotine, and in every French outpost which is captured or destroyed.

We must not therefore be content with delving into the past of a people in order to find coherent elements which will counteract colonialism's attempts to falsify and harm. We must work and fight with the same rhythm as the people to construct the future and to prepare the ground where vigorous shoots are already springing up. A national culture is not a folklore, nor an abstract populism that believes it can discover the people's true nature. It is not made up of the inert dregs of gratuitous actions, that is to say actions which are less and less attached to the ever-present reality of the people. A national culture is the whole body of efforts made by a people in the sphere of thought to describe, justify, and praise the action through which that people has created itself and keeps itself in existence. A national culture in underdeveloped countries should therefore take its place at the very heart of the struggle for freedom which these countries are carrying on. Men of African cultures who are still fighting in the name of African-Negro culture and who have called many congresses in the name of the unity of that culture should today realize that all their efforts amount to is to make comparisons between coins and sarcophagi.

There is no common destiny to be shared between the national cultures of Senegal and Guinea; but there is a common destiny between the Senegalese and Guinean nations which are both dominated by the same French colonialism. If it is wished that the national culture of Senegal should come to resemble the national culture of Guinea, it is not enough for the rulers of the two peoples to decide to consider their problems—whether the problem of liberation is concerned, or the trade-union question, or economic difficulties—from similar viewpoints. And even here there does not seem to be complete identity, for the rhythm of the people and that of their rulers are not the same. There can be no two cultures which are completely identical. To believe that it is possible to create a black culture is to forget that niggers are disappearing, just as those people who brought them into being are seeing the breakup of their economic and cultural supremacy.[3] There will never be such a thing as black culture because there is not a single politician who feels he has a vocation to bring black republics into being. The problem is to get to know the place that these men mean to give their people, the kind of social relations that they decide to set up, and the conception that they have of the future of humanity. It is this that counts; everything else is mystification, signifying nothing.

In 1959, the cultured Africans who met at Rome never stopped talking about unity. But one of the people who was loudest in the praise of this cultural unity, Jacques Rabemananjara, is today a minister in the Madagascan government, and as such has decided, with his government, to oppose the Algerian people in the General Assembly of the United Nations. Rabemananjara, if he had been true to himself, ought to have resigned from the government and denounced those men who claim to incarnate the will of the Madagascan people. The ninety thousand dead of Madagascar have not given Rabemananjara authority to oppose the aspirations of the Algerian people in the General Assembly of the United Nations.

It is around the peoples' struggles that African-Negro culture takes on substance, and not around songs, poems, or folklore. Senghor, who is also a member of the Society of African Culture and who has worked with us on the question of African culture, is not afraid for his part either to give the order to his delegation to support French proposals on Algeria. Adherence to African-Negro culture and to the cultural unity of Africa is arrived at in the first place by upholding unconditionally the peoples' struggle for freedom. No one can truly wish for the spread of African culture if he does not give practical support to the creation of the conditions necessary to the existence of that culture; in other words, to the liberation of the whole continent.

I say again that no speech-making and no proclamation concerning culture will turn us from our fundamental tasks: the liberation of the national territory; a continual struggle against colonialism in its new forms; and an obstinate refusal to enter the charmed circle of mutual admiration at the summit.

Reciprocal Bases of National Culture and the Fight for Freedom

Colonial domination, because it is total and tends to oversimplify, very soon manages to disrupt in spectacular fashion the cultural life of a conquered people. This cultural obliteration is made possible by the negation of national reality, by new legal relations introduced by the occupying power, by the banishment of the natives and their customs to outlying districts by colonial society, by expropriation, and by the systematic enslaving of men and women.

Three years ago at our first congress I showed that, in the colonial situation, dynamism is replaced fairly quickly by a substantification of the attitudes of the colonizing power. The area of culture is then marked off by fences and signposts. These are in fact so many defense mechanisms of the most elementary type, comparable for more than one good reason to the simple instinct for preservation. The interest of this period for us is that the oppressor does not manage to convince himself of the objective non-existence of the oppressed nation and its culture. Every effort is made to bring the colonized person to admit the inferiority of his culture which has been transformed into instinctive patterns of behavior, to recognize the unreality of his "nation," and, in the last extreme, the confused and imperfect character of his own biological structure.

Vis-à-vis this state of affairs, the native's reactions are not unanimous. While the mass of the people maintain intact traditions which are completely different from those of the colonial situation, and the artisanal style solidifies into a formalism which is more and more stereotyped, the intellectual throws himself in frenzied fashion into the frantic acquisition of the culture of the occupying power and takes every opportunity of unfavorably criticizing his own national culture, or else takes refuge in setting out and substantiating the claims of that culture in a way that is passionate but rapidly becomes unproductive.

The common nature of these two reactions lies in the fact that they both lead to impossible contradictions. Whether a turncoat or a substantialist, the native is ineffectual precisely because the analysis of the colonial situation is not carried out on strict lines. The colonial situation calls a halt to national culture in almost every field. Within the framework of colonial domination there is not and there will never be such phenomena as new cultural departures or changes in the national culture. Here and there valiant attempts are sometimes made to reanimate the cultural dynamic and to give fresh impulses to its themes, its forms, and its tonalities. The immediate, palpable, and obvious interest of such leaps ahead is nil. But if we follow up the consequences to the very end we see that preparations are being thus made to brush the cobwebs off national consciousness, to question oppression, and to open up the struggle for freedom.

A national culture under colonial domination is a contested culture whose destruction is sought in systematic fashion. It very quickly becomes a culture condemned to secrecy. This idea of a clandestine culture is immediately seen in the reactions of the occupying power which interprets attachment to traditions as faithfulness to the spirit of the nation and as a refusal to submit. This persistence in following forms of cultures which are already condemned to extinction is already a demonstration of nationality; but it is a demonstration which is a throwback to the laws of inertia. There is no taking of the offensive and no redefining of relationships. There is simply a concentration on a hard core of culture which is becoming more and more shrivelled up, inert, and empty.

By the time a century or two of exploitation has passed there comes about a veritable emaciation of the stock of national culture. It becomes a set of automatic habits, some traditions of dress, and a few broken-down institutions. Little movement can be discerned in such remnants of culture; there is no real creativity and no overflowing life. The poverty of the people, national oppression, and the inhibition of culture are one and the same thing. After a century of colonial domination we find a culture which is rigid in the extreme, or rather what we find are the dregs of culture, its mineral strata. The withering away of the reality of the nation and the death pangs of the national culture are linked to each other in mutual dependence. This is why it is of capital importance to follow the evolution of these relations during the struggle for national freedom. The negation of the native's culture, the contempt for any manifestation of culture whether active or emotional, and the placing outside the pale of all specialized branches of organization contribute to breed aggressive patterns of conduct in the native. But these patterns of conduct are of the reflexive type; they are poorly differentiated, anarchic, and ineffective. Colonial exploitation, poverty, and endemic famine drive the native more and more to open, organized revolt. The necessity for an open and decisive breach is formed progressively and imperceptibly, and comes to be felt by the great majority of the people. Those tensions which hitherto were non-existent come into being. International events, the collapse of whole sections of colonial empires and the contradictions inherent in the colonial system strengthen and uphold the native's combativity while promoting and giving support to national consciousness.

These new-found tensions which are present at all stages in the real nature of colonialism have their repercussions on the cultural plane. In literature, for example, there is relative overproduction. From being a reply on a minor scale to the dominating power, the literature produced by natives becomes differentiated and makes itself into a will to particularism. The intelligentsia, which during the period of repression was essentially a consuming public, now themselves become producers. This literature at first chooses to confine itself to the tragic and poetic style; but later on novels, short stories, and essays are attempted. It is as if a kind of internal organization or law of expression existed which wills that poetic expression become less frequent in proportion as the objectives and the methods of the struggle for liberation become more precise. Themes are completely altered; in fact, we find less and less of bitter, hopeless recrimination and less also of that violent, resounding, florid writing which on the whole serves to reassure the occupying power. The colonialists have in former times encouraged these modes of expression and made their existence possible. Stinging denunciations, the exposing of distressing conditions and passions which find their outlet in expression are in fact assimilated by the occupying power in a cathartic process. To aid such processes is in a certain sense to avoid their dramatization and to clear the atmosphere.

But such a situation can only be transitory. In fact, the progress of national consciousness among the people modifies and gives precision to the literary utterances of the native intellectual. The continued cohesion of the people constitutes for the intellectual an invitation to go further than his cry of protest. The lament first makes the indictment; and then it makes an appeal. In the period that follows, the words of command are heard. The crystallization of the national consciousness will both disrupt literary styles and themes, and also create a completely new public. While at the beginning the native intellectual used to produce his work to be read exclusively by the oppressor, whether with the intention of charming him or of denouncing him through ethnic or subjectivist means, now the native writer progressively takes on the habit of addressing his own people.

It is only from that moment that we can speak of a national literature. Here there is, at the level of literary creation, the taking up and clarification of themes which are typically nationalist. This may be properly called a literature of combat, in the sense that it calls on the whole people to fight for their existence as a nation. It is a literature of combat, because it molds the national consciousness, giving it form and contours and flinging open before it new and boundless horizons; it is a literature of combat because it assumes responsibility, and because it is the will to liberty expressed in terms of time and space.

On another level, the oral tradition—stories, epics, and songs of the people— which formerly were filed away as set pieces are now beginning to change. The storytellers who used to relate inert episodes now bring them alive and introduce into them modifications which are increasingly fundamental. There is a tendency to bring conflicts up to date and to modernize the kinds of struggle which the stories evoke, together with the names of heroes and the types of weapons. The method of allusion is more and more widely used. The formula "This all happened long ago" is substituted with that of "What we are going to speak of happened somewhere else, but it might well have happened here today, and it might happen tomorrow." The example of Algeria is significant in this context. From 1952–53 on, the storytellers, who were before that time stereotyped and tedious to listen to, completely overturned their traditional methods of storytelling and the contents of their tales. Their public, which was formerly scattered, became compact. The epic, with its typified categories, reappeared; it became an authentic form of entertainment which took on once more a cultural value. Colonialism made no mistake when from 1955 on it proceeded to arrest these storytellers systematically.

The contact of the people with the new movement gives rise to a new rhythm of life and to forgotten muscular tensions, and develops the imagination. Every time the storyteller relates a fresh episode to his public, he presides over a real invocation. The existence of a new type of man is revealed to the public. The present is no longer turned in upon itself but spread out for all to see. The storyteller once more gives free rein to his imagination; he makes innovation and he creates a work of art. It even happens that the characters, which are barely ready for such a transformation—highway robbers or more or less antisocial vagabonds—are taken up and remodeled. The emergence of the imagination and of the creative urge in the songs and epic stories of a colonized country is worth following. The storyteller replies to the expectant people by successive approximations, and makes his way, apparently alone but in fact helped on by his public, toward the seeking out of new patterns, that is to say national patterns. Comedy and farce disappear, or lose their attraction. As for dramatization, it is no longer placed on the plane of the troubled intellectual and his tormented conscience. By losing its characteristics of despair and revolt, the drama becomes part of the common lot of the people and forms part of an action in preparation or already in progress.

Where handicrafts are concerned, the forms of expression which formerly were the dregs of art, surviving as if in a daze, now begin to reach out. Woodwork, for example, which formerly turned out certain faces and attitudes by the million, begins to be differentiated. The inexpressive or overwrought mask comes to life and the arms tend to be raised from the body as if to sketch an action. Compositions containing two, three, or five figures appear. The traditional schools are led on to creative efforts by the rising avalanche of amateurs or of critics. This new vigor in this sector of cultural life very often passes unseen; and yet its contribution to the national effort is of capital importance. By carving figures and faces which are full of life, and by taking as his theme a group fixed on the same pedestal, the artist invites participation in an organized movement.

If we study the repercussions of the awakening of national consciousness in the domains of ceramics and pottery-making, the same observations may be drawn. Formalism is abandoned in the craftsman's work. Jugs, jars, and trays are modified, at first imperceptibly, then almost savagely. The colors, of which formerly there were but few and which obeyed the traditional rules of harmony, increase in number and are influenced by the repercussion of the rising revolution. Certain ochres and blues, which seemed forbidden to all eternity in a given cultural area, now assert themselves without giving rise to scandal. In the same way the stylization of the human face, which according to sociologists is typical of very clearly defined regions, becomes suddenly completely relative. The specialist coming from the home country and the ethnologist are quick to note these changes. On the whole such changes are condemned in the name of a rigid code of artistic style and of a cultural life which grows up at the heart of the colonial system. The colonialist specialists do not recognize these new forms and rush to the help of the traditions of the indigenous society. It is the colonialists who become the defenders of the native style. We remember perfectly, and the example took on a certain measure of importance since the real nature of colonialism was not involved, the reactions of the white jazz specialists when after the Second World War new styles such as the be-bop took definite shape. The fact is that in their eyes jazz should only be the despairing, broken-down nostalgia of an old Negro who is trapped between five glasses of whiskey, the curse of his race, and the racial hatred of the white men. As soon as the Negro comes to an understanding of himself, and understands the rest of the world differently, when he gives birth to hope and forces hack the racist universe, it is clear that his trumpet sounds more clearly and his voice less hoarsely. The new fashions in jazz are not simply born of economic competition. We must without any doubt see in them one of the consequences of the defeat, slow but sure, of the southern world of the United States. And it is not utopian to suppose that in fifty years time the type of jazz howl hiccuped by a poor misfortunate Negro will be upheld only by the whites who believe in it as an expression of negritude, and who are faithful to this arrested image of a type of relationship.

We might in the same way seek and find in dancing, singing, and traditional rites and ceremonies the same upward-springing trend, and make out the same changes and the same impatience in this field. Well before the political or fighting phase of the national movement, an attentive spectator can thus feel and see the manifestation of new vigor and feel the approaching conflict. He will note unusual forms of expression and themes which are fresh and imbued with a power which is no longer that of invocation but rather of the assembling of the people, a summoning together for a precise purpose. Everything works together to awaken the native's sensibility and to make unreal and inacceptable the contemplative attitude, or the acceptance of defeat. The native rebuilds his perceptions because he renews the purpose and dynamism of the craftsmen, of dancing and music, and of literature and the oral tradition. His world comes to lose its accursed character. The conditions necessary for the inevitable conflict are brought together.

We have noted the appearance of the movement in cultural forms and we have seen that this movement and these new forms are linked to the state of maturity of the national consciousness. Now, this movement tends more and more to express itself objectively, in institutions. From thence comes the need for a national existence, whatever the cost.

A frequent mistake, and one which is moreover hardly justifiable, is to try to find cultural expressions for and to give new values to native culture within the framework of colonial domination. This is why we arrive at a proposition which at first sight seems paradoxical: the fact that in a colonized country the most elementary, most savage, and the most undifferentiated nationalism is the most fervent and efficient means of defending national culture. For culture is first the expression of a nation, the expression of its preferences, of its taboos and of its patterns. It is at every stage of the whole of society that other taboos, values, and patterns are formed. A national culture is the sum total of all these appraisals; it is the result of internal and external tensions exerted over society as a whole and also at every level of that society. In the colonial situation, culture, which is doubly deprived of the support of the nation and of the state, falls away and dies. The condition for its existence is therefore national liberation and the renaissance of the state.

The nation is not only the condition of culture, its fruitfulness, its continuous renewal, and its deepening. It is also a necessity. It is the fight for national existence which sets culture moving and opens to it the doors of creation. Later on it is the nation which will ensure the conditions and framework necessary to culture. The nation gathers together the various indispensable elements necessary for the creation of a culture, those elements which alone can give it credibility, validity, life, and creative power. In the same way it is its national character that will make such a culture open to other cultures and which will enable it to influence and permeate other cultures. A non-existent culture can hardly be expected to have bearing on reality, or to influence reality. The first necessity is the re-establishment of the nation in order to give life to national culture in the strictly biological sense of the phrase.

Thus we have followed the breakup of the old strata of culture, a shattering which becomes increasingly fundamental; and we have noticed, on the eve of the decisive conflict for national freedom, the renewing of forms of expression and the rebirth of the imagination. There remains one essential question: what are the relations between the struggle—whether political or military—and culture? Is there a suspension of culture during the conflict? Is the national struggle an expression of a culture? Finally, ought one to say that the battle for freedom however fertile *a posteriori* with regard to culture is in itself a negation of culture? In short, is the struggle for liberation a cultural phenomenon or not?

We believe that the conscious and organized undertaking by a colonized people to re-establish the sovereignty of that nation constitutes the most complete and obvious cultural manifestation that exists. It is not alone the success of the struggle which afterward gives validity and vigor to culture; culture is not put into cold storage during the conflict. The struggle itself in its development and in its internal progression sends culture along different paths and traces out entirely new ones for it. The struggle for freedom does not give back to the national culture its former value and shapes; this struggle which aims at a fundamentally different set of relations between men cannot leave intact either the form or the content of the people's culture. After the conflict there is not only the disappearance of colonialism but also the disappearance of the colonized man.

This new humanity cannot do otherwise than define a new humanism both for itself and for others. It is prefigured in the objectives and methods of the conflict. A struggle which mobilizes all classes of the people and which expresses their aims and their impatience, which is not afraid to count almost exclusively on the people's support, will of necessity triumph. The value of this type of conflict is that it supplies the maximum of conditions necessary for the development and aims of culture. After national freedom has been obtained in these conditions, there is no such painful cultural indecision which is found in certain countries which are newly independent, because the nation by its manner of coming into being and in the terms of its existence exerts a fundamental influence over culture. A nation which is born of the people's concerted action and which embodies the real aspirations of the people while changing the state cannot exist save in the expression of exceptionally rich forms of culture.

The natives who are anxious for the culture of their country and who wish to give to it a universal dimension ought not therefore to place their confidence in the single principle of inevitable, undifferentiated independence written into the consciousness of the people in order to achieve their task. The liberation of the nation is one thing; the methods and popular content of the fight are another. It seems to us that the future of national culture and its riches are equally also part and parcel of the values which have ordained the struggle for freedom.

And now it is time to denounce certain pharisees. National claims, it is here and there stated, are a phase that humanity has left behind. It is the day of great concerted actions, and retarded nationalists ought in consequence to set their mistakes aright. We however consider that the mistake, which may have very serious consequences, lies in wishing to skip the national period. If culture is the expression of national consciousness, I will not hesitate to affirm that in the case with which we are dealing it is the national consciousness which is the most elaborate form of culture.

The consciousness of self is not the closing of a door to communication. Philosophic thought teaches us, on the contrary, that it is its guarantee. National consciousness, which is not nationalism, is the only thing that will give us an international dimension. This problem of national consciousness and of national culture takes on in Africa a special dimension. The birth of national consciousness in Africa has a strictly contemporaneous connection with the African consciousness. The responsibility of the African as regards national culture is also a responsibility with regard to African Negro culture. This joint responsibility is not the fact of a metaphysical principle but the awareness of a simple rule which wills that every independent nation in an Africa where colonialism is still entrenched is an encircled nation, a nation which is fragile and in permanent danger.

If man is known by his acts, then we will say that the most urgent thing today for the intellectual is to build up his nation. If this building up is true, that is to say if it interprets the manifest will of the people and reveals the eager African peoples, then the building of a nation is of necessity accompanied by the discovery and encouragement of universalizing values. Far from keeping aloof from other nations, therefore, it is national liberation which leads the nation to play its part on the stage of history. It is at the heart of national consciousness that international consciousness lives and grows. And this two-fold emerging is ultimately only the source of all culture.

NOTES

1 "The political leader as the representative of a culture." Address to the second Congress of Black Writers and Artists, Rome, 1959.

2 The lady was not alone; she had a most respectable husband, who knew how to quote Racine and Corneille, Voltaire and Rousseau, Victor Hugo and Mussel, Gide, Valéry and as many more again. (René Depestre: "Face à la Nuit.")

3 At the last school prize giving in Dakar, the president of the Senegalese Republic, Léopold Senghor, decided to include the study of the idea of negritude in the curriculum. If this decision was due to a desire to study historical causes, no one can criticize it. But if on the other hand it was taken in order to create black self-consciousness, it is simply a turning of his back upon history which has already taken cognizance of the disappearance of the majority of Negroes.

16

PAUL GILROY

The Tyrannies of Unanimism

I read every account of the Fascist movement in Germany I could lay my hands on, and from page to page I encountered and recognized familiar emotional patterns. What struck me with particular force was the Nazi preoccupation with the construction of a society in which there would exist among all people (*German* people, of course!) *one* solidarity of ideals, *one* continuous circulation of fundamental beliefs, notions, and assumptions. I am not speaking of the popular idea of regimenting people's thought; I'm speaking of the implicit, almost unconscious, or pre-conscious, assumptions and ideals upon which whole nations and races act and live.　　　　—Richard Wright

The narrower the scope of a community formed by collective personality, the more destructive does the experience of fraternal feeling become. Outsiders, unknowns, unlikes become creatures to be shunned; the personality traits the community shares become ever more exclusive; the very act of sharing becomes ever more centred on decisions about who can belong and who cannot. . . . Fraternity has become empathy for a select group of people allied with rejection of those not within the local circle. This rejection creates demands for autonomy from the outside world, for being left alone by it rather than demanding that the outside world itself change. . . . Fragmentation and division is the very logic of this fraternity, as the units of people who really belong get smaller and smaller. It is a version of fraternity which leads to fratricide.

—Richard Sennet

This is an especially important period in the political lives and consciousness of the African-descended peoples of the overdeveloped countries. Their journeys through modernity have recently reached a significant staging-post as Africa's struggle against colonial domination, which defined so many political aspirations in the period after slavery, has reached its conclusion. African countries are still exploited and excluded, but the quality of their marginalization has changed. The distinctive patterns of nineteenth-century imperialism have receded. New battles over health, technology, ecology, and particularly debt have emerged to expand and adapt our

220

understanding of colonial and possibly postcolonial political conflicts. The world's richest countries remain deeply divided over the desirability of writing off the debts held by African governments.

In this nominally postcolonial period, the desire for freedom, which was for so long the center of the modern black political imaginary, must pause and reflect seriously when confronted by the deceptively simple questions: "freedom from what?" "liberty to accomplish what?" The emancipation of South Africa from Apartheid's criminal governance, incomplete though it may be, provides a timely opportunity to reconsider the wider relationship between Africa's New World diaspora and Africa's future. This reflection involves pondering the politics of decolonization in an age without colonies, and seeking the possibility of anti-imperialist consciousness in an era without triumphant empires arranged along bold, racist, nineteenth-century lines. It confronts the historical and philosophical limits of the idea of liberation and promotes a reevaluation of those fundamental modern notions freedom and revolution.

A language of revolution may persist, but these days it is more likely to turn away from the complexities of wholesale societal transformation and promote an "inward," New Age turn. This timely orientation is something quite different from the historic process of self-possession that James Brown famously identified during the Black Power era as a "revolution of the mind." We have seen that it involves a changed understanding of the racial self articulated exclusively through the body and its imaginary power to determine human social destiny. This revolution, if revolution it be, is a biopolitical project that not only produces new common-sense truths about "race" but, in doing so, sets mind and body in a distinctive relationship so that managing and training the latter become the key to regulating the former.

The genocide in Rwanda and the continuing conflicts in Congo, Burundi, and elsewhere are only the most notable recent events to have endowed inquiries made by diaspora blacks into the status of racial difference, solidarity, and democracy with further disquiet about the limits of *racialized* particularity. Recall here that the first people ever to be convicted of the crime of genocide were the Africans Jean-Paul Akayesu and Jean Kambamba. This should not obscure the fact that tribalism, though it has been manifestly invented rather than transmitted seamlessly from the precolonial past, and asserts itself as a supremely powerful force for "ethnic" solidarity and sectarian division, is very ambiguously placed in relation to modern ideas of "race."[1]

To complicate matters even more, the political and ideological divisions set down in earlier times are becoming blurred. The black puppet leaders of the Apartheid pseudo-state Bophutatswana disastrously summoned the white supremacist Afrikaner Weerstandsbeweging (AWB) to protect them, bonded across the color line in spite of their political differences by deeply fascistic investments in mythologies of masculinism, the fiction of purity, and a common hatred for the dilution of their sacred distinctiveness. Closer to home, the Strasserite ideologues who first forged a "third position" for the neo-fascist British National Front during the late 1980s presented Louis Farrakhan in their publications as "a God-send to all races and cultures," distributed leaflets in support of his Nation of Islam, and visited its #4 Mosque in Washington, D.C., in order to study its antidrug programs.

Around the same time, the National Front magazine, *Nationalism Today,* interviewed another ultranationalist African-American, Osiris Akkebala, "an elder of the Pan African International Movement (P.A.I.N)," based in Florida. He told them that his organization invested the separation of the races with a sacred significance in keeping with its status as part of the law of God, and that members opposed intermarriage between black and white because it "results in racial genocide."[2] Fraternal relations between these two ultranationalist groups appeared to be intact ten years later, when Akkebala reappeared in Britain. This time, he served as a witness for the defense in the 1998 trial of the British National Party (BNP) activist Nick Griffin, the publisher of *The Rune,* who had been charged with incitement to racial hatred. On this occasion, he told the British black newspaper *New Nation:* "We see the B.N.P. as our natural allies. We both see the necessity of preserving our distinct races."[3] The BNP may have been eager to recover its position after suggestions that it had been implicated in the murder of Stephen Lawrence. But that is not enough to explain its active support for the family of an unemployed, twenty-six-year-old Bermuda-born chef and Rastafarian, Archie O'Brien, whom BNP members joined in a demonstration outside the Home Office in September 1996. O'Brien was seeking the financial sponsorship of the British Government for his plan to emigrate and settle in Africa, preferably Ghana. Interviewed by *The Guardian,* he said that, unlike his BNP associates, he was not advocating a compulsory return to Africa for all black people. He explained: "I can't express myself here. I can only express myself in Africa, surrounded by my own people and by nature . . . It's not for everyone. You have to reach a certain level of consciousness and be able to live off the land before you go there. Black people have to be prepared before they return to Africa."[4]

These contacts contribute to a pattern of disturbing events that precipitates further anxiety about the changing nature of the claims that modern ideas about "race" can make upon a world in which racial solidarities no longer enjoy an automatic allegiance or uncontested priority over other competing collectivities based on age, religion, language, region, health, gender, or sexual preference. These worries have been rendered all the more troubling in a new geopolitical context that increasingly lacks even the possibility of imagining an alternative to capitalism, the regulating mechanisms of the market, and the vicious logic of economic rationality. It is not yet an issue of whether blacks in the overdeveloped world, who are likely to be substantially cushioned from the brute scarcity that defines the developing areas, will want to go on associating themselves with Africa. Though that outcome remains a distinct possibility in the medium term, at present it is more a matter of how tenuous, precious connections might be maintained or enhanced in the interest of economic justice, political democracy, ecological equilibrium, and ongoing battles against white supremacism and other forms of absolutism. In this climate, it becomes important to consider how the vital symbolic and cultural links between Africa and its modern diaspora might be protected. They might even be made to mean something important for the future development of both locations at a time when the material and experiential gulf between overdeveloped and underdeveloped zones of the planet is being widened by accelerated technological change and new modes of exploitation typified by punitive, interminable debt and the burgeoning trade in hazardous waste.[5]

This apprehension of a deep change in the location and significance of Africa for the political imaginary of its most recent diaspora is also being registered at a time when black communities inside the overdeveloped zones are experiencing both an unprecedented degree of internal differentiation and new levels of economic immiseration. The metropolitan areas where those populations have been concentrated can be characterized by the demise of that common lifeworld once shared by the poor and the privileged. These groups no longer cluster in integrated cross-class communities and may no longer even reside in the same physical space, let alone dwell in the same undifferentiated "culture" or experience racism in essentially the same ways. This divergence in black experience and history has fed the underlying crisis in understanding racial particularity sketched in earlier chapters. Increasingly desperate assertions of a common, invariant racial identity cannot plausibly be projected through the idea of a common culture; rather, they find alternative expression in a significant return to aspects of an older racial science. Identity, understood only as sameness, is once more lodged in and signified by special properties discernible in black bodies. Interest in the biochemical properties of melanin and in the workings of distinct racialized forms of memory have been two of the most prominent themes in this revival. The biological codes of the eighteenth century have been brought back in inverted form. Leavened with New Age and occult themes, they have been made to produce tantalizing glimpses of a redemptive and compensatory black superiority. These tropes are part of a powerful new racial poetics, but it has not been sufficient to complete a cosmetic procedure capable of concealing the scars of intracommunal division that are visible through economic lenses and confirmed by disputes surrounding the moral, behavioral, and carnal rather than corporeal attributes of blackness. Well-publicized panics over the decadence, misogyny, and nihilism of slackness, gangsta rap, booty rap, and the subversive vulgarity of the Jamaican dancehall (which now circulates in eddies far from its Caribbean ghetto sources) have provided valuable insights into the class and gender-based pathologies of the black body politic.

The multiple controversies surrounding the conduct of the former heavyweight boxing champion and convicted rapist Mike Tyson are instructive. During the summer of 1995, to mark his release from jail, where he had served time for the rape of Desiree Washington, and well before Tyson developed his tragic taste for the raw flesh of his opponents, it was proposed that he should make a heroic "homecoming" to Harlem. The proposed public celebration would have enabled him to "declare that he intends to lead a positive life, following in the footsteps of Joe Louis and Muhammad Ali." The event, which was also set to involve a street parade and a major gala event at the Apollo Theatre, was immediately denounced by a wide range of political figures. An organization called African Americans against Violence attacked the event's complicity with "the merchandizing of violence" and its "breath-taking display of black-woman hate, greed and collective irresponsibility." This forgotten episode neatly symbolized the deepening divisions that had appeared in earlier controversies over the nihilism, cynicism, and violence of gangsta rap. The muscled and tattooed body of yet another black male athletic hero, recast here as a victim of conspiracy by unsavory antiblack forces, was placed at the center of this drama. Many of the same elements would be replayed in a major key around the figure of O. J. Simpson.

It is only a slight oversimplification to suggest that in the United States, Britain, and parts of the Caribbean, two opposed but strangely complementary definitions of black nationalism have been confronting each other. The first was putatively streetwise, working-class, and habitually gendered male. It often answered the accusation of cynical commercialism by claiming for itself the role of the war correspondent who reports vividly, but as dispassionately as possible, the unacceptable realities visible from the frontlines of the ghetto. The other formation, for whom Dr. C. Delores Tucker, the head of the National Political Congress of Black Women, provided one convenient figurehead, was assertively feminist, unselfconsciously bourgeois, undoubtedly moralistic, and clearly confident in its core belief that however much money popular forms might bring to those who peddled them, they were trafficking in the most base and destructive stereotypes, which could only be detrimental to communal interests.[6]

Where this chronic binary conflict took root, it created a new sickness that has proved resistant to the simple remedies once supplied by the sweet-tasting medicines of nationalism and essentialism. To bolster their declining effectiveness, these failing therapies must now be supplemented by an austere corrective regime centered on the regulation of personal and interpersonal conduct between men and women and, to an increasing degree, between parents and children. In both versions of this strategy, the black family is seen as the principal object of the technologies of racial selfhood that aim to rebuild black people and remake black households, training them toward a common national consciousness and a suitable gender hierarchy.

Family defines the limits of the forms of political agency that are deemed integral to rebuilding the fading nation. Ominous New Age rhetoric conditions the ambitions of this Afrocentrism even as it disavows Europe and its devilry.[7]

Black feminist analysis has rightly repudiated the identification of the race's fortunes with the public integrity of its masculinities. The impact of its critiques has added substantially to uncertainty about collective particularity and the conditions in which racialized solidarity can emerge and be sustained. Political conflicts over the compatibility of black homosexuality with the favored masculinist patterning of racial identity have also underlined the absence of spontaneous or automatic solidarity and the disappearance of an ethics of care from intraracial interaction.

A cultural elite in which black intellectuals and academics have been prominent, though by no means dominant, has also appeared during this fateful period, operating as something like the vanguard of a new middle-class minority that has substantially improved its own position. Whether it is located in the engine room of the entertainment industries or is clinging by its toehold in the older, more respectable professions, this influential group enjoys a deeply conflictual response to the black poor whose fate it has escaped, but upon whom it remains dependent for its understanding of the difference that "race" makes. Its advent, at a time when the words "exclusion" and "underclass" are never very far from the lips of policy-makers and political opinion formers, points once more toward the vexed issue of that stubborn order of class differences that can be identified inside what can no longer be credibly called a single racial community.

De-industrialization ensures that the economic predicament of these divided black communities is bleak, particularly where their subaltern social world is circumscribed by a high degree of spatial segregation.[8] At the same time, elements of globalization and the centrality of black cultures to popular culture, youth cultures, advertising, cinema, and sports have never been greater. However, this enhanced visibility does not mean that the black body is imaged in postures or roles that would be chosen as a means to articulate or complement black political interests. It can be argued that novel communicative technologies and the faceless forms of appropriation they foster impact negatively upon solidarity-building tactics devised in earlier periods and refined where black subculture moved above ground during the 1960s and 1970s. Consciousness of kind and synchronized action previously mediated by print and sound have been changed and have begun to break down in the different atmosphere created by communicative and representational regimes dominated by images. The growing power of visuality tips the balance away from sound and even from print to create new forms of minstrelsy and new remote audiences hungry for the pleasures they display and orchestrate. Music and dance, so long the core of the alternative public world in which dissidence was worked into a counterculture, reluctantly yield their traditional places of authority to pseudo-performances and video-based simulations. Black culture is not just commodified but lends its special exotic allure to the marketing of an extraordinary range of commodities and services that have no connection whatever to these cultural forms or to the people who have developed them. So much for the good news.

The Limits of Revolutionary Conservatism

From one angle, the following observations on the place of "revolutionary conservatism" in contemporary black political culture might be read as an extended commentary upon rapper Ice Cube's role in selling the movies *Street Fighter, Dangerous Ground,* and *Anaconda.* The first movie caught my attention because it seemed to represent a highly developed instance of multiformat marketing. Hip-hop, computer games, and cinema were suggestively cross-linked in a way that foregrounded Cube and his official marginality as much as the changed profile of a youth culture in which music was no longer the central element. It was also interesting that no contradictions were perceived between Cube's informal Nation of Islam affiliations and the variety of Hollywood mainstreaming represented by *Anaconda* and *Dangerous Ground* and his collaboration with that well-known "cave bitch" the English actress and model Elizabeth Hurley. The apparent ease with which he could move through these mainstream Hollywood projects prompted me toward a reassessment of the currency of racial marginality in youth culture's economy of rebel signs. It initiated a different kind of speculation about the compatibility of powerful revolutionary political rhetoric with the more conventional if not explicitly conservative forms of economic thinking. It is important to appreciate that Cube's assertive espousal of racial separation as both a necessary therapy and a positive politics apparently relates exclusively to the realm of *interpersonal* conduct. This convenient restriction also exempts from consideration any issues arising from the sale of his own art to the legions of young white males who are—officially at least—hip-hop's major consumers. No problems there. Transracial intimacy is not considered insurmountable in the corporate spaces that he inhabits and that are essential to the scale of his cross-over stardom. In the commercial world, just as in the dark space of the performance venue, contact across the color line can be tolerated and legitimized as an unexceptional though possibly regrettable fact of economic life. In more intimate locations it becomes much more of a problem:

> One thing I believe we need to do, we got to separate. We really have to say, "O.K. white folks. You wanna help us? You go to your community and break down the walls." When they're in there talking in the boardroom talking about us, you go correct them. Don't come here picking up trash.[9]

This strategy was summed up in another statement Ice Cube made in the same conversation: "You handle yours, we'll handle ours." In his characteristically eloquent speech, these pessimistic words are part of a precise indictment. They help to animate a discourse that identifies the treacherous role and inadequate conduct of black political leaders. It is deeply significant that the compromised actions of that reviled group are conceived along lines analogous to the improper and inadequate role of fathers in unstable black families and unsustainable households from which masculine authority has been absent. The replacement of these leaders and fathers is necessary in the process of building racial recovery. Fatherhood becomes the principal means of communal reconstruction. Its primary characteristic is not tenderness, insight, patience, love, sympathy, or care but strength—preferably the same variety that is currently lacking from the actions of those "spineless" black leaders who "took their eyes off the prize in the 70s" and, again according to Cube, committed the grave mistake of "trying to make the public schools better instead of building our own schools." This remark reveals the logic of privatization operating here. Racial identity is being privatized in exactly the same way as education should be. The motif of withdrawal—civic and interpersonal—governs this new form of segregation that is being proposed.

Cube's public relations spin reveals repeatedly that he takes pride in his own activities as a father. But fatherhood has another resonance here. It affirms the naturalness of hierarchy. Complete separation is only an issue for those who occupy the subordinate roles in this ideal scheme. The dads (who presumably will be the ones to enforce these rules) can themselves pass at will across the line of color. They move to and fro freely, as the needs of their cross-over careers dictate. They offer their subordinates and followers a fantasy of segregation while themselves consolidating its absolute opposite: a network of economic, cultural, and political relationships that is driven only by the exigencies of the market and the strictest delineation between private and public worlds. Everything is to be politicized but only for those at the bottom of the heap.

It seems to me that in order to locate this type of thinking in its sorry modernist political lineage, we require a topography that operates in more dimensions than the one defined by the outmoded opposition between Left and Right. The chain of fundamental(ist) meanings established here—strength, masculinity, fraternity, self-reliance, discipline, hierarchy—is articulated above all through and by appeals to the value of racial purity. It is not powered by its own hermeneutic capacity, but is rendered believable nonetheless thanks to a default that operates all the more effectively in the absence of any alternative interpretative language that could challenge the overwhelmingly catastrophic value placed on mixture, intercultural, and "transracial" contacts. Its triumph underscores that we lack an adequate language for comprehending mixture outside of jeopardy and catastrophe. Finding this valuable new idiom does not require merely inverting the polarity of hybridity's internal circuits so that what was previously seen in terms of loss, dilution, and weakness becomes valuable instead and offers an opportunity to celebrate the vigorous cosmopolitanism endowed in modernity by transgressive and creative contacts with different people. Perhaps, pending a more complex organicity that comprehends difference in the forms of interarticulation and unremarkable interdependence suggested by the idea of symbiosis, we might begin to comprehend what is still best named "transcultural" mixture, and the assumptions about alterity that it promotes, as phenomena without any necessary or fixed value at all. This transitional but possibly radical suggestion could also be useful when linked to a plea for what might be termed an "indifferent modernity." Under that promising sign, antiracist democracy, care, and viable notions of civic reciprocity could thrive in the absence of an obligation to possess or even completely comprehend the forms of otherness signified by that narrow band of phenotypical variations that produces racialized difference.

These modest aspirations can be connected to the idea that we should take the *scale* upon which the calculus of human difference is to be judged more carefully into account. The shift away from a Euclidean geometry (which operates within closely bounded scalar limits that are anything but natural) and its analytic Cartesian successor, which links perception to a deterministic rationalism, and toward a fractal geometry that problematizes the questions of scale and scaling in a radical fashion offers a useful analogy here. Bodily scale is certainly important, but it is not the only possible basis for calculation and interaction. Varieties of solidarity other than the local and the national assert their presence and have to be placed within an explicit hierarchy of scales with multiple patterns of determination. In Chapter 1 I argued that this attention to scale and its effects is demanded by the emergence of the human genome as a "code of codes" and the principal focus of concern with human distinctiveness. What Fanon called the "epidermalization" of difference operates only at one scale, which will not always be able to claim priority over other, less readily visible modes of differentiation and determination. The varying degrees of melanin in the body seem a poor alternative vehicle for these biosocial speculations and the radically realist epistemology through which they must work.

Biologists like Richard Lewontin and Steven Rose have reminded us that we stand on the threshold of a transformed understanding of the visible differences coded inside human bodies. The old notions of "race" are likely to look very different, less natural, and more unstable than they now do when confronted with a pattern of predispositions to health, illness, and longevity that does not obey the predictive rules of Linnean racial typology. Perhaps a new, as it were "postracial," genetic science will appear before long. It is already being prefigured in several forms, not all of which will respect a vestigial racial theory as the frontier of some enhanced eugenic ambitions. In the meantime, the complexities of separating somatic cells from germ cells and the problems involved in distinguishing "periphrastic" from fully functional genetic information can only confirm the contingent but inescapable wisdom which stipulates that human beings are more alike than unalike and asserts the overwhelming natural and biological unity of the human species where polymorphism is enhanced but not diminished once we shift to this nano-political scale.

The Fraternity of Purity-Seekers

In Britain, the United States, South Africa, Bosnia, and elsewhere, politically opposed purity-seekers have been prepared to bury their differences and become partners in the dismal dance of absolutism. It is therefore important to repeat that contemporary conflicts over the status of racialized difference have taken shape in an area far beyond the grasp of simplistic distinctions between the Left and the Right, radical and conservative. I would suggest that at root, these confluences are manifestations not of *political* ideology at all but of something anterior to it that challenges the rules and assumptions of modern politics by exalting particularistic ontology and primordial kinship above the distinctive blend of solidarity and autonomy for which the word modernity has long been emblematic. However much melanin is present in their cells, these purists voice a distinctive understanding of culture, tradition, self; kinship, ethnicity, nation, and "race" that blurs the lines between views formerly located at opposite ends of the spectrum of modern political ideologies. To recognize this is not to capitulate to the old—and in my view misguided—liberal assertion that intolerant and antidemocratic extremes merge readily into one another to found an anti-ideological or pragmatic totalitarianism. This is not an organic blending of ideologies or some inevitable closing of the narrow circuits of human frailty, imagination, and evil. For politically opposed groups to discover common cause, things have to happen—meetings must be conducted, language adjusted, objectives redefined, and purpose and solidarity reconfigured.

I am asking you to venture into the unstable location where white supremacists and black nationalists, Klansmen, Nazis, neo-Nazis and ethnic absolutists, Zionists and anti-semites have been able to encounter each other as potential allies rather than sworn foes. In the words of Primo Levi, it "is a grey zone, with ill defined outlines which both separate and join the two camps of masters and servants. It possesses an incredibly complicated internal structure, and contains within itself enough to confuse our need to judge."[10] Understanding the forms of complicity that arise there is not only a matter of recognizing the possibility that enemies can, in exceptional circumstances, acquire a common political interest.[11] It involves accepting the possibility that, interests apart, they may share parallel ways of understanding the meaning of their own particularity, of responding to the idea of transgressive contact between groups and of conceptualizing ethnicity and "race" as general, even necessary, principles of human differentiation. For example, the common investment in the idea of segregation that marks many of these encounters should not then be read as some spontaneous eruption of fundamental human antipathy toward otherness. It is better understood as a negotiated political outcome that has been produced through regimes of seeing and knowing the world that have a history.

I would like to recognize the existence of these gray and ambiguous zones in order to assess the value of linking a variety of different historical and cultural phenomena that are not normally associated. The common features of the political forces that join hands secretly there are overlooked because the groups involved in this tacit contact appear, from one angle of vision, to be politically opposed. This overly narrow conceptualization of their politics can be misleading. The situation is compounded when racial, religious, or cultural differences are invoked as a reason to place similar actions or attitudes in different moral categories. For example, it has sometimes been argued that only white people can be judged racist because racism is a defining attribute of whiteness or an intrinsic property of the power it holds. Racism can only be a consequence of power and so, the argument runs, since blacks have no power—as a "race"—they cannot, by definition, be racist. The tautology passes unnoticed and the jump between individual action and societal patterning is glossed over. I would argue that it might be better to interpret these and other similar statements as a means to solicit racial identification and endorse the principle of racialized difference as a valid means to classify and divide human beings. Attempting to adjust the scale upon which human interests are calculated so that it is no longer compatible with raciology reveals disturbing patterns that demand a reassessment of where the lines between revolutionary and conservative, modern and antimodern are deemed to fall. This situation becomes even more difficult when a favored group seeks or is endowed with a special or unique ethical status because of past experiences of victimage. On these historical grounds, normal standards of judgment can be suspended as restitution or reparation for past suffering. The idea that victims of racism are immunized against the appeal of racism precisely because they have been victims, or the idea that prior victimage renders victims and their descendants exempt from normal standards of conduct and judgment, are typical of these types of argument. This kind of reasoning was reduced to nonsense in the vulgar formula that suggested racism could be defined as the simple sum of prejudice and power. The proposition that only white people could be racist became confused with the different notion that black people could not be racist. The slippage between these two interlinked propositions is a symptom that should alert us to the pernicious power of racializing categories to reassert themselves even in the moment of their supposed erasure.

The capacity to do the wrong thing is an omnipresent possibility for which modernity afforded unprecedented opportunities. Exploring the linkage between various modern forms of authoritarianism, absolutism, masculinism, belligerence, intolerance, and genocidal hatred is important now because it has become abundantly dear that the fascisms of the past have not exhausted the palette of barbarity and the syntax of evil. Those histories of suffering can be used to bring a counter-anthropological, strategic universalism into view.

The revolutionary rhetoric sometimes employed in interaction between black nationalists and separatists and their white-supremacist associates is misleading. To be conservative is to be engaged in a politics of cultural conservation. It is to subscribe to a doggedly positive and always over-integrated sense of culture and/or biology as the essential reified substances of racial, national, and ethnic difference. In this view, rather than being a product of profane politics and complex history, an obvious, biologically based, and natural apprehension of "race" initiates the development of both culture and identity. The junction of those two foundational terms—"race" and "culture"—indexes something so important and yet so fragile and brittle that it is in ceaseless jeopardy and can be readily destroyed. Whether the social and psychological processes we term culture and identity are really so insubstantial cannot be debated here. The idea that priceless, essential identities are in perpetual danger from the difference outside them and that their precious purity is always at risk from the irrepressible power of heteroculture has certainly supplied the pivot for some unlikely political alliances. Those formal connections are extremely important, but the word "alliance" suggests links that are too deliberate and too self-conscious to capture the tacit convergences and common habits of mind that should be recognized as equally significant. Perhaps the retreat into the spurious certainties that were once the exclusive stock in trade of European raciological thinking itself conveys the extent to which political tactics produced in the struggle against racial slavery, for democratic political rights and beyond those rights for a measure of social autonomy and cultural recognition, have become utterly exhausted.

The Malcolm X cult was one early symptom of a process in which the recent past of the black liberation movement was recycled and reimagined as well as actively reinvented. The Nation of Islam now provides the most significant model of solidarity here. It is important precisely because, though it buys heavily into the idea of Nationhood,[12] its own ideology is based not on nationalism, notions of citizenship, or rights but on an older and more straightforwardly authoritarian form of kinship that is masculinist, intolerant, and militaristic and shares important features with other "fraternalist" and "fratriarchal" political cultures. To find the substantive reasons for this enduring pattern requires an extensive historical detour by way of Garveyism and its antecedents. It would also have to take in the neglected phenomena that Wilson Moses has called the "pseudo-militarism of the Hampton-Tuskeegee traditions, where uniforms and drill practice re-emphasized the importance of a New Negro who would repudiate the legendary cultural soft-ness of an excessively languid and aesthetic people."[13] Further dues can be drawn from the work of Frederick Douglass, who, surveying the predicament of his racial siblings in July 1848, ten years after his own escape from slavery, first asked the famous, endlessly repeated question: "What Are the Colored People Doing for Themselves?" His characteristically bold plea for more black self-activity in the cause of antislavery was delivered more in sorrow than in anger and, he tells us, was addressed primarily to "comparatively idle and indifferent" free African-American men. He measured their local failures against the energetic way in which "the oppressed of the old world were holding public meetings, putting forth addresses, passing resolutions and in various other ways making their wishes known to the world." Contrasting their indifference to their political welfare with their great enthusiasm for the grand fraternal rituals of freemasonry and odd-fellowship, and the follies of the latter with the attainment of real character, Douglass's lament is worth quoting at length:

> If we put forth a call for a National Convention, for the purpose of considering our wrongs, asserting our rights, and adopting measures for our mutual elevation and the emancipation of our enslaved fellow countrymen, we shall bring together about *fifty;* but if we call a grand celebration of odd-fellowship, or free-masonry, we shall assemble, as was the case a few days ago in New York, from *four to five thousand*— the expense of which alone would be from seventeen to twenty thousand dollars, a sum sufficient to maintain four or five efficient presses, devoted to our elevation and improvement. We should not say this of odd-fellowship and free-masonry, but that it is swallowing up the best energies of many of our best men, contenting them with the glittering follies of artificial display, and indisposing them to seek for solid and important realities. The enemies of our people see this tendency in us, and encour-age it. The same persons who would puff such demonstrations in the newspapers, would mob us if we met to adopt measures for obtaining our rights. They see our weak points, and avail themselves of them to crush us. We are imitating the infe-rior qualities of and examples of white men, and neglecting superior ones. We do not pretend that all the members of odd-fellow societies and masonic lodges are indifferent to their rights and means of obtaining them; for we know the fact to be otherwise. Some of the best and brightest among us are numbered with those soci-eties; and it is on this account that we make these remarks. We desire to see these

noble men expending their time, talents and strength for higher and nobler objects than any that can be attained by the weak and glittering follies of odd-fellowship and freemasonry.[14]

Some of Douglass's frustration may have been aimed at his close associate Martin Delany, an enthusiastic mason who would publish a pamphlet on the legitimacy of the movement among colored men just five years later. Delany's arguments in favor of masonic activities are notable, but he was only one of many distinguished nationalists who found the segregated fraternal milieu of Prince Hall masonry,[15] with its rituals, hierarchies, secrecy, and military associations, a suitable environment in which to advance their social and political ambitions. Unlike Douglass, he had been freeborn and was therefore untroubled by the convention that freedom was an essential precondition of masonic membership.

The history of black masonry has been carefully surveyed by a number of historians who have pondered the movement's class character, identified its military roots, and recognized the valuable space it provided for building forms of moral solidarity, formal sociality, and political ideology among its black practitioners. The masons' advocacy of the centrality of ancient Egypt to the advance of civilization has been appreciated as a source of later nationalist theologies and ideologies, but their enduring impact upon subsequent patterns of political style and organization has been curiously overlooked.[16]

Prince Hall masonry was a profound if sometimes indirect influence on the thinking of Marcus Garvey and Noble Drew All (the founder of the Moorish Science Temple), two fundamental figures who inspired the later work of W. D. Fard and Elijah Muhammad.[17] The institutional foundations of the fraternal movements would collapse in the 1930s amid the same economic turmoil that witnessed the birth of the Nation of Islam, but their cultural, psychological, and political impact has continued into the present and is all the more pernicious where it is unrecognized.[18] The Nation of Islam certainly made use of the Prince Hall tradition, transforming its teachings so that masonry could be seen to be based upon the truths of Islam. Thus the masonic association of so many of America's founding fathers is employed as a way to specify the world conspiracy to which they contributed.

Where the ideal of fraternity shaped a distinctive political style, it raises still more difficult cross-cultural puzzles, both genealogical and interpretative. These puzzles demand an unconventional historical understanding of fascist groups and the traditional brotherhoods that shaped their development, and require new approaches to the conspiracy theories on which they relied.[19] Fraternal and fratriarchal movements ask us fundamental questions about the power of secrecy, particularly when combined with homosocial hierarchy and ritual. Analyzing them requires a more detailed historical sociology and psychology of movement behavior than is currently available, something that can extend the preliminary agenda set long ago by Simmel's invaluable speculations in this field: "the secret society must seek to create a sort of life totality. For this reason, it builds round its sharply emphasized purposive content a system of formulas, like a body round a soul, and places both alike under the protection of secrecy, because only thus does it become a harmonious whole in which one part protects the other."[20]

The resurgence of the fraternalist Nation of Islam has been central to notable recent changes in the black political imaginary, but the quest for a mechanical, pre-modern form of racialized solidarity that underpins its popularity takes a number of other forms, some of which manage to be much less forbidding and obviously fascistic. Though superficially more attractive, they are still connected to the authoritarian revision of community less by their investments in the fraternal style than by the widespread belief that working on maleness is the primary means to racial restoration and national reconstruction.[21] Simmel's observations on the appeal of secret societies and the absolute but necessarily temporary protection they afford their members linked a discussion of secrecy and betrayal to a sociology of adornment. His approach alerts us to the possibility that the magical production and simulation of community by means of uniform clothing can take diverse forms. It is as likely to be accomplished these days by a pair of boots or a hat supplied by "101% black-owned" Karl Kani™ as it is by the campy, bourgeois dignity of a bow tie or the bright embellishment of a colorful Kente cloth. These days, the role of uniforms is different because adequate proof of identity is not provided by a would-be state machine to which Garveyite or even Black Power uniforms tied their wearers. The privatized uniforms of the 1990s come with the multiple blessings of the corporate world. Donning them in pursuit of solidarity is a largely self-motivated gesture of submission to or immersion in a virtual community that cannot be socially confirmed by a radically fragmented everyday world.

The same breakdown of a political culture in which the contending values of solidarity and autonomy could be held in an unstable equilibrium is also conveyed in the disaggregation of embattled, alternative public spheres and the notions of freedom that were created there, often under the ambivalent protection of the black Protestant church. These and other factors have produced the anxieties that we routinely name as a crisis of "identity." Hankering after identity and the related desire to acquire the certainty and legitimacy that its possession supposedly confers has become associated with some spectacular disavowals of modernity. These patterns mark the black populations of the overdeveloped world rather unexpectedly as full participants in some mainstream cultural currents. Today, identity and its characteristic discontents are not marginal concerns at all, but phenomena that appear at the very center of the contemporary political agenda. This drive to resolve critical problems of social solidarity via a technology of the self is not the only point where an abject minority has been bound by the same assumptions and cultural processes as those who dominate it.

Universal Fascism

The word fascism is a surprisingly recent and imprecise term seemingly remote from the concerns of black cultural politics. Its short, contested life has made it hard to use, and there is a strong and entirely appropriate inhibition about setting the concept to work in analyzing phenomena that are remote in space and time from the site of its original usage to describe one recent phase in Europe's barbarities.[22] I prefer to see the dispute about its character as part of what is useful about it. It draws us into a valuable confrontation with the moral and political limits of both democracy and modernity. Let us work within the flexible framework established by two contentious hypotheses. The first suggests that a generic fascism can be identified;[23] the second that, even though there are real problems about isolating its ideological and conceptual signatures, fascism does have a coherent ideological shape born, to put it crudely, in the articulation of nationalism and a form of socialism.[24] Of course, this pseudo-socialism is an anti-marxist variety, but it retains certain utopian and indeed revolutionary attributes that play with and distort the ideal of fraternity into an anti-democratic and viciously hierarchical caricature that silences the competing claims of its sibling term—"equality."

Although extreme nationalism underlines the affinity of this generic fascism with the Right, it need not be seen as their exclusive ideological property. In some of its earlier forms, this fascism suggested a third way between the twin evils of socialism and capitalism. Though I recognize the danger that contemporary critics may end up taking the ideological pretensions of fascist doctrine far more seriously than many of its adherents, I reject the suggestion that recognizing the overarching power of the will to deception and destruction relieves critics of the unpleasant task of delving into fascist morality, law, aesthetics, and science.[25] It is unavoidable and indeed useful that the concept should remain enveloped in all sorts of disputes: political, ethical, and historical. For a long time, it became a debased coinage through being employed as a vague and general term of abuse. Lines drawn around analyses of its specific historical incarnations became entangled in debates about the attributes of the fascist state, the activities of fascist movements, the quality of fascist ideologies, and their complex and shifting relation to the normal forms, rules, and institutional patterns of color-coded bourgeois democracy, especially in the United States, where raciology and eugenic social policy were loudly articulated. However, fascism is more than just a political system, and there is far more involved in defining it than undoubtedly important inquiries into the characteristics of fascist states and governments. Distinctions between fascist ideology and culture, fascist governmentality, and fascist economic and political strategy are indispensable, but if a generic fascism is to appear plausible, we must also be alive to fascism in its prepolitical, cultural, and psychological aspects. Fascism remote from state power and distant from the possibility of its acquisition is different from fascism in government, being rationally practiced as a means of modern political administration. Though relatively few fascist movements have actually taken power, these different dimensions of fascist politics can become linked, particularly in situations of civil war.

The lines of descent from 1930s fascists shamelessly claimed by some contemporary neo-fascists precluded the necessity of working to define which elements of earlier incarnations were being retained by today's adherents and supporters. This has been an acute problem, not where the Nazi label was conveniently applied to their own activities by contemporary subscribers to fascist doctrine, but where post-Hitlerian nationalism, racism, anti-semitism, and other related doctrines obscured the purity of their lineage. The antiracist and anti-fascist movement in Britain was, for example, constantly challenged to demarcate where legitimate patriotism ended and callous neo-Nazism began. Whatever one may think of his politics, Alain Finkielkraut's *Remembering in Vain* [26] had the virtue of focusing with some clarity on the exceptional nature of fascist crimes against humanity and the contested reconstruction of that exceptional status in the light of French colonialism's catastrophic consequences. Because these judgments have presented substantial political problems, it is not banal to recall that the history of Nazism and of Italian fascism associates them intellectually and organizationally with other forms of nationalism, traditionalism, and authoritarianism, as well as with syndicalism, socialism, and environmentalism. [27] We need to be able to see precisely where the practitioners of racial science became enmeshed with the normal practice of eugenics and euthanasia in Europe and the United States. Similarly, without becoming overly protective or defensive, we should be prepared to acknowledge the forms of linkage (in my view neither wholly necessary nor wholly contingent) that can be shown to connect to the Nazi cause the works of important figures like Heidegger, Reifenstahl, Mies Van der Rohe, Paul de Man, Carl Gustav Jung, and a host of other profound and stimulating artists and thinkers. Each of these celebrated examples has generated an extensive literature that cannot be reconstructed here, though it may be useful to note a certain similarity in the postures assumed by those who have sought to redeem these figures and their genius from the taint of Nazism, which is understood in all these cases to be external to whatever they had to say that is enduring or valuable.

Taking these observations on board should not mean that the specificities of fascism are allowed to disappear, merging into what is familiar. If that were to happen, the normal imperfections of capitalist democracy would become indistinguishable from the exceptional governmental state for which the concept of fascism provides a vital signature. Fascism is not to be separated from normality by a question of degree. And yet, the modes of cultural expression and the practices of everyday life under the Nazi regime so tellingly reconstructed in the priceless labor of historians like George Mosse, Detlev Peukert, Gisela Bock, Jill Stephenson, Alison Owings, Peter Adam, Michael Kater, and Robert Wistrich have a very familiar look.[28] Volumes of moving testimony from other genocidal war zones demonstrate how swiftly an exceptional brutality can be triggered from the seeming stability of normal interaction. Stefan Kuhl and Edward Larson[29] have provided a means to emphasize the kinship between white supremacist regimes in different places and their recruitment of eugenic racial science into social policy. Recognizing the complexity of these interconnections, we must work harder to find fascism's characteristic features in philosophy, aesthetics, and cultural criticism as well. This vigilance should not just be directed toward the possibility that past forms may recur but should also recognize the danger that fascism is still somehow pending—a possibility that remains inherent in all attempts to organize social life according to orderly modern, raciological principles. It is inappropriate, then, to seek a final extrahistorical formula for fascism that would enable us to devise a simple test for its presence or absence. To desire a device of that type is also to trivialize the complexity and mutability of these unsavory political phenomena that we cannot reduce to being either modernity's repudiation or its fulfillment, reason's betrayal or its immoral affirmation.

Events in Latin America and Indo-China as well as in Southern Africa and the Middle East testify that Hitlerism did not exhaust the forms that fascism can take. Emmanuel Levinas pointed long ago to the difference between the philosophy of Hitlerism and the philosophy of the Hitlerians. We would do well to reflect on similar distinctions and employ their correlates in all considerations of the contemporary phenomena that we want to identify as wholly fascist or, with even greater difficulty, as tendentially fascistic. There are additional obstacles in trying to determine exactly what the status of the unspeakable past should be in defining the meaning of the concept today. Irreconcilable memories of fascism are articulated and projected by fascists and their opponents. This appears in gross form where the scholarship of the Holocaust "negationists" faces the testimony of survivors, their families, and other moral advocates, but there are numerous other, less dramatic instances of the same sort of conflict. To seek to open and utilize debates over what counts as fascist is not to downplay the importance of knowing with as much detail as possible what really happened in the past. It is to recognize that both easy exceptionalism and simplistic notions of repetition offer unsatisfactory ways of facing the enduring power of fascisms and racisms: scientific, pseudo-scientific, and antiscientifically cultural. This line of inquiry might also play a role in cultivating the special skills necessary to recognize and oppose fascism when it appears without the convenience of an identifying label and in inhospitable circumstances far outside the overdeveloped countries where we might be most attuned to the possibility of its reappearance. This endeavor has been made urgent not only by the intermittent denial of fascist crimes against humanity but more controversially by the emergence of respectable forms of nationalism and patriotism that have been able to accommodate "strong" versions of ethnicity and invite comparison with fascist discourses but that bid for a legitimate place in official political institutions.

The categories that have emerged from detailed historical analyses of fascist movements become somewhat fudged in the transition to more general and abstract thinking. Perhaps it is better not to attempt to pronounce finally upon the balance between reason and occultism outside of any particular historical example or to try to make general estimations from material relating to concrete issues like the place of racist ideologies in any particular fascist "polity."

Emphasis on the genocidal processes in which fascisms have culminated should not diminish our sensitivity to the proto-fascist potentials secreted inside familiar everyday patterns of government, justice, thought, and action. The notions of absolute ethnicity that have created a sense of culture as something organic that can be grown or husbanded by the state and owned as a form of property by individual subjects are an interesting example of this possibility. They suggest that members of the dominant social group in a racialized social hierarchy do not have to imagine themselves to be superior; they need only assert unbridgeable difference to awaken the possibility of a fascistic solidarity.

I recognize that while there are still plenty of openly active, self-confessed fascists around, this degree of reflexivity may be seen as a luxury that antiracist politics cannot afford. It may be criticized as a dangerous distraction because its speculative tone could divert attention away from their actions and toward more problematic areas where the label will be unproductively contested. There will also be a risk of diluting opposition to fascistic political activity by finding fascism and its preconditions everywhere, but this need not be the case. By confining the term and restricting it to those cases in which unbroken continuity with past fascisms can be established, we may also minimize contemporary dangers and diminish our sense of what antiracist and antifascist action might mean as a future-oriented politics rather than an essentially defensive operation against violence and terror.

Those of us tied by affinity as well as kinship to histories of suffering and victimage have an additional responsibility not to betray our capacity to imagine democracy and justice in indivisible, nonsectarian forms. Perhaps because of what we have witnessed or chosen to commemorate we have a special obligation to be vigilant and alert to the possibility that barbarity can appear anywhere, at any time, not only where economic rationality or the logic of capital dictates it as the preferred outcome. These qualifications ensure that histories of suffering are not reduced to the private experience of their victims. Mourning is only one of many practices of memory, and it involves more than remembering. Bolstered by the cautious, strategic universalism toward which the history of fascism inclines us, diverse stories of suffering can be recognized as belonging to anyone who dares to possess them and in good faith employ them as interpretative devices through which we may clarify the limits of our selves, the basis of our solidarities, and perhaps pronounce upon the value of our values.

Whether or not you agree with the attempt to apply the concept of fascism to these different phenomena, ask yourself this: What, in the face of the proliferating chronicles of human barbarity, would it mean to seek to contrive a pastoral and permanently innocent ethnic or racial identity? What is at stake in the desire to find an entirely pure mode of particularized being, and to make it the anchor for a unique culture that is not just historically or contingently divorced from the practice of evil but permanently fortified against that very possibility by its essential constitution? Perhaps the desire for that fiction of particularity is an especially problematic feature of contemporary black politics but one that supplies ironic confirmation of its distinctively modern lineage. It seeks to shield its supposed beneficiaries from the effects of the complex moral choices that define human experience and to insulate them from the responsibility to act well and choose wisely: favoring negotiation over violence and the will to justice over the will to dominate. It would usher black politics into a desert, a flattened moral landscape bereft of difficult choices where cynicism would rule effortlessly in the guise of naturalized morality. Secreted inside that exaltation of biologically grounded innocence and its over-identification with moral legitimation is a promise that the political agenda set by the innocent will, at some future point, be emancipated from moral constraints. The institution of innocent identity makes the difficult work of judgment and negotiation irrelevant. Fascism will flourish where that innocence is inflated by the romances of "race," nation, and ethnic brotherhood.

Black Fascists?

Writing in 1938, in "A History of Negro Revolt," a political and theoretical coda to *The Black Jacobins*, C.L.R. James had the following to say about Marcus Garvey:

> All the things that Hitler was to do so well later, Garvey was doing in 1920 and 1921. He organized storm troopers, who marched, uniformed in his parades, and kept order and gave colour to his meetings.[30]

James revised the tone of this prewar evaluation in later work, but these words summon up not the least of the many historiographical controversies buried in the analysis of the Garveyite movement. Did Garvey's ideology of fundamental race con-sciousness incline him toward a version of the generic fascism sketched above, or was his sympathy for the activities of the European dictators won by their practical achievements and his similar enthusiasm for the career of powerful, heroic figures like Napoleon? What matters more than these undecideable though absorbing inquiries is a consideration of whether Garvey's militaristic movement, with its exhortation to manhood and repeatedly stated desire to "purify and standardize" the race, can be understood as a family member to the other, similar movements of that period and whether the variety of authoritarian leadership that Garvey practiced was akin to the type that was being developed by fascists in Italy and Germany. James was only one of the many political commentators to have compared Marcus Garvey and the United Negro Improvement Association (UNIA) to the fascists. To draw attention to this is not to undermine any of the extraordinary and important achievements of the Garvey movement. It is, however, to entertain the possibility of a profound kinship between the UNIA and the fascist political movements of the period in which it grew. These affinities can be approached via the idea of a common political style that usefully shades simplistic distinctions between ideology on the one hand and organizational techniques and strategies on the other. According to the his-torian J. A. Rogers, in a 1937 interview quoted in what has become a celebrated passage from the second volume of *The World's Great Men of Color*, Garvey himself compared his organization's activities to those of Hitler and Mussolini:

> We were the first Fascists. We had disciplined men, women and children in training
> for the liberation of Africa. The black masses saw that in this extreme nationalism
> lay their only hope and readily supported it. Mussolini copied fascism from me but
> the Negro reactionaries sabotaged it.[31]

Robert A. Hill, a perceptive commentator on Garvey,[32] has offered an especially valuable exposition of his authoritarian political philosophy and its explicitly antide-mocratic and Spartan conceptions of law, self, nationality, and duty. Hill describes Garvey's identification with fascism as "naive" but notes that it was able to merge with Garvey's explicit anti-semitism, something Hill does not minimize. The point at issue here is not whether Garvey's claims to have been an inspiration to Mussolini and Hitler are true but rather what it means for us today that Garvey, "the master propagandist," may have believed them to be so. Though it takes us into even more perilous territory, it seems worthwhile to attempt to situate Garvey's own account of his project in relation to his early associations with the Ku Klux Klan and other white supremacist ideologues, something that did not draw unequivocal support from members of the UNIA. The symbolic summit of these connections was a two-hour meeting between Garvey and Edward Clarke, the Klan's second in command, that took place in Atlanta in June 1922. However, before that, Garvey had spoken favorably of the organization's having "lynched race pride into the Negroes"[33] and applauded its segregationism. These positions went hand in hand with support for the activities of other individual segregationists and white supremacist organizations in the North and the South:

> In our desire to achieve greatness as a race, we are liberal enough to extend to others a similar right. . . . All races should be pure in morals and in outlook, and for that we, as Negroes, admire the leaders and members of the Anglo-saxon clubs. They are honest and honorable in their desire to purify and preserve the white race even as we are determined to purify and standardize our race.[34]

Purify and standardize: Garvey is saying that racial purity and standardization have to be fashioned. The combined, deadly weight of racial difference, subordination, and oppression is insufficient to generate them spontaneously. The martial technologies of racial becoming—drill, uniforms, medals, titles, massed display—have to be set to work to generate these qualities that are not immediately present. Garvey's views were framed and sanctioned by a version of nationalism figured through the familiar masculinist values of conquest and military prowess:

> This is a white man's country. He found it, he conquered it and we can't blame him because he wants to keep it. I'm not vexed with the white man of the South for Jim Crowing me because I am black. I never built any street cars or railroads. The white man built them for their own convenience. And if I don't want to ride where he's willing to let me then I'd better walk.

It has been suggested that these arguments may have been produced to aid Garvey's long-term strategy for building the UNIA in the Southern states. Tony Martin, another distinguished historian of the UNIA and Garvey biographer, who is more sympathetic than Hill to the call for separatist politics, has described the Garvey movement's relationship with the Klan and other white supremacist and segregationist individuals and organizations during this period as a symbiotic one. Dismissing as "simplistic" any understanding of these connections that sees them as an alliance based solidly on a common desire for racial purity, enthusiasm for emigration, and hostility to integration, Martin notes the emergence of areas of "common concern" between these political constituencies and quotes with approval Garvey's own defense of the contacts between the two organizations. Martin ends his extremely valuable historical study of Garvey and his organization with Garvey's telling description of that famous encounter with the Klan leader: "I was speaking to a man who was brutally a white man, and I was speaking to him as a man who was brutally a Negro."

This suggestive moment of transracial symmetry pivots on two recurrent attributes of what I feel can be justifiably named fascism: brutalism and masculinism.

Some version of a shared and appropriately gendered humanity is ironically confirmed by their presence even as the a priori significance of racial codes is being asserted. Garvey's implied superiority is communicated only by the way that he monopolizes the role of speaker in the encounter.

Another troubling example from the same interwar period can be built around Zora Neale Hurston's anthropological trips to Haiti in 1936 and 1937. Hurston explains that she was captivated not only by a well-dressed Haitian colonel who was "the number one man in the military forces in Haiti" but also by his authoritarian and populist plans to reintroduce something like slavery into the country:

> He is a tall, and slender black man around forty with the most beautiful hands and feet that I have ever beheld on a man. He is truly loved and honored by the three thousand men under him. . . . There is no doubt that the military love their chief.
> . . . Anyway, there is Colonel Calixe with his long tapering fingers and his beautiful slender feet, very honest and conscientious and doing a beautiful job of keeping order in Haiti . . . he is a man of arms and wishes no other job than the one he has. In fact we have a standing joke between us that when I become president of Haiti, he is going to be my chief of the army and I am going to allow him to establish state farms in all the departments . . . a thing he has long wanted to do in order to eliminate the beggars from the streets of Port Au Prince, and provide food for the hospitals, jails and other state institutions. . . . He is pathetically eager to clear the streets of Haiti of beggars and petty thieves. . . . What a beautifully polished Sam Brown belt on his perfect figure and what lovely, gold looking buckles on his belt![35]

There is something about a man in uniform! Hurston is clearly swept up in the erotic charge attached to the charismatic figure of this man of destiny. Her extraordinary enthusiasm is also an important moment in which some of the psychoanalytic issues involved in being invited to identify with the would-be dictator might also be noted. Her suggestion that he is an object of love for his subordinates is, for example, striking. What variety of love is this that blends the heterosexual and homosexual and delicately flavors the blend with fear and coercion? The colonel's conspicuous physical attributes symbolize the innocence of his political inclinations. The combination of bodily perfection and a firm political hand on the beggars and thieves is not, of course, enough to damn him as a fascist, but the resonance is a strong one, and it is significant that Hurston also articulates a contempt for the moribund political system that, in her view, fetters Haitian progress. This view is shared with the young Caribbean men of action who captivated her.

In numerous settings, fascism has involved precisely this idea that political solutions can be imposed upon the mass of people by an elite group. Its populist character is thus circumscribed and directed. Its primary political goal is defined by a restless exaltation to act toward the institution of a national community. The process of national becoming must of course be perpetually deferred because on the day that it dawns, much of the distinctiveness of fascist politics will be lost. Superficially at least, Malcolm X's repudiation of the Nation of Islam's later contacts with the Klan presents even more fissile material than the Garvey and Hurston cases. Malcolm has himself been represented as a charismatic and authoritarian leader, but he differs sharply from Garvey in that he repudiated the links with the Klan and the Nazis that were a central part of his complete break from the Nation of Islam. Though Malcolm's comprehension of these contacts is couched in terms of a conspiracy theory, his open contempt for the immoral outcome they represent comes across very strongly:

> I know for a fact that there is a conspiracy between, among the Muslims and the Lincoln Rockwell Nazis and also the Ku Klux Klan. There is a conspiracy. . . . Well, the Ku Klux Klan made a deal with Elijah Muhammad in 1960 in the home of Jeremiah X, the minister in Atlanta at that time, in the presence of the minister in Philadelphia. They were trying to make a deal with him to make available to Elijah Muhammad a county-size tract of land in Georgia or South Carolina where Elijah Muhammad could then induce Negroes to migrate and make it appear that his program of a segregated state or separated state was feasible. And to what extent these negotiations finally developed, I do not know. Because I was not involved in them beyond the period of December 1960. But I do know that after that, Jeremiah, who was the minister throughout the South, could roam the entire South and the Klan not bother him in any way shape or form, nor would they bother any of the Black Muslims from then on. Nor would the Black Muslims bother the Klan.[36]

Just as in the case of Ice Cube, it would seem that practical implementation of that longed-for separation essential to racial rebirth actually requires, indeed legitimates, transgressive contact with the forbidden Other in a strange but entirely predictable act of fraternalist mirroring. The segregationists and purifiers who are located on both sides of the fatal boundary between "races" claim monopoly of the useful capacity to handle those contacts with the enemy that would be damaging to everybody else. The enemy who announces himself to be your enemy ceases to be an enemy. He becomes an ally, and a more authentic and treacherous foe is produced in the form of the enemy who tells you he can be your ally in the coalitional struggles that can bring about justice and rights for all. The Nazi and the Klansman are preferable because they are open and honest about their racialized beliefs. You know where you are with a Klansman.

Perhaps, recognizing the problems in seeking to apply the label fascist to the Klan, we should consider what justifies an association between an openly Nazi organization and a spiritual movement dedicated to the emancipation, uplift, and protection of Africans abroad. It is, of course, the acquisition of sovereign territory: a national homeland, a piece of ground, that legitimates these aspirations. Garvey's oldest son, Marcus Garvey, Jr., put this point with a brutal and disarming clarity in a 1974 anthology organized as a tribute to his father:

> African National Socialism postulates that the children of the Black God of Africa have a date with destiny. We shall recreate the glories of ancient Egypt, Ethiopia and Nubia. It is natural that the children of mother Africa scattered in the great diaspora will cleave together once more. It seems certain that the world will one day be faced with the black cry for an African "Anschluss" and the resolute demand for African "Lebensraum."[37]

The idea that fascism involved making politics aesthetic also raises the question of its exceptional status and relationship to the normal business of the bourgeois nation-state in which politics has had to become aesthetic to hold the attention of people sensitized to the accelerated communicative pace of advertising. The recent bloody histories of authoritarian regimes in Iran, Greece, Latin America, Indo-China, and Africa all suggest that fascism is not productively grasped as Europe's own private and internal drama. Though it is neither the flipside of a Europe-centered modernity nor something eternal and evil, outside of history and secular morality altogether, it does have something to do with the pathologies of modern development that Rousseau called "the fatal ingenuities of civilized man." The capacity to perpetrate evil is not itself modern, but the metaphysics of modernity brought a special tone to it. The scale and power of the nation-state condition it. We have to deal, not only with the old dangers of occultism and irrationality, but with the new evils represented by the rational application of irrationality. There is a utopian element here, too, and it is signaled in the antidemocratic but nonetheless modern value of fraternity and projected through the desire for a simpler world premised on racial sameness and racial certainties. Homogeneity and hypersimilarity become the principles of a hierarchical, authoritarian, and antimodern bonding. Solidarity is simulated in silent, spectacular rituals that must remain voiceless in order to mask the differentiation within the totality. The modern impulse to recreate and perfect the world is trivialized by being reduced to a narrowly racial project. We must concede today that making politics aesthetic has become harder to distinguish from Walter Benjamin's alternative—the politicization of art—and that both possibilities exist together, embedded in the more benign but decidedly volatile forms of authoritarian populism to which we have grown accustomed in the overdeveloped countries.

It bears repeating that a susceptibility to the appeal of authoritarian irrationalism has become part of what it means to be a modern person. It is bound to the dreams of enlightenment and autonomy as an ever-present alternative. To recognize that blacks are not after all a permanently innocent people, forever immune to this dismal allure, is, perversely, to embrace our status as modern folk who can think and act for ourselves.

NOTES

1 Edith Sanders, "The Hamitic Hypothesis: Its Origins and Functions in Time Perspective," *Journal of African History*, 10 (1969), pp. 524–526.

2 "A Call to Arms, a Call to Sacrifice," *Nationalism Today* (not dated).

3 Ross Slater, "Revealed: the B.N.P.'s Black Buddies," *New Nation*, June 1998.

4 *The Guardian*, September 11, 1996, p. 5.

5 Marian A. L. Miller, *The Third World in Global Environmental Politics* (Open University Press, 1995).

6 Kiema Mayo Dawsey, "Caught Up in the (Gangsta) Rapture: Dr. C. Del Tucker's Crusade Against 'Gangsta Rap'" and "Reality Check," both in *The Source* (June 1994).

7 Richard King, M.D., *African Origin of Biological Psychiatry* (U.B. and U.S. Communications Systems, 1990).

8 Douglass S. Massey and Nancy A. Denton, *American Apartheid: Segregation and the Making of the Underclass* (Harvard University Press, 1993).

9 *New York Times Magazine*, April 3, 1994, p. 45.

10 Primo Levi, *The Drowned and the Saved*, trans. R. Rosenthal (Summit Books, 1988), p. 27.

11 Yehuda Bauer, *Jews for Sale? Nazi-Jewish Negotiations, 1933–1945* (Yale University Press, 1994).

12 "Frankly it ain't none of your business. What have you got to say about it? Did you teach Malcolm? Did you clean up Malcolm? Did you put Malcolm out before the world? Was Malcolm your traitor or was he ours? And if we dealt with him like a nation deals with a traitor, what the hell business is it of yours? You just shut your mouth and stay out of it. Because in the future, we are going to become a nation. And a nation gotta be able to deal with traitors, cutthroats and turncoats. The white man deals with his. The Jews deal with theirs. Salman Rushdie wrote a nasty thing about the Prophet, and Imam Khomeini put a death thing on him." These words were delivered by Minister Farrakhan at a closed meeting in his mosque in February 1993. They are quoted in the film *Brother Minister* made by Jefri Aalmuhammed, Jack Baxter, and Lewis Kesten (phone 516–625–5561).

13 Wilson J. Moses, *The Golden Age of Black Nationalism, 1850–1925* (Oxford University Press, 1988), p. 197.

14 Frederick Douglass, "What Are the Coloured People Doing for Themselves?" in H. Brotz, ed., *African-American Social and Political Thought* (Transaction, 1992), pp. 204–205; Martin Delany, *The Origins and Objects of Ancient Freemasonry: Its Introduction into the United States and Legitimacy among Colored Men* (Pittsburgh, 1853).

15 Prince Hall masonry was the black system of freemasonry in the eighteenth century. See Donn A. Cass, *Negro Freemasonry and Segregation* (Ezra A. Cook Publications, 1957); William A. Muraskin, *Middle Class Blacks in a White Society: Prince Hall Freemasonry in America* (University of California Press, 1975); Harry E. Davis, *A History of Freemasonry Among Negroes in America* (United Supreme Council, Ancient and Accepted Scottish Rite of Freemasonry, 1946); Loretta J. Williams, *Black Freemasonry and Middle-Class Realities* (University of Missouri Press, 1980).

16 Steven Howe's *Afrocentrism: Mythical Pasts and Imagined Homes* (Verso, 1998), is a notable exception to this pattern; see chapter 6, "The Masonic Connection."

17 Claude Andrew Clegg III, *An Original Man: The Life of Elijah Muhammad* (St. Martin's Press, 1997).

18 The important issue of continuities between these movements is complex, with interaction and overlap to be found at different levels, and thus it cannot be settled here. The perils of attempting to deal superficially with the topic are amply illustrated by the failures of Mattias Gardell's *Countdown to Armageddon: Louis Farrakhan and the Nation of Islam* (Hurst and Co., 1996).

19 Nicholas Goodrick-Clarke, *The Occult Roots of Nazism: Secret Aryan Cults and Their Influence on Nazi Ideology* (I. B. Tauris, 1992); and *Hitler's Priestess: Savitri Devi, the Hindu-Aryan Myth and Neo-Nazism* (New York University Press, 1998); Daniel Pipes, *Conspiracy: How the Paranoid Style Flourishes and Where It Comes From* (Free Press, 1997).

20 Georg Simmel, "The Secret and the Secret Society," in *The Sociology of Georg Simmel*, ed. and trans. Kurt H. Wolff (Free Press, 1950), pp. 307–376.

21 Marita Golden, *Saving Our Sons: Raising Black Children in a Turbulent World* (Anchor, 1995); Haki R. Madhubuti, *Black Men: Obsolete, Single, Dangerous? The Afrikan American Family in Transition* (Third World Press, 1990).

22 Roberto Vivarelli, "Interpretations of the Origins of Fascism," *Journal of Modern History*, 63 (March 1991), pp. 29–43.

23 Roger Griffin, *The Nature of Fascism* (Routledge, 1993).

24 Zeev Sternhell, *The Birth of Fascist Ideology* (Princeton University Press, 1993).

25 Max Weinreich, *Hitler's Professors: The Part of Scholarship in Germany's Crimes Against the Jewish People* (Yiddish Scientific Institute, 1948); Henry Friedlander, *The Origins of Nazi Genocide: From Euthanasia to the Final Solution* (University of North Carolina Press, 1995); Hans Peter Bluel, *Sex and Society in Nazi Germany* (J. B. Lippincott Co., 1973); Michael Stolleis, *The Law under the Swastika: Studies on Legal History in Nazi Germany*, trans. Thomas Dunlap (University of Chicago Press, 1998).

26 Alain Finkielkraut, *Remembering in Vain: The Klaus Barbie Trial and Crimes against Humanity* (Columbia University Press, 1992).

27 Anna Bramwell, *The Ecological Movement in the Twentieth Century: A History* (Yale University Press, 1989); Janet Biehl, " 'Ecology' and the Modernization of Fascism in the German Ultra-Right," *Society and Nature*, 5 (1994), pp. 130–170.

28 George Mosse, *Toward the Final Solution: A History of European Racism* (University of Wisconsin Press, 1985), and Mosse, ed., *Nazi Culture: Intellectual, Cultural, and Social Life in the Third Reich* (Schocken, 1966); Alison Owings, *Frauen: German Women Recall the Third Reich* (Penguin, 1995); Detlev Peukert, *Inside Nazi Germany: Conformity, Opposition, and Racism in Everyday Life* (Penguin Books, 1993); Jill Stephenson, *Women in Nazi Society* (Croom Helm, 1975); Peter Adam, *The Arts of the Third Reich* (Thames and Hudson, 1992); Michael Kater, *Different Drummers: Jazz in the Culture of Nazi Germany* (Oxford University Press, 1992), and *The Twisted Muse: Musicians and Their Music in the Third Reich* (Oxford University Press, 1997); Robert Wistrich, *Weekend in Munich: Art, Propaganda, and Terror in the Third Reich* (Pavilion Books, 1995).

29 Stefan Kuhl, *The Nazi Connection. Eugenics, American Racism, and German National Socialism* (Oxford University Press, 1994); Edward J. Larson, *Sex, Race, and Science: Eugenics in the Deep South* (Johns Hopkins University Press, 1995).

30 C.L.R James, *A History of Negro Revolt* (Fact Ltd., 1985 [1938]), p. 53.

31 J. A. Rogers, *The World's Great Men of Color* (J. A. Rogers, c. 1947), p. 420; see also Robert A. Hill, introduction to Robert A. Hill and Barbara Bair, eds., *Marcus Garvey, Life and Lessons: A Centennial Companion to the Marcus Garvey and Universal Negro Improvement Association Papers* (University of California Press, 1987), p. lviii.

32 Robert A. Hill, "Making Noise: Marcus Garvey Dada, August 1922," in Deborah Willis, ed., *Picturing Us: African American Identity in Photography* (The New Press, 1994).

33 Judith Stein, *The World of Marcus Garvey* (Louisiana State University Press, 1986), p. 154.

34 Marcus Garvey, "The Ideals of Two Races," *Philosophy and Opinions of Marcus Garvey*, vol. 2 (Frank Cass, 1967), p. 338.

35 Zora Neale Hurston, *Tell My Horse: Voodoo and Life in Haiti and Jamaica* (Harper, 1990), p. 89.

36 Malcolm X, *The Last Speeches* (Pathfinder Press, 1989), pp. 135–136.

37 Marcus Garvey, Jr., "Garveyism: Some Reflections on Its Significance for Today," in John Henrik Clarke, ed., with the assistance of Amy Jacques Garvey, *Marcus Garvey and the Vision of Africa* (Vintage, 1974), p. 387.

V

Hybrid Identities

Thomas Babington Macaulay's attempt to anglicize the colonial Indian subject, to create "a class of persons, Indian in blood and colour, but English in taste, in opinions," explicitly acknowledges the formidable capacity of the colonial apparatus and of education, in particular, to transform a potentially alien and recalcitrant subject into a useful intermediary, even an expedient ally (see chapter 9). But it also tacitly signals the possibility that the gulf between the colonizer and the colonized is not as unbridgeable as it might seem, setting the stage, as the scholars in part V demonstrate, for anxieties and ambivalences on both sides. Although the colonial encounter involved more than a simple clash of civilizations, there was undoubtedly a transformation of identities through cultural contact, a process of uneven psychic exchange between the dominant and the subordinate groups that was inevitable in the circumstances. Frantz Fanon, for instance, would agree with his fellow Martinican and teacher Aimé Césaire that the psychological effects on the colonizers were intense (and he himself conducted studies on French soldiers in Algeria), but he was understandably more invested in examining the traumatic effects of colonialism on its subjects. In a diagnosis that combined the political with the psychological, Fanon concluded that colonialism had pathological effects that must be expelled in order to heal the colonized personality. So severe was the damage, according to an increasingly militant Fanon, that nothing short of apocalyptic violence would dislodge the colonial stranglehold and fully liberate the colonial subject.

Octave Mannoni, who was as interested as Fanon in the psychic dynamics of colonial relations and the ways in which they were expressed or enacted, writes after just such a violent insurrection predicted by Fanon. Mannoni, a French ethnologist and administrator who spent twenty years in Madagascar, uses psychoanalysis to explain, among other things, the widespread anticolonial insurgency of 1947 by the Mouvement Démocratique de la Rénovation Malgache (MDRM) and its ferocious repression by the

French authorities and their Seneghalese conscripts, leading to the death of about a hundred thousand Malagasy. In *Psychologie de la colonisation* (translated into English as *Prospero and Caliban: The Psychology of Colonization*), Mannoni formulates two personality types to account for both colonial rule and the conflict that followed. In his account, the Europeans, here specifically the French, have evolved through various stages from feudalism to independence. But with individualism and republicanism comes an inferiority complex that drives them to overcompensate psychologically by seeking to control others, here the Malagasy. The Malagasy, in contrast, though more evolved than the "primitive" Africans, were still at the feudal stage, and so depended on forceful authority to dominate them. The colonial situation, then, seems to resolve both neuroses (read as cause rather than as effect), since those who had inferiority complexes find their match in needy others whom they colonize.

As disturbing as this neat historical outcome is, what is even more unsettling is Mannoni's explanation for why the "Caliban" types, the partially assimilated Malagasy, ultimately revolt from colonial authority. Rather than understanding this act as the logical outcome of a desire for political independence by those who resent its absence, Mannoni finds it analogous to the fit thrown by Caliban upon his "abandonment" by Prospero in Shakespeare's *The Tempest*, a play that was to be interpreted to different ends by anticolonial intellectuals such as Roberto Fernández Retamar and George Lamming (see part II). To be fair, Mannoni went on to revise, even reject, some of the premises of his early work, but we include the controversial analysis since it has been the subject of much debate among its detractors, notably Césaire and Fanon, and as Mannoni's defenders would argue, it has been subject to some misunderstanding as well.

Despite the problems in Mannoni's analysis, some of his early work is still worth salvaging. For instance, suggesting that colonizers suffered from an inferiority complex was radical for his time, raising the possibility that colonial power was neither as stable nor as superior as it was made out to be. Likewise, Mannoni's complex readings of assimilation and his critique of French responses, including the inability of the French to accept the fact that some Malagasy chose not to adapt to or mimic the Europeans, or did so only partly, anticipate Homi Bhabha's poststructuralist and psychoanalytic scrutiny of the process of mimicry presented in this section.

Derek Walcott anticipates Bhabha in emphasizing agency rather than passive assimilation in the tactics of mimicry. Walcott's lecture "The Caribbean: Culture or Mimicry?" is a response to V. S. Naipaul's scathing dismissals of Caribbean cultures as poor copies, pathetic imitations of European and more recently North American prototypes. According to Walcott, Naipaul's construction of "mimic men," the title of one of his novels, condemns the Caribbean to being an inauthentic, repetitive, hollow echo of more vital and creative cultures. Walcott, however, refuses to give the "conqueror" complete power over the "victim," or to assume that power alone determines a unidirectional pattern to mimicry. Instead he argues not only that mimicry is a creative and subversive defense mechanism (a camouflage, as in the epigraph from Jacques Lacan in Bhabha's essay), but also, as poststructuralists were to insist, that repetition always involves difference. Signifying on Naipaul's indictment, Walcott twists it around to claim famously, "Nothing will always be created in the West Indies, for quite a long time, because what will come out of there is like nothing one has ever seen before." Mindful of the fact that he is giving his lecture in Miami, Walcott also aligns the Caribbean with the rest of the Americas, seizing on the possibilities of the New World, reading it not as an inferior and infantile version but as a regenerative space that exceeded the prescribed and stagnant limits of the Old World. If, as Mannoni advises, one does not look for the repetition of the same and find grotesque failure in its incomplete appearance (partial assimilation), then, in Walcott's view, what might seem merely imitative—the Carnival, the calypso, the steel drum—may actually have inventive potential.

Interestingly, Homi Bhabha's perspective on Naipaul attributes more critical, parodic force to the latter's portrayal of mimicry than allowed for by Walcott, even as Bhabha would agree that mimicry is not only failed imitation; that, as Walcott puts it, "there is something else going on." In an assessment of insecure power that echoes Mannoni, Bhabha argues that various colonial exploits are not just incited by the colonized subjects, but induced by "the twin figures of narcissism and paranoia that repeat furiously, uncontrollably" in the unraveling psyche of the colonizers. For Bhabha as for Walcott, the colonial subject is never all-powerful and the object of colonial control is never completely passive. Undermined from within by instability, double standards, and contradictory articulations and from without by the threatening "success of colonial appropriation," the Self/Other binary of the colonial equation has a more conflicted relationship than expected. As Bhabha concludes, the "ambivalence of colonial authority repeatedly turns from *mimicry*—a difference that is almost nothing but not quite—to *menace*—a difference that is almost total but not quite."

The Créolité intellectuals Jean Bernabé, Patrick Chamoiseau, and Raphaël Confiant use a different term to reject both Europe and Africa as authentic, originary models for their creolized islands. Using exteriority rather than mimicry to signify the morbid turn outward, the trio insist in their essay "Éloge de la créolité" (translated into English in 1990) that the epigonous history of Caribbean production must give way to a sustained, inward-flowing, hybrid sense of "Caribbeanness." In a rather circular formulation, Creoleness, they declare, is what determines their Caribbeanness. "Creoleness is the *interactional or transactional aggregate* of Caribbean, European, African, Asian, and Levantine cultural elements, united on the same soil by the yoke of [colonial] history." Although their poetic declamations tend to make the precise understanding of creolized identity slippery and sometimes too broad, stretching across the Atlantic and Pacific Rims, the ultimate common ground seems to be the plantation economy, the shared experience of slavery and indentured labor. But neither the United States nor the Trinidadian East

Indians serve as successful creolized communities for these intellectuals, since both are insular in different ways. The North Americans and the East Indians have the potential to be creolized, however, once they adapt to the new environment and open up to a "mixed culture" in which no single component is individually or hierarchically valued. The term "Creole" has a wide and complex provenance, which might account for its elastic use by its advocates here. Much work still remains to be done in the theory of creolization over a decade after the publication of "Éloge de la créolité," when Bernabé, Chamoiseau, and Confiant together made a plea for the particular identity of the Caribbean to be given its own unique name.

Of all the writers in part V, Jana Sequoya is the most attentive to the precise material conditions that dictate how some identities are formed or reshaped. The title of her essay, "How (!) Is an Indian," which she adapts from a wryly comic anecdote relating a series of misunderstandings of Native American cultures, incorporates the other question of "who" is an Indian. In other words, the cultural and psychic factors of identity formation can never fully be separated from the material and historical realities. Inadequate access to their ancestral land and indigenous resources constantly affect "who" Native Americans see themselves as, and they are often forced to resort to the mythical, undifferentiated affiliation imposed upon them by the majority culture. Their very presence in a "postcolonial" society is itself inauthentic, Sequoya claims, both because it troubles the complacently conventional spaces and temporalities of colonial history and because the "Indian" who miraculously survives is an "unreadable sign." Critiquing the role of the academy and the revelations by "native informants" of what should be carefully guarded tribe lore, Sequoya draws attention to the paradox of sacrilegious disclosures that provide the authentic foundation for "the secular humanist and popular cultures of the Euroamerican tradition." But Sequoya is not opposed to the use of archaeological and archival research for the purpose of "recuperation." Nor is she trying to disinter a pure, untouched Indian "expert" who could best speak for her people. Acknowledging that mixed blood and bicultural identities are the tangible outcomes after years of colonization, Sequoya, herself of mixed descent, suggests that blood alone is no indication of commitment to the community or adherence to its customs. Like some of the other writers in this section, she admits that "syncretic" cultures and "emergent subjectivities" challenge "the relation of opposition between colonizer and colonized." But her desctiption of the ambivalence that accelerates the breakdown of the binary opposition is considerably more sobering than the accounts of any of the other writers in part V, who, as their critics have pointed out, sometimes get carried away by the discursive flamboyance of their otherwise brilliant insights into relational identities.

17

OCTAVE MANNONI

The Threat of Abandonment

To return to my main theme—when the Malagasy, with his dependent personality, is confronted with someone whose personality is free and independent, like that of the adult European, he cannot easily adapt himself to it.

The first attempt at adaptation takes place on the mythical level by means of a process of rationalization which I must mention because it is still 'true' in the eyes of the Malagasies. They think that the European has no soul. This is a living belief which they do not attempt to reduce to a formula, and it is firmly held because it is linked with the belief in the dead. To them it seems self-evident—a fact which gives us some insight into their concept of the soul. Ironically enough, of course, the very people the Malagasies accuse of having no soul are precisely those who thought to bring them the doctrine of the immortality of the spiritual substance.

The fact is that to the Malagasies the soul is virtually identical with dependence: it is that which requires the observance of the customs and respect for the *fady*; it is that which unites the family and the tribe; it is that which reappears, after death, in the dreams of the living, and so on. Proof of the Europeans' lack of soul is the fact that they have no cult of the dead and no white ghosts. To say that the white man has no conscience, that he does what he likes, that he has no soul, or that he has no ancestors is, for the Malagasy, to say the same thing in four different ways. I have never obtained from a Malagasy an account of a dream in which a white man figured —although this is not conclusive, for a Malagasy would never relate such a dream to a European.

The Malagasy in his way is unhappily aware of the white man's inferiority complex, just as the white man dimly—though to his advantage—comprehends the Malagasy's dependence complex. The Malagasy realizes that there is in the white man some force which drives him to seek constant change, to try out novelties, to make incessant demands, and to accomplish extraordinary things just to 'show off.' He understands it the more easily since the inferiority complex, though masked in him by his acceptance of dependence, is not entirely absent and in some circumstances becomes clearly apparent. On such occasions his Malagasy comrades say he is 'trying to play the *vazaha*,' and make fun of him. Playing the *vazaha* and swanking are virtually synonymous, and the Malagasy who begins to act in this way will not get very far or derive any great satisfaction from it unless he has been uprooted from his environment at an early age—for assuredly there is nothing to prevent a Malagasy acquiring a personality of the European type if he has been brought up from infancy in a European environment. But such a Malagasy will be a European and will have the complexes of a European. There may be some traits of character linked with the physical temperament, the manner of expressing emotion, for instance, which persist by way of racial characteristics—but even that is doubtful.

The situation is quite different in those cases, and they are not a few, where a Malagasy has during his youth—and not, be it noted, in infancy—acquired a European personality which is superimposed upon the Malagasy personality he already possessed. If he represses his Malagasy personality he is to all outward appearances a European, but his original personality has not been destroyed and will continue to manifest itself in disguise. If he returns to his own people his repressed personality will be awakened again by the environment. He is then rather in the position of a repressed homosexual among overt homosexuals, a situation which, as is well known, is liable to give rise to hatred, either conscious or otherwise. This explains why 'assimilated' natives have so very little influence, why the policy of bringing back to Madagascar Malagasies who have been thoroughly Europeanized in Europe, in the hope of fostering Franco-Malagasy, friendship, does not pay off as well as might, *a priori,* be expected. The complexes of the 'assimilated' drive them to seek the company of Europeans, but they are never received by them as equals. They are ill at ease in all societies, and the failure they embody heightens rather than diminishes consciousness of racial differences.[1]

If the Europeanized Malagasy is not to repress his Malagasy personality he must integrate his European elements into it—a difficult task for which his own goodwill and skilfulness are not enough; it is necessary in addition that the European and Malagasy environments should not place insurmountable obstacles in his way. If he fails in his task, his European personality will probably be just a slender *persona* and our 'civilized' man will have but a thin European veneer. The unenlightened would see this veneer as the cause of the familiar displays of vanity and manifestations of degradation; their observation of the facts would be correct but their explanation of them wrong: vanity is the price that is paid for failure and is a compensation for inferiority. The Malagasy is better off if he is deliberately hypocritical—and this, too, happens at times. Usually, however, things are less simple, for the original personality does not remain intact under its mask: in place of an almost megalomaniac vanity, resentment and hostility appear. These traits—vanity, hypocrisy, resentment—have sometimes been attributed to the Malagasies as a whole, but this is a mistake, for they are the consequence of unsuccessful Europeanization. Unfortunately, as things are at present—at any rate in Madagascar—Europeanization fails more often than it succeeds. It is more successful in Europe, for European society offers fewer obstacles, and there in any case the Malagasy personality is eventually repressed.

The Malagasy who can be most useful to us in forwarding Franco-Malagasy collaboration is the one who has preserved his Malagasy personality intact, adapting it, but not concealing it. A real understanding of this fact would lead to a total revision of our teaching methods, for all we do at present is to instruct the masses without adapting them to our civilization, and to cultivate the *élite* while suppressing their personalities, neither of which methods really improves the situation.

It is worthy of note that disturbances broke out at the very time when a number of Europeanized Malagasies were returning to Madagascar. Some of them—those who had been truly assimilated—broke with their compatriots, and thereafter had no influence on them. Others, whose assimilation had been incomplete, fomented and led the revolts, for they are the people most likely to develop a real hatred of Europeans. Caliban's dictum:

> You taught me language; and my profit on't
> Is, I know how to curse. . . ,

though it over-simplifies the situation, is true in essence. It is not that Caliban has savage and uneducable instincts or that he is so poor so that even good seed would bring forth bad plants, as Prospero believes. The real reason is given by Caliban himself:

> . . . When thou camest first,
> Thou strok'dst me, and mad'st much of me . . .
> . . . and then I lov'd thee

—and then you abandoned me before I had time to become your equal. . . . In other words: you taught me to be dependent, and I was happy; then you betrayed me and plunged me into inferiority. It is indeed in some such situation as this that we must look for the origin of the fierce hatred sometimes shown by 'evolved' natives; in them the process of civilization has come to a halt and been left incomplete.

In contrast, the Malagasy whose personality has been neither repressed nor masked, who has preserved his original dependence complex in all its purity, is not generally a prey to hostility towards the European. During the recent rebellion there was a number of cases where Malagasies who came to assassinate isolated

Europeans explained that they did so with regret in obedience to their chiefs, to whom they had sworn oaths of allegiance, and not out of any hatred.

NOTES

1 This failure is a good example of those false verifications by experience which are so frequently met with in the study of inter-racial relations.

To all appearances, in fact, these Europeanized Malagasies differ from Europeans proper only by the racial characteristics determined by their genetic stock, the most obvious of these being the colour of the skin. Thus it appears that the conditions are present for a verification by the 'method of difference' as conceived by inductive logic. The difference in skin-colour is enough, in fact, for the European colonial society to refuse to receive these evolved natives into its midst (though it finds room for them in the administration). The Malagasy reacts to these difficulties with symptoms of inferiority, a need for compensation, feelings of abandonment, and so on. But his reaction is taken by the European for a racial characteristic, and racialism, which was at first spontaneous, becomes deliberate, and claims to be based on impartial observation. Typical Malagasies, for their part, noticing what happens to Europeanized Malagasies, draw their conclusions too. Thus, paradoxically, the more 'civilized' the colonial inhabitants become, the greater is the awareness on both sides of irremovable racial differences. These differences acquire exactly the importance attributed to them. Seen in this light, our old claim that we wanted to assimilate the Malagasies seems somewhat hypocritical, since in fact we denied them social assimilation. We may conclude that but for this hypocrisy assimilation would have been perfectly possible. But there is no doubt to-day that as a result of new unconscious convictions, this possibility has quite disappeared.

18

DEREK WALCOTT

The Caribbean

Culture or Mimicry?

We live in the shadow of an America that is economically benign yet politically malevolent. That malevolence, because of its size, threatens an eclipse of identity, but the shadow is as inescapable as that of any previous empire. But we were American even while we were British, if only in the geographical sense, and now that the shadow of the British Empire has passed through and over us in the Caribbean, we ask ourselves if, in the spiritual or cultural sense, we must become American. We have broken up the archipelago into nations, and in each nation we attempt to assert characteristics of the national identity. Everyone knows that these are pretexts of power if such power is seen as political. This is what the politician would describe as reality, but the reality is absurd. In the case of my own identity, or my realness if you like, it is an absurdity that I can live with; being both American and West Indian is an ambiguity without a crisis, for I find that the more West Indian I become, the more I can accept my dependence on America as a professional writer, not because America owes me a living from historical guilt, nor that it needs my presence, but because we share this part of the world, and have shared it for centuries now, even as conqueror and victim, as exploiter and exploited. What has happened here has happened to us. In other words that shadow is less malevolent than it appears, and we can absorb it because we know that America is black, that so much of its labor, its speech, its music, its very style of living is generated by what is now cunningly and carefully isolated as "black" culture, that what is most original in it has come out of its ghettos, its river-cultures, its plantations. Power itself is ephemeral, unstable. It is the least important aspect of any culture, who rules.

So, in the Caribbean, we do not pretend to exercise power in the historical sense. I think that what our politicians define as power, the need for it, or the lack of it should have another name; that, like America, what energizes our society is the spiritual force of a culture shaping itself, and it can do this without the formula of politics.

To talk about the contribution of the black man to American culture or civilization is absurd, because it is the black who energized that culture, who styles it, just as it is the black who preserved and energized its faith. The most significant experience in America's recent past is this revolution, and it is a revolution that was designed by the poets and intellectuals of our powerless archipelago, by West Indians like Garvey, Césaire, Fanon, Padmore, and Stokely if you wish, and so our definitions of power must go beyond the immediately political. We can see this and still keep distinctions. In fact it is only because these leaders could make distinctions that they could see the necessity for certain actions. And that is what I mean by being both West Indian and American. This is not schizophrenia. Remember our experience of different empires. Those experiences have been absorbed. To us, in many ways, America is a young country, and that is why the metaphor exists in the minds of every revolutionary. Many of us in the Caribbean still hold the ideal of the archipelago, just as you here hold to the metaphor named America. If I speak in the tone of metaphor among men who are more practical in their approach to problems, it is because I do not think that as men of the Americas, we are different. Our society may be less complex. It is obviously powerless. What I hope to explore is that society's validity, its reality.

To begin with, we are poor. That gives us a privilege. The poor always claim intimacy with God over the rich. Emergent countries simplify man's political visions in like manner because they are reduced to essentials. Like faith, it remains the American problem, how to be rich and still good, how to be great and exercise compassion.

Perhaps powerlessness leaves the Third World, the ex-colonial world, no alternative but to imitate those systems offered to or forced on it by the major powers, their political systems which must alter their common life, their art, their language, their philosophy. On the other hand, the bitterness of the colonial experience, its degradations of dependency and its cynicism of older "values" tempts the Third World with spiritual alternatives. These alternatives will be violent, the total rejection through revolution, for example, or cunning, or conservative, by which I mean the open assimilation of what is considered from the metropolitan center to be most useful. But whichever method is applied, it is obvious that the metamorphosis is beginning. Large sections of the population of this earth have nothing to lose after their history of slavery, colonialism, famine, economic exploitation, patronage, contempt. But the tragedy is that most of its politicians are trapped in the concept of a world proposed by those who rule it, and these politicians see progress as inevitability. They have forgotten the desperate authority of the man who has nothing. In that sense Naipaul is right, that their mimicry of power defrauds their own people. Such politicians insist on describing potential in the same terms as those whom they must serve; they talk to us in the bewildering code of world markets, and so forth. They use, in short, the calculus of contemporary history, and that gives them and us the illusion that we really contribute to the destiny of mankind, to foreign policy. We align ourselves to this bloc or that, to that way of life or the other, and it is this tiredness, which falls so quickly on the powerless, that horrifies Naipaul; but the truth is that there is something else going on, that this is not the force of the current, and that its surface may be littered with the despairs of broken systems and of failed experiments, that the river, stilled, may reflect, mirror, mimic other images, but that is not its depth.

It could not be. You see, the degradations have already been endured; they have been endured to the point of irrelevancy. In the Caribbean history is irrelevant, not because it is not being created, or because it was sordid; but because it has never mattered, what has mattered is the loss of history, the amnesia of the races, what has become necessary is imagination, imagination as necessity, as invention.

The phrase "the mimic men," which so many English-speaking West Indian intellectuals have so eagerly, almost masochistically taken to themselves, originates in the East Indian novelist Vidia Naipaul, who uses it as the title for one of his novels. Mr. Naipaul's epitaph on all West Indian endeavor has not aborted the passion with which West Indian culture continues to procreate this mimicry, because life, if we can call it that in the archipelago, defiantly continues.

To mimic, one needs a mirror, and, if I understand Mr. Naipaul correctly, our pantomime is conducted before a projection of ourselves which in its smallest gestures is based on metropolitan references. No gesture, according to this philosophy, is authentic, every sentence is a quotation, every movement either ambitious or pathetic, and because it is mimicry, uncreative. The indictment is crippling, but, like all insults, it contains an astonishing truth. The only thing is that it is not, to my mind, only the West Indies which is being insulted by Naipaul, but all endeavor in this half of the world, in broader definition: the American endeavor.

I use the word American regardless of genetic variety and origin. Once the meridian of European civilization has been crossed, according to the theory, we have entered a mirror where there can only be simulations of self-discovery. The civilized virtues on the other side of this mirror are the virtues of social order, a lineally clear hierarchy, direction, purpose, balance. With these things, so we were taught, come social justice and the exercise of racial memory which is tradition. Somehow, the cord is cut by that meridian. Yet a return is also impossible, for we cannot return to what we have never been. The truth in all this is, of course, the amnesia of the American, particularly of the African. Most of our definitions of American culture are fragmentary, based on the gleam of racial memory which pierces this amnesia. The Old World, whether it is represented by the light of Europe or of Asia or of Africa, is the rhythm by which we remember. What we have carried over, apart from a few desultorily performed customs, is language. When language itself is condemned as mimicry, then the condition is hopeless and men are no more than jackdaws, parrots, myna birds, apes.

The idea of the American as ape is heartening, however, for in the imitation of apes there is something more ancient than the first human effort. The absurdity of pursuing the anthropological idea of mimicry then, if we are to believe science, would lead us to the image of the first ape applauding the gestures of what we must call the first man. Here the contention crumbles because there is no scientific distinction possible between the last ape and the first man, there is no memory or history of the moment when man stopped imitating the ape, his ancestor, and became human. Therefore, everything is mere repetition. Did the first ape look at his reflection in the mirror of a pond in astonishment or in terror? Could it, or he, identify its or himself, and what name was given to that image? And was it at that moment of the self-naming grunt, a grunt delivered either in terror or in amusement, that the ape became man? And was that the beginning of the human ego and our history?

Advance some thousand years, protract the concept of evolution to the crossing of the mirror and the meridian of Alexander VI, and, like that instant of self-recognition or self-disgust, which are the same, what was the moment when the old ape of the Old World saw himself anew and became another, or, was paralyzed with the knowledge that henceforth, everything he did in the New World, on the other side of the mirror, could only be a parody of the past? Of course there is no such moment, just as there is no such moment for science of the transition from ape to man.

Columbus kneels on the sand of San Salvador. That is a moment. Bilbao, or Keats's Cortez looks on the Pacific. That is another moment. Lewis and Clark behold whatever they beheld, and that is yet another moment. What do they behold? They behold the images of themselves beholding. They are looking into the mirror of the sea (the phrase is mimicked from Joseph Conrad), or the mirror of the plain, the desert, or the sky. We in the Americas are taught this as a succession of illuminations, lightning moments that must crystallize and irradiate memory if we are to believe in a chain of such illuminations known as history. To make a swift leap, probably without the mimicry of Aristotelian logic; because these illuminations are literary and not in the experience of American man, they are worthless. We cannot focus on a single ancestor, that moment of ape to man if you wish, or its reverse, depending on what side of the mirror you are favoring, when the black felt that he had crossed the meridian, when the East Indian had, or the Portugese, or the Chinese, or the Old World Jew. There was no line in the sea which said, this is new, this is the frontier, the boundary of endeavor, and henceforth everything can only be mimicry. But there was such a moment for every individual American, and that moment was both surrender and claim, both possession and dispossession. The issue is the claim.

The moment then, that a writer in the Caribbean, an American man, puts down a word—not only the first writer whoever he was, in Naipaul's view, but every writer since—at that moment he is a mimic, a mirror man, he is the ape beholding himself. This is supposed to be true as well of the dancer, the sculptor, the citizen, anyone in the Caribbean who is fated to unoriginality. So, of course, is Mr. Naipaul, whose curse extends to saying of this place that "nothing has ever been created in the West Indies, and nothing will ever be created." Precisely, precisely. We create nothing, but that is to move from anthropological absurdity to pseudo-philosophical rubbish, to discuss the reality of nothing, the mathematical conundrum of zero and infinity. Nothing will always be created in the West Indies, for quite a long time, because what will come out of there is like nothing one has ever seen before.

The ceremony which best exemplifies this attitude to history is the ritual of Carnival. This is a mass art form which came out of nothing, which emerged from the sanctions imposed on it. The banning of African drumming led to the discovery of the garbage can cover as a potential musical instrument whose subtlety of range, transferred to the empty oil drum, increases yearly, and the calypso itself emerged from a sense of mimicry, of patterning its form both on satire and self-satire. The impromptu elements of the calypso, like the improvisation and invention of steelband music, supersedes its traditional origins, that is, the steeldrum supersedes the attempt to copy melody from the xylophone and the drum, the calypso supersedes its ancient ritual forms in group chanting. From the viewpoint of history, these forms originated in imitation if you want, and ended in invention; and the same is true of the Carnival costume, its intricate, massive, and delicate sculpture improvised without a self-conscious awe of reality, for the simple duplication of ancient sculptures is not enough to make a true Carnival costume. Here are three forms, originating from the mass, which are original and temporarily as inimitable as what they first attempted to copy. They were made from nothing, in their resulting forms it is hard to point to mere imitation.

But more significant than this is the attitude to such a prolixity of creative will that is jeered at as the "Carnival mentality." The carnival mentality seriously, solemnly dedicates itself to the concept of waste, of ephemera, of built-in obsolescence, but this is not the built-in obsolescence of manufacture but of art, because in Carnival the creative energy is strictly regulated to its own season. Last year's intricate sculptures are discarded as immediately valueless when it is midnight on Shrove Tuesday, last year's songs cannot be sung this year, nor last year's tunes, and so an entire population of craftsmen and spectators compel themselves to this regeneration of perpetually making it new, and by that rhythm create a backlog of music, design, song, popular poetry which is as strictly observed as the rhythm of cane harvest and cane-burning, of both industry and religion. The energy alone is overwhelming, and best of all, on one stage, at any moment, the simultaneity of historical legends, epochs, characters, without historical sequence or propriety is accepted as a concept.

Mimicry is an act of imagination, and, in some animals and insects, endemic cunning. Lizards, chameleons, most butterflies, and certain insects adapt the immediate subtleties of color and even of texture both as defense and as lure. Camouflage, whether it is in the grass-blade stripes of the tiger or the eyed hide of the leopard, is mimicry, or more than that, it is design. What if the man in the New World needs mimicry as design, both as defense and as lure? We take as long as other fellow creatures in the natural world to adapt and then blend into our habitats, whether we possess these environments by forced migration or by instinct. That is genetics. Culture must move faster, defensively. Everyone knows that there are differences between, say, plains cultures and sea cultures, or mountain cultures and jungle cultures, and if we see that in the Caribbean particularly, creatures from these different regions, forced into a common environment, still carry over their genetic coloring, their racial or tribal camouflage, the result, for a long time, can only be a bewildering variety that must race its differences rapidly into stasis, into recognition. The rapidity with which this is happening in the Caribbean looks like confusion.

But those who see only disorder, futility, and chaos must look for the patterns which they produce, and they will find in those patterns contradicting strains which often were not meant to adapt, far more survive. There were those who did not survive, not by weakness but by a process of imperialistic defoliation which blasted defiance; and this process, genocide, is what destroyed the original, destroyed the Aztec, and American Indian, and the Caribbean Indian. All right, let us say what these had was not a culture, not a civilization, but a way of life, then, a way with their own gods and language and domestic or marital customs. The point is that they broke, that they were resilient for a while but were broken. These have gone. They left few ruins, since the ego was tribal, not individualistic, pagan if you want, not Christian. We can praise them for not imitating, but even imitation decimated them, or has humiliated them like the aborigine and the American Indian. What have we been offered here as an alternative but suicide? I do not know if apes commit suicide—their mimicry is not that far advanced—but men do, and it appears too, certain cultures.

That is the process by which we were Christianized. The imitation of Christ, the mimicry of God as a man. In that sense the first Christian is also not only the first man but the first ape, since before that everything was hearsay. The imitation of Christ must be carried into human life and social exchange, we are responsible for our brother, we are not responsible to ourselves but to God, and while this is admirable and true, how true is it that the imitation of God leads to human perfectibility, how necessary is it for us to mimic the supreme good, the perfect annihilation of present, past, and future since God is without them, so that a man who has achieved that spiritual mimicry immediately annihilates all sense of time. "Take no thought of the morrow" is the same as "history is bunk"; the first is from Christ, the second from Henry Ford. But Ford is the divine example of American materialist man. Ford is an inventor, Ford created cars, Edison created light, and so it goes. What surrounds all of us as mimic men is that gratitude which acknowledges those achievements as creation. We are thus taught specific distances between the word invention and the word creation, between the inventor and the creator. We invent nothing, that is, no object. We do not have the resources, we can argue. Well, neither did Ford, neither did Edison. But electricity and light and even the idea of the car existed before they were discovered. They were not creations, they are also mimicry, originating from the existence and the accidents of natural elements. We continue far enough and we arrive at Voltaire confronting Nietzsche: "It is necessary to invent God," and "God is dead." Join both, and that is our twentieth-century credo. "It is necessary to invent a God who is dead."

Where have cultures originated? By the force of natural surroundings. You build according to the topography of where you live. You are what you eat, and so on; you mystify what you see, you create what you need spiritually, a god for each need.

If religion is not a life, if it is not itself mere mimicry of some unappeasable fear, then is not the good man a man who needs nothing? And I do not mean a man who does not need a car, nor electricity, nor television or whatever else we have failed to invent in the Caribbean, but a man who does not need them in the religious sense, a man who is dependent on the elements, who inhabits them, and takes his life from them. Even further, the ideal man does not need literature, religion, art, or even another, for there is ideally only himself and God. What he needs he makes, and what he makes will become more subtle in its uses, dependent on the subtlety of his needs or the proliferation of his creature comforts. That pursuit takes him further away from his mystical relation to the universe, thins its mystery, distances the idea of prayer, awe, spiritual necessity, until he can ask, surrounded by his own creations, "who needs God?"

No, cultures can only be created out of this knowledge of nothing, and in deeper than the superficial, existential sense, we in the Caribbean know all about nothing. We know that we owe Europe either revenge or nothing, and it is better to have nothing than revenge. We owe the past revenge or nothing, and revenge is uncreative. We may not even need literature, not that we are beyond it, but in the archipelago particularly, nature, the elements if you want, are so new, so overpowering in their presence that awe is deeper than articulation of awe. To name is to contradict. The awe of God or of the universe is the unnameable, and this has nothing to do with literacy. It is better for us to be a race of illiterates who retain this awe than to be godless, without mystery. A pygmy is better than an atheist. Sophistication is human wisdom and we who are the dregs of that old history, its victims, its transients, its dispossessed know what the old wisdom brought. What is called mimicry is the painful, new, laborious uttering that comes out of belief, not out of doubt. The votive man is silent, the cynical is articulate. Ask any poet which he would prefer, poetry or silence, poetry or wisdom, and he would answer wisdom. It is his journey to self-annihilation, to beginning again.

History, taught as morality, is religion. History, taught as action, is art. Those are the only uses to which we, mocked as a people without history, can put it. Because we have no choice but to view history as fiction or as religion, then our use of it will be idiosyncratic, personal, and therefore, creative. All of this is beyond the sociological, even beyond the "civilized" assessment of our endeavor, beyond mimicry. The stripped and naked man, however abused, however disabused of old beliefs, instinctually, even desperately begins again as craftsman. In the indication of the slightest necessary gesture of ordering the world around him, of losing his old name and rechristening himself, in the arduous enunciation of a dimmed alphabet, in the shaping of tools, pen or spade, is the whole, profound sigh of human optimism, of what we in the archipelago still believe in: work and hope. It is out of this that the New World, or the Third World, should begin.

Theoretical and idealistic though this sounds, it is our duty as poets to reiterate it. The embittered despair of a New World writer like Naipaul is also part of that impatience and irascibility at the mere repetition of human error which passes for history, and that irascibility is also a belief in possibility. The New World originated in hypocrisy and genocide, so it is not a question for us, of returning to an Eden or of creating Utopia; out of the sordid and degrading beginning of the West Indies, we could only go further in decency and regret. Poets and satirists are afflicted with the superior stupidity which believes that societies can be renewed, and one of the most nourishing sites for such a renewal, however visionary it may seem, is the American archipelago.

19

HOMI BHABHA

Of Mimicry and Man

The Ambivalence of Colonial Discourse

Mimicry reveals something in so far as it is distinct from what might be called an itself that is behind. The effect of mimicry is camouflage. . . . It is not a question of harmonizing with the background, but against a mottled background, of becoming mottled—exactly like the technique of camouflage practised in human warfare.

—Jacques Lacan, "The Line and Light," *Of the Gaze*

It is out of season to question at this time of day, the original policy of conferring on every colony of the British Empire a mimic representation of the British Constitution. But if the creature so endowed has sometimes forgotten its real insignificance and under the fancied importance of speakers and maces, and all the paraphernalia and ceremonies of the imperial legislature, has dared to defy the mother country, she has to thank herself for the folly of conferring such privileges on a condition of society that has no earthly claim to so exalted a position. A fundamental principle appears to have been forgotten or overlooked in our system of colonial policy—that of colonial dependence. To give to a colony the forms of independence is a mockery; she would not be a colony for a single hour if she could maintain an independent station.

—Sir Edward Cust, "Reflections on West African Affairs . . . addressed to the Colonial Office," Hatchard, London, 1839

The discourse of post-Enlightenment English colonialism often speaks in a tongue that is forked, not false. If colonialism takes power in the name of history, it repeatedly exercises its authority through the figures of farce. For the epic intention of the civilizing mission, "human and not wholly human" in the famous words of Lord Rosebery, "writ by the finger of the Divine"[1] often produces a text rich in the traditions of *trompe l'oeil*, irony, mimicry, and repetition. In this comic turn from the high ideals of the colonial imagination to its low mimetic literary effects, mimicry emerges as one of the most elusive and effective strategies of colonial power and knowledge.

Within that conflictual economy of colonial discourse which Edward Said[2] describes as the tension between the synchronic panoptical vision of domination—the demand for identity, stasis—and the counter-pressure of the diachrony of history—change, difference—mimicry represents an *ironic* compromise. If I may adapt Samuel Weber's formulation of the marginalizing vision of castration,[3] then colonial mimicry is the desire for a reformed, recognizable Other, as *a subject of a difference that is almost the same, but not quite*. Which is to say, that the discourse of mimicry is constructed around an *ambivalence; in* order to be effective, mimicry must continually produce its slippage, its excess, its difference. The authority of that mode of colonial discourse that I have called mimicry is therefore stricken by an indeterminacy: mimicry emerges as the representation of a difference that is itself a process of disavowal. Mimicry is, thus, the sign of a double articulation; a complex strategy of reform, regulation, and discipline, which "appropriates" the Other as it visualizes power. Mimicry is also the sign of the inappropriate, however, a difference or recalcitrance which coheres the dominant strategic function of colonial power, intensifies surveillance, and poses an immanent threat to both "normalized" knowledges and disciplinary powers.

The effect of mimicry on the authority of colonial discourse is profound and disturbing. For in "normalizing" the colonial state or subject, the dream of post-Enlightenment civility alienates its own language of liberty and produces another knowledge of its norms. The ambivalence which thus informs this strategy is discernible, for example, in Locke's Second Treatise which *splits* to reveal the limitations of liberty in his double use of the word "slave": first simply, descriptively as the locus of a legitimate form of ownership, then as the trope for an intolerable, illegitimate exercise of power. What is articulated in that distance between the two uses is the absolute, imagined difference between the "Colonial" State of Carolina and the Original State of Nature.

It is from this area between mimicry and mockery, where the reforming, civilizing mission is threatened by the displacing gaze of its disciplinary double, that my instances of colonial imitation come. What they all share is a discursive process by which the excess or slippage produced by the *ambivalence* of mimicry (almost the same, *but not quite*) does not merely "rupture" the discourse, but becomes transformed into an uncertainty which fixes the colonial subject as a "partial" presence. By "partial" I mean both "incomplete" and "virtual." It is as if the very emergence of the "colonial" is dependent for its representation upon some strategic limitation or prohibition *within* the authoritative discourse itself. The success of colonial appropriation depends on a proliferation of inappropriate objects that ensure its strategic failure, so that mimicry is at once resemblance and menace.

A classic text of such partiality is Charles Grant's "Observations on the State of Society among the Asiatic Subjects of Great Britain" (1792)[4] which was only superseded by James Mills's *History of India* as the most influential early nineteenth-century account of Indian manners and morals. Grant's dream of an evangelical system of mission education conducted uncompromisingly in English was partly a belief in political reform along Christian lines and partly an awareness that the expansion of company rule in India required a system of "interpellation"—a reform of manners, as Grant put it, that would provide the colonial with "a sense of personal identity as we know it." Caught between the desire for religious reform and the fear that the Indians might become turbulent for liberty, Grant implies that it is, in fact the "partial" diffusion of Christianity, and the "partial" influence of moral improvements which will construct a particularly appropriate form of colonial subjectivity. What is suggested is a process of reform through which Christian doctrines might collude with divisive caste practices to prevent dangerous political alliances. Inadvertently, Grant produces a knowledge of Christianity as a form of social control which conflicts with the enunciatory assumptions which authorize his discourse. In suggesting, finally, that "partial reform" will produce an empty form of "the imitation of English manners which will induce them [the colonial subjects] to remain under our protection,"[5] Grant mocks his moral project and violates the Evidences of Christianity—a central missionary tenet—which forbade any tolerance of heathen faiths.

The absurd extravagance of Macaulay's *Infamous Minute* (1835)—deeply influenced by Charles Grant's *Observations*—makes a mockery of Oriental learning until faced with the challenge of conceiving of a "reformed" colonial subject. Then the great tradition of European humanism seems capable only of ironizing itself. At the intersection of European learning and colonial power, Macaulay can conceive of nothing other than "a class of interpreters between us and the millions whom we govern—a class of persons, Indian in blood and colour, but English in taste, in opinions, in morals, and in intellect"[6]—in other words a mimic man raised "through our English School," as a missionary educationist wrote in 1819, "to form a corps of translators and be employed in different departments of Labour."[7] The line of descent of the mimic man can be traced through the works of Kipling, Forester, Orwell, Naipaul, and to his emergence, most recently, in Benedict Anderson's excellent essay on nationalism, as the anomalous Bipin Chandra Pal.[8] He is the effect of a flawed colonial mimesis, in which to be Anglicized, is *emphatically* not to be English.

The figure of mimicry is locatable within what Anderson describes as "the inner incompatibility of empire and nation."[9] It problematizes the signs of racial and cultural priority, so that the "national" is no longer naturalizable. What emerges between mimesis and mimicry is a *writing,* a mode of representation, that marginalizes the monumentality of history, quite simply mocks its power to be a model, that power which supposedly makes it imitable. Mimicry *repeats* rather than *re-presents* and in that diminishing perspective emerges Decoud's displaced European vision of Sulaco as the endlessness of civil strife where folly seemed even harder to bear than its ignominy . . . the lawlessness of a populace of all colours and races, barbarism, irremediable tyranny. . . . America is ungovernable.[10]

Or Ralph Singh's apostasy in Naipaul's *The Mimic Men:*

We pretended to be real, to be learning, to be preparing ourselves for life, we mimic men of the New World, one unknown corner of it, with all its reminders of the corruption that came so quickly to the new.[11]

Both Decoud and Singh, and in their different ways Grant and Macaulay, are the parodists of history. Despite their intentions and invocations they inscribe the colonial text erratically, eccentrically across a body politic that refuses to be representative, in a narrative that refuses to be representational. The desire to emerge as "authentic" through mimicry—through a process of writing and repetition—is the final irony of partial representation.

What I have called mimicry is not the familiar exercise of *dependent* colonial relations through narcissistic identification so that, as Fanon has observed,[12] the black man stops being an actional person for only the white man can represent his self-esteem. Mimicry conceals no presence or identity behind its mask: it is not what Césaire describes as "colonization-thingification"[13] behind which there stands the essence of the *présence Africaine.* The *menace* of mimicry is its *double* vision which in disclosing the ambivalence of colonial discourse also disrupts its authority. And it is a double-vision that is a result of what I've described as the partial representation/recognition of the colonial object. Grant's colonial as partial imitator, Macaulay's translator, Naipaul's colonial politician as play-actor, Decoud as the scene setter of the *opéra bouffe* of the New World, these are the appropriate objects of a colonialist chain of command, authorized versions of otherness. But they are also, as I have shown, the figures of a doubling, the part-objects of a metonymy of colonial desire which alienates the modality and normality of those dominant discourses in which they emerge as "inappropriate" colonial subjects. A desire that, through the repetition of *partial presence,* which is the basis of mimicry, articulates those disturbances of cultural, racial, and historical difference that menace the narcissistic demand of colonial authority. It is a desire that reverses "in part" the colonial appropriation by now producing a partial vision of the colonizer's presence. A gaze of otherness, that shares the acuity of the genealogical gaze which, as Foucault describes it, liberates marginal elements and shatters the unity of man's being through which he extends his sovereignty.[14]

I want to turn to this process by which the look of surveillance returns as the displacing gaze of the disciplined, where the observer becomes the observed and "partial" representation rearticulates the whole notion of *identity* and alienates it from essence. But not before observing that even an exemplary history like Eric Stokes's *The English Utilitarians in India* acknowledges the anomalous gaze of otherness but finally disavows it in a contradictory utterance:

> Certainly India played *no* central part in fashioning the distinctive qualities of English civilisation. In many ways it acted as a disturbing force, a magnetic power placed at the periphery tending to distort the natural development of Britain's character. . . .[15]

What is the nature of the hidden threat of the partial gaze? How does mimicry emerge as the subject of the scopic drive and the object of colonial surveillance? How is desire disciplined, authority displaced?

If we turn to a Freudian figure to address these issues of colonial textuality, that form of difference that is mimicry—*almost the same but not quite*—will become clear. Writing of the partial nature of fantasy, caught *inappropriately,* between the unconscious and the preconscious, making problematic, like mimicry, the very notion of "origins," Freud has this to say:

> Their mixed and split origin is what decides their fate. We may compare them with individuals of mixed race who taken all round resemble white men but who betray their coloured descent by some striking feature or other and on that account are excluded from society and enjoy none of the privileges.[16]

Almost the same but not white: the visibility of mimicry is always produced at the site of interdiction. It is a form of colonial discourse that is uttered *inter dicta:* a discourse at the crossroads of what is known and permissible and that which though known must be kept concealed; a discourse uttered between the lines and as such both against the rules and within them. The question of the representation of difference is therefore always also a problem of authority. The "desire" of mimicry, which is Freud's *striking feature* that reveals so little but makes such a big difference, is not merely that impossibility of the Other which repeatedly resists signification. The desire of colonial mimicry—an interdictory desire—may not have an object, but it has strategic objectives which I shall call the *metonymy of presence.*

Those inappropriate signifiers of colonial discourse—the difference between being English and being Anglicized; the identity between stereotypes which, through repetition, also become different; the discriminatory identities constructed across traditional cultural norms and classifications, the Simian Black, the Lying Asiatic— all these are metonymies of presence. They are strategies of desire in discourse that make the anomalous representation of the colonized something other than a process of "the return of the repressed," what Fanon unsatisfactorily characterized as collective catharsis.[17] These instances of metonymy are the nonrepressive productions of contradictory and multiple belief. They cross the boundaries of the culture of enunciation through a strategic confusion of the metaphoric and metonymic axes of the cultural production of meaning. For each of these instances of "a difference that is almost the same but not quite" inadvertently creates a crisis for the cultural priority given to the *metaphoric* as the process of repression and substitution which negotiates the difference between paradigmatic systems and classifications. In mimicry, the representation of identity and meaning is rearticulated along the axis of metonymy. As Lacan reminds us, mimicry is like camouflage, not a harmonization or repression of difference, but a form of resemblance that differs/defends presence by displaying it in part, metonymically. Its threat, I would add, comes from the prodigious and strategic production of conflictual, fantastic, discriminatory "identity effects" in the play of a power that is elusive because it hides no essence, no "itself." And that form of *resemblance* is the most terrifying thing to behold, as Edward Long testifies in his *History of Jamaica* (1774). At the end of a tortured, negrophobic passage, that shifts anxiously between piety, prevarication, and perversion, the text finally confronts its fear; nothing other than the repetition of its resemblance "in part":

> (Negroes) are represented by all authors as the vilest of human kind, to which they have little more pretension of resemblance *than what arises from their exterior forms* (my italics).[18]

From such a colonial encounter between the white presence and its black semblance, there emerges the question of the ambivalence of mimicry as a problematic of colonial subjection. For if Sade's scandalous theatricalization of language repeatedly reminds us that discourse can claim "no priority," then the work of Edward Said will not let us forget that the "ethnocentric and erratic will to power from which texts can spring"[19] is itself a theater of war. Mimicry, as the metonymy of presence is, indeed, such an erratic, eccentric strategy of authority in colonial discourse. Mimicry does not merely destroy narcissistic authority through the repetitious slippage of difference and desire. It is the process of the *fixation* of the colonial as a form of cross-classificatory, discriminatory knowledge in the defiles of an interdictory discourse, and therefore necessarily raises the question of the *authorization* of colonial representations. A question of authority that goes beyond the subject's lack of priority (castration) to a historical crisis in the conceptuality of colonial man as an *object* of regulatory power, as the subject of racial, cultural, national representation.

"This culture . . . fixed in its colonial status," Fanon suggests, "(is) both present and mummified, it testified against its members. It defines them in fact without appeal."[20] The ambivalence of mimicry—almost but not quite—suggests that the fetishized colonial culture is potentially and strategically an insurgent counter-appeal. What I have called its "identity-effects," are always crucially *split*. Under cover of camouflage, mimicry, like the fetish, is a part-object that radically revalues the normative knowledges of the priority of race, writing, history. For the fetish mimes the forms of authority at the point at which it deauthorizes them. Similarly, mimicry rearticulates presence in terms of its "otherness," that which it disavows. There is a crucial difference between this *colonial* articulation of man and his doubles and that which Foucault describes as "thinking the unthought"[21] which, for nineteenth-century Europe, is the ending of man's alienation by reconciling him with his essence. The colonial discourse that articulates an *interdictory* "otherness" is precisely the "other scene" of this nineteenth-century European desire for an authentic historical consciousness.

The "unthought" across which colonial man is articulated is that process of classificatory confusion that I have described as the metonymy of the substitutive chain of ethical and cultural discourse. This results in the *splitting* of colonial discourse so that two attitudes towards external reality persist; one takes reality into consideration while the other disavows it and replaces it by a product of desire that repeats, rearticulates "reality" as mimicry.

So Edward Long can say with authority, quoting variously, Hume, Eastwick, and Bishop Warburton in his support, that:

> Ludicrous as the opinion may seem I do not think that an orangutang husband would be any dishonour to a Hottentot female.[22]

Such contradictory articulations of reality and desire—seen in racist stereotypes, statements, jokes, myths—are not caught in the doubtful circle of the return of the repressed. They are the effects of a disavowal that denies the differences of the other but produces in its stead forms of authority and multiple belief that alienate the assumptions of "civil" discourse. If, for a while, the ruse of desire is calculable for the uses of discipline, soon the repetition of guilt, justification, pseudoscientific theories, superstition, spurious authorities, and classifications can be seen as the desperate effort to "normalize" *formally* the disturbance of a discourse of splitting that violates the rational, enlightened claims of its enunciatory modality. The ambivalence of colonial authority repeatedly turns from *mimicry*—a difference that is almost nothing but not quite—to *menace*—a difference that is almost total but not quite. And in that other scene of colonial power, where history turns to farce and presence to "a part," can be seen the twin figures of narcissism and paranoia that repeat furiously, uncontrollably.

In the ambivalent world of the "not quite/not white," on the margins of metropolitan desire, the *founding objects* of the Western world become the erratic, eccentric, accidental *objets trouvés* of the colonial discourse—the part-objects of presence. It is then that the body and the book loose their representational authority. Black skin splits under the racist gaze, displaced into signs of bestiality, genitalia, grotesquerie, which reveal the phobic myth of the undifferentiated whole white body. And the holiest of books—the Bible—bearing both the standard of the cross and the standard of empire finds itself strangely dismembered. In May 1817 a missionary wrote from Bengal:

> Still everyone would gladly receive a Bible. And why?—that he may lay it up as a curiosity for a few pice; or use it for waste paper. Such it is well known has been the common fate of these copies of the Bible. . . . Some have been bartered in the markets, others have been thrown in snuff shops and used as wrapping paper.[23]

NOTES

This paper was first presented as a contribution to a panel on "Colonialist and Post-Colonialist Discourse," organized by Gayatri Chakravorty Spivak for the Modern Language Association Convention in New York, December 1983. I would like to thank Professor Spivak for inviting me to participate on the panel and Dr. Stephan Feuchtwang for his advice in the preparation of the paper.

1 Cited in Eric Stokes, *The Political Ideas of English Imperialism*, Oxford, Oxford University Press, 1960, pp. 17–18.

2 Edward Said, *Orientalism*, New York, Pantheon Books, 1978, p. 240.

3 Samuel Weber: "The Sideshow, Or: Remarks on a Canny Moment," *Modern Language Notes*, vol. 88, no. 6 (1973), p. 1112.

4 Charles Grant, "Observations on the State of Society among the Asiatic Subjects of Great Britain," *Sessional Papers 1812–13*, X (282), East India Company.

5 *Ibid.*, chap. 4, p. 104.

6 T. B. Macaulay, "Minute on Education," in *Sources of Indian Tradition*, vol. II, ed. William Theodore de Bary, New York, Columbia University Press, 1958, p. 49.

7 Mr. Thomason's communication to the Church Missionary Society, September 5, 1819, in *The Missionary Register*, 1821, pp. 54–55.

8 Benedict Anderson, *Imagined Communities*, London, Verso, 1983, p. 88.

9 *Ibid.*, pp. 88–89.

10 Joseph Conrad, *Nostromo*, London, Penguin, 1979, p. 161.

11 V. S. Naipaul, *The Mimic Men*, London, Penguin, 1967, p. 146.

12 Frantz Fanon, *Black Skin, White Masks*, London, Paladin, 1970, p. 109.

13 Aimé Césaire, *Discourse on Colonialism*, New York, Monthly Review Press, 1972, p. 21.

14 Michel Foucault, "Nietzsche, Genealogy, History," in *Language, Counter-Memory, Practice*, trans. Donald F. Bouchard and Sherry Simon, Ithaca, Cornell University Press, p. 153.

15 Eric Stokes, *The English Utilitarians and India*, Oxford, Oxford University Press, 1959, p. xi.

16 Sigmund Freud, "The Unconscious" (1915), *SE*, XIV, pp. 190–191.

17 Fanon, *Black Skin*, p. 103.

18 Edward Long, *A History of Jamaica*, 1774, vol. II, p. 353.

19 Edward Said, "The Text, the World, the Critic," in *Textual Strategies*, ed. J. V. Harari, Ithaca, Cornell University Press, 1979, p. 184.

20 Frantz Fanon, "Racism and Culture," in *Toward the African Revolution*, London, Pelican, 1967, p. 44.

21 Michel Foucault, *The Order of Things,* New York, Pantheon, 1970, part II, chap. 9.

22 Long, *History,* p. 364.

23 *The Missionary Register,* May 1817, p. 186.

20

JEAN BERNABÉ, PATRICK CHAMOISEAU,
AND RAPHAËL CONFIANT

In Praise of Creoleness

Prologue

Neither Europeans, nor Africans, nor Asians, we proclaim ourselves Creoles. This
will be for us an interior attitude—better, a vigilance, or even better, a sort of mental envelope in the middle of which our world will be built in full consciousness of the
outer world. These words we are communicating to you do not stem from theory, nor
do they stem from any learned principles. They are, rather, akin to testimony. They
proceed from a sterile experience which we have known before committing ourselves
to reactivate our creative potential, and to set in motion the expression of what we
are. They are not merely addressed to writers, but to any person of ideas who conceives our space (the archipelago and its foothills of firm land, the continental
immensities), in any discipline whatsoever, who is in the painful quest for a more fertile thought, for a more precise expression, for a truer art. May this positioning serve
them as it serves us. Let it take part of the emergence, here and there, of verticali-
ties which would maintain their Creole identity and elucidate it at the same time,
opening thus for us the routes of the world and of freedom.

Caribbean literature does not yet exist. We are still in a state of preliterature:
that of a written production without a home audience, ignorant of the authors/read-
ers interaction which is the primary condition of the development of a literature. This
situation is not imputable to the mere political domination, it can also be explained
by the fact that our truth found itself behind bars, in the deep bottom of ourselves,
unknown to our consciousness and to the artistically free reading of the world in
which we live. We are fundamentally stricken with exteriority. This from a long time
ago to the present day. We have seen the world through the filter of western values,
and our foundation was "exoticized" by the French vision we had to adopt. It is a terrible condition to perceive one's interior architecture, one's world, the instants of

one's days, one's own values, with the eyes of the other. All along overdetermined, in history, in thoughts, in daily life, in ideals (even the ideals of progress), caught in the trick of cultural dependence, of political dependence, of economic dependence, we were deported out of ourselves at every moment of our scriptural history. This determined a writing for the Other, a borrowed writing, steeped in French values, or at least unrelated to this land, and which, in spite of a few positive aspects, did nothing else but maintain in our minds the domination of an elsewhere. . . . A perfectly noble elsewhere, of course, ideal ore to look forward to, in the name of which we were supposed to break the gangue of what we were. Against a controversial, partisan, and anachronistic appreciation of history, however, we want to reexamine the terms of this indictment and to promote the people and facts of our scriptural continuum, a true idea. Neither obliging, nor conniving, but supportive.

Toward Interior Vision and Self-Acceptance

During the first periods of our writing, this exteriority provoked a mimetic expression, both in the French language and in the Creole language. We unquestionably had our clock-makers of the sonnet and the alexandrine. We had our fabulists, our romantics, our parnassians, our neoparnassians, not to mention the symbolists. Our poets used to indulge in bucolic drifts, enraptured by Greek muses, polishing up the ink tears of a love not shared by the olympian Venus. This was, said the critics and they had a point, more than secondhand cultural dealing: it was the quasi-complete acquisition of another identity. These zombies were ousted by those who wanted to be part of their native biotope—those who planted their eyes on themselves and our environment, but with a strong exteriority as well, with the eyes of the Other. They saw of their being what France saw through its preachers-travellers, its chroniclers, its visiting painters or poets, or its great tourists. Between the blue sky and the coconut trees blossomed a heavenly writing, first naive and then critical, after the fashion of the indigenists of Haiti. The local cultural coloration was sung in a scription which deserted totality, the truths then depreciated of what we were. It was desperately perceived in subsequent militant criticism as a regional writing, so-called doudouist, and therefore thin: another way of being exterior. However, if, like Jack Corzani in his *Histoire de la littérature des Antilles-Guyane* (Editions Désormaux 1978), we were to examine this writing (from René Bonneville to Daniel Thaly, from Victor Duquesnay to Salavina, from Gilbert de Chambertrand to Jean Galmot, from Léon Belmont to Xavier Eyma, from Emmanuel Flavia-Léopold to André Thomarel, from Auguste Joyau to Paul Baudot, from Clément Richer to Raphaël Tardon, from Mayotte Capécia to Marie-Magdeleine Carbet . . .), it would appear that it actually kept a reserve of wicks capable of bringing sparks to our obscurities.

The best evidence is that given us by the Martinican writer Gilbert Gratiant throughout his monumental Creole work: *Fab Compè Zicaque* (Editions Horizons Caraïbes 1958). A visionary of our authenticity, Gratiant soon placed his scriptural expression on the poles of both languages, both cultures, French and Creole, which magnetized from opposite directions the compasses of our consciousness. And though he was in many respects a victim of the unavoidable exteriority, *Fab Compè Zicaque* remains nonetheless an extraordinary investigation of the vocabulary, the forms, the proverbs, the mentality, the sensibility, in a word, of the intelligence of this cultural entity in which we are attempting, today, a salutary submersion. We call Gilbert Gratiant and many other writers of this period the precious keepers (often without their knowing) of the stones, of the broken statues, of the disarranged pieces of pottery, of the lost drawings, of the distorted shapes: of this ruined city which is our foundation. Without all these writers, we would have had to achieve this return *"to the native land"* with no signs of support of any kind, not even that of scattered fireflies which in bluish nights guide the grim hope of the lost traveller. And we believe that all these writers, especially Gilbert Gratiant, understood enough of our reality to create the conditions of the emergence of a multidimensional phenomenon which (totally, therefore unfairly, threatening but necessary, and spreading over several generations) was to overshadow them; *Negritude*.

To a totally racist world, self-mutilated by its own colonial surgeries, Aimé Césaire restored mother Africa, matrix Africa, the black civilization. He denounced all sorts of dominations in the country, and his writing, which is committed and which derives its energy from the modes of war, gave severe blows to postslavery sluggishness. Césaire's Negritude gave Creole society its African dimension, and put an end to the amputation which generated some of the superficiality of the so-called doudouist writing.

This brings us to free Aimé Césaire of the accusation—with Oedipal overtones—of hostility to the Creole language. We have committed ourselves to understand why, despite an advocated return *"to the deserted hideousness of our wounds"* Césaire did not seriously associate Creole to a scriptural practice forged on the anvils of the French language. There is no need to stir up this crucial question, and to quote the contrapuntal approach of Gilbert Gratiant who tried to invest both languages of our ecosystem. It is important, however, that our reflection becomes phenomenological and considers the very roots of the Césairian phenomenon. A man of both *"initiation"* and *"ending,"* Aimé Césaire had exclusively the formidable privilege of symbolically reopening and closing again the circle in which are clasped two incumbent monsters: Europeanness and Africanness, two forms of exteriority which proceed from two opposed logics—one monopolizing our minds submitted to its torture, the other living in our flesh ridden by its scars, each inscribing in us after its own way its keys, its codes, its numbers. No, these two forms of exteriority could not be brought to the same level. Assimilation, through its pomps and works of Europe, tried unrelentingly to portray our lives with the colors of Elsewhere. Negritude imposed itself then as a stubborn will of resistance trying quite plainly to embed our identity in a denied, repudiated, and renounced culture. Césaire, an anti-Creole? Indeed not, but rather an *ante-Creole*. It was Césaire's Negritude that opened to us the path for the actuality of a Caribbeanness which from then on could be postulated, and which itself is leading to another yet unlabelled degree of authenticity. Césairian Negritude is a baptism, the primal act of our restored dignity. We are forever Césaire's sons.

We had adopted Parnassus. With Césaire and Negritude we were steeped in Surrealism.[1] It was obviously unfair to consider Césaire's handling of the "Miraculous Weapons" of Surrealism as a resurgence of literary bovarism. Indeed, Surrealism blew to pieces ethnocentrist cocoons, and was in its very foundations the first reevaluation of Africa by Western consciousness. But, that the eyes of Europe should in the final analysis serve as a means for the rising of the buried continent of Africa, such was the reason for fearing risks of reinforced alienation which left few chances to escape from it except by a miracle: Césaire, thanks to his immense genius, soaked in the fire of a volcanic idiom, never paid tribute to Surrealism. On the contrary, he became one of the most burning figures of this movement, one of these figures we cannot understand without referring to the African substrate resuscitated by the operating powers of the verb. Yet African tropism did not prevent Césaire from very deeply embedding himself in the Caribbean ecology and referential space. And if he did not sing in Creole, the language he uses remains, as revealed namely by a recent reading of *Et les chiens se taisaient*,[2] nonetheless more open than generally thought to the Creole emanations of these native depths.

Apart from the prophetic blaze of speech, Negritude did not set out any pedagogy of the Sublime. In fact, it never had any intention of doing so. Indeed, the prodigious power of Negritude was such that it could do without a poetics. Its brilliance shone, marking out with blinding signs the space of our blinkings, and it defused every thaumaturgic repetition much to the dismay of epigones. So that, even if it stimulated our energies with unheard of fervors, Negritude did not solve our aesthetic problems. At some point, it even might have worsened our identity instability by pointing at the most pertinent syndrome of our morbidities: self-withdrawal, mimetism, the natural perception of local things abandoned for the fascination of foreign things, etc., all forms of alienation. A violent and paradoxical therapy, Negritude replaced the illusion of Europe by an African illusion. Initially motivated by the wish of embedding us into the actuality of our being, Negritude soon manifested itself in many kinds of exteriority: *the exteriority of aspirations* (to mother Africa, mythical Africa, impossible Africa) and *the exteriority of self-assertion* (we are Africans).[3] It was a necessary dialectical moment, an indispensable development. But it remains a great challenge to step out of it in order to finally build a new yet temporary synthesis on the open path of history, our history.

Epigones of Césaire, we displayed a committed writing, committed to the anticolonialist struggle,[4] but consequently committed also outside any interior truth, outside any literary aesthetics. With screams. With hatred. With denunciations. With great prophecies and pedantic concepts. In that time. Screaming was good. Being obscure was a sign of depth. Strangely enough, it was necessary and did us much good. We sucked at it as if it was a breast of Tafia. We were freed on the one hand, and enslaved on the other as we grew more and more involved in French ways. For if, during the Negrist rebellion, we protested against French colonization, it was always in the name of universal generalities thought in the Western way of thinking, and with no consideration for our cultural reality.[5] And yet Césairian Negritude allowed for the emergence of those who were to express the envelope of our Caribbean thought: abandoned in a dead end, some had to jump over the barrier (as did Martinican writer Edouard Glissant), others had to stay where they were (as did many), turning around the word Negro, dreaming of a strange black world, feeding on denunciations (of colonization or of Negritude itself), and were exhausted indulging in a really suspended writing,[6] far from the land, far from the people, far from the readers, far from any authenticity except for an accidental, partial, and secondary one.

With Edouard Glissant we refused the trap of Negritude, and spelled out Caribbeanness,[7] which was more a matter of vision than a concept. As a project it was not just aimed at abandoning the hypnoses of Europe and Africa. We had yet to keep a clear consciousness of our relations with one and the other: in their specificities, their right proportions, their balances, without obliterating or forgetting anything pertaining to the other sources conjugated with them; thus, to scrutinize the chaos of this new humanity that we are, *to understand* what the Caribbean is; to perceive the meaning of this Caribbean civilization which is still stammering and immobile; to embrace, like René Depestre, this American dimension, our space in the world; to explore, like Frantz Fanon, our reality from a cathartic perspective; to decompose what we are while purifying what we are by fully exhibiting to the *sun of consciousness* the hidden mechanisms of our alienation; to plunge in our singularity, to explore it in a projective way, to reach out for what we are . . . these are Edouard Glissant's words. The objective was prominent; if we wanted to apprehend this Caribbean civilization in its American space, we had to abandon screams, symbols, sensational comminations, and turn away from the fetishist claim of a universality ruled by Western values in order to begin the minute exploration of ourselves, made of patiences, accumulations, repetitions, stagnations, obstinacies, where all literary genres (separately or in the negation of their limits) as well as the transversal (and not just pedantic) use of all human sciences would take their share. Somewhat like with the process of archeological excavations: when the field was covered, we had to progress with light strokes of the brush so as not to alter or lose any part of ourselves hidden behind French ways.

This was easier to say than to do, because the paths of penetration in Caribbeanness were not marked out. We went around them for a long time with the helplessness of dogs on board a skiff. Glissant himself did not really help us, being taken by his own work, by his own rhythm, and persuaded that he is writing for future generations. We received his texts like hieroglyphics in which we were able somehow to perceive the quivering of a voice, the oxygen of a perspective. In his novel *Malemort* (Sevil 1975), however, (through the alchemy of the language, the structure, the humor, the themes, the choice of characters, the preciseness) he suddenly and singularly revealed Caribbean reality. On the other hand, Haitian writer Frankétienne, taking part in the first buddings of a Creoleness centered around its native depths, proved, in his work *Dézafi* (Port-au-Prince 1975), to be both the blacksmith and the alchemist of the central nervure of our authenticity: Creole re-created by and for writing. So that *Malemort* and *Dézafi*—strangely published in the same year, 1975—were the works which, in their deflagrating interaction, released for new generations the basic tool of this approach of self-knowledge: interior vision.

To create the conditions of authentic expression meant also to exorcise the old fatality of exteriority. Having only the Other's pupils under one's eyelids invalidated the fairest approaches, processes, and procedures. Opening one's eyes on oneself, like the regionalists, was not enough. Neither was scrutinizing this *"fondal-natal"* culture, as did the Haitian indigenists, in order to keep the essence of our creativity. We had yet to wash our eyes, to turn over the vision we had of our reality in order to grasp its truth: a new look capable of taking away our nature from the secondary or peripheral edge so as to place it again in the center of ourselves, somewhat like the child's look, questioning in front of everything, having yet no postulates of its own, and putting into question even the most obvious facts. This is the kind of free look which, having no outside spectators, can do without self-explanations or comments. It emerges from the projection of our being and considers each part of our reality as an event in order to break the way it is traditionally viewed, in this case the exterior vision submitted to the enchantment of alienation. . . . This is why interior vision is revealing, therefore revolutionary.[8] To learn again how to visualize our depths. To learn again how to look positively at what revolves around us. Interior vision defeats, first of all, the old French imagery which covers us, and restores us to ourselves in a mosaic renewed by the autonomy of its components, their unpredictability, their now mysterious resonances. It is an inner disruption, and, like Joyce's, a sacred one. That is to say: a freedom. But, having tried to enjoy it with no success, we realized that there could be no interior vision without a preliminary self-acceptance. We could even go so far as to say that interior vision is a result of self-acceptance.

French ways forced us to denigrate ourselves: the common condition of colonized people. It is often difficult for us to discern what, in us, might be the object of an aesthetic approach. What we accept in us as aesthetic is the little declared by the Other as aesthetic. The noble is generally elsewhere. So is the universal. And our artistic expression has always taken its sources from the far open sea. And it was always what it brought from the far open sea that was kept, accepted, studied, for our idea of aesthetics was elsewhere. What good is the creation of an artist who totally refuses his unexplored being? Who does not know who he is? Or who barely accepts it? And what good is the view of a critic who is trapped in the same conditions? We had to bring an exterior look to our reality which was refused more or less consciously. Our ways of laughing, singing, walking, living death, judging life, considering bad luck, loving and expressing love, were only badly considered in literature, or in the other forms of artistic expression. Our imaginary was forgotten, leaving behind this large desert where the fairy Carabossa dried Manman Dlo. Our refused bilingual richness remained a diglossic pain. Some of our traditions disappeared without being questioned by any inquiring mind,[9] and even though we were nationalists, progressivists, independentists, we tried to beg for the universal in the most colorless and scentless way, i.e. refusing the very foundation of our being, a foundation which, today, we declare solemnly as the major aesthetic vector of our knowledge of ourselves and the world: Creoleness.

Creoleness

We cannot reach Caribbeanness without interior vision. And interior vision is nothing without the unconditional acceptance of our Creoleness. We declare ourselves Creoles. We declare that Creoleness is the cement of our culture and that it ought to rule the foundations of our Caribbeanness.[10] Creoleness is the *interactional or transactional aggregate* of Caribbean, European, African, Asian, and Levantine cultural elements, united on the same soil by the yoke of history. For three centuries the islands and parts of continents affected by this phenomenon proved to be the real forges of a new humanity, where languages, races, religions, customs, ways of being from all over the world were brutally uprooted and transplanted in an environment where they had to reinvent life. Our Creoleness was, therefore, born from this extraordinary "migan," wrongly and hastily reduced to its mere linguistic aspects,[11] or to one single element of its composition. Our cultural character bears both the marks of this world and elements of its negation. We conceived our cultural character as a function of acceptance and denial, therefore permanently questioning, always familiar with the most complex ambiguities, outside all forms of reduction, all forms of purity, all forms of impoverishment. Our history is a braid of histories. We had a taste of all kinds of languages, all kinds of idioms. Afraid of this uncomfortable muddle, we tried in vain to anchor it in mythical shores (exterior vision, Africa, Europe, and still today, India or America), to find shelter in the closed normality of millennial cultures, ignoring that we were the anticipation of the relations of cultures, of the future world whose signs are already showing. We are at once Europe, Africa, and enriched by Asian contributions, we are also Levantine, Indians, as well as pre-Columbian Americans, in some respects. Creoleness is *"the world diffracted but recomposed,"* a maelstrom of signifieds in a single signifier: a Totality. And we think that it is time to give a definition of it. To define would be here a matter of taxidermy. This new dimension of man, whose prefigured shadow we are, requires notions which undoubtedly we still don't know. So that, concerning Creoleness, of which we have only the deep intuition or the poetic knowledge, and so as not to neglect any one of its many possible ways, we say that it ought to be approached as *a question to be lived,* to be lived obstinately in each light, in each shadow of our mind. To live a question is already to enrich oneself of elements besides the answer. To live the question of Creoleness, at once freely and prudently, is finally to penetrate insensibly the immense unknown vastitudes of its answer. *Let live (and let us live!) the red glow of this magma.*

Because of its constituent mosaic, Creoleness is an open specificity. It escapes, therefore, perceptions which are not themselves open. Expressing it is not expressing a synthesis, not just expressing a crossing or any other unicity. It is expressing a kaleidoscopic totality,[12] that is to say: *the nontotalitarian consciousness of a preserved diversity.* We decided not to resist its multiplicity just as the Creole garden does not resist the different forms of yam which inhabit it. We shall live its discomfort as a mystery to be accepted and elucidated, a task to be accomplished and an edifice to be inhabited, a ferment for the imagination and a challenge for the imagination. We shall conceive it as a central reference and as a suggestive explosion demanding to be aesthetically organized. For it has no value in itself; in order to be pertinent, its expression must be the result of a serious aesthetic approach. Our aesthetics cannot exist (cannot be authentic) without Creoleness.

Creoleness is an annihilation of false universality, of monolingualism, and of purity. It is in harmony with the *Diversity* which inspired the extraordinary momentum of Victor Segalen. Creoleness is our primitive soup and our continuation, our primeval chaos and our mangrove swamp of virtualities. We bend toward it, enriched by all kinds of mistakes and confident of the necessity of accepting ourselves as complex. For complexity is the very principle of our identity. Exploring our Creoleness must be done in a thought as complex as Creoleness itself. The need for clarification based on two or three laws of normality, made us consider ourselves as abnormal beings. But what seemed to be a defect may turn out to be the indeterminacy of the new, the richness of the unknown. That is why it seems that, for the moment, *full knowledge of Creoleness will be reserved for Art,* for Art absolutely. Such will be the precondition of our identity's strengthening. But it goes without saying that Creoleness is inclined to irrigate all the nervures of our reality in order to become gradually its main principle. In multiracial societies, such as ours, it seems urgent to quit using the traditional raciological distinctions and to start again designating the people of our countries, regardless of their complexion, by the only suitable word: *Creole.* Socioethnic relations in our society ought to take place from now on under the seal of a common creoleness, without, not in the least, obliterating class relations or conflicts. In literature, the now unanimous recognition of the poet Saint-John Perse by our people as one of the most prestigious sons of Guadeloupe—in spite of his belonging to the Béké ethnoclass—is indeed an advance of Creoleness in Caribbean consciousness. It is delighting. Accordingly, in architecture, in culinary art, in painting,[13] in economics (as proven by the example of the Seychelles), in the art of clothing, etc., the dynamics of an accepted, questioned, elated Creoleness seem to us to be the best way toward self-acceptance.

It is necessary to make a distinction between Americanness, Caribbeanness, and Creoleness, all concepts which might at first seem to cover the same realities. First, the sociohistorical processes which produced Americanization are different in nature from those which were at work in Creolization. Indeed, Americanization and its corollary, the feeling of Americanness, describes the progressive adaptation, and with no real interaction with other cultures, of Western populations in a world they baptized new. Thus, the Anglo-Saxons who formed the thirteen colonies, embryo of the future American state, displayed their culture in a new environment, almost barren, if we consider the fact that the native redskins, who were imprisoned in reservations or massacred, did not virtually influence their initial culture. In the same way, the Boni and Saramak blacks of Guyana, who remained yet relatively closed to the tribes of the Amazonian forest, were Americanized through their interaction with the forest environment. Just as the Italians who emigrated massively to Argentina during the nineteenth century, or the Hindus who replaced the black slaves in the plantations of Trinidad, adapted their original culture to new realities without completely modifying them. *Americanness is, therefore, in many respects, a migrant culture,* in a splendid isolation.

Altogether different is the process of Creolization, which is not limited to the American continent (therefore, it is not a geographic concept) and which refers to the brutal interaction, on either insular or landlocked territories—be it immense territories such as Guyana or Brazil—of culturally different populations: Europeans and Africans in the small Caribbean islands; Europeans, Africans, and Indians in the Mascarene islands; Europeans and Asians in certain areas of the Philippines or in

Hawaii; Arabs and black Africans in Zanzibar, etc. Generally resting upon a plantation economy, *these populations are called to invent the new cultural designs allowing for a relative cohabitation between them.* These designs are the result of a
nonharmonious (and unfinished therefore nonreductionist) mix of linguistic, religious, cultural, culinary, architectural, medical, etc. practices of the different people
in question. Of course there are more or less intense Creolizations depending on
whether the peoples in question are exogenous as is the case in the Caribbeans of
the Mascarene islands, or whether one of these people is autochthonous as in the
island of Cape Verde or in Hawaii. So, Creoleness is the fact of belonging to an original human entity which comes out of these processes in due time. There are a
Caribbean Creoleness, a Guyanese Creoleness, a Brazilian Creoleness, an African
Creoleness, an Asian Creoleness, and a Polynesian Creoleness, which are all very
different from one another but which all result from the matrix of the same historical maelstrom. Creoleness encompasses and perfects Americanness because it
involves a double process:

—*the adaption of Europeans, Africans, and Asians to the New World; and*
—*the cultural confrontation of these peoples within the same space, resulting
in a mixed culture called Creole.*

There are obviously no strict frontiers separating zones of Creoleness from zones
of Americanness. We might find them juxtaposed or interpenetrated within the same
country: thus in the U.S.A., Louisiana and Mississippi are predominantly Creole,
whereas New England, which was initially inhabited by Anglo-Saxons only, is just
American. After the abolition of slavery, however, and the rise of black people in the
North, and during the twentieth-century arrival of Italians, Greeks, Chinese, and
Puerto-Ricans, one might rightly think that the conditions are ripe for a process of
Creolization to start presently in New England.

After this distinction between Creoleness and Americanness, what can we say
of the relations between Caribbeanness and Creoleness? We consider Caribbeanness
to be the only process of Americanization of Europeans, Africans, and Asians in the
Caribbean Archipelago. Thus, it is, so to speak, a province of Americanness like
Canadianness or Argentineness. Indeed, it leaves out the fact that in certain islands
there was, more than mere Americanization, a phenomenon of Creolization (and
therefore Creoleness). For example, entire regions in the north of Cuba were affected
only by an Americanization of Andalusian colonists, Canarians or Galicians, and
knew no Creolization whatsoever. In certain sugar cane areas of Trinidad, Hindu culture adapted itself to the new environment without getting involved in a process of
Creolization as opposed to the *bondyékouli* of the small Caribbean islands, which is
a Creole cult based in Hinduism. Thus, we believe that Caribbeanness is first of all a
geopolitical concept. The word "Caribbean" says nothing of the human situation of

Martinicans, Guadeloupeans, or Haitians. As Creoles, we are as close, if not closer, anthropologically speaking, to the people of the Seychelles, of Mauritius, or the Reunion, than we are to the Puerto Ricans or the Cubans. On the contrary there are little things in common between someone from the Seychelles and a Cuban. We, the Caribbean Creoles, enjoy, therefore, a double solidarity:

> —a Caribbean solidarity (geopolitical) with all the peoples of our Archipelago regardless of our cultural differences-our Caribbeanness; and
> —a Creole solidarity with all African, Mascarin, Asian, and Polynesian peoples who share the same anthropological affinities as we do—our Creoleness.

Interior vision at the service of the unconditional acceptance of our Creoleness (as the very vitality of our creativity) must feed and reinforce, in a completely new way, the temporary conditions of the literary expression of Caribbeanness defined by Glissant.

. . .

Constant Dynamics

One of the hindrances to our creativity has been the obsessional concern with the Universal. Old syndrome of the colonized: afraid of being merely his depreciated self and ashamed of wanting to be what his master is, the colonized accepts therefore—supreme subtlety—the values of his master as the ideal in the world. Hence exteriority vis-à-vis ourselves. Hence the defamation of the Creole language and the deep mangrove swamp of Creoleness. Hence—except for unique miracles—our aesthetic shipwreck. Creole literature will have nothing to do with the Universal, or this disguised adherence to Western values, it will have nothing to do with this concern with exhibiting the transparency of oneself, exhibiting oneself to the attractiveness of the obvious. We want to deepen our Creoleness in full consciousness of the world. *It is through Creoleness that we will be Martinicans. Becoming Martinicans, we will be Caribbeans, therefore Americans, in our own way.* It is through Creoleness that we will crystalize Caribbeanness, the ferment of a Caribbean civilization. We want to think the world as a polyphonic harmony: rational/irrational, finished/complex, united/diffracted. . . . The complex thought of a Creoleness, itself complex, can and should help us in so doing. The Whole-world's life quivers with expressed Creoleness. It is the Whole-world in a particular dimension, and a particular form of the Whole-world.

The world is evolving into a state of Creoleness. The old national immovable organizations are being replaced by federations which in turn might not survive for long. Under the totalitarian universal crust, Diversity maintained itself in small peoples, small languages, small cultures.[14] The world standardized bristles, paradoxically, with Diversity. Everything being in relation with everything, visions embrace more, provoking the paradox of a general consensus around and a celebration of differences. And we believe that Babel is unlivable only for narrow spaces. That it won't bother the great voice of Europe if Breton is spoken in Britanny and Corsican in Corsica, that it won't be a concern for the unified Maghreb if Berber is spoken in Kabylia, if the Touaregs assert their ways. The capacity to incorporate Diversity has always been the privilege of great powers. Cultures melt and spread into subcultures which in turn generate other aggregates. To perceive the world today, a man or woman's identity, the principle of a people or a culture with the values of the eighteenth century or those of the nineteenth century would be an impoverishment. A new humanity will gradually emerge which will have the same characteristics as our Creole humanity: all the complexity of Creoleness. The son or daughter of a German and a Haitian, born and living in Peking, will be torn between several languages, several histories, caught in the torrential ambiguity of a mosaic identity. To present creative death, one must perceive that identity in all its complexity. *He or she will be in the situation of a Creole*. That is what we have prefigured. Our submersion into our Creoleness, by means of Art, is one of the most extraordinary and fairest ways of entering in relation with the world. Expressing Creoleness will be expressing the very *beings* of the world.[15] What we felt, our emotional experience, our pains, our uncertainties, the strange curiosity of what was thought to be our defects, will help in our achieved expression to build in diversity the harmonious Being of the world.

Creoleness liberates us from the ancient world. But, in this new turn, we will look for the maximum of communicability compatible with the extreme expression of a singularity. We call Creole the work of art which, celebrating within its coherence the diversity of meanings, will preserve the mark which justifies its pertinence regardless of how it is understood,[16] where it is culturally perceived, or to what issues it is associated. Our submersion into Creoleness will not be incommunicable, but neither will it be completely communicable. It will not go without its opaqueness, the opaqueness we restore to the processes of communication between men.[17] Shutting ourselves in Creoleness would have contradicted its constitutive principle, and denied it. It would have transformed the initial emotion into some kind of hollow machinery, working uselessly, and in doing so getting poorer and poorer like those dominating civilizations, nowadays shattered. One of the conditions of our survival as Creoles (open-complex) is to maintain a consciousness of the world while constructively exploring our initial cultural complexity, and to insure that such a consciousness celebrates and enriches this exploration. Our primary diversity will be part of an integrating process of world diversity, recognized and accepted as permanent. Our Creoleness will have to recover itself, structure itself, and preserve itself, while changing and absorbing. *It will have to survive in Diversity*.[18] Applying this double move will automatically favor our creative vitality. It will also prevent us from returning to the totalitarian order of the old world, fixed by the temptation of the unified and definitive. At the heart of our Creoleness, we will maintain the modulation of new laws, of illicit blendings. For we know that each culture is never a finished product but rather the constant dynamics on the lookout for genuine issues, new possibilities, and interested in relating rather than dominating, in exchanging rather than looting. Respectful. Cultures would have continued living such a dynamics if it wasn't for Western madness. Clinical sign: colonizations. A living culture, and especially Creoleness, is a permanent stimulation of convivial desire. And if we recommend to our artists this exploration of our singularities, that is because it brings back to what is natural in the world, outside the *Same* and the *One*, and because it opposes to Universality the great opportunity of a world diffracted but recomposed, the conscious harmonization of preserved diversities: DIVERSALITY.

Appendix: Creoleness and Politics

The claims of Creoleness are not just aesthetic in nature, as we saw, they also have important ramifications touching on all fields of activity in our societies, and especially the most fundamental ones: politics and economics. Indeed, Creoleness claims a full and entire sovereignty of our peoples without, however, identifying with the different ideologies which have supported this claim to date. This means that it distrusts, in the first place, some sort of primary Marxism which has it that cultural and therefore identity-related issues will find a solution once the revolution is achieved. Thus expressed, often in good faith, this theory, we must insist, has often prevented our political leaders and organizations from thinking seriously about the contents of a true Martinican, Guadeloupean, or Guyanese culture. We also want to distance ourselves from this somewhat narrow nationalism that perceives the Martinican as a stranger to the Guadeloupean, and vice versa. Without denying the differences between our peoples, we would like to say that what unites them is vaster than what opposes them, and that the task of a defender of the Martinican people's sovereignty is also to reconcile his struggle as much as possible with that of the Guadeloupean or Guyanese peoples, and vice versa.

Creoleness sketches the hope for the first possible grouping within the Caribbean Archipelago: that of the Creolophone peoples of Haiti, Martinique, Saint Lucia, Dominica, Guadeloupe, and Guyana, grouping which is only the prelude of a larger union of our Anglophone and Hispanophone neighbors. This is to say that, for us, the acquisition of an eventual mono-insulary sovereignty will be but a stage (a very brief one, we hope) in the process toward a Caribbean federation or confederation, the only way to stand up efficiently to the different hegemonic blocks that share the planet among them. In this perspective, we maintain our opposition to the present process of integration without popular consultation of the people of the so-called "départments français d'Amérique" to the European community. Our solidarity is first with our brothers of the neighboring islands and secondly with the nations of South America.

We remain persuaded that, having failed to incorporate in their strategy the reinstallation of our peoples within this Creole culture, miraculously forged during three centuries of humiliation and exploration, our political leaders are preparing us for a grim future—states devoid of the most basic democratic principles, the only guarantee of economic development. This allows us to say that our preference is for a multipartisan, multiunionist, and pluralist regime, which breaks radically with the fantasies that are the providential man or the nation's father who did so much harm in many countries of the Third World and Eastern Europe. By this we are not adhering to the Western political models, we are simply recognizing that equality between people cannot be obtained in a durable fashion without the freedom of thinking, of writing, and of traveling that goes with it. For us, there are no *formal freedoms*. All liberties, provided they do not stand in the way of the functioning of society, are good.

Translated by Mohamed B. Taleb Khyar

NOTES

1 "Surrealism" appeared "positively" as bringing a questioning of the Western Society, a verbal liberation, a power for scandal; "negatively" it appeared as a factor of passivity (André Breton as master), a place of uncertain references (life, fire, the poet), the absence of critical thought in social issues, the belief in elect men. The relation was noted between the powers of the imaginary, the irrational, of madness and the blacks' power of the "elementary" *(Tropiques)*. It was also pointed out that Surrealism tends to reduce "particularities" and specificity, that it tends to erase, by simply negating them, the racial issues, that it maintains, therefore, paradoxically (and by a generous but abusive generalization) a tendency for Europeocentrism. See E. Glissant, *Le Discours Antillais* (Edition du Sueil, 1981).

2 Vernacular in *Et les chiens se taisaient* by Aimé Césaire; cf. the work in progress of Annie Dyck, Ph.D. diss., L'Université des Antilles et de la Guyane.

3 Which, in fact, amounted to placing oneself outside the black dimension of our Creole being. But what a chance it was at the time to find a soul better suited to the dominants of our topology! . . . It was the time when many of our writers and artists flew to Africa thinking they were going to meet their selves.

4 Commitment which, in the final analysis, was one of the manifestations of exteriority: "The majority of the people questioned about literature in Haiti demand a commitment from the Haitian writer; very few of them had actually read be it a single book of this literature. And despite the writers' efforts, they had changed very little things in Haiti. The communication is constantly interrupted for lack of readers: why in such conditions doesn't a writer modify the scope of his text, or simply abandon his means of expression? Only a single answer comes

to mind: the writer had met the demands of the foreign literary world by choosing to adopt recognized forms of expression. He had also met the demands of a public who wanted him to deal with their problems. He fails on both sides for he is neither recognized nor read by his people . . ." (U. Fleishmann, *Ecrivain et société en Haiti*, Centre de Rocherches Caraibe, 1976).

5 The revolt probably went along with the following type of argumentation of the colonialists: Before we arrived here, there was just an island and a few savages. We were the ones who brought you here. Here, there were no people, no culture, no civilization for us to colonize. You exist only by colonization, so where is colonization?

6 "Generally speaking the literature of a society spreads the models according to which the society perceives and evaluates itself. These models, at least in principle, support the actions of individuals and groups, and push them to espouse the images they draw. But for this to happen, a coherence between the ideal models and reality is necessary; in other words these models must, at least partially, actualize in accessible time and space. The emergence of a committed literature is in relation with a society's refusal of its current reality: solicited by the public, the writer expresses models capable of guiding the audience toward the apprehension of a new reality. As for the Haitian writer . . . he shapes his ideal on that of the ex-metropole or another society, to the point of completely identifying with it. If Haitian reality is to become accessible to him, it must transform itself until it resembles this other reality. This divorce between daily life and the dreamed ideal prevents consequently the models from having any impact on reality" (Fleishmann).

7 It was, explains Glissant, during a lecture by Danile Guérin read for the students of the Association générale des étudiants martiniquais in 1957 or 1958. Daniel Guérin who had just pleaded for a federation of the Caribbeans in his book *Les Antilles décolonisées,* was nonetheless surprised by this neologism which alluded to more than just a political agreement between Caribbean countries. "Reality is irrefutable: cultures springing up from the system of plantations, insulary civilization (where the Caribbean sea defracts, when, for example, it may be believed that a sea, also civilizing, such as the Mediterranean sea had, before all, powers of attraction and concentration); pyramidal population with African or Hindu origins at the base, European ones at the summit; languages of compromise; general cultural phenomenon of creolization; a vocation for reunion and synthesis; persistence of African facts; sugar cane, corn, and spice agriculture; place of the combination of rhythms; people of orality. This reality is virtual. Caribbeanness needs: to achieve the passage from the common lived experiences to the expressed consciousness; to go beyond the intellectual postulation of the elites and to go along with the collective assertion supported by the actions of peoples" (Glissant).

8 "The first ones who will rise and take off from your mouths the gag of a meaningless inquisition described as knowledge—and an exhausted sensibility, sign of our times, who will take all the room to the benefit of the sole poetic truth which is constantly fighting against imposture and permanently revolutionary, to you" (René Char, *Recherche de la base et du sommet. Bandeau des matinaux,* Gallimard, 1950).

9 The work of folklorists is absolutely necessary for the simple conservation of the elements of national heritage. People like Loulou Boislaville and others did a wonderful job in that respect.

10 The word "creole" seems to come from the Spanish word "crillo," itself deriving from the Latin verb "criare," which means "to raise, to educate." The Creole is the person who was born and raised in the Americas and who is not a native like American Indians. Very soon this term was applied to all the human races, all the animals and plants transported to America from 1492 on. There was, therefore, a mistake in French dictionaries which from the beginning of the nineteenth century reserved the word "Creole" for the white Creoles (or Béké) only. Anyway, etymology is, as everyone knows, a dangerous and uncertain field. There is, therefore, no need to refer to it in order to approach the idea of Creoleness.

11 Creole appears as the best data allowing, in a dynamic and progressive way, *to frame* the identity of the Caribbean people and the Guyanese. Indeed, there is, beyond Creole languages and cultures, a Creole *matrix* (bway) which, on the universal level, transcends their diversity. See GEREC, *Charte culturelle créole,* 1982.

12 The approach of the GEREC is, in this respect, interesting: "Creoleness dismisses all the 'back-worlds' without pronouncing in favour of either one in order to construct the future on *transracial and transcultural bases.* . . . Not just a network of cultures, Creoleness is the concrete expression of a civilization in the making. Its rough and harsh genesis is at work in each of us. . . . Creoleness is a magnetic pole to the attraction of which we—unless we want to lose our souls—are called to align our reflection and our sensibility. Its deepening at all levels of individual and social commitment might allow our societies to accomplish their *third great breech,* and this time not just on the mode of exclusion, but also on the community mode. . . . (ibid.).

13 Martinican painter José Clavot demonstrated during a symposium devoted to Lafcadio Hearn (in 1987) that there could be a Creole perception of the chromatic range, which could be the foundation of a Creole pictorial aesthetics.

14 "I find it convenient to call 'Diversity' all that, until today, was called strange, unusual, unexpected, surprising, mysterious, amorous, superhuman, heroic, and even divine. All that is Other" (Victor Segalen, *Essai sur l'exotisme,* livre de poche, 1986).

"Diversity which is not chaos or sterility, is the effort of the human mind toward a transversal relation, without any universalist transcendence. Diversity needs the presence of peoples, not as an object to sublimate, but as a project to relate. As Sameness began with the expansionist plundering in the West, Diversity saw the light of day with the armed political violence of peoples. As sameness reaches a peak *in* the ecstasy of individuals, Diversity is spread by the momentum of communities. As Otherness is the temptation of Sameness, Wholeness is the demand of Diversity" (Glissant).

15 "Even as a hypothesis, totality becomes easily totalitarian when it doesn't take *beings* into account" (Glissant).

16 "In fact, a form is esthetically valid precisely when it is considered from and understood according to many perspectives, when it manifests a great variety of aspects and resonances and still remains itself" (Eco).

17 "Let us begin with admitting this impenetrability. Let us not flatter ourselves for assimilating customs, races, nations, others; but on the contrary let us take pleasure in never being able to assimilate them; for then we will eternally secure the pleasure of feeling Diversity" (Segalen).

"The transliteration of works of arts operates according to rules which change so much that one does not really know how to express them. Some writers who might appear as hardly exportable because of the heavy foreign accent they keep even in the best translations, or because they owe their singularity to their narrowly local conditions of life and creation, end up crossing the borders easily, and spreading in the vast world—sometimes at once, sometimes, on the contrary, well before they were recognized and understood in their national boundaries (as was the case for Kafka . . .). Other writers, on the other hand, who appear to be addressing men everywhere, thanks to a work devoid of local coloring and subtle idiotisms, stall indefinitely at the gates of the Universal Library and find no reception, not even from their nearest neighbors" (Marthe Robert, *Livre de lectures,* Grasset, 1977).

18 "Unity represents itself to itself only in diversity" (Segalen).

21

JANA SEQUOYA

How (!) Is an Indian?

A Contest of Stories

The question of who and how is an Indian is an ongoing contest of stories in North America, a contest in many ways emblematic of global struggles to contain and control difference in modern societies. At stake are the social, political, and economic conditions of possibility for Indian identity within the encompassing national context. Who, what, where, and when can that Indian be, which the founding narratives of the North American nation construed as either absent—the empty land scenario—or inauthentic. Inauthentic, that is, by comparison with the imagined "original" Indian, whether of the Golden Age or demonic variety; inauthentic because rather than vanishing, American Indians in all our diversity are still here, alive and kicking against the odds.

Although the figure of the "authentic" Indian is a figment of the imagination—a symbolic identity invested with meanings of temporal inequality vis-à-vis the colonizing real(m)—it has real consequences for contemporary American Indian people. Among the most obvious of these is that we must respond to the question of Indian identity in terms of that figure. And because Native Americans must understand themselves in relation to conventional images of "Indianness," and therefore, in relation to the false question of authenticity—a "red-herring" discourse, one might say—even our own versions of who and how is an Indian are not so much the antithesis of the imaginary Indian, as its echo. The key paradox of Indian identity, then, is that it is when we least contradict the familiar images that Native American stories will seem most articulate and true. For in order to be perceived as speaking subjects American Indians must adopt categories of meaning and codes of representation that convey an implicit set of social goals in many ways contrary to those that articulate their own stories.

The grammar of identity, identification, and affiliation presents a logical and ethical problem at the outset of this essay, as the shifting standpoint of the foregoing paragraph demonstrates. For in order to constitute ourselves as bicultural subjectivities, Indian-identified writers must negotiate a politics of position and of representation. And in order to do so adequately, we must sharpen our awareness of the multiple relationships out of and into which we write. Each subject position occupied in relation to Indian/non-Indian identity has its own story. Each perspective is critiqued by its other at the borders of its particular discourse along the social axis of "inside-outside." Thus the ambiguous positionality that complicates my own use of pronouns in speaking of Indian identification mirrors the subject-object under discussion—the relationship of narratives of identity and modes of identification as they respond to, accommodate, and resist the master narratives of national culture. For in contrast to the range of Euroamerican identities, self-evident to a degree in the dominant political and economic institutions, the discursive codes that constrain Native American interventions in the story of Indianness neither reflect traditional (resistant) Native American identities nor adequately mediate their responses to interpellation by those institutions.

Although the category "Indian" is a colonial one, having its roots in British expansion into Ireland as well as in the imaginary "Indios" of Spanish colonialism, because the name signified an elusive and threatening population "beyond the pale" of the colonizing system, Native Americans themselves adopted the name. As Roger Williams records in the early seventeenth century,

> They have often asked me, why we call them Indians [. . . .] And understanding the reason, they will call themselves Indians, in opposition to English, &c.
>
> (Berkhofer 1979:15)

The imaginary Indian has its roots, of course, in material relationships, as well as in colonizing fantasies of timeless origins. When our bicultural forebears became obsolete as active intermediaries between the unmapped wilderness and the civilizing market, the fledgling economy of "manifest destiny" sold the concept of the Indian as Art before the product was on the streets, both figuratively and literally. In the earliest commodity form of the Vanishing Indian, tribal remnants of westward expansion were befeathered, furred, and frozen in attitudes of sorrowful nobility. The resulting iconograph, an image at once of land and soul, represented an ideal integral to the American self-image: all the wilderness that had been overcome, all the wildness waiting in the heart, ready to spring into action should the occasion demand (and occasions continue to demand: sporting occasions, occasions of warfare, confrontations between good and evil, right and wrong).

Although the displacement and control of that sorrowful wildness seemed to the young America a guarantee of its future, the contest with uncertainty was won at a certain cost. For freedom is not to be thought of as cheap; sacrifices must be made. As an iconograph of the cost, images of the Vanishing Indian (in contrast to narratives of democracy as an unending process of "becoming") constitute both the authenticating sign of "Indianness" and an alibi for usurpation of the territorial and cultural space indicated by that sign. Thus, essentialist images of Indianness fetishize that which would be preserved under the rubric of cultural revitalization. And the Indian who refuses that paradoxical legitimation—for whom, for example, tribal religion is vital practice rather than abstract belief—such an Indian is framed not as Art but as Outlaw.[1]

This is all to say that the problem indicated by questions of who and how is an Indian is that the material conditions of being Indian have changed over time, while the images of Indianness have not. The conditions of being Indian have changed, of course, for a variety of reasons, and many of those changes are directly related to differing degrees of access to land and resources among Native American peoples, as well as to corresponding restrictions on traditional religious and economic practices which depend on such access. Real, as distinct from imaginary, answers to the question of "how" is an Indian, then, must depend in part on whether one is Indian in the city or the country; whether in the ways of tradition or of modernization; whether drawing more on old or on new cultural influences.

But the question of "who" is an Indian is subject to other conditions as well, and these are indirectly related to federal restrictions on non-capital intensive access to the land. For it is one of the paradoxes of democratic government that without the appearance of a homogeneous political identity—an identity constituted in terms of the dominant system of representation—the issues crucial to Native American survival as regionally diverse peoples cannot be heard.

Thus under the auspices of legal, educational, esthetic, and popular representations, colonizing imperatives in many instances are not "post" but ongoing. Because each of those arenas is a site of struggle in the contesting stories of "who and how" is an Indian, the question entails a problem of disjunction between its rhetorical and material terms. Insofar as American Indians have been defined generically in terms of the past (but whose?) by tellers of tall and self-serving tales, whatever our own standpoints in the contest (and they will be many according to tribal and family histories), our presence in relationship to those terms must necessarily be equivocal. For our sense of who we are in relation to the majority society, as well as our judgment of other Indian-identified people, is conditioned by what continues to be at stake—the replacement of traditional Native American structures of identity with those of Euro-America. And because of the complexity of Indian identification in all its varied determinants and permutations, no matter how deeply bicultural Indians "know" who we are—as we are quick to avow when our identities are in question, the question of Indian identity itself is often a matter that goes with the territory. It is at this impasse then, that Native Americans must become particularly inventive.

The paradoxical situation of Native American discourse is evident in the emergent literary genre exemplified by the early work of N. Scott Momaday and Leslie Marmon Silko in the 1960s and 1970s. These syncretic works created great public and academic interest, to the extent that in the 1990s both authors are included in most standard American anthologies. Because the poetry, novels, and autobiographies of these two writers articulate perspectives that resonate with a growing movement in the schools and universities to reclaim the standpoints of those who continue to have much at stake but little say in North American culture and society, they continue to influence a new generation of writers and to encourage the development of critical commentary on all forms of Native American literature.

Although the works of Momaday and Silko are stylistically different, they share many similarities: both are concerned with the recuperation of indigenous sources of identity, and to this end both writers draw upon tribal oral stories. Most significantly for the focus of this essay, the first novels of both directly incorporate elements of traditional sacred story cycles—a practice constituting, along with an emergent literary form, an ethical question vis-à-vis the particular communities of which these authors write.[2] It is a question that arises out of the dual social contexts of these syncretic works, yet which tends to be answered in terms of academic interests. Because for the most part neither the university nor the mainstream reading public has regarded ethical considerations as relevant to the category of fiction, critical commentary has tended to follow the lead of the authors in effacing the communal sanctions that restrict the use of sacred oral stories in traditional tribal communities. This essay therefore is part of an ongoing project to include in discussions of contemporary Native American literature not only those canonical esthetics of the privileged imagination mediated by reified ethnographic material, but a sense of responsibility to the lived relationships in which culture functions as a connected way of life—connected, that is, to varied modes of continuity and emergence. For to many Indian-identified students it seems ironic at best that the literary incorporation of sacred story fragments is cited by critics of these novels as evidence of their particularly Native American character.

The problem, of course, is precisely one of context: what is misuse in relation to the sacred cultures of particular tribal communities evokes authentic atmosphere in relation to the secular humanist and popular cultures of the Euroamerican tradition. The prerogative of a cross-cultural preserve exempt from accountability to the tribal community whose worldviews it purports to represent is justified in the name of "fiction"; the category of esthetics is invoked to dismiss as impertinent any protest in the name of a politics of representation.

Perhaps one might consider such dismissive strategies as an institutional residue of the paradigm of the vanishing Indian by which traditional tribal communities are perceived less as subjects than as objects of knowledge, and hence as terminally up for grabs. But despite disciplinary pressures to dismiss the ethical issues attending academic and popular appropriations of Native American sacred cultures, those issues are slowly becoming a matter of public record as tribal spokespeople on behalf of traditional ethos are finding their voices in cross-cultural forums.

One example among many is an article published in the Northern Arizona University newspaper *The Lumberjack* (Feb. 1, 1991), in which Hopi tribal spokesman Vernon Masayesva protests that "[a]s people we have been studied as artifacts." Aside from documenting the elder's objections "to NAU's attempts to publish information concerning what [the Hopi] call their 'religious privacy,'" the article illustrates a common editorial practice that tends to put into question the validity of the speaker within the representational space. Accordingly, Masayesva's claim for Hopi "'religious privacy'" is framed by an ironic boundary within which the tribal elder's voice is contained and controlled by the normalizing gaze of the writer. The quotation marks function simultaneously to represent and to deny the Hopi elder's words, withholding the validity that objections to a violation of Judeo-Christian proscriptions would be granted. Similarly, the marks setting off Masayesva's protest that there have been "too many instances where our elders have been betrayed" make his protest seem strange, even a bit paranoid. They signal an idiosyncratic space of difference that speaks to the mainstream imagination of a field of otherness—like the tribal lands set apart from the dominant modes of property. In consequence of the relations of power always in contention between dominant and subordinate groups, only a speaker authorized by the former can legitimate the Hopi elder's voice. Thus the director of cultural preservation for the tribe, Leigh Jenkins, is obliged to confirm and explain the elder's objection. And according to Jenkins, "The conflict arises when non-Indians want to preserve the Hopi culture by means of publishing their secrets [. . .] the tribe would prefer to lose its traditions."[3]

Although, in the context of the academy, such a position may be difficult to comprehend, self-destructive even, invoking as it does an ethic which is contrary to the prerogatives of the institution (i.e., the capitalization of knowledge), Hopi traditionalists may yet have some say in defense of tribal secrets; for Masayesva's protest on behalf of the tribe resulted, we are informed, in a "committee [that] will investigate guidelines on the limits and freedoms in Indian research." And to the extent that the committee sincerely questions the limits of academic freedom to interfere with ways of life based upon a different system of cultural values and practices, it is likely to become an arena of struggle in the contest of stories.

For all that Western narrative practices of displacement and distance have been internalized as convention and celebrated as style, they are nevertheless practices that deprecate contestatory points of view. They are not only the editorial practices of journalists, nor only the appropriative practices of anthropologists, but, more problematically, literary practices in defense of a corner on the market for local color and pedagogical practices converting knowledge of "others" to institutional power. A related issue was addressed by Vine Deloria (as cited by Ward Churchill in "A Little Matter of Genocide: Native American Spirituality & New Age Hucksterism," *The Bloomsbury Review,* Sept./Oct. 1988). Deloria raises the question of non-Indian "experts" employed by the universities to train young Native Americans how to be Indian, and asserts that "[t]hese students are being trained to view themselves and their cultures in the terms prescribed by such 'experts' rather than in the traditional terms of the tribal elders." The Lakota scholar points to an important (but, of course, contestable) consequence of this aspect of the contest of stories:

> The process automatically sets the members of Indian communities at odds with one another, while outsiders run around picking up the pieces for themselves. In this way the "experts" are perfecting a system of self-validation in which all semblance of honesty and accuracy are lost.

He concludes that this situation "is not only a travesty of scholarship but it is absolutely devastating to Indian societies." Similarly, Pam Colorado, an Oneida poet (cited by Churchill and in turn citing his article in a 1989 conference on Native American spirituality), warned the audience that "the process is ultimately intended to supplant Indians, even in areas of their own customs and spirituality."

The ontogeny of a mostly immigrant nation approves, perhaps, the displacement of indigenous systems of belief, of material culture, of political forms. But if you are the "host" in this relationship, you see the situation of culture differently, as Colorado warns:

> We are talking here about an absolute ideological/conceptual subordination of Indian people in addition to the total physical subordination they already experience. When this happens, the last vestiges of real Indian society and Indian rights will disappear. Non-Indians will then "own" our heritage and ideas as thoroughly as they now claim to own our land and resources.

The alarm sounded by these Native American social critics is easily dismissed by both non-Indian and Indian-identified academics according to postmodern perspectives that question claims to authenticity (or to reality, for that matter). Thus Colorado's invocation of "real Indian society" may be wrested from its communal context and repositioned in Anglo-American and other immigrant histories of diaspora, transgression of boundaries, and cultural assimilation of difference. From these standpoints, the ironic sense of "expert" in matters Indian implied by Churchill's gloss of both Deloria and Colorado is very much in question: do the ironizing marks imply that people most fully Indian by blood are automatically expert, or more expert than those with less genetic heritage? That is, to paraphrase more than one Indian "expert," does American Indian culture travel in the blood?

This is unlikely to be the meaning since all three critics are of mixed racial as well as cultural heritage.

Instead the issue of these warnings is more likely to refer to the fact that since Native American communities and traditions have in many instances been shattered, the young must reinvent viable conditions of being Indian. And because the process of reinvention entails recuperation of cultural fragments from many sources, including recourse to the alienated forms of archive material—often the purview of non-Indian "experts"—the dangers of "ideological/conceptual subordination" for young Indians in universities will be mitigated by a teacher whose knowledge is well grounded in a Native American community. Despite the often disrupted and interpellated condition of such communities, the preferred teacher of Indian students would be one who has internalized the perspectives of a Native American culture, as well as those of the dominant society. The best teacher for American Indian students, that is, would be fully bicultural. The problem of training young Indians in the critical issues of their own cultures thus becomes one of gaining informed perspectives on, in James Clifford's phrase, "the predicament of culture" (the title of his 1988 study of ethnography, literature, and art) from the standpoints of the more traditional American Indian social goals,[4] rather than from those of Euro-America.

Traditional Native American social goals are in many ways different from the general aims of the majority culture, and foremost among these differences is the function and meaning of culture itself. While experiences of diaspora, transgression of boundaries, and incorporation of difference inform both Indian and non-Indian societies, American Indians are more likely to designate culture as a system of alignment with the shifting forces of the environment—whether those forces be elemental or social—and that system is embodied in the living mediators of the ceremonial traditions. Rather than defining culture according to an evaluative set of binary oppositions to the geophysical surroundings, as is more characteristic of Judeo-Christian social systems, those raised in (or more influenced by) Native American traditions are more likely to point to the hill or river and say, "This is our culture." When the place which embodies the traditional culture is fenced off as "sacrifice" or "developed" for its material resources (for whom?), the social system that responded simultaneously to its symbolic and pragmatic value is effectively erased. And that is what is at stake in the predicament of American Indian culture.

A geocentric sense of identity may be understood from Western standpoints if it is considered in light of similar self-confirmation in reference to classical Greece, for example, or—as my French-Welsh grandmother avows—to Paris. Just as Western cultural traditions, embodied in its literature and art, located in museums and libraries, depend on access to those institutions, so indigenous cultural practices based on symbolic responses to the natural environment depend on physical access to those places in which tribal traditions are embodied. Contemporary Native American literature may be understood, in part, as a response to the threat of cultural extinction due to the capitalization of the environment—but it is a response that entails its own series of paradoxes as a function of the different social goals of Western and tribal story.

Literary forms of "cultural revitalization" are paradoxical forms in that they are necessarily not constituted in the cultural terms of the traditions which they would vitalize. "Necessarily not," that is, because in contrast to the centrifugal functions of displacement and substitution enacted by the print technologies attending stories in modern Western societies—a social practice underwriting the atomized individual in the interests of expanding the ground of dominant values—the social role of traditional tribal story is communally centripetal and integrative. In order to hear the stories that tell them who they are, that is to say, dispersed members of the tribal community must return to their elders; in order to receive the tribal knowledge encoded in the traditional stories, they must submit to the social terms of which the stories are a vital part. Thus, communal sanctions on the oral stories counter the disintegrative tendencies of the dominant society, encouraging the reintegration of acculturated (or deculturated) Indians with the community.

By contrast, the technologies of mechanical reproduction belong to the cultural logic of the colonial story—a logic of space rather than of place. As such, colonial technologies lend themselves to the *dis*placement of differently organized cultures. Moreover, because print literature reframes geocentric symbolic relationships in terms of commodity forms of culture, it enables the assimilation (and effective sacrifice) of traditional American Indian narrative and evaluative forms to those alien and alienating cultural modes.

Thus, in the same way that well-meaning academics may disparage as superstitious the objections of Native American traditionalists like Hopi elder Vernon Masayesva, or the warnings of social critics like Deloria, Churchill, and Colorado, authors and scholars of Native American literature may unwittingly denigrate or dispense with the specificity of tribal histories by assimilating the materiality of place and community to the representational esthetics of distance and displacement. Similarly, despite the best intentions, theories that are benevolent in the context of the academy may have negative consequences for those tribal people to whom the old ways of having stories are vital to the continuity of their social order. For according to the political climate in which theories of culture find their concrete expressions in state and federal policies, theoretical emphases on the provisional character of twentieth-century identities may be adapted to the ideology of "progress" through the self-evidence of "modernity" in support of the dominant mode of having stories. However, the dark side of those truths the U.S. Constitution holds to be self-evident is their justification of the continuing erasure of indigenous lifeways, a process that was nearly concluded in the United States in 1871 when Charles Darwin wrote, in

The Descent of Man, "At some future period, not very distant as measured by centuries, the civilized races of man will almost certainly exterminate, and replace, the savage races throughout the world."

In pointing to the differences between ways of having stories (cultures), I intend a reminder that theoretical emphases on the expedient reinventions of culture in Western literary forms, for example, while functional for standpoints grounded in colonizing perspectives, override American Indian conceptions of identity with the landscape and the ancestors, conceptions every bit as determining for the cultures of indigenous people as Euroamerican institutions are for the people they serve.[5] And I hope to emphasize that the primary distinction between the indigenous and Western ethos turns on the divergent social aims of their different cultural institutions (without forgetting that the particularity of the former have been penetrated and altered by the economic dominance of the latter). Thus where the secular humanist definition of culture celebrates the creative capacities of the individual—and the development of the notion of the sovereign individual through the history of the European Enlightenment is itself a response to a particular set of political and economic circumstances—in contrast, traditional American Indian identities are not determined by the centrality of the ego. Instead, such identities include the interactive participation of sacred beings embodied in that geography, the plant and animal life of the region, its elemental characteristics, as well as ancestors and kin whose histories constitute a part of the place. In the words of Jack Forbes, the difference between Western and tribal identities consists fundamentally of the experience of our selves as "inside each other rather than outside." The goal-seeking drive of Native American systems of cultural organization, then, is different from that of European systems in its emphasis on preserving identification with ancestral events, customs, and values; and these are located as story and song, ritual, and memory in the members of living Indian communities, as well as in the territorial features of the homeplace. The system, therefore, is not fundamentally motivated by expansionist goals, but by conservative ones.

These differences have powerful consequences for the ways of having stories in both cultures. Therefore, this essay must engage (in a necessarily general way) the social realities of those Native American communities upon whose traditional stories Momaday's *House Made of Dawn* and Silko's *Ceremony* draw. While a common aim of tribal communities is to persist and to flourish as distinct national entities within the dominant economic and legal structures of American society, most are tenuously poised against assimilative pressures—whether they be the atomistic forces of economic necessity or of Western ideas of education; of changing federal policies and legal proscriptions on traditional practices or the multicorporate devastation of ancestral land bases. Indeed, the influences of global capitalism and its institutional expressions reach deeply into most tribal societies despite their often disproportionate poverty. Although the more conservative Pueblo communities are perhaps less internally divided by these influences than many others, there is nevertheless a tension along the lines of revitalizing tradition and selective modernization—imprecise terms that signify the divergent social goals I have attempted to clarify.

Those disparate influences and goals are differently engaged according to the relative material and social bases of regional tribal communities in general, altering customary values and practices, positioning some members at the center of traditional ways and others more at the margins of the community, nearer to mainstream culture. (The spatial metaphor of center–periphery understood from the tribal perspective refers to asymmetrical relationships to antithetical systems of power: traditionally based resources of power and knowledge, on the one hand, metaphysically encoded in ritual and oral traditions; the material technologies of the dominant society, on the other, transmitted through state or parochial education systems. Both entail problems of access to social resources: the former restricts specialized knowledge through clan and gender roles, the latter through evaluative criteria based on formal testing and informal "gatekeeping" relationships.)

In general, then, traditional or conservative forms of social organization are penetrated through economic, legal, and health-care systems, while the more permeable "modernizing" periphery enters the mainstream through the educational system. The latter prepares the way for increasing identification with the homogenizing influences of popular entertainment and advertising media. Institutions of capital define what it takes to be fully human in terms of those institutions—money and things—while the nostalgic soul of those global economic-cultural systems sees the Indian in terms of an imagined past. The elders have some say in all this, but again, conditions have changed and the situation is not all that clear. It is revealing of the problems for Native American identity in this contest of stories that Indian children who grew up with the genre of American frontier movies identified with the cowboy heroes rather than with the Indian bad guys; of course, Indians could not recognize themselves in the self-reflexive mirror held up by the popular media.

The emergence of syncretic cultures among American Indian peoples is related not only to federal pressures to replace tribal modes of social organization with dominant forms of representation, nor only to economic pressures to replace traditional evaluative narratives with those of modern capitalism, but also to the common practice of "mixed" marriage—a matter that itself reflects paradoxically on the idea of the racial basis of ethnicity. Most Native American communities define members on the basis of kinship affiliations and social acuity rather than blood quantum,[6] so that the key to being Native American in terms of a given community does not depend on the degree of Indian blood, but on the degree of incorporation into the social network of that community. Thus a full-blood may be thoroughly acculturated to the dominant society, while a mixed-blood may identify and function entirely as a member of a tribal group that has assimilated biological non-Indians over genera-tions. However, the criterion of social incorporation may be a Catch-22 proposition, for the Pueblos depicted in *House Made of Dawn* and *Ceremony* tend to be conser-vatively organized communities, exclusive rather than inclusive, despite (or because of) centuries of Spanish and then U.S. colonialism and the corresponding religious and economic influences of each regime.[7]

The relationship of both Momaday and Silko to the tribal communities in which their first novels are set is similar, then, in that both write out of dual cultural con-texts: dual in the sense that they are of mixed Native American and Euroamerican descent, and dual in that they did not grow up within the tribal traditions on which their early works draw. Rather, as their autobiographical writings indicate, both were raised in families with strong connections to the dominant society's educational and economic practices, and somewhat peripheral relationships with the tribal societies among whom they lived. Furthermore, while both writers identify with particular tribal traditions, that identification is conflicted in terms of their writing.[8] Although the syncretic and dual cultural influences to which their novels respond are in some respects complementary, in others they are at significant odds. Nevertheless, the works of both writers articulate the social forces contending for dominance within the tribal societies of which they write, as well as those of the mainstream reading public for whom they write.

Most importantly, the literary innovations of which Momaday's *House Made of Dawn* and Silko's *Ceremony* are exemplary attest at once to the assimilation of American Indian structures of identity to the mainstream[9] and to the "Indianization" of appropriated cultural forms. However, the apparent duality of social assimilation and resistance entails a metacommunication[10] at the cultural level of which James Clifford speaks as a moment of "hesitation" (*The Predicament of Culture,* 343). Sim-ilarly, but with an emphasis on Western—specifically Roman—notions of legendary moments of foundation, Hannah Arendt (*On Revolution,* 180–214), traces the politi-cal significance of "the hiatus between the end of the old order and the beginning of the new" (205), the relationship, that is, of narratives of exodus to the legitimation of the U.S. Constitution as an act of foundation that circumvents recourse to prior authority. The principle of revolutionary beginning, according to Arendt, is one of "a new event breaking into the continuous sequence of historical time" (205). She inter-prets these legends as indicating that "freedom is no more the automatic result of liberation than the new beginning is the automatic consequence of the end" (205). Rather, agents of change must undergo a period of transition prior to the inaugura-tion of the new social order.

That transitional stage or—in Clifford's phrase, "hesitation"—preceding social change, is also theorized by Victor Turner (*The Ritual Process,* 94–130) as "liminal-ity," an anti- or extrastructural phase characterized by disengagement with the social order. While hesitation marks a withdrawal that effectively places the subject outside of the system under consideration, it is a hiatus capable of fostering alternative standpoints in the contest of stories. That is, under conducive conditions, "hesitation" may enable conceptual reorganization preceding a new engagement, with more than a rhetorical difference, on the part of those who, like Momaday and Silko, are already positioned by existing educational and economic institutions to operate dominant forms for emergent class goals.

Although at the individual level innovations of dominant cultural forms in terms of American Indian narrative styles may be a means of negotiating mainstream bases of power under cover of currently valorized representations of difference, privileged bicultural mediators nevertheless reflect changing configurations of identity occurring simultaneously in mainstream and tribal cultures. Thus, to the extent that both Momaday and Silko write out of and into these differently empowered social conditions, their works respond to the conflicted subject positions that are generated between traditional modes of social organization and adaptive tribal responses to the dominant society.

Yet because the tribally based aspects of their literary identities—as distinct from those aspects based in the esthetic values of mainstream society—are at odds with the more traditional tribal ethos, both *House Made of Dawn* and *Ceremony* might be considered not only as contemporary examples of Native American storytelling (as direct manifestations and transformations of the continuity of those traditions), but also in the more ambiguous light of the overlay of one set of social values by another.

In particular, they must be considered in relationship to the counterculture movement of the '60s and '70s when many white, middle-class Americans began looking for alternative modes of spirituality, since the popularity of these novels is more than incidental to that context. These works, therefore, may be more accurately understood as hybrid forms arising out of the general tendencies of North American culture to confrontation, alienation, and discontinuity. That is to say, the mixed-blood,[11] or "half-breed,"[12] authors of the syncretic literature exemplified by *House Made of Dawn* and *Ceremony* mediate cross-cultural traditions for the disaffected, at the same time that they engage in metacommunication about their own existential condition.

However, in so doing, they inevitably betray the "origins" (in the sense of communally sanctioned traditions) from which they derive their canonical status as representative Native American writers in the first place. Insofar, that is, as the traditional culture is not up for grabs, as Masayesva's objection witnesses, the bicultural author of North American Indian literature inscribes for the canonical record an ambiguous sign of Indianness—a fossilized trace of numinous passage, perhaps, though certainly not the mystic critter itself. The quite co-opted analogy to the infamous Trickster suggests itself in this regard, as Gerald Vizenor and others have noted, though the Trickster is in no way constrained by analogies. (This essay got its title from one such Coyote who told his tale at a recent powwow: Two Mescalero Apaches were hanging out in a park, said Lorenzo Baca, when they were approached by a hippie speaking what he believed to be their native tongue. "How!" said the hippie to the Indians. Coyote looked at his friend, Ramon, and said "What?" Ramon looked back and said "Where?" Coyote asked "Who?" Ramon, "Why?" The hippie walked away muttering "Wow!" Lorenzo Baca has included this tale in his collection *Songs, Poems, and Lies*.)

The syncretic works of Momaday and Silko articulate a paradoxical presence/absence in the general currency of representations: they invoke familiar images of the exotic, while giving the comfortable a peculiar twist. They may raise the art level a notch beyond our comfort zone, as—according to some tastes—in Momaday's early works; or may descend to tedium in their condensed or complicated syntax. Then again, fragments of the sacred may be recuperated from the already alienated context of anthropological archives—a sort of textual necrophilia. All this may comprise a double jeopardy, but whatever it is, it's not what it appears to be. In this forest of ambiguity the hermeneutical project of American literary criticism must contend with an unreadable sign like that legendary inscription carved into the tree in the abandoned Roanoke colony, composed only of the local Indian name designating a neighboring tribe, a sign that would seem to indicate distress, yet not punctuated by the agreed-upon mark. That sign—of what if not of distress?—was perhaps the first move in such literature.

However, the category of Native American fiction may be clarified by placing it in the theoretical framework of colonial discourse, for aside from the phenotypal blending of formerly discrete gene pools characteristic of colonial societies, the "half-breed" protagonist articulates the range of emergent subjectivities generated by colonial dependence and postcolonial dissolution of those relationships. The biological offspring of that historical antinomy embodies a third term which, in some respects, mediates and, in others, negates the relation of opposition between colonizer and colonized. The mixed-blood in its ideal form (a form to be taken with a grain of salt) forges new openings in existing social relations, shifting the balance of power by constellating new categories of meaning out of the dissolution of the old. On the one hand, because the "half-breed" position is neither of the binaries constituting its condition of partiality, it may mark the site of a synchronic mediation of diachronic relationships of oppression and subordination;[13] yet insofar as it articulates simultaneously the excluded middle term of the historical antinomy *and,* as a function of its privileged relationship to hegemonic institutions, displaces that excluded position which would enter into representation, it writes itself over that along side which it would take its ethical and politicized stand. Consequently, if the privileged position of mediation is not to emerge as a new form of domination, bicultural mediators must explicitly critique both the ambivalence and the privilege of the positions we occupy.

In Mexico and the Americas to the south, and to varying degrees in Canada, the category of the mestizo or the métis refers to historically cohesive cultures. In North America, by contrast, pressures for assimilation tend to produce fragmentation and dispersal of identity and identification rather than cohesiveness. And though the Native American half-breed experience in the United States is an often painful one (cf. Paula Gunn Allen's essay in *The Sacred Hoop,* "A Stranger in My Own Life"), the tropological force of the mixed-blood position refers as much to contemporary resistance to nationalistic meltdown as to quantum of Indian "blood." In any case, the latter may be difficult to determine due to the powerful assimilative pressures exerted on our predecessors by federal policies. Racism, institutionalized as political and economic restrictions, and internalized as self-hatred, inclined our mixed-blood parents (speaking of my Chickasaw father, born in Oklahoma in 1914) more toward denial than to claiming what was generally considered to be a stigma. Unlike those to the north and south who are able to develop socially stable mixed identities, many of us embody a genealogical blank, filled with secondhand bits of information, partially uncovered tracks, fragments of photos in which we strain to recognize our own features and those of our children.

Our ancestors were ambivalent; caught between the lines of powerfully contending stories of origin and aim, they attempted to blend into the anonymous niches between, in Homi Bhabha's phrase, "almost, but not quite, (not white)." That legacy is as determining for mixed-bloods as was the more forthright horror of those who were rounded up and confined to reservations, or the resignation of others allotted eighty acres of poor land in exchange for a way of life that had long sustained and satisfied them.

Yet even moving nearer to the main currents of the dominant society, we will be hard pressed to find anyone who considers his or her identity to be an unproblematic unity appropriately integrated in available social structures. Without a doubt therefore, contemporary mixed-blood literature presents new paradigms of self-knowledge to the general public. At their best, instead of subject positions based on binary either/or oppositions, these works articulate relational subjectivities in the analogic mode of both-and, more-less, forging multiple sites of invention without collapsing the tension of difference back into a merely oppositional stance.[14]

Nevertheless, while these partial identifications may provide considerable flexibility in the context of mainstream society, such provisional strategies of self-constitution can be a problem from the point of view of the tribes on which syncretic novels are based. For to the extent that Native American fiction draws upon sacred oral traditions in order to satisfy the expectations of the reading public for local color—that is, insofar as it explicitly uses culturally proscribed narratives—it immediately becomes unrepresentative of the very communities it is taken to represent. However, at issue is not the colonial question of authenticity, but the ethical question of transgression of communal sanctions by cultural mediators.

Although the explicit incorporation of sacred oral stories in the novel form was initiated by N. Scott Momaday, Leslie Marmon Silko's *Ceremony* presents a network of issues immediately relevant to the conflicting ethos of tribal ceremonials and Western esthetics at the conjunction of sacred and secular orientations. *Ceremony*'s thematic concern with mixed subjectivities, its motif of the spotted and the commingled, and its call for transcendence of boundaries—"no boundaries, only transitions through all distances and time" (258)—the complex relationships of these multiple subject positions are foreshadowed in the prologue's suggestion of a continuity between Silko's authorship of the novel and Thought-Woman's creation of the world: "Thought-Woman, the spider, named all things and as she named them they appeared," the clan story begins. Shifting from the mediate to the immediate, the narrator adds, "She is sitting in her room thinking of a story now. I'm telling you the story she is thinking" (1).

From the standpoint of the outsider then, the narrator's identification with the Pueblo creatrix seems to authorize the novel's representation of that tradition. At the same time, the prologue's effacement of the contradictions between secular and sacred ways of having stories seems to legitimate the reader's access to the traditional narratives of the Pueblo. However, in the real terms of traditional communal functions, recourse to the clan stories presupposes conditions that are difficult to honor within the secular context of the novel. If, as according to Paula Gunn Allen, these clan stories are "not to be told outside of the clan" (1990:383), the narrator's shifting perspective from the communitarian context to that of the atomized writer defines the author's place as a site of transgression rather than of continuity between traditional tribal and Western storytelling traditions.

While the issue may be and probably is perceived differently among different Pueblo—Allen's standpoint is disputed by some (see note 2)—to the extent that it is generally upheld, as I have been told that it is, the prologue's admonishment (1) acquires a particular resonance:

> "They aren't just entertainment.
> Don't be fooled.
> They are all we have, you see,
>   all we have to fight off illness and death."

For if the clan stories aren't "just entertainment," but have a survival function in sustaining the identity of the community—a function threatened by "they [who] try to destroy the stories / let the stories be confused or forgotten," then the problem introduced at the outset of the novel, that of defending the stories and hence their social relations against "the mighty evil," pivots on the paradox of their expropriation for the literary market by the cultural mediator. For by seeming to define an identity, the possessive "our" in reference to the clan stories effaces, but does not dispose of, the actual contradictions in ways of having stories—the different relations of production and distribution between tribal oral traditions and those of Native American novels. Thus the conflicted context in which we encounter the clan stories equivocally positions the reader in their defense.[15]

It is relevant to the present argument to observe that in the prologue's formulation of the threat to the clan stories as consisting in the possibility of their confusion, and its alternate (but related) threat to the stories constituted by the possibility of forgetting them, the narrator collapses distinct perspectives—those inside and outside the context of traditional sanctions—into an internally divided identity (a form which itself mirrors the bicultural subject). Thus, when we take on the subject position offered by the prologue in identification with traditional sanctions on the performative contexts of the clan stories—for "they are all we have"—and if the pronoun "we" and the possessive "our" refers to the *clan* whose stories these are and not to we readers who appropriate them in the context of the novel, we occupy a culturally familiar double-bind. For if the stories are confused, they will be forgotten. That is, if they lose significance for the lifeways of the Pueblo (as they may, for example, if they are disconnected from the ethical and symbolic contexts of traditional clan roles), they will cease to be told by those for whom they functioned to maintain those role allocations. And, on the other hand, if the stories are forgotten because of an ensuing confusion of their social function, the tribal identity which they once embodied and articulated will be lost. Underlying these related propositions is an irresolvable conflict in which *Ceremony* is caught up: that if the stories are told outside the sanctions of their communal context, as indeed they are in the commodity form of the novel, they will be confused in the terms of their communal context and hence forgotten because in the secular domain of the novel they *are* "just entertainment."

The ethical problem I am narrating in terms of a paradox would seem to have two possible solutions: either traditional sanctions are respected and the stories are entrusted to the internal vitality of those traditions, or they are assimilated as fragments of an exotic subculture into the dominant institutions which serve a different system of cultural values and social organization. The consequences of the latter transformation is that the clan stories cease to be what they were in their former context—the socially integrative means by which tribal communities maintain the structures of their identity—and the community itself will be ever more vulnerable to assimilation by the dominant society. And this is where agents of social change must become not only innovative but ethically accountable to the communities they purport to represent.

Because consideration of the ethical contexts of tribal cultures would call into question one of the presumed rights of the academy—that of pursuing knowledge for its own sake (for the sake, that is, of control and the legitimation of control), Silko's novel and its critical commentary reprise an historical dilemma: to the extent that authors and critics alike deny the real differences between the cultures in ways of having stories—differences in relations of production, in modes of circulation, in social functions—they silence crucial aspects of those tribal traditions they would reclaim. And insofar as the literary presence of bicultural Native Americans (as exemplified in its emergent phase) is predicated on an absence of the ethical context of the tribal communities on which they draw, that disjunctive space becomes the arena—at once place and space—of the contesting stories of who and how is an Indian.

The multiple perspectives brought to bear in this discussion attest to the material and ideological ambiguities alternately supporting and subverting my own critique of the misappropriation of communally proscribed traditions. They demonstrate, as well, that purist paradigms that impose either/or fictions on the question of "how" is an Indian unrealistically circumscribe lived narratives of "who" is an Indian. No single point of view can be said to be more valid than another; each reflects historically changing conditions constituting Indian (and in this case) specifically Pueblo identity. Each standpoint represents a particular set of relationships to the dominant order's narratives of individual freedom; each is differentially constituted in relation to the more traditional values of tribal community; and each perspective critiques the other along the social axis of "inside-outside."

Yet the bicultural arena is not only the permeable intersection of contesting narratives of identity and identification. What is at issue in the contest of stories entails far more than esthetic or rhetorical consequences. At stake is precisely the issue of viable material conditions for sustaining Indian identity. That the problem is critical is confirmed by the recent Greenpeace report informing the public of fifty-three proposals to locate incinerators, landfills, and nuclear waste repositories on Native American lands. It is well known among tribal people everywhere that their councils are being approached with financial "incentives" and employment "possibilities" that include lease agreements stipulating that the tribes waive their sovereign rights in relation to these sites of economic exploitation.[16] What is at stake in these devastating propositions compels the conclusion that the question of "how" is an Indian is increasingly crucial to the question of "who" is an Indian.[17]

NOTES

1 The 1990 Supreme Court decision in the case of *Employment Division, Department of Human Resources of Oregon v. Alfred Smith* states that it is an "unavoidable consequence of demo-

cratic government" that majority interests "must be preferred to a system in which each conscience is a law unto itself. . . ." That is, insofar as minority religious practices infringe on the
laws of the majority society, those practices will be judged illegal by the superior rights of the
latter. The decision reverses previous positions on religious freedom by saying that while we
may believe whatever we wish, if we try to practice what we believe (in this case, using sacra-
mental Peyote in the Native American church), we may not only lose our jobs, as did Al Smith,
but can be thrown in jail. All this would sound quite familiar to the Pilgrims. In the words of
Justice Scalia, "we cannot afford the luxury of deeming . . . invalid, as applied to the religious
objector, every regulation of conduct that does not protect an interest of the highest order."
The conflicting contexts in which this contest of stories is being fought out are reduced to the
interests of dominant power, and the sense of ethical poverty expressed by the decision reflects
badly on the status of democratic principles in the United States.

2 Paula Gunn Allen (1990). Critics of this article tend to consider the position Allen takes up
against unsanctioned use of tribal stories problematic in view of her own appropriations of
sacred material for the commercial market, a practice that she apparently did not forego following her critique of that practice. Despite her own contributions to the contradiction she critiques, the critique itself is valid to the extent that it does indeed reflect traditional sanctions
on the use of sacred stories. But questions remain as to the status of the particular oral story
fragments that Silko incorporates into *Ceremony*. According to the perspectives of two insiders, Tony and Wilma Purley of Mesita—the village to which the traditionals moved after Silko's
great grandfather, Robert Marmon, became governor of Laguna, Silko's use of the oral stories
is in no way transgressive because the stories she incorporates were always "like T.V.—just for
entertainment." Moreover, they were already in the "public" domain thanks to their prior textualization by anthropologist Elsie Clews Parsons. As an outsider I am not in a position to confirm or deny the syncretic cultural effects resulting from the particular Christian interventions
(some say disruptions) in Laguna traditions instituted by Silko's paternal forebears, beyond
offering a reminder of the distinction between the traditional structures of Pueblo social roles
and the mediating symbolic *narratives* that those roles articulate in response to historically
changing influences.

3 The article explains that "because the university supports many students' and professors' dissertations and research on the Indian reservation, the issue of disrespect for sacred Indian traditions has been a serious one in the past few years." NAU's confrontation was brought about
"largely by a book written by NAU professor Ekkehart Malotki, *The Hopi Salt Journey*, [that]
contains secrets the tribe does not want revealed," according to director of cultural preservation Jenkins. One might ask, If the Hopi are united in wishing to preserve their tribal secrets,
how did Malotki get his information? Those possibilities include payments to a needy individual for his store of secrets and the mediation of an individual tribal member largely acculturated to the exchange value of knowledge.

4 I am using the term traditional in the way generally used by Native Americans to indicate a
distinction between "modernizing" factions within tribal communities and those seeking to
retain or revitalize cultural practices and values that sustained collective identity prior to conquest, relocation, and interpellation by dominant economic and social formations. For an analysis of "modernization" see Marshall Berman's *All That Is Solid Melts into Air*, as well as
Raymond Rocco's essay in *Culture Studies* 4:3 (October 1991) "The Theoretical Construction
of the 'Other' in Postmodern Thought," in which modernization "implies the progressive economic and administrative rationalization and differentiation of the social world: processes
which brought into being the modern capitalist-industrial state" (1988:325). The distinction
between Native American traditionalist and modernizing modes of social organization tends to
become an opposition at the level of politics when the latter are closely associated with, or otherwise an ideological extension of, federal policies to capitalize tribal land bases. Conversely,
although the more traditional enclaves within many tribal communities tend to be the most
economically impoverished precisely because their priorities are survival to the seventh generation rather than economic exploitation of the land base, their cultural practices constitute

an invaluable resource for assuring the continuity of perspectives able to counter the commodification of every value characteristic of global capitalism.

5   However, this is not to suggest that Native American identities constitute an 'Other' to contemporary social conditions. Rather, the various forms of colonization to which Native American societies were (and continue to be) subject, and our diverse histories of domination and subordination, are common to native as well as non-native populations. Both sides of the 'self-notself' paradigm are thoroughly implicated in the paradoxical injunctions colonial histories entail. (I am thinking here of one of the first Native American authors—the early-seventeenth-century Andean Guaman Poma's translation of his side of the story into the language and form of the colonizer in an effort to influence King Philip III of Spain on behalf of his community. Like Poma, North American Indians necessarily and regularly appropriate the technological and discursive forms, as well as the representational ideologies, of the dominant society, in order to negotiate the prevailing social conditions.) (See Adorno 1986.)

6   Because of generally resilient practices, and despite disruptive pressures on cohesive social formations, the influences of 'modernity' may disperse but do not entirely disrupt these traditionally centripetal communities. Tribal assimilation of the offspring of mixed marriages varies widely among Indian communities and even among the same tribe on a regional basis: for instance for one branch of the Lakota the word *Iyeska* in contemporary usage conveys a strongly pejorative attitude toward mixed-bloods, while in others, its earlier sense of 'translator' continues to retain traces of the spiritual roots of precontact meanings. The particular communities of which both Momaday and Silko write traditionally denied full participation in community life to outsiders—a condition defined by transgression of customary practices—including marriages outside the boundaries of sanctioned kinship affiliations. Particularly when these writers were growing up, the tribes of which they write tended to exclude outsiders from traditional tribal structures. The bias toward members of mixed descent is currently undergoing a transition to relative permeability of boundaries due to the tenacity of kinship ties. The ambiguous situation of mixed-blood children among these tribes is the topic of much of the writing by Allen (for example, "A Stranger in My Own Life," *The Sacred Hoop,* 1986 and "Special Problems in Teaching Leslie Marmon Silko's *Ceremony,*" 1991, cited below).

7   The bicultural orientation of the Laguna Pueblo consequent on the influences of its multiply interpellated history is addressed by A. LaVonne Ruoff Brown in *MELUS* 5 (1978). Ruoff quotes Elsie Clews Parson's account of the history of Laguna: "Laguna was the first of the Pueblos to Americanize through intermarriage . . . and Silko's great grandfather, Robert Marmon, led the Americanization faction, resulting in the exodus of the traditional Laguna to Mesita and then to Isleta" (2–3). However, Tony and Wilma Purley of Mesita, cited above, caution that it is a mistake to apply both the notion of relative "Americanization" and the counter-notion of "resistance" to the cultural situation of the main village at Laguna. They point out that all the villages partake of T.V. and other 'mainstream' cultural practices. They disagree, however, that such incorporation constitutes "Americanization." Because the national and global market economy has intervened in the symbolic meanings of Pueblo identity and identification, rather than resistance to national symbolic tropes and cultural practices, they emphasize that the Pueblos incorporate those structures of modernization into the old traditions. Nevertheless, the village "has its secrets" that outsiders should respect (but have notoriously betrayed).

8   Momaday, one might assume, identifies more particularly with the Kiowa of his paternal heritage than with the Jemez Pueblo and Navajo depicted in *House Made of Dawn,* and yet he also deeply identifies with the latter as he observes in *The Names* (New York: Harper Colophon Books, 1977). "My parents lived and taught at the Jemez Day School for more than a quarter of a century. It was my home from the time I was twelve until I ventured out to seek my fortune in the world. My most vivid and cherished boyhood memories are centered upon that place" (1977:117–118).

9   Arnold Krupat in Gerald Vizenor's *Narrative Chance* (1989). Speaking of a thematic movement in Native American autobiography from history and science to art, Krupat observes that "Native Americans have had to make a variety of accommodations to the dominant culture's

forms, capitulating to them, assimilating them, sometimes dramatically transforming them, but never able to proceed independent of them" (1989:57).

10 My formulation of bicultural mediation extrapolates from the distinction between use and exchange value in Anthony Wilden (1980): "In the constitution of exchange value out of use value, the primary necessity is a 'point of contact' with the exterior." Similarly, the bicultural mediator, an exchange value of sorts, is constituted in relation to "external contact at a boundary which . . . brings about internal reorganization AFTER THE EVENT" (1980:252, glossed from Kojeve, 1947a: 372ff.). As such, the mediating subject articulates "a system of higher order complexity," than that on either side of the mediated boundary. The tension between assimilation and resistance consequently entails a third level metacommunication about the rearticulation of boundary relationships by representatives of some aspect of Native American culture in the terms of some corresponding aspect of dominant culture. Although the representative dual subject functions as a translator between the two cultural systems, in so doing, he/she inevitably betrays some of the social rules of the former, just as does translation between languages. Thus the bicultural subject as translator for the dominant culture signals the paradoxical presence/absence of the temporal 'Other' imagined by that culture. The discourse of the bicultural mediator, then, refers to an aura of originary value in much the same way that economic exchange value functions in relationship to use value.

11 While I will use the term *mixed-blood* in order to define a site of strategic articulation of both Western and indigenous perspectives, I wish to problematize the category. The category of blood is not an indigenous one, but circulates among the borrowings from Western ideologies, and like the appropriation of the horse or of firearms, functions to signify a resistant 'Indianness' that persists despite the encroachments of the colonizing cultures. Although the ideology of race derives from medieval Europe, constituting the self-affirmation of the nobility in its attempt to secure itself against gathering peasant and mercantile pressures, the same strategy is appropriated and transposed by indigenous peoples in order to affirm their resistance to the assimilative pressures of colonization. Thus the conceptual category of genealogy is reified in both European and indigenous contexts to describe a quality that travels in the blood: the notion of "blue blood" is adapted by post-"contact" Indian-identified peoples as the valorization of "red blood." (As an aside: the reader should be alert to the proliferation of tropes commonly resorted to in order to convey information concerning "red" and "white" relations. While the tropological basis of the notion of mixed blood must be foregrounded and the irony of its use registered, it is well to keep in mind the brute facts of colonization within which the signifier "mixed-blood" functions.)

12 The term *half-breed* is commonly used by Native Americans of mixed descent both as affirmation of our sense of ambiguity and as a pejorative appelation (legitimating, by contrast, those whose identities are less ambiguously constituted). In its affirmative function, it belongs to the same category of resistance to assimilation as that earlier designation appropriated by indigenous peoples—Indian—to assert difference from their namers.

13 Anthony Wilden (1980:354) understands the synchronic perspective as "an overdetermined communication about some (overdetermined) relationship or other at another level." One can extrapolate the representative mixed-blood position, then, as consisting in a "metacommunication about a referent communication," that is, the crises of subjectivities generated by simultaneously identifying with contradictory systems of cultural organization and aim. The mixed-blood position can be understood as a communication, in a sense, about the double-bind experience consequent on internalizing conflicting messages regarding origins that form the underlying evaluative criteria of these systems. Yet the mixed-blood position, insofar as it presents itself as representative of the tribal community, can only speak with 'forked tongue,' and it is precisely that doubleness that is required by the multi-leveled contradictions, denials, and selective affirmations within the messages in circuit.

14 Anthony Wilden (1980:174).

15 I discuss the matter in detail in *Revising the Ethnic Canon* (University of Minnesota Press, forthcoming 1994), edited by David Palumbo-Liu.

16 See, for example, an article in *The Amicus Journal* (Fall 1991) by Dick Russell, "Dances with Waste," which reports the efforts of Pine Ridge resident, Joann Tall, to organize resistance to this facet of "modernization."

17 Special thanks to my fellow graduate students at Stanford, Mike Morales, Arturo Heredia, and Heather Zwicker, for taking time out from their own work to offer editorial suggestions in the various stages of this essay.

REFERENCES

Adorno, Rolena. 1986. *Guaman Poma: Writing and Resistance in Colonial Peru*. Austin: University of Texas Press.

Allen, Paula Gunn. 1986. *The Sacred Hoop: Recovering the Feminine in American Indian Traditions*. Boston: Beacon Press.

———. 1990. "Special Problems in Teaching Leslie Marmon Silko's *Ceremony.*" Berkeley: *The American Indian Quarterly: Journal of American Indian Studies* 14:4:379–386.

Arendt, Hannah. 1963. *On Revolution*. London and New York: Penguin Books.

Bhabha, Homi. 1984. "Of Mimicry and Man: The Ambivalence of Colonial Discourse." *October,* number 28.

Clifford, James. 1988. *The Predicament of Culture: Twentieth-Century Ethnography. Literature, and Art*. Cambridge, Mass.: Harvard University Press.

Kojeve, Alexandre. 1947. *Introduction à la lecture de Hegel*, ed. Raymond Queneau, Paris: Gallimard.

Momaday, N. Scott. 1968. *House Made of Dawn*. New York: Harper and Row.

Silko, Leslie Marmon. 1977. *Ceremony*. New York: Viking Press.

Turner, Victor. 1969. *The Ritual Process: Structure and Anti-Structure*. Chicago: Aldine.

Vizenor, Gerald. 1989. *Narrative Chance: Postmodern Discourse on Native American Indian Literatures*. Albuquerque: University of New Mexico Press

Wilden, Anthony. 1980. *System and Structure*. London and New York: Tavistock.

VI

Genders and Sexualities

Whatever the internal disputes regarding the mechanics of colonial governance among the administrators, the insistent myth of colonialism as immediately or in the long run beneficial to its subject populations was taken for granted in virtually every domain of colonial intervention. According to this myth, the necessity of substituting Western-style democracy for "Oriental despotism," revolutionizing stagnant societies, and liberalizing conservative cultures through external force was justified by the comforting piety that the natives needed someone to show them the way of the colonizers, either to the one, true God or to the most ideal sociopolitical structure. Women's rights played not an incidental, but a major role in the rhetoric and practice of empire. The general belief that colonialists rescued native women from the brutality of their men went on to gain a new avatar in the assumption that Western feminisms galvanized moribund (or nonexistent) indigenous feminisms in the so-called Third World. However problematic the terminology just used, feminists such as Chandra Talpade Mohanty have rightly critiqued what was once a dominant trend: the concurrent homogenization and ghettoization of "Third World women" through which the "West" claimed the terrain of modern feminism for itself. This is not to disclaim the incidental benefits of colonialism or even to dismiss the significant contributions of white, heterosexual, and middle-class feminism to colonized societies. But as some of the writers in part VI argue, both the European male subject and the First World woman were often constituted and legitimized at the expense of a monolithically designated Third World woman. The first three scholars in this section, Leila Ahmed, Oyèrónké Oyěwùmí, and Gayatri Chakravorty Spivak, fundamentally challenge the enduring myth of the feminist benevolence of colonialism in three different cultural contexts that share the same historical ground in the nineteenth century. Timothy Chin, in contrast, explores the effects of gendered and sexual binaries, partly inherited through colonialism but also channeled through native ethnocentrism in the contemporary Caribbean.

Leila Ahmed explores the function of the veil, one of the most contentious symbols of Islamic women, in what she would say is a largely misguided "contest over culture." The veiled woman in colonial and modern discourse has largely symbolized the hapless female body trapped in virulent patriarchy, and was appropriated as such by the British who occupied Egypt in 1882. But Ahmed argues that contrary to British claims of liberating passive Arab women from their shrouded prison, nineteenth-century administrators were no more feminist than the Arab men they saw themselves challenging. Nor, says Ahmed, were Arab men who called for an emulation of liberal, supposedly superior British values necessarily advocating a feminist revolution. Citing the controversial work *Tahrir Al-Mar'a* (The Liberation of Woman) by the Egyptian intellectual Qassim Amin, published in 1899, Ahmed concludes that the "book merely called for the substitution of Islamic-style male dominance by Western-style male dominance." As she goes on to say, "for neither side was male dominance ever in question."

If, in some ways, Amin sounds like the conventional "mimic man," consuming and reproducing the refrain of colonial excellence as a model to aspire toward, his access to middle-class, colonial education and class hierarchy not only enabled his endorsement but also rewarded it. Despite their invocation of oppressed Islamic women to confirm the Orientalist discourse of Arab inferiority, administrators such as Lord Cromer were themselves heirs to "Victorian theories of the biological inferiority of women and the naturalness of the Victorian ideal of the female role of domesticity." The ostensible project of liberating Middle Eastern women that such figures were apparently engaged in was ultimately, according to Ahmed, a "colonial feminism, or feminism as used against other cultures in the service of colonialism," which invariably tainted feminist movements in the region. Ahmed's point is not to defend Arab patriarchy or even to insist that the veil is an appropriate receptacle for the cultural baggage assigned to it either by Orientalist discourse or by nativist resistance to Western influences. She reveals, instead, how the veil functioned as a convenient alibi for the justification of colonial intervention, which did not really have the benign motives it claimed.

Oyèrónké Oyěwùmí goes even further to argue that the Victorian "bio-logic" of gender was imposed, through British colonization of Yorùbáland from 1862 to 1960, on the Oyo-Yorùbá society, which did not discriminate against men and women on the basis of what Spivak elsewhere refers to as "genitalism." Also qualifying her claims, Oyěwùmí does not suggest that her observation applies to all African cultures or that the Yorùbá peoples had no social hierarchy before British rule. The community was simply not organized along the lines of gender but used other factors such as age and seniority. She points out that while precolonial Yorùbá culture obviously recognized anatomical sex differences (anasex, anamale, anafemale), such distinctions were not used to read women biblically as inferior mates of men. Although bourgeois, individualist capitalism was touted as an improvement that followed colonial rule, Oyěwùmí demonstrates how it also had negative effects in which newly autocratic male chieftainship, male individualism, land ownership, wage access, and legal rights all combined to make Yorùbá women lose their traditional rights while struggling to gain access to modern ones in a system that required adjustment to a different worldview and different means of gaining privilege.

"Central to colonial rule was the question of how to extract wealth from the colonies for the benefit of the occupying European powers," Oyěwùmí sums up. Once the profit motive, rather than any noble aspiration for uplifting natives, is recognized as the primary motivation behind colonialism, the "woman question," despite its appropriation, becomes as tangential to colonial power as it was to Victorian patriarchy. But Oyěwùmí also reminds us that not only did the colonizers not liberate Yorùbá women from oppressive native structures, they actually reduced them to "the unenviable position of European women" in that century. Like Ahmed, Oyěwùmí emphasizes the contaminated process of research when layers of colonialist misreadings and misunderstandings have made what is "customary" or "traditional" difficult to trace. So "natural" did their own system of gender distinction and subordination seem to the British, that Yorùbá women in positions of power became "invisible" to them in a process that Spivak calls the "general epistemic violence of imperialism."

Spivak's rereadings of the construction of native subjects—white Creole Bertha Mason in *Jane Eyre* and freed black house slave Christophine in *Wide Sargasso Sea*, the imaginative supplement to Charlotte Brontë's novel published in 1966 but set in the nineteenth-century Caribbean and England, implicates both the authors and the literary critics in the "imperialist project." However sensitive critics may be to class and gender issues in Brontë's novel, Spivak insists that they also have to recognize what enables the individualist feminism of Brontë's protagonist, Jane. A racialized demonization of Bertha and her madness produces what many readers find a satisfying denouement in which Bertha commits suicide by leaping from the flaming battlements, and Jane marries a suitably chastened Rochester. In her later revisionist account, Dominican author Jean Rhys portrays Antoinette Bertha Mason more sympathetically, but here Christophine functions as her enabling vehicle that now conveniently disappears from the text. "It is the active ideology of imperialism that provides the discursive field," says Spivak, revealing a critical blindness in earlier analyses of the novels to the colonial contexts of India, the Middle East, and the Caribbean.

Spivak cautions against the "reverse ethnocentrism" of Caliban, the trope of the rebellious, masculinized native justly opposed to colonial power, but not quite sensitive to ways in which gender difference was employed, or repressed, in colonial transactions. Timothy Chin goes on to elaborate the risks involved in such a process, revealing the homophobia and sexism in postcolonial cultures that threaten the potential of decolonization. Along with the rest of the writers in part VI, Chin targets literary production that is complicitous with colonial formulations, but like Ahmed, he implicates the native populations as well. The belief that homosexuals are unevolved human beings, for instance, echoes and displaces the racist ideology that once said the same of all natives. Chin also explores the double bind of anticolonial or nationalist intellectuals who need to reject the universal assertion of metropolitan enlightenment and progressiveness, but not dismiss the accusations of homophobic or sexist behavior in their communities. He notes that the necessary critique of racism and colonialism sometimes "reinscribes certain dominant sexual ideologies," of what is constructed as natural black heterosexuality, for instance, unspoiled by what is presumed to be the colonial introduction of homosexuality. The "companionate love" plot between Jane and Rochester which excludes Bertha is repeated with a difference in the compulsory heterosexual coupling ultimately sanctified by the Caribbean writers Chin critiques. "Rather than choosing between readings that emphasize either colonial or sexual politics," Chin prefers to articulate an anticolonial position that is necessarily critical toward normative discourses of gendered bodies and varied sexualities.

22

LEILA AHMED

The Discourse of the Veil

Qassim Amin's *Tahrir Al-mar'a* (The Liberation of Woman), published in 1899, during a time of visible social change and lively intellectual ferment, caused intense and furious debate. Analyses of the debate and of the barrage of opposition the book provoked have generally assumed that it was the radicalness of Amin's proposals with respect to women that caused the furore. Yet the principal substantive recommendations that Amin advocated for women—giving them a primary-school education and reforming the laws on polygamy and divorce—could scarcely be described as innovatory. As we saw in the last chapter, Muslim intellectuals such as al-Tahtawi and 'Abdu had argued for women's education and called for reforms in matters of polygamy and divorce in the 1870s and 1880s and even earlier without provoking violent controversy. Indeed, by the 1890s the issue of educating women not only to the primary level but beyond was so uncontroversial that both state and Muslim benevolent societies had established girls' schools.

The anger and passion Amin's work provoked become intelligible only when one considers not the substantive reforms for women that he advocated but rather, first, the symbolic reform—the abolition of the veil—that he passionately urged and, second, the reforms, indeed the fundamental changes in culture and society, that he urged upon society as a whole and that he contended it was essential for the Egyptian nation, and Muslim countries generally, to make. The need for a general cultural and social transformation is the central thesis of the book, and it is within this thesis that the arguments regarding women are embedded: changing customs regarding women and changing their costume, abolishing the veil in particular, were key, in the author's thesis, to bringing about the desired general social transformation. Examining how Amin's recommendations regarding women formed part of his general thesis and how and why he believed that unveiling was the key to social transformation is essential to unraveling the significance of the debate that his book provoked.

Amin's work has traditionally been regarded as marking the beginning of feminism in Arab culture. Its publication and the ensuing debate certainly constitute an important moment in the history of Arab women: the first battle of the veil to agitate the Arab press. The battle inaugurated a new discourse in which the veil came to comprehend significations far broader than merely the position of women. Its connotations now encompassed issues of class and culture—the widening cultural gulf between the different classes in society and the interconnected conflict between the culture of the colonizers and that of the colonized. It was in this discourse, too, that the issues of women and culture first appeared as inextricably fused in Arabic discourse. Both the key features of this new discourse, the greatly expanded signification of the veil and the fusion of the issues of women and culture, that made their formal entry into Arab discourse with the publication of Amin's work had their provenance in the discourses of European societies. In Egypt the British colonial presence and discursive input constituted critical components in the situation that witnessed the emergence of the new discourse of the veil.

————————

The British occupation, which began in Egypt in 1882, did not bring about any fundamental change in the economic direction in which Egypt had already embarked—the production of raw material, chiefly cotton, to be worked in European, mainly British, factories. British interests lay in Egypt's continuing to serve as a supplier of raw materials for British factories; and the agricultural projects and administrative reforms pursued by the British administration were those designed to make the country a more efficient producer of raw materials. Such reforms and the country's progressively deeper implication in European capitalism brought increased prosperity and benefits for some classes but worse conditions for others. The principal beneficiaries of the British reform measures and the increased involvement in European capitalism were the European residents of Egypt, the Egyptian upper classes, and the new middle class of rural notables and men educated in Western-type secular schools who became the civil servants and the new intellectual elite. Whether trained in the West or in the Western-type institutions established in Egypt, these new "modern" men with their new knowledges displaced the traditionally and religiously trained 'ulama as administrators and servants of the state, educators, and keepers of the valued knowledges of society. Traditional knowledge itself became devalued as antiquated, mired in the old "backward" ways. The 'ulama class was adversely affected by other developments as well: land-reform measures enacted in the nineteenth century led to a loss of revenue for the 'ulama, and legal and judicial reforms in the late nineteenth century took many matters out of the jurisdiction of the shari'a courts, over which the 'ulama presided as legislators and judges, and transferred them to the civil courts, presided over by the "new men."

The law reforms, under way before the British occupation, did not affect the position of women. The primary object of the reforms had been to address the palpable injustice of the Capitulary system, whereby Europeans were under the jurisdiction of their consular powers and could not be tried in Egyptian courts. (The Capitulations were concessions gained by European powers, prior to colonialism, which regulated the activities of their merchants and which, with the growing influence of their consuls and ambassadors in the nineteenth century, were turned into a system by which European residents were virtually outside the law.) The reforms accordingly established Mixed Courts and promulgated civil and penal codes applicable to all communities. The new codes, which were largely based on French law, bypassed rather than reformed shari'a law, although occasionally, concerning homicide, for instance, shari'a law, too, was reformed by following an Islamic legal opinion other than the dominant opinion of the Hanafi school, the school followed in Egypt. This method of reforming the shari'a, modifying it by reference to another Islamic legal opinion, was followed in Turkey and, later in the twentieth century, in Iraq, Syria, and Tunisia—but not Egypt—in order to introduce measures critically redefining and amending the law on polygamy and divorce in ways that fundamentally curtailed male license.[1]

Other groups besides the 'ulama were adversely affected by Western penetration and the local entrenchment of Western power. Artisans and small merchants were unable to compete with Western products or were displaced by the agents of Western interests. Others whose circumstances deteriorated or whose economic advancement was blocked by British administrative policies were rural workers who, as a result of peasant dispossession, flocked to the cities, where they swelled the ranks of urban casual laborers. A growing lower-middle class of men who had received a Western-type secular education up to primary level and who filled the lower ranks of the administration were unable to progress beyond these positions because educational facilities for further training were not available. The British administration not only failed to provide more advanced facilities but responded to the problem by increasing fees at primary level to cut enrollment. Measures such as these, which clearly discriminated in favor of the well-to-do and frustrated the hopes and ambitions of others, accentuated class divisions.[2]

The British administration pursued its educational policy in the teeth of both a popular demand for education for boys and for girls and the urgings of intellectuals of all political and ideological complexions that the administration give priority to providing more educational facilities because of the importance of education to national development. The British administration espoused its restrictive policy partly for political reasons. Cromer, the British consul general, believed that providing subsidized education was not the province of government, and he also believed that education could foster dangerous nationalist sentiments.[3]

Even this brief outline of the consequences of the increasing economic importance of the West and of British colonial domination suggests how issues of culture and attitudes toward Western ways were intertwined with issues of class and access to economic resources, position, and status. The lower-middle and lower classes, who were generally adversely affected by or experienced no benefits from the economic and political presence of the West, had a different perspective on the colonizer's culture and ways than did the upper classes and the new middle-class intellectuals trained in Western ways, whose interests were advanced by affiliation with Western culture and who benefited economically from the British presence. Just as the latter group was disposed by economic interests as well as training to be receptive to Western culture, the less prosperous classes were disposed, also on economic grounds, to reject and feel hostile toward it. That attitude was exacerbated by the blatant unfairness of the economic and legal privileges enjoyed by the Europeans in Egypt. The Capitulations—referred to earlier—not only exempted Europeans from the jurisdiction of Egyptian law but also virtually exempted them from paying taxes; Europeans consequently engaged in commerce on terms more favorable than those applied to their native counterparts, and they became very prosperous.

Conflicting class and economic interests thus underlay the political and ideological divisions that began ever more insistently to characterize the intellectual and political scene—divisions between those eager to adopt European ways and institutions, seeing them as the means to personal and national advancement, and those anxious to preserve the Islamic and national heritage against the onslaughts of the infidel West. This states somewhat simply the extremes of the two broad oppositional tendencies within Egyptian political thought at this time. The spectrum of political views on the highly fraught issues of colonialism, westernization, British policies, and the political future of the country, views that found expression in the extremely lively and diverse journalistic press, in fact encompassed a wide range of analyses and perspectives.

Among the dominant political groups finding voice in the press at the time Amin's work was published was a group that strongly supported the British administration and advocated the adoption of a "European outlook." Prominent among its members were a number of Syrian Christians who founded the pro-British daily *Al-muqattam*. At the other extreme was a group whose views, articulated in the newspaper *Al-mu'ayyad*, published by Sheikh 'Ali Yusuf, fiercely opposed Western encroachment in any form. This group was also emphatic about the importance of preserving Islamic tradition in all areas. The National party (Al-hizb al-watani), a group led by Mustapha Kamil, was equally fierce in its opposition to the British and to westernization, but it espoused a position of secular rather than Islamic nationalism. This group, whose organ was the journal *Al-liwa*, held that advancement for Egypt must begin with the expulsion of the British. Other groups, including the Umma party

(People's party), which was to emerge as the politically dominant party in the first decades of the twentieth century, advocated moderation and an attitude of judicious discrimination in identifying political and cultural goals. Muhammad 'Abdu, discussed in chapter 7, was an important intellectual influence on the Umma party, though its members were more secular minded; he had advocated the acquisition of Western technology and knowledge and, simultaneously, the revivification and reform of the Islamic heritage, including reform in areas affecting women. The Umma party advocated the adoption of the European notion of the nation-state in place of religion as the basis of community. Their goals were to adopt Western political institutions and, at the same time, to gradually bring about Egypt's independence from the British. Umma party members, unlike Mustapha Kamil's ultranationalists or the Islamic nationalists, consequently had an attitude, not of hostility to the British, but rather of measured collaboration. Among its prominent members were Abmad Lutfi al-Sayyid and Sa'd Zaghloul.

The colonial presence and the colonizer's economic and political agenda, plus the role that cultural training and affiliation played in widening the gap between classes, provided ample ground for the emergence at this moment of the issue of culture as fraught and controversial. Why the contest over culture should center on women and the veil and why Amin fastened upon those issues as the key to cultural and social transformation only becomes intelligible, however, by reference to ideas imported into the local situation from the colonizing society. Those ideas were interjected into the native discourse as Muslim men exposed to European ideas began to reproduce and react to them and, subsequently and more pervasively and insistently, as Europeans—servants of empire and individuals resident in Egypt—introduced and actively disseminated them.

The peculiar practices of Islam with respect to women had always formed part of the Western narrative of the quintessential otherness and inferiority of Islam.[4] A detailed history of Western representations of women in Islam and of the sources of Western ideas on the subject has yet to be written, but broadly speaking it may be said that prior to the seventeenth century Western ideas about Islam derived from the tales of travelers and crusaders, augmented by the deductions of clerics from their readings of poorly understood Arabic texts. Gradually thereafter, through the seventeenth and eighteenth centuries, readings of Arabic texts became slightly less vague, and the travelers' interpretations of what they observed approximated more closely the meanings that the male members of the visited societies attached to the observed customs and phenomena. (Male travelers in Muslim societies had extremely limited access to women, and the explanations and interpretations they brought back, insofar as they represented a native perspective at all, essentially, therefore, gave the male point of view on whatever subject was discussed.)

By the eighteenth century the Western narrative of women in Islam, which was drawn from such sources, incorporated elements that certainly bore a resemblance to the bold external features of the Islamic patterns of male dominance, but at the same time it (1) often garbled and misconstrued the specific content and meaning of the customs described and (2) assumed and represented the Islam practiced in Muslim societies in the periods in which the Europeans encountered and then in some degree or other dominated those societies to be the only possible interpretation of the religion. Previous chapters have already indicated the dissent within Islam as to the different interpretations to which it was susceptible. And some sense of the kinds of distortions and garbling to which Muslim beliefs were subject as a result of Western misapprehension is suggested by the ideas that a few more perceptive Western travelers felt themselves called upon to correct in their own accounts of Muslims. The eighteenth-century writer and traveler Lady Mary Wortley Montagu, for example, attacked the widespread belief among her English contemporaries that Muslims believed that women had no souls, an idea that she explained was untrue. (Montagu believed that many of the misapprehensions of her contemporaries about Islam arose from faulty translations of the Quran made by "Greek Priests, who would not fail to falsify it with the extremity of Malice.") She also said that having herself not only observed veiled women but also used the veil, she was able to assert that it was not the oppressive custom her compatriots believed it to be and in fact it gave women a kind of liberty, for it enabled them not to be recognized.[5]

But such rebuttals left little mark on the prevailing views of Islam in the West. However, even though Islam's peculiar practices with respect to women and its "oppression" of women formed some element of the European narrative of Islam from early on, the issue of women only emerged as the centerpiece of the Western narrative of Islam in the nineteenth century, and in particular the later nineteenth century, as Europeans established themselves as colonial powers in Muslim countries.[6]

The new prominence, indeed centrality, that the issue of women came to occupy in the Western and colonial narrative of Islam by the late nineteenth century appears to have been the result of a fusion between a number of strands of thought all developing within the Western world in the latter half of that century. Thus the reorganized narrative, with its new focus on women, appears to have been a compound created out of a coalescence between the old narrative of Islam just referred to (and which Edward Said's *Orientalism* details) and the broad, all-purpose narrative of colonial domination regarding the inferiority, in relation to the European culture, of all Other cultures and societies, a narrative that saw vigorous development over the course of the nineteenth century. And finally and somewhat ironically, combining with these to create the new centrality of the position of women in the colonial discourse of Islam was the language of feminism, which also developed with particular vigor during this period.[7]

In the colonial era the colonial powers, especially Britain (on which I will focus my discussion), developed their theories of races and cultures and of a social evolutionary sequence according to which middle-class Victorian England, and its beliefs and practices, stood at the culminating point of the evolutionary process and represented the model of ultimate civilization. In this scheme Victorian womanhood and mores with respect to women, along with other aspects of society at the colonial center, were regarded as the ideal and measure of civilization. Such theories of the superiority of Europe, legitimizing its domination of other societies, were shortly corroborated by "evidence" gathered in those societies by missionaries and others, whose observations came to form the emergent study of anthropology. This same emergent anthropology—and other sciences of man—simultaneously served the dominant British colonial and androcentric order in another and internal project of domination. They provided evidence corroborating Victorian theories of the biological inferiority of women and the naturalness of the Victorian ideal of the female role of domesticity. Such theories were politically useful to the Victorian establishment as it confronted, internally, an increasingly vocal feminism.[8]

Even as the Victorian male establishment devised theories to contest the claims of feminism, and derided and rejected the ideas of feminism and the notion of men's oppressing women with respect to itself, it captured the language of feminism and redirected it, in the service of colonialism, toward Other men and the cultures of Other men. It was here and in the combining of the languages of colonialism and feminism that the fusion between the issues of women and culture was created. More exactly, what was created was the fusion between the issues of women, their oppression, and the cultures of Other men. The idea that Other men, men in colonized societies or societies beyond the borders of the civilized West, oppressed women was to be used, in the rhetoric of colonialism, to render morally justifiable its project of undermining or eradicating the cultures of colonized peoples.

Colonized societies, in the colonial thesis, were alike in that they were inferior but differed as to their specific inferiority. Colonial feminism, or feminism as used against other cultures in the service of colonialism, was shaped into a variety of similar constructs, each tailored to fit the particular culture that was the immediate target of domination—India, the Islamic world, sub-Saharan Africa. With respect to the Islamic world, regarded as an enemy (and indeed as *the* enemy) since the Crusades, colonialism—as I have already suggested—had a rich vein of bigotry and misinformation to draw on.

Broadly speaking, the thesis of the discourse on Islam blending a colonialism committed to male dominance with feminism—the thesis of the new colonial discourse of Islam centered on women—was that Islam was innately and immutably oppressive to women, that the veil and segregation epitomized that oppression, and that these customs were the fundamental reasons for the general and comprehensive backwardness of Islamic societies. Only if these practices "intrinsic" to Islam (and therefore Islam itself) were cast off could Muslim societies begin to move forward on the path of civilization. Veiling—to *Western* eyes, the most visible marker of the differentness and inferiority of Islamic societies—became the symbol now of both the oppression of women (or, in the language of the day, Islam's degradation of women) and the backwardness of Islam, and it became the open target of colonial attack and the spearhead of the assault on Muslim societies.

The thesis just outlined—that the Victorian colonial paternalistic establishment appropriated the language of feminism in the service of its assault on the religions and cultures of Other men, and in particular on Islam, in order to give an aura of moral justification to that assault at the very same time as it combated feminism within its own society—can easily be substantiated by reference to the conduct and rhetoric of the colonizers. The activities of Lord Cromer are particularly illuminating on the subject, perfectly exemplifying how, when it came to the cultures of other men, white supremacist views, androcentric and paternalistic convictions, and feminism came together in harmonious and actually entirely logical accord in the service of the imperial idea.

Cromer had quite decided views on Islam, women in Islam, and the veil. He believed quite simply that Islamic religion and society were inferior to the European ones and bred inferior men. The inferiority of the men was evident in numerous ways, which Cromer lists at length. For instance: "The European is a close reasoner; his statements of fact are devoid of ambiguity; he is a natural logician, albeit he may not have studied logic; he loves symmetry in all things . . . his trained intelligence works like a piece of mechanism. The mind of the Oriental on the other hand, like his picturesque streets, is eminently wanting in symmetry. His reasoning is of the most slipshod description."[9]

Cromer explains that the reasons "Islam as a social system has been a complete failure are manifold." However, "first and foremost," he asserts, was its treatment of women. In confirmation of this view he quotes the words of the preeminent British Orientalist of his day, Stanley Lane-Poole: "The degradation of women in the East is a canker that begins its destructive work early in childhood, and has eaten into the whole system of Islam" (2:134, 134n).

Whereas Christianity teaches respect for women, and European men "elevated" women because of the teachings of their religion, Islam degraded them, Cromer wrote, and it was to this degradation, most evident in the practices of veiling and segregation, that the inferiority of Muslim men could be traced. Nor could it be doubted that the practices of veiling and seclusion exercised "a baneful effect on Eastern society. The arguments in the case are, indeed, so commonplace that it is unnecessary to dwell on them" (2:155). It was essential that Egyptians "be persuaded or forced into imbibing the true spirit of western civilisation" (2:538), Cromer stated, and to achieve this, it was essential to change the position of women in Islam, for it was Islam's degradation of women, expressed in the practices of veiling and seclusion, that was "the fatal obstacle" to the Egyptian's "attainment of that elevation of thought and character which should accompany the introduction of Western civilisation" (2:538–39); only by abandoning those practices might they attain "the mental and moral development which he [Cromer] desired for them."[10]

Even as he delivered himself of such views, the policies Cromer pursued were detrimental to Egyptian women. The restrictions he placed on government schools and his raising of school fees held back girls' education as well as boys'. He also discouraged the training of women doctors. Under the British, the School for Hakimas, which had given women as many years of medical training as the men received in the School of Medicine, was restricted to midwifery. On the local preference among women for being treated by women Cromer said, "I am aware that in exceptional cases women like to be attended by female doctors, but I conceive that throughout the civilised world, attendance by medical men is still the rule."[11]

However, it was in his activities in relation to women in his own country that Cromer's paternalistic convictions and his belief in the proper subordination of women most clearly declared themselves. This champion of the unveiling of Egyptian women was, in England, founding member and sometime president of the Men's League for Opposing Women's Suffrage.[12] Feminism on the home front and feminism directed against white men was to be resisted and suppressed; but taken abroad and directed against the cultures of colonized peoples, it could be promoted in ways that admirably served and furthered the project of the dominance of the white man.

Others besides the official servants of empire promoted these kinds of ideas: missionaries, for example. For them, too, the degradation of women in Islam legitimized the attack on native culture. A speaker at a missionary conference held in London in 1888 observed that Muhammad had been exemplary as a young man but took many wives in later life and set out to preach a religion whose object was "to extinguish women altogether"; and he introduced the veil, which "has had the most terrible and injurious effect upon the mental, moral and spiritual history of all Mohammedan races." Missionary women delivered themselves of the same views. One wrote that Muslim women needed to be rescued by their Christian sisters from the "ignorance and degradation" in which they existed, and converted to Christianity. Their plight was a consequence of the nature of their religion, which gave license to "lewdness." Marriage in Islam was "not founded on love but on sensuality," and a Muslim wife, "buried alive behind the veil," was regarded as "prisoner and slave rather than . . . companion and help-meet." Missionary-school teachers actively attacked the custom of veiling by seeking to persuade girls to defy their families and not wear one. For the missionaries, as for Cromer, women were the key to converting backward Muslim societies into civilized Christian societies. One missionary openly advocated targeting women, because women molded children. Islam should be undermined subtly and indirectly among the young, and when children grew older, "the evils of Islam could be spelled out more directly." Thus a trail of "gunpowder" would be laid "into the heart of Islam."[13]

Others besides officials and missionaries similarly promoted these ideas, individuals resident in Egypt, for example. Well-meaning European feminists, such as Eugénie Le Brun (who took the young Huda Sha'rawi under her wing), earnestly inducted young Muslim women into the European understanding of the meaning of the veil and the need to cast it off as the essential first step in the struggle for female liberation.

Whether such proselytizers from the West were colonial patriarchs, then, or missionaries or feminists, all essentially insisted that Muslims had to give up their native religion, customs, and dress, or at least reform their religion and habits along the recommended lines, and for all of them the veil and customs regarding women were the prime matters requiring reform. And all assumed their right to denounce native ways, and in particular the veil, and to set about undermining the culture in the name of whatever cause they claimed to be serving—civilizing the society, or Christianizing it, or saving women from the odious culture and religion in which they had the misfortune to find themselves.

Whether in the hands of patriarchal men or feminists, the ideas of Western feminism essentially functioned to morally justify the attack on native societies and to support the notion of the comprehensive superiority of Europe. Evidently, then, whatever the disagreements of feminism with white male domination within Western societies, outside their borders feminism turned from being the critic of the system of white male dominance to being its docile servant. Anthropology, it has often been said, served as a handmaid to colonialism. Perhaps it must also be said that feminism, or the ideas of feminism, served as its other handmaid.

The ideas to which Cromer and the missionaries gave expression formed the basis of Amin's book. The rationale in which Amin, a French-educated upper-middle-class lawyer, grounded his call for changing the position of women and for abolishing the veil was essentially the same as theirs. Amin's text also assumed and declared the inherent superiority of Western civilization and the inherent backwardness of Muslim societies: he wrote that anyone familiar with "the East" had observed "the backwardness of Muslims in the East wherever they are." There were, to be sure, local differences: "The Turk, for example, is clean, honest, brave," whereas the Egyptian is "the opposite."[14] Egyptians were "lazy and always fleeing work," left their children "covered with dirt and roaming the alleys rolling in the dust like the children of animals," and were sunk in apathy, afflicted, as he put it, "with a paralysis of nerves so that we are unmoved by anything, however beautiful or terrible" (34). Nevertheless, over and above such differences between Muslim nationals, Amin asserted, the observer would find both Turks and Egyptians "equal in ignorance, laziness and backwardness" (72).

In the hierarchy of civilizations adopted by Amin, Muslim civilization is represented as semicivilized compared to that of the West.

> European civilization advances with the speed of steam and electricity, and has even overspilled to every part of the globe so that there is not an inch that he [European man] has not trodden underfoot. Any place he goes he takes control of its resources . . . and turns them into profit and if he does harm to the original inhabitants, it is only that he pursues happiness in this world and seeks it wherever he may find it. . . . For the most part he uses his intellect, but when circumstances require it, he deploys force. He does not seek glory from his possessions and colonies, for he has enough of this through his intellectual achievements and scientific inventions. What drives the Englishman to dwell in India and the French in Algeria . . . is profit and the desire to acquire resources in countries where the inhabitants do not know their value nor how to profit from them.
>
> When they encounter savages they eliminate them or drive them from the land, as happened in America . . . and is happening now in Africa. . . . When they encounter a nation like ours, with a degree of civilization, with a past, and a religion . . . and customs and . . . institutions . . . they deal with its inhabitants kindly. But they do soon acquire its most valuable resources, because they have greater wealth and intellect and knowledge and force. (69–70)

Amin said that to make Muslim society abandon its backward ways and follow the Western path to success and civilization required changing the women. "The grown man is none other than his mother shaped him in childhood," and *this is the essence of this book. . . . It is impossible to breed successful men if they do not have mothers capable of raising them to be successful.* This is the noble duty that advanced civilisation has given to women in our age and which she fulfills in advanced societies" (78; emphasis in original).

In the course of making his argument, Amin managed to express not just a generalized contempt for Muslims but also contempt for specific groups, often in lavishly abusive detail. Among the targets of his most dismissive abuse were the rulers of Egypt prior to the British, whom he called corrupt and unjust despots. Their descendants, who still constituted the nominal rulers of the country, were championed by some nationalist anti-British factions, including Mustapha Kamil's party, as the desirable alternative to British rule. Amin's abuse thus angered nationalists opposed to the British as well as the royal family. Not surprisingly, Khedive Abbas, compelled to govern as the British wished him to, refused to receive Amin after the publication of his book. And Amin's eager praise of the British also inflamed the anti-British factions: he represented British dominion in Egypt as bringing about an age of unprecedented justice and freedom, when "knowledge spread, and national bonding appeared, and security and order prevailed throughout the country, and the basis of advancement became available" (69).

In Amin's work only the British administration and European civilization receive lavish praise. Among those singled out as targets of his abuse were the 'ulama. Amin characterizes them as grossly ignorant, greedy, and lazy. He details the bleakness of their intellectual horizons and their deficiencies of character in unequivocal terms.

> Our 'ulama today . . . takes no interest in . . . the intellectual sciences; such things are of no concern to them. The object of their learning is that they know how to parse the bismillah [the phrase "in the name of God"] in no fewer than a thousand ways, and if you ask them how the thing in their hands is made, or where the nation to which they belong or a neighboring nation or the nation that occupied their country is located geographically and what its strengths and weaknesses are, or what the function of a bodily part is, they shrug their shoulders, contemptuous of the question; and if you talk with them about the organization of their government and its laws and economic and political condition, you will find they know nothing. Not only are they greedy . . . they always want to escape hard work, too.   (74)

Those for whom Amin reserved his most virulent contempt—ironically, in a work ostensibly championing their cause—were Egyptian women. Amin describes the physical habits and moral qualities of Egyptian women in considerable detail. Indeed, given the segregation of society and what must have been his exceedingly limited access to women other than members of his immediate family and their retinue, and perhaps prostitutes, the degree of detail strongly suggests that Amin must have drawn on conceptions of the character and conduct of women based on his own and other European or Egyptian men's self-representations on the subject, rather than on any extensive observation of a broad-enough segment of female society to justify his tone of knowledgeable generalization.[15] Amin's generalizations about Egyptian women include the following.

> Most Egyptian women are not in the habit of combing their hair everyday . . . nor do they bathe more than once a week. They do not know how to use a toothbrush and do not attend to what is attractive in clothing, though their attractiveness and cleanliness strongly influence men's inclinations. They do not know how to rouse desire in their husband, nor how to retain his desire or to increase it. . . . This is because the ignorant woman does not understand inner feelings and the promptings of attraction and aversion. . . . If she tries to rouse a man, she will usually have the opposite effect.   (29)

Amin's text describes marriage among Muslims as based not on love but on ignorance and sensuality, as does the missionary discourse. In Amin's text, however, the blame has shifted from men to women. Women were the chief source of the "lewdness" and coarse sensuality and materialism characterizing Muslim marriages. Because only superior souls could experience true love, it was beyond the capacity of the Egyptian wife. She could know only whether her husband was "tall or short, white or black." His intellectual and moral qualities, his sensitive feelings, his knowledge, whatever other men might praise and respect him for, were beyond her grasp. Egyptian women "praise men that honorable men would not shake hands with, and hate others that we honor. This is because they judge according to their ignorant minds. The best man to her is he who plays with her all day and night . . . and who has money . . . and buys her clothes and nice things. And the worst of men is he who spends his time working in his office; whenever she sees him . . . reading . . . she . . . curses books and knowledge" (29–30).

One further passage about Egyptian women is worth citing for its surely unwarranted tone of authority. It is also interesting for the animus against women, perhaps even paranoia, that it betrays.

> Our women do nothing of housework, and work at no skill or art, and do not engage themselves in the pursuit of knowledge, and do not read and do not worship God, so what do they do? I will tell you, and you know as I do that what occupies the wife of the rich man and the poor, the learned and the ignorant, master and servant, is one thing . . . which takes many forms and that is her relationship with her husband. Sometimes she will imagine he hates her, and then that he loves her. At times she compares him with the husbands of her neighbors. . . . Sometimes she sets herself to finding a way to change his feelings toward his relatives. . . . Nor does she fail to supervise his conduct with the servant girls and observe how he looks when women visitors call . . . she will not tolerate any maid unless the maid is hideous. . . . You see her with neighbors and friends, . . . raising her voice and relating all that occurs between herself and her husband and her husband's relatives and friends, and her sorrows and joys, and all her secrets, baring what is in her heart till no secret remains—even matters of the bed. (40)

Of course, not many women would have had the wealth to be as free of housework as Amin suggests, and even wealthy women managed homes, oversaw the care of their children, and saw to their own business affairs, as I described in an earlier chapter, or took an active part in founding and running charities, as I will discuss in the following chapter. But what is striking about Amin's account (addressed to male readers) of how he imagined that women occupied themselves is that even as he describes them as obsessed with their husband and with studying, analyzing, and discussing his every mood and as preoccupied with wondering whether he hates them and whether he is eyeing the maid or the guest, Amin does not have the charity to note that indeed men had all the power and women had excellent reason to study and analyze a husband's every mood and whim. On a mood or a whim, or if a maid or a guest caught his fancy, they could find themselves, at any age, divorced, and possibly destitute. To the extent, then, that Amin was right in his guess as to what women discussed when no men were present—and some women did endlessly talk about their husbands—perhaps those that did, did indeed need to be vigilant about their husbands' moods and conduct and to draw on their women friends for ideas.

On the specific measures for the "liberation" of woman that Amin called for, and even what he meant by liberation, the text is turgid and contradictory to a degree attributable variously to intellectual muddle on the part of the writer, to the intrinsic confusion and speciousness inherent in the Western narrative, which he adopted, and to the probability that the work was the fruit of discussions on the subject by several individuals, whose ideas Amin then threw together. Indeed, the contribution of other individuals to the work was apparently more than purely verbal: certain chapters, suggests Muhammad 'Amara, editor of Amin's and 'Abdu's works, were written by Abdu. One chapter that 'Amara argues was 'Abdu's is distinctly different in both tone and content and consequently will be discussed here separately. It may be noted in this context that one rumor in circulation when the book was published was that it had been written at Cromer's urgings. Given the book's wholehearted reproduction of views common in the writings of the colonizers, that idea was not perhaps altogether far-fetched.[16]

Amin's specific recommendations regarding women, the broad rhetoric on the subject notwithstanding, are fairly limited. Among his focuses is women's education. He was "not among those who demand equality in education," he stated firmly, but a primary-school education was necessary for women (36). Women needed some education to enable them to fulfill their function and duty in life as wives. As Amin spelled it out: "It is the wife's duty to plan the household budget . . . to supervise the servants . . . to make her home attractive to her husband, so that he may find ease when he returns to it and so that he likes being there, and enjoys the food and drink and sleep and does not seek to flee from home to spend his time with neighbors or in public places, and it is her duty—and this is her first and most important duty—to raise the children, attending to them physically, mentally, and morally" (31).

Clearly there is nothing in this definition to which the most conservative of patriarchs could not readily assent. Amin's notion that women should receive a primary-school education similarly represented the conservative rather than the liberal point of view among intellectuals and bureaucrats of his day. After all, Amin's book was published in 1899, thirty years after a government commission had recommended providing government schools for both boys and girls and toward the end of a decade in which the demand for education at the primary and secondary level far exceeded capacity. In the 1890s girls, it will be recalled, were already attending schools—missionary schools and those made available by Muslim benevolent societies as well as government schools—and they flooded the teacher-training college with applications when it opened in 1900. In 1891 one journal had even published essays on the role of women by two women from the graduating class of the American College for Girls. Amin's call for a primary-school education for women was far from radical, then; no one speaking out in the debate sparked by his book contested this recommendation.

The demand that was most vehemently and widely denounced was his call for an end to segregation and veiling. Amin's arguments, like the discourse of the colonizers, are grounded in the presumption that veiling and seclusion were customs that, in Cromer's words, "exercised a baneful effect on Eastern society." The veil constituted, wrote Amin, "a huge barrier between woman and her elevation, and consequently a barrier between the nation and its advance" (54). Unfortunately, his assault on the veil represented not the result of reasoned reflection and analysis but rather the internalization and replication of the colonialist perception.

Pared of rhetoric, Amin's argument against seclusion and veiling was simply that girls would forget all they had learned if they were made to veil and observe seclusion after they were educated. The age at which girls were veiled and secluded, twelve to fourteen, was a crucial age for the development of talents and intellect, and veiling and seclusion frustrated that development; girls needed to mix freely with men, for learning came from such mixing (55–56). This position is clearly not compatible with his earlier statement that anything beyond a primary-school education was "unnecessary" for girls. If intellectual development and the acquisition of knowledge were indeed important goals for women, then the rational recommendation would be to pursue these goals directly with increased schooling, not indirectly by ending segregation and veiling so that women could associate with men.

Even more specious—as well as offensive to any who did not share Amin's uncritical and wholesale respect for European man and his presumption of the inferiority of native practices—was another argument he advanced for the abandonment of the veil. After asserting that veiling and seclusion were common to all societies in ancient times, he said: "Do Egyptians imagine that the men of Europe, who have attained such completeness of intellect and feeling that they were able to discover the force of steam and electricity . . . these souls that daily risk their lives in the pursuit of knowledge and honor above the pleasures of life, . . . these intellects and these souls that we so admire, could possibly fail to know the means of safeguarding woman and preserving her purity? Do they think that such a people would have abandoned veiling after it had been in use among them if they had seen any good in it?" (67).

In one section of the book, however, the argument against veiling is rationally made: the chapter which 'Amara suggests was composed by 'Abdu. 'Abdu points out the real disadvantages to women of segregation and veiling. These customs compel them to conduct matters of law and business through an intermediary, placing poor women, who need to earn a living in trade or domestic service, in the false and impossible position of dealing with men in a society that officially bans such dealings (47–48).

The section as a whole is distinctly different in tone and ideas from the rest of the work, and not just in the humane rather than contemptuous prose in which it frames its references both to women and to the Islamic heritage. As a result, some of the views expressed there contradict or sit ill with those expressed elsewhere in the book. There is surely some discrepancy, for example, between Amin's view that women are "deficient in mind, strong in cunning" (39) and need no more than a primary-school education, on the one hand, and the sentiments as to the potential of both sexes that finds expression in the following passage, on the other: "Education is the means by which the individual may attain spiritual and material happiness. . . . Every person has the natural right to develop their talents to the limit.

"Religions address women as they do men. . . . Arts, skills, inventions, philosophy . . . all these draw women as they do men . . . . What difference is there between men and women in this desire, when we see children of both sexes equal in their curiosity about everything falling within their ken? Perhaps that desire is even more alive in girls than in boys" (22–23).

Passages suggestive of careful thought are the exception rather than the rule in this work, however.[17] More commonly the book presented strident criticism of Muslim, particularly Egyptian, culture and society. In calling for women's liberation the thoroughly patriarchal Amin was in fact calling for the transformation of Muslim society along the lines of the Western model and for the substitution of the garb of Islamic-style male dominance for that of Western-style male dominance. Under the guise of a plea for the "liberation" of woman, then, he conducted an attack that in its fundamentals reproduced the colonizer's attack on native culture and society. For Amin as for the colonizers, the veil and segregation symbolized the backwardness and inferiority of Islamic society; in his discourse as in theirs, therefore, the veil and segregation came in for the most direct attack. For Amin as for Cromer, women and their dress were important counters in the discourse concerning the relative merits of the societies and civilizations of men and their different styles of male domination; women themselves and their liberation were no more important to Amin than to Cromer.

Amin's book thus represents the rearticulation in native voice of the colonial thesis of the inferiority of the native and Muslim and the superiority of the European. Rearticulated in native upper-middle-class voice, the voice of a class economically allied with the colonizers and already adopting their life-styles, the colonialist thesis took on a classist dimension: it became in effect an attack (in addition to all the other broad and specific attacks) on the customs of the lower-middle and lower classes.

The book is reckoned to have triggered the first major controversy in the Arabic press: more than thirty books and articles appeared in response to its publication. The majority were critical, though the book did please some readers, notably members of the British administration and pro-British factions: the pro-British paper *Al-muqattam* hailed the book as the finest in years.[18] There were evidently many reasons for Muslims and Egyptians, for nationalists of all stripes, to dislike the work: Amin's adulation of the British and of European civilization, his contempt for natives and native ways, his insulting references to the reigning family and to specific groups and classes, such as the 'ulama (who were prominent among the critics of his book), and his implied and indeed explicit contempt for the customs of the lower classes. However, just as Amin had used the issue of women and the call for their unveiling to conduct his generalized assault on society, so too did the rebuttals of his work come in the form of an affirmation of the customs that he had attacked—veiling and segregation. In a way that was to become typical of the Arabic narrative of resistance, the opposition appropriated, in order to negate them, the terms set in the first place by the colonial discourse.

Analysts routinely treat the debate as one between "feminists," that is, Amin and his allies, and "antifeminists," that is, Amin's critics. They accept at face value the equation made by Amin and the originating Western narrative: that the veil signified oppression, therefore those who called for its abandonment were feminists and those opposing its abandonment were antifeminists.[19] As I have suggested, however, the fundamental and contentious premise of Amin's work was its endorsement of the Western view of Islamic civilization, peoples, and customs as inferior, whereas the author's position on women was profoundly patriarchal and even somewhat misogynist. The book merely called for the substitution of Islamic-style male dominance by Western-style male dominance. Far from being the father of Arab feminism, then, Amin might more aptly be described as the son of Cromer and colonialism.

Opponents with a nationalist perspective were therefore not necessarily any more antifeminist than Amin was feminist. Some who defended the national custom had views on women considerably more "feminist" than Amin's, but others who opposed unveiling, for nationalist and Islamist reasons, had views on women no less patriarchal than his. For example, the attacks on Amin's book published in *Al-liwa,* Mustapha Kamil's paper, declared that women had the same right to an education as men and that their education was as essential to the nation as men's—a position considerably more liberal and feminist than Amin's. The writers opposed unveiling not as antifeminists, it seems, but as cogent analysts of the current social situation.

They did not argue that veiling was immutable Islamic custom, saying, on the contrary, that future generations might decree otherwise. They argued that veiling was the current practice and that Amin's call to unveil was merely part of the hasty and unconsidered rush to imitate the West in everything.[20] This perspective anticipates an incisive and genuinely feminist analysis of the issue of the veil and the accompanying debate offered a few years later by Malak Hifni Nassef, discussed in the next chapter.

Tal'at Harb's nationalist response to Amin, in contrast, defended and upheld Islamic practices, putting forward a view of the role and duties of women in society quite as patriarchal as Amin's; but where Amin wanted to adopt a Western-style male dominance, describing his recommendation as a call for women's liberation, Harb argued for an Islamic patriarchy, presenting his views quite simply as those of traditional, unadorned, God-ordained patriarchy. Harb invoked Christian and Muslim scriptures and Western and Muslim men of learning to affirm that the wife's duty was to attend to the physical, mental, and moral needs of her husband and children[21]— the same duty that Amin ascribed to her. Their prescriptions for women differed literally in the matter of garb: Harb's women must veil, and Amin's unveil. The argument between Harb and Amin centered not on feminism versus antifeminism but on Western versus indigenous ways. For neither side was male dominance ever in question.

Amin's book, then, marks the entry of the colonial narrative of women and Islam— in which the veil and the treatment of women epitomized Islamic inferiority—into mainstream Arabic discourse. And the opposition it generated similarly marks the emergence of an Arabic narrative developed in resistance to the colonial narrative. This narrative of resistance appropriated, in order to negate them, the symbolic terms of the originating narrative. The veil came to symbolize in the resistance narrative, not the inferiority of the culture and the need to cast aside its customs in favor of those of the West, but, on the contrary, the dignity and validity of all native customs, and in particular those customs coming under fiercest colonial attack—the customs relating to women—and the need to tenaciously affirm them as a means of resistance to Western domination. As Frantz Fanon was to say of a later battle of the veil, between the French and the Algerians, the Algerians affirmed the veil because "tradition demanded the rigid separation of the sexes" and because *"the occupier was bent on unveiling Algeria"* (emphasis in original).[22] Standing in the relation of antithesis to thesis, the resistance narrative thus reversed—but thereby also accepted—the terms set in the first place by the colonizers. And therefore, ironically, it is Western discourse that in the first place determined the new meanings of the veil and gave rise to its emergence as a symbol of resistance.

Amin's book and the debate it generated, and the issues of class and culture with which the debate became inscribed, may be regarded as the precursor and prototype of the debate around the veil that has recurred in a variety of forms in a number of Muslim and Arab countries since. As for those who took up Amin's call for unveiling in Egypt (such as Huda Sha'rawi), an upper-class or upper-middle-class background, and to some degree or other a Western cultural affiliation, have been typical of those who became advocates of unveiling. In Turkey, for example, Ataturk, who introduced westernizing reforms, including laws affecting women, repeatedly denounced the veil in terms that, like Amin's, reproduced the Western narrative and show that his concern was with how the custom reflected on Turkish men, allowing them to appear "uncivilized" and objects of "ridicule." In one speech Ataturk declared: "In some places I have seen women who put a piece of cloth or a towel or something like that over their heads to hide their faces, and who turn their backs or huddle themselves on the ground when a man passes by. What are the meaning and sense of this behaviour? Gentlemen, can the mothers and daughters of a civilised nation adopt this strange manner, this barbarous posture? It is a spectacle that makes the nation an object of ridicule. It must be remedied at once."[23]

Similarly, in the 1920s the Iranian ruler Reza Shah, also an active reformer and westernizer, went so far as to issue a proclamation banning the veil, a move which had the support of some upper-class women as well as upper-class men. The ban, which symbolized the Westerly direction in which the ruling class intended to lead the society and signaled the eagerness of the upper classes to show themselves to be "civilized," was quite differently received by the popular classes. Even rumors of the move provoked unrest; demonstrations broke out but were ruthlessly crushed. For most Iranians, women as well as men, the veil was not, as a historian of Iranian women has observed, a "symbol of backwardness," which members of the upper classes maintained it was, but "a sign of propriety and a means of protection against the menacing eyes of male strangers." The police had instructions to deal harshly with any woman wearing anything other than a European-style hat or no headgear at all, and many women chose to stay at home rather than venture outdoors and risk having their veils pulled off by the police.[24]

In their stinging contempt for the veil and the savagery with which they attack it, these two members of the ruling class, like Amin, reveal their true motivation: they are men of the classes assimilating to European ways and smarting under the humiliation of being described as uncivilized because "their" women are veiled, and they are determined to eradicate the practice. That is to say, theirs are the words and acts of men exposed to the Western discourse who have accepted its representation of their culture, the inferiority of its practices, and the meaning of the veil. Why Muslim men should be making such statements and enacting such bans is only intelligible against the background of the global dominance of the Western world and the authority of its discourses, and also against the background of the ambiguous position of men and women of the upper classes, members of Muslim societies whose economic interests and cultural aspirations bound them to the colonizing West and who saw their own society partly through Western eyes.

———————

The origins and history, just described, of the idea of the veil as it informs Western colonial discourse and twentieth-century Arabic debate have a number of implications. First, it is evident that the connection between the issues of culture and women, and more precisely between the cultures of Other men and the oppression of women, was created by Western discourse. The idea (which still often informs discussions about women in Arab and Muslim cultures and other non-Western world cultures) that improving the status of women entails abandoning native customs was the product of a particular historical moment and was constructed by an androcentric colonial establishment committed to male dominance in the service of particular political ends. Its absurdity and essential falseness become particularly apparent (at least from a feminist point of view) when one bears in mind that those who first advocated it believed that Victorian mores and dress, and Victorian Christianity, represented the ideal to which Muslim women should aspire.

Second, these historical origins explain another and, on the face of it, somewhat surprising phenomenon: namely, the peculiar resemblance to be found between the colonial and still-commonplace Western view that an innate connection exists between the issues of culture and women in Muslim societies and the similar presumption underlying the Islamist resistance position, that such a fundamental connection does indeed exist. The resemblance between the two positions is not coincidental: they are mirror images of each other. The resistance narrative contested the colonial thesis by inverting it—thereby also, ironically, grounding itself in the premises of the colonial thesis.

The preceding account of the development of a colonial narrative of women in Islam has other implications as well, including that the colonial account of Islamic oppression of women was based on misperceptions and political manipulations and was incorrect. My argument here is not that Islamic societies did not oppress women. They did and do; that is not in dispute. Rather, I am here pointing to the political uses of the idea that Islam oppressed women and noting that what patriarchal colonialists identified as the sources and main forms of women's oppression in Islamic societies was based on a vague and inaccurate understanding of Muslim societies. This means, too, that the feminist agenda for Muslim women as set by Europeans—and first devised by the likes of Cromer—was incorrect and irrelevant. It was incorrect in its broad assumptions that Muslim women needed to abandon native ways and adopt those of the West to improve their status; obviously, Arab and Muslim women need to reject (just as Western women have been trying to do) the androcentrism and misogyny of whatever culture and tradition they find themselves in, but that is not at all the same as saying they have to adopt Western culture or reject Arab culture and Islam comprehensively. The feminist agenda as defined by Europeans was also incorrect in its particularities, including its focus on the veil. Because of this history of struggle around it, the veil is now pregnant with meanings. As an item of clothing, however, the veil itself and whether it is worn are about as relevant to substantive matters of women's rights as the social prescription of one or another item of clothing is to Western women's struggles over substantive issues. When items of clothing—be it bloomers or bras—have briefly figured as focuses of contention and symbols of feminist struggle in Western societies, it was at least Western feminist women who were responsible for identifying the item in question as significant and defining it as a site of struggle and not, as has sadly been the case with respect to the veil for Muslim women, colonial and patriarchal men, like Cromer and Amin, who declared it important to feminist struggle.

That so much energy has been expended by Muslim men and then Muslim women to remove the veil and by others to affirm or restore it is frustrating and ludicrous. But even worse is the legacy of meanings and struggles over issues of culture and class with which not only the veil but also the struggle for women's rights as a whole has become inscribed as a result of this history and as a result of the cooptation by colonialism of the issue of women and the language of feminism in its attempt to undermine other cultures.

This history, and the struggles over culture and between classes, continues to live even today in the debates on the veil and on women. To a considerable extent, overtly or covertly, inadvertently or otherwise, discussions of women in Islam in academies and outside them, and in Muslim countries and outside them, continue either to reinscribe the Western narrative of Islam as oppressor and the West as liberator and native classist versions of that narrative or, conversely, to reinscribe the contentions of the Arabic narrative of resistance as to the essentialness of preserving Muslim customs, particularly with regard to women, as a sign of resistance to imperialism, whether colonial or postcolonial.[25]

Further, colonialism's use of feminism to promote the culture of the colonizers and undermine native culture has ever since imparted to feminism in non-Western societies the taint of having served as an instrument of colonial domination, rendering it suspect in Arab eyes and vulnerable to the charge of being an ally of colonial interests. That taint has undoubtedly hindered the feminist struggle within Muslim societies.

In addition, the assumption that the issues of culture and women are connected —which informed and to an extent continues to inform Western discussions of women in Islam and which, entering Arabic discourse from colonialist sources, has become ensconced there—has trapped the struggle for women's rights with struggles over culture. It has meant that an argument for women's rights is often perceived and represented by the opposing side as an argument about the innate merits of Islam and Arab culture comprehensively. And of course it is neither Islam nor Arab culture comprehensively that is the target of criticism or the objects of advocated reform but those laws and customs to be found in Muslim Arab societies that express androcentric interests, indifference to women, or misogyny. The issue is simply the humane and just treatment of women, nothing less, and nothing more— not the intrinsic merits of Islam, Arab culture, or the West.

I suggested in an earlier chapter that Western economic penetration of the Middle East and the exposure of Middle Eastern societies to Western political thought and ideas, though undoubtedly having some negative consequences for women, nonetheless did lead to the dismantling of constrictive social institutions and the opening up of new opportunities for women. In the light of the evidence reviewed in the present chapter it appears that a distinction has to be made between, on the one hand, the consequences for women following from the opening of Muslim societies to the West and the social changes and the expansion of intellectual horizons that occurred as a result of the interest within Arab societies in emulating Western technological and political accomplishments and, on the other hand, the quite different and apparently essentially negative consequences following from the construction and dissemination of a Western patriarchal discourse targeting the issue of women and co-opting the language of feminism in the service of its strategies of domination.

True, reforms introduced by upper- and middle-class political leaders who had accepted and internalized the Western discourse led in some countries, and specifically Turkey, to legal reforms benefiting women. Ataturk's programs included the replacement of the shari'a family code with a code inspired by the Swiss family code, which at once outlawed polygamy, gave women equal rights to divorce, and granted child-custody rights to both parents. These reforms benefited primarily women of the urban bourgeoisie and had little impact beyond this class. Moreover, and more importantly, whether they will prove enduring remains to be seen, for even in Turkey, Islam and the veil are resurgent: militant Turkish women have staged sit-ins and hunger strikes to demand the right to veil.[26] Reforms in laws governing marriage and divorce that were introduced in Iran in the 1960s and 1970s, though not as far-reaching as Turkish reforms, have already been reversed. Possibly, reforms pursued in a native idiom and not in terms of the appropriation of the ways of other cultures would have been more intelligible and persuasive to all classes and not merely to the upper and middle classes, and possibly, therefore, they would have proved more durable.

NOTES

1 See J. N. Anderson, "Law Reform in Egypt: 1850–1950," in *Political and Social Change in Modern Egypt,* ed. P. M. Holt (London: Oxford University Press, 1968), 209–30; and Noel J. Coulson and Doreen Hinchcliffe, "Women and Law Reform in Contemporary Islam," in *Women in the Muslim World,* ed. Lois Beck and Nikki Keddie (Cambridge: Harvard University Press, 1978), 37–51.

2 Robert L. Tignor, *Modernisation and British Colonial Rule in Egypt, 1882–1914* (Princeton: Princeton University Press, 1966), 324.

3 Ibid., 324–26.

4 In Dante's *Divine Comedy,* for instance, in which Muhammad is relegated to one of the lowest circles of hell, Muhammad is associated with a figure whose transgressions similarly were in the area of what he preached with respect to women. See *The Comedy of Dante Alighieri,* trans. Dorothy Sayers (Penguin Books, 1949), Canto 28, 346–47, 251. For some accounts of early Western representations of Islam see Norman Daniel, *Islam and the West* (Edinburgh: Edinburgh University Press, 1966); and R. W. Southern, *Western Views of Islam in the Middle Ages* (Cambridge: Harvard University Press, 1962).

5 *The Complete Letters of Lady Mary Wortley Montagu,* 2 vols., ed. Robert Halsband (Oxford: Clarendon Press, 1965), 1:318. She corrects "our Vulgar Notion that they do not own women to have any Souls" but perpetuates a modified version of that error in writing, " 'Tis true, they say they [women's souls] are not of so elevated a kind, and therefore must not hope to be admitted into the paradise appointed for the Men." Ibid., 1:363. For her statements on polygamy and the parallel "inconstancy" of European men see ibid., 1:329. Montagu also points out in this context that Muslim women of the upper classes owned property in their own right and thus were less at the mercy of men than their Christian sisters. For her remarks on the veil see ibid., 1:328.

6 Timothy Mitchell's *Colonising Egypt* (Cambridge: Cambridge University Press, 1988) offers an interesting and valuable exploration of the issues of colonialism and its discursive designs.

7 Edward Said, *Orientalism* (London: Routledge and Kegan Paul, 1978).

8 For discussions of the uses of anthropology to colonial theory and its uses in reinforcing sexist views of women see Mona Etienne and Eleanor Leacock, "Introduction," in *Women and Colonisation: Anthropological Perspectives,* ed. Etienne and Leacock (New York: Praeger Publishers, 1980), 1–24; Susan Carol Rogers, "Women's Place: A Critical Review of Anthropological Theory," *Comparative Studies in Society and History* 20, no. 1 (1978): 123–62; Elizabeth Fee, "The Sexual Politics of Victorian Social Anthropology," in *Clio's Consciousness Raised,* ed. M. Hartman and L. Banner (New York: Harper Torchbooks, 1974), 86–102.

9 Earl of Cromer, *Modern Egypt,* 2 vols. (New York: Macmillan, 1908), 2:146; hereafter cited in the text.

10 A. B. De Guerville, *New Egypt* (London: William Heinemann, 1906), 154.

11 Cromer Papers, cited in Judith E. Tucker, *Women in Nineteenth-Century Egypt* (Cambridge: Cambridge University Press, 1985), 122.

12 Cromer was so prominent in the antisuffrage movement that it was sometimes called the Curzon-Cromer combine after Cromer and Lord Curzon, first marquis of Keddleston. See Constance Rover, *Women's Suffrage and Party Politics in Britain, 1866–1914* (London: Routledge and Kegan Paul; Toronto: University of Toronto Press, 1967), 171–73; see also Brian Harrison, *Separate Spheres: The Opposition to Women's Suffrage in Britain* (New York: Holmes and Meier Publishers, 1978).

13 Rev. Robert Bruce, in *Report of the Centenary Conference on Protestant Missions of the World Held in Exeter Hall, London (June 9–19th),* 2 vols., ed. James Johnston (New York: F. H. Revell, [1889]), 1:18–19; Annie van Sommer and Samuel M. Zwemer, eds., *Our Moslem Sisters: A Cry of Need from Lands of Darkness Interpreted by Those Who Heard It* (New York:

F. H. Revell, 1907), 27–28; van Sommer and Zwemer, eds., *Daylight in the Harem* (Edinburgh: Oliphant, Anderson and Ferrier, 1911), 149–50.

14 Qassim Amin, *Tahrir al-mar'a,* in *Al-a'mal al-kamila li Qassim Amin,* 2 vols., ed. Muhammad 'Amara (Beirut: Al-mu'assasa al-'arabiyya lil-dirasat wa'lnashr, 1976), 2:71–72; hereafter cited in the text. All quotations from *Tahrir al-mar'a* are from vol. 2.

15 For a discussion of Amin's family life see Mary Flounders Arnett, "Qassim Amin and the Beginnings of the Feminist Movement in Egypt" (Ph.D. diss., Dropsie College, 1965).

16 'Amara, "Hadith 'an al-a'mal al-kamila" (Discussion of the works of Amin), in *Al-a'mal al-kamila li Qassim Amin,* ed. 'Amara, 1:133. 'Amara mentions that the work was the outcome of a gathering in Geneva in 1897 attended by Muhammad 'Abdu, Sa'd Zaghloul, Lutfi al-Sayyid, and Qassim Amin. Indeed, 'Amara points to particular sections that he believes were written by Muhammad 'Abdu. Ibid., 1:139.

17 Perhaps passages such as the above were contributed by 'Abdu or by others—Sa'd Zaghloul or Lutfi al-Sayyid—who have also been mentioned as collaborating with Amin. See Afaf Lutfi al-Sayyid Marsot, *Egypt and Cromer* (London: John Murray, 1968), 187.

18 Mukhtar Tuhami, *Al-sahafa wa'l-fikr wa'l-thawra, thalath ma'ariq fikriyya* (Baghdad: Dar ma'mun lil-tiba'a, 1976), 28.

19 Among the more interesting pieces on the subject are Judith Gran, "Impact of the World Market on Egyptian Women," *Middle East Research and Information Report,* no. 5 8 (1977): 3–7; and Juan Ricardo Cole, "Feminism, Class, and Islam in Turn-of-the-Century Egypt," *International Journal of Middle East Studies* 13, no. 4 (1981): 394–407.

20 Tuhami, *Thalath ma'ariq fikriyya,* 42–45.

21 Tal'at Harb, *Tarbiyet al-mar'a wa'l-hijab,* 2d ed. (Cairo: Matba'at al-manar, 1905), e.g., 18, 19, 25, 29.

22 Frantz Fanon, *A Dying Colonialism,* trans. Haakon Chevalier (New York: Grove Press, 1967), 65. A useful discussion of the interconnections between thesis and antithesis and the ways in which antithesis may become locked in meanings posed by the thesis may be found in Joan W. Scott, "Deconstructing Equality-versus-Difference: Or, the Uses of Poststructuralist Theory for Feminism," *Feminist Studies* 14, no. 1 (1988): 33–49.

23 Ataturk, speech at Kastamonu, 1925, quoted in Bernard Lewis, *The Emergence of Modern Turkey* (London: Oxford University Press, 1961), 165. For further discussions of Turkish articulations of the issue see S. Mardin, *The Genesis of Young Ottoman Thought* (Princeton: Princeton University Press, 1962); and O. Ozankaya, "Reflections of Semsiddin Sami on Women in the Period before the Advent of Secularism," in *Family in Turkish Society,* ed. T. Erder (Ankara: Turkish Social Science Association, 1985).

24 Guity Nashat, "Women in Pre-Revolutionary Iran: A Historical Overview," in *Women and Revolution in Iran,* ed. Nashat (Boulder, Colo.: Westview Press, 1982), 27.

25 One problem with rebuttals of the Islamicist argument voiced by women of Muslim background (and others) generally, but not exclusively, based in the West is the extent to which they reproduce the Western narrative and its iteration in native upper-class voice without taking account of the colonialist and classist assumptions in which it is mired. This silent and surely inadvertent reinscription of racist and classist assumptions is in rebuttals offered from a "Marxist" perspective as much as in rebuttals aligned with the Western liberal position. See, for example, Mai Ghoussoub, "Feminism—or the Eternal Masculine—in the Arab World," *New Left Review* 161 (January–February 1987): 3–18; and Azar Tabari, "The Women's Movement in Iran: A Hopeful Prognosis," *Feminist Studies* 12, no. 2 (1986): 343–60. The topic of Orientalism and the study of Arab women is addressed with particular acumen in Rosemary Sayigh, "Roles and Functions of Arab Women: A Reappraisal of Orientalism and Arab Women," *Arab Studies Quarterly* 3, no. 3 (1981): 258–74.

26 See Deniz Kandiyoti, "Women and the Turkish State: Political Actors or Symbolic Pawns?" in *Women—Nation—State,* ed. Nira Yuval-Davis (London: Macmillan, 1989), 126.

23

OYÈRÓNKÉ OYĚWÙMÍ

Colonizing Bodies and Minds

Gender and Colonialism

Theorists of colonization like Frantz Fanon and Albert Memmi tell us that the colonial situation, being a Manichaean world,[1] produces two kinds of people: the colonizer and the colonized (also known as the settler and the native), and what differentiates them is not only skin color but also state of mind.[2] One similarity that is often overlooked is that both colonizers and colonized are presumed male. Colonial rule itself is described as "a manly or husbandly or lordly prerogative."[3] As a process, it is often described as the taking away of the manhood of the colonized. While the argument that the colonizers are men is not difficult to sustain, the idea of the colonized being uniformly male is less so. Yet the two following passages from Fanon are typical of the portrayal of the native in the discourses on colonization: "Sometimes people wonder that the native rather than give his wife a dress, buys instead a transistor radio."[4] And, "The look that the native turns on the settler's town is a look of lust, a look of envy; it expresses *his* dreams of possession—all manner of possession: to sit at the settler's table, to sleep in the settler's bed, with *his wife* if possible. The colonized man is an envious man."[5] But what if the native were female, as indeed many of them were? How is this feeling of envy and desire to replace the colonizer manifested or realized for women? Or, for that matter, does such a feeling exist for women?

The histories of both the colonized and the colonizer have been written from the male point of view—women are peripheral if they appear at all. While studies of colonization written from this angle are not necessarily irrelevant to understanding what happened to native females, we must recognize that colonization impacted males and females in similar and dissimilar ways. Colonial custom and practice stemmed from "a world view which believes in the absolute superiority of the human over the nonhuman and the subhuman, the *masculine* over the *feminine* . . . , and the modern or progressive over the traditional or the savage."[6]

Therefore, the colonizer differentiated between male and female bodies and acted accordingly. Men were the primary target of policy, and, as such, they were the natives and so were visible. These facts, from the standpoint of this study, are the justification for considering the colonial impact in gender terms rather than attempting to see which group, male or female, was the most exploited. The colonial process was sex-differentiated insofar as the colonizers were male and used gender identity to determine policy. From the foregoing, it is clear that any discussion of hierarchy in the colonial situation, in addition to employing race as the basis of distinctions, should take into account its strong gender component. The two racially distinct and hierarchical categories of the colonizer and the native should be expanded to four, incorporating the gender factor. However, race and gender categories obviously emanate from the preoccupation in Western culture with the visual and hence physical aspects of human reality (see above). Both categories are a consequence of the bio-logic of Western culture. Thus, in the colonial situation, there was a hierarchy of four, not two, categories. Beginning at the top, these were: men (European), women (European), native (African men), and Other (African women). Native women occupied the residual and unspecified category of the Other.

In more recent times, feminist scholars have sought to rectify the male bias in the discourses on colonization by focusing on women. One major thesis that emerged from this effort is that African women suffered a "double colonization": one form from European domination and the other from indigenous tradition imposed by African men. Stephanie Urdang's book *Fighting Two Colonialisms* is characteristic of this perspective.[7] While the depth of the colonial experience for African women is expressed succinctly by the idea of doubling, there is no consensus about what is being doubled. From my perspective, it is not colonization that is two, but the forms of oppression that flowed from the process for native females. Hence, it is misleading to postulate two forms of colonization because both manifestations of oppression are rooted in the hierarchical race/gender relations of the colonial situation. African females were colonized by Europeans as Africans and as African women. They were dominated, exploited, and inferiorized as Africans together with African men and then separately inferiorized and marginalized as African women.

It is important to emphasize the combination of race and gender factors because European women did not occupy the same position in the colonial order as African women. A circular issued by the British colonial government in Nigeria shows the glaringly unequal position of these two groups of women in the colonial system. It states that "African women should be paid at 75% of the rates paid to the European women."[8] Furthermore, whatever the "status" of indigenous customs, the relations between African men and women during this period can be neither isolated from the colonial situation nor described as a form of colonization, particularly because

African men were subjects themselves.[9] The racial and gender oppressions experienced by African women should not be seen in terms of addition, as if they were piled one on top of the other. In the context of the United States, Elizabeth Spelman's comment on the relationship between racism and sexism is relevant. She writes: "How one form of oppression is experienced is influenced by and influences how another form is experienced."[10] Though it is necessary to discuss the impact of colonization on specific categories of people, ultimately its effect on women cannot be separated from its impact on men because gender relations are not zero-sum—men and women in any society are inextricably bound.

This chapter will examine specific colonial policies, practices, and ideologies and ascertain how they impacted males and females in different ways. In this regard, the gender identity of the colonizers is also important. At the level of policy, I shall look at administrative, educational, legal, and religious systems. It will become clear that certain ideologies and values flowed out of these policies and practices, and in an often unstated, but no less profound, way they shaped the behavior of the colonized. Colonization was a multifaceted process involving different kinds of European personnel, including missionaries, traders, and state officials. Hence, I treat the process of Christianization as an integral part of the colonial process. Finally, colonization was, above all, the expansion of the European economic system in that "beneath the surface of colonial political and administrative policy lay the unfolding process of capital penetration."[11] The capitalist economic system shaped the particular ways in which colonial domination was effected.

The State of Patriarchy

The imposition of the European state system, with its attendant legal and bureaucratic machinery, is the most enduring legacy of European colonial rule in Africa. The international nation-state system as we know it today is a tribute to the expansion of European traditions of governance and economic organization. One tradition that was exported to Africa during this period was the exclusion of women from the newly created colonial public sphere. In Britain, access to power was gender-based; therefore, politics was largely men's job; and colonization, which is fundamentally a political affair, was no exception. Although both African men and women as conquered peoples were excluded from the higher echelons of colonial state structures, men were represented at the lower levels of government. The system of indirect rule introduced by the British colonial government recognized the male chief's authority at the local level but did not acknowledge the existence of female chiefs. Therefore, women were effectively excluded from all colonial state structures. The process by which women were bypassed by the colonial state in the arena of politics—an arena in which they had participated during the precolonial period—is of particular interest in the following section.

The very process by which females were categorized and reduced to "women" made them ineligible for leadership roles. The basis for this exclusion was their biology, a process that was a new development in Yorùbá society. The emergence of women as an identifiable category, defined by their anatomy and subordinated to men in all situations, resulted, in part, from the imposition of a patriarchal colonial state. For females, colonization was a twofold process of racial inferiorization and gender subordination. In chapter 2, I showed that in pre-British Yorùbá society, anafemales, like the anamales, had multiple identities that were not based on their anatomy. The creation of "women" as a category was one of the very first accomplishments of the colonial state.

In a book on European women in colonial Nigeria, Helen Callaway explores the relationship between gender and colonization at the level of the colonizer. She argues that the colonial state was patriarchal in many ways. Most obviously, colonial personnel was male. Although a few European women were present in a professional capacity as nurses, the administrative branches, which embodied power and authority, excluded women by law.[12] Furthermore, she tells us that the Colonial Service, which was formed for the purpose of governing subject peoples, was

> a male institution in all its aspects: its "masculine" ideology, its military organisation and processes, its rituals of power and hierarchy, its strong boundaries between the sexes. It would have been "unthinkable" in the belief system of the time even to consider the part women might play, other than as nursing sisters, who had earlier become recognised for their important "feminine" work.[13]

It is not surprising, therefore, that it was unthinkable for the colonial government to recognize female leaders among the peoples they colonized, such as the Yorùbá.

Likewise, colonization was presented as a "man-sized" job—the ultimate test of manhood—especially because the European death-rate in West Africa at this time was particularly high. Only the brave-hearted could survive the "white man's grave," as West Africa was known at the time. According to Callaway, Nigeria was described again and again as a man's country in which women[14] (European women) were "out of place" in a double sense of physical displacement and the symbolic sense of being in an exclusively male territory. Mrs. Tremlett, a European woman who accompanied her husband to Nigeria during this period, lamented about the position of European women: "I often found myself reflecting rather bitterly on the insignificant position of a woman in what is practically a man's country. . . . If there is one spot on earth where a woman feels of no importance whatever, it is in Nigeria at the present day."[15] If the women of the colonizer were so insignificant, then one could only imagine the position of the "other" women, if their existence was acknowledged at all.

Yet on the eve of colonization there were female chiefs and officials all over Yorùbáland. Ironically, one of the signatories to the treaty that was said to have ceded Ìbàdàn to the British was Lànlátù, an *iyálóde,* an anafemale chief.[16] The transformation of state power to male-gender power was accomplished at one level by the exclusion of women from state structures. This was in sharp contrast to Yorùbá state organization, in which power was not gender-determined.

The alienation of women from state structures was particularly devastating because the nature of the state itself was undergoing transformation. Unlike the Yorùbá state, the colonial state was autocratic. The African males designated as chiefs by the colonizers had much more power over the people than was vested in them traditionally. In British West Africa in the colonial period, (male) chiefs lost their sovereignty while increasing their powers over the people,[17] although we are to believe that their powers derived from "tradition" even where the British created their own brand of "traditional chiefs." Martin Chanock's astute comment on the powers of chiefs in colonial Africa is particularly applicable to the Yorùbá situation: "British officials, . . . where they came across a chief, . . . intended to invest *him* retroactively not only with a greater range of authority than he had before but also with authority of a different type. There seemed to be no way of thinking about chiefly authority . . . which did not include judicial power."[18] Thus male chiefs were invested with more power over the people while female chiefs were stripped of power. Through lack of recognition, their formal positions soon became attenuated.

At another level, the transfer of judicial power from the community to the council of male chiefs proved to be particularly negative for women at a time when the state was extending its tentacles to an increasing number of aspects of life. In pre-British Yorùbá society, adjudication of disputes rested with lineage elders. Therefore, very few matters came under the purview of the ruler and the council of chiefs. But in the colonial administration, the Native Authority System, with its customary courts, dealt with all civil cases including marriage, divorce, and adultery.

It is precisely at the time that the state was becoming omnipotent that women were excluded from its institutions. This omnipotence of the state was a new tradition in Yorùbá society, as it was in many African societies. The omnipotence of the state has deep roots in European politics. Fustel De Coulanges's analysis of the Greek city-states in antiquity attests to this fact:

> There was nothing independent in man; his body belonged to the state, and was devoted to its defence. . . . If the city had need of money, it could order the women to deliver up their jewels. Private life did not escape the omnipotence of the state. The Athenian law, in the name of religion, forbade men to remain single. Sparta punished not only those who remained single, but those who married late. At

Athens, the state could prescribe labor, and at Sparta idleness. *It exercised its tyranny in the smallest things;* at Locri the laws forbade men to drink pure wine; at Rome, Miletus and Marseilles, wine was forbidden to women.[19]

Remarkably, Edward Shorter, writing about European societies, echoes De Coulanges's earlier observations: "Traditional European communities regulated such matters as marital sexuality or the formation of the couple. What may be startling, however, is the extent to which these affairs were removed from informal regulation by public opinion and *subjected to public policy.*"[20] To mention a few examples: there was a "fornication penalty" against women who were pregnant out of wedlock—no bridal crowns for pregnant brides; and before a man was allowed to join a guild, the guild insisted "not only that [the] man himself not be illegitimate (or even conceived before marriage), but that his parents be respectably born as well."[21] Above all, the community had the power to halt marriages.[22] We must not forget that in Europe at this time women were largely excluded from formal public authority; therefore, the public policy referred to by Shorter was male-constituted. No doubt, some of these matters were regulated by African societies, but the regulation was in the hands of the lineage and possibly nonfamilial opinion. Consequently, the probability that any one category of people, such as anafemales, could have been excluded from the decision-making process of the family was much less than in Europe.

It was into this unfortunate tradition of male dominance that Africans were drafted—this was particularly disadvantageous to women because marriage, divorce, and even pregnancy came under the purview of the state. Given the foregoing, it is clear that the impact of colonization was profound and negative for women. Appraisals of the impact of colonization that see certain "benefits" for African women are mistaken in light of the overarching effect of the colonial state, which effectively defined females as "women" and hence second-class colonial subjects unfit to determine their own destiny. The postindependence second-class status of African women's citizenship is rooted in the process of inventing them as women. Female access to membership in the group is no longer direct; access to citizenship is now mediated through marriage, through the "wifization of citizenship."

Yet a group of scholars maintains that colonization was of some benefit to African women. Let us consider two scholars who hold that, in some way, African women in relation to African men benefited from colonial rule. According to Jane Guyer, the idea that African women experienced a decline in status under European rule is misrepresented; in reality, according to her, the status gap between men and women actually narrowed due to a "decline in men's status."[23] For one thing, Guyer assumes that gender identities existed for males and females as groups. Furthermore, this is obviously another way of expressing the male-biased notion that colonization is experienced as loss of manhood by the colonized, thereby projecting the erroneous belief that females had nothing (or nothing as valuable) to lose. This is a narrow interpretation of the effect of colonization in terms of something intangible (called manhood). The colonized also lost their capacity to make their own history without foreign interference; they lost their labor and their land; many lost their lives; and because the colonized comprised both males and females, women, too, evidently suffered these losses. Furthermore, an analysis of the notion of manhood, which is usually left undefined, suggests that it is a masculinized version of the concept of the self. Ashis Nandy has written about the colonial experience as the loss of self for the native.[24] From Nandy's more inclusive standpoint, we can begin to analyze the experience of females on the same terms as that of males.

Nina Mba is another scholar who sees some advantages for African women in colonization. In her study of the effects of British rule on women in southwestern Nigeria, she concludes that the colonial marriage ordinance increased women's legal status because it enhanced women's right to marital property.[25] This view is inaccurate for a number of reasons. To start with, her assumption of the status of wives as identical with the "status of women" leads to her inability to grasp the fact that in the cultures of southwestern Nigeria, the rights of anafemales as wives, as daughters, and as sisters derived from different bases. For example, lack of access to their husband's property did not constitute secondary status for "women" because as daughters and sisters they had rights to both lineages—that is, to their father's, their mother's, and their brothers' properties. In the past, conjugal oko could not inherit their aya's property either. So the apparent provision of "marital property" rights in colonial law was not necessarily a good thing for women because the constitution of a new category of property called marital property meant that wives lost their independent property rights and that, by the same token, husbands could now take over their wives' property. Moreover, the positioning of wives as the beneficiaries of husbands also meant that the rights of some other women, such as mothers, sisters, and daughters, were abrogated as well. We must also remember that many Nigerian societies had polygamous marriage systems, which raises the complex question as to which wives inherited what property, given that some wives had been married to the same husband longer than others. Mba does not deal with any of these issues. Finally, her faith in the legal system as a way of "improving women's status" is unwarranted given that the same colonial system had constituted women into second-class subjects. Legal systems do not work in a vacuum, and men, for reasons that will be discussed later, were in a better position to take advantage of the newfangled legal systems. In sum, the idea that women, or for that matter any category of people among the colonized, benefited from colonial rule does not reflect reality.

. . .

No Woman's Land

Another landmark of European penetration of indigenous societies, whether in Africa or in the Americas, was the commercialization of land. Land became a commodity to be bought and sold. The focus of this section is to analyze the effect of the commodification of land and how females were shortchanged in the transition from collective rights of access to private ownership.

In nineteenth-century Yorùbáland, as in most parts of Africa, land was not a commodity to be individually owned, bought, and sold. The following statement from the memoirs of Anna Hinderer, a European missionary living in Ìbàdàn at the time, shows the Yorùbá conception of property and ownership: "When Mr. Hinderer, on first settling at Ìbàdàn, asked what price he must pay for some land . . . , the chief said laughing, 'Pay! Who pays for the ground? All the ground belongs to God; you cannot pay for it.'"[26] If there was any claim to land, it was lineage-based and communally based.[27] Land was never sold—it was given to newcomers either by the *ọba* or by representatives of lineages. The lineage was the landholding unit, and all members of the family, male and female, had rights of usage. As Samuel Johnson noted, "No portion of such farms can be alienated from the family without the unanimous consent of all the members thereof."[28]

Use rights to land were universal. However, in recent literature on women and development, attempts have been made to reinterpret women's use rights as inferior to men's rights in some way. For example, M. Lovett states that in many precolonial societies in Africa, "women possessed no independent, autonomous rights to land; rather their access was mediated through men."[29] This interpretation of the precolonial right of access to land through lineage membership (by birth) as access through the father, and access to land through marriage as access through the husband, shifts the focus of discussion from rights as communally derived and guaranteed to rights as based on the individual. In this way, the concept of individualism is transposed onto societies where communal rights superseded the rights of individuals. Furthermore, such a statement misses the point, in that it interpolates the relative scarcity of land in the colonial period, when land had become commodified and therefore valuable and more restricted, to the precolonial period, when it was plentiful. Statements like Lovett's also go astray by failing to understand that even in traditional African societies in which women gained access to land through marriage, such access was secure because it was guaranteed by the community. Moreover, one's right to be a member of the lineage was derived not from being the son or daughter of one's parents but from being born into the lineage. One must remember that *the lineage was conceived as being composed of the living, the dead, and the unborn*. Marriage, being an interlineage affair, meant that the lineage (not just the particular husband) guaranteed the right to land.

In the Yorùbá case, *obìnrin* and *okùnrin* members of the family had the same routes of access; membership in the lineage was based on birth, not marriage—thus, anafemales marrying into a lineage had no rights to the land of their husbands' lineage. Their right to land was held and guaranteed by the lineage of their birth. G.B.A. Coker, writing on the rights of Yorùbá lineage members to immovable property such as land, states: "The rights of the members of a family are equal *inter se,* and it is not possible to have interests differing in quality and quantity."[30] Colonial anthropologist P. C. Lloyd, writing on Yorùbá society in a similar vein, asserts: "The rights of management [of family lands] can only be exercised by the family acting as a corporate group and not by any individual member, unless he [or she] is so authorized."[31] To assume, as writers like Lovett have, that men (as a group) had a supervisory right that women (as a group) did not have is to misrepresent the facts. In precolonial Yorùbáland, the rights of the individual derived from group membership. This is an expression of the classic African conception of the individual in relation to the community, ever so beautifully expressed by the dictum, "We are, therefore I am," in contradistinction to the Europe-identified Cartesian pronouncement, "I think, therefore I am."

Furthermore, in the Yorùbá case, if corporate land was to be partitioned, it was not done on the basis of anasex-distinction. As I noted earlier, Yorùbá did not make a social distinction between anafemale and anamale members of the family. To pose questions about the quality of male versus female rights is to assume individual rights to land, which is the cornerstone of Western notions of property ownership. More importantly, it is to assume that females have a gender identity that assured or jeopardized their access to land. As I showed in the previous chapter, Yorùbá anafemales' rights as offspring (members of the lineage) were different from their rights as in-marrying females. Thus, the duality and divergence of African female identity as members of the lineage through birth (offspring) and members of the lineage through marriage were, in fact, the first casualty of the European notion of "the status of women" (the idea that all women had one common condition).

This Yorùbá "no man's land" system of land tenure thus started to undergo transformation in the colonial period, to the detriment of women. Their land rights were affected by a number of developments, best illustrated by the case of Lagos, which was occupied by the British in 1861. Changes there were indicative of what was to take place in other Yorùbá towns following European rule.

Land sales evolved quite early in Lagos because of the presence of European merchants and a Westernized class of Yorùbá—the Sàró. Land grants to European merchants from the *ọba* of Lagos were understood as outright sales. In the case of the Sàró, their Western education and values predisposed them to the buying and selling of land. More directly, the system of crown grants of land was used in which local "owners of property held their land as a grant from the British Crown."[32] For example, an ordinance was issued in 1869 that provided for property ownership for any person who "had been in occupation either by *himself* or his subtenant."[33] This Crown grant system served to propagate further the idea of land for sale. The idea that persons occupying land had a right of ownership must have turned many a family property into private property, usually male-owned. First, the movement from collective ownership of land to private and individual ownership was stacked against women because by colonial definition (as the wording of the ordinance suggests) only men could be individuals. Second, given that marriage residence in Yorùbáland was in general patrilocal, it is not likely that a woman occupied land *"by himself."* I should be quick to note that the apparent disadvantage in this case stemmed not from the Yorùbá tradition of patrilocality but from the colonial law that occupation of land constituted ownership, thereby abrogating the precolonial rights of access conferred by birth. After all, the idea that a man occupied land by himself and not on behalf of the lineage was a result of the new dispensation and could only be sustained by the European idea of a male household head whose authority was absolute. More significantly, relative to men, many women lacked both cultural capital and currency that had become necessary for accumulation in Victorian Lagos.

Social historian Kristin Mann is correct when she articulated that in Victorian Lagos,

> the ability to read and write in English ensured the early educated Christians advantages in a community where the government and private citizens increasingly wrote down, in the language of colonial rulers, important communications and commercial and legal transactions. . . . Illiterate merchants soon found they had to hire literate clerks.[34]

Among the Sàró, the number of educated women was far less than men; and besides, the Victorian values of such women meant that they saw the business of acquiring property and breadwinning as properly within the sphere of men. Nevertheless, Sàró women benefited from their privileged status, and in fact some of them took advantage of their education. The situation in Abẹ́òkúta was almost identical to that of Lagos, as the former was the other locality where the Sàró were concentrated. The sale of land in Abẹ́òkúta became so rapid and generated so many problems that in 1913 the council issued an order limiting sale to indigenes of the town.[35]

The production of cash crops such as cocoa proved to be another factor that increased the value of land. In gender terms, it is also important because it generated new wealth from which women were by and large marginalized. This process can be seen further inland. In Ìbàdàn, Ife, and Ondo, the commercialization of land and its rapid sale were due to the expansion of cocoa cultivation. Though the British did not introduce cocoa into Yorùbáland, they quickly recognized the potential of its exploitation for the benefit of the colonial government. They promoted its spread and subsequently monopolized its marketing. The major impact of cocoa cultivation on women was that they were marginal to the biggest opportunity for gaining wealth that opened up during this period. According to Sara Berry, the pioneers of the cocoa cultivation were Yorùbá men who had been exposed to Christianity.[36] The literature has assumed a link between women's marginality in cocoa production and their lack of association with farming in the precolonial period. However, in chapter 2, I demonstrated that the evidence shows that farming was not a gender-defined occupation in precolonial Yorùbáland. Even if we accept the notion of a gender division of labor, the disadvantage of women still needs to be accounted for considering that even in societies where females were recognized as farmers and took part in the cocoa boom, as among the Ashanti of Ghana, women did not seem to do as well as men during the colonial period; despite the claim that Yorùbá women had been dominant in trade, this did not guarantee their continued dominance in the colonial period. No comparable opportunity for accumulating wealth opened up to women. Therefore, we begin to see a gender gap in access to wealth. This gap was heightened because cocoa production gave men an advantage in trade and provided them with capital. Again, this fact shows that the polarization of trade and farming as distinct occupational types is misleading.

The individuation of land ownership and the scarcity attendant upon commercialization did not augur well for women's rights. Simi Afonja has documented that in Ondo since the colonial period, women's rights have been abrogated, especially in the case of children who want to enforce their rights of access based on their mother's membership in a lineage.[37] Jane Guyer found that in another Yorùbá locality, as a result of the value placed on land used to grow cocoa, patrilineages were unwilling to pass it down through females. They preferred to pass this land through males in the second generation, though they remained willing to pass food-crop land through both male and female members of the lineage.[38]

Perhaps the most serious development resulting from land sale was the ideology explaining the new reality of land sales and abrogation of women's rights as "our custom" rather than as a "tradition" that developed in the colonial period. Gavin Kitching, in his discussion of the impact of the European land-tenure system on the Kikuyu of Kenya, points out that it was in the colonial period that Africans started to conceptualize their land-use patterns in terms of Western notions of land purchase, sale, and tenancy.[39] Such developments were also evident in Yorùbáland. Fadipe notes that by the 1930s, there existed an erroneous belief in some Yorùbá localities that "the sale of land has been a long tradition among them."[40] In the same way, the marginalization of females from family land has also been presented as a "long tradition." Simi Afonja cites a seventy-year-old man in the town of Ife who stated that "it was unheard of for the commoner women to own landed property and houses in the past."[41] However, Afonja did not raise the next logical question as to which "past" he was referring to, particularly because private property in land and houses for any person was unknown in Yorùbáland until the nineteenth century in Lagos and Abẹ́òkúta and much later in the hinterland.

Making Customary Law Customary

The process of reinventing the past to reflect the present is critical to my analysis of gender-formation in colonial Yorùbáland. In the previous chapter, I showed the way it operated with regard to the writing of history. The treatment of land sale and property ownership was another example of this process, and there were still other institutional sites in which this process was glaring. The making of customary law also illustrates how traditions were reinvented in this period. In the process of the constitution of customary law, women were excluded; their rights steadily eroded as new customs were fashioned mainly to serve male interests. Customary law is a contradiction in terms because there was nothing "customary" in the way it came into being. Here I am making a distinction between the recording of customary norms and mores as laws, on the one hand, and the construction of new traditions as customary law, on the other. The ultimate source of the "new customary law" was not custom but the British colonial government. As part of the colonial administrative machinery, it set up a native court system in which civil cases were to be adjudicated as long as the law applied was "not repugnant to justice, equity and good conscience."[42] Male local rulers became salaried officials of the colonial government, and one of their functions was to "adjudicate" customary law. The dual nature of colonial-initiated customary law as something new and something old (its appeal to the Yorùbá past for legitimacy) is captured by T. M. Aluko's description of a native court in Idasa, a fictional town in colonial Yorùbáland:

> At last they saw the Court House from a distance. The father approached it with awe and diffidence, the son with curiosity and excitement. It had traditional mud walls but was plastered and white-washed both inside and out. The thatched roof had recently been replaced by corrugated-iron sheets, a sign that justice was at the vanguard of the march of civilization in this important town.[43]

That justice had a house all its own was a new tradition in Yorùbáland, and this realization is the reason the father approached it with "awe and diffidence" and the son with "curiosity and excitement."

The establishment of native courts in Yorùbáland was not about taking preexisting courts and updating them, as legal scholars tend to explain—it was the development of a new way of thinking about justice and a new place for administering it. In pre-British Yorùbáland, judicial power inhered in various courts (in the sense of a quorum), not just the council of chiefs. But the colonial government imposed a European view of justice that would be in the hands of male chiefs to the exclusion of all other groups. The exclusion of female officials was one of the sure signs that custom had nothing much to do with the fashioning of "customary court." The *aláké* (ruler) of Abẹ̀òkúta (a Yorùbá polity) was to acknowledge the glaring omission of women when during discussion of marriage and divorce in 1937 he lamented that the women of Egbaland (Abẹ̀òkúta) had not even been consulted on a matter that concerned them so closely.[44] As Martin Chanock argues, "from the British point of view, . . . the customary law would have been what the chiefs [male chiefs] did in their courts, while what happened outside the courts was 'extra-legal.' But in real village life there was no such clear-cut distinction between the realms of public and private."[45] Nina Mba exhibits this Western point of view when she states that in precolonial Yorùbáland "the dissolution of a marriage was extra-judicial: It was effected *merely* by the mutual consent of the parties involved."[46] She suggests that this was a simple and nonjudicial way of settling conflicts, a curious notion in light of the fact that the "parties involved" in a Yorùbá marriage could include a large number of people, since marriage was an interlineage affair. Why lineage adjudication of marriage is extrajudicial is unclear except, of course, if one accepts the colonial definition of the public and private spheres.

Another way the colonial government tailored the making of customary law was through the administration of native law and custom by the higher courts, which meant that such administration was in the hands of colonial officials born and bred in England, although they were supposed to be assisted by indigenous assessors in the person of "traditional chiefs." Consequently, it was the English judicial approach that was applied. The use of the "repugnancy law" led to the abolition of some customary laws.[47] A good example of colonial construction of customary law is cited by Coker. Analyzing a case on Yorùbá women's property rights, he writes: "Evidence was taken first from both parties in the case, and secondly from chiefs summoned as expert witnesses. The learned Chief Justice [an Englishman], who heard the matter, preferred the evidence of the Lagos chiefs to the evidence given by the Yorùbá (hinterland) chiefs."[48] Although they used chiefs as assessors, the British officials reserved the right to dispense with their evidence, as shown by this example. The criterion for selecting which sets of evidence were more "customary" than the other sets was not clear. Therefore, the process was fraught with misinterpretation and misrepresentation, if not outright nonsense, as exemplified in this pronouncement attributed to the Honorable Justice Paul Graham, in reference to a case about Yorùbá women's property rights in colonial Lagos:

> The defendant called as witness an old man. . . . The evidence he gave was a perfectly clear *reductio ad absurdum* of the defendant's case. . . . I have heard a good

deal of nonsense talked in the witness box about Yorùbá custom but seldom anything more ridiculous than this. Even the defendant's counsel himself had to throw over this witness.[49]

How the British judges distinguished custom from the process of "customizing" newfangled social practices is not always that obvious, although it was quite clear that personal and sectional interests were being promoted that did not augur well for both tradition and women. As Coker concludes in regard to rights of Yorùbá females in family property:

> It should be borne in mind that although it has been suggested that under native law and custom in olden days the rights of females were restricted, there seems to be no authority for this suggestion, for the cases did not contain any instance in which such a proposition of native law and custom had been propounded by independent assessors. Any suggestion on those lines could only have come from the parties themselves, and especially from the *party who stands to win if such propositions were accepted as law*.[50]

The issue of interested parties was the crux of the matter. Unfortunately for women, they were marginalized by the process through which flexible customary rules were encoded into legal principles after "the nonsense" and the "biased" had been supposedly weeded out. Customs are produced through repetition. The constant challenge to female rights during this period created an impression that such rights were newly created. Furthermore, the appearance of women in the court system as mere litigants, never assessors or judges, served to propagate the idea that men are the custodians of tradition and women its hapless victims.

The Wages of Colonization

Central to colonial rule was the question of how to extract wealth from the colonies for the benefit of the occupying European powers. To this end, by the turn of the century, the British colonial administration started to build a railway line that would link various parts of their three colonies that were to become Nigeria. For this study, the railways are important because railway service pioneered wage labor and proved to be the largest employer of labor in colonial Nigeria. Women were largely excluded from the wage-labor force (although there have been relatively large improvements since independence, female representation in the formal sector remains much lower than that of men).

By 1899, over ten thousand men were employed in the construction of the railways. Later, more men were employed to operate the system. Most of the original workers were Yorùbá. According to W. Oyemakinde, unlike other parts of Nigeria and indeed other areas of Africa, there was no labor shortage for the construction of the railways in Yorùbáland because there was already in existence a "floating population" of men.[51] These were displaced persons who had been enslaved in the wake of the Yorùbá civil wars in the nineteenth century. This population was easily recruited as labor by the colonial government. However, despite the presence of females among this population, and in spite of the fact that some of the initial work on the railways involved head-loading supplies, which was no different from what males and females did in the nineteenth century, women were not employed in any considerable numbers. It is not clear what happened to the "floating" female population.

More importantly, the introduction of capitalist relations in the form of wage labor was a novelty in the Yorùbá economy and was to have major repercussions, particularly in the definition of work. All through the nineteenth century, in spite of the expansion of trade with Europe, no free-market developed in Yorùbáland as regards labor. In fact, domestic slavery (as distinct from the Atlantic slave trade) expanded during this period due to the increased demand for labor, as trade with Europe in agricultural produce expanded. Oyemakinde notes that in colonial Yorùbáland wage labor became the avenue for former slaves to buy their freedom.[52] The implications of this statement are far-reaching in light of the fact that females did not have access to wages. Does it then mean that female enslavement was prolonged? This is an interesting question that cannot be answered in this study. Historical studies of slavery and the slave trade in Africa remain trapped in Eurocentric concerns and misrepresentations.

Apart from access to cash, which wage labor meant for men, there were other more subtle but equally profound effects. Because men were paid a wage, their labor acquired exchange value while women's labor retained only its use value, thereby devaluing work that became associated with women. Walter Rodney's analysis of work in the colonial situation is elucidating:

> Since men entered the money sector more easily and in greater numbers than women, women's work became greatly inferior to that of men within the new value system of colonialism: men's work was "modern" and women's work was "traditional" and "backward." Therefore, the deterioration in the status of African women was bound up with the consequent loss of the right to set indigenous standards of what work had merit and what did not.[53]

This gender distinction was to lead to the perception of men as workers and women as nonworkers and therefore appendages of men. Women's work became invisible. Yet in reality the starvation wages that men were paid by the colonial government were insufficient to reproduce the family, and women's labor remained as necessary as ever for the survival of the community. It is well documented that African men, unlike their European counterparts, were paid a single and not a family wage. In fact, by 1903, the initial attraction of wage work on the railways in Nigeria gave way to a labor shortage and trade union organization by disgruntled workers.[54]

In addition, wage labor involved migration away from places of origin to centers of government and commerce that were developing all over the colony at the time. It meant that women moved with their husbands away from kin groups. The case of Madame Bankole, a subject in an ethnographic study of Yorùbá migrant families, is not atypical:

> In 1949 she married . . . another Ijebu man who was a supervisor in the telegraph office and had recently been widowed. He was transferred frequently from place to place, and she went with him, changing her trade each time. From Warri in the western Niger delta she transported palm oil to Ìbàdàn and re-sold it there to retailers. Then from Jos and Kano she sent rice and beans to a woman to whom she sublet her . . . stall, and received crockery in return that she sold in the North. She also cooked and sold food in the migrant quarters of those towns. From 1949 to 1962 she moved around with him.[55]

What is most striking about Madame Bankole's experience is her resourcefulness and entrepreneurial spirit, responding to the market and her situation. But on a more subtle note, Madame Bankole had become a wife, an appendage whose situation was *determined* by her husband's occupation. Although she retained one of the dominant indigenous occupations of Yorùbáland, the focus of her existence appears to have shifted from trade to marriage as an occupation. The combination of male wage labor and migration produced a new social identity for females as dependents and appendages of men. Regardless of the fact that in precolonial Ọ̀yọ́ the position of an *aya* was junior to that of her conjugal partner, the perception of an *aya* as a dependent and an appendage was a new one. For example, in spite of the fact that Madame Bankole was not dependent in economic terms, there is a perception of her dependency built into the new family situation. The anafemales had moved from being *aya* to *wife*.

A corollary of women's exaggerated identity as wives was that other identities became muted. As couples moved away from kin groups, women's identity as offspring (daughters) and members of the lineage became secondary to their identities as wives. Though Madame Bankole retained a dominant precolonial occupation in Yorùbáland (i.e., trading), the fact that she had to fold up shop whenever her husband's job demanded shows that she and her occupation were secondary. The family itself was slowly being redefined as the man plus his dependents (wife/wives and children) rather than as the "extended" family, including siblings and parents. The emergence of men as apparent sole breadwinners was to shape the kind of opportunities and resources that were made available by both the colonial and the neo-colonial state that followed. For example, the reason why men had more educational opportunities is often ascribed to the notion that they were the "breadwinners." The symbolism of bread is particularly apt since both bread and the male as sole bread-winner are colonial infusions into Yorùbá culture. The definition of men as the "breadwinners" resulted in discrimination against women in the taxation system, which has continued to the present. Women cannot claim any exemptions for chil-dren as long as the fathers of such children are still alive. As Fola Ighodalo notes, one of the first female permanent secretaries in the Nigerian civil service said about the tax regulation: "This particular regulation has completely disregarded the social cir-cumstances of Nigeria where polygamy is a way of life and under which many women have to carry solely the responsibility for the maintenance, education and every care of their children."[56]

The notion that only men really work shows up in the compilation of national sta-tistics on labor force participation. The percentage of women in the formal sector remains small.[57] This is accounted for by the fact that most women are self-employed and their engagements are not defined as work, despite their participation in the cash economy. It is important to point out that I am not referring here to their con-tribution of goods and services in the home but employment outside the home as traders and farmworkers, to give two examples. From the standpoint of national statistics-accounting, Madame Bankole was unemployed.

Becoming Women, Being Invisible

We can discern two vital and intertwined processes inherent in European coloniza-tion of Africa. The first and more thoroughly documented of these processes was the racializing and the attendant inferiorization of Africans as the colonized, the natives. The second process, which has been the focus of this chapter, was the infe-riorization of females. These processes were inseparable, and both were embedded in the colonial situation. The process of inferiorizing the native, which was the essence of colonization, was bound up with the process of enthroning male hege-mony. Once the colonized lost their sovereignty, many looked to the colonizer for direction, even in the interpretation of their own history and culture. Many soon abandoned their own history and values and embraced those of the Europeans. One of the Victorian values imposed by the colonizers was the use of body-type to delin-eate social categories; and this was manifested in the separation of sexes and the presumed inferiority of females. The result was the reconceptualization of the his-tory and customs of the natives to reflect this new race and gender bias of the Euro-peans. Thus, in Yorùbá society we see this demonstrated in the dialogue on women between two male characters in T. M. Aluko's novel set in colonial Yorùbáland:

"This woman, Sister Rebecca, is a good woman. But you cannot always rely on the evidence of a woman, . . . 'Daughter of Eve, Tempter of Adam'—Jeremiah dug up woman's unenviable ancestry."[58]

There is no question in the mind of this character that Eve was the legitimate "ancestress" of Yorùbá women. Why and how? These questions are not raised precisely because the character—reflecting the attitude of many people—believes that the colonized had become part and parcel of the history of the colonizer, and as such there was only one set of ancestors for both native and colonizer (though there were different ancestors [i.e., Adam and Eve] for males and females, in keeping with the Victorian notion of separation of the sexes). The point about the natives' loss of control over their history has been succinctly made by Albert Memmi when he notes that "the most serious blow suffered by the colonized is being removed from history."[59] In a similar vein, Frantz Fanon calls on the native to "put an end to the history of colonization . . . and to bring into existence the history of the nation—the history of decolonisation."[60] Fanon's rallying call very clearly situates the question of resistance and the necessity and possibility of the colonized transforming the state of things.

For African women, the tragedy deepened in that the colonial experience threw them to the very bottom of a history that was not theirs. Thus, the unenviable position of European women became theirs by imposition, even as European women were lifted over Africans because their race was privileged. More specifically, in the Yorùbá case, females became subordinated as soon as they were "made up" into women—an embodied and homogenized category. Thus by definition they became invisible. The precolonial Yorùbá seniority system was displaced by a European system of hierarchy of the sexes in which the female sex is always inferior and subordinate to the male sex. The ultimate manifestation of this new system was a colonial state that was patriarchal and that has unfortunately survived the demise of "the empire." Whatever the values, history, and world-sense of any cultural group in Africa, the colonial government held political control and "the specifically symbolic power to impose the principles of the construction of reality."[61] The reality created and enforced was the inferiority of Africans and the inferiority of females until the colonized chart their own reality.

Germane to the emergence of both men and women as identifiable and hierarchical categories is the creation of separate spheres of operation for the sexes. A new public sphere was created just for males. The creation of a public sphere in which only men could participate was the hallmark and symbol of the colonial process. This gender-based division into spheres was not, however, the only segmentation of society going on at the time. In fact, what we see in Africa in the colonial and neocolonial periods is the reality of a number of public spheres. In an essay on the nature of the state in postcolonial Africa, Peter Ekeh posits the existence of two public realms as a legacy of colonization.[62] The first he designates the primordial-public, as it is based on primordial groupings, sentiments, and activities. The other, the civic-public, is associated with colonial administration and is based on civil structure, the military, the police, and the civil service.[63] For Ekeh, the difference between the two has to do with their moral bases: the primordial-public being moral and the civic-public being amoral. From the standpoint of the present work, an important distinction between the two publics that is often overlooked is that the civic-public is male-dominant and the primordial-public is gender-inclusive. These two ways of labeling the colonial segmentation of society thus point in the same direction. As I have shown, the exclusion of women officials from the structures of the colonial state overrode the precolonial practice of politics being the province of all adults. In precolonial Yorùbáland, anafemales had not been excluded from leadership positions, but this changed drastically in the colonial period.

The indigenous, primordial realm did not collapse into the civic-public realm; it continued to exist orally and in social practice. However, it tended to be subordinated to the newer civic-public realm because most of the resources and wealth of the society were concentrated in the state arena. The two realms were not rigidly separate. In fact, they flowed into each other precisely because the actors were one and the same, particularly after the departure of the colonizers. The European colonial officials during the colonial period did not directly participate in the primordial-public realm, but their control of state power often determined what went on in that realm. Further, different groups of people were articulated into these two realms differently. The Western-educated, emergent elite tended to be affected more directly by the civic-public realm because they were the "inheritors" of the colonial state, with all its privileges and ideologies. Consequently, we tend to find ideas of male superiority and African inferiority more prevalent within this privileged class—they were (and are) in closer and more extended contact with the civic-public sphere. The civic-public realm expanded in the sense that more people were drawn directly into it, and its greatest manifestation was in the Western educational system that was a bequest of the colonial experience. In the section on education, I showed what a determinant education was in the stratification of colonial society. In the arena of education, there is still a perception within certain sections of the population that females are not as capable as their male counterparts.

Today, the participation of females in this privileged system remains very low, a fact that is of itself perceived as evidence of their inability to function in this "all-male world." Seemingly paradoxically, it is precisely the women who are embedded in this realm who realize their subordination. Nevertheless, there are certain class privileges that accrue to both men and women of this most patriarchalized class—the elite. Therefore, it is important that even as we acknowledge the construction of women as a homogenized, subordinated group by the colonizer, we recognize the class hierarchy that cross-cut the gender hierarchy that developed in the colonial

period. Ultimately, the process of gender-formation is inseparable from that of institutionalizing race and class hierarchies.

The paradox of the imposition of Western hegemony on African women is that the
elite women who derive class privileges from the legacy of the colonial situation
appear to suffer from the ill-effects of male dominance the most. For the women in
the lower classes, their experience of male dominance is muted, probably because it
is overshadowed by socioeconomic disadvantages. Obviously, socioeconomic disadvantage and gender subordination are intertwined, feeding on each other. But it
appears that the difference between the experiences of the elite and lower-class
women of male dominance is important as a determinant of their consciousness and
hence what sorts of action they take (or do not take) against the system. This distinction is particularly important in the contemporary period.

One important concern in this study is the role of intellectuals in the construction of reality. In the colonial period, it was not only colonial officials and policies that
were determinant. Western writers have also played a role in the construction of
reality, which in turn determines our views of what we see or do not see on the
ground. Note that the apprehension process now privileges the visual. One very concrete example of the invisibility of African women (or is it an example of the blindness of researchers?) is illustrated by the experience of R. S. Rattray, an eminent
colonial anthropologist of the Ashanti of Ghana. In 1923, Rattray, after many years
of studying the Ashanti, was surprised to "discover" the important "position of
women" in the state and family. Puzzled that after many years of being the expert on
the Ashanti this most significant fact had escaped him, he asked the Ashanti elders
why. In his words:

> I have asked the old men and women why I did not know all this—I had spent many
> years in Ashanti. The answer is always the same: "The white man never asked us
> this; you have dealings with and recognize only the men; we supposed the *Euro-
> pean considered women of no account,* and we know you do not recognize them as
> we have always done."[64]

In Yorùbáland, the transformation of *obìnrin* into women and then into "women of no
account" was at the essence of the colonial impact as a gendered process. Colonization, besides being a racist process, was also a process by which male hegemony
was instituted and legitimized in African societies. Its ultimate manifestation was the
patriarchal state. The specificities of how Yorùbá anafemales were "rendered of no
account" have been the focal point of this chapter. However, the recognition of the
profound impact of colonization does not preclude the acknowledgment of the survival of indigenous structures and ideological forms. Colonial and neocolonial Yorùbá
society was not Victorian England in gender terms because both men and women
actively resisted cultural changes at different levels. Indigenous forms did not dis-

appear, though they were battered, subordinated, eroded, and even modified by the colonial experience. It is important to note that gender hierarchies in Yorùbá society today operate differently than they do in the West. Undoubtedly, there are similarities founded on the fact that in the global system, white males continue to set the agenda of the modern world and white women, because of their race privileges, are the second most powerful group in this international program. Recall the UN conferences on women. In the West, to paraphrase Denise Riley, the challenge of feminism is how to proceed from the gender-saturated category of "women" to the "fullness of an unsexed humanity."[65] For Yorùbá *obìnrin* the challenge is obviously different because at certain levels in the society and in some spheres, the notion of an "unsexed humanity" is neither a dream to aspire to nor a memory to be realized. It exists, albeit in concatenation with the reality of separate and hierarchical sexes imposed during the colonial period.

NOTES

1 This is a bifurcated world—a world cut in two. Abdul Jan Mohammed elaborates the idea of Manichaeanism in the colonial world as "a field of diverse yet interchangeable oppositions between White and Black, good and evil, superiority and inferiority, civilization and savagery, intelligence and emotion, rationality and sensuality, self and Other, subject and object" ("The Economy of Manichean Allegory: The Function of Racial Difference in Colonialist Literature," in *Race, Writing, and Difference,* ed. Henry Louis Gates Jr. [Chicago: University of Chicago Press, 1988], 82).

2 Frantz Fanon, *The Wretched of the Earth* (New York: Grove Weidenfeld, 1963); Albert Memmi, *The Colonizer and the Colonized* (Boston: Beacon Press, 1965).

3 Ashis Nandy, *The Intimate Enemy: Loss and Recovery of Self under Colonialism* (Delhi: Oxford University Press, 1983), 5. Dominance is often expressed in sexual terms; consequently, colonization is seen as a process of taking away the manhood of the colonized, and national liberation seen as a step toward its restoration.

4 Fanon, *Wretched of the Earth,* 63.

5 Ibid., 39; emphasis added.

6 Nandy, *Intimate Enemy,* x; emphasis added.

7 Stephanie Urdang, *Fighting Two Colonialisms: Women in Guinea-Bissau* (London: Zed Press, 1979); Elizabeth Schmidt, *Peasants, Traders, and Wives: Shona Women in the History of Zimbabwe, 1870–1939* (Portsmouth, N.H.: Heinemann Educational Books, 1992), makes the claim that Shona women of Zimbabwe were beholden to two patriarchies—indigenous and European.

8 Cited in Nina Mba, *Nigerian Women Mobilized: Women's Political Activity in Southern Nigeria, 1900–1965* (Berkeley: University of California, Institute of International Studies, 1982), 65.

9 It is misleading to assume that the relationship between African men and women was untouched by colonization. After all, according to Memmi, "I discovered that few aspects of my life and personality were untouched by the fact of colonization. Not only my own thoughts, my passions and my conduct, but the conduct of others towards me was affected" (*Colonizer,* viii).

10 Elizabeth Spelman, *Inessential Woman: Problems of Exclusion in Feminist Thought* (Boston: Beacon Press, 1988), 123.

11 Bill Freund, *The Making of Contemporary Africa* (Bloomington: Indiana University Press, 1984), 111.

12 Helen Callaway, *Gender, Culture, Empire: European Women in Colonial Nigeria* (Oxford: Macmillan Press in association with St. Anthony's College, 1987), 4.

13 Ibid., 5–6.

14 Callaway appears to be impervious to the fact that there were gender distinctions among the Africans, despite the fact that part of her motivation for writing was to restore a gendered analysis of colonization.

15 Quoted in Callaway, *Gender,* 5.

16 Samuel Johnson, *The History of the Yorubas* (New York: Routledge and Kegan Paul, 1921), 656.

17 M. Crowder and O. Ikime, *West African Chiefs* (Ife: University of Ife Press, 1970), xv.

18 Martin Chanock, "Making Customary Law: Men, Women and the Courts in Colonial Rhodesia," in *African Women and the Law: Historical Perspectives,* ed. M. J. Hay and Marcia Wright (Boston: African Studies Center, Boston University, 1982), 59; emphasis added.

19 Fustel De Coulanges, *The Ancient City: A Study on the Religion, Laws and Institutions of Greece and Rome* (n.p., 1983 [1987]), 293–94; emphasis added.

20 Edward Shorter, *The Making of the Modern Family* (New York: Vintage Books, 1983), 50; emphasis added.

21 Ibid., 51.

22 Ibid., 52.

23 Jane Guyer, *Family and Farm in Southern Cameroon* (Boston: Boston University, African Studies Center, 1984), 5.

24 Nandy, *Intimate Enemy*.

25 Nina Mba, *Nigerian Women Mobilized: Women's Political Activity in Southern Nigeria, 1900–1965* (Berkeley: University of California, Institute of International Studies, 1982), 54.

26 Anna Hinderer, *Seventeen Years in the Yoruba Country : Memorials of Anna Hinderer* (London: Seeley, Jackson and Halliday, 1877), 60.

27 N. A. Fadipe, *Sociology of the Yoruba* (Ìbàdàn: Ìbàdàn University Press, 1970), 169.

28 Johnson, *History of the Yorubas,* 96.

29 M. Lovett, "Gender Relations, Class Formation, and the Colonial State in Africa," in *Women and the State in Africa,* ed. Kathleen A. Staudt and Jane L. Parpar (Boulder, Colo.: Lynne Rienner Publishers, 1989), 25.

30 G.B.A. Coker, *Family Property among the Yoruba* (London: Sweet and Maxwell, 1958), 48.

31 P. C. Lloyd, *Yoruba Land Law* (New York: Oxford University Press, 1962), 80.

32 Coker, *Family Property*.

33 Ibid., 189–90; emphasis added.

34 Kristin Mann, *Marrying Well: Marriage, Status, and Social Change among the Educated Elite in Colonial Lagos* (Cambridge: Cambridge University Press, 1985), 19–20.

35 T. O. Elias, *Nigerian Land Law and Custom* (London: Routledge and Kegan Paul, 1951), 186.

36 Sara Berry, *Cocoa, Custom and Socio-economic Change in Rural Western Nigeria* (Oxford: Clarendon Press, 197S), 46–49.

37 Simi Afonja, "Land Control: A Critical Factor in Yorùbá Gender Stratification," in *Women and Class in Africa,* ed. C. Robertson and I. Berger (New York: Africana Publishing, 1986).

38 Cited in ibid.

39 Gavin Kitching, *Class and Economic Change in Kenya: The Making of an African Petit Bourgeoisie* (New Haven, Conn.: Yale University Press, 1980), 285.

40 Fadipe, *Sociology of the Yoruba,* 171.

41 Simi Afonja, "Changing Modes of Production and the Sexual Division of Labor among the Yoruba," in *Women's Work, Development and Division of Labor by Gender,* ed. H. Safa and E. Leacock (South Hadley, Mass.: Bergin and Garvey, 1986), 131.

42 O. Adewoye, "Law and Social Change in Nigeria," *Journal of Historical Society of Nigeria* 3, no. 1 (December 1973): 150.

43 T. M. Aluko, *One Man, One Wife* (London: Heinemann, 1959), 40.

44 Cited in Mba, *Nigerian Women,* 40.

45 Chanock, "Making Customary Law," 60.

46 Mba, *Nigerian Women,* 56; emphasis added.

47 Adewoye, "Law and Social Change," 156.

48 Coker, *Family Property,* 113.

49 Ibid., 162.

50 Ibid., 159; emphasis added.

51 W. Oyemakinde, "Railway Construction and Operation in Nigeria, 1895–1911," *Journal of Historical Society of Nigeria* 7, no. 2 (1974): 305.

52 Ibid., 305.

53 Walter Rodney, *How Europe Underdeveloped Africa* (Washington, D.C.: Howard University Press, 1972), 227.

54 Oyemakinde, "Railway Construction," 312.

55 Dan Aronson, *The City Is Our Farm: Seven Migrant Yoruba Families* (Cambridge, Mass.: Schenkman Publishing Co., 1978), 128–29.

56 Fola Ighodalo, "Barriers to the Participation of Nigerian Women in the Modern Labor Force," in *Nigerian Women and Development,* ed. O. Ogunsheye et al. (Ìbàdàn: Ìbàdàn University Press, 1988), 363.

57 Ibid., 356.

58 Aluko, *One Man,* 42.

59 Memmi, *Colonizer.*

60 Fanon, *Wretched,* 41.

61 Callaway, *Gender,* 55.

62 Peter Ekeh, "Colonialism and the Two Publics: A Theoretical Statement," *Journal of Comparative Studies in Society and History* 17, no. 1 (1975): 91–112.

63 Ibid., 92.

64 R. S. Rattray, *The Ashanti* (reprint; Oxford: Clarendon Press, 1969), 84.

65 Denise Riley, *Am I That Name? Feminism and the Category of Women in History* (Minneapolis: University of Minnesota Press, 1988), 65.

24

GAYATRI CHAKRAVORTY SPIVAK

Three Women's Texts and a Critique of Imperialism

It should not be possible to read nineteenth-century British literature without remembering that imperialism, understood as England's social mission, was a crucial part of the cultural representation of England to the English. The role of literature in the production of cultural representation should not be ignored. These two obvious "facts" continue to be disregarded in the reading of nineteenth-century British literature. This itself attests to the continuing success of the imperialist project, displaced and dispersed into more modern forms.

If these "facts" were remembered, not only in the study of British literature but in the study of the literatures of the European colonizing cultures of the great age of imperialism, we would produce a narrative, in literary history, of the "worlding" of what is now called "the Third World." To consider the Third World as distant cultures, exploited but with rich intact literary heritages waiting to be recovered, interpreted, and curricularized in English translation fosters the emergence of "the Third World" as a signifier that allows us to forget that "worlding," even as it expands the empire of the literary discipline.[1]

It seems particularly unfortunate when the emergent perspective of feminist criticism reproduces the axioms of imperialism. A basically isolationist admiration for the literature of the female subject in Europe and Anglo-America establishes the high feminist norm. It is supported and operated by an information-retrieval approach to "Third World" literature which often employs a deliberately "nontheoretical" methodology with self-conscious rectitude.

In this essay, I will attempt to examine the operation of the "worlding" of what is today "the Third World" by what has become a cult text of feminism: *Jane Eyre*.[2] I plot the novel's reach and grasp, and locate its structural motors. I read *Wide Sargasso Sea* as *Jane Eyre*'s reinscription and *Frankenstein* as an analysis—even a deconstruction—of a "worlding" such as *Jane Eyre*'s.[3]

I need hardly mention that the object of my investigation is the printed book, not its "author." To make such a distinction is, of course, to ignore the lessons of deconstruction. A deconstructive critical approach would loosen the binding of the book, undo the opposition between verbal text and the biography of the named subject "Charlotte Brontë," and see the two as each other's "scene of writing." In such a reading, the life that writes itself as "my life" is as much a production in psychosocial space (other names can be found) as the book that is written by the holder of that named life—a book that is then consigned to what is most often recognized as genuinely "social": the world of publication and distribution.[4] To touch Brontë's "life" in such a way, however, would be too risky here. We must rather strategically take shelter in an essentialism which, not wishing to lose the important advantages won by U.S. mainstream feminism, will continue to honor the suspect binary oppositions book and author, individual and history—and start with an assurance of the following sort: my readings here do not seek to undermine the excellence of the individual artist. If even minimally successful, the readings will incite a degree of rage against the imperialist narrativization of history, that it should produce so abject a script for her. I provide these assurances to allow myself some room to situate feminist individualism in its historical determination rather than simply to canonize it as feminism as such.

Sympathetic U.S. feminists have remarked that I do not do justice to Jane Eyre's subjectivity. A word of explanation is perhaps in order. The broad strokes of my presuppositions are that what is at stake, for feminist individualism in the age of imperialism, is precisely the making of human beings, the constitution and "interpellation" of the subject not only as individual but as "individualist."[5] This stake is represented on two registers: childbearing and soul making. The first is domestic-society-through-sexual-reproduction cathected as "companionate love"; the second is the imperialist project cathected as civil-society-through-social-mission. As the female individualist, not-quite/not-male, articulates herself in shifting relationship to what is at stake, the "native female" as such (*within* discourse, as a signifier) is excluded from any share in this emerging norm.[6] If we read this account from an isolationist perspective in a "metropolitan" context, we see nothing there but the psychobiography of the militant female subject. In a reading such as mine, in contrast, the effort is to wrench oneself away from the mesmerizing focus of the "subject-constitution" of the female individualist.

To develop further the notion that my stance need not be an accusing one, I will refer to a passage from Roberto Fernández Retamar's "Caliban."[7] José Enrique Rodó had argued in 1900 that the model for the Latin American intellectual in relationship to Europe could be Shakespeare's Ariel.[8] In 1971 Retamar, denying the possibility of an identifiable "Latin American Culture," recast the model as Caliban. Not surprisingly, this powerful exchange still excludes any specific consideration of the civilizations of the Maya, the Aztecs, the Incas, or the smaller nations of what is now called Latin America. Let us note carefully that, at this stage of my argument, this "conversation" between Europe and Latin America (without a specific consideration of the political economy of the "worlding" of the "native") provides a sufficient thematic description of our attempt to confront the ethnocentric and reverse-ethnocentric benevolent double bind (that is, considering the "native" as object for enthusiastic information-retrieval and thus denying its own "worlding") that I sketched in my opening paragraphs.

In a moving passage in "Caliban," Retamar locates both Caliban and Ariel in the postcolonial intellectual:

> There is no real Ariel-Caliban polarity: both are slaves in the hands of Prospero, the foreign magician. But Caliban is the rude and unconquerable master of the island, while Ariel, a creature of the air, although also a child of the isle, is the intellectual.

> The deformed Caliban—enslaved, robbed of his island, and taught the language by Prospero—rebukes him thus: "You taught me language, and my profit on't / Is, I know how to curse." ["C," pp. 28, 11]

As we attempt to unlearn our so-called privilege as Ariel and "seek from [a certain] Caliban the honor of a place in his rebellious and glorious ranks," we do not ask that our students and colleagues should emulate us but that they should attend to us ("C," p. 72). If, however, we are driven by a nostalgia for lost origins, we too run the risk of effacing the "native" and stepping forth as "the real Caliban," of forgetting that he is a name in a play, an inaccessible blankness circumscribed by an interpretable text.[9] The stagings of Caliban work alongside the narrativization of history: claiming to *be* Caliban legitimizes the very individualism that we must persistently attempt to undermine from within.

Elizabeth Fox-Genovese, in an article on history and women's history, shows us how to define the historical moment of feminism in the West in terms of female access to individualism.[10] The battle for female individualism plays itself out within the larger theater of the establishment of meritocratic individualism, indexed in the aesthetic field by the ideology of "the creative imagination." Fox-Genovese's presupposition will guide us into the beautifully orchestrated opening of *Jane Eyre*.

It is a scene of the marginalization and privatization of the protagonist: "There was no possibility of taking a walk that day. . . . Out-door exercise was now out of the question. I was glad of it," Brontë writes (*JE*, p. 9). The movement continues as Jane breaks the rules of the appropriate topography of withdrawal. The family at the center withdraws into the sanctioned architectural space of the withdrawing room or drawing room; Jane inserts herself—"I slipped in"—into the margin—"A small breakfast-room *adjoined* the drawing room" (*JE*, p. 9; my emphasis).

The manipulation of the domestic inscription of space within the upwardly mobilizing currents of the eighteenth- and nineteenth-century bourgeoisie in England and France is well known. It seems fitting that the place to which Jane withdraws is not only not the withdrawing room but also not the dining room, the sanctioned place of family meals. Nor is it the library, the appropriate place for reading. The breakfast room "contained a book-case" (*JE,* p. 9). As Rudolph Ackerman wrote in his *Repository* (1823), one of the many manuals of taste in circulation in nineteenth-century England, these low bookcases and stands were designed to "contain all the books that may be desired for a sitting-room without reference to the library."[11] Even in this already triply off-center place, "having drawn the red moreen curtain nearly close, I [Jane] was shrined in double retirement" (*JE,* pp. 9–10).

Here in Jane's self-marginalized uniqueness, the reader becomes her accomplice: the reader and Jane are united—both are reading. Yet Jane still preserves her odd privilege, for she continues never quite doing the proper thing in its proper place. She cares little for reading what is *meant* to be read: the "letter-press." *She* reads the pictures. The power of this singular hermeneutics is precisely that it can make the outside inside. "At intervals, while turning over the leaves of my book, I studied the aspect of that winter afternoon." Under "the clear panes of glass," the rain no longer penetrates, "the drear November day" is rather a one-dimensional "aspect" to be "studied," not decoded like the "letter-press" but, like pictures, deciphered by the unique creative imagination of the marginal individualist (*JE,* p. 10).

Before following the track of this unique imagination, let us consider the suggestion that the progress of *Jane Eyre* can be charted through a sequential arrangement of the family/counterfamily dyad. In the novel, we encounter, first, the Reeds as the legal family and Jane, the late Mr. Reed's sister's daughter, as the representative of a near incestuous counter-family; second, the Brocklehursts, who run the school Jane is sent to, as the legal family and Jane, Miss Temple, and Helen Burns as a counter-family that falls short because it is only a community of women; third, Rochester and the mad Mrs. Rochester as the legal family and Jane and Rochester as the illicit counter-family. Other items may be added to the thematic chain in this sequence: Rochester and Céline Varens as structurally functional counter-family; Rochester and Blanche Ingram as dissimulation of legality—and so on. It is during this sequence that Jane is moved from counter-family to the family-in-law. In the next sequence, it is Jane who restores full family status to the as-yet-incomplete community of siblings, the Rivers. The final sequence of the book is a *community of families,* with Jane, Rochester, and their children at the center.

In terms of the narrative energy of the novel, how is Jane moved from the place of the counter-family to the family-in-law? It is the active ideology of imperialism that provides the discursive field.

(My working definition of "discursive field" must assume the existence of discrete "systems of signs" at hand in the socius, each based on specific axiomatics. I am identifying these systems as discursive fields. "Imperialism as social mission" generates the possibility of one such axiomatics. How the individual artist taps the discursive field at hand with a sure touch, if not with transhistorical clairvoyance, in order to make the narrative structure move I hope to demonstrate through the following example. It is crucial that we extend our analysis of this example beyond the minimal diagnosis of "racism.")

Let us consider the figure of Bertha Mason, a figure produced by the axiomatics of imperialism. Through Bertha Mason, the white Jamaican Creole, Brontë renders the human/animal frontier as acceptably indeterminate, so that a good greater than the letter of the Law can be broached. Here is the celebrated passage, given in the voice of Jane:

> In the deep shade, at the further end of the room, a figure ran backwards and forwards. What it was, whether beast or human being, one could not . . . tell: it grovelled, seemingly, on all fours; it snatched and growled like some strange wild animal: but it was covered with clothing, and a quantity of dark, grizzled hair, wild as a mane, hid its head and face. [*JE,* p. 295]

In a matching passage, given in the voice of Rochester speaking to Jane, Brontë presents the imperative for a shift beyond the Law as divine injunction rather than human motive. In the terms of my essay, we might say that this is the register not of mere marriage or sexual reproduction but of Europe and its not-yet-human Other, of soul making. The field of imperial conquest is here inscribed as Hell:

> "One night I had been awakened by her yells . . . it was a fiery West Indian night. . . .
>
> "'This life,' said I at last, 'is hell!—this is the air—those are the sounds of the bottomless pit! *I have a right* to deliver myself from it if I can. . . . Let me break away, and go home to God!' . . .
>
> "A wind fresh from Europe blew over the ocean and rushed through the open casement: the storm broke, streamed, thundered, blazed, and the air grew pure. . . . It was true Wisdom that consoled me in that hour, and showed me the right path. . . .
>
> "The sweet wind from Europe was still whispering in the refreshed leaves, and the Atlantic was thundering in glorious liberty. . . .
>
> "'Go,' said Hope, 'and live again in Europe. . . . You have done all that God and Humanity require of you.'" [*JE,* pp. 310–11; my emphasis]

It is the unquestioned ideology of imperialist axiomatics, then, that conditions Jane's move from the counter-family set to the set of the family-in-law. Marxist critics such as Terry Eagleton have seen this only in terms of the ambiguous *class* position of governess.[12] Sandra Gilbert and Susan Gubar, on the other hand, have seen Bertha Mason only in psychological terms, as Jane's dark double.[13]

I will not enter the critical debates that offer themselves here. Instead, I will develop the suggestion that nineteenth-century feminist individualism could conceive of a "greater" project than access to the closed circle of the nuclear family. This is the project of soul making beyond "mere" sexual reproduction. Here the native "subject" is not almost an animal but rather the object of what might be termed the terrorism of the categorical imperative.

I am using "Kant" in this essay as a metonym for the most flexible ethical moment in the European eighteenth century. Kant words the categorical imperative, conceived as the universal moral law given by pure reason, in this way: "In all creation every thing one chooses and over which one has any power, may be used *merely as means;* man alone, and with him every rational creature, is an *end in himself.*" It is thus a moving displacement of Christian ethics from religion to philosophy. As Kant writes: "With this agrees very well the possibility of such a command as: *Love God above everything, and thy neighbor as thyself.* For as a command it requires respect for a law which commands love and does not leave it to our own arbitrary choice to make this our principle."[14]

The "categorical" in Kant cannot be adequately represented in determinately grounded action. The dangerous transformative power of philosophy, however, is that its formal subtlety can be travestied in the service of the state. Such a travesty in the case of the categorical imperative can justify the imperialist project by producing the following formula: *make* the heathen into a human so that he can be treated as an end in himself.[15] This project is presented as a sort of tangent in *Jane Eyre,* a tangent that escapes the closed circle of the *narrative* conclusion. The tangent narrative is the story of St. John Rivers, who is granted the important task of concluding the *text.*

At the novel's end, the *allegorical* language of Christian psychobiography— rather than the textually constituted and seemingly *private* grammar of the creative imagination which we noted in the novel's opening—marks the inaccessibility of the imperialist project as such to nascent "feminist" scenario. The concluding passage of *Jane Eyre* places St. John Rivers within the fold of *Pilgrim's Progress.* Eagleton pays no attention to this but accepts the novel's ideological lexicon, which establishes St. John Rivers' heroism by identifying a life in Calcutta with an unquestioning choice of death. Gilbert and Gubar, by calling *Jane Eyre* "Plain Jane's progress," see the novel as simply replacing the male protagonist with the female. They do not notice the distance between sexual reproduction and soul making, both actualized by the unquestioned idiom of imperialist presuppositions evident in the last part of *Jane Eyre:*

Firm, faithful, and devoted, full of energy, and zeal, and truth, [St. John Rivers] labours for his race. . . . His is the sternness of the warrior Greatheart, who guards his pilgrim convoy from the onslaught of Apollyon. . . . His is the ambition of the high master-spirit[s] . . . who stand without fault before the throne of God; who share the last mighty victories of the Lamb; who are called, and chosen, and faithful.

[*JE*, p. 455]

Earlier in the novel, St. John Rivers himself justifies the project: "My vocation? My great work? . . . My hopes of being numbered in the band who have merged all ambitions in the glorious one of bettering their race—of carrying knowledge into the realms of ignorance—of substituting peace for war—freedom for bondage—religion for superstition—the hope of heaven for the fear of hell?" (*JE*, p. 376). Imperialism and its territorial and subject-constituting project are a violent deconstruction of these oppositions.

When Jean Rhys, born on the Caribbean island of Dominica, read *Jane Eyre* as a child, she was moved by Bertha Mason: "I thought I'd try to write her a life."[16] *Wide Sargasso Sea,* the slim novel published in 1965, at the end of Rhys' long career, is that "life."

I have suggested that Bertha's function in *Jane Eyre* is to render indeterminate the boundary between human and animal and thereby to weaken her entitlement under the spirit if not the letter of the law. When Rhys rewrites the scene in *Jane Eyre* where Jane hears "a snarling, snatching sound, almost like a dog quarrelling" and then encounters a bleeding Richard Mason (*JE*, p. 210), she keeps Bertha's humanity, indeed her sanity as critic of imperialism, intact. Grace Poole, another character originally in Jane Eyre, describes the incident to Bertha in *Wide Sargasso Sea:* "So you don't remember that you attacked this gentleman with a knife? . . . I didn't hear all he said except 'I cannot interfere legally between yourself and your husband'. It was when he said 'legally' that you flew at him' " (*WSS*, p. 150). In Rhys' retelling, it is the dissimulation that Bertha discerns in the word "legally"—not an innate bestiality—that prompts her violent *re*action.

In the figure of Antoinette, whom in *Wide Sargasso Sea* Rochester violently renames Bertha, Rhys suggests that so intimate a thing as personal and human identity might be determined by the politics of imperialism. Antoinette, as a white Creole child growing up at the time of emancipation in Jamaica, is caught between the English imperialist and the black native. In recounting Antoinette's development, Rhys reinscribes some thematics of Narcissus.

There are, noticeably, many images of mirroring in the text. I will quote one from the first section. In this passage, Tia is the little black servant girl who is Antoinette's close companion: "We had eaten the same food, slept side by side, bathed in the same river. As I ran, I thought, I will live with Tia and I will be like her. . . . When I was close I saw the jagged stone in her hand but I did not see her throw it. . . . We stared at each other, blood on my face, tears on hers. It was as if I saw myself. Like in a looking glass" (*WSS*, p. 38).

A progressive sequence of dreams reinforces this mirror imagery. In its second occurrence, the dream is partially set in a *hortus conclusus*, or "enclosed garden"—Rhys uses the phrase (*WSS*, p. 50)—a Romance rewriting of the Narcissus topos as the place of encounter with Love.[17] In the enclosed garden, Antoinette encounters not Love but a strange threatening voice that says merely "in here," inviting her into a prison which masquerades as the legalization of love (*WSS*, p. 50).

In Ovid's *Metamorphoses*, Narcissus' madness is disclosed when he recognizes his Other as his self: "Iste ego sum."[18] Rhys makes Antoinette see her *self* as her Other, Bronte's Bertha. In the last section of *Wide Sargasso Sea*, Antoinette acts out *Jane Eyre*'s conclusion and recognizes herself as the so-called ghost in Thornfield Hall: "I went into the hall again with the tall candle in my hand. It was then that I saw her—the ghost. The woman with streaming hair. She was surrounded by a gilt frame but I knew her" (*WSS*, p. 154). The gilt frame encloses a mirror: as Narcissus' pool reflects the selfed Other, so this "pool" reflects the Othered self. Here the dream sequence ends, with an invocation of none other than Tia, the Other that could not be selfed, because the fracture of imperialism rather than the Ovidian pool intervened. (I will return to this difficult point.) "That was the third time I had my dream, and it ended. . . . I called 'Tia' and jumped and woke" (*WSS*, p. 155). It is now, at the very end of the book, that Antoinette/Bertha can say: "Now at last I know why I was brought here and what I have to do" (*WSS*, pp. 155–56). We can read this as her having been brought into the England of Brontë's novel: "This cardboard house"—a book between cardboard covers—"where I walk at night is not England" (*WSS*, p. 148). In this fictive England, she must play out her role, act out the transformation of her "self" into that fictive Other, set fire to the house and kill herself, so that Jane Eyre can become the feminist individualist heroine of British fiction. I must read this as an allegory of the general epistemic violence of imperialism, the construction of a self-immolating colonial subject for the glorification of the social mission of the colonizer. At least Rhys sees to it that the woman from the colonies is not sacrificed as an insane animal for her sister's consolation.

Critics have remarked that *Wide Sargasso Sea* treats the Rochester character with understanding and sympathy.[19] Indeed, he narrates the entire middle section of the book. Rhys makes it clear that he is a victim of the patriarchal inheritance law of entailment rather than of a father's natural preference for the firstborn: in *Wide Sargasso Sea*, Rochester's situation is clearly that of a younger son dispatched to the colonies to buy an heiress. If in the case of Antoinette and her identity, Rhys utilizes the thematics of Narcissus, in the case of Rochester and his patrimony, she touches on the thematics of Oedipus. (In this she has her finger on our "historical moment."

If, in the nineteenth century, subject-constitution is represented as childbearing and soul making, in the twentieth century psychoanalysis allows the West to plot the itinerary of the subject from Narcissus [the "imaginary"] to Oedipus [the "symbolic"]. This subject, however, is the normative male subject. In Rhys' reinscription of these themes, divided between the female and the male protagonist, feminism and a critique of imperialism become complicit.)

In place of the "wind from Europe" scene, Rhys substitutes the scenario of a suppressed letter to a father, a letter which would be the "correct" explanation of the tragedy of the book.[20] "I thought about the letter which should have been written to England a week ago. Dear Father . . ." (*WSS,* p. 57). This is the first instance: the letter not written. Shortly afterward:

> Dear Father. The thirty thousand pounds have been paid to me without question or condition. No provision made for her (that must be seen to). . . . I will never be a disgrace to you or to my dear brother the son you love. No begging letters, no mean requests. None of the furtive shabby manoeuvres of a younger son. I have sold my soul or you have sold it, and after all is it such a bad bargain? The girl is thought to be beautiful, she is beautiful. And yet . . . [*WSS,* p. 59]

This is the second instance: the letter not sent. The formal letter is uninteresting; I will quote only a part of it:

> Dear Father, we have arrived from Jamaica after an uncomfortable few days. This little estate in the Windward Islands is part of the family property and Antoinette is much attached to it. . . . All is well and has gone according to your plans and wishes. I dealt of course with Richard Mason. . . . He seemed to become attached to me and trusted me completely. This place is very beautiful but my illness has left me too exhausted to appreciate it fully. I will write again in a few days' time.
>
> [*WSS,* p. 63]

And so on.

Rhys' version of the Oedipal exchange is ironic, not a closed circle. We cannot know if the letter actually reaches its destination. "I wondered how they got their letters posted," the Rochester figure muses. "I folded mine and put it into a drawer of the desk. . . . There are blanks in my mind that cannot be filled up" (*WSS,* p. 64). It is as if the text presses us to note the analogy between letter and mind.

Rhys denies to Brontë's Rochester the one thing that is supposed to be secured in the Oedipal relay: the Name of the Father, or the patronymic. In *Wide Sargasso Sea,* the character corresponding to Rochester has no name. His writing of the final version of the letter to his father is supervised, in fact, by an image of the *loss* of the patronymic: "There was a crude bookshelf made of three shingles strung together over the desk and I looked at the books, Byron's poems, novels by Sir Walter Scott,

Confessions of an Opium Eater . . . and on the last shelf, *Life and Letters of* . . . The rest was eaten away" (*WSS,* p. 63).

Wide Sargasso Sea marks with uncanny clarity the limits of its own discourse in Christophine, Antoinette's black nurse. We may perhaps surmise the distance between *Jane Eyre* and *Wide Sargasso Sea* by remarking that Christophine's unfinished story is the tangent to the latter narrative, as St. John Rivers' story is to the former. Christophine is not a native of Jamaica; she is from Martinique. Taxonomically, she belongs to the category of the good servant rather than that of the pure native. But within these borders, Rhys creates a powerfully suggestive figure.

Christophine is the first interpreter and named speaking subject in the text. "The Jamaican ladies had never approved of my mother, 'because she pretty like pretty self' Christophine said," we read in the book's opening paragraph (*WSS,* p. 15). I have taught this book five times, once in France, once to students who had worked on the book with the well-known Caribbean novelist Wilson Harris, and once at a prestigious institute where the majority of the students were faculty from other universities. It is part of the political argument I am making that all these students blithely stepped over this paragraph without asking or knowing what Christophine's patois, so-called incorrect English, might mean.

Christophine is, of course, a commodified person. " 'She was your father's wedding present to me' " explains Antoinette's mother, " 'one of his presents' " (*WSS,* p. 18). Yet Rhys assigns her some crucial functions in the text. It is Christophine who judges that black ritual practices are culture-specific and cannot be used by whites as cheap remedies for social evils, such as Rochester's lack of love for Antoinette. Most important, it is Christophine alone whom Rhys allows to offer a hard analysis of Rochester's actions, to challenge him in a face-to-face encounter. The entire extended passage is worthy of comment. I quote a brief extract:

> "She is Creole girl, and she have the sun in her. Tell the truth now. She don't come to your house in this place England they tell me about, she don't come to your beautiful house to beg you to marry with her. No, it's you come all the long way to her house—it's you beg her to marry. And she love you and she give you all she have. Now you say you don't love her and you break her up. What you do with her money, eh?" [And then Rochester, the white man, comments silently to himself] Her voice was still quiet but with a hiss in it when she said "money." [*WSS,* p. 130]

Her analysis is powerful enough for the white man to be afraid: "I no longer felt dazed, tired, half hypnotized, but alert and wary, ready to defend myself" (*WSS,* p. 130).

Rhys does not, however, romanticize individual heroics on the part of the oppressed. When the Man refers to the forces of Law and Order, Christophine recognizes their power. This exposure of civil inequality is emphasized by the fact that, just before the Man's successful threat, Christophine had invoked the emancipation of slaves in Jamaica by proclaiming: "No chain gang, no tread machine, no dark jail either. This is free country and I am free woman" (*WSS*, p. 131).

As I mentioned above, Christophine is tangential to this narrative. She cannot be contained by a novel which rewrites a canonical English text within the European novelistic tradition in the interest of the white Creole rather than the native. No perspective *critical* of imperialism can turn the Other into a self, because the project of imperialism has always already historically refracted what might have been the absolutely Other into a domesticated Other that consolidates the imperialist self.[21] The Caliban of Retamar, caught between Europe and Latin America, reflects this predicament. We can read Rhys' reinscription of Narcissus as a thematization of the same problematic.

Of course, we cannot know Jean Rhys' feelings in the matter. We can, however, look at the scene of Christophine's inscription in the text. Immediately after the exchange between her and the Man, well before the conclusion, she is simply driven out of the story, with neither narrative, nor characterological explanation or justice. " 'Read and write I don't know. Other things I know.' She walked away without looking back" (*WSS*, p. 133).

Indeed, if Rhys rewrites the madwoman's attack on the Man by underlining of the misuse of "legality," she cannot deal with the passage that corresponds to St. John Rivers' own justification of his martyrdom, for it has been displaced into the current idiom of modernization and development. Attempts to construct the "Third World Woman" as a signifier remind us that the hegemonic definition of literature is itself caught within the history of imperialism. A full literary reinscription cannot easily flourish in the imperialist fracture or discontinuity, covered over by an alien legal system masquerading as Law as such, an alien ideology established as only Truth, and a set of human sciences busy establishing the "native" as self-consolidating Other.

In the Indian case at least, it would be difficult to find an ideological clue to the planned epistemic violence of imperialism merely by rearranging curricula or syllabi within existing norms of literary pedagogy. For a later period of imperialism—when the constituted colonial subject has firmly taken hold—straightforward experiments of comparison can be undertaken, say, between the functionally witless India of *Mrs. Dalloway*, on the one hand, and literary texts produced in India in the 1920s, on the other. But the first half of the nineteenth century resists questioning through literature or literary criticism in the narrow sense, because both are implicated in the project of producing Ariel. To reopen the fracture without succumbing to a nostalgia for lost origins, the literary critic must turn to the archives of imperial governance.

In conclusion, I shall look briefly at Mary Shelley's *Frankenstein*, a text of nascent feminism that remains cryptic, I think, simply because it does not speak the language of feminist individualism which we have come to hail as the language of high feminism within English literature. It is interesting that Barbara Johnson's brief study tries to rescue this recalcitrant text for the service of feminist autobiography.[22] Alternatively, George Levine reads *Frankenstein* in the context of the creative imagination and the nature of the hero. He sees the novel as a book about its own writing and about writing itself, a Romantic allegory of reading within which Jane Eyre as unself-conscious critic would fit quite nicely.[23]

I propose to take *Frankenstein* out of this arena and focus on it in terms of that sense of English cultural identity which I invoked at the opening of this essay. Within that focus we are obliged to admit that, although *Frankenstein* is ostensibly about the origin and evolution of man in society, it does not deploy the axiomatics of imperialism.

Let me say at once that there is plenty of incidental imperialist sentiment in *Frankenstein*. My point, within the argument of this essay, is that the discursive field of imperialism does not produce unquestioned ideological correlatives for the narrative structuring of the book. The discourse of imperialism surfaces in a curiously powerful way in Shelley's novel, and I will later discuss the moment at which it emerges.

Frankenstein is not a battleground of male and female individualism articulated in terms of sexual reproduction (family and female) and social subject-production (race and male). That binary opposition is undone in Victor Frankenstein's laboratory —an artificial womb where both projects are undertaken simultaneously, though the terms are never openly spelled out. Frankenstein's apparent antagonist is God himself as Maker of man, but his real competitor is also woman as the maker of children. It is not just that his dream of the death of mother and bride and the actual death of his bride are associated with the visit of his monstrous homoerotic "son" to his bed. On a much more overt level, the monster is a bodied "corpse," unnatural because bereft of a determinable childhood: "No father had watched my infant days, no mother had blessed me with smiles and caresses; or if they had, all my past was now a blot, a blind vacancy in which I distinguished nothing" (*F*, pp. 57, 115). It is Frankenstein's own ambiguous and miscued understanding of the real motive for the monster's vengefulness that reveals his own competition with woman as a maker:

> I created a rational creature and was bound towards him to assure as far as was in my power, his happiness and well-being. This was my duty, but there was another still paramount to that. My duties towards the beings of my own species had greater claims to my attention because they included a greater proportion of happiness or misery. Urged by this view, I refused, and I did right in refusing, to create a companion for the first creature. [*F*, p. 206]

It is impossible not to notice the accents of transgression inflecting Frankenstein's demolition of his experiment to create the future Eve. Even in the laboratory, the woman-in-the-making is not a bodied corpse but "a human being." The (il)logic of the metaphor bestows on her a prior existence which Frankenstein aborts, rather than an anterior death which he reembodies: "The remains of the half-finished creature, whom I had destroyed, lay scattered on the floor, and I almost felt as if I had mangled the living flesh of a human being" (*F*, p. 163).

In Shelley's view, man's hubris as soul maker both usurps the place of God and attempts—vainly—to sublate woman's physiological prerogative.[24] Indeed, indulging a Freudian fantasy here, I could urge that, if to give and withhold to/from the mother a phallus is *the* male fetish, then to give and withhold to/from the man a womb might be the female fetish.[25] The icon of the sublimated womb in man is surely his productive brain, the box in the head.

In the judgment of classical psychoanalysis, the phallic mother exists only by virtue of the castration-anxious son; in *Frankenstein*'s judgment, the hysteric father (Victor Frankenstein gifted with his laboratory—the womb of theoretical reason) cannot produce a daughter. Here the language of racism—the dark side of imperialism understood as social mission—combines with the hysteria of masculism into the idiom of (the withdrawal of) sexual reproduction rather than subject-constitution. The roles of masculine and feminine individualists are hence reversed and displaced. Frankenstein cannot produce a "daughter" because "she might become ten thousand times more malignant than her mate . . . [and because] one of the first results of those sympathies for which the demon thirsted would be children, and a race of devils would be propagated upon the earth who might make the very existence of the species of man a condition precarious and full of terror" (*F*, p. 158). This particular narrative strand launches a thoroughgoing critique of the eighteenth-century European discourses on the origin of society through (Western Christian) man. Should I mention that, much like Jean-Jacques Rousseau's remark in his *Confessions*, Frankenstein declares himself to be "by birth a Genevese" (*F*, p. 31)?

In this overly didactic text, Shelley's point is that social engineering should not be based on pure, theoretical, or natural-scientific reason alone, which is her implicit critique of the utilitarian vision of an engineered society. To this end, she presents in the first part of her deliberately schematic story three characters, childhood friends, who seem to represent Kant's three-part conception of the human subject: Victor Frankenstein, the forces of theoretical reason or "natural philosophy"; Henry Clerval, the forces of practical reason or "the moral relations of things"; and Elizabeth Lavenza, that aesthetic judgment—"the aerial creation of the poets"—which, according to Kant, is "a suitable mediating link connecting the realm of the concept of nature and that of the concept of freedom . . . (which) promotes . . . *moral* feeling" (*F*, pp. 37, 36).[26]

This three-part subject does not operate harmoniously in *Frankenstein*. That Henry Clerval, associated as he is with practical reason, should have as his "design . . . to visit India, in the belief that he had in his knowledge of its various languages, and in the views he had taken of its society, the means of materially assisting the progress of European colonization and trade" is proof of this, as well as part of the incidental imperialist sentiment that I speak of above (*F,* pp. 151–52). I should perhaps point out that the language here is entrepreneurial rather than missionary:

> He came to the university with the design of making himself complete master of the Oriental languages, as thus he should open a field for the plan of life he had marked out for himself. Resolved to pursue no inglorious career, he turned his eyes towards the East as affording scope for his spirit of enterprise. The Persian, Arabic, and Sanskrit languages engaged his attention. [*F,* pp. 66–67]

But it is of course Victor Frankenstein, with his strange itinerary of obsession with natural philosophy, who offers the strongest demonstration that the multiple perspectives of the three-part Kantian subject cannot co-operate harmoniously. Frankenstein creates a putative human subject out of natural philosophy alone. According to his own miscued summation: "In a fit of enthusiastic madness I created a rational creature" (*F,* p. 206). It is not at all farfetched to say that Kant's categorical imperative can most easily be mistaken for the hypothetical imperative—a command to ground in cognitive comprehension what can be apprehended only by moral will—by putting natural philosophy in the place of practical reason.

I should hasten to add here that just as readings such as this one do not necessarily accuse Charlotte Brontë the named individual of harboring imperialist sentiments, so also they do not necessarily commend Mary Shelley the named individual for writing a successful Kantian allegory. The most I can say is that it is possible to read these texts, within the frame of imperialism and the Kantian ethical moment, in a politically useful way. Such an approach presupposes that a "disinterested" reading attempts to render transparent the interests of the hegemonic readership. (Other "political" readings—for instance, that the monster is the nascent working class—can also be advanced.)

Frankenstein is built in the established epistolary tradition of multiple frames. At the heart of the multiple frames, the narrative of the monster (as reported by Frankenstein to Robert Walton, who then recounts it in a letter to his sister) is of his almost learning, clandestinely, to be human. It is invariably noticed that the monster reads *Paradise Lost* as true history. What is not so often noticed is that he also reads Plutarch's *Lives,* "the histories of the first founders of the ancient republics," which he compares to "the patriarchal lives of my protectors" (*F,* pp. 123, 124). And his *education* comes through "Volney's *Ruins of Empires,*" which purported to be a prefiguration of the French Revolution, published after the event and after the author had rounded off his theory with practice (*F,* p. 113). It is an attempt at an enlightened universal secular, rather than a Eurocentric Christian, history, written from the perspective of a narrator "from below," somewhat like the attempts of Eric Wolf or Peter Worsley in our own time.[27]

This Caliban's education in (universal secular) humanity takes place through the monster's eavesdropping on the instruction of an Ariel—Safie, the Christianized "Arabian" to whom "a residence in Turkey was abhorrent" (*F,* p. 121). In depicting Safie, Shelley uses some commonplaces of eighteenth-century liberalism that are shared by many today: Safie's Muslim father was a victim of (bad) Christian religious prejudice and yet was himself a wily and ungrateful man not as morally refined as her (good) Christian mother. Having tasted the emancipation of woman, Safie could not go home. The confusion between "Turk" and "Arab" has its counterpart in present-day confusion about Turkey and Iran as "Middle Eastern" but not "Arab."

Although we are a far cry here from the unexamined and covert axiomatics of imperialism in *Jane Eyre,* we will gain nothing by celebrating the time-bound pieties that Shelley, as the daughter of two antievangelicals, produces. It is more interesting for us that Shelley differentiates the Other, works at the Caliban/Ariel distinction, and *cannot* make the monster identical with the proper recipient of these lessons. Although he had "heard of the discovery of the American hemisphere and *wept with Safie* over the helpless fate of its original inhabitants," Safie cannot reciprocate his attachment. When she first catches sight of him, "Safie, unable to attend to her friend [Agatha], rushed out of the cottage" (*F,* pp. 114 [my emphasis], 129).

In the taxonomy of characters, the Muslim-Christian Safie belongs with Rhys' Antoinette/Bertha. And indeed, like Christophine the good servant, the subject created by the fiat of natural philosophy is the tangential unresolved moment in *Frankenstein.* The simple suggestion that the monster is human inside but monstrous outside and only provoked into vengefulness is clearly not enough to bear the burden of so great a historical dilemma.

At one moment, in fact, Shelley's Frankenstein does try to tame the monster, to humanize him by bringing him within the circuit of the Law. He "repair[s] to a criminal judge in the town and . . . relate[s his] history briefly but with firmness"—the first and disinterested version of the narrative of Frankenstein—"marking the dates with accuracy and never deviating into invective or exclamation. . . . When I had concluded my narration I said, 'This is the being whom I accuse and for whose seizure and punishment I call upon you to exert your whole power. It is your duty as a magistrate'" (*F,* pp. 189, 190). The sheer social reasonableness of the mundane voice of Shelley's "Genevan magistrate" reminds us that the absolutely Other cannot be selfed, that the monster has "properties" which will not be contained by "proper" measures:

"I will exert myself [he says], and if it is in my power to seize the monster, be assured that he shall suffer punishment proportionate to his crimes. But I fear, from what you have yourself described to be his properties, that this will prove impracticable; and thus, while every proper measure is pursued, you should make up your mind to disappointment."
[*F,* p. 190]

In the end, as is obvious to most readers, distinctions of human individuality themselves seem to fall away from the novel. Monster, Frankenstein, and Walton seem to become each other's relays. Frankenstein's story comes to an end in death; Walton concludes his own story within the frame of his function as letter writer. In the *narrative* conclusion, he is the natural philosopher who learns from Frankenstein's example. At the end of the *text,* the monster, having confessed his guilt toward his maker and ostensibly intending to immolate himself, is borne away on an ice raft. We do not see the conflagration of his funeral pile—the self-immolation is not consummated in the text: he too cannot be contained by the text. In terms of narrative logic, he is "lost in darkness and distance" (*F,* p. 211)—these are the last words of the novel—into an existential temporality that is coherent with neither the territorializing individual imagination (as in the opening of *Jane Eyre*) nor the authoritative scenario of Christian psychobiography (as at the end of Brontë's work). The very relationship between sexual reproduction and social subject-production—the dynamic nineteenth-century topos of feminism-in-imperialism—remains problematic within the limits of Shelley's text and, paradoxically, constitutes its strength.

Earlier, I offered a reading of woman as womb holder in *Frankenstein.* I would now suggest that there is a framing woman in the book who is neither tangential, nor encircled, nor yet encircling. "Mrs. Saville," "excellent Margaret," "beloved Sister" are her address and kinship inscriptions (*F,* pp. 15, 17, 22). She is the occasion, though not the protagonist, of the novel. She is the feminine *subject* rather than the female individualist: she is the irreducible *recipient*-function of the letters that constitute *Frankenstein.* I have commented on the singular appropriative hermeneutics of the reader reading with Jane in the opening pages of *Jane Eyre.* Here the reader must read with Margaret Saville in the crucial sense that she must *intercept* the recipient-function, read the letters *as* recipient, in order for the novel to exist.[28] Margaret Saville does not respond to close the text as frame. The frame is thus simultaneously not a frame, and the monster can step "beyond the text" and be "lost in darkness." Within the allegory of our reading, the place of both the English lady and the unnamable monster are left open by this great flawed text. It is satisfying for a postcolonial reader to consider this a noble resolution for a nineteenth-century English novel. This is all the more striking because, on the anecdotal level, Shelley herself abundantly "identifies" with Victor Frankenstein.[29]

I must myself close with an idea that I cannot establish within the limits of this essay. Earlier I contended that *Wide Sargasso Sea* is necessarily bound by the reach of the European novel. I suggested that, in contradistinction, to reopen the epistemic fracture of imperialism without succumbing to a nostalgia for lost origins, the critic must turn to the archives of imperialist governance. I have not turned to those archives in these pages. In my current work, by way of a modest and inexpert "reading" of "archives," I try to extend, outside of the reach of the European novelistic tradition, the most powerful suggestion in *Wide Sargasso Sea:* that *Jane Eyre* can be read as the orchestration and staging of the self-immolation of Bertha Mason as "good wife." The power of that suggestion remains unclear if we remain insufficiently knowledgeable about the history of the legal manipulation of widow-sacrifice in the entitlement of the British government in India. I would hope that an informed critique of imperialism, granted some attention from readers in the First World, will at least expand the frontiers of the politics of reading.

NOTES

1 My notion of the "worlding of a world" upon what must be assumed to be uninscribed earth is a vulgarization of Martin Heidegger's idea; see "The Origin of the Work of Art," in *Poetry, Language, Thought*, trans. Albert Hofstadter (New York, 1977), pp. 17–87.

2 See Charlotte Brontë, *Jane Eyre* (New York, 1960); all further references to this work, abbreviated *JE*, will be included in the text.

3 See Jean Rhys, *Wide Sargasso Sea* (Harmondsworth, 1966); all further references to this work, abbreviated *WSS*, will be included in the text. And see Mary Shelley, *Frankenstein; or, The Modern Prometheus* (New York, 1965); all further references to this work, abbreviated *F*, will be included in the text.

4 I have tried to do this in my essay "Unmaking and Making in *To the Lighthouse*," in *Women and Language in Literature and Society*, ed. Sally McConnell-Ginet, Ruth Borker, and Nelly Furman (New York, 1980), pp. 310–27.

5 As always, I take my formula from Louis Althusser, "Ideology and Ideological State Apparatuses (Notes towards an Investigation)," in *"Lenin and Philosophy" and Other Essays*, trans. Ben Brewster (New York, 1971), pp. 127–86. For an acute differentiation between the individual and individualism, see V. N. Volosinov, *Marxism and the Philosophy of Language*, trans. Ladislav Matejka and I. R. Titunik, Studies in Language, vol. 1 (New York, 1973), pp. 93–94 and 152–53. For a "straight" analysis of the roots and ramifications of English "individualism," see C. B. MacPherson, *The Political Theory of Possessive Individualism: Hobbes to Locke* (Oxford, 1962). I am grateful to Jonathan Rée for bringing this book to my attention and for giving a careful reading of all but the very end of the present essay.

6 I am constructing an analogy with Homi Bhabha's powerful notion of "not-quite/not-white" in his "Of Mimicry and Man: The Ambiguity of Colonial Discourse," *October* 28 (Spring 1984): 132. I should also add that I use the word "native" here in reaction to the term "Third World Woman." It cannot, of course, apply with equal historical justice to both the West Indian and the Indian contexts nor to contexts of imperialism by transportation.

7 See Roberto Fernández Retamar, "Caliban: Notes towards a Discussion of Culture in Our America," trans. Lynn Garafola, David Arthur McMurray, and Robert Marquez, *Massachusetts*

Review 15 (Winter–Spring 1974): 7–72; all further references to this work, abbreviated "C," will be included in the text.

8 See José Enrique Rodó, *Ariel,* ed. Gordon Brotherston (Cambridge, 1967).

9 For an elaboration of "an inaccessible blankness circumscribed by an interpretable text," see my "Can the Subaltern Speak?" in *Marxist Interpretations of Culture,* ed. Cary Nelson (Urbana, Ill., forthcoming).

10 See Elizabeth Fox-Genovese, "Placing Women's History in History," *New Left Review* 133 (May–June 1982): 5–29.

11 Rudolph Ackerman, *The Repository of Arts, Literature, Commerce, Manufactures, Fashions, and Politics* (London, 1823), p. 310.

12 See Terry Eagleton, *Myths of Power: A Marxist Study of the Brontës* (London, 1975); this is one of the general presuppositions of his book.

13 See Sandra M. Gilbert and Susan Gubar, *The Madwoman in the Attic: The Woman Writer and the Nineteenth-Century Literary Imagination* (New Haven, Conn., 1979), pp. 360–62.

14 Immanuel Kant, *Critique of Practical Reason, The "Critique of Pure Reason," the "Critique of Practical Reason" and Other Ethical Treatises, the "Critique of Judgement,"* trans. J.M.D. Meiklejohn et al. (Chicago, 1952), pp. 328, 326.

15 I have tried to justify the reduction of sociohistorical problems to formulas or propositions in my essay "Can the Subaltern Speak?" The "travesty" I speak of does not befall the Kantian ethic in its purity as an accident but rather exists within its lineaments as a possible supplement. On the register of the human being as child rather than heathen, my formula can be found, for example, in "What Is Enlightenment?" in Kant, *"Foundations of the Metaphysics of Morals," "What Is Enlightenment?" and a Passage from "The Metaphysics of Morals,"* trans. and ed. Lewis White Beck (Chicago, 1950). I have profited from discussing Kant with Jonathan Rée.

16 Jean Rhys, in an interview with Elizabeth Vreeland, quoted in Nancy Harrison, *An Introduction to the Writing Practice of Jean Rhys: The Novel as Women's Text* (Rutherford, N.J., forthcoming). This is an excellent, detailed study of Rhys.

17 See Louise Vinge, *The Narcissus Theme in Western European Literature Up to the Nineteenth Century,* trans. Robert Dewsnap et al. (Lund, 1967), chap. 5.

18 For a detailed study of this text, see John Brenkman, "Narcissus in the Text," *Georgia Review* 30 (Summer 1976): 293–327.

19 See, e.g., Thomas F. Staley, *Jean Rhys: A Critical Study* (Austin, Tex., 1979), pp.108–16; it is interesting to note Staley's masculist discomfort with this and his consequent dissatisfaction with Rhys' novel.

20 I have tried to relate castration and suppressed letters in my "The Letter As Cut Edge," in *Literature and Psychoanalysis; The Question of Reading: Otherwise,* ed. Shoshana Felman (New Haven, Conn., 1981), pp. 208–26.

21 This is the main argument of my "Can the Subaltern Speak?"

22 See Barbara Johnson, "My Monster/My Self," *Diacritics* 12 (Summer 1982): 2–10.

23 See George Levine, *The Realistic Imagination: English Fiction from Frankenstein to Lady Chatterley* (Chicago, 1981), pp. 23–35.

24 Consult the publications of the Feminist International Network for the best overview of the current debate on reproductive technology.

25 For the male fetish, see Sigmund Freud, "Fetishism," in *The Standard Edition of the Complete Psychological Works of Sigmund Freud,* ed. and trans. James Strachey et al., 24 vols. (London, 1953–74), 21:152–57. For a more "serious" Freudian study of *Frankenstein,* see Mary Jacobus, "Is There a Woman in This Text?" *New Literary History* 14 (Autumn 1982): 117–41. My "fantasy" would of course be disproved by the "fact" that it is more difficult for a woman to assume the position of fetishist than for a man; see Mary Ann Doane, "Film and the Masquerade: Theorising the Female Spectator," *Screen* 23 (Sept.–Oct. 1982): 74–87.

26 Kant, *Critique of Judgement*, trans. J. H. Bernard (New York, 1951), p. 39.

27 See [Constantin Francois Chasseboeuf de Volney], *The Ruins; or, Meditations on the Revolutions of Empires*, trans. pub. (London, 1811). Johannes Fabian has shown us the manipulation of time in "new" secular histories of a similar kind; see *Time and the Other: How Anthropology Makes Its Object* (New York, 1983). See also Eric R. Wolf, *Europe and the People without History* (Berkeley and Los Angeles, 1982), and Peter Worsley, *The Third World,* 2d ed. (Chicago, 1973); I am grateful to Dennis Dworkin for bringing the latter book to my attention. The most striking ignoring of the monster's education through Volney is in Gilbert's otherwise brilliant "Horror's Twin: Mary Shelley's Monstrous Eve," *Feminist Studies* 4 (June 1980): 48–73. Gilbert's essay reflects the absence of race-determinations in a certain sort of feminism. Her present work has most convincingly filled in this gap; see, e.g., her recent piece on H. Rider Haggard's *She* ("Rider Haggard's Heart of Darkness" *Partisan Review* 50, no. 3 [1983]: 444–53).

28 "A letter is always and *a priori* intercepted. . . . the 'subjects' are neither the senders nor the receivers of messages. . . . The letter is constituted . . . by its interception" (Jacques Derrida, "Discussion," after Claude Rabant, "Il n'a aucune chance de l'entendre," in *Affranchissement: Du transfert et de la lettre,* ed. René Major [Paris, 1981], p. 106; my translation). Margaret Saville is not made to appropriate the reader's "subject" into the signature of her own "individuality."

29 The most striking "internal evidence" is the admission in the "Author's Introduction" that, after dreaming of the yet-unnamed Victor Frankenstein figure and being terrified (through, yet not quite through, him) by the monster in a scene she later reproduced in Frankenstein's story, Shelley began her tale "on the morrow . . . with the words 'It was on a dreary night of November'" (*F*, p. xi). Those are the opening words of chapter 5 of the finished book, where Frankenstein begins to recount the actual making of his monster (see *F*, p. 56).

25

TIMOTHY S. CHIN

"Bullers" and "Battymen"

Contesting Homophobia in Black Popular Culture and Contemporary Caribbean Literature

The recent controversy surrounding Buju Banton, the Jamaican dancehall "don"—which, like so many contemporary debates about race, gender, and sexuality, has been played out in the theater of popular culture—demonstrates the high ideological stakes as well as the discursive limits that determine current discussions of gay and lesbian sexuality and Caribbean culture. Occasioned by the circulation over North American airwaves of Banton's popular dancehall tune "Boom Bye Bye," the controversy provides a prime example of the cross-cultural conflicts and contradictions that are often generated by the increasingly globalized markets of the culture industry. The debate, as it was staged in the pages of the popular press (the *New York Post*, the *Village Voice*) and periodicals associated with the music industry *(VIBE, Billboard)*, concerned the alleged homophobia displayed in the lyrics of Banton's song.[1] According to an article that appeared in the *Village Voice*, two groups—GLAAD (Gay and Lesbian Alliance Against Defamation) and GMAD (Gay Men of African Descent)—joined forces in 1992 to "decode Buju Banton's bullet-riddled patois" and "embarked on a media campaign to have 'Boom Bye Bye' removed from the playlists of radio stations WBLS and WRKS." Peter Noel and Robert Marriot, the co-authors of the *Village Voice* article, applauded GLAAD for boldly defining the meaning of "diversity" and "tolerance" for Banton (35). Insisting on a literal reading of Banton's lyrics, Noel and Marriot state that the song "advocates the execution of gay men" and, consequently, reflects the especially virulent forms of homophobia that are rampant in Caribbean culture generally and Jamaican culture specifically (31).

Interestingly enough, the critics who have—to varying degrees—defended Banton also tend to rely primarily on culturally based arguments. However, these critics typically assert that Banton's lyrics should be understood metaphorically and that metropolitan critics have therefore misread both Banton's song and the "indigenous" culture from which it springs. For example, in a piece written for *VIBE,* Joan Morgan criticizes certain North American reviewers for their "ignorance of Jamaican street culture" and their inability or unwillingness to "grasp the metaphoric richness of Jamaican patois" (76). In addition, Morgan contends that Buju Banton's refusal to apologize for "Boom Bye Bye" "makes the most sense" given his first and ultimate commitment to the "hardcore dancehall audience" to whom Banton owes his success. According to Morgan, Banton's loyalty to this (cultural) constituency has been rewarded—unlike what is conversely seen as Shabba Ranks' capitulation to the powers that be—with an even greater adulation from his "true" fans (82).

Carolyn Cooper, a well-known Jamaican literary and cultural critic, has likewise insisted that Buju's gun is essentially a "lyrical" one that is meant to illustrate "the function of metaphor and role play in contemporary Jamaican dancehall culture."[2] Consequently, Cooper argues that critics who are unfamiliar with the metaphorical qualities of the Jamaican vernacular have misread Buju's song by taking his words all too literally: "Thus, taken out of context, the popular Jamaican Creole declaration, 'aal bati-man fi ded,' may be misunderstood as an unequivocal, literal death-sentence: 'all homosexuals must die.'" In contrast, Cooper suggests that Buju's "lyrical gun" should be understood primarily as a "symbolic penis" and, therefore, "[i]n the final analysis, the song can be seen as a symbolic celebration of the vaunted potency of heterosexual men who know how to use their lyrical gun to satisfy their women" (438).

Although critics like Cooper and Morgan have rightfully exposed the ethnocentrism that typically informs dominant accounts of the controversy—which often suggest, for example, that North American culture is more advanced and therefore less homophobic than its Caribbean counterpart—their arguments, nevertheless, tend to reinforce a notion of culture that relies on certain fixed oppositions between native and foreign, indigenous and metropolitan, us and them, etc. Even if we concede that their arguments do not seek "to legitimate homophobia on so-called cultural grounds,"[3] as one response to Morgan's *VIBE* piece alleges, these critics have nevertheless missed a crucial opportunity to challenge the deeply rooted homophobia that is unmistakably reflected in Banton's lyrics and that, more importantly, pervades Caribbean societies, as it does most Third and First World cultures. In contrast to the reactive and/or defensive postures implied by such arguments, it is necessary—especially given the complex ideological issues currently surrounding the question of black cultural production—to formulate modes of cultural criticism that can account for the differences within as well as between cultures. In addition, our contemporary situation calls for a cultural politics that can critique as well as affirm—a politics that recognizes, in other words, the heterogeneous and contradictory (as opposed to homogeneous and monolithic) nature of all cultural formations.

In the words of Jamaican anthropologist Charles V. Carnegie, "Even as we seek to restore 'indigenous knowledge' systems, we must simultaneously seek to sharpen an 'indigenous' criticism."[4]

Despite the limitations that currently define the terms in which the debate has been carried out, the Banton controversy—as Cooper ironically notes—nevertheless opens a critical space for talking about questions of gay and lesbian sexuality and homophobia as they pertain to Caribbean culture.[5] Using this critical space as a point of departure, I would like to continue and extend this dialogue by exploring the representation of gay and lesbian sexuality in contemporary Anglophone Caribbean narratives. Such an exploration implicitly assumes that the texts in question inevitably reflect and, indeed, participate in (by reinforcing or contesting) the sexual ideologies that pervade the wider culture.

If the Buju Banton controversy represents a manifestation of how such questions have recently erupted in the realm of the popular, Caribbean literary production has traditionally maintained a conspicuous silence around issues of gay and lesbian sexuality. In this case, the absence of representation is perhaps the most telling factor, especially when we consider the earlier decades of literary activity. Nevertheless, there are writers—like Claude McKay and Paule Marshall, for instance—for whom gay and lesbian sexuality or "homosexuality" remains an important subtextual issue and one that is intimately and inextricably intertwined with other, more explicit narrative preoccupations. In addition, there are more recent writers—emerging particularly within the last two decades—who have broken the taboo that has previously surrounded the question of gay and lesbian sexuality and homophobia in Caribbean culture. These writers have vigorously challenged the patriarchal and heterosexual ideologies that have resulted in the marginalization of women and gay men at the same time that they have continued to expose the social and political structures that serve to perpetuate the region's colonial legacy. Consequently, these writers have made the critique of homophobic and sexist ideologies an integral component of what we might call a decolonized Caribbean discourse.

Claude McKay and the Construction of Un/Natural Sexualities

A pioneering Jamaican writer who migrated to the U.S. in 1912, Claude McKay was, needless to say, a product of his time. In his biography of McKay, Wayne Cooper notes that although there is ample evidence to confirm his homosexuality, McKay never publicly identified himself as a homosexual and "like many homosexual writers of his day, did not seriously challenge the rule that such subjects were not to be discussed openly in creative literature."[6] Therefore, it is not surprising that McKay's most successful narratives—*Home to Harlem*, *Banjo*, and *Banana Bottom*—do not deal, at least in any explicit way, with the subject of homosexuality or contain any overt homosexual characters. On the contrary, *Home to Harlem* (1928) and *Banjo* (1929) both feature swaggering, good-natured, hypermasculine protagonists who are emphatically and unequivocally heterosexual. Passionate, sensual, and instinctive, Jake and Banjo, respectively, embody the African-American folk spirit that the narratives celebrate, representing what Bernard Bell calls "romantic prototypes of the rootlessness, creativity, and spiritual resilience of the common people of the race."[7]

Nevertheless, *Home to Harlem* and *Banjo* construct what is, in effect, a "homosocial" world of men interacting predominantly with other men.[8] This exclusively male domain is defined by the gamblers, musicians, hustlers, sailors, soldiers, pullman porters, cooks, and waiters who typically populate McKay's novels. Although women are frequently objects of the protagonist's sexual desire—Jake's "tantalizing brown" in *Home to Harlem*, for example—the values and codes of this masculine domain are the ones that Jake and Banjo must strive to uphold and that the novel ultimately reinscribes and celebrates. However, despite the vitality and passion with which McKay's protagonists are typically imbued, the forms of masculinity that the narratives inscribe do not ultimately depart from traditional notions of maleness and masculine behavior. Indeed, McKay's folk heroes reflect and even reinforce dominant sexual ideologies by asserting a masculinity that is predicated on both sexism and homophobia. For example, during one of his stints as a cook working in a railroad dining car, Jake encounters a waiter reading a "French" (clearly a code for homosexual) novel. While questioning the waiter about the book—a story by Alphonse Daudet entitled *Sappho*—he begins to hum a tune that makes explicit the link between the novel's particular figuration of masculine identity and the sexist and homophobic values on which it depends:

> And it is ashes to ashes and dust to dust,
> Can you show me a woman a man can trust?
> And there is two things in Harlem I don't understan'
> It is a bulldycking woman and a faggotty man.[9]

In addition, McKay's participation in a discourse of primitivism that prevailed in both black and white literary circles of the era resulted in the replication of certain essentialist notions about blackness and black sexuality in particular. Reflecting tendencies that were more or less prevalent in the major literary and cultural movements that distinguished the period—the Harlem Renaissance in the U.S. and Negritude in Africa and the Caribbean, for example—McKay's texts constructed a notion of blackness that reinscribed a racial binary in which blacks were once again associated—albeit in a positive sense—with the realm of the instincts, emotions, and passions, with sensuality, sexuality, and all that was considered "natural."

McKay's depictions of black urban life undoubtedly worked to disrupt class-bound notions of appropriateness and respectability—a fact that the negative response of certain black intellectuals to his work only serves to confirm.[10] In addition, his novels broke new ground in the sense that they challenged the taboo surrounding the representation of black sexuality. At the same time, however, his reinscription of a racial binary—especially one that depends so crucially on a category of the "natural"—implicitly articulates the very terms that have historically been used not only to devalue black cultures but also to marginalize gay and lesbian sexualities. The Caribbean feminist scholar Jacqui Alexander has demonstrated, for example, how the "naturalization" of heterosexuality as state law has traditionally depended on the designation of gay and lesbian sex as "unnatural." Furthermore, Alexander points out that "there is no absolute set of commonly understood or accepted principles called the 'natural' which can be invoked definitionally except as they relate to what is labelled 'unnatural.'"[11]

The reinscription of this category of the "natural" and its implicit corollary the "unnatural" is implicated even more explicitly in McKay's third novel, *Banana Bottom,* which is set in his native Caribbean. McKay's narrative is structured around a series of oppositions that include the native vs. the European, Obeah vs. Christianity, the primitive vs. the civilized, instinct vs. intellect, folk culture vs. high culture, spontaneous warmth vs. cultivated refinement, natural growth vs. artificial growth, and so on. Within this schema, the female protagonist, Bita Plant—a name which is clearly meant to suggest the character's rootedness in the "native" soil of Jamaican folk culture—represents the triumph of "indigenous" cultural values over the metropolitan ones that have been imposed upon her. Consequently, Bita—despite her European education and the "seven years of polite upbringing" that the Craigs have provided—maintains an inherent and "instinctive" connection to the language, culture, and folk ways of the rural peasantry from which she springs.

Moreover, McKay's valorization of "indigenous" culture also entails the affirmation of a "native" sexuality, specifically coded as "natural" and therefore necessarily counterposed to the possibility of an "unnatural" or "aberrant" sexuality. Bita's marriage to Jubban the drayman—instead of Herald Newton Day, the Craigs' choice for Bita—at the end of the novel signals the triumph of this "natural" sexuality as much as it represents the affirmation of an indigenous Jamaican folk culture. Like Jordan Plant, Bita's father—over whose (literal) dead body Bita and Jubban consummate their love—Jubban "possessed a deep feeling for the land" and he was "a lucky-born cultivator."[12] Jubban's sexual desires for Bita—and hers for him—are thus associated with the "natural" cycles of birth and death, growth and decay that determine the rhythms of peasant life. Furthermore, the sexuality that their union affirms is consequently linked to the reproductive laws that supposedly govern nature as well as humankind.

In contrast to Jubban's "natural" sexuality, Herald Newton Day, the promising young deacon who tragically "defiled himself with a nanny goat," represents the epitome of an "unnatural" sexuality. Whether explained as an "aberration" within nature as Teacher Fearon suggests or "the result of too much exclusive concentration on sacred textbooks and holy communion" as Squire Gensir conjectures (176–77), Herald's behavior constitutes a deviation from the (reproductive and heterosexual) norm that defines the "instinctive" sexuality of the black peasantry. In addition to reinforcing notions about racial atavism that circulate throughout the text, Herald Newton Day's "aberrant" behavior also serves to confirm the novel's premise about the potentially degenerating effects of an overcivilized, sexually repressed, Western (European) civilization that privileges intellect over instinct, reason over emotions.

McKay's construction of a dichotomy between "natural" and "unnatural" sexualities consequently fixes "native" sexuality within certain narrow terms—restricting it to an exclusively reproductive function, for example—at the same time that it seems to link "aberrant" or "unnatural" sexual behavior (bestiality, rape, and presumably, other forms of non-procreative sex) to the effects of either miscegenation or foreign "decadence and degeneracy."[13] Indeed, McKay's depiction of Squire Gensir—the eccentric Englishman who befriends Bita—prefigures, to a certain extent, the representation (in Paule Marshall's *The Chosen Place, The Timeless People,* for example) of homosexuality and the homosexual as products of foreign "contamination."

As Cooper points out in his biography, Squire Gensir represents the "fictional prototype" for Walter Jekyll—the eccentric Englishman who served as one of McKay's literary patrons. Although Cooper acknowledges Jekyll's homosexuality, he cautiously asserts that in all probability "Jekyll's admiration and love . . . expressed itself wholly in his role as mentor and friend" (32). Given the unspoken taboo that in McKay's time precluded the explicit representation of homosexual characters, it is certainly not surprising that Jekyll's homosexuality is sublimated in the portrayal of Squire Gensir. Nevertheless, the traces of this repressed homosexuality are discernible in Gensir's so-called "eccentricity," his life-long bachelorhood, and his admission that he was "not a marrying man" (126). Indeed, the complete de-sexualization of Gensir within the novel underscores—by way of its conspicuous absence—what the narrative is unable to name. According to the text, Gensir "lived aloof from sexual contact" and was, as Mrs. Craig often remarked, "a happy old bachelor with . . . not the slightest blemish upon his character—a character about which nothing was whispered either *naturally* or otherwise" [emphasis mine] (92). To the extent that Gensir remains an outsider whose appreciation of Jamaican folk culture is ultimately "merely cerebral" (85), the homosexuality (however latent) implied in his characterization is likewise encoded as non-native and therefore "foreign."

(Neo)colonialism and (Homo)sexuality in Paule Marshall's
The Chosen Place, The Timeless People

In an exchange that in many ways echoes the cultural politics of the Buju Banton controversy, Hortense Spillers takes issue with Judith Fetterley's claim that Paule Marshall's novel *The Chosen Place, The Timeless People* is "homophobic." Fetterley's allegation is presumably based on her reading of the brief lesbian affair that takes place between Merle, the novel's protagonist, and a wealthy white woman who serves as her "London patroness." In an attempt to account for the divergence between her interpretation and that of Fetterley, Spillers suggests that the disagreement represents "an illustration of the sorts of conflicts that arise among discontinuous reading and interpretive communities." In addition, Spillers argues that Merle's lesbian encounter is not "a major thematic issue in the novel" and suggests instead that Marshall is more concerned in the episode with "the particular dynamics of colonial politics and its involvement on the intimate ground of feeling."[14]

Although Spillers' reading of the ways in which the relationship between Merle and her London patroness reflects the inequities of the colonial relation is certainly astute, the question of the novel's "homophobia" is not (or should not be) so easily dismissed. Rather than choosing between readings that emphasize either colonial *or* sexual politics, I would argue that the two are inextricably linked in Marshall's text and that Merle's encounter with the white lesbian functions as a trenchant critique of colonialism at the same time that it reinscribes certain dominant sexual ideologies. In fact, I would argue that this particular conjunction of the sexual and the colonial in Marshall's 1969 novel reflects the terms within which anti-colonial arguments were often constructed in certain "Afrocentric" or black nationalist discourses that characterized the period. Consequently, Marshall's formulation demonstrates how such discourses—especially insofar as they rely on notions of family or "race" as family—are always already gendered, always already, in Stuart Hall's words, "underpinned by a particular sexual economy, a particular figured masculinity [or femininity], a particular class identity," and so on.[15]

Although the "lesbian episode" may not appear to occupy a central place in the thematic scheme of the novel—Spillers points out, for example, that the encounter is only retrospectively recalled by Merle—it can (and should) be read alongside other episodes where the question of homosexuality is either implicitly or explicitly raised. A pattern of representation might, thus, be established in terms of the recirculation of certain ideologies of gender and sexuality within the narrative. These ideologies have to do not only with positioning gay and lesbian sexuality as "foreign" and/or "unnatural" but also with prescribing normative boundaries for male and female gender identity in general.

The affair between Merle and her London patroness is clearly meant to signify as a metaphor for the asymmetries of the colonial relationship itself. This link between sexual and imperial motives is made explicit when Merle recalls her patroness' preference for "foreigners": "During the time I lived there I met people from every corner of the globe: India, Asia, Africa . . . all over the place. The sun, you might say, never set on the little empire she had going in her drawing room."[16] In addition, Merle's account of the indebtedness and dependency that the wealthy white woman would deliberately and strategically encourage exposes one of the primary mechanisms by which post-independence Caribbean states—like the fictitious Bourne Island—are kept under the crush of the neo-colonial heel. However, at the same time that the portrayal of Merle's encounter with the English woman enacts an insightful critique of (neo)colonial politics, it simultaneously reinscribes a rhetoric that positions gay and lesbian sexuality as "unnatural" and "foreign." Describing the "wild crowd" she fell in with, Merle states that they (the English) were "experts at making anything they do seem perfectly *natural,* and getting you to think so, too." In addition, she describes her patroness as "one of those upper-class types you hear of over there who don't seem to mind having produced a *degenerate* or two" [emphases added] (327–28).

This association of gay/lesbian sexuality with the "unnatural" also informs Marshall's characterization of the gay tourists who frequent Sugar's, the local nightclub. Like Merle's patroness, the gay men are portrayed as predators; their exploitation of "native" sexuality serves as an emblem of the economic exploitation that defines the neo-colonial regime. Pointing out this group of affluent gay white men to Saul, Merle exclaims: "As for that bunch out on the balcony . . . Not a boy child over the age of three is safe since they arrived on the island" (87). Nevertheless, at the same time that it reflects an acute and subtle understanding of the way that the colonial dynamic permeates all levels of "indigenous" life—including what Spillers calls "the intimate ground of feeling"—this characterization also reinforces certain stereotypical notions about the "unnaturalness" of gay sexuality. The narrator states that these men "had the overstated gestures of their kind, as well as the *unnaturally* high voices that called attention to themselves and the laugh that was as shrill and sexless as a eunuch's, and which never ceased" [emphasis mine] (88).

As Jacqui Alexander points out, these narrative figurations that position gay and lesbian sexuality as "unnatural" also serve to "naturalize" heterosexuality as an implicit norm (5–6). In addition to ensnaring her in a cycle of debt and dependency, Merle's liaison with the English lesbian has the effect of destabilizing her identity as a woman. Merle admits that the "business between her and myself . . . had me so I didn't know who or what I was." And she confesses to Saul that when she finally decided to sever the ties with her patroness it was because "most of all . . . I was curious to see if a man would maybe look at me twice" (329). In other words, Merle's recuperation of a stable black female identity seems to hinge on her ability to attract the sexual attentions of a (heterosexual) male. In fact, Merle is eventually "saved" from the corrupting influence of the white lesbian not only by a man, but also through marriage and motherhood—in other words, the type of sexual relationship that epitomizes the heterosexual norm, what Alexander calls "conjugal heterosexuality" (10).

Recalling her brief marriage to Ketu—the committed Ugandan nationalist she met in London—Merle states that "most of all, he made me know I was a woman. . . . After years of not being sure what I was, whether fish or fowl or what, I knew with him I was a woman and no one would ever again be able to make me believe otherwise. I still love him for that" (332). In the novel, Merle's lesbian affair represents a betrayal not only of her "true womanhood"—the "great wrong" that Ketu finds it impossible to forgive—but also of her anti-colonial politics, her family, and ultimately her "race." Afraid that Merle's touch might somehow "contaminate" their child, Ketu eventually abandons Merle and returns to Africa, taking their daughter with him. Demonstrating the degree to which she has internalized the supposed "naturalness" of the heterosexual norm, Merle herself is convinced that Ketu's actions are entirely justified. From another perspective, one might convincingly argue that Ketu leaves primarily because the knowledge of Merle's lesbian affair threatens his own sense of masculinity.

Similarly, Marshall's portrait of Allen Fuso, Saul Amron's young assistant, implicitly assumes the universality or "naturalness" of a normative heterosexual masculinity. Although Allen's (latent) homosexuality is more complexly delineated than that of Merle's London patroness or the gay men at Sugar's, the resolution (or the lack thereof) of his "identity crisis" ultimately reveals the narrative's refusal to imagine anything other than a heterosexual solution to his "problem." Allen's crisis is precipitated by the homosexual feelings that are occasioned by his growing friendship with Vere, the "native son" who has returned home to Bourne Island after a brief stint on a labor scheme in the U.S. Moreover, Allen's homosexuality is represented in the narrative as a kind of arrested development—i.e. the consequence of an unresolved castration anxiety. Allen is unable to perform (hetero)sexually with Elvita—the date that Vere arranges for him during Carnival—not only because he finds women's bodies which "lacked purity of line with the up-jutting breasts and buttocks" distasteful, but also because of "his fear, borne of a recurrent phantasy of his as a boy, that once he entered that dark place hidden away at the base of their bodies, he would not be able to extricate himself" (309).

Alone on the settee, with Vere and Milly making love on the other side of the screen, Allen performs a solitary sexual act that signifies in the text not only as a substitute for intercourse but also as a parody of the (heterosexual) sex act itself. As Allen masturbates to the sounds of the unseen lovers, the image of Vere looms large in his imagination:

> The girl was faceless, unimportant, but he saw Vere clearly: his dark body rising and falling, advancing and retreating, like one of the powerful Bournehills waves they sometimes rode together in the early evening. (312)

Allen, in effect, erases Milly from the scene and puts himself in her place, thus becoming what he has subconsciously longed to be—namely, Vere's lover:

> His cry at the end, which he tried to stifle but could not, broke at the same moment the girl uttered her final cry, and the two sounds rose together, blending one into the other, becoming a single complex note of the most profound pleasure and release. (312)

Given the ambiguity of the text—especially where issues of gay/lesbian sexuality are concerned—it is difficult to determine the extent to which Allen is aware (consciously, at least) of his own homosexuality. Nevertheless, he admits to Merle—in an attempt to explain the deep depression that had overtaken him since the events of Carnival and the subsequent death of Vere—that he longs for "something that wasn't so safe and sure all the time" or even "something people didn't approve of so they no longer thought of me as such a nice, respectable type." The obvious inadequacy of Merle's response—she recommends "a nice girl and some children"—is not surprising, given the guilt she has internalized as a result of her own lesbian affair (378–81). However, her response also reflects the novel's investment in and re-circulation of an ideology that naturalizes heterosexuality while it positions gay/lesbian sexuality as deviant or "unnatural." Furthermore, as Merle's inability to imagine anything other than a conventional heterosexual (and reproductive) solution to Allen's "problem" not only defines the limits of the novel's discourse on questions of homosexuality, it also exposes one of the consequences—inherent in certain black nationalist discourses, for example—of uncritically conflating "race" with notions (especially "naturalized" ones) of family.

Michelle Cliff, H. Nigel Thomas, and the Contradictions of Representing the "Indigenous" Gay/Lesbian Subject

> We are always in negotiation, not with a single set of oppositions that place us always in the same relation to others, but with a series of different positionalities. Each has for us its point of profound subjective identification. And that is the most difficult thing about this proliferation of the field of identities and antagonisms: they are often dislocating in relation to one another. (Hall 31)

In an essay in which he attempts to map the critical challenges presented by the current historical conjuncture, Stuart Hall suggests that "it is to the diversity, not the homogeneity, of black experience that we must now give our undivided creative attention." Hall argues that, given the emergence of what he refers to as "a new kind of cultural politics," it is necessary now more than ever to "recognize the other kinds of difference [those of gender, sexuality, and class, for example] that place, position, and locate black people" (30). Two recent Caribbean writers—Michelle Cliff (Jamaica) and H. Nigel Thomas (St. Vincent)—have produced texts which reflect the way anti-colonial/imperial discourses need to be conceptualized in the context of the present historical and cultural situation. Attending to the differences that operate within as well as between cultures, these texts simultaneously critique the sexist/homophobic and colonial/neo-colonial structures that continue to pervade contemporary Caribbean societies. By posing an implicit challenge to the binary oppositions that often define discussions of "native" sexuality, writers like Cliff and Thomas have cleared a discursive space for the articulation of an "indigenous" gay/lesbian subjectivity.

In contrast to these binary structures—which often imply the mutually exclusive choice of an either/or—these writers frequently deploy narrative strategies that privilege ambiguity and the ability to negotiate contradictions. For example, in an essay entitled "If I Could Write This in Fire, I Would Write This in Fire," Michelle Cliff relates an incident that underscores the contradictions generated by a Caribbean lesbian identity—contradictions that illustrate, in Hall's terms, how the multiple "positionalities" that inevitably constitute such an identity "are often dislocating in relation to one another." Cliff becomes justifiably enraged when she and a distant cousin who is "recognizably black and speaks with an accent" are refused service in a London bar. Although she is light-skinned enough to "pass" for white, Cliff states that she has "chosen sides." However, the lines suddenly become blurred—and allegiances begin to shift—when the cousin joins his white colleagues in a "sustained mockery" of the waiters in a gay-owned restaurant.[17] The conflicting feelings of anger (at his homophobia/sexism) and solidarity (because he is also a victim of racism and colonial oppression) that exemplify Cliff's response to Henry mirror the profound ambivalence she feels towards Jamaica itself—the "killing ambivalence" (103) that comes with the realization that home (especially for the "lesbian of color") is often a site of alienation as well as identification.

This ambivalence is also reflected in the dual strategy that informs Cliff's first novel, *Abeng*. On one hand, the narrative affirms the value of an "indigenous" Jamaican culture—especially the oral traditions and folk practices that embody the island's long history of anti-colonial resistance. On the other, the novel elaborates an incisive critique of the oppressive ideological structures that continue to pervade the postcolonial state—a deeply entrenched color-caste system, homophobia, and sexism, for example. Exemplifying the formal and stylistic innovations that are characteristic of her work, Cliff deliberately disrupts the narrative continuity of *Abeng* by intercutting the story of Clare Savage—the novel's young female protagonist—with fragments of history, myth, and legend. In her attempt to reconstruct what the critic Simon Gikandi calls a "repressed Afro-Caribbean history,"[18] Cliff inscribes a revisionary account that challenges not only the Eurocentric premises of conventional historiography but also its phallocentric and heterosexist assumptions as well. In other words, in addition to representing a female-centered tradition of resistance, *Abeng* also attempts to posit an historical or "genealogical" precedent for an "indigenous" lesbian/gay subjectivity.

Although it would perhaps be a historical misnomer to label Mma Alli—the mythical figure who plays a part in the novel's reconstruction of Caribbean slave resistance—a lesbian character per se, she clearly represents the possibility of an "indigenous" or even "Afrocentric" precedent for a non-heterosexual orientation:

> Mma Alli had never lain with a man. The other slaves said she loved only women in that way, but that she was a true sister to the men—the Black men: her brothers. They said that by being with her in bed, women learned all manner of the magic of passion. How to become wet again and again all through the night. How to soothe and excite at the same time. How to touch a woman in her deep-inside and make her womb move within her.[19]

Descended from a line of "one-breasted warrior women," Mma Alli is spiritually if not biologically related to Maroon Nanny—the slave leader who, according to local legend, "could catch a bullet between her buttocks and render the bullet harmless" (14)—and all the other female figures who function as historical precursors in a tradition from which Clare ("colonized child" that she is) has become tragically disconnected.

In addition to inscribing a "proto-lesbian" figure within the reconstructed mythology of an Afro-Caribbean past, Cliff exposes the homophobia that results in the marginalization and persecution of lesbians and gay men within contemporary Jamaican culture. These deeply-ingrained homophobic attitudes—which reflect a fear of "difference"—represent one of the primary means by which a normative heterosexuality is consolidated and, indeed, enforced. For example, the story of Clinton, the son of "Mad Hannah," demonstrates what can happen if one is even suspected of being homosexual. When Clinton is "taken with a cramp while . . . swimming in the river," he is left to drown while "shouts of 'battyman, battyman' echoed off the rocks and across the water of the swimming hole" (63). Likewise, the fate of an uncle who was rumoured to be "funny" serves as an implicit warning to Clare against the dangers of transgressing the boundaries of what is culturally sanctioned as acceptable or "normal" sexual behavior. Although Clare was "not sure what 'funny' meant," she "knew that Robert had caused some disturbance when he brought a dark man home from Montego Bay and introduced him to his mother as 'my dearest friend.'"

Stigmatized and ostracized by his family, Robert finally "did what Clare understood many 'funny' 'queer' 'off' people did: He swam too far out into Kingston Harbor and could not swim back. He drowned just as Clinton—about whom there had been similar whispers—had drowned" (125–26).

In Cliff's second novel, *No Telephone to Heaven,* the ambivalence of the Caribbean gay/lesbian subject is literally embodied by the character Harry/Harriet—the "boy-girl" who serves as the friend, confidant, and alter-ego of an older Clare Savage. In the very indeterminacy of his/her name, Harry/Harriet reflects the unresolved (and perhaps unresolvable) contradictions that are inevitably generated by an "indigenous" gay and/or lesbian identity. Constantly transgressing the boundaries that supposedly separate male from female, upper from lower classes, insider from outsider, self from "other," "natural" from "unnatural" sexuality, Harry/Harriet inhabits an "interstitial" space—designated by the conjunction "both/and" rather than "either/or"—that, as he/she asserts, is "not just sun, but sun and moon."[20] In addition, Cliff clearly disrupts the discursive positioning of homosexuality as a "foreign contamination" by de-allegorizing the rape of Harry/Harriet when he was a child by a British officer. Although Harry/Harriet admits to Clare that he/she is often tempted to think "that what he [the officer] did to me is but a symbol for what they did to all of us," he/she asserts that the experience was not the "cause" of his ambiguous sexuality. Instead, Harry/Harriet insists on the concrete and literal brutality of the rape: "Not symbol, not allegory . . . merely a person who felt the overgrown cock of a big whiteman pierce the asshole of a lickle Black bwai" (129–30).

In his first novel, *Spirits in the Dark,* H. Nigel Thomas deploys a narrative construct that functions—especially in its utopian gestures—much like the band of "revolutionaries" that Clare joins in *No Telephone to Heaven*. Jerome Quashee, the protagonist of Thomas' narrative, is initiated into an obscure and vaguely "Afrocentric" religious sect known as the Spiritualists. As a consequence, Jerome undergoes a ritual experience during the course of the novel that ultimately transforms and redeems him. Moreover, this redemptive experience becomes a way for Thomas to imagine and represent what might be called a decolonized Caribbean reality. In his attempt to articulate the ideological conditions of this decolonized Caribbean reality, Thomas insists on the need to dismantle not only oppressive political structures but restrictive sexual ones as well. Demonstrating an implicit understanding of how, as Stuart Hall puts it, "a transgressive politics in one domain is constantly sutured and stabilized by reactionary or unexamined politics in another" (31), Thomas simultaneously confronts the patriarchal, heterosexist, and Eurocentric ideologies that constitute the particular legacy of the Caribbean colonial experience. Jerome's descent into "madness"—he suffers a series of "breakdowns" prior to his initiation—consequently reflects his unstable status as both a colonial subject and a homosexual.

Jerome's initiation entails a period of self-imposed isolation and sensory depri-vation that enables him to reflect on and thereby come to terms with his experiences within a deeply flawed colonial school system, the expectations and disappointments of his parents, and his sexual feelings for other men. Assisted by Pointer Francis, who serves as his spiritual guide, Jerome emerges with a newfound understanding of his "African heritage" as well as an acceptance of his homosexuality. Jerome finally realizes that he had "put the sex part of [his] life 'pon a trash heap just fo' please society" and that "madness" was the price he paid for "hiding and sacrificing [his] life like that."[21]

However, if Jerome's spiritual rebirth constitutes a utopian gesture that reflects Thomas' desire to inscribe a decolonized "indigenous" gay subject within his text, that gesture is necessarily tempered by the pervasive homophobia that the novel also exposes. Although Pointer Francis tells Jerome that there is "[n]othing sinful 'bout sex" even if Jerome is "a case of a pestle needing a pestle" (as opposed to a pestle needing a mortar or vice versa), he nevertheless reminds Jerome that he is "going back to live in the real world, with real people" and that "most o' the brethren ain't grown enough fo' understand why you is how yo' is and fo' accept yo' as yo' is" (198, 212–13). In the course of his spiritual journey, Jerome recalls various incidents that were decisive in terms of his subconscious decision to repress his homosexual-ity. Chief among these are his memories of Boy Boy, the gay cousin who "was a con-stant point of reference for what the society would not accept" (94). The ridicule and humiliation that Boy Boy was forced to endure confirmed the unacceptability of Jerome's homosexual feelings. In addition, the fate that Boy Boy suffered when he "arranged with a young man to meet him in one of the canefields" demonstrated how physical violence was often used by the community in order to enforce a normative heterosexuality:

> When he [Boy Boy] got there, there were ten of them. They took turns buggering him; one even used a beer bottle; then they beat him into unconsciousness and left him there. He'd refused to name the young men. But everyone knew who they were because they'd bragged about what they'd done—everything but the buggering.
>
> (199)

Jerome also recalls a more recent incident that illustrates how the community often acted in complicity with such violence by condoning or at least refusing to challenge these virulent displays of homophobic behavior. Jerome remembers that when Albert Brown, a cashier in the post office where he worked, was slapped by a co-worker because he dared to offer a strikingly effective riposte to the mail sorter's crude homophobic insult, "no one, not even Jerome, reprimanded Brill." Moreover, when Jerome is called as a witness, the postmaster seems almost unwilling to believe his account which leads Jerome to wonder if "perhaps the postmaster would have preferred that he lie and save him from having to take action against Brill" (200). Despite the postmaster's apparent reluctance, Brill is eventually dismissed—it seems he was on probation at the time for "telling a female clerk that he didn't have to 'take orders from a cunt.'" Nevertheless, many of Jerome's co-workers were "angry with Albert, saying that he did not know how to take a joke as a man, that he had caused Brill to lose his job, and didn't he know that Brill had a wife and two children to feed?" Jerome is likewise criticized for not knowing "how to see and not see and hear and not hear" (200). The obvious implication is, of course, that homophobia and sexism are not considered serious offenses—since they uphold an apparently "natural" order—and therefore hardly warrant such severe censure. From this perspective, it is unimaginable that Brill would lose his job simply because "he slap a buller."

However, at the same time that it exposes the complicity of the community, Thomas' text, like Cliff's, demonstrates an acute sensitivity to the ambiguous and sometimes contradictory spaces that inevitably exist in any culture. These sites of ambiguity and contradiction—which often reflect how "differences" are actually lived and negotiated—are, paradoxically perhaps, the ones that can potentially enable new forms of social and cultural relations. For example, at one point in his meditations, Jerome finds himself contemplating an episode that reveals the surprising capacity for tolerance that also exists alongside the homophobia pervading all levels of Caribbean society. Jerome recalls that among the female food vendors who plied their trade in the open-air market, there was also "a man whom the buyers and non-buyers said was the biggest woman of the lot. They called him Sprat." Because he "got more customers than the women," Sprat often became the target of homophobic insults in the quarrels that frequently broke out as a result of the fierce competition among the vendors. However, despite the caustic nature of these exchanges, Jerome observes that Sprat nevertheless "loaned Melia [a vendor with whom he had previously argued] ten dollars to buy some ground provisions somebody was selling at a bargain." Noting Sprat's absence on another occasion, Jerome learns that he had the flu and that "three of the women had been to see him. One said he would be out the next week and she was buying supplies for him that day" (21–22). What Jerome comes to understand, then, is that there are relations of professional and personal reciprocity binding Sprat and the other vendors together—existing social relations which pose a contradiction to the homophobic ideologies that serve to position him as "other."

Indeed, Thomas' novel seems to suggest that the willingness to accept the indeterminacy associated with such contradictions—the opposite of rigid binary thinking, in other words—is often the first step in undoing the homophobia that continues to marginalize lesbians and gay men in contemporary Caribbean cultures. For example, Pointer Francis reminds Jerome that it "is only when most people have a son or a daughter that is like that [that] they stop ridiculing and start thinking" (213). Once again, it is particularly within the context of concrete affiliative social relations that the potential for negotiating these contradictions can exist. Consequently, Jerome singles out his brother, Wesi, as the one "he would tell . . . everything about himself" mainly because Wesi "was the first person he knew that understood and accepted contradictions" (156). In fact, one of the central insights that Jerome gleans from his initiation has to do precisely with the importance of this "non-binary" mode of thinking: "Jerome knew that by the time the spirit called you, you knew that life itself was a contradiction" (177).

In the context of an "indigenous" criticism, the need for "non-binary" modes of thinking that resist the totalizing impulses implicit in both the "universalist" and "nativist" positions—the impasse between which the Buju Banton controversy so clearly exemplifies—is equally urgent. Given the alarming persistence of anti-gay violence in contemporary Caribbean societies and the reproduction in literature and popular culture of ideologies that condone or legitimate such violence, we clearly need a critical practice that goes beyond simple dichotomies—us/them, native/foreign, natural/unnatural—a practice that can not only affirm but also critique "indigenous" cultures in all of their varied and inevitably contradictory forms.

NOTES

1 See Ransdell Pierson, "'Kill Gays' Hit Song Stirs Fury," *The New York Post*, 24 Oct. 1992; Joan Morgan, "No Apologies, No Regrets," *VIBE*, Oct. 1993; Peter Noel and Robert Marriott, "Batty Boys in Babylon," *Village Voice*, 12 Jan. 1993. Subsequent references appear parenthetically within the text.

2 Carolyn Cooper, "'Lyrical Gun': Metaphor and Role Play in Jamaican Dancehall Culture," *The Massachusetts Review* (Autumn-Winter 1994): 437. Cooper borrows the notion of the "lyrical gun" from Shabba Ranks' dancehall tune "Gun Pon Me." Subsequent references appear parenthetically within the text.

3 See the "Open Letter" that was published alongside Morgan's *VIBE* piece and collectively signed by many prominent "lesbians, gay men, and transgendered persons of African, Afro-American, Afro-Caribbean, and Afro-Latin descent."

4 The quote is taken from an unpublished paper that the author was kind enough to share with me. Entitled "On Liminal Subjectivity," the paper was presented at the "National Symposium on Indigenous Knowledge and Contemporary Social Issues" in March 1994, Tampa, Florida.

5 According to Cooper, plans for a protest to be led by a group of "local homosexuals" failed to materialize because "on the day of the rumoured march, men of all social classes gathered in the square, armed with a range of implements—sticks, stones, machetes—apparently to defend their heterosexual honor." Nevertheless, Cooper states that the aborted attempt paradoxically generated a public discourse on homosexuality when, in the wake of the non-event, "[n]umerous callers on various talk show programs aired their opinions in defence of, or attack on the homosexual's right to freedom of expression" (440). In addition, the recent film by Isaac Julien, *The Darker Side of Black,* explores these very issues in relation to Rap, Hip Hop, and African-American popular culture in general as well as its diasporic counterpart in the Caribbean, the culture of the Dancehall.

6   Wayne Cooper, *Claude McKay: Rebel Sojourner in the Harlem Renaissance* (Baton Rouge: Louisiana State University Press, 1987), 75. Subsequent references appear parenthetically within the text.

7   Bernard Bell, *The Afro-American Novel and Its Tradition* (Amherst: University of Massachusetts Press, 1987), 118.

8   I am indebted to my colleague Charles Nero for helping me to clarify this concept of the homosocial in McKay's novels.

9   Claude McKay, *Home to Harlem* (New York: Harper & Brothers, 1928), 129.

10 For example, see Wayne Cooper's discussion on the critical reception—especially on the part of Black American intellectuals like W.E.B. Du Bois—of McKay's *Home to Harlem* (238–48).

11 M. Jacqui Alexander, "Not Just (Any)Body Can Be a Citizen: The Politics of Law, Sexuality and Postcoloniality in Trinidad and Tobago and the Bahamas," *Feminist Review* 48 (Autumn 1994): 9. Subsequent references appear parenthetically within the text.

12 Claude McKay, *Banana Bottom* (1933; New York: Harcourt, Brace, Jovanovich, 1961), 291. Subsequent references appear parenthetically within the text.

13 Early in the novel, Bita is raped by Crazy Bow Adair, a third generation descendant of a "strange Scotchman who had emigrated to Jamaica in the eighteen-twenties." Although the narrator states that the mixed-race progeny of this "strange liberator" were, for the most part, "hardy peasants," he nevertheless admits that there are those who believe "the mixing of different human strains" had less salutary effects (2–4). In addition, the novel suggests that Patou, the "cripple-idiot" son of the missionary couple, Priscilla and Malcolm Craig, is both a product and a reflection of the repressed sexuality that is associated with their Englishness.

14 Hortense Spillers, "*Chosen Place, Timeless People:* Some Figurations on the New World," in *Conjuring: Black Women, Fiction, and Literary Tradition,* ed. Marjorie Pryse and Hortense Spillers (Bloomington: Indiana University Press, 1985), footnote 6, 172–73.

15 Stuart Hall, "What Is This 'Black' in Black Popular Culture?" in *Black Popular Culture,* ed. Gina Dent (Seattle: Bay Press, 1992), 31. Subsequent references appear parenthetically within the text. See also Paul Gilroy's article, "It's a Family Affair," in the same anthology and Anne McClintock's essay, "Family Feuds: Gender, Nationalism and the Family," *Feminist Review* 44 (Summer 1993).

16 Paule Marshall, *The Chosen Place, The Timeless People* (1969; New York: Vintage, 1992), 328. Subsequent references appear parenthetically within the text.

17 Michelle Cliff, *The Land of Look Behind* (Ithaca, NY: Firebrand Books, 1985), 68. Subsequent references appear parenthetically within the text.

18 Simon Gikandi, *Writing in Limbo: Modernism and Caribbean Literature* (Ithaca: Cornell University Press, 1992), 233.

19 Michelle Cliff, *Abeng* (1984; New York: Penguin Books, 1991), 35. Subsequent references appear parenthetically within the text.

20 Michelle Cliff, *No Telephone to Heaven* (1987; New York: Vintage, 1989), 171. Subsequent references appear parenthetically within the text.

21 H. Nigel Thomas, *Spirits in the Dark* (1993; Oxford: Heinemann Publishers, 1994), 198. Subsequent references appear parenthetically within the text.

VII

Reading the Subaltern

The power dynamics in a crudely formulated colonizer-colonized equation can mis-leadingly signal an obvious binary, unruffled by internal splits, nuance, or tension. While Homi Bhabha borrows from poststructuralist and psychoanalytic models in chal-lenging the uniformity of the individual combatants and the taken-for-granted assump-tions about the power of the colonizer and the powerlessness of the colonized, the Subaltern Studies group has used Marxist theories to split the colonized into heteroge-neous groups divided along multiple lines, none of them necessarily united by shared interests and agendas. However indebted the group has been to British and Marxist social scientists whose work was deeply engaged in class and labor history, it would be a mistake to categorize Subaltern Studies as an appendage to European Marxism (filtered through Michel Foucault). Although group members have been deeply influ-enced by the Italian Marxist Antonio Gramsci's "Notes on Italian History" and have even adopted his use of the term "subaltern," Subaltern Studies began in the 1980s pri-marily as a revisionist intervention in modern Indian historiography. The group came into being as a scholarly collective based in India, the UK, and Australia, led by Rana-jit Guha, an Indian historian then teaching in the UK but who has since retired from the collective. In subsequent years Subaltern Studies has expanded its disciplinary and national boundaries, influencing scholarship on Latin America and inspiring similar projects in literature and anthropology.

The first volume of *Subaltern Studies: Writings on South Asian History and Society* was published in 1981, with Guha's "On Some Aspects of the Historiography of Colonial India" as the lead essay. In his preface to the volume, Guha cites the *Concise Oxford Dictionary*'s definition of subaltern as someone of "inferior rank." He goes on to say that the term, as used by the collective, will indicate "the general attribute of subor-dination in South Asian society whether this is expressed in terms of class, caste, age, gender and office or in any other way." Subordination, however, functions more as a processual relationship in the dynamics of power rather than as a static condition of being. Thus the colonially educated middle-class elites of India were subordinate to English colonial regimes, but dominant, in their local contexts, over illiterate and landless peasants with whom they possibly interacted more than the English administrators ruling from urban/metropolitan areas. The Subaltern Studies project chooses as its subject the peasant and lower-class masses that were the lowest common denominator of the colonial equation in accounts by a group of Cambridge historians as well as in other narratives by Indian nationalists. According to both these groups, Indian nationalism was either the product of a small and collaborationist, even opportunistic, elite or a fiery movement for independence inspired by statesmen-heroes like Gandhi and Nehru who mobilized all Indians in a homogeneous anticolonial revolution against British occupation.

What these narratives of modern Indian history ignore, to quote Guha, is "the contribution made by the people *on their own*, that is, *independently of the elite* to the making and development of this nationalism." One-sided accounts that privilege the Indian bourgeoisie as the lead actors and primary agents in nationalist movements not only misread what they interpret as unruly and ineffective peasant insurgencies, but gloss over the fact that some of the insurgents revolted, for instance, not simply against British policies but also against Indian landlords. Although there were strategic and unplanned alliances between the native elites and the subaltern masses, the conclusion Guha reaches in his essay highlights the failure of the Indian nationalist movement to eradicate more comprehensively the traditional structures of feudal inequality. Ironically, while the Subaltern Studies group is critical of conventional Marxist approaches to seemingly regressive, unorganized peasant rebellions and seeks to reinscribe the agency of the latter, Guha echoes the deterministic temporal scheme of insufficiently "mature" subaltern groups that "waited in vain for a leadership to raise them above localism and generalize them into a nationwide anti-imperialist campaign." Guha echoes Gramsci's belief that subaltern histories, with few self-ascriptions or sympathetic interpretations of what does get documented in elite historiography, appear fragmented and discontinuous.

David Lloyd's essay shows the influence of the Subaltern Studies group but also records a significant departure in the Irish context, where revisionist historiography tends to read Ireland's history as one continuous with the larger history of Europe. Lloyd challenges attempts by the Irish historians who conjure a convenient graph of Ireland's Europeanized "progress" into democratic modernity, industrial advancement, and civil society in order to silence the colonial comparisons that some scholars find odious. Against this enabling constitution of modern Irish subjectivity terminally liberated from an earlier history of colonial subordination, Lloyd posits the "subalternity effect," which seeks to offer, through "differently constituted objects of research," opposing accounts of Ireland's continuing domination by British interests. Although

Lloyd notes that subaltern subjects are both constituted and marginalized by the discursive effects of dominant and unitary historiography, he also draws attention to the interruption of this narrative by the "episodic and fragmentary" nature of Irish history. The teleological history of state formation and bureaucracy is broken by "the emergence of a large corpus of non-elite histories: histories of agrarian movements, local histories, social histories of the complex intersections of class and colonization in rural Ireland, women's history," and so on. Rather than any singular sense of historical progress, Lloyd emphasizes a constant tension, a series of manipulations of and reactions to the subjectivities enforced or recommended by the postcolonial Irish state. Significantly, Lloyd rejects any deterministic teleology of subaltern hegemony but foregrounds the "persistent inassimilability [of these discontinuous histories] to the state."

John Beverley discusses the unexpected consequences of the subaltern's rise to hegemony, a possibility pessimistically denied in the present but hopefully anticipated in the future by Guha. Focusing on the unprecedented success of the testimonial narrative *I, Rigoberta Menchú*, by the Guatemalan activist Rigoberta Menchú, a figure now well known in the American academy, Beverley considers the risks and potential of what happens when a subaltern not only speaks but also becomes a dominant voice. Beverley invokes the oft-cited essay by Gayatri Chakravorty Spivak, "Can the Subaltern Speak," in which Spivak, though commonly understood as having answered the question in the negative (thereby making her the target of charges that she was silencing the subaltern and denying the latter any agency), pointedly suggests that the subaltern voice is rarely heard or properly understood in dominant power structures. Menchú's canonization in North American universities as the authentic native informant in the Guatemalan peasant struggles earned the disapproval of conservative intellectuals such as Dinesh D'Souza and of the anthropologist David Stoll for quite different reasons. D'Souza has worried over elevating "inferior" literature (read propaganda) and romanticizing the oppressed; Stoll has unearthed various inaccuracies in Menchú's testimony that give the lie to her speaking truth to power and render suspect, in his analysis, her entire agenda.

Although in earlier accounts Beverley insists on the truth-telling value of Menchú's *testimonio*, in this essay he comes to grips with the fictional liberties Menchú takes as she manipulates her audience for *her* purposes, a striking contrast to liberal fears about subordinating lower-class voices to bourgeois interests. While those in the academy are generally seen as complicitous with dominating mechanisms of state power, here the subaltern as trickster figure disarms the patronizing academics. Invoking the fragmentary and episodic in a different sense, Beverley ultimately acknowledges the "internal rivalries, contradictions, [and] different ways of telling" in a community, all driven by the diverse agendas of competing interests. In a move similar to Lloyd's, Beverley notes that the social facticity of events need not have the last word on historical relevance and insists on the necessary fragmentation of subaltern cultural practice. His "deconstructive ethics," however, do not preclude solidarity and affiliations across class and national boundaries, leaving room for the subaltern to transform the academic space.

If Beverley maps a process, through Menchú, of the subaltern's "becoming not-subaltern," Nicholas Thomas returns us to the reverse process of academic and dominant "constructions of the exotic and primitive," including the settler's "going native" phase. Thomas examines the various ways in which the subaltern, the aboriginal, is *spoken for* in settler cultures. In becoming the subaltern through New Age appropriation, the dominant subject of settler society erases the historically existing natives, who tend to show up in cultural representations as conveniently disappeared or dead in the "fatal impact" plots. Like other critics in settler contexts, Thomas underlines the temporal complacency of the term "postcolonial," which does not take into account indigenous peoples who see themselves as still colonized, including in the United States, where, ironically, Thomas finds them to be more institutionally silenced and invisible than in Australia, New Zealand, and Canada.

Primitivist constructions of the natives as antimaterialistic euphemize their material dispossession, including the loss of their ancestral lands. Reading them as prelapsarian enables their being written out of history. And finally, idealizing the aboriginal inhabitants as purely connected to their traditional past ignores their appropriation of Western technologies or reduces them to contaminated mimics. As in Menchú's case, liberal ideologies tend to appropriate the voices (and sometimes identities, as in the case of the popular film *Dances with Wolves*) of the "primitives," but unlike Beverley, Thomas does not discuss strategic alliances between them. He does conclude, however, with an affirmation of subaltern agency, including the use of nativist and essentialist discourses to stage resistance as well as, on occasion, a pragmatic exploitation of the very primitivist stereotypes inflicted by white settler society. Finally, what bears repeating is a point that each of the scholars in part VII makes in different ways. As Thomas puts it, "just as colonial culture needs to be understood, not as an essence, but as a plurality of projects including, most recently, the primitivist renovation of white identity via indigenous culture, anti- and postcolonial culture cannot be taken as a unitary set of meanings or a stable position."

REFERENCE

Spivak, Gayatri Chakravorty. 1988. "Can the Subaltern Speak?" In *Marxism and the Interpretation of Culture*, ed.Cary Nelson and Lawrence Grossberg, 271–313. Urbana: University of Illinois Press.

26

RANAJIT GUHA

On Some Aspects of the Historiography of Colonial India

1. The historiography of Indian nationalism has for a long time been dominated by elitism—colonialist elitism and bourgeois-nationalist elitism.[1] Both originated as the ideological product of British rule in India, but have survived the transfer of power and been assimilated to neo-colonialist and neo-nationalist forms of discourse in Britain and India respectively. Elitist historiography of the colonialist or neo-colonialist type counts British writers and institutions among its principal protagonists, but has its imitators in India and other countries too. Elitist historiography of the nationalist or neo-nationalist type is primarily an Indian practice but is not without imitators in the ranks of liberal historians in Britain and elsewhere.

2. Both these varieties of elitism share the prejudice that the making of the Indian nation and the development of the consciousness—nationalism—which informed this process, were exclusively or predominantly elite achievements. In the colonialist and neo-colonialist historiographies these achievements are credited to British colonial rulers, administrators, policies, institutions and culture; in the nationalist and neo-nationalist writings—to Indian elite personalities, institutions, activities and ideas.

3. The first of these two historiographies defines Indian nationalism primarily as a function of stimulus and response. Based on a narrowly behaviouristic approach this represents nationalism as the sum of the activities and ideas by which the Indian elite responded to the institutions, opportunities, resources, etc. generated by colonialism. There are several versions of this historiography, but the central modality common to them is to describe Indian nationalism as a sort of 'learning process' through which the native elite became involved in politics by trying to negotiate the maze of institutions and the corresponding cultural complex introduced by the colonial authorities in order to govern the country. What made the elite go through this process was, according to this historiography, no lofty idealism addressed to the

general good of the nation but simply the expectation of rewards in the form of a share in the wealth, power and prestige created by and associated with colonial rule; and it was the drive for such rewards with all its concomitant play of collaboration and competition between the ruling power and the native elite as well as between various elements among the latter themselves, which, we are told, was what constituted Indian nationalism.

4. The general orientation of the other kind of elitist historiography is to represent Indian nationalism as primarily an idealist venture in which the indigenous elite led the people from subjugation to freedom. There are several versions of this historiography which differ from each other in the degree of their emphasis on the role of individual leaders or elite organizations and institutions as the main or motivating force in this venture. However, the modality common to them all is to uphold Indian nationalism as a phenomenal expression of the goodness of the native elite with the antagonistic aspect of their relation to the colonial regime made, against all evidence, to look larger than its collaborationist aspect, their role as promoters of the cause of the people than that as exploiters and oppressors, their altruism and self-abnegation than their scramble for the modicum of power and privilege granted by the rulers in order to make sure of their support for the Raj. The history of Indian nationalism is thus written up as a sort of spiritual biography of the Indian elite.

5. Elitist historiography is of course not without its uses. It helps us to know more about the structure of the colonial state, the operation of its various organs in certain historical circumstances, the nature of the alignment of classes which sustained it; some aspects of the ideology of the elite as the dominant ideology of the period; about the contradictions between the two elites and the complexities of their mutual oppositions and coalitions; about the role of some of the more important British and Indian personalities and elite organizations. Above all it helps us to understand the ideological character of historiography itself.

6. What, however, historical writing of this kind cannot do is to explain Indian nationalism for us. For it fails to acknowledge, far less interpret, the contribution made by the people *on their own,* that is, *independently of the elite* to the making and development of this nationalism. In this particular respect the poverty of this historiography is demonstrated beyond doubt by its failure to understand and assess the mass articulation of this nationalism except, negatively, as a law and order problem, and positively, if at all, either as a response to the charisma of certain elite leaders or in the currently more fashionable terms of vertical mobilization by the manipulation of factions. The involvement of the Indian people in vast numbers, sometimes in hundreds of thousands or even millions, in nationalist activities and ideas is thus represented as a diversion from a supposedly 'real' political process, that is, the grinding away of the wheels of the state apparatus and of elite institutions geared to it, or it is simply credited, as an act of ideological appropriation, to

the influence and initiative of the elite themselves. The bankruptcy of this historiography is clearly exposed when it is called upon to explain such phenomena as the anti-Rowlatt upsurge of 1919 and the Quit India movement of 1942—to name only two of numerous instances of popular initiative asserting itself in the course of nationalist campaigns in defiance or absence of elite control. How can such one-sided and blinkered historiography help us to understand the profound displacements, well below the surface of elite politics, which made Chauri-Chaura or the militant demonstrations of solidarity with the RIN mutineers possible?

7. This inadequacy of elitist historiography follows directly from the narrow and partial view of politics to which it is committed by virtue of its class outlook. In all writings of this kind the parameters of Indian politics are assumed to be or enunciated as exclusively or primarily those of the institutions introduced by the British for the government of the country and the corresponding sets of laws, policies, attitudes and other elements of the superstructure. Inevitably, therefore, a historiography hamstrung by such a definition can do no more than to equate politics with the aggregation of activities and ideas of those who were directly involved in operating these institutions, that is, the colonial rulers and their *élèves*—the dominant groups in native society—to the extent that their mutual transactions were thought to be all there was to Indian nationalism, the domain of the latter is regarded as coincident with that of politics.

8. What clearly is left out of this un-historical historiography is the *politics of the people*. For parallel to the domain of elite politics there existed throughout the colonial period another domain of Indian politics in which the principal actors were not the dominant groups of the indigenous society or the colonial authorities but the subaltern classes and groups constituting the mass of the labouring population and the intermediate strata in town and country—that is, the people. This was an *autonomous* domain, for it neither originated from elite politics nor did its existence depend on the latter. It was traditional only in so far as its roots could be traced back to pre-colonial times, but it was by no means archaic in the sense of being outmoded. Far from being destroyed or rendered virtually ineffective, as was elite politics of the traditional type by the intrusion of colonialism, it continued to operate vigorously in spite of the latter, adjusting itself to the conditions prevailing under the Raj and in many respects developing entirely new strains in both form and content. As modern as indigenous elite politics, it was distinguished by its relatively greater depth in time as well as in structure.

9. One of the more important features of this politics related precisely to those aspects of mobilization which are so little explained by elitist historiography. Mobilization in the domain of elite politics was achieved vertically whereas in that of subaltern politics this was achieved horizontally. The instrumentation of the former was characterized by a relatively greater reliance on the colonial adaptations of British

parliamentary institutions and the residua of semi-feudal political institutions of the pre-colonial period; that of the latter relied rather more on the traditional organization of kinship and territoriality or on class associations depending on the level of the consciousness of the people involved. Elite mobilization tended to be relatively more legalistic and constitutionalist in orientation, subaltern mobilization relatively more violent. The former was, on the whole, more cautious and controlled, the latter more spontaneous. Popular mobilization in the colonial period was realized in its most comprehensive form in peasant uprisings. However, in many historic instances involving large masses of the working people and petty bourgeoisie in the urban areas too the figure of mobilization derived directly from the paradigm of peasant insurgency.

10. The ideology operative in this domain, taken as a whole, reflected the diversity of its social composition with the outlook of its leading elements dominating that of the others at any particular time and within any particular event. However, in spite of such diversity one of its invariant features was a notion of resistance to elite domination. This followed from the subalternity common to all the social constituents of this domain and as such distinguished it sharply from that of elite politics. This ideological element was of course not uniform in quality or density in all instances. In the best of cases it enhanced the concreteness, focus and tension of subaltern political action. However, there were occasions when its emphasis on sectional interests disequilibrated popular movements in such a way as to create economistic diversions and sectarian splits, and generally to undermine horizontal alliances.

11. Yet another set of the distinctive features of this politics derived from the conditions of exploitation to which the subaltern classes were subjected in varying degrees as well as from its relation to the productive labour of the majority of its protagonists, that is, workers and peasants, and to the manual and intellectual labour respectively of the non-industrial urban poor and the lower sections of the petty bourgeoisie. The experience of exploitation and labour endowed this politics with many idioms, norms and values which put it in a category apart from elite politics.

12. These and other distinctive features (the list is by no means exhaustive) of the politics of the people did not of course appear always in the pure state described in the last three paragraphs. The impact of living contradictions modified them in the course of their actualization in history. However, with all such modifications they still helped to demarcate the domain of subaltern politics from that of elite politics. The co-existence of these two domains or streams, which can be sensed by intuition and proved by demonstration as well, was the index of an important historical truth, that is, *the failure of the Indian bourgeoisie to speak for the nation*. There were vast areas in the life and consciousness of the people which were never integrated into their hegemony. The *structural dichotomy* that arose from this is a datum of Indian

history of the colonial period, which no one who sets out to interpret it can ignore without falling into error.

13. Such dichotomy did not, however, mean that these two domains were hermetically sealed off from each other and there was no contact between them. On the contrary, there was a great deal of overlap arising precisely from the effort made from time to time by the more advanced elements among the indigenous elite, especially the bourgeoisie, to integrate them. Such effort when linked to struggles which had more or less clearly defined anti-imperialist objectives and were consistently waged, produced some splendid results. Linked, on other occasions, to movements which either had no firm anti-imperialist objectives at all or had lost them in the course of their development and deviated into legalist, constitutionalist or some other kind of compromise with the colonial government, they produced some spectacular retreats and nasty reversions in the form of sectarian strife. In either case the braiding together of the two strands of elite and subaltern politics led invariably to explosive situations indicating that the masses mobilized by the elite to fight for their own objectives managed to break away from their control and put the characteristic imprint of popular politics on campaigns initiated by the upper classes.

14. However, the initiatives which originated from the domain of subaltern politics were not, on their part, powerful enough to develop the nationalist movement into a full-fledged struggle for national liberation. The working class was still not sufficiently mature in the objective conditions of its social being and in its consciousness as a class-for-itself, nor was it firmly allied yet with the peasantry. As a result it could do nothing to take over and complete the mission which the bourgeoisie had failed to realize. The outcome of it all was that the numerous peasant uprisings of the period, some of them massive in scope and rich in anti-colonialist consciousness, waited in vain for a leadership to raise them above localism and generalize them into a nationwide anti-imperialist campaign. In the event, much of the sectional struggle of workers, peasants and the urban petty bourgeoisie either got entangled in economism or, wherever politicized, remained, for want of a revolutionary leadership, far too fragmented to form effectively into anything like a national liberation movement.

15. It is the study of this *historic failure of the nation to come to its own,* a failure due to the inadequacy of the bourgeoisie as well as of the working class to lead it into a decisive victory over colonialism and a bourgeois-democratic revolution of either the classic nineteenth-century type under the hegemony of the bourgeoisie or a more modern type under the hegemony of workers and peasants, that is, a 'new democracy'—*it is the study of this failure which constitutes the central problematic of the historiography of colonial India.* There is no one given way of investigating this problematic. Let a hundred flowers blossom and we don't mind even the weeds. Indeed we believe that in the practice of historiography even the elitists have a part

to play if only by way of teaching by negative examples. But we are also convinced that elitist historiography should be resolutely fought by developing an alternative discourse based on the rejection of the spurious and un-historical monism characteristic of its view of Indian nationalism and on the recognition of the co-existence and interaction of the elite and subaltern domains of politics.

16. We are sure that we are not alone in our concern about the present state of the political historiography of colonial India and in seeking a way out. The elitism of modern Indian historiography is an oppressive fact resented by many others, students, teachers and writers like ourselves. They may not all subscribe to what has been said above on this subject in exactly the way in which we have said it. However, we have no doubt that many other historiographical points of view and practices are likely to converge close to where we stand. Our purpose in making our own views known is to promote such a convergence. We claim no more than to try and indicate an orientation and hope to demonstrate in practice that this is feasible. In any discussion which may ensue we expect to learn a great deal not only from the agreement of those who think like us but also from the criticism of those who don't.

ACKNOWLEDGMENTS

The author is grateful to all the other contributors to this volume as well as to Gautam Bhadra, Dipesh Chakrabarty, and Raghabendra Chattopadhyay for their comments on an earlier version of this statement.

NOTES

1 A note on the terms 'elite,' 'people,' 'subaltern,' etc. as used above.

The term 'elite' has been used in this statement to signify *dominant* groups, foreign as well as indigenous. The *dominant foreign* groups included all the non-Indian, that is, mainly British officials of the colonial state and foreign industrialists, merchants, financiers, planters, landlords and missionaries.

The *dominant indigenous* groups included classes and interests operating at two levels. At the *all-India level* they included the biggest feudal magnates, the most important representatives of the industrial and mercantile bourgeoisie and native recruits to the uppermost levels of the bureaucracy

At the *regional and local levels* they represented such classes and other elements as were *either* members of the dominant all-India groups included in the previous category or if belonging to social strata hierarchically inferior to those of the dominant all-India groups still *acted in the interests of the latter and not in conformity to interests corresponding truly to their own social being.*

Taken as a whole and in the abstract this last category of the elite was *heterogeneous* in its composition and thanks to the uneven character of regional economic and social developments, *differed from area to area*. The same class or element which was dominant in one area according to the definition given above, could be among the dominated in another. This could and did create many ambiguities and contradictions in attitudes and alliances, especially among the lowest strata of the rural gentry, impoverished landlords, rich peasants and upper-middle peasants all of whom belonged, *ideally speaking,* to the category of 'people' or 'subaltern classes,' as defined below. It is the task of research to investigate, identify and measure the *specific* nature and degree of the *deviation* of these elements from the ideal and situate it historically.

The terms 'people' and 'subaltern classes' have been used as synonymous throughout this note. The social groups and elements included in this category represent *the demographic difference between the total Indian population and all those whom we have described as the 'elite.'* Some of these classes and groups such as the lesser rural gentry, impoverished landlords, rich peasants and upper-middle peasants who 'naturally' ranked among the 'people' and the 'subaltern,' could under certain circumstances act for the 'elite,' as explained above, and therefore be classified as such in some local or regional situations—an ambiguity which it is up to the historian to sort out on the basis of a close and judicious reading of his evidence.

27

DAVID LLOYD

Outside History

Irish New Histories and the 'Subalternity Effect'

This essay has a threefold agenda. I hope first to provide an account of recent shifts in Irish historiography that align some of its practitioners, implicitly if not programmatically, with the kinds of questioning that have been associated with *Subaltern Studies*. Secondly, I wish to explore the implications of such historical work for Irish cultural studies, concentrating on the ways in which the study of subaltern groups in Ireland as elsewhere has entailed equally a critique of the 'modernizing' or enlightenment assumptions that structure a state formation largely inherited from British imperial institutions. Thirdly, I want to engage with criticisms of such a critique of enlightenment, in particular with those from a feminist perspective, in order to nuance the kinds of exploration that may be undertaken under the rubrics of subalternity or 'post-colonialism.'

That some of these issues will seem familiar to readers of *Subaltern Studies* and of associated work helps to underscore two linked remarks of a theoretical nature that from the outset I wish to make. The first relates to the designation of Ireland as 'post-colonial.' This cannot, under present political conditions, be an innocent categorization, since it implies that that portion of the island under British rule is, properly speaking, still colonized. This assertion will be hotly, if not always rigorously, contested by some, and particularly by those who seek to defend the normative status of British 'civil society' in Ireland. Clearly, for them the expression 'post-colonial' used of any part of the island seems to legitimate the view that the current conflict is a final stage in the history of Ireland's decolonization and must accordingly be contested. In so far as it relates to contemporary issues, this chapter will take as its premise that Ireland has been and remains a site of colonialism and anti-colonial struggle but will suggest that that struggle needs to be articulated around a far broader interpretation of the concept of the 'post-colonial' than one defined principally by national independence or unification. I will return to this point in greater detail below.

But the designation 'post-colonial' will also be contested for different reasons, especially by those who would argue that Ireland's location on the western edge of Europe properly links its history to European national struggles, to Young Italy, or to Polish and Hungarian nationalism, for example, rather than to those of the so-called Third World. By the same token, Ireland's increasing participation in the European trading block seems a strong argument against any analysis of its current condition as 'post-colonial.' There are indeed strong arguments on any side of this debate; too many to explore fully here, and it is part of Ireland's anomalous state to have the social and cultural forms of both a small European country and a decolonizing nation.[1] The social contradictions consequent on this anomaly have inspired a number of recent projects in various cultural and intellectual spheres that seek to explore Irish history in the comparative frames offered by Third World experiences. Such projects can evidently be read as antagonistic to recent trends towards increasing integration into Europe, and accordingly to both the economic logic of integration sponsored by the Irish state and the political logic of regionalism as a solution to partition; a solution espoused by the British and Irish states as also some Northern Irish nationalists.[2] Historiography informed by the lessons of dependency theory, by critiques of neo-colonialism and, indeed, by subaltern histories is less sanguine about the implications of super-state formations and the fate of regions within them. It would, accordingly, be disingenuous to pretend that the debate about Ireland's colonial history could be resolved through empirical means: what is at stake in the terminology is at once political, that is, regarding the ends of the state, and always already methodological.

This brings me to the second point: the apparent familiarity to subaltern historians of Irish discussions derives not from any given analogies between Irish and Indian history or historiography (though at some level of analysis such analogies may certainly be maintained) but from what we might call a 'subalternity effect.'[3] That is, the social space of the 'subaltern' designates not some sociological datum of an objective and generalizable kind, but is an effect emerging in and between historiographical discourses. Those of us who have been interested in learning from *Subaltern Studies* in some form have been so interested precisely because that lesson transforms the kind of questions we pose to Irish history and culture, and enables a rearticulation of political possibilities. Both the terms 'post-colonial' and 'subaltern' designate in different but related ways the desire to elaborate social spaces that are recalcitrant to any straightforward absorption—ever more inevitable though this often seems—of Ireland into European modernity. A project of historical representation or denotation addressed to differently constituted objects of research combines with a performative engagement which could be seen, borrowing Raymond

Williams's triadic structure, to desire the derivation of emergent from residual practices.[4] This is not, however, to seek to legitimate contemporaneous acts or practices by appealing to past forms, opposing thereby an alternative but no less spurious mode of historical continuity to that of dominant narratives. Indeed, the interesting question to pose, to take one forceful example, would be not whether the Provisional Irish Republican Army (PIRA) is in fact continuous with the nineteenth-century Fenian movement, but how non-elite struggles, including these, operate through discontinuities. The object is, accordingly, to reapprehend social processes in terms of the uncloseable struggle between the 'self-evidence' and continuity of dominant representations and those other cultural forms whose apparent 'irrationality' and sporadic temporality is as much the effect as the cause of their marginalization. The study, for example, of popular movements for their forms of practice as well as for their simple occurrence not only recalls instances of resistance that have often been erased from canonical narratives, but also questions the temporality that underpins dominant historiography. I shall argue later that this question of forms of temporality is crucial to the political dimension of historiography in a post-nationalist moment.[5]

I

Ranajit Guha, in his well-known preface to *Subaltern Studies,* projects subaltern historiography as the elaboration of precisely such spaces, constituted ambiguously by previous modes of historiography and/or by the statist orientation of colonial and nationalist politics as marginal. In this sense, the preface partially follows its ostensible mentor, Antonio Gramsci, in understanding the intimate relation between elite historiography and the state formation. In another sense, as I have argued elsewhere, the subaltern project thus described deviates significantly from Gramsci's Hegelian Marxist one in refusing to reinscribe the end of subalternity in the capture of the state (Guha and Spivak, 1988:35; Gramsci, 1971: 52–5; Lloyd, 1993: 126–8). No less than Indian historiography, the course of Irish history writing has been bound to state formations. Irish cultural nationalism could be said to have articulated itself from the 1840s around the contestation of a Whig historiography for which Ireland's successive civil struggles culminated in its benevolent absorption into the British constitution. But nationalist historians, lacking perhaps Gramsci's elegant interpretation of their dilemma, were unable to produce Irish history without remarking constantly on its peculiarly *discontinuous* narrative, on its untotalizable tale of spasmodic uprisings and defeats, or its 'fragmentary and episodic' cultural forms. As Gramsci might have predicted, only the admittedly partial capture of an independent state ushers in the heyday of nationalist histories whose teleological version of the Irish national struggle became the staple of the national curriculum. To quote from one such text, Edmund Curtis's standard *A History of Ireland,* first published in 1936:

> To make a country's history intelligible, the historian naturally seeks for some point of unity, and this has been long deferred in Ireland's history. . . . For the establishment of a central government representing the nation and able to rule justly over all its elements, Ireland has had to wait till the present generation.
>
> (Curtis, 1961: vi)

Henceforth, however, Irish historiography has not followed the pattern ascribed by Guha to Indian historiography. For the contestation of nationalist histories, until relatively recently, came not from anything akin to *Subaltern Studies* but rather from a large and impressive body of historical work that has become known as 'revisionist history.'[6] The focus of this work has been less on the epic of national struggle and more on the emergence under British administration of modern state institutions in Ireland: the national education system, national police force, the legal apparatus, and so forth. Though it has perhaps been superseded by R. F. Foster's *Modern Ireland, 1600–1972* (1989), F.S.L. Lyons's *Ireland since the Famine* (1971) is still a summary instance of the tendencies of this group of historians, synthesizing into a larger narrative much of the work on nineteenth- and twentieth-century institution building that had been produced in individual monographs. The methodological and political underpinnings of this historiography are inextricable from the consolidation in Ireland of institutions of higher education and the revisionist emphasis on the emergence of modern state institutions as the proper object of history is itself an instance of the material parameters of discursive formations. Indeed, the supersession of an avowedly political nationalist historiography by a professionalized and empirically sceptical methodology occurred for the most part through the retraining of Irish historians in British institutions (Dunne, 1992; Stewart, 1993).

In the wake of a still dominant 'revisionist' history, Irish historiography has yet to produce anything as self-conscious and theoretically reflective as *Subaltern Studies*. Nevertheless, it is clear that the last fifteen years or so has seen the emergence of a large corpus of non-elite histories: histories of agrarian movements, local histories, social histories of the complex intersections of class and colonization in rural Ireland, women's history, in the form both of biographical work and, more recently, of studies of women's movements and social history. The historiographical influences and analogues of these studies have been various, but include in particular the 'history from below' of Thompson and Hobsbawm or the social and gender history of journals like *History Workshop,* on the one hand, and French everyday and local histories, on the other. It would thus be wrong to seek to homogenize either the impulses behind or the products of the new Irish histories.[7]

The cumulative effect of this historical work has, however, been to shift significantly the narrative axes of Irish history. The concentration of nationalist and revisionist historiography on state seizure and state building is displaced by histories (the plural is deliberate) whose narrative telos has ceased to be the state. Clearly, for example, the 'ends' of the Irish labour movement have not been, nor were ever assumed to be, coincident with the foundation of the Irish state. The same holds true for the various movements for women's emancipation that have emerged since the mid-nineteenth century: it is probably no accident that the major feminist contributions to Irish history of the past decade have been biographies of the principal women figures of the first quarter of this century whose active involvement in the national, labour, and women's movements issued in their corresponding opposition to the conservative Catholic state that actually came into being. It is indeed precisely the inadequacy of the organizing narrative of state formation to represent such struggles, and the failure of the state itself to respond even to that dimension of feminist and labour demands whose expression takes shape within the forms of legal discourses on rights and citizenship, that has required the opening of further studies in the longer duration of labour and women's history. What such studies may yet clarify is the extent to which the failures of the state lie in the peculiar conjunction of modernity and non-modernity that forms the cultural substrata of the post-1922 Irish states. To the implications of such contradictory formations for the understanding of a gender history of Ireland we will return later.

II

But it is at this point that the significance, at once political and epistemological, if that distinction still has any meaning, of invoking Ireland's *post-colonial* status makes itself felt and that the performative nature of historical discourse, including that of subalternity, manifests itself. For the *anti-colonial* nature of the Irish nationalist struggle is not expressed through any 'objective' decision as to the political status of Ireland within the United Kingdom or the British Empire. It is located rather in the peculiarity, within the Western European frame, or the typicality within the context of global anti-colonial struggles, of Irish nationalism's appeal to its premodernity as the site of significant cultural differences on which to found a distinct but no less *modern* state formation, equivalent to if not identical with that of Britain. Or, to put it differently, Irish nationalism appealed to the very characteristics that were, to imperial eyes, the marks of the people's underdevelopment and inherent dependence to provide the very grounds of its claim to independence. The state is, accordingly, founded upon a fetishization of invented traditions that are constitutively rather than contingently (as might be argued for the 'traditions' of metropolitan states) in contradiction to the state's need to form abstract political subjects as citizens. Many of the social contradictions that have attended Ireland's entry into the European Community circulate around this ideological necessity by which the state was constituted around a conservative cultural identity whose traditionalism conflicts with concepts of abstract individual rights that are fundamental to the idea of the modern state.

The conclusion to be drawn from these observations is not, however, that Ireland accordingly must be seen to have undergone a so far incomplete modernization, as if modernity had some discernible if Platonic ideal as its telos.[8] On the contrary, we can recognize that the form in which Ireland entered its modernity was constitutively contradictory, on both sides of the border. One of the most striking symptoms of Ireland's colonial history is the virtually chiasmic relation between the two post-treaty states: where the Republic constituted itself around conservative traditionalism in order to forge a modern democratic state, Northern Ireland sought to legitimate its separation by appeal to the values of civil society, yet, since these values were explicitly derived from Protestantism, succeeded in constituting a violently sectarian state.[9] Not untypical of the dynamic of colonial history generally, this instance of contradictory modernity helps us to trouble the distinction usually made, and constantly invoked in Irish debates, between the matrix of modernity, state institutions, rationality and historiography itself, on the one hand, and that of traditionalism, tribalism or localism, irrationality and mythology, on the other. For if the state relies in the post-colonial moment on the canonization of a certain selection of practices then termed tradition, and forges that canon through nationalist histories, it relies equally on a violence proportional in intensity and kind to the resistance it meets in order to repress or erase the traces of other practices and narratives. In Northern Ireland that violence has been manifest in the massive deployment of the repressive state apparatuses; in the Republic, due to the eventual incorporation after a brief civil war of the political opposition to the Free State under De Valera and, no less significantly, to massive and continuing emigration, the violence has been largely a function of the ideological state apparatuses.

Cliona Murphy has remarked that 'The controversy regarding revisionism in Irish history is ironic considering the narrowness of the history that has been at the centre of the dispute—nationalist history' (Murphy, 1992:21). While the focus of both nationalist history and revisionism has been on nation-state formation, with a shift of focus from heroes to bureaus, the multiple foci of the new histories have been on the sites and narratives that state formation constitutively occludes. The shift of focus entails equally the production of various subjects and various temporalities while simultaneously bringing into play the ideological location of the historian. As Murphy herself points out, the very project of women's history, even before the question of a specifically feminist perspective, questions not only the contents of previous histories and their principally male protagonists, but also the institutional construction of objectivity: what is objective is not merely a function of empirical method but is bound to the modes of narrative verisimilitude which, as with the literary canon, divide significant from insignificant, major from minor subjects. Crucial to the self-evidences of historiography, as she elsewhere points out, is the normativity of historical 'periods' (Luddy and Murphy, 1990: 3). To take up an earlier point, women's history in Ireland as elsewhere has had to move gradually from studies devoted to figures active in the arena of the state—nationalists and suffragists—to studies increasingly devoted to the 'daily life' of women in Ireland, as if the former studies legitimated the latter (Luddy and Murphy, 1990:2; Cullen, 1994). A not dissimilar set of observations about the institutional construction of histories that matter can be made in relation to the recent upsurge of local histories, many, if not most, of which have been undertaken by non-professional historians, or by academics from other disciplines. In this case too, the subjects of history, in the sense of its writers as of its agents, have changed together with implicit assumptions both regarding what counts as history and what historical processes 'seem like.'[10]

The shifts in perspective that the new histories imply are numerous, and akin to many with which readers of *Subaltern Studies* will be familiar. Among these might be included a rethinking of popular culture not in terms of tradition or its 'betrayal,' but in terms of its capacity to conjoin processes of adaptation and resistance, the refunctioning of printed ballads or of melodramas—commodity forms principally emanating from Britain—for purposes of agitation being but two instances; the study of social formations that proved insusceptible to absorption into the state formation or the nationalist movements that shaped it, such as the agrarian movements of the eighteenth and nineteenth centuries and the short-lived soviets of the 1920s; the examination of the ways in which the daily lives, especially of working class women, cut across the neat division of gendered social spheres on which the Republic's constitution itself is founded.[11] It is for this reason that any hard and fast distinction between the 'new histories' and cultural studies is difficult to maintain.

In each of the above instances, what is troubling is not merely a set of assumptions as to the 'proper' content or object of history, but its narrative ends. Popular culture can no longer be seen in relation to a putative adherence to or deviation from a resurgence of national consciousness embodied in traditions, nor can its insurgencies be seen merely, in Hobsbawm's terms, as 'proto-nationalist,' awaiting their full significance in absorption into the nationalist struggle for the state (Hobsbawm, 1990). Whether we are speaking of agrarian struggles, women's history, or of non-élite cultural forms, what this implies is the recalcitrance of each of these historical sites to the formation of abstract political subjectivity in which, for all its ideological traditionalism, official Irish nationalism conjoins with the project of modernity. At the same time, however, it is also the case that in the final analysis it is equally impossible to narrate the histories of non-élite social and cultural formations in abstraction from the narrative of state formation. For the latter narrative certainly relates, from the perspective of state and modernity, the story of successive attempts to incorporate recalcitrant formations, implying that the history of non-élite formations is always at least partially the history of their constitution and emergence as resistant, if not always openly, to state formation. I emphasize this in order to insist on the *contemporaneity* of non-élite formations to those that are taken by élite historiography to represent modern forms that supersede outmoded or primitive 'traditions' (Lloyd, 1993:149). In contradiction to such narratives, we may assert that the practices of non-élite groups represent, no less than those canonized in state-oriented histories, responses of adjustment and resistance to the 'modern' social transformations whose institutions they may often have provoked, and as such constitute spaces outside and adjacent to rather than 'prior' to the state formation itself.

It is in this sense that we can begin to comprehend a phenomenon that we might term 'oscillation' that Luke Gibbons captures so well in reference to popular understandings of traditional ballads like 'The Lass of Aughrim.' Discussing this and similar ballads, Gibbons points to the difficulty of knowing when such a figure is to be seen as an individual and historical person, and when as a refunctioning of traditional allegories (Gibbons, 1992: 366–7). The oscillation between allegorical and historical interpretations of the latter takes place precisely in the shift of social location that the interpreting subject occupies at any given moment. The fading of the allegorical mode of understanding is, as it were, a function of the accession of the subject to the symbolic modes proper to the representative histories of the nation-state formation. But it is important to stress that it is a fading that takes place in time with the emergence of a dominant social narrative and from the latter's perspective: the space occupied by the non-élite social formation is occluded rather than erased or superseded by the dominant and persists even in that occlusion. Rey Ileto's work on the Philippines is analogously instructive here in ways that might be useful to the furthering of new Irish histories. As he argues in 'Outlines of a Non-Linear Emplotment of Philippine History,' in the shadow of the dominant national and imperial narratives of modernity, and, specifically, outside the colonial formations of the metropolis and the pueblo, existed another social space and formation, depicted from the centre as 'banditry.' The bandit, accordingly, becomes 'the emblem of disorder, of the fundamental discontinuity of any pueblo-based history,' and must be re-incorporated by 'linear history' as 'an inchoate form of peasant unrest' that will give rise to a nationalist-oriented peasant movement later in the century (Ileto, 1988: 145–6). It is important, however, not to dissolve the formal discontinuity emblematized by the bandit (or in the Irish context, agrarian movements or women's culture, for example) in emphasizing their 'always already thereness.' Constituted in simultaneity with and difference from modern civil society, and representing in a certain sense the 'constitutive other' of modernity, these spaces that are the object of 'new histories' are not therefore to be conceived as alternative continuities, parallel to dominant narratives and only awaiting, in Gramsci's sense, to attain hegemony in order to be completed. On the contrary, and at the risk of deliberate hypostasization, we might argue that the apparent discontinuity of popular or non-élite history furnishes indications of alternative social formations, difficult as these may be to document and decipher for the disciplined historian, as well as the formal grounds for their persistent inassimilability to the state. Of course, the sporadic appearance of popular resistance is always in part a function of the historians' own perspectives, but I would argue, if tentatively, for the more substantive claim that popular memory constitutes a repertoire of narratives, mythemes, rumours, retained and reconstellated, that flash up, like Benjamin's dialectical images, in moments of danger (Benjamin, 1973). Like Benjamin's image, the constellations of popular memory are spatial more than temporal formations, whose very 'failure' to totalize and whose formal hybridity allow for the accommodation of multiple locations among which the non-élite subject oscillates. Among those locations are those sites in which that subject is indeed interpellated, if incompletely, as citizen-subject. The insubordination of such formations is in precise differentiation to the narrative forms of official histories.[12] For the latter, faced with the impossibility of totalizing societies whose mode of rationalization is simultaneously and paradoxically disintegrative and homogenizing, endow totality with a narrative structure that, though never itself finally closed, continually subordinates social groups which cannot be included systemically to the status of the pre-rational and primitive. The recurrent insurgence of those groups correspondingly appears as sporadic and irrational violence and as an index of the failure of Irish society, in this instance, to have fully emerged into modernity. It is the implicit and explicit project, on the other hand, of post-colonial, subaltern, or simply 'new' histories to open the spaces within which unsubordinated narratives can resonate. That resonance is the effect of the excess of possible histories, subject positions, affects, affiliations or memories over the singular history through which the state seeks to incorporate and regulate its political subjects.

III

The position on modernity and the state formation that I have been drawing out of the Irish new histories has been contested from a number of positions, of which the feminist version is the most coherent. Such critiques generally have a dual focus: on the one hand, on the conservatism of both the Irish states, on the other, the presumed conservatism of Irish communities. Although the former focus targets appropriately the deployment of tradition and sectarianism, respectively, by hegemonic state nationalisms, the latter focus firstly presumes the accuracy of representations of Irish communities as conservative and secondly misreads what I would term the *performative* intervention of the critique of modernity.[13]

Among the effects of the new histories has been to challenge both the assumption of the inherent conservatism of the Irish populace and that of the traditionalism of Irish republicanism in general; assumptions that structure, to different ends, both nationalist and revisionist historiographies. As one of two salient instances, the long-standing understanding of the 1798 uprising as resulting from an incongruous alliance between enlightened and mostly middle-class Protestant republicans, on the one hand, and a traditionally minded Gaelic and Catholic peasantry, on the other, has recently begun to crumble as more research has been done not only on the social composition of the 'peasant' rebels but also on intellectual contacts, through priests and schoolteachers, between Ireland and the continent outside élite circles.[14] The implications of this research may well be carried forward to new understandings of subaltern radicalism through the nineteenth century and into the post-Independence period.

A second instance of the questioning of such assumptions involves continuing research on the effects of emigration on the social and political composition of rural Ireland during the post-Famine consolidation of larger landholdings that enabled the emergence of what Emmet Larkin referred to as the 'nation-building class,' the small farmers. The relation between this class and the social and cultural conservatism of the Irish nationalism that founded the Irish Free State in 1922 is not far to seek, but cannot be extended to Irish society as a whole.[15] As the historian Joseph Lee has recently been arguing, the apparent relative economic and political success of Ireland with regard to other decolonizing societies must necessarily be understood in relation to decades of emigration that have maintained Irish population levels at around five million rather than the fourteen million that might have been reasonably projected at the moment of Independence. Given that circumstance, the degree of Ireland's continuing structural dependence and underdevelopment becomes all the more remarkable, even as the social stability of the Republic becomes more explicable for reasons indicated above. Again, despite the predominant image of the Irish male emigrant, recent research indicates that the impact of emigration may have been greater on Irish women than on Irish men, although partially disguised by the vocational nature of much female emigration: missionary, educational and nursing work dominating alongside domestic service.

The patriarchal conservatism of the post-Independence state accordingly needs to be understood in terms of a longer history involving the pre-Independence class formations that brought bourgeois nationalism into dominance, the contradictions of post-1920s populism through which De Valera gained and maintained power despite the often socially disastrous effects of his isolationist economic policies, and the persisting importance of emigration as the means to maintaining social and economic stability by diffusing conflict. In the light of such histories, it might become apparent that, however paradoxically, a socially conservative or 'traditionalist' state was the instrument by which post-Independence Ireland negotiated its entry into global capitalism and modernity. In a certain sense, this very paradox permitted Ireland's rapid transition through the 1960s and 1970s from an isolated economy to a classic instance of 'dependence': the depletion of organized labour and the 'traditionally' highly gendered division of labour furnished ideal conditions for multinational corporate investment akin to those of other Third World sites, but advantageously located within the European Community. The impact of the cycle of state-subsidized foreign investment in largely assembly-oriented industry, short-term surplus-value extraction and subsequent plant-closure has been especially severe on a predominantly female workforce in a fashion strikingly correspondent to the situation of women elsewhere within the larger structures of post-Fordist global capitalism.[16] And, as in those other locations in the Third World, the Irish post-colonial state's sponsorship of traditionalist social relations, especially in the domain of gender relations, has contributed substantially to the possibility of hyperexploitation of labour in general and women's labour in particular in the present.

Currently the increasing integration of Ireland within the political and legal as well as economic framework of the European Community is accentuating the contradictions between the state's traditional ideology and its modernizing forms. The European Court at Strasbourg offers a court of appeal for civil liberties beyond the Irish (and, it must be noted, British) courts. In this respect, Europe certainly offers the possibility of extending the realization of those civil rights promised by the modern political state into domains of the family and sexuality where they have largely been denied both by the Irish constitution, as in the case of abortion and divorce, and by related legislation. Accordingly, the completion of a project of modernity and the full extension of rights of citizenship are linked in the struggle against patriarchal conservatism. As Clara Connolly put it in her review of recent Irish critiques of the universalism of western modernity:

> We know that all over the contemporary world, these notions [of abstract humanity] are being replaced by the most frightening forms of communalism, and 'difference'-based ethnic exclusivism. In that scenario, women are merely the property of the group, the symbol of the nation's future, to be protected or defiled according to their belonging. The concept of equality enshrined in 'citizenship' offers more to women than that.
>
> (Connolly, 1993:109)

However, the long history of modernity and of nationalism in Ireland has not involved any simple opposition between abstract universalism and reactionary particularism. On the contrary, as much of the new history is already demonstrating, each enfolds the other while producing contemporaneous and resistant alternatives. That is, in certain respects, the universalizing project of imperial modernity, so well detailed in much revisionist history, is at one with the needs of nationalism to produce the modern citizen-subject as the subject of the nation-state. Hence the assiduous preservation of the apparatuses, ideological and repressive, of the British state after 1922. At the same time, that state nationalism has redeployed ideas of tradition and racial stereotypes that were equally crucial to the maintenance of an imperial discourse on modernity and identity, redefining them only to mark its difference within the same forms. The consequence has been an effort, common to imperialism and the national state, to marginalize inassimilable and recalcitrant social groups, cultural forms, and political projects.

Nowhere has this been more apparent than in the complex history of gender in Ireland. Briefly, since the full history of gender relations in modern Ireland has scarcely been broached, Irish nationalism and British imperialism largely concur in the late nineteenth century in associating self-government and 'manliness,' at the level of the individual person as at that of the nation. In reaction to 'celticist' stereotypes of the 'feminine Celt' produced by Matthew Arnold and others, Irish nationalism reacts by seeking to produce a rigorous re-engendering of social spaces in Ireland, culminating in the constitution of 1937 with its explicit division of masculine and feminine spheres. The process is clearly analogous to processes that Ashis Nandy has described within the Indian context in *The Intimate Enemy*. That project, however, would appear to have worked against the grain of Irish sociality and to have failed to grasp the social and economic consequences of imperialism. The stereotype of Irish 'femininity' is not merely an invention, but is a refraction into terms that legitimate empire of what must have been marked differences in the codings of gender, its economic and social significance, and the articulation of affect or what Williams has termed 'structures of feeling' (Williams, 1977:128–35). At the same time, given the terms of Victorian and modern constructions of gender, the structural position of Irish males, as dispossessed and disenfranchised, corresponds in part to the position generally designated feminine, while few women can have simply occupied domestic spaces. The contradiction between the assumptions and project of the modern state, as indeed of capitalist gender relations, and the historical and material conditions of Irish men and women has been profoundly productive of anomic masculinity in Ireland. What has yet to be adequately documented and analysed is the emergence of differently articulated male and female homosocial spheres in colonial and post-colonial Ireland, though these doubtless exist and have probably profoundly affected political and social life in Ireland. It is an open question whether these spheres will appear to historical research merely as effects of colonial damage or as resources for alternative visions of cultural and social life.

The consideration that in fact social forms regarded as damaged, whether from a perspective that sees them as remnants or residues of past forms or from one that sees them as inadequately developed, may nonetheless represent resources for alternative projects, is fundamental to the possibilities I am seeking to draw from Irish subaltern historiography. The implication of the new Irish histories is that the resistances inscribed in non-élite histories represent not a mere adherence to often outmoded cultural traditions, but sites of a complex intersection of individual and communal locations that resist reduction to the form of civil subjectivity which dominant narratives prioritize. The *performativity* that I seek to draw from this currently fluid, and by no means integrated, body of researches involves the attempt to produce and theorize dialectically out of such materials the possibility that social and cultural forms that are necessarily relegated to residual status by dominant historiography might generate forms for emergent practices even where their apparent content may be in some views simply conservative.[17] Where the emancipatory claims of both nationalism and Marxism have been predicated effectively on the need to erase and surpass contemporary social and cultural forms and to seek the resources for social transformation in a dialectical relation to the deep past, it may be possible to locate in the marginalized forms of lived social relations the contours of radical imaginaries. The insistence of the new histories on the *contemporaneity* of marginal and dominant social forms, and on their differential construction, is in this respect a profoundly instructive corrective to the self-evidences of developmental historiographies which over and again relegate difference to anteriority.

NOTES

1 For a critical approach to the term 'colonial' as used of Ireland, see Bartlett (1988). See also Tom Dunne's summary (1992) of arguments that Ireland's condition is that of an outlying territory gradually absorbed into an expanding European monarchy rather than a colony, and of counter-arguments that to view Irish history thus is to risk omitting the traumatic effects of British rule. For strong contrary arguments, based primarily on cultural grounds, see MacSiomoin (1994) and Kiberd (1994); Crotty (1986) provides a thorough economic analysis of relations between Ireland and other countries that have undergone what he terms 'capitalist colonial underdevelopment.' India is his principal comparative instance. Lustick (1993)'s comparison of Ireland with Algeria in the process of state formation, while taking issue with the 'internal colonialism' model developed by Hechter (1975), implicitly relates Irish history to that of one of the most striking instances of post-war decolonization; one that gave rise to Frantz Fanon's foundational texts on colonialism.

2 John Hume, leader of the moderate Northern Irish nationalist party, Social Democratic and Labour Party (SDLP), has for some time been arguing the regionalist position. See, for example, his long article entitled 'Time for all sectors to reflect deeply on the legacy of Irish nationalism,' *Irish Times,* 13 April 1994. For an overview of 'regional' solutions, see Kearney and Wilson (1994).

3 On parallels between Ireland and India, see Cook (1993) and Crotty (1986). I use the term 'subalternity effect' by analogy with the late Joel Fineman's use of the term 'subjectivity effect'

in relation to the emergence of the western subject, as he argues, in literature and especially in Shakespeare. See Fineman (1992).

4 On these terms and their historical relations, see Williams (1977:121–7).

5 A crucial precursor for such historiography in Ireland may well be James Connolly. Though, like Gramsci, he was an activist intellectual rather than a professional historian, his historical works, especially *Labour in Irish History* and *The Re-Conquest of Ireland,* are pioneering attempts to trace the episodic insurgencies of working-class elements within and beneath the more familiar history of nationalist movements. Also like Gramsci, he sees working-class history as one that ultimately overcomes the 'episodic and fragmentary' nature of Irish history:

> Without this key to the meaning of events, this clue to unravel the actions of 'great men,' Irish history is but a welter of unrelated facts, a hopeless chaos of sporadic outbreaks, treacheries, intrigues, massacres, murders, and purposeless warfare. With this key all things become understandable and traceable to their primary origin . . . .
>
> (Connolly, 1922:215)

As with Gramsci, however, the implications of his critique of orthodox historiography may be more suggestive in the present moment than his desire to recreate a unitary history.

6 For a fuller survey of this tradition and its recent critics, see Dunne (1992). For a defence of revisionism, see Michael Laffan's essay 'Insular Attitudes: The Revisionists and their Critics,' in Ni Dhonnchadha and Dorgan (1991:106–21); for critical positions, especially in relation to Roy Foster's recent work, see Seamus Deane, 'Wherever Green is Read,' in ibid., 91–105, Brian P. Murphy, 'Past Events and Present Politics: Roy Foster's *Modern Ireland*,' in O Ceallaigh (1994:72–93) and Donal McCartney, 'History Revisions: Good and Bad,' in ibid., 134–56.

7 For a useful survey of such new histories and the current historical debates, see the section 'New Histories: Visions and Revisions' of *The Irish Review*, no. 12 (Spring/Summer 1992).

8 For a critique of the notion of 'incomplete modernity' in the Indian context, see Chakrabarty (1994).

9 For some of the contradictions attendant on the close relation between sectarianism and the secular claims of the Northern Irish state, see Todd (1988).

10 Kevin Whelan pointed out to me that this disdain for local histories is closely related to the traditional historiographer's suspicion of non-written sources such as ballads and tales, that are, nonetheless, crucial to subaltern historiography.

11 For some instances of these conjunctions between cultural studies and new history, see Herr (1991), Lloyd (1993), O'Connor (1988), Cahill (1990), Luddy and Murphy (1990).

12 See Ranajit Guha, 'The Prose of Counter-Insurgency,' in Guha and Spivak (1988), for a magisterial analysis of the formal elements of dominant historiography. I would want to suggest here, in the spirit of Ileto's work on the *pasyon* (Ileto, 1979), that the formal analysis of popular or subaltern cultural forms suggests equally the outline of other semiotics of organization and movement.

13 It should also be remarked that the often unintended tendency of the criticism of both states is to legitimate unionist arguments for preferring the association with a 'more modern' British civil society to unification with the conservative Irish Republic.

14 For some recent work on 1798 and the United Irishmen, see, for example, Smyth (1992) and Dickson et al. (1993).

15 Continuing resistance by conservative if rural-based parties to the Irish Labour Party's moves to extend voting rights to recent emigrants is a pragmatic acknowledgement both of the radicalizing effects of emigration on many and of the way in which the emigration of the working classes has historically consolidated conservativism in 'independent' Ireland. On patterns of emigration and their relation to Irish politics, see Mac Laughlin (1991, 1993a, and 1993b). Irish music, which has in any case historically emerged from and been transformed by the experience of emigration from the mid-nineteenth century, continues to be an

excellent register of the radicalizing potential of migration. For two notable instances, see the London-based group Marxman, *33 Revolutions per minute* (Phonogram, London, 1993) and the New York–based Black 47, *Fire of Freedom* (SBK, New York, 1993).

16 For a survey of the history of women's labour in modern Ireland, see Beale(1987:139–63).

17 The attempt to derive the forms of radical ideologies from actual social relations has been a long-standing tradition of Irish national Marxism and feminism. James Connolly, again, is a principal figure here. For some preliminary explorations of these traditions, see Gibbons (1991 and 1992); Lloyd, 'Nationalisms against the State'; Coulter (1993).

SELECT BIBLIOGRAPHY

Althusser, Louis, 'Ideology and Ideological State Apparatuses (Notes towards an investigation),' in *Lenin and Philosophy and other Essays*, Ben Brewster (trans.) (New York: Monthly Review Press, 1971).

Bartlett, Thomas, 'An End to Moral Economy: The Irish Militia Disturbances of 1793,' *Past and Present*, no. 99 (May 1983), pp. 76–136.

———, '"What Ish My Nation?": Themes in Irish History 1550–1850,' in *Irish Studies: A General Introduction*, ed. Thomas Bartlett et al. (Dublin: Gill and Macmillan, 1988), pp. 44–59.

Beale, Jenny, *Women in Ireland: Voices of Change* (Bloomington: Indiana University Press, 1987).

Beames, Michael R., *Peasants and Power: The Whiteboy Movements and their Control in Pre-Famine Ireland* (New York: 1983).

Benjamin, Walter, 'Theses on the Philosophy of History,' in *Illuminations*, ed. Hannah Arendt, trans. Harry Zohn (London: Fontana, 1973), pp. 256–66.

Boland, Eavan, *Outside History: Selected Poems, 1980–90* (New York: Norton, 1990).

Cahill, Liam, *Forgotten Revolution: Limerick Soviet, 1919, a Threat to British Power in Ireland* (Dublin: O'Brien Press, 1990).

Chakrabarty, Dipesh, 'Hindu Extremism and Post-modernism: An Indian Debate on the Politics of Knowledge' (TSS 1994; forthcoming in David Lloyd and Lisa Lowe, eds., *Other Circuits*).

Connolly, Clara, 'Culture or Citizenship? Notes from the "Gender and Colonialism" Conference, Galway, Ireland, May 1992,' *Feminist Review* 44 (Summer 1993), pp. 104–11.

Connolly, James, *Labour in Irish History and The Reconquest of Ireland* (Dublin: Maunsel and Roberts, 1922).

Cook, S. B., *Imperial Affinities: Nineteenth-Century Analogies and Exchanges between India and Ireland* (New Delhi: Sage, 1993).

Coulter, Carol, *The Hidden Tradition: Feminism, Women and the State in Ireland* (Cork: Cork University Press, 1993).

Crotty, Raymond, *Ireland in Crisis: A Study in Capitalist Colonial Underdevelopment* (Dingle: Brandon Books, 1986).

Cullen, Mary, 'History Women and History Men: The Politics of Women's History,' in O Ceallaigh, 1994, pp. 113–33.

Curtis, Edmund, *A History of Ireland* (London: Methuen, 1961).

Dickson, D. et al., eds., *The United Irishmen: Republicanism, Radicalism and Rebellion* (Dublin: Lilliput, 1993).

Donnelly, James S. Jr., 'The Whiteboy Movement, 1761–5,' *Irish Historical Studies*, 21, no. 81 (March 1978), pp. 20–54.

Dunne, Tom, 'New Histories: Beyond "Revisionism,"' *The Irish Review*, no. 12 (Spring/Summer 1992), pp. 1–12.

Fineman, Joel, *The Subjectivity Effect in Western Literature* (Cambridge, Mass.: M.I.T. Press, 1992).

Foster, R. F., *Modern Ireland, 1600–1972* (New York: Penguin, 1989).

Gibbons, Luke, 'Race against Time,' *Oxford Literary Review*, no. 13 (Spring 1991).

——, 'Identity without a Centre: Allegory, History and Irish Nationalism,' *Cultural Studies*, 6.3 (Oct. 1992), pp. 358–75.

Gramsci, Antonio, 'Notes on Italian History,' in *Selections from the Prison Notebooks*, ed. and trans. Quintin Hoare and Geoffrey Nowell Smith (New York: International Publishers, 1971), pp. 52–120.

Guha, Ranajit, and Gayatri Chakravorty Spivak, *Selected Subaltern Studies* (Oxford: Oxford University Press, 1988).

Hechter, Michael, *Internal Colonialism: The Celtic Fringe in British National Development, 1536–1966* (Berkeley: University of California Press, 1975).

Herr, Cheryl, ed., *For the Land They Loved: Irish Political Melodramas, 1890–1925* (New York: Syracuse University Press, 1991).

Hobsbawm, E. J., *Nations and Nationalism since 1780: Programme, Myth, Reality* (Cambridge: Cambridge University Press, 1990).

Ileto, Reynaldo Clemena, *Pasyon and Revolution: Popular Movements in the Philippines, 1840–1910* (Manila: Ateneo de Manila, 1979).

——, 'Outlines a Non-Linear Emplotment of Philippine History,' in Lim Teck Ghee, ed., *Reflections on Development in Southeast Asia* (ASEAN Economic Research Unit: Institute of Southeast Asian Studies, 1988), pp. 130–59.

Kearney, Richard, and Robin Wilson, 'Northern Ireland's Future as a European Region,' *Irish Review* 15 (Spring 1994), pp. 51–69.

Kiberd, Declan, 'Post-colonial Ireland: "Being Different,"' in O Ceallaigh, 1994, pp. 94–112.

Lloyd, David, *Anomalous States: Irish Writing and the Post-Colonial Moment* (Dublin: Lilliput Press, 1993).

Luddy, Maria, and Cliona Murphy, eds., *Women Surviving: Studies in Irish Women's History in the 19th and 20th Centuries* (Dublin: Poolbeg, 1990).

Lustick, Ian, *Unsettled States, Disputed Lands: Britain and Ireland, France and Algeria, Israel and the West Bank-Gaza* (Ithaca: Cornell University Press, 1993).

Lyons, F.S.L., *Ireland since the Famine* (London: Weidenfeld & Nicolson, 1971).

Mac Laughlin, Jim, 'Social Characteristics and Destination of Recent Emigrants from Selected Regions in the West of Ireland,' *Geoforum*, 22.3 (1991), pp. 319–31.

——, 'Ireland: An "Emigrant Nursery" in the World Economy,' *International Migration Quarterly Review*, 31.1 (1993), pp. 149–70 (1993a).

——, 'Place, Politics and Culture in Nation-Building Ulster: Constructing Nationalist Hegemony in Post-Famine Donegal,' *Canadian Review of Studies in Nationalism*, 20.1–2 (1993), pp. 97–111 (1993b).

MacCurtain, Margaret, and Donncha O'Corrain, eds., *Women in Irish Society: The Historical Dimension* (Westport, Conn.: Greenwood Press, 1979).

MacSiomoin, Tomas, 'The Colonized Mind: Irish Language and Society,' O Ceallaigh, 1994, pp. 42–71.

Markievicz, Constance, *Prison Letters*, with a Biographical Sketch by Esther Roper and Preface by President De Valera (London: Longmans Green & Co., 1934).

Murphy, Cliona, 'Women's History, Feminist History, or Gender History?,' *The Irish Review*, no. 12 (Spring/Summer 1992), pp. 21–6.

Ni Dhonnchadha, Mairin, and Theo Dorgan, eds., *Revising the Rising* (Derry: Field Day, 1991).

Norman, Diana, *Terrible Beauty: A Lift of Constance Markievicz* (Dublin: Poolbeg, 1991).

O Ceallaigh, Daltun, ed., *Reconsiderations of Irish History and Culture* (Dublin: Leirmheas, 1994).

O'Connor, Emmet, *Syndicalism in Ireland, 1917–1923* (Cork: Cork University Press, 1988).

O'Neill, James W., 'A Look at Captain Rock: Agrarian Rebellion in Ireland 1815–45,' *Eire-Ireland*, 17.1 (Autumn 1982), pp. 17–34.

Smyth, Jim, *The Men of No Property: Irish Radicals and Popular Politics in the Late Eighteenth Century* (London: Macmillan, 1992).

Stewart, A.T.Q., 'A Scholar and a Gentleman,' interview with Hiram Morgan, *History Ireland*, 1.2 (Summer 1993), pp. 55–8.

Todd, Jennifer, 'The Limits of Britishness,' *Irish Review*, no. 5 (Autumn 1988), pp. 11–16.

Ward, Margaret, *Maud Gonne: Ireland's Joan of Arc* (London: Pandora, 1990).

Whelan, Kevin, 'Come All Ye Blinkered Nationalists: A Post-Revisionist Agenda for Irish History,' *Irish Reporter* 2 (2nd Quarter, 1991), pp. 24–6.

——, 'The Power of Place,' *The Irish Review*, no. 12 (Spring/Summer 1992), pp. 13–20.

Williams, Raymond, *Marxism and Literature* (Oxford: Oxford University Press, 1977).

28

JOHN BEVERLEY

Our Rigoberta?

I, Rigoberta Menchú, Cultural Authority, and the Problem of Subaltern Agency

The epistemological and ethical authority of testimonial narratives like *I, Rigoberta Menchú* is said to depend on their appeal to personal experience. Thus, for example (in my own account of the form):

> By *testimonio* I mean . . . a narrative . . . told in the first person by a narrator who is also the real protagonist or witness of the events he or she recounts. . . . The word *testimonio* translates literally as testimony, as in the act of testifying or bearing witness in a legal or religious sense. . . . The situation of narration in testimonio has to involve an urgency to communicate, a problem of repression, poverty, subalternity, imprisonment, struggle for survival, and so on, implicated in the act of narration itself. The position of the reader of testimonio is akin to that of a jury member in a courtroom. Unlike the novel, testimonio promises by definition to be primarily concerned with sincerity rather than literariness.[1]

"What if much of Rigoberta's story is not true?" the anthropologist David Stoll asks in a book about *I, Rigoberta Menchú* and the uses to which it has been put, a book that attracted considerable international media attention when it appeared late in 1998 (coincident with the final stages of the impeachment trial of President Clinton, which also hinged on questions of evidence and credibility).[2] Referring in part to my own remarks on testimonio quoted above, Stoll argues that "[j]udging by such definitions, *I, Rigoberta Menchú* does not belong in the genre of which it is the most famous example, because it is not the eyewitness account it purports to be" (242). In truth, what Stoll is able to show is that *some* rather than *much* of Menchú's story involves what he calls "mythic inflation" (232). But the point remains: if the power of testimonio is ultimately grounded in the presumption of witnessing and speaking truth to power, then any evidence of "invention" should be deeply troubling.

Gayatri Spivak anticipates one possible reply to Stoll's question when she remarks—in the course of an interview published in 1990—that "perhaps the proper question of someone who has not been allowed to be the subject of history is to say: What is man that he was obliged to produce such a text of history?"[3] As I noted in the introduction, Spivak's notorious claim that the subaltern cannot speak as such is meant to underline the fact that if the subaltern could speak in a way that really mattered to us, that we would feel compelled to listen to, it would not be subaltern. Spivak is saying, in other words, that one of the things being subaltern means is not mattering, not being worth listening to. Stoll's argument with Rigoberta Menchú, by contrast, is precisely with the way in which her book in fact "matters." It concerns how the canonization of *I, Rigoberta Menchú* was used by academics like myself and solidarity and human rights activists to mobilize international support for the Guatemalan guerrilla movement in the 1980s, long after (in Stoll's view) that movement had lost whatever support it might have initially enjoyed among the Mayan peasants whom Menchú claims to speak for (and about). The inaccuracies and omissions Stoll claims to find in Menchú's account lend themselves, he feels, "to justify violence" (274). That issue—"how outsiders were using Rigoberta's story to justify continuing a war at the expense of peasants who did not support it" (241)— is the main problem for Stoll, rather than the inaccuracies or omissions themselves. By making Menchú's story seem, in her own words, "the story of all poor Guatemalans," *I, Rigoberta Menchú* misrepresented a more complex and ideologically contradictory situation among the indigenous peasants.

In one sense, of course, there is a coincidence between Spivak's concern, in "Can the Subaltern Speak?," with the production in metropolitan academic and theoretical discourse of a "domesticated Other" and Stoll's concern with the conversion of Menchú into an icon of political correctness in order to sustain a vanguardist political strategy he thinks is profoundly flawed. In a way that seems to echo Spivak, Stoll notes that "books like *I, Rigoberta Menchú* will be exalted because they tell academics what they want to hear. . . . What makes *I, Rigoberta Menchú* so attractive in universities is what makes it misleading about the struggle for survival in Guatemala. We think we are getting closer to understanding Guatemalan peasants when actually we are being borne away by the mystifications wrapped up in an iconic figure" (227). But his argument is also explicitly with Spivak, as a practitioner of the very "postmodern scholarship" that privileges a text like *I, Rigoberta Menchú* (247). I will come back to this point. But for the moment it may be enough to note that where Spivak is concerned with the way in which elite representation effaces the effective presence of the subaltern, Stoll's case against Menchú is precisely that: a way of, so to speak, *re-subalternizing* a narrative that aspired to (and achieved) hegemony. In this sense, Stoll's book could be seen as a contemporary case of what Ranajit Guha means by "the prose of counter-insurgency"—that is, a discourse that captures the fact of insurgency precisely through the cultural assumptions and practices of the elite and the state agencies that the insurgency is directed against.

Stoll foregrounds in his discussion the elevation of Rigoberta Menchú into a kind of secular saint for politically correct academics and solidarity activists. That concern may explain in part his curious insistence in referring to her familiarly by her first name, even though the force of his book is precisely to discredit her personal authority. Why does it seem proper to refer, as we habitually do, to Rigoberta Menchú as Rigoberta? The use of the first name is appropriate to address, on the one hand, a friend or significant other, or, on the other, a servant, child, or domestic animal—that is, a subaltern. But is it that we are addressing Rigoberta Menchú as a friend or familiar in the work we do on her testimonio? We would not say with such ease, for example, Fred for Fredric Jameson, or Gayatri for Gayatri Spivak, unless we wanted to signal that we have or want to claim a personal relationship with them. Jameson himself observes that while testimonio involves the displacement of the "master subject" of modernist narrative, it does so paradoxically via the insistence on the first-person voice and proper name of the narrator (Jameson nevertheless continues to speak of Rigoberta).[4]

The question of name—of the authority of a proper name—is embedded in the title of Menchú's testimonio, which reproduces its opening lines, *Me llamo Rigoberta Menchú, y así me nació la conciencia* ("My name is Rigoberta Menchú, and this is how my consciousness was formed"), dramatically mistranslated in the English edition as *I, Rigoberta Menchú: An Indian Woman in Guatemala*. In an interview some years ago, Menchú was asked about her relationship with Elisabeth Burgos, the Venezuelan anthropologist (ex-wife of Regis Debray) who initiated the conversations in Paris that produced the testimonio. In most editions of the book Burgos appears as the author, and she has been the recipient of the royalties (though she claims to have turned over at least part of these to Menchú). Menchú, however, insists on her right to appear as the author or coauthor: "What is in fact an absence in the book is the rights of the author. . . . Because the authorship of the book, in fact, should have been more precise, shared, no?" ("[L]o que si efectivamente es un vacío en el libro es el derecho de autor. . . . Porque la autoría del libro, efectivamente, debío ser más precisa, compartida, ¿verdad?").[5]

In deference to political correctness, not to say politeness or respect for a person I have met only formally, I make it a point to say Rigoberta Menchú or Menchú. But I have to keep reminding myself on this score. My inclination is also to say Rigoberta. What is at stake in the question of how to address Menchú is the status of the testimonial narrator as a subject in her own right, rather than as someone (or some thing) who exists essentially for us. What I have to say here is located in the tension between the injunction to grant Menchú the respect and autonomy she deserves in these terms, and the desire to see myself (my own projects and desires) in or through her.

Does Rigoberta Menchú have a psyche, or is the unconscious itself a form of white-skin privilege? The question seems on the face of it ironic or perverse, given the testimonial narrator's own insistence on the public and collective dimension of his or her narrative persona and social function. In "The Storyteller," Walter Benjamin makes storytelling as such impermeable to psychological introspection, which is instead the province of the bildungsroman.[6] Nevertheless, there is a way in which *I, Rigoberta Menchú* could (should?) itself be read as an oedipal bildungsroman, along fairly familiar lines. The sequence of the narration, which corresponds both to the narrator's coming of age and to the emergence of revolutionary armed struggle among the Mayan communities of Guatemala, goes from an initial rejection of the Mother and motherhood in favor of an Athena-like identification with the Father, Vicente, the *campesino* organizer;[7] to an authority struggle with the Father, who does not want his daughter to learn how to read and write, because he believes that will mean her alienation from the community and traditional women's roles; then to the death of the Father (in 1979, along with other demonstrators, he occupied the Spanish embassy in Guatemala City to protest military violence; the army surrounded the embassy and set fire to it, killing everyone inside), which leads to a recognition that her Mother is also someone who controls the subversive arts of subaltern speech and rumor; then to the killing of the Mother, again at the hands of the army (she is kidnapped and tortured to death in a military camp); then to the emergence of Menchú as a full speaking subject, an organizer and leader in her own right, represented in the act of narrating the testimonio itself.

Perhaps it might be useful to see the testimonio as such as involving a kind of narrative hybridity: a fusion between what Benjamin means by "storytelling" as a premodern form of wisdom and authority, and the bildungsroman or autobiography, which are paradigmatic forms of "modern," transcultured subjectivity. Like Richard Rodriguez's *Hunger of Memory, I, Rigoberta Menchú* not only narrates but also embodies in its textual aporias the tensions involved in this almost classic coming-of-age sequence, which also marks the transition (or, perhaps more correctly, the oscillation) between the orders of tradition and modernity, the local and the global, oral and print culture (Menchú telling her story orally and its textualization by Elisabeth Burgos), ethnographic narrative and literature, the subaltern and hegemony, and—in the Lacanian schema of subject formation—the Imaginary and the Symbolic. For Rodriguez, Spanish is the maternal language of the private sphere that has to be rejected in order to gain full access to the authority (governed by the Law of the Father) of the Symbolic order represented by English—so that *Hunger of Memory* is among other things a celebration of English writing programs and a critique of bilingualism. By contrast, it is Menchú's contradictory and shifting relationship to her Mother, who represents the authority of oral culture and Mayan languages, as much as any specifically political experience, that is at the core of her own process of *concientización* as well as her ability to authorize herself as a narrator.[8]

At the (apparent) cost of relativizing the political and ethical claims a text like *I, Rigoberta Menchú* makes on its readers, my improvised psychoanalytic reading foregrounds its complexity, the fact that its analysis is interminable, that it resists simply being the mirror that reflects our narcissistic assumptions about what it should be. Despite all the misunderstandings her essay has provoked, this was surely Spivak's point in answering the question "Can the Subaltern Speak?" in the negative. She was trying to show that behind the good faith of the liberal academic or the committed ethnographer or solidarity activist in allowing or enabling the subaltern to speak lies the trace of the colonial construction of an other—an other who is conveniently available to speak to us (with whom we *can* speak or feel comfortable speaking with). This neutralizes the force of the reality of difference and antagonism our own relatively privileged position in the global system might give rise to.

Elzbieta Sklodowska has in mind something similar when she argues that, despite its appeal to the authority of an actual subaltern voice, testimonio is in fact a staging of the subaltern by someone who is not subaltern, as in Lyotard's notion of the *differend* (where a dispute is carried out according to the terms and language of one of the parties to the dispute). In particular, testimonio is not, in Sklodowska's words, "a genuine and spontaneous reaction of a 'multiform-popular subject' in conditions of postcoloniality, but rather continues to be a discourse of elites committed to the cause of democratization."[9] The appeal to authenticity and victimization in the critical validation of testimonio stops the semiotic play of the text, Sklodowska implies, fixing the subject in a unidirectional gaze that deprives it of its reality. Fixes the testimonial narrator as a subject, that is, but also fixes us as subjects in what Althusser would have called a relation of double specularity created by the idealization or sublimation of subaltern otherness, which in the end also isolates us from *our* reality.

At the same time, the deconstructive appeal to the "many-leveled, unfixable intricacy and openness of a work of literature"—the phrase is Spivak's,[10] but it captures the position on testimonio assumed by Sklodowska—also has to be suspect, given that this "unfixable intricacy and openness" happens only in a historical matrix in which written literature itself is one of the social practices which generate the difference that is registered as subalternity in the testimonial text. The limit of deconstruction in relation to testimonio is that it reveals (or produces) a textual unfixity or indeterminacy which not only misrepresents but itself produces and reproduces as a reading effect the fixity of actual relations of power and exploitation in the "real" social text.

Is testimonio then simply another chapter in the history of the "lettered city" in Latin America: the assumption, tied directly to the class interests of the creole elites and their own forms of cultural self-authorization, that literature and the literary intellectual and the urban public sphere they define are or could be adequate signifiers of the national? The question is relevant to the claim made by Dinesh D'Souza, in the throes of the controversy over the Stanford Western Culture requirement, that *I, Rigoberta Menchú* is not good or great literature. D'Souza wrote, to be precise: "To celebrate the works of the oppressed, apart from the standard of merit by which other art and history and literature is judged, is to romanticize their suffering, to pretend that it is naturally creative, and to give it an esthetic status that is not shared or appreciated by those who actually endure the oppression."[11]

I happen to think that *I, Rigoberta Menchú* is one of the most important works of literature produced in Latin America in the last twenty years. But I would rather have it be a provocation in the academy, a radical otherness, as D'Souza feels it to be, than something smoothly integrated into a curriculum for multicultural citizenship at an elite university like Stanford. I would like students at Stanford, or for that matter at the University of Pittsburgh, where I teach (although the stakes in terms of class privilege and intellectual authority are somewhat different), to feel uncomfortable rather than virtuous when they read a text like *I, Rigoberta Menchú*. I would like them to understand that almost by definition the subaltern, which will in some cases be a component of their own personal identity, is not, and cannot be, adequately represented by literature or in the university, that literature and the university are among the practices that create and sustain subalternity.[12] At the same time, of course, it is precisely the academic canonization of *I, Rigoberta Menchú* that contributes to its ideological force, as Stoll notes.

Menchú herself is of course also an intellectual, whose formation as such includes a period of training as a lay catechist charged with explaining stories from the Bible to her people. But she is an intellectual in a sense clearly different than what Gramsci called the traditional intellectual—that is, someone who meets the standards and carries the authority of high culture, philosophy, and science—and a sometimes explicit hostility to intellectuals, the state education system, and the authority of book-learning is one of the leitmotifs of her testimonio.[13] The concern with the question of subaltern agency in testimonio depends on the suspicion, noted in chapter 2, that intellectuals and writing itself are themselves complicit in relations of domination and subalternity. Testimonio presents itself to us (that is, to the reading public) as a written text, but it also grants a certain authority or epistemic privilege to orality in the context of processes of modernization that privilege literacy and writing in European languages as cultural norms.

Sklodowska and Spivak are concerned with what Gareth Williams calls the "disciplinary fantasies" implied in the academic staging of testimonio.[14] But perhaps the more urgent question is not so much how intellectuals like ourselves appropriate testimonial narrators like Menchú as, in David Stoll's view, a kind of icon that tells us what we want to hear, as how those narrators appropriate *us* for their purposes. Sklodowska misunderstands the nature of the claim I am making for testimonio by treating it as if it were an appeal to the documentary authenticity of a subaltern voice. She is, of course, correct to point out that the voice in testimonio is a textual construct, put together by an editor who exists in a very different locus of enunciation than the one represented by the testimonial narrative-voice itself. Her implication is that we should beware of a metaphysics of presence perhaps even more in testimonio, where the convention of fictionality has been suspended, than in other texts. But something of the experience of the body in pain or hunger or danger—what René Jara calls "a trace of the Real"—also inheres in testimonio.[15]

That is certainly the sense of the extraordinary passage in which Menchú narrates the torture and execution of her brother by the army in the town plaza of Chajul. She describes how, at the climax of the massacre, the witnesses experience an almost involuntary shudder of revulsion and anger, which the soldiers sense and which puts them on their guard:

> After he'd finished talking the officer ordered the squad to take away those who'd been "punished," naked and swollen as they were. They dragged them along, they could no longer walk. Dragged them to this place, where they lined them up all together within sight of everyone. The officer called to the worst of the criminals— the *Kaibiles*, who wear different clothes from other soldiers. They're the ones with the most training, the most power. Well, he called the *Kaibiles* and they poured petrol over each of the tortured. The captain said, "This isn't the last of their punishments, there's another one yet. This is what we've done with all the subversives we catch, because they have to die by violence. And if this doesn't teach you a lesson, this is what'll happen to you too. The problem is that the Indians let themselves be led by the communists. Since no-one's told the Indians anything, they go along with the communists." He was trying to convince the people but at the same time he was insulting them by what he said. Anyway, they [the soldiers] lined up the tortured and poured petrol on them; and then the soldiers set fire to each one of them. Many of them begged for mercy. Some of them screamed, many of them leapt but uttered no sound—of course, that was because their breathing was cut off. But— and to me this was incredible—many of the people had weapons with them, the ones who'd been on their way to work had machetes, others had nothing in their hands, but when they saw the army setting fire to the victims, everyone wanted to strike back, to risk their lives doing it, despite all the soldiers' arms. . . . Faced with its own cowardice, the army itself realized that the whole people were prepared to fight. You could see that even the children were enraged, but they didn't know how to express their rage. (178–79)

Reading this passage, we also experience this rage—and possibility of defiance even in the face of the threat of death—through the mechanism of identification, just as we do at the moment in *Schindler's List* when the women in the Krakow concentration camp, who have been congratulating each other on surviving the selection process, suddenly realize that their children have been rounded up in the meantime and are being taken to the gas chambers in trucks. These are instances of what Lacan calls *tuché:* moments where the experience of the Real breaks through the repetitious passivity of witnessing imposed by the repression itself. By contrast, romanticizing victimization would tend to confirm the Christian narrative of suffering and redemption that underlies colonial or imperialist domination in the first place. In practice such a representation would lead more to a posture of benevolent paternalism or liberal guilt rather than effective solidarity, which presumes in principle a relation of equality and reciprocity between the parties involved.[16]

As it happens, however, the narration of the death of Menchú's brother is precisely one of the passages in *I, Rigoberta Menchú* whose literal veracity Stoll contests, claiming on the basis of his own interviews in the area Menchú comes from (where he spent several years doing fieldwork) that the torture and massacre of her brother by the army happened in a different way, that Menchú herself could not have been an eyewitness to it (63–70), and that therefore her description is, in his words, a "mythic inflation" (232). It is important to distinguish this claim from the claim subsequently made by some right-wing commentators that *I, Rigoberta Menchú* is fraudulent. Stoll is not saying that Menchú is making it all up. He does not contest the fact of the murder of Menchú's brother by the army. And he stipulates in his preface that "[t]here is no doubt about the most important points [in her story]: that a dictatorship massacred thousands of indigenous peasants, that the victims included half of Rigoberta's immediate family, that she fled to Mexico to save her life, and that she joined a revolutionary movement to liberate her country" (viii). But, as noted, he does argue, that the inaccuracies, omissions, or misrepresentations in her account make her less than a reliable representative of the interests and beliefs of the people she claims to be speaking for.

Menchú has publicly conceded that she grafted elements of other people's experiences and stories onto her own account. In particular, she has admitted that she was not herself present at the massacre of her brother and his companions in Chajul and that the account of the event came instead from her mother, who (she claims) was there. She says that these interpolations were a way of making her story a collective account, rather than an autobiography.[17] Her remarks, posed against Stoll's questioning of the representativity of her testimonio, allow a new way of reading certain passages in the text: for example, the famous opening paragraph, where Menchú declares that her story "is not only my life, it's also the testimony of my people."

But, in a way, the argument between Menchú and Stoll is not so much about what really happened as about who has the authority to narrate. What seems to bother Stoll above all is that Menchú *has* an ideological agenda. He wants her to be in effect a "native informant," who will lend herself to his purposes (of information gathering and evaluation), but she is instead an organic intellectual concerned with producing a text of "local history" (to recall Florencia Mallon's term)—that is, with elaborating hegemony. Though Stoll talks about objectivity and facts, it turns out he also has an ideological agenda. He believes that the attempt of the Marxist left to wage an armed struggle against the military dictatorship in Guatemala put the majority of the highland indian population "between two fires," driven to support the guerrillas mainly by the ferocity of the army's counterinsurgency measures rather than by a belief in the justice or strategic necessity of armed struggle.[18] By contrast, the narrative logic of *I, Rigoberta Menchú* suggests that the Guatemalan armed struggle grew necessarily out of the conditions of repression the indigenous communities faced in their attempts to hold the line against land seizures and exploitation by the army, paramilitary death squads, and ladino landowners. For Stoll to sustain his hypothesis, he has to impeach the force of Menchú's testimony, in other words. As he makes clear at the end of his book, Stoll intends not only a retrospective critique of the armed struggle in Guatemala; he also means his book as a caution against enthusiasm for contemporary movements like the Zapatistas in Mexico. Indeed, for Stoll, rural guerrilla strategies as such "are an urban romance, a myth propounded by middle-class radicals who dream of finding true solidarity in the countryside," a myth which has "repeatedly been fatal for the left itself, by dismaying lower-class constituents and guaranteeing a crushing response from the state" (282). The misrepresentation or simplification of indigenous life and rural realities that a text like *I, Rigoberta Menchú* performs colludes with this urban romance.

But is the problem for Stoll the verifiability of Menchú's story or the wisdom of armed struggle as such? If it could be shown that all the details in Menchú's account are in fact verifiable or plausible, would it follow for Stoll that the armed struggle was justified? Obviously not. But, by the same token, the gaps, inaccuracies, "mythic inflations," and so on that he finds in Menchú's account do not necessarily add up to an indictment of the armed struggle. Maybe the armed struggle was a mistake: Stoll observes that Menchú has sought in recent years to place some distance between herself and the umbrella organization of the left, the UNRG. But that judgment does not itself follow from his impeachment of Menchú's narrative authority. In other words, the question of verifiability is subordinate to the question of Stoll's ideological disagreement with the strategy of armed struggle.

My own view is that under conditions of military and paramilitary rule in which even the most cautious trade unionists and social-democratic or Christian-

Democratic elected officials were liable to be "disappeared" and in the context of the Sandinista victory in 1979, it is not surprising that armed resistance came to seem to many people in Guatemala as a desperate but plausible strategy. In particular, it is a long way from saying that not all highland peasants supported the armed struggle to claiming that the guerrilla movement lacked, or lost, significant popular roots among them, that it was imposed on them against their will and interests. But Stoll gives us no more convincing "hard" evidence to support this contention than Menchú does to argue the contrary. Other observers have argued that the guerrillas were in fact relatively successful in recruiting highland indigenous peasants, that the integration of the previously predominantly ladino and Marxist guerrilla groups with significant elements of this population constituted a powerful challenge to the military dictatorship, that it was precisely that possibility that the army was seeking to destroy in the genocidal counter-insurgency war that Menchú describes in her narrative. Who are we to believe? As in the impeachment trial of president Clinton, it comes down to a matter of "he said, she said," which in the end will be decided on *political* rather than epistemological grounds.[19]

Referring to the tasks of the truth commissions established as part of the peace process in Guatemala, Stoll notes that "[i]f identifying crimes and breaking through regimes of denial has become a public imperative in peacemaking, if there is a public demand for establishing 'historical memory,' then *I, Rigoberta Menchú* cannot be enshrined as true in a way it is not" (273). Fair enough. But if the Guatemalan army had simply destroyed the guerrillas and imposed its will on the population, then there would be no truth commissions in the first place. Yet Stoll faults Menchú's story among other things precisely for helping guerrilla leaders "finally obtain the December 1996 peace agreement" (278).

In the process of constructing her narrative and articulating herself around its circulation, Menchú is becoming not-subaltern, in the sense that she is functioning as a "subject of history" (to recall Spivak's point at the beginning of this chapter). But the conditions of her becoming-not-subaltern—her narrative choices, silences, "mythic inflation," "reinvention," and so on entail necessarily that there are versions of "what really happened" that she does not or cannot represent without relativizing the authority of her own account. It goes without saying that in any social situation, indeed even within a given class or group identity, it is always possible to find a variety of narratives, points of view that reflect contradictory agendas and interests. "A frank account of Chimel [the region Menchú's family is from] would have presented an uninspiring picture of peasants feuding with each other," Stoll notes. "[T]ellers of life stories tend to downplay the incoherence, accident, discontinuity, and doubt that characterize actual lived experience. . . . In Rigoberta's case, she achieved coherence by omitting features of the situation that contradicted the ideology of her new organization, then substituting appropriate revolutionary themes" (192–93).

The existence of "other" voices in Stoll's account makes Guatemalan indigenous communities—indeed even Menchú's own immediate family—seem irremediably riven by internal rivalries, contradictions, different ways of telling. "Obviously," Stoll writes, "Rigoberta is a legitimate Mayan voice. So are all the young Mayas who want to move to Los Angeles or Houston. So is the man with a large family who owns three worn-out acres and wants me to buy him a chain saw so he can cut down the last forest more quickly. Any of these people can be picked to make misleading generalizations about Mayas" (247). But, in a way, this is to deny the possibility of political struggle as such, since a hegemonic project by definition points to a possibility of collective will and action that depends precisely on transforming the conditions of cultural and political disenfranchisement that underlie these contradictions. The appeal to heterogeneity—"any of these people"—leaves intact the authority of the outside observer—that is, Stoll—who is alone in the position of being able to both hear and sort through the various testimonies (but the "outside" observer also has his own social, political, and cultural agendas, and his actions have effects "inside" the situation he pretends to describe from a position of neutral objectivity). It also leaves intact the *existing* structures of political-military domination and cultural authority. The existence of "contradictions among the people"—for example, the interminable internecine fights over land and natural resources within and between peasant communities that Stoll puts so much emphasis on—does not deny the possibility of contradiction between the "people" as such and an ethnic, class, and state formation felt as deeply alienating and repressive (I will return to this issue in the next chapter).

But Stoll's argument, as we have seen, is not only about Guatemala. It is also with the discourses of multiculturalism and postmodernism in the North American academy, which he feels consciously or unconsciously colluded to perpetuate armed struggle, therefore promoting *I, Rigoberta Menchú* as a text and making Menchú into an international icon. Thus, for example: "It was in the name of multiculturalism that *I, Rigoberta Menchú* entered the university reading lists" (243). Or, "[u]nder the influence of postmodernism (which has undermined confidence in a single set of facts) and identity politics (which demands acceptance of claims to victimhood), scholars are increasingly hesitant to challenge certain kinds of rhetoric" (2). Or, "the identity needs of Rigoberta's academic constituency play into the weakness of rules of evidence in postmodern scholarship" (247). Or, "with postmodern critiques of representation and authority, many scholars are tempted to abandon the task of verification, especially when they construe the narrator as a victim worthy of their support" (274).

What starts off as a critique of the truth claims of Rigoberta Menchú's testimonio and the *foquista* strategy of the Guatemalan guerrilla movement metamorphoses into an attack on what the neoconservative writer Roger Kimball calls "tenured radicals" in European and North American universities, including myself. The connection between postmodernism and multiculturalism that Stoll is bothered about is predicated on the fact that multiculturalism (and Menchú's book is, among other things, an argument for understanding Guatemala itself as a deeply multicultural and multilinguistic nation) implies a demand for epistemological relativism that coincides with the postmodernist critique of science. If there is no one universal standard for truth, then claims about truth are contextual: they have to do with how people construct different understandings of the world and historical memory from the same set of facts in situations of radical social inequality, exploitation, and repression. The truth claims for a testimonial narrative like *I, Rigoberta Menchú* depend on conferring on the form a certain special kind of epistemological authority as embodying subaltern experience. But for Stoll this amounts to a "mythic inflation" of the subaltern to favor the prejudices of a metropolitan academic audience, in the interest of a solidarity politics that (in his view) is doing more harm than good. Against such inflation, Stoll wants to affirm the authority of the fact-gathering procedures of anthropology and journalism, in which testimonial accounts like Menchú's will be treated simply as raw material that must be processed by more objective techniques of assessment. "If we focus on text, narrative, or voice, it is not hard to find someone to say what we want to hear—just what we need to firm up our sense of moral worth or our identity as intellectual rebels," he writes (247). But Stoll's own basis for questioning Menchú's account of the massacre of her brother and other details of her story are interviews with people from the region where the massacre occurred, interviews he conducted many years afterward. That is, the only evidence he can put in the place of what he considers Menchú's unrepresentative testimony are *other* testimonies, in which (it will come as no surprise) he can also find things that *he* might want to hear.

There is a section in Shoshana Felman and Don Laub's book on testimonial representations of the Holocaust that relates to this quandary. It has to do with a woman survivor who gave an eyewitness account of the Auschwitz uprising for the Video Archive for Holocaust Testimonies at Yale. At one point in her narrative the survivor recalls that in the course of the uprising, in her own words, "All of a sudden, we saw four chimneys going up in flames, exploding. The flames shot into the sky, people were running. It was unbelievable."[20] Months later, at a conference on the Holocaust that featured a viewing of the videotape of the woman's testimony, this sequence became the focus of a debate. Some historians of the Holocaust pointed out that only one chimney had been destroyed in the uprising, and that the woman had not mentioned in her account the fact that the Polish underground had betrayed the uprising. Given that the narrator was wrong about these crucial details, they argued, it might be best to set aside her whole testimony, rather than give credence to the revisionists who want to deny the reality of the Holocaust altogether by questioning the reliability of the factual record.

Laub and Felman note that, on that occasion,

[a] psychoanalyst who had been one of the interviewers of the woman profoundly disagreed. "The woman was testifying," he insisted, "not to the number of the chimneys blown up, but to something else more radical, more crucial: the reality of an unimaginable occurrence. One chimney blown up at Auschwitz was as incredible as four. The number mattered less than the fact of the occurrence. . . . The woman testified to an event that broke the all compelling frame of Auschwitz, where Jewish armed revolts just did not happen, and had no place. She testified to the breakage of a framework. That was historical truth."   (60)

The psychoanalyst was in fact Laub, who goes on to explain:

In the process of the testimony to a trauma, as in psychoanalytic practice, in effect, you often do not want to know anything except what the patient tells you, because what is important in the situation is the *discovery* of knowledge—its evolution, and its very *happening*. Knowledge in the testimony is, in other words, not simply a factual given that is reproduced and replicated by the testifier, but a genuine advent, an event in its own right. . . . [The woman] was testifying not simply to empirical historical facts, but to the very secret of survival and of resistance to extermination. The historians could not hear, I thought, the way in which her silence was itself part of the testimony, an essential part of the historical truth she was precisely bearing witness to. . . . This was her way of being, of surviving, of resisting. It is not merely her speech, but the very boundaries of silence which surround it, which attest, today as well as in the past, to this assertion of resistance.   (62)

We know something about the nature of this problem. There is not, outside of human discourse itself, a level of social facticity that can guarantee the truth of this or that representation, given that the facts of memory are not essences prior to representation, but rather themselves the consequence of struggles to represent and over representation. That is the meaning of Benjamin's aphorism "Even the dead are not safe": even the memory of the past is conjunctural, relative, perishable. Testimonio is both an art and a strategy of subaltern memory.

It would be yet another version of the "native informant" to grant testimonial narrators like Rigoberta Menchú only the possibility of being witnesses, but not the power to create their own narrative authority and negotiate its conditions of truth and representativity. This amounts to saying that the subaltern can of course speak, but only through us, through our institutionally sanctioned authority and pretended objectivity as intellectuals, which gives us the power to decide what counts in the narrator's raw material. But it is precisely that institutionally sanctioned authority and objectivity that, in a less benevolent form, but still claiming to speak from the place of Truth, the subaltern must confront every day in the form of war, economic exploitation, development schemes, obligatory acculturation, police and military repression, destruction of habitat, forced sterilization, and the like.[21]

Since (in a way that recalls Florencia Mallon's point about the "dust of the archives") Stoll raises directly the question of the authority of anthropology—which, in his view, has the disciplinary franchise of representing the other to us—against what is, for him, its corruption by "postmodernist scholarship," let me say a few words about the relation of Menchú to Mayan tradition. Though it is founded on a notion of the recuperation of tradition, which her interlocutor, Elisabeth Burgos (also an anthropologist), underlines by inserting passages from the *Popol Vuh* at the beginning of some chapters, there is nothing particularly "traditional" about Menchú's narrative: this is not what makes it the representation of "toda la realidad de un pueblo" ("the whole reality of a people"), because there is nothing particularly traditional about the community and way of life that the narrative describes either. Nothing more "postmodern," nothing more traversed by the economic and cultural forces of transnational capitalism—nothing that we can claim anyway—than the social, economic, and cultural contingencies Menchú and her family and friends live and die in. Even the communal mountain *aldea* or village that her narrative evokes so compellingly, with its collective rituals and economic life, turns out on closer inspection as not so much an ancestral Mayan gemeinschaft as a quite recent settlement, founded by Menchú's father, Vicente, on unoccupied lands in the mountains in the wake of its inhabitants' displacement from their previous places of residence, much as squatters from the countryside have created the great slums around Latin American cities, or returned refugees in Central America have tried to reconstruct their former communities.[22]

I do not mean by this to diminish the force of Menchú's insistent appeal to the authority of her ancestors and tradition, but want simply to indicate that it is an appeal that is being activated and, at the same time, continuously revised *in the present,* that it is a response to the conditions of proletarianization and semi-proletarianization that subjects like Menchú and her family are experiencing in the context of the same processes of globalization that affect our own lives. In some ways, a Latino postmodernist performance artist like Gloria Anzaldúa or Guillermo Gómez Peña might be a more reliable guide to Menchú's world than anthropologists like David Stoll or Elisabeth Burgos, who assume they are authorized or authorize themselves to represent that truth for us.

Readers of *I, Rigoberta Menchú* will remember in particular Burgos's perhaps unintentionally condescending remarks in her introduction about Menchú's cooking and clothing ("she was wearing traditional costume, including a multicoloured *hupil* with rich and varied embroidery," and so on [xiv]), and will probably tend to see these as illustrating the self-interested benevolence of the hegemonic intellectual toward the subaltern. But Menchú's clothes are not so much an index of her authenticity as a subaltern, which would confirm the ethical and epistemological virtue of the *bien pensant* intellectual in the first world: both as a field worker in the coffee plantations and as a maid in Guatemala City she had to learn how to dress very differently, as she tells us herself in her narrative. They speak rather to a kind of performative transvestism on her part, a conscious use of traditional Mayan women's dress as a cultural signifier to define her own identity and her allegiance to the community and values she is fighting for.[23]

There is a question of subaltern agency here, just as there is in the construction of the testimonial text itself. Asked, in the same interview where she claims her right to appear as the coauthor of *I, Rigoberta Menchú*, if she thinks that her struggles will have an end, Menchú answers: "I believe that the struggle does not have an end. . . . I believe that democracy does not depend on the implantation of something, but rather that it is a process in development, that it will unfold in the course of History" ("Yo si creo que la lucha no tiene fin. . . . yo creo que la democracia no depende de una implantación de algo, sino que va a ser un proceso en desarrollo, se va a desenvolver a lo largo de la Historia") (Britten and Dworkin 213; my translation). She sees her own testimonio in similar terms as a conjunctural intervention that responded to a certain strategic urgency, now relativized by what was not or could not be included in it—an imperfect metonym of a different, potentially more complete or representative text, open to the contingencies of memory and history. Except for wanting to be recognized as coauthor, it is not so much that she objects to the way Elisabeth Burgos edited the transcripts of her narrative. Rather, her concern takes the form of a self-criticism:

> Reading it [*I, Rigoberta Menchú*] now, I have the impression that it's a part, that there are fragments of history itself, no? So many stories one comes across in life, in our experiences with the family, with the land, with so many things. What the book has are fragments and I hope that one day we could redo it, maybe for our grandchildren, maybe after putting in a series of other stories, testimonies, experiences, beliefs, prayers that we learned as children, because the book has a lot of limitations.

> Ahora, al leerlo, me da la impresión que es una parte, que son fragmentos de la historia misma, ¿verdad? Tantas anécdotas que uno tiene en la vida, especialmente la convivencia con los abuelos, con la familia, con la tierra, con muchas cosas. Son fragmentos los que tiene el libro y ójala que algún día pudieramos redocumentarlo para publicarlo, tal vez para nuestros nietos, posiblemente después de poner una

serie de otras leyendas, testimonios, vivencias, creencias, oraciones, que aprendi-
mos de chiquitos, porque el libro tiene una serie de limitaciones.

(Britten and Dworkin 217; my translation)

Note that Menchú distinguishes in this passage between a testimonio—the book
I, Rigoberta Menchú ("son fragmentos los que tiene el libro")—and *testimonios* in the
plural as heterogenous and primarily oral acts or practices of witnessing and recounting in her own community, as in "una serie de otras leyendas, testimonios, vivencias,
creencias, oraciones." Testimonio in the singular is for her only one, audience-specific
(to use the jargon of Communications) form of a much broader *testimonial practice*
in subaltern cultures, a practice which includes the arts of oral memory, storytelling,
gossip, and rumor. Where her primary identification in the early part of her narrative is with her father, Vicente—the organizer or public man—these are precisely
the arts Menchú acknowledges learning from her mother, whose own life she calls
toward the end of her story a "testimonio vivo," or living testimony.[24]

Testimonio in the singular is, of course, the form of this communal practice that
we get to experience, since we have no direct access to (and, in general, no interest
in) that larger practice. Hence the essentially metonymic character of the testimonial text. However, it is not only the voice/experience of the narrator in testimonio
that is a metonym of a larger community or group, as in Menchú's claim that her personal story is the story of "todo un pueblo"; the testimonio itself is also a metonym
of the complex and varied cultural practices and institutions of that community or
group.

What *I, Rigoberta Menchú* forces us to confront is not the subaltern as a "represented" victim of history, but rather as agent of a transformative historical project
that aspires to become hegemonic in its own right. Although we can enter into relations of understanding and solidarity with this project, it is not ours in any immediate sense and may in fact imply structurally a contradiction with our own position of
relative privilege and authority in the global system. Becoming a writer, making a literary text out of an oral narration, using testimonial material to construct a historical narrative in the way Mallon does in *Peasant and Nation,* reading and discussing
the text in a classroom, cannot be the solution the "situation of urgency" that generates the telling of the testimonio in the first place requires, although Burgos,
Menchú, and the others involved in creating her testimonio were aware from the
start that it would be used as a weapon against the counter-insurgency war being
waged by the Guatemalan army. But Menchú's own interest in creating the testimonio is not to have it become part of "Western Culture," which in any case she distrusts deeply, so that it can become an object *for us,* a means of getting the whole
truth—"toda la realidad"—of her people. It is rather to act strategically in a way she
hopes will advance the interests of the people she "represents"—whom she calls

"poor" Guatemalans. That is why her testimonio can never be "great literature" in the sense this has for D'Souza: the response it elicits falls necessarily outside of the fields of both literature and anthropology in their present form.[25]

This seems obvious enough, but it is a hard lesson for us to absorb, because it forces us to recognize that it is not the intention of subaltern cultural practice simply to signify more or less artfully, more or less sincerely, its subalternity to us. If that is what testimonio does, then Sklodowska and Spivak are right in seeing it as a kind of postmodernist *costumbrismo*. While she speaks in the passage quoted above of the possibility of redoing her text, Menchú also makes it clear that returning to testimonio is now beside the point for her, that there are other stories she needs, or wants, to tell. That is as it should be, because it is not only our desires and purposes that should count in relation to testimonio.

But we—the we of "*our* desires and purposes" above—are not exactly in the position of the dominant in the dominant/subaltern binary. While we serve the ruling class, we are not (necessarily) part of it. To leave things simply at a celebration of difference and alterity, therefore, is to leave things in the space of a liberal multiculturalism. It is to replace politics with a deconstructive ethics. Part of the appeal of *I, Rigoberta Menchú* that David Stoll objects to resides in the fact that it both symbolizes and enacts concretely a relation of active solidarity between ourselves—as members of the professional middle class and practitioners of the human sciences—and subaltern social subjects. Testimonio implies more than simply being onlookers and reporters of the struggles of others built around identity politics and new points of contention in globalization. We also have a stake in those struggles. Both the economic and ethical bases of our professional lives depend on the idea of *service* and on a network of publicly supported or subsidized institutions and activities. As a class or class-fraction, with local, national, and transnational parameters, intellectuals and professionals have very little to gain and a lot to lose from privatization and the pressure to erode wages and living standards. That realization argues for a tactical alliance between the middle strata and the global/local "poor."

Similarly, though it is based on an affirmation of Mayan identity and culture against a "great narrative" (which has both Marxist and bourgeois-liberal versions) of acculturation and modernization, *I, Rigoberta Menchú* is not so much an appeal to Mayan exceptionalism as a gesture toward a potentially hegemonic political formation in Guatemala that would also include elements of the ladino working class and middle class (and beyond Guatemala, engage the support of progressive forces in the world at large). What Menchú comes to understand, in other words, is that the very possibility of Mayan identity politics and cultural survival has come to depend on an alliance with (what is for her) an other.[26]

The possibility of building such a political formation, based on a coincidence of interests between subaltern subjects and intellectuals and professionals like ourselves who seek to represent them in some way, is also something that David Stoll's argument against Rigoberta Menchú seeks to preclude. In that way too it functions as a text of counter-insurgency. What we share with Rigoberta Menchú, beyond the contradictions that separate our interests and projects, is the desire and need for a *new kind of state* along with new kinds of transnational political-economic institutionality. How do we activate this possibility in the face of the overwhelming ideological hegemony of neoliberalism? That is the question I would like to address in the second half of this book, which concerns in a general way the relation between subaltern studies and cultural studies.

NOTES

1 John Beverley, "The Margin at the Center: On *Testimonio*," in *The Real Thing: Testimonial Discourse and Latin America,* ed. Georg Gugelberger (Durham: Duke Univ. Press, 1996), 24, 26.

2 David Stoll, *Rigoberta Menchú and the Story of All Poor Guatemalans* (Boulder: Westview, 1999).

3 Gayatri Spivak, *The Post-Colonial Critic: Interview, Strategies, Dialogues,* ed. Sarah Harasym (New York: Routledge, 1990), 33. My thanks to Therese Tardio for this citation.

4 "[T]he anonymity of the counterautobiography, which is among other things the testimonial novel, is then in that sense not the loss of a name, but—quite paradoxically—the multiplication of proper names." Fredric Jameson, "On Literary and Cultural Import-Substitution in the Third World: The Case of Testimonio," in *The Real Thing,* 185. "Master subject" is from Jameson's earlier interview with Anders Stephanson: "I always insist on a third possibility beyond the old bourgeois ego and the schizophrenic subject of our organization society today: a *collective subject,* decentered but not schizophrenic. It emerges in certain forms of storytelling that can be found in third-world literature, in testimonial literature, in gossip and rumors and things of this kind. . . . It is decentered since the stories you tell there as an individual subject don't belong to you; you don't control them in the way the master subject of modernism would. But you don't just suffer them in the schizophrenic isolation of the first-world subject of today." Anders Stephanson, "Regarding Postmodernism—A Conversation with Fredric Jameson," *Social Text* 17 (1987): 45.

5 Alice Britten and Kenya Dworkin, "Rigoberta Menchú: 'Los indígenas no nos quedamos como bichos aislados,'" *Nuevo Texto Crítico* 6, no. 11 (1993): 214 (my translation). Ironically, the reverse of what Menchú is complaining about happens in the recent English translation of her new book, *Crossing Borders,* which continues the story begun in *I, Rigoberta Menchú* up to the present (London: Verso, 1998). Though Menchú prepared the book in close collaboration with an Italian editor, Giani Mina, and the Guatemalan literary scholar Dante Liano, both Mina and Liano are eliminated entirely from the English edition, which appears as the sole product of Menchú, transcribed and edited by the translator, Ann Wright. Elisabeth Burgos has continued to insist in various interviews that she is the "sole" author of *I, Rigoberta Menchú,* even as she has sought to distance herself from Menchú's politics. In one way or another, the issue of authorship in testimonio is often a point of conflict between the parties involved in its production. For example, in the first edition of *Biografía de un cimarrón,* published in Cuba, Miguel Barnet appeared as the author, even though the text itself is a first-person narrative by his subaltern informant, Esteban Montejo. In the subsequent English translation (London: Bodley Head, 1968; New York: Meridian, 1969), now out of print, the work was retitled, more accurately in my opinion, *Autobiography of a Runaway Slave,* and the author was designated as Esteban Montejo, with Barnet appearing as the editor. In a new English translation recently

published by Curbstone Press (1995), prepared with Barnet's approval, the book is again titled *Biography of a Runaway Slave* and Barnet again appears as the author (I owe this information to Goffredo Diana).

6 "There is nothing that commends a story to memory more effectively than that chaste compactness which precludes psychological analysis. And the more natural the process by which the storyteller foregoes psychological shading, the greater becomes the story's claim to a place in the memory of the listener, the more completely is it integrated into his own experience, the greater will be his inclination to repeat it to someone else someday, sooner or later." Walter Benjamin, *Illuminations,* trans. Harry Zohn (New York: Shocken, 1969), 91.

7 "Figures like the goddess Athena—'father's daughters self-professedly uncontaminated by the womb'—are useful for establishing women's ideological self-debasement, which is to be distinguished from a deconstructive attitude toward the essentialist subject." Gayatri Spivak, "Can the Subaltern Speak?" in *Marxism and the Interpretation of Culture,* ed. Cary Nelson and Lawrence Grossberg (Urbana: Univ. of Illinois Press, 1988), 308.

8 I often return to Walter Mignolo's observation that the violence of the Spanish practice of segregating the children of the indian aristocracy from their families in order to teach them literacy and Christianity "is not located in the fact that the youngsters have been assembled and enclosed day and night. It comes, rather, from the interdiction of having conversations with their parents, particularly with their mothers. In a primary oral society, in which virtually all knowledge is transmitted by means of conversation, the preservation of oral contact was contradictory with the effort to teach how to read and write. Forbidding conversations with the mother meant, basically, depriving the children of the living culture imbedded in the language and preserved and transmitted in speech." Walter Mignolo, "Literacy and Colonization: The New World Experience," in *1482–1992: Re/Discovering Colonial Writing,* ed. René Jara and Nicholas Spadaccini (Minneapolis: Prisma Institute, 1989), 67.

9 "No representa una reacción genuina y espontánea del 'sujeto-pueblo multiforme' frente a la condición postcolonial, sino que sigue siendo un discurso de las élites comprometidas a la causa de la democratización." Elzbieta Sklodowska, "Hacia una tipología del testimonio hispanoamericano," *Siglo XX/Twentieth Century 8,* nos. 1–2 (1990–1991): 113. The concept of "sujeto-pueblo multiforme" Sklodowska alludes to comes from the Chilean critic Jorge Narvaéz.

10 Gayatri Spivak, *In Other Worlds* (New York: Methuen, 1987), 95.

11 Dinesh D'Souza, *Illiberal Education* (New York: Free Press, 1991), 87.

12 Mary Louise Pratt tells me that a poll of undergraduates at Stanford shows that *I, Rigoberta Menchú* was the book that had the greatest impact on them. A similar poll at the University of Pittsburgh would, I think, yield a very different result, in part because many of the students here are themselves from working-class or lower-middle-class backgrounds, and (on the whole) are destined for middle-management or low-level professional jobs, rather than the elite. On the contradictions of teaching *I, Rigoberta Menchú* in U.S. classrooms, see the essays in Allen Carey-Webb and Stephen Benz, *Teaching and Testimony* (New York: SUNY Press, 1996).

13 For example, "They have tried to take our things away and impose others on us, be it through religion, through dividing up the land, through schools, through books, through radio, through all things modern." Rigoberta Menchú, with Elisabeth Burgos-Debray, *I, Rigoberta Menchú: An Indian Woman in Guatemala,* trans. Ann Wright (London: Verso, 1994), 170–71. Or: "When teachers come into the villages, they bring with them the ideas of capitalism and getting on in life. They try and impose these ideas on us. I remember that in my village there were two teachers for awhile and they began teaching the people, but the children told their parents everything they were being taught in school and the parents said: 'We don't want our children to become like *ladinos*.' And they made the teachers leave. . . . For the indian, it is better not to study than to become like *ladinos*" (Menchú 205).

14 Gareth Williams, "Fantasies of Cultural Exchange in Latin American Subaltern Studies," in *The Real Thing*, 225–53.

15 René Jara, "Prólogo," in *Testimonio y literatura*, ed. René Jara and Hernán Vidal (Minneapolis: Institute for the Study of Ideologies and Literature, 1986), 2.

16 I owe this observation to Pat Seed. Romanticizing victimization was the strategy of the anti-slave narrative produced by liberal elites or would-be elites in the nineteenth century in both Latin America and the United States. It is also a problem in *Schindler's List*, as the emerging critical discussion of the film has begun to register. Steven Spielberg's use of the Schindler story personalizes the Holocaust and brings it closer to the viewer: it differentiates his film from a modernist film treatment of the Holocaust such as Alain Resnais's *Night and Fog*. The price, however, is that the Jews (as a group) can be represented in the film only as victims, dependent on Schindler and on the character played by Ben Kingsley, who symbolizes the role of the traditional Jewish leadership of the *Judenrats*, for their salvation. A Zionist or Communist representation would have critiqued the role of the *Judenrats* and stressed the possibility of Jewish self-organization from below and armed struggle against the Nazi system, instead of their reliance on the benevolence of both Jewish and non-Jewish elites. Even the representation of the Holocaust, in other words, is taken away in *Schindler's List* from the actual victims or participants. The film as a capitalist enterprise mirrors Schindler's business venture (arms manufacture) as the *necessary* vehicle for Jewish salvation. It is instructive to contrast Spielberg's narrative strategy in the film with the collective montage of direct testimonios by Holocaust survivors presented in the Holocaust Museum in Washington or with the similar video produced under his auspices, *Voices of the Holocaust*.

17 See the text of her interview with Juan Jesús Aznárez, "Los que me atacan humillan alas víctims," for the Spanish newspaper *El País*. A translation of the interview, together with documents, journalistic articles, interviews, and essays representing a variety of positions in the Stoll/Menchú debate, including Stoll's own response to his critics, are forthcoming in *The Properties of Words: Rigoberta Menchú, David Stoll, and Identity Politics in Central America*, ed. Arturo Arias (Minneapolis: Univ. of Minnesota Press, 2000). A balanced general account of the controversy may be found in Peter Canby, "The Truth about Rigoberta Menchú," *New York Review of Books*, April 8, 1999: 28–34.

18 David Stoll, *Between Two Armies in the Ixil Towns of Guatemala* (New York: Columbia Univ. Press, 1993).

19 For the counter-case to Stoll, see, for example, Carol Smith, "Why Write an Exposé of Rigoberta Menchú," in Arias, *The Properties*, and Canby, "The Truth."

20 Shoshana Felman and Don Laub, *Testimony: Crises of Witnessing in Literature, Psychoanalysis, and History* (New York: Routledge, 1992), 59.

21 "Any statement of authority has no other guarantee than its very enunciation, and it is pointless for it to seek another signifier, which could not appear outside this locus in any way. Which is what I mean when I say that no metalanguage can be spoken, or, more aphoristically, that there is no Other of the Other. And when the Legislator (he who claims to lay down the Law) presents himself to fill the gap, he does so as an imposter." Jacques Lacan, *Ecrits: A Selection* (New York: Norton, 1977), 310–11.

22 See Beth and Steve Cagan's meticulous account of one such community, *This Promised Land, El Salvador* (New Brunswick: Rutgers Univ. Press, 1991).

23 Menchú notes that, "[i]n the eyes of the community; the fact that anyone should even change the way they dress shows a lack of dignity. Anyone who doesn't dress as our grandfathers, our ancestors, dressed, is on the road to ruin" (Menchú, 37). But I have been told by the Guatemalan writer Arturo Arias, who has worked with her, that outside the public eye Menchú has been known to wear blue jeans and T-shirts. Guha has several lucid passages on the semiotics of dress as a form of subaltern negativity in *Elementary Aspects of Peasant Insurgency in Colonial India* (Delhi: Oxford Univ. Press, 1983); see, e.g., 6–66.

24 I noted in the last chapter some examples of the work of the subaltern studies historians on orality in South Asian peasant cultures. What is relevant to *I, Rigoberta Menchú* is that the mode of transmission of oral culture is dependent on the highly socialized character of everyday community life, in which women play a key role.

25 Mary Louise Pratt's idea of testimonio as "ethnobiography" is pertinent here. Where in oral history or ethnographic "life history" it is the intentionality of the interlocutor which is paramount, in ethnobiography a subaltern subject finds an interlocutor from the hegemony who is in a position to make her story known to a wider, "lettered" audience. In the "life history" the text is the product of a form of hegemonic agency; in ethnobiography it is the product of subaltern agency. Menchú's *Nuevo Texto Crítico* of the transcript of *I, Rigoberta Menchú* was done not only by Elisabeth Burgos but also by a team of Menchú's *compañeros* from the military-political organization she was associated with in Guatemala, the ERP, including the historian Arturo Taracena, working together with her after the sessions with Burgos in Paris. *I, Rigoberta Menchú* is, in this sense, the proverbial text written by a committee (and a central committee at that!).

26 On this point, see Mario Roberto Morales, *La articulación de las diferencias: Los discursos literarios y políticos del debate interétnico en Guatemala* (Guatemala City: FLACSO, 1999). I should note, however, that I disagree with Morales's polemic against Mayan identity politics in Guatemala. The reasons for my disagreement are at the core of my argument about multiculturalism in chapter 6.

29

NICHOLAS THOMAS

The Primitivist and the Postcolonial

Of the forms that colonialism takes in the present, the development projects and military interventions on the part of First World states are perhaps the most conspicuous. Though development takes many forms, some of which are no doubt as constructive as others are pernicious, and though arguments about the Gulf war or Panama might be rather different to those around Vietnam, both military interventions and 'economic assistance' are manifestly linked with investments and spheres of informal political control. If global power has certainly undergone numerous displacements and destabilizations over the second half of the twentieth century, its dynamics and asymmetries remain recognizably imperialist; if this colonialism seeks to convert 'newly industrialized' or 'less developed' economies, rather than pagan souls, it nevertheless retains the intrusive character that missionary interventions always possessed, even when local people had their own reasons for adopting whatever introduced practices or discourses were at issue.

This chapter explores neither economic neo-colonialism nor the New World Order that cost so many Iraqi lives.[1] I pass over these topics partly because they have been extensively discussed by many others, but mostly because I wish to focus on forms of contemporary cultural colonialism which left-liberal culture in the West is not dissociated from, but deeply implicated in. It is easy to denounce government policies and bodies such as the IMF, but perhaps more difficult to explore constructions of the exotic and the primitive that are superficially sympathetic or progressive but in many ways resonant of traditional evocations of others. Though these, in their time, may similarly have appeared enlightened, they often now look restrictive and exploitative. One of the tasks of cultural critique can be an exposure of the tension between the apparent strategic value of these rhetorical forms and their underlying or longer-term limitations.

I have argued that colonialism's culture should not be seen as a singular enduring discourse, but rather as a series of projects that incorporate representations, narratives and practical efforts. Although competing colonizing visions at particular times often shared a good deal, as the racist discourses of one epoch superficially resembled those of others, these projects are best understood as strategic reformulations and revaluations of prior discourses, determined by their historical, political and cultural contexts, rather than by allegedly eternal properties of self-other relations, or by any other generalized discursive logic. Accordingly, contemporary primitivisms possess a good deal in common with earlier reifications and fetishizations of notionally simple ways of life, but have a distinctive character that derives from the politics of identity in the present.

The primitivist discourses I describe here cannot be straightforwardly located in particular, institutionally circumscribed colonizing projects such as that of the Australasian Methodist mission or the British administration in Fiji; rather, like the capital-I Imperialism which Rhodes, Buchan and Milner championed, contemporary primitivism is diffused through consumer culture and a variety of class and interest groups. However, the variants that I am concerned to explore are located in societies of a distinct type, that is, settler colonies. While eighteenth-century primitivism is associated mainly with French and British Enlightenment writers who were reflecting on accounts from remote America or the South Pacific, whites in Australia, New Zealand, Canada and elsewhere are now idealizing indigenous peoples in similar terms, but with reference to Australian Aborigines, Maori and native Americans.[2] The key question is whether affirmations of native spirituality and harmony with the environment (of the sort exemplified by the furniture mentioned in chapter 1) actually entail a consequential revaluation of indigenous culture (or in what contexts, and for whom?), or whether they instead merely recapitulate appropriations familiar from the history of settler colonies, in which Australians and others have defined themselves as 'natives' by using boomerang motifs and Aboriginal designs and by claiming similar attachments to land.

These issues are rendered more complicated by the range of indigenous statements in the debate. 'Primitivist' idealizations are advanced not only by whites but also by some Aborigines and some Maori, and their evident strategic value in advancing the recognition of indigenous cultures clearly precludes any categorical rejection of the whole discourse. What is at issue is not whether current representations match some check-list of what is or is not politically correct, but the play between essentialist and hybridized identities in a field of affirmations and contests.

My main reason for concluding *Colonialism's Culture* with these themes is that they loom large in public debate around the scene of its composition. However, a book about the directions and techniques of colonial cultural studies might have another reason for privileging the construction of indigenous identities in this way: because it redresses the marginalization of these issues—and these people—in the contemporary discourses of critical multiculturalism and postcolonial theory, especially as they are fashioned in the United States, which (despite all the talk of 'decentering') remains the key arena for the legitimization and the marketing of scholarship and theory. It is understandable, but regrettable, that debates about race, minority identities, representations of ethnicity and cognate questions are almost always about Afro-Americans, Hispanics and other immigrant people of colour within the United States or about histories of colonialism in other regions. In U.S. journals that address race,[3] more reference is made to racism and colonial conflicts elsewhere—in South Africa or Britain—than to native American struggles, and there is no widely read theoretical text that speaks from the indigenous perspective in the way that the work of Gates, bell hooks, Cornel West and many others speak from Afro-American experience, or as Said's *Orientalism* and Spivak's work present the positions of diasporic intellectuals from the Middle East and south Asia respectively.

If this is readily explicable on the grounds of the limited presence of native Americans in the academy, it is in other ways puzzling: native Americans and narratives of conquest are prominent in major popular genres such as Hollywood Westerns, but scarcely enter into the literature on colonial discourse and the 'representation of the other.' While the blindness may have been partially ameliorated by the debates around native American issues in the Quincentenary year, it remains to be seen whether contemporary issues and localized protests receive as much enduring attention as work on the conquest itself by prominent theorists such as Stephen Greenblatt. It is notable that *Marvelous Possessions* relates the violence and wonder of cross-cultural contact gesturally to Zionism, and in more detail to the paradigmatically exotic Bali, but not to the encounter that continues between the indigenous peoples and the dominant society within North America.[4] It is no doubt desirable for the fifteenth- and sixteenth-century histories to be reinterpreted, but it is a pity if an emphasis on that period paradoxically reinforces the marginalization of contemporary native Americans.[5] There thus seems scope for the marginal societies of Australia, New Zealand and Canada, in which indigenous assertions and identities are far more powerfully present, to write something back into the debates in the United States. This is simply that American societies are settler societies too, and that indigenous perspectives and histories cannot be equivalized with those of other 'others.'

———

Although the 'primitive' and the 'exotic' are sometimes conflated, exoticism has more to do with difference and strangeness than an antithetical relation to modernity. The Middle East, India and China were often constructed as 'feudal' or otherwise premodern, but their significance in Western representation tended to derive from emblematic customs such as the harem, caste, footbinding and so on, rather than from their archaism as such. The importance of difference—as opposed to sheer inversion—is manifest for instance in the interest in Indian architecture shown in Salt's engraving, reproduced in chapter 2 (plate 3). The potential disconnection of exoticism from evolutionary time is marked also by the fact that Japan, Korea, Singapore and Hong Kong remain exotic for Europeans and Americans, even though their modernity can hardly be in doubt. The primitive, on the other hand, is not generally significant because of some specific attributes that say Australian Aborigines possess and 'Hottentots' do not, but above all because of an originary, socially simple and natural character.

Even in eighteenth-century expressions, this simplicity can be understood in terms of a lack of the material possessions by which Europeans are corrupted or dulled, rather than enhanced.

> [N]ature in her more simple modes is unable to furnish a rich European with a due portion of pleasurable sensations. He is obliged to have recourse to masses of inert matter, which he causes to be converted into a million of forms, far the greatest part solely to feed that incurable craving known by the name of vanity. All the arts are employed to amuse him, and expel the *tedium vita,* acquired by the stimulus of pleasure being used till it will stimulate no more; and all the arts are insufficient. Of this disease, which you are here so terribly afflicted, the native Americans know nothing. When war and hunting no longer require their exertions, they can rest in peace. After satisfying the more immediate wants of nature, they dance, they play; —weary of this, they bask in the sun, and sing. If enjoyment of existence be happiness, they seem to possess it; not indeed so high raised as yours sometimes, but more continued and more uninterrupted.[6]

'Primitivism,' typified by this sort of contrast, is something more specific than an interest in the primitive: it attributes an exemplary status to simple or archaic ways of life, and thus frequently shares the progressivist understanding of tribal society as an original and antecedent form, but revalues its rudimentary character as something to be upheld. At this level of generality, it is the conformity of contemporary primitivism with the longer tradition that seems striking.

In *Voices of the First Day: Awakening in the Aboriginal Dreaming* (1991), Robert Lawlor argues that Aboriginal culture is everything that the West is not. In particular, he emphasizes that Aboriginal dreaming constructs the world as a unified field of psychic energy, and that in many fundamental respects this worldview has been conducive to higher forms of happiness and sociality than those 'we' are able to experience. Western civilization, associated with the 'puritanical oppression' of Christianity, colonialism, 'capitalism and its socialistic variations,' scientific thinking and so on amounts to a massive detour from healthy human development; it is fortunately one that we appear now to be in a position to rectify. Although Lawlor had earlier pursued his interests in ancient civilization in south India, living among 'Dravidian people whose language and way of life had remained virtually unchanged for the last four thousand years,' he was drawn away from that 'land blanketed with layers of history and burdened with overpopulation' toward 'the most ancient of all cultures.'[7]

Not content with the standard archaeological view that Aborigines have been in Australia for 40,000 or 50,000 years, or even the more speculative claim that occupation may extend back to around 150,000 years before the present, Lawlor finds mounting evidence for an Australian origin for humanity; the facts have been neglected by archaeologists predisposed to look to Africa. Aborigines are seen to have developed a kind of pre–Stone Age wood-based culture, which has persisted to the present day without evolving perhaps 'because their revelations, or Dreamtime laws, prevented them from doing so.' In many respects, for Lawlor, 'The Australian Aborigines seem to be a predecessor or prototype in that they exhibit, throughout their populations, distinctive characteristics of all the other four major races.'[8] Some points of Lawlor's argument lend themselves more readily to quotation than paraphrase.

> It is as if the Aborigines are the quintessence of the primary fourfold division of the races [White, Yellow, Black, and Red, or Caucasian, Mongoloid, Negroid, and Capoid]. . . . It may seem to be a coincidence that modern astronomers have designated the four major phases in the life cycles of stars as black holes, red giants, white dwarfs, and yellow suns. However, their respective qualities are related to and consistent with other symbologies of the four colors.[9]

Aboriginal culture is thus original in a radical and absolute sense. Lawlor asserts again and again that what can be witnessed of Aboriginal life in the present expresses and recapitulates a truth that humanity has otherwise lost: a typical caption to an 1890s photograph reproduced by Lawlor reads 'The ceremonies of the Aborigines call us back to the primal origins of creation.' Many particular aspects of Aboriginal sociality thus compare favourably with Western practices because the former preserve a sense of the interconnectedness of all things. Even the domain of gender relations, generally thought to entail domination and a variety of social and ritual asymmetries across most of the continent, illustrates for Lawlor the superiority of 'early societies' that escaped 'the crackdown on fertility rites by state religions.' He finds that 'The bestowal of women in Aboriginal society supports a stable social order based on nonpossessive attitudes. It also fulfills a more positive function than the repressive pornographic forms found in our own society.'[10]

While the idea that 'our society' possesses any unitary form of sexuality is untenable (where would this place the voguing of Jenny Livingstone's film *Paris Is Burning*?) the idea that non-European sexualities might be preferable to the objectifications of pornography and advertising is entirely reasonable, as is the thesis that non-industrial forms of production make the obscenity of pollution and overproduction visible. This is commonplace, of course, but may be justified if juxtaposition with other societies somehow adds rhetorical force to the denunciation of modernity; we need not only to see that Los Angeles would be nicer if there were fewer cars, but also that Aborigines got on very well without cars at all.

If this was only silly it would hardly warrant discussion. What is problematic is the extent to which this New Age primitivism reiterates the negative as well as the potentially positive features of the archaism attributed to Aborigines. Constructing them as culturally stable since the beginning of humanity does imply an ahistorical existence, an inability to change and an incapacity to survive modernity; this essentialism also entails stipulations about what is and what is not appropriately and truly Aboriginal, which marginalizes not only urban Aboriginal cultures, but any forms not closely associated with traditional bush gathering. The book's interest in contemporary Aboriginality may be judged from the fact that nearly all the photographs of people are from the Baldwin Spencer collection of outback images from the turn of the century, that are said to provide 'an authentic glimpse into the oldest known human society.'[11] The other images include exploration-period engravings and numerous drawings based on colonial images, and a range of colour photographs of dot and x-ray animal paintings (it nowhere being made explicit that these are distinctively modern styles). Other recent photographs feature the landscape, the desert, kangaroos and other wildlife; only one is of an Aboriginal person, a head-and-torso portrait of a girl, dots painted across her forehead, apparently not wearing any European clothing, and naturalized by a bird standing on her hand. The caption reads 'Wild birds bring messages from unknown realms.'

The anthropologist Spencer's images are thus decontextualized from the history of contact between the people depicted and Europeans; despite the fact that some were clearly posed on Spencer's request, what we see reflects not a particular population, but a generic Aboriginal culture which has existed since the beginning of time. Lawlor is, of course, ignoring the archaeological evidence for various shifts in technology, art and production systems—evidence which is often frustratingly inconclusive, but which presumably reflects wider social and cultural changes and a larger dynamism. But it is hardly surprising to find this undiscussed: were the historical vigour of Aboriginal societies acknowledged, their prelapsarian status would of course be prejudiced.

Being radically anti-modern, it is not surprising that Aborigines are profoundly threatened by modernity. The worn and misleading 'fatal impact' thesis is aired again in passing allusions such as those to the destructive effects of alcohol and to an old man who is 'the last member of his tribe' still able to make stone tools. More problematically, it is asserted that the Tasmanian Aborigines (especially attractive to

Lawlor because of their ecologically sound nudity and alleged inability to light fires) were in fact eliminated: 'by 1850, the extermination of this primeval people had swept from the earth the last rituals of human innocence.'[12] This kind of statement is of course offensive to modern indigenous Tasmanians (though no doubt from Lawlor's point of view they are half-castes and hence not 'real' Aborigines).

Aboriginality can thus be cherished only in so far as it is a stable form that can be made to correspond with New Age metaphysics; Aboriginal history contributes to the picture only by showing that the relation of white Western culture to Aboriginal life was purely destructive. In so far as histories might establish that Aborigines resisted colonization, or accommodated themselves to it, or appropriated Christianity, Western art styles and other objects, discourses and institutions to serve Aboriginal needs and ends, they are irrelevant, and are occluded. This celebration of Aboriginality is thus limited to the traditional, and presents contemporary Aboriginal life through works of art that can be construed as traditional by a primarily American readership unfamiliar with the postwar history of Aboriginal painting. Though alluding to the oppressed and damaged character of Aboriginal society, the book has no space for Aboriginal political movements, not even for the Land Rights struggle which in fact establishes the enduring importance of attachments to country. Is it possible to avoid concluding that this evocation is little more than a rip-off, that the 'Aboriginal Dreamtime' here is like the woman in the glossy pornographic photograph, construed 'appreciatively' in terms specified by the image-maker?

Kevin Costner's *Dances with Wolves* was more than just another movie. It was widely applauded; its sympathetic treatment of American Indians was regarded as unprecedented;[13] it took a lion's share of the 1991 Oscars; and despite being long and very predictable, it was rereleased in a director's cut with an additional 40 minutes of footage in late 1991.[14] In production, the film was in fact progressive to the extent that native American actors, rather than white stars, took the Indian parts. Beyond this, and the realist device of presenting subtitled speech in the native languages, the film is strikingly unoriginal in its reiteration of primitivist tropes and the stereotypic understanding of colonial histories that I evoked in chapter 1.

As several commentators have pointed out, *Dances,* like a number of earlier 'liberal' Westerns, merely inverts the Manichean oppositions associated with the more conventional triumph of 'how the West was won.'[15] The frontier whites are degenerate and evil; the Indians are noble and courageous, and live in harmony with the land and with one another. What is remarkable is not the reappearance of these terms in a Hollywood film, or the New Age re-emphasis on indigenous spirituality, but the way in which the master-caption of Costner's voice-over reduces the complexities and ambiguities of characters to categorical truths. In fact, there is some tension within the Lakota Sioux community which the alienated Lieutenant Dunbar joins, between Indians favouring hostile and more accommodating responses to whites, and though this energizes much of the film's implicit emotional dynamism, the voice-over resists the implication that the native community is divided by any inequity or conflict: 'It seems every day ends with a miracle here. . . . I've never known a people so eager to laugh; so devoted to family, and so dedicated to each other, and the only word that came to mind was harmony.'

This reinforces the sense noted earlier in which primitivism, unlike exoticism, is concerned less with difference than sheer inversion and juxtaposition: the specificity of Indian cultures (marked by the canonical teepees and feather headdresses) serves no narrative function, but merely authenticates a portrait of a type of society opposed to our own, which possesses virtues that are plainly absent from a rapacious and expanding white modernity. This primitivism is therefore distinct from the anthropological tradition dedicated to the itemization of cultural difference, which informed a colonial governmentality that operated in Fiji and elsewhere upon the various native societies or cultures that it defined. While neutralizing those differences through idealization, primitivism however shares with that anthropological project a legislation of authenticity: others are acceptable in so far as they conform to their proper natures, but are degenerate and improper in 'acculturated' or hybridized forms. *Dances* refrains from presenting the inauthentic Indian, but accords with familiar primitivist logic in displacing the negative attributes of savagery onto another tribal population, in this case the Pawnee, whose characterization as lawless barbarians has been overlooked by those who celebrate the film. Hence, as with the Cook voyage responses to Pacific islanders, discussed in chapter 3, it is not the case that a romantic noble savage discourse has been opposed to another set of representations that denigrated ignoble savages; rather a unitary discourse could deploy both figures in different contexts or for different narrative purposes. The ambiguity that Marianna Torgovnick noted in very different Western reflections on the primitive is again manifest: while overtly aiming to displace ideas of savagery and white superiority, liberal texts air and deploy the very notions that they notionally question, and in the end perhaps do more to reaffirm than subvert them.[16]

Dances naturalizes the Sioux by revealing them within a remarkable, brilliantly photographed landscape. The 'big screen' is as crucial here as it is in David Lean's *Lawrence of Arabia,* creating an image of heroic proportions, a cinematic equivalent to the history painting that, despite the film's unoriginality, is not remotely to be seen as a succession of generic allusions or postmodern ironies, but a fatal-impact narrative saturated with human meaning, morality and tragedy.

The lamentation of the fatal impact is perhaps the film's profoundest subterfuge. The idealization of the Sioux entails their incompatibility with colonial society and makes their elimination inevitable. Dunbar explains near the beginning that he wants 'to see the frontier . . . before it's gone,' and though the viewer is spared any horrific massacre, the closing text frames, over the smouldering fires of an abandoned camp, record that 'Thirteen years later, their homes destroyed, their buffalo gone, the last band of free Sioux submitted to white authority at Fort Robinson, Nebraska. The great horse culture of the Plains was gone and the American frontier was soon to pass into history.' This conclusion thus affirms what Dunbar's initial statement anticipates, and privileges the indigenized Dunbar as a resourceful backwoodsman, striding off into the snow with his wife and child, in a principled action aimed to draw the military's attention away from the tribe that has hosted him. The evocation of the native Americans has a conditional quality: not 'here they are,' but 'here is their passing.' As in E. S. Curtis's classic images of noble Indians vanishing into the mists, the landscape or their own melancholy, so also in Lindt's studio portrait, Raffles's print of the Papuan slave staring toward his homeland and many settler-colonial representations of 'The last of the . . . ,' this fading to absence is determined by the presence of another figure, a white protagonist who is in some cases a settler, in others a writer able to record the truth of an extinguished culture.[17]

While *Dances* denigrates actual settlers and is not centrally preoccupied with ethnographic authority, it does ennoble the figure that Lieutenant Dunbar exemplifies. In its allegory of accomplishment and identity, the film may possess a singularity which its conformity with a long and diversified primitivist lineage would leave us unprepared for. In other words, and in terms of the argument I have advanced earlier in this book, the film is not merely another specimen of an enduring colonialist discourse, but a distinctive project that resonates with wider peculiarities of the present.

One of the more powerful sections of the film is the opening display of the sheer insanity of the Civil War, which is followed by the corruption and cowardice of frontier officers Dunbar encounters on his way into Sioux country. Just as the Vietnam experience has been revealed cinematically as a debased madness from which nationalist truths of emancipation and military honour had been evacuated, both the Union's war and the civilizing mission in the West are exposed as struggles devoid of principled motive and expression, as corruptions from which Dunbar can only be alienated. Though initially deeply disorientated and confused, he is therefore not so much an agent of conquest, as a traveller; unlike Crawfurd in *Prester John,* he goes not to bring a people within the ambit of colonial order and power, but to prejudice his own customary truths, to transgress and experiment. With help from firearms appropriated from the military outpost he has abandoned, Dunbar aids his community in fighting off Pawnee raiders; as the chaos of the conflict subsides around him, Dunbar's voice-over tells us:

It was hard to know how to feel. I'd never been in a fight like this one . . . there was no dark political objective. . . . It had been fought to preserve the foodstores that would see us through the winter. . . . I gradually began to look at it in a new way. I felt a pride I'd never felt before. I'd never really known who John Dunbar was. Perhaps the name itself had no meaning. As I heard my Sioux name being called over and over, I knew for the first time who I really was.

Dunbar's nominal indigenization is also a moment of conquest in two senses. Not only does he help defeat the Pawnee, but he establishes himself as a champion among the Sioux, who recognize the power of the weapons he has introduced and make him the hero of the moment, calling his name over and over. This interpellation does not identify Dunbar as a Sioux, and this is not what his self-discovery consists in. Instead, his prior self-recognition as a soldier in battles possessing 'dark' political significance is transmuted into his recognition by the Sioux as a heroic warrior; he never becomes a common member of their community, but retains the privilege of the colonizer to act forcefully and with historical effect, yet his individual heroism is stripped of its associations with conquest and authenticated by the Sioux. This is, in fact, the only narrative work that the Indians can accomplish; everything else in the story is done to them or for them.

The simultaneity of Dunbar's self-assertion and partial indigenization is allegorized by his 'dancing with wolves,' his mystical association with an intractably wild creature that he paradoxically succeeds in partially domesticating and feeding, that becomes a kind of mascot and guardian spirit, occasionally visible and audible even after it is callously shot by the soldiers attempting to police Dunbar's dereliction of duty and reabsorb him to their side of the frontier. Costner/Dunbar, dissociated from the flaws of modernity and white society, as an indigenized white man, is a profoundly different figure to the acculturated Indian; while the latter can only acquire the corruption of white society and the half-caste morality typified by Henriques in *Prester John,* the white traveller retains the authority of presence that the passing Indian perforce lacks, while substituting integrity and an identification with the land for the discredited expansionist narratives of conquest and environmental destruction. What *Dances with Wolves* re-dresses is not history but a dominant masculine identity, and it does this not by narrating the other side of the story, but through the appropriation of Indian garb that lacks the stains of discarded uniforms.

At any time a plethora of narratives of national identity are no doubt circulating in a conflicted field. It would be unwise to claim any emblematic status for *Dances with Wolves,* but the film may typify a liberal response to the declining appeal of modernization, patriotism and civic conservatism. With the rise and institutionalization of multiculturalism, 'identity' is associated increasingly with cultural difference and minority status, which is unavailable to the dominant culture, or at least to men. Liberal men, who cannot take the option of overtly denigrating minority identities and reaffirming the value of imperialism, environmentally destructive modernization and so on, are therefore prompted to reconstruct their own identities on the model of a minority. This curious, recursive reformulation, or moment of 'symbolic obviation' in Roy Wagner's terms, seems to lie behind such projects as the New Age redefinition of male sexuality, the 'Men's Movement' presided over by primitivist intellectuals like Robert Bly and the refashioned American individual of *Dances with Wolves*. Kevin Costner, dissociated from the Vietnam–Civil War, having discovered the Sioux in himself, and sanctimoniously lamented their departure from a land that now constitutes a vacant space for his own achievements, can re-emerge as a crusader for honesty and freedom in Oliver Stone's *JFK*.

This marks another sense in which 'the primitive' is profoundly different from 'the exotic.' The force of the primitive in Costner's appropriation, and in similar operations in Canadian, Australian and New Zealand culture, derives precisely from the fact that the native is not foreign but indigenous: self-fashioning via the Sioux or the Aborigines does not exoticize oneself, but makes one more American or more Australian. (This is precisely what Paul Hogan, the folkloricized Australian hero, does in *Crocodile Dundee,* as is manifested particularly by his participation in a corroboree.) In this mode, primitivism has something in common with the long tradition of white settler appropriations of indigenous names and motifs—the use of the boomerang as an Australian emblem, for example—but augments these by defining ethos and being, rather than merely the icons of identity, through indigenous models. If the legitimacy of traditional narratives of nationhood is destabilized to the point that the epoch can be characterized as 'posthistorical,' primitivism can now serve not only the generalized New Age interest in spirituality and new masculinity, but also a specifically national truth.

It is difficult to tell this tale without recapitulating the vanishing trick that *Dances with Wolves* itself performs upon native Americans. The cultural dynamic seems to establish the permanence of colonial asymmetry, the fact that dominant white cultures seem to abandon one form of exploitation only to proceed to another: having stolen Aboriginal land, Australians are now stealing the Dreamtime. Depressingly plausible as it is, this pessimism might leave us unprepared for the distinct dynamics of these transactions, and the potentially empowering aspect of even their 'New Age' manifestations. The example of Aotearoa New Zealand reinforces the argument that there is a new appropriative dynamic of nationalized indigenous identity, but would undermine the view that this is no more that a further tactic of white dominance.

New Zealand, like Australia, is a 'postcolonial' society in the sense that it is no longer formally a British colony. It is also conspicuous that Maori culture now possesses a degree of prestige and legitimacy unprecedented in the period of colonization: even over a period of right-wing backlash and National (conservative) Party government, the notion that New Zealand should be a 'bicultural' society is gaining acceptance. But in what form is Maori culture recognized and celebrated?

One telling expression is the projection of Maori identity in major exhibitions of *taonga* (valuables or treasures); the success of the *Te Maori* exhibition in New York in 1984 was regarded as a major boost for the Maori 'cultural renaissance' of the last decade, and a subsequent, related exhibition, *Taonga Maori,* more recently toured Australia and formed a long-term display in the National Museum in Wellington. What is striking about this collection of fine carvings, weaving, featherwork and nephrite is a radical aesthetic decontextualization that excludes non-traditional contexts of production, colonial processes and European influences of all kinds. Despite the fact that most of the material was nineteenth century, and was therefore made and collected during a period of intensive contact and rapid change, it was unambiguously associated through display captions and in the catalogue with a stable, authentic and radically different social universe that is characterized particularly by its holism, archaism and spirituality.

> Being a Maori, therefore, is knowing who we are and where we come from. It is about our past, present and future. Our kinship ties and descent expressed through our *whakapapa* (genealogy) are what binds us to our past and to our ancestors, and where our *mana* (power), *ihi* (prestige), *wehi* (fear) and *tapu* (sacredness) come from. This is our identity; without it we have no foundation, no refuge. It is expressed in the following words:
>
> *He mana Maori motuhake*
> *He mana tuku iho ki a tatou.*
> (Maori spirituality set apart
> A spirituality that has been handed down to us).

> The answer to the question 'Who are the Maori people?' is about the separation of . . . the two primal parents of the Maori. . . . It is about the many tribal traditions, myths, and stories which provide a solid foundation for our lives . . . it is about love and respect for our culture, our fellow man, and our environment.[18]

On the face of it, this evocation has a good deal in common with the discourse of *Voices of the First Day*. A number of objections to its content might be rehearsed, but it is important then to consider what the effect of *Taonga Maori* has been in its context.

Certainly, the catalogue's larger description of Maori culture cannot be seen as an unproblematic self-presentation on the part of Maori: the section on kinship, for example, is highly reminiscent of anthropological systematizations, such as those of Sir Raymond Firth, that happen to be consistent with the projection of a cohesive kin-structured world because they emphasize the nesting together of descent lines, clans, and tribes. Similarly, though it should not be denied that categories such as *mana* and *tapu* were important notions in precolonial Maori culture, the descriptions in the catalogue do owe something to the traditional colonialist and anthropological representations, and on the whole they lean toward a construction of Maoriness as mystical and spiritual: 'The Maori psyche revolves around tribal roots, origins, and identity.'[19] George French Angas, in *New Zealanders Illustrated* (1847), in his captions to depictions of a variety of artefacts, carvings, weapons and the like often alluded to the 'sacred' character of particular objects but associated this with irrational and constrained superstition: some *tiki* represented 'the supposed *taniwa* or river god'; 'so strict is the law of *tapu* that no one dare touch these valuable relics.'[20] The *Taonga Maori* catalogue reproduces this emphasis on the mystical associations of the objects, supplanting a rationalist progressivism with white society's craving for non-industrial authenticity.

The critique that might be put forward is not that this projection of identity is merely a derivative discourse, but that it partakes of a cultural essentialism that construes Maoriness primarily in terms of its difference from pakeha (white New Zealander) identity, and thus reduces it to terms that complement white society's absences: against the alienations of modernity are 'intimate connections' that constitute 'roots, origins, and identity.' In the discussion of the *marae,* the meeting ground that was and is the site of various formal celebrations, that is generally central to tribal affairs, it is stated that the *marae* 'is intimately connected with the ceremonial experiences in life crises such as birth, death, and marriage. To return to the *marae* from the brashness of urban life is to return to a simpler time, to a place of enduring human values.'[21] What is oddly elided here is one of the most significant developments of the Maori renaissance, namely the great expansion of urban *marae* to serve the interests of Maori now remote from rural tribal homelands.

The Maoriness evoked here, like some representations of Aboriginality, is available to white settlers seeking to establish national identities that are not merely impoverished versions of Britishness or limited to the pioneer experience to which relatively few can directly relate.[22] The *Taonga Maori* show was part of a surge of interest that received particular impetus in the mid-1980s from the earlier *Te Maori* exhibition and the success of Keri Hulme's Booker-Prizewinning novel, *The Bone People*. The exhibitions might be criticized through similar arguments to those I adduced against Lawlor's *Voices of the First Day:* the construction of authentic spirituality marginalizes most Maori who, though not part of a homogeneous pakeha society, must negotiate identities in urban contexts, with non-traditional social relations, institutions, jobs and so on. In relation to folkloricized identities such as that paraded in the *Taonga Maori* exhibition, they stand as poor copies of a correct ethnic authenticity that is at once inaccessible to many urban Maori and inappropriate in so far as it is associated strongly with the past, rather than with the contemporary circumstances within which they, like everyone else, have to operate. In the specific domain of art, this excludes or marginalizes innovations, non-traditional media and any forms of modernist style: the few contemporary pieces that figured in the *Taonga Maori* exhibition were either modern examples of wholly traditional forms, such as weavings and carvings, or other works that manifested the persistence of traditional patterns and designs.[23] The extensive body of modernist and post-modernist Maori art was excluded.

In the Maori case, however, this kind of critique would neglect the extent to which characterizations of Maori tradition, spirituality and mythology have played a crucial empowering role in a wider struggle that has not been limited to the legitimization of traditional culture. This struggle has involved many campaigns against the desecration of tribal lands, against development or for compensation, and for better services and funding for Maori development and education programmes, such as Kohanga Reo, which aims to reverse the long-term decline in Maori language use through teaching programmes directed especially at primary school children.[24] These efforts have ranged from occupations of land and direct action against anti-Maori racists to lobbying and bureaucratic reforms. In many cases the issues and objectives are not directly linked with tribes or with Maori culture and language, but nevertheless draw inspiration and legitimacy from the same range of symbols and traditions that seem to be reprimitivized in exhibitions such as *Taonga Maori*. In Alan Duff's remarkable novel *Once Were Warriors,* an urban Maori population devastated by alcohol and violence is shown to redeem itself through the organization of pragmatic local projects that are not themselves essentially or peculiarly indigenous, but that derive their coherence from a sense of continuity with Maori ways, and are inspired by the dignity and power of the elders' oratory.[25]

The issue here resonates with one raised earlier, in chapter 1. I referred to James Clifford's criticisms of Edward Said, whose rejection of the Orientalist postulate of radical difference between East and West was seen to rest sometimes upon the evocation of a 'real' Orient and common humanity. Clifford suggests that Said's work 'frequently relapses into the essentializing modes it attacks' and proposes that Said's hybridized position as an Arab-American intellectual typifies the question that needs now to be explored: 'What processes rather than essences are involved in present experiences of cultural identity?'[26] For his part, Said has more recently attacked nativism on much the same grounds that I have criticized primitivism: it reinforces the imperialist notion that there is a clear-cut and absolute difference between ruler and ruled by merely 'revaluating the weaker or subservient partner.' He claims that such manifestations of nativism as Leopold Senghor's negritude, Wole Soyinka's explorations of the African past and Rastafarianism lead to 'compelling but often demagogic assertions about a native past, history, or actuality that seems to stand free not only of the colonizer but of worldly time itself.' He accuses this 'abandonment of history' of degenerating into millenarianism, craziness and 'an unthinking acceptance of stereotypes.'[27]

What both these critiques pass over is the extent to which humanism and essentialism have different meanings and effects in different contexts. Clifford writes as though the problem were merely intellectual: difference and hybridity are more appropriate analytically to the contemporary scene of global cultural transposition than claims about human sameness or bounded types. I would agree, but this does not bear upon the uses that essentialist discourses may have for people whose projects involve mobilization rather than analysis. Said might be able to argue that nativism as a political programme or government ideology has been largely pernicious, but nativist consciousness cannot be deemed undesirable merely because it is historical and uncritically reproduces colonialist stereotypes. The main problem is not that this imposes academic (and arguably ethnocentric) standards on non-academic and non-Western representations, but that it paradoxically essentializes nativism by taking its politics to be historically uniform. On the contrary, I suggest that representations of identity such as the *Taonga Maori* exhibition, which certainly inverts colonialist stereotypes and reproduces the idea of essential difference, have different meanings at different times, and for different audiences. My initial response to the show arose from an aesthetic similar to Clifford's: I was disturbed by its fetishization of an unacculturated authenticity. However, the exhibition, and more particularly the broader reputation of its predecessor *Te Maori,* was clearly enabling and empowering for many Maori. Just as Aboriginal art and the Dreamtime mythology helped promote the legitimacy of Aboriginal culture at a time when it was not widely respected by the dominant population, this essentialism played a progressive role by capitalizing on white society's primitivism and creating a degree of prestige and power for Maori that did not exist before the 1980s.

Discourses of this kind must thus be understood as ambiguous and historically mutable instruments, as projects that possess one value at one time and another subsequently. In the 1970s and 1980s the gains produced by nativism were probably more significant than the drawbacks arising from the recapitulation of a restrictive primitivism; complemented by other political movements and discourses concerned more directly with contemporary indigenous lives and needs, essentialist constructions of native identity are likely to continue to play a part in gaining ground for indigenous causes among conservative populations, whose ideas of authenticity are generally still defined by the 'anthropological' tradition traced in chapter 3: particular peoples are the bearers of distinct characters or cultures, and hybridized natives (unless models of perfect assimilation) are seen as degenerate and untrue to their natures. Nativism may remain even more important for native Americans in the United States, who remain considerably more marginal than Australian Aborigines, Maori and native Americans within Canada. Nativist-primitivist idealizations can only be politically productive, however, if they are complemented by here-and-now concerns, and articulated with histories that do not merely recapitulate the 'imperialist nostalgia' of the fatal-impact narrative. Thus, for all its elisions, *Taonga Maori* can be empowering, while the positive effects of *Dances with Wolves* seem limited to the point of being negligible.

Like James Clifford, Paul Gilroy is attracted to a pluralist view of identity— specifically in the context of black diasporic cultural creativity—but points out that both essentialist and pluralist identities have limitations. The latter, which emphasizes divisions internal to ethnicities based on 'class, sexuality, gender, age and political consciousness,' tends towards an 'uneasy but exhilarating' libertarianism. The emphasis on the constructed and shifting character of race 'has been insufficiently alive,' Gilroy suggests, 'to the lingering power of specifically 'racial' forms of power and subordination.'[28] While this is a comment specifically on the British scene, it perhaps has the broader correlate that a preoccupation with divisions and hybridity may often be more compatible with individual artistic creativity than the forms of collective representation and mobilization that remain crucial in many political domains.

These difficulties however seem less significant in the present than those arising from the opposed position. An 'over-integrated sense of cultural and ethnic particularity' has led in Gilroy's view to 'a volkish political outlook,' particularly among artists and middle-class blacks claiming to speak for communities while mystifying the differences within them.[29] Again, the specific observations resonate with problems which arise elsewhere: like most other codifications, such as the colonial administration's representation of Fijian sociality, constructions of indigenous identities almost inevitably privilege particular fractions of the indigenous population who correspond best with whatever is idealized: the chiefly elites of certain regions, bush Aborigines rather than those living in cities, even those who appear to live on ancestral lands as opposed to groups who migrated during or before the colonial period. Such asymmetries are transposed in various ways from colonial discourses to nativist assertions, frequently through being opportunistically refashioned by the privileged codifiers of nativist identity. These constructions notably often rigidify gender and age relationships that were formerly more fluid; in Aotearoa New Zealand, for example, despite the evidence concerning nineteenth-century practice, it has become traditionalist dogma that women were not permitted to speak at *marae*. This 'fact' of Maori culture has been significant not only for contemporary practice on those meeting grounds but has been drawn into other domains: conservative Maori clerics, for instance, have used it to oppose the ordination of women. Similarly, while elders gain prestige from the nativist representation of Maori culture, others find the association with archaism problematic and constricting: 'Being Maori doesn't come from my heart. I think that in Maoritanga everything is going backwards instead of going forwards. I just want to go forward.'[30]

I have suggested that modern colonial discourses have represented native peoples in a number of ways: as heathens but potential Christians, as savages to be wished away, as primitives defined through the negation of modernity and as distinct 'races' or 'cultures' possessing particular natures. While the evangelists purveying the first of these constructions were often racist or at least paternalistic and ethnocentric in their attitudes, it is significant that the basic model was anti-essentialist: the mutability of people, not a fixity in their character, was pivotal to its narrative of conversion and improvement. It is, of course, this anti-essentialism which makes it possible for Christianity to be appropriated by anti-racist movements, such as the struggle against apartheid. Both primitivism and anthropological typification, in contrast, are deeply essentialist, and the projects that Gilroy refers to, that affirm identities in non-nativist, pluralistic terms, are at the same time struggles against the fixed types projected by colonial cultures.

Just as colonial culture needs to be understood, not as an essence, but as a plurality of projects including, most recently, the primitivist renovation of white identity via indigenous culture, anti- and postcolonial culture cannot be taken as a unitary set of meanings or a stable position. The ways of subverting limiting constructions of Maoriness and Aboriginality are thus as diverse as the practices, media and genres through which such subversions are effected. While colonialist preoccupations with fixed boundaries and authentic types were once undone by millennial movements which appropriated European symbols, books, banknotes and rituals, hybridized performances that assert above all the positions and presence of indigenous actors can be expressed through graffiti, tattoos and reggae music, or novels, theatre, photography and painting.

One such performance is *Bran Nue Dae,* a remarkable, very funny and very sexy musical written by Jimmy Chi of the Aboriginal community of Broome, in the far northwest of Western Australia, and performed mostly by actors from that community.[31] In a range of parodic and amusing but sometimes also haunting songs, the story works through mission station experiences, presided over by terrifyingly orderly German Lutherans, and presents a series of people coming back together in their country. Tadpole has been in and out of gaol—'I bin drovin' I bin drinkin' I bin christian I bin everything and now it's time I gotta go home see old people'; young

Willie has been brought up on the mission and knows little of bush life. They meet up with an urban dropout, Marijuana Annie, and her German hippy boyfriend Slippery, both of whom discover that they are in fact part-Aborigines who had been fostered into white society during the notorious period of assimilation in the 1950s and 1960s. Slippery, it turns out, is son of the German missionary: 'Ich bin Ine Aborig- ine!!' he proclaims, mimicking to ambiguous effect Kennedy's famous assertion in Berlin. The Broome community is an unusually hybrid one, reflecting various phases of Asian immigration associated with fishing and pearling, as well as white settle- ment, but *Bran Nue Dae* presents histories and predicaments that have counterparts across Australia. In particular it defines Aboriginality through the experience of assimilation and its rejection, as something that can be recovered through self- identification, rather than a quantity that 'authentic' Aborigines possess more of than others. The musical evoked not stable cultural differences but experiential predicaments, some of which (to do with drugs and drink) are rendered through the character of Marijuana Annie to belong to urban youth rather than one 'race' or the other. Through its north Australian kriol (Aboriginal English), the performance had an unmistakable cultural location, but appealed to commonalities and shared aspi- rations rather than differences. As Tadpole says, 'He's a Christian, I'm a Christian, she's a Christian, We all bloody Christian'; and as the chorus concludes 'On the way to a Bran Nue Dae, everybody, everybody say.' The sheer zest of *Bran Nue Dae* is difficult to convey in a text of this kind (suffice it to say that rather than merely advo- cating safe sex in one song, the chorus facilitated it by distributing condoms to the audience). Against the humourlessness of colonialist and nativist codifications of identity alike, Chi's work conveys truths of biography and identity that stabilized cul- tures cannot.

. . .

NOTES

1 For the critical literature on 'development,' see Hamza Alavi and Teodor Shanin, eds., *Intro- duction to the Sociology of 'Developing Societies'* (London: Macmillan, 1982). Though it seems hardly necessary to cite commentaries on the Gulf war, some comments that relate to the the- oretical perspectives I have discussed in this book appear in *Public Culture* (section entitled 'War talk,' 3 (2), (1991), 119–64); see also W.J.T. Mitchell's 'Culture wars,' *London Review of Books,* 23 April 1992, 7–10.

2 It might be noted in passing that Marianna Torgovnick's useful and readable discussion of twentieth-century primitivism (*Gone Primitive: Savage Intellects, Modern Lives* (Chicago: Uni- versity of Chicago Press, 1990) neglects representations of contemporary native peoples, focusing instead on literary and ethnographic discourses such as the writings of Michel Leiris, Bronislaw Malinowski, D. H. Lawrence and Roger Fry. The issue that I am concerned with, of the significance of representations of native peoples in (former) colonies of settlement, thus does not enter into her discussion.

3 In the new series of *Transition,* for example, the first five numbers (51–5) ranged widely over postcolonial literature and film, AIDS, southern Africa, the Caribbean, Britain, Israel, Lebanon, Japan and so on, but included no articles whatsoever on native Americans. Gates's collection, *'Race,' Writing, and Difference* (Chicago: University of Chicago Press, 1985) did slightly better in including one essay, Jane Tompkins's ' "Indians": textualism, morality, and the problem of history.'

4 Stephen Greenblatt, *Marvelous Possessions: The Wonder of the New World* (Chicago: University of Chicago Press, 1991), pp. ix, 3–5.

5 An honourable exception is Clifford's chapter on 'Identity in Mashpee' *in The Predicament of Culture* (Cambridge, Mass.: Harvard University Press, 1988). There is of course an enormous range of other literature in the ethnohistory and anthropology of native Americans; what I am drawing attention to is their marginalization in cultural studies and critical theory, not of course a total absence from current discourse.

6 Robert Bage, *Hermsprong, or Man as He Is Not* (London: William Lane, 1796), ii, p. 21.

7 Robert Lawlor, *Voices of the First Day: Awakening in the Aboriginal Dreaming* (Rochester, Vermont: Inner Traditions International, 1991), pp. 19, 51–9, 20, 10.

8 Ibid., p. 30.

9 Ibid., p. 30–1.

10 Ibid., pp. 211, 213. It is important to note that Australian patterns of gender relations varied considerably: see Diane Bell, *Daughters of the Dreaming* (Melbourne: McPhee Gribble and Allen and Unwin, 1983) and Fay Gale, ed., *Woman's Role in Aboriginal Society* (Canberra: Australian Institute of Aboriginal Studies, 1970).

11 Lawlor, *Voices of the First Day,* p. x.

12 Ibid., p. 137.

13 A caption to an article in *Le Monde* entitled 'Hollywood focus on the real Indians' read 'The film showed the American Indians in their true light for the first time' (*Guardian Weekly,* 5 July 1992, p. 15).

14 For one of the few more critical comments in the mainstream press, see Michael Dorris, 'Indians in Aspic,' *New York Times,* 24 February 1991, section 4, p. 17.

15 See, for example, Jean Fisher, 'Dancing with words and speaking with forked tongues,' *Third Text* 14 (1991), pp. 29–30. Although Fisher offers a somewhat different argument to that presented here, I have drawn on this useful article at several points. It should be pointed out that while the revisionist view of frontier history seems an unsophisticated inversion from some points of view, it nevertheless remains contentious, as was attested by the controversy over the 1991 exhibition 'The West as America—Reinterpreting Images of the Frontier,' at the Smithsonian Institution (see Martin Walker, 'Westward Oh!,' *Guardian Weekly,* 30 June 1991, pp. 25–6).

16 Torgovnick, *Gone Primitive,* pp. 88–9.

17 See Florence Curtis Graybill and Victor Boesen, *Edward Sherriff Curtis: Visions of a Vanishing Race* (New York: Thomas Crowell, 1976).

18 *Taonga Maori: Treasures of the New Zealand Maori People* (Sydney: Australian Museum, 1989), pp. 20–1.

19 Ibid., p. 25.

20 George French Angas, *New Zealanders Illustrated* (London: Thomas M'Lean, 1847), caption to pl. xxxiv.

21 *Taonga Maori,* p. 27.

22 Cf. Ruth Brown, 'Maori spirituality as Pakeha construct,' *Meanjin* 48 (2) (1989), 252–8.

23 *Taonga Maori,* pp. 62–3.

24 For a useful overview see Ranginui Walker, *Ka Whaiwhai Tonu Matou: Struggle without End* (Auckland: Penguin, 1990).

25 Alan Duff, *Once Were Warriors* (St. Lucia, Queensland: University of Queensland Press, 1991).

26 Clifford, *Predicament of Culture,* pp. 271, 275.

27 Edward W. Said, 'Yeats and decolonization,' in *Remaking History,* ed. Barbara Kruger (Seattle: Bay Press, 1989), pp. 15–16.

28 Paul Gilroy, 'It ain't where you're from, it's where you're at: the dialectics of diasporic identification,' *Third Text* 13 (1990), 5.

29 Gilroy, 'It ain't where you're from,' 3–6. See also Paul Gilroy, *There Ain't no Black in the Union Jack* (London: Hutchinson, 1987; Chicago: University of Chicago Press, 1991).

30 Maori woman quoted in Toon van Meiji, 'Political paradoxes and timeless traditions: Ideology and development among the Tainui Maori, New Zealand,' Ph.D. thesis, Australian National University, 1990, p. 140.

31 Published as *Bran Nue Dae: A Musical Journey,* by Jimmy Chi and Kuckles (Sydney: Currency Press/Broome: Magabala Books, 1991). Tom Zubrycki made a film about the musical, also entitled *Bran Nue Dae,* released through Ronin Films, Canberra, 1991.

VIII

Comparative (Post)colonialisms

Postcolonial theory, like most other theoretical fields, has self-reflexively interrogated its own assumptions and structures of thought. There is currently an extensive literature about the usefulness and appropriateness of the term "postcolonial" as a necessarily limited label for a voluminous and unruly index of histories, geographies, and cultures. Some would argue for a narrower, more rigorously exclusionary set of qualifiers for what does or does not count as postcolonial; others tend to find in the term an infinitely elastic capacity to fit a range of diverse chronologies and categories. But the question of the label's "fit" to this or that area is far from settled in all cases. In contexts such as Ireland, attempts to claim a postcolonial status have been rejected on the grounds that Ireland is tied to a European trajectory of development rather than to the underdeveloped, non-Western, and Third World designations that more commonly suggest postcoloniality (see Lloyd in chapter 27). Conversely, Native American contexts tend to resist an easy imposition of the label given the absence of independence and the continuation of colonial inequalities, the irreparable loss of land being the most obvious one (see Sequoya in chapter 21).

Even if some of these communities have regained limited sovereign status, the issue itself is highly contentious, since critics of sovereignty movements tend to demonize them as the racial and ethnic balkanization of the modern, democratic, presumably unified nation rather than as a reassertion of lost rights by the descendants of those who were colonized. The marginalization of these peoples is then perceived as self-inflicted and their grievances reduced to the sour grapes syndrome of those who were conquered by an implacable but generally impartial history. So, for instance, Hawai'i and Puerto Rico are seen as legitimate territorial expansions, gaining rather than losing when the mantle of Manifest Destiny was thrown over them. Even within geographic coastal borders, the First Nations are also "annexed," as in the case of the United States, Canada, and Australia, to a blanket First World label, although it is hardly indicative of the actual lifestyles and limited, if any, privileges of many indigenous and aboriginal peoples. The terminology is further confounded when, as Pal Ahluwalia discusses here, strict separations between settlers and natives are not always rigidly maintained. So when exactly does the term "postcolonial" seem appropriate if not precise? The texts in part VIII set out some of the parameters in contexts not traditionally conceived of as the properly postcolonial: Hawai'i, Australia, and even the post-Soviet Union.

This section begins with the unusual Public Law 103–150, which acknowledges publicly the imperialist pretensions—and success—of the United States. Virtually all the "whereas" clauses reproduce what Linda Tuhiwai Smith calls the "grammar" of imperialism, strikingly not in its defense, as we saw in the documents earlier, but in the convention of the apologies that have become the rage in recent times. It is worth noting that neither the writers of the bill nor the members of the U.S. Congress who passed it in 1993 seem to accept that "the illegal overthrow of the Kingdom of Hawai'i" and the forced abdication of Queen Lili'uokalani in 1893 constitute sufficient criminality on the part of the United States to warrant legal retribution. Instead, despite the keywords "reconciliation" and "acknowledgment and apology," the careful disclaimer that concludes the documented sketch of events leading to the overthrow and annexation of Hawai'i renders the apology itself nominal and more a case of "feel-good" politics. In the copy of the bill provided by the Office of Hawaiian Affairs, Senator Slade Gorton is quoted as saying that "the logical consequences of this resolution would be independence," but this logic is defied when the whereas clauses are apparently prevented by the disclaimer from erupting into the "therefore" of legal recompense. The bill thus reads as a masterpiece of irony, in which the detailed acknowledgment of an explicitly colonial sequence of events slips away into discursive legislation emptied of any material reprisals, although there is the consolation of "reconciliation efforts between the United States and the Native Hawaiian people." However, the bill is a rare document in the colonial archives: it significantly complicates dominant discourse by endorsing what would otherwise be dismissed as native gripes.

Amy Kaplan's brief but pithy title, "Manifest Domesticity," not only signifies on the doctrine that legitimated the imperial expansion of the United States but also examines the role of nineteenth-century American women writers who enthusiastically embraced the expansionist ideology of Manifest Destiny. Influenced by the work of critics such as Nancy Armstrong who have focused on the nationalist and bourgeois complicities of white, middle-class, Victorian women writers, Kaplan extends her project to consider more fully the "racialized national subjectivity" that white, middle-class, American women played out in a more international setting. (Her analysis bears some similarities to Gayatri Spivak's critique of nineteenth-century English women writers as well. See chapter 24.) Rejecting the notion of separate spheres that relegated women to a strictly domestic interior, "primarily at the center of the home," Kaplan argues instead that women's novels of the 1850s are embedded in the discourse of "empire and nation building," leading to the paradox of what she calls "imperial domesticity."

The moralizing bent of this particular literature lent itself easily to reproduce the paternal (and maternal) benevolence of colonial ideology as something with the best interests of the natives at heart. The domesticating potential of Anglo-Saxon women was mobilized not only to characterize the original inhabitants of the Americas as threatening and alien but also to transform the Anglo-Saxon settlers into the legitimate natives of the New World. Sarah Josepha Hale's novels go further in proposing a neat plan to send the region's black people back to Africa, rendering the area more comfortably the terrain of white Americans. As Alexander Crummell hoped, Americanized Africans (never more safely and thoroughly American in Hale's work than when they were in Africa, Kaplan points out) would then convey civilized values back to Africa (see chapter 10).

Kaplan's critical reading of domesticity as enabling the nativization of colonial Americans anticipates Pal Ahluwalia's questions about "citizenship and identity in a settler society." Ahluwalia notes that in the context of postcolonial Australia (formally distinct from the British Commonwealth), authentic national identity is structurally configured through the state and civil society of the dominant white settlers. By this account, migrations from Asia, Africa, and the Pacific islands have been considered marginal, and the very category "aboriginal native" has been used not to sanctify national origins, but to exclude the Aboriginal and other minority populations from so-called "universal liberal values of equality, citizenship and justice." The term "natives" shows some slippage from its derogatory reference to those of dusky complexion who had been displaced by British imperialism to the inherited entitlement of white people born in the colonies—the settler becomes native in the Australian colony. Indigenous structures and genealogies become invisible, irrelevant in their systematic erasure by new civic requirements built upon the primary foundation of *terra nullius* (see Mudimbe in chapter 4).

Even as new considerations of citizenship challenge the founding myth and Aboriginal populations have become increasingly militant in their claims, Ahluwalia demonstrates the instability of categories such as settler, native, citizen, and subject. Nor is postcolonialism an essential state of being. "In the battle over post-colonialism, what is perhaps forgotten is that the very subjects of empire have endured different forms of colonialism." White settlers may have issues of their own embattled sovereignty with the mother country, but their postcolonial accounts, Ahluwalia reminds us, have often been articulated, enacted, and idealized at the expense of other populations they have in turn colonized.

For those who find objectionable the idea of white settlers occupying the colonized end of the postcolonial continuum, David Chioni Moore further muddies the waters by speculating whether any part of the world, even England, can be emphatically *not* postcolonial. Although postcolonialists have thus rightly considered the "postcoloniality" of a variety of global contexts, Moore notes a significant "blank" space: "the post-Soviet sphere—the Baltic states, Central and Eastern Europe (including former Soviet republics and independent 'East Bloc' states), the Caucasus, and Central Asia." Moore points to an interesting reversal in the general reluctance to include this region in configurations of the postcolonial. While countries such as England, read as the prime instigators of genocide and dispossession, are less likely to be accepted as nations with a postcolonial past of their own, the left-leaning politics of most postcolonial scholars make them unwilling to identify "the Soviet Union [as] a French- or British-style villain." In the three-worlds paradigm that influenced postcolonial scholarship, argues Moore, the Second World offered a utopian alternative to the First and Third World histories of exploitation and abuse (with the First as perpetrator and the Third as victim). The socialist achievements of this intermediary space redeem the Second World in the eyes of the Left, but Moore nevertheless points out that the Soviet Union—despite the complex variations and nuances that distinguished it from the Western European nations—engaged in its own expansion and dominion over neighboring areas. The challenge of recasting postcolonial relations and remapping their geographies is a daunting task. Acknowledging the risk that stretching "postcolonial" too thin may make it "lose all analytic bite," becoming flaccid and losing its tension, Moore concludes that such a bold global reinterpretation also has the potential to "add richness to studies of place or literature."

30

Apology Bill

Public Law 103-150

To acknowledge the 100th anniversary of the January 17, 1893 overthrow of the Kingdom of Hawai'i, and to offer an apology to Native Hawaiians on behalf of the United States for the overthrow of the Kingdom of Hawai'i.

Whereas, prior to the arrival of the first Europeans in 1778, the Native Hawaiian people lived in a highly organized, self-sufficient, subsistent social system based on communal land tenure with a sophisticated language, culture, and religion;

Whereas, a unified monarchical government of the Hawaiian Islands was established in 1810 under Kamehameha I, the first King of Hawai'i;

Whereas, from 1826 until 1893, the United States recognized the independence of the Kingdom of Hawai'i, extended full and complete diplomatic recognition to the Hawaiian Government, and entered into treaties and conventions with the Hawaiian monarchs to govern commerce and navigation in 1826, 1842, 1849, 1875, and 1887;

Whereas, the Congregational Church (now known as the United Church of Christ), through its American Board of Commissioners for Foreign Missions, sponsored and sent more than 100 missionaries to the Kingdom of Hawai'i between 1820 and 1850;

Whereas, on January 14, 1893, John L. Stevens (hereafter referred to in this Resolution as the "United States Minister"), the United States Minister assigned to the sovereign and independent Kingdom of Hawai'i conspired with a small group of non-Hawaiian residents of the Kingdom of Hawai'i, including citizens of the United States, to overthrow the indigenous and lawful Government of Hawai'i;

Whereas, in pursuance of the conspiracy to overthrow the Government of Hawai'i, the United States Minister and the naval representatives of the United States caused armed naval forces of the United States to invade the sovereign

Hawaiian nation on January 16, 1893, and to position themselves near the Hawaiian Government buildings and the Iolani Palace to intimidate Queen Liliuokalani and her Government;

Whereas, on the afternoon of January 17, 1893, a Committee of Safety that represented the American and European sugar planters, descendants of missionaries, and financiers deposed the Hawaiian monarchy and proclaimed the establishment of a Provisional Government;

Whereas, the United States Minister thereupon extended diplomatic recognition to the Provisional Government that was formed by the conspirators without the consent of the Native Hawaiian people or the lawful Government of Hawai'i and in violation of treaties between the two nations and of international law;

Whereas, soon thereafter, when informed of the risk of bloodshed with resistance, Queen Lili'uokalani issued the following statement yielding her authority to the United States Government rather than to the Provisional Government:

"I Lili'uokalani, by the Grace of God and under the Constitution of the Hawaiian Kingdom, Queen, do hereby solemnly protest against any and all acts done against myself and the Constitutional Government of the Hawaiian Kingdom by certain persons claiming to have established a Provisional Government of and for this Kingdom.

"That I yield to the superior force of the United States of America whose Minister Plenipotentiary, His Excellency John L. Stevens, has caused United States troops to be landed at Honolulu and declared that he would support the Provisional Government.

"Now to avoid any collision of armed forces, and perhaps the loss of life, I do this under protest and impelled by said force yield my authority until such time as the Government of the United States shall, upon facts being presented to it, undo the action of its representatives and reinstate me in the authority which I claim as the Constitutional Sovereign of the Hawaiian Islands."

Done at Honolulu this 17th day of January, A.D. 1893.;

Whereas, without the active support and intervention by the United States diplomatic and military representatives, the insurrection against the Government of Queen Lili'uokalani would have failed for lack of popular support and insufficient arms;

Whereas, on February 1, 1893, the United States Minister raised the American flag and proclaimed Hawai'i to be a protectorate of the United States;

Whereas, the report of a Presidentially established investigation conducted by former Congressman James Blount into the events surrounding the insurrection and overthrow of January 17, 1893, concluded that the United States diplomatic and military representatives had abused their authority and were responsible for the change in government;

Whereas, as a result of this investigation, the United States Minister to Hawai'i was recalled from his diplomatic post and the military commander of the United States armed forces stationed in Hawai'i was disciplined and forced to resign his commission;

Whereas, in a message to Congress on December 18, 1893, President Grover Cleveland reported fully and accurately on the illegal acts of the conspirators, described such acts as an "act of war, committed with the participation of a diplomatic representative of the United States and without authority of Congress," and acknowledged that by such acts the government of a peaceful and friendly people was overthrown;

Whereas, President Cleveland further concluded that a "substantial wrong has thus been done which a due regard for our national character as well as the rights of the injured people requires we should endeavor to repair" and called for the restoration of the Hawaiian monarchy;

Whereas, the Provisional Government protested President Cleveland's call for the restoration of the monarchy and continued to hold state power and pursue annexation to the United States;

Whereas, the Provisional Government successfully lobbied the Committee on Foreign Relations of the Senate (hereafter referred to in this Resolution as the "Committee") to conduct a new investigation into the events surrounding the overthrow of the monarchy;

Whereas, the Committee and its chairman, Senator John Morgan, conducted hearings in Washington, D.C., from December 27,1893, through February 26, 1894, in which members of the Provisional Government justified and condoned the actions of the United States Minister and recommended annexation of Hawai'i;

Whereas, although the Provisional Government was able to obscure the role of the United States in the illegal overthrow of the Hawaiian monarchy, it was unable to rally the support from two-thirds of the Senate needed to ratify a treaty of annexation;

Whereas, on July 4, 1894, the Provisional Government declared itself to be the Republic of Hawai'i;

Whereas, on January 24, 1895, while imprisoned in Iolani Palace, Queen Lili'uokalani was forced by representatives of the Republic of Hawai'i to officially abdicate her throne;

Whereas, in the 1896 United States Presidential election, William McKinley replaced Grover Cleveland;

Whereas, on July 7, 1898, as a consequence of the Spanish-American War, President McKinley signed the Newlands Joint Resolution that provided for the annexation of Hawai'i;

Whereas, through the Newlands Resolution, the self-declared Republic of Hawai'i ceded sovereignty over the Hawaiian Islands to the United States;

Whereas, the Republic of Hawai'i also ceded 1,800,000 acres of crown, government and public lands of the Kingdom of Hawai'i, without the consent of or compensation to the Native Hawaiian people of Hawai'i or their sovereign government;

Whereas, the Congress, through the Newlands Resolution, ratified the cession, annexed Hawai'i as part of the United States, and vested title to the lands in Hawai'i in the United States;

Whereas, the Newlands Resolution also specified that treaties existing between Hawai'i and foreign nations were to immediately cease and be replaced by United States treaties with such nations;

Whereas, the Newlands Resolution effected the transaction between the Republic of Hawai'i and the United States Government;

Whereas, the indigenous Hawaiian people never directly relinquished their claims to their inherent sovereignty as a people or over their national lands to the United States, either through their monarchy or through a plebiscite or referendum;

Whereas, on April 30, 1900, President McKinley signed the Organic Act that provided a government for the territory of Hawai'i and defined the political structure and powers of the newly established Territorial Government and its relationship to the United States;

Whereas, on August 21, 1959, Hawai'i became the 50th State of the United States;

Whereas, the health and well-being of the Native Hawaiian people is intrinsically tied to their deep feelings and attachment to the land;

Whereas, the long-range economic and social changes in Hawai'i over the nineteenth and early twentieth centuries have been devastating to the population and to the health and well-being of the Hawaiian people;

Whereas, the Native Hawaiian people are determined to preserve, develop and transmit to future generations their ancestral territory, and their cultural identity in accordance with their own spiritual and traditional beliefs, customs, practices, language, and social institutions;

Whereas, in order to promote racial harmony and cultural understanding, the Legislature of the State of Hawai'i has determined that the year 1993, should serve Hawai'i as a year of special reflection on the rights and dignities of the Native Hawaiians in the Hawaiian and the American societies;

Whereas, the Eighteenth General Synod of the United Church of Christ in recognition of the denomination's historical complicity in the illegal overthrow of the Kingdom of Hawai'i in 1893 directed the Office of the President of the United Church of Christ to offer a public apology to the Native Hawaiian people and to initiate the process of reconciliation between the United Church of Christ and the Native Hawaiians; and

Whereas, it is proper and timely for the Congress on the occasion of the impending 100th anniversary of the event, to acknowledge the historic significance of the illegal overthrow of the Kingdom of Hawai'i, to express its deep regret to the Native Hawaiian people, and to support the reconciliation efforts of the State of Hawai'i and the United Church of Christ with Native Hawaiians;

Now, therefore, be it

Resolved by the Senate and House of Representatives of the United States of America in Congress assembled,

Section 1. Acknowledgment and Apology.

The Congress

(1) on the occasion of the 100th anniversary of the illegal overthrow of the Kingdom of Hawai'i on January 17, 1893, acknowledges the historical significance of this event which resulted in the suppression of the inherent sovereignty of the Native Hawaiian people;

(2) recognizes and commends efforts of reconciliation initiated by the State of Hawai'i and the United Church of Christ with Native Hawaiians;

(3) apologizes to Native Hawaiians on behalf of the people of the United States for the overthrow of the Kingdom of Hawai'i on January 17, 1893 with the participation of agents and citizens of the United States, and the deprivation of the rights of Native Hawaiians to self-determination;

(4) expresses its commitment to acknowledge the ramifications of the overthrow of the Kingdom of Hawai'i, in order to provide a proper foundation for reconciliation between the United States and the Native Hawaiian people; and

(5) urges the President of the United States to also acknowledge the ramifications of the overthrow of the Kingdom of Hawai'i and to support reconciliation efforts between the United States and the Native Hawaiian people.

Sec. 2. Definitions.

As used in this Joint Resolution, the term "Native Hawaiians" means any individual who is a descendent of the aboriginal people who, prior to 1778, occupied and exercised sovereignty in the area that now constitutes the State of Hawai'i.

Sec. 3. Disclaimer.

Nothing in this Joint Resolution is intended to serve as a settlement of any claims against the United States.

—Approved November 23, 1993

LEGISLATIVE HISTORY—S.J. Res. 19

SENATE REPORTS: No. 103–125 (Select Comm. on Indian Affairs)

CONGRESSIONAL RECORD, Vol. 139 (1993):

October 27, considered and passed Senate.

November 15, considered and passed House.

31

AMY KAPLAN

Manifest Domesticity

The "cult of domesticity," the ideology of "separate spheres," and the "culture of sentiment" have together provided a productive paradigm for understanding the work of white women writers in creating a middle-class American culture in the nineteenth century. Most studies of this paradigm have revealed the permeability of the border that separates the spheres, demonstrating that the private feminized space of the home both infused and bolstered the public male arena of the market, and that the sentimental values attached to maternal influence were used to sanction women's entry into the wider civic realm from which those same values theoretically excluded them. More recently, scholars have argued that the extension of female sympathy across social divides could violently reinforce the very racial and class hierarchies that sentimentality claims to dissolve.[1]

This deconstruction of separate spheres, however, leaves another structural opposition intact: the domestic in intimate opposition to the foreign. In this context *domestic* has a double meaning that not only links the familial household to the nation but also imagines both in opposition to everything outside the geographic and conceptual border of the home. The earliest meaning of *foreign*, according to the *Oxford English Dictionary*, is "out of doors" or "at a distance from home." Contemporary English speakers refer to national concerns as domestic in explicit or implicit contrast with the foreign. The notion of domestic policy makes sense only in opposition to foreign policy, and uncoupled from the foreign, national issues are never labeled domestic. The idea of foreign policy depends on the sense of the nation as a domestic space imbued with a sense of at-homeness, in contrast to an external world perceived as alien and threatening. Reciprocally, a sense of the foreign is necessary to erect the boundaries that enclose the nation as home.

Reconceptualizing domesticity in this way might shift the cognitive geography of nineteenth-century separate spheres. When we contrast the domestic sphere with the market or political realm, men and women inhabit a divided social terrain, but when we oppose the domestic to the foreign, men and women become national allies against the alien, and the determining division is not gender but racial demarcations of otherness. Thus another part of the cultural work of domesticity might be to unite men and women in a national domain and to generate notions of the foreign against which the nation can be imagined as home. The border between the domestic and foreign, however, also deconstructs when we think of domesticity not as a static condition but as the process of domestication, which entails conquering and taming the wild, the natural, and the alien. Domestic in this sense is related to the imperial project of civilizing, and the conditions of domesticity often become markers that distinguish civilization from savagery. Through the process of domestication, the home contains within itself those wild or foreign elements that must be tamed; domesticity not only monitors the borders between the civilized and the savage but also regulates traces of the savage within itself.[2]

If domesticity plays a key role in imagining the nation as home, then women, positioned at the center of the home, play a major role in defining the contours of the nation and its shifting borders with the foreign. Those feminist critics and historians whose work has been fundamental in charting the paradigm of separate spheres, however, have for the most part overlooked the relationship of domesticity to nationalism and imperialism. Their work is worth revisiting here because their language, echoing that of their sources, inadvertently exposes these connections, which scholars have just recently begun to pursue. Jane Tompkins, for example, lauds Catharine Beecher's *Treatise on Domestic Economy* as "the prerequisite of world conquest" and claims of a later version that "the imperialistic drive behind the encyclopedism and determined practicality of this household manual . . . is a blueprint for colonizing the world in the name of the 'family state' under the leadership of Christian women."[3] As her title indicates, Mary P. Ryan's *Empire of the Mother: American Writing about Domesticity, 1830–1860* employs empire as a metaphor framing her analysis; yet she never links this pervasive imperial metaphor to the contemporaneous geopolitical movement of imperial expansion or to the discourse of Manifest Destiny. This blind spot, I believe, stems from the way that the ideology of separate spheres has shaped scholarship; until recently it has been assumed that nationalism and foreign policy lay outside the concern and participation of women. Isolating the empire of the mother from other imperial endeavors, however, runs two risks: First, it may reproduce in women's studies the insularity of an American Studies that imagines the nation as a fixed, monolithic, and self-enclosed geographic and cultural whole; second, the legacy of separate spheres that sees women as morally superior to men can lead to the current moralistic strain in feminist criticism, which has shifted from celebrating the liberatory qualities of white women's writing to condemning their racism. In this essay I try instead to understand the vexed and contradictory relations between race and domesticity as an issue not solely of individual morality nor simply internal to the nation but as structural to the institutional and discursive processes of national expansion and empire-building.[4]

My essay poses the question of how the ideology of separate spheres in antebellum America contributed to creating an American empire by imagining the nation as a home at a time when its geopolitical borders were expanding rapidly through violent confrontations with Indians, Mexicans, and European empires. Scholars have overlooked the fact that the development of domestic discourse in America is contemporaneous with the discourse of Manifest Destiny. If we juxtapose the spatial representations of these discourses, they seem to embody the most extreme form of separate spheres: The home as a bounded and rigidly ordered interior space is opposed to the boundless and undifferentiated space of an infinitely expanding nation. Yet these spatial and gendered configurations are linked in complex ways that are dependent on racialized notions of the foreign. According to the ideology of separate spheres, domesticity can be viewed as an anchor, a feminine counterforce to the male activity of territorial conquest. I argue, to the contrary, that domesticity is more mobile and less stabilizing; it travels in contradictory circuits both to expand and contract the boundaries of home and nation and to produce shifting conceptions of the foreign. This form of traveling domesticity can be analyzed in the writings of Catharine Beecher and Sara Josepha Hale, whose work, despite their ideological differences as public figures, reveals how the internal logic of domesticity relies on, abets, and reproduces the contradictions of nationalist expansion in the 1840s and 1850s. An analysis of Beecher's *A Treatise on Domestic Economy* demonstrates that the language of empire both suffuses and destabilizes the rhetoric of separate spheres, while an analysis of Hale's work uncovers the shared racial underpinnings of domestic and imperialist discourse through which the separateness of gendered spheres reinforces the effort to separate the races by turning blacks into foreigners. The essay concludes with suggestions about how understanding the imperial reach of domestic discourse might remap the way we read women's novels of the 1850s by interpreting their narratives of domesticity and female subjectivity as inseparable from narratives of empire and nation building.

Domesticity dominated middle-class women's writing and culture from the 1830s through the 1850s, a time when national boundaries were in violent flux; during this period the United States doubled its national territory, completed a campaign of Indian removal, fought its first prolonged foreign war, wrested the Spanish borderlands from Mexico, and annexed Texas, Oregon, and California. As Thomas Hietala has shown, this convulsive expansion was less a confident celebration of Manifest Destiny than a response to crises of confidence about national unity, the expansion of slavery, and the racial identity of citizenship—crises that territorial expansion exacerbated.[5] Furthermore, these movements evoked profound questions about the conceptual border between the domestic and the foreign. In the 1831 Supreme Court decision *Cherokee Nation v. the State of Georgia,* for example, Indians were declared members of "domestic dependent nations," neither foreign nationals nor United States citizens.[6] This designation makes the domestic an ambiguous third realm between the national and the foreign, as it places the foreign inside the geographic boundaries of the nation. The uneasy relation between the domestic and the foreign can also be seen in the debates over the annexation of new territory. In the middle of the Mexican War President Polk insisted that slavery was "purely a domestic question" and not a "foreign question" at all, but the expansion he advocated undermined that distinction and threatened domestic unity by raising the question of slavery's extension into previously foreign lands.[7] In debates about the annexation of Texas and later Mexico, both sides represented the new territories as women to be married to the United States; Sam Houston, for example, wrote of Texas presenting itself "to the United States as a bride adorned for her espousals"; and President Taylor accused annexationists after the Mexican War of trying to "drag California into the Union before her wedding garment has yet been cast about her person."[8] These visions of imperial expansion as marital union carried within them the specter of marriage as racial amalgamation. While popular fiction about the Mexican War portrayed brave American men rescuing and marrying Mexican women of Spanish descent, political debate over the annexation of Mexico hinged on what was agreed to be the impossibility of incorporating a foreign people marked by their racial intermixing into a domestic nation imagined as Anglo-Saxon.[9] One of the major contradictions of imperialist expansion was that while it strove to nationalize and domesticate foreign territories and peoples, annexation incorporated nonwhite foreign subjects in a way perceived to undermine the nation as a domestic space.

My point here is not to survey foreign policy but to suggest how deeply the language of domesticity suffused the debates about national expansion. Rather than stabilizing the representation of the nation as home, this rhetoric heightened the fraught and contingent nature of the boundary between the domestic and the foreign, a boundary that breaks down around questions of the racial identity of the nation as home. If we begin to rethink woman's sphere in this context, we have to ask how the discourse of domesticity negotiates the borders of an increasingly expanding empire and a divided nation. Domestic discourse both redresses and reenacts the contradictions of empire through its own double movement to expand female influence beyond the home and the nation while simultaneously contracting woman's sphere to police domestic boundaries against the threat of foreignness both within and without.

At this time of heightened national expansion, proponents of a "woman's sphere" applied the language of empire to both the home and women's emotional lives. "Hers is the empire of the affections," wrote Sarah Josepha Hale, influential editor of *Godey's Lady's Book,* who opposed the women's rights movement as "the attempt to take woman away from her empire of home."[10] To educational reformer Horace Mann, "the empire of the Home" was "the most important of all empires, the pivot of all empires and emperors."[11] Writers who counseled women to renounce politics and economics, "to leave the rude commerce of camps and the soul hardening struggling of political power to the harsher spirit of men," urged them in highly political rhetoric to take up a more spiritual calling, "the domain of the moral affections and the empire of the heart."[12] Catharine Beecher gives this calling a nationalist cast in *A Treatise on Domestic Economy* when, for example, she uses Queen Victoria as a foil to elevate the American "mother and housekeeper in a large family," who is "the sovereign of an empire demanding as varied cares, and involving more difficult duties, than are exacted of her, who wears the crown and professedly regulates the interests of the greatest nation on earth, [yet] finds abundant leisure for theaters, balls, horse races, and every gay leisure."[13] This imperial trope might be interpreted as a compensatory and defensive effort to glorify the shrunken realm of female agency, in a paradox of what Mary Ryan calls "imperial isolation," whereby the mother gains her symbolic sovereignty at the cost of withdrawal from the outside world.[14] For these writers, however, metaphor has a material efficacy in the world. The representation of the home as an empire exists in tension with the notion of woman's sphere as a contracted space because it is in the nature of empires to extend their rule over new domains while fortifying their borders against external invasion and internal insurrection. If, on the one hand, domesticity draws strict boundaries between the home and the world of men, on the other, it becomes the engine of national expansion, the site from which the nation reaches beyond itself through the emanation of woman's moral influence.

The paradox of what might be called "imperial domesticity" is that by withdrawing from direct agency in the male arena of commerce and politics, woman's sphere can be represented by both women and men as a more potent agent for national expansion. The outward reach of domesticity in turn enables the interior functioning of the home. In her introduction to *A Treatise on Domestic Economy,* Beecher inextricably links women's work at home to the unfolding of America's global mission of "exhibiting to the world the beneficent influences of Christianity, when carried into every social, civil, and political institution" (12). Women's maternal responsibility for molding the character of men and children has global repercussions: "To American women, more than to any others on earth, is committed the exalted privilege of extending over the world those blessed influences, that are to renovate degraded man, and 'clothe all climes with beauty' " (14). Beecher ends her introduction with an extended architectural metaphor in which women's agency at home is predicated on the global expansion of the nation:

> The builders of a temple are of equal importance, whether they labor on the foundations, or toil upon the dome. Thus also with those labors that are to be made effectual in the regeneration of the Earth. The woman who is rearing a family of children; the woman who labors in the schoolroom, the woman who, in her retired chamber, earns with her needle, the mite to contribute for the intellectual and moral elevation of her country; even the humble domestic, whose example and influence may be molding and forming young minds, while her faithful services sustain a prosperous domestic state;—each and all may be cheered by the consciousness that they are agents in accomplishing the greatest work that ever was committed to human responsibility. It is the building of a glorious temple, whose base shall be coextensive with the bounds of the earth, whose summit shall pierce the skies, whose splendor shall beam on all lands, and those who hew the lowliest stone, as much as those who carve the highest capital, will be equally honored when its top-stone shall be laid, with new rejoicing of the morning stars, and shoutings of the sons of God. (14)

One political effect of this metaphor is to unify women of different social classes in a shared project of construction while sustaining class hierarchy among women.[15] This image of social unity both depends on and underwrites a vision of national expansion, as women's varied labors come together to embrace the entire world. As the passage moves down the social scale, from mother to teacher to spinster, the geographic reach extends outward from home to schoolroom to country, until the "humble domestic" returns back to the "prosperous domestic state," a phrase that casts the nation in familial terms. Women's work at home here performs two interdependent forms of national labor; it forges the bonds of internal unity while impelling the nation outward to encompass the globe. This outward expansion in turn enables the internal cohesiveness of woman's separate sphere by making women agents in constructing an infinitely expanding edifice.

Beecher thus introduces her detailed manual on the regulation of the home as a highly ordered space by fusing the boundedness of the home with the boundlessness of the nation. Her 1841 introduction bears a remarkable resemblance to the rhetoric of Manifest Destiny, particularly to this passage by one of its foremost proponents, John L. O'Sullivan:

> The far-reaching, the boundless future will be the era of American greatness. In its magnificent domain of space and time, the nation of many nations is destined to manifest to mankind the excellence of divine principles; to establish on earth the

noblest temple ever dedicated to the worship of the most high—the Sacred and the True. Its floor shall be a hemisphere—its roof the firmament of the star-studded heavens, and its congregation an Union of many Republics, comprising hundreds of happy millions, calling, owning no man master, but governed by God's natural and moral law of equality.[16]

While these passages exemplify the stereotype of separate spheres (one describes work in the home and the other the work of nation building), both use a common architectural metaphor from the Bible to build a temple coextensive with the globe. O'Sullivan's grammatical subject is the American nation, which is the implied medium in Beecher's text for channeling women's work at home to a Christianized world. The construction of an edifice ordinarily entails walling off the inside from the outside, but in both these cases there is a paradoxical effect whereby the distinction between inside and outside is obliterated by the expansion of the home/nation/temple to encompass the globe. The rhetorics of Manifest Destiny and domesticity share a vocabulary that turns imperial conquest into spiritual regeneration to efface internal conflict or external resistance in visions of geopolitical domination as global harmony.

Although imperial domesticity ultimately imagines a home co-extensive with the entire world, it also continually projects a map of unregenerate outlying foreign terrain that both gives coherence to its boundaries and justifies its domesticating mission. When in 1869 Catharine Beecher revised her *Treatise* with her sister, Harriet Beecher Stowe, as *The American Woman's Home,* they downplayed the earlier role of domesticity in harmonizing class differences while enhancing domesticity's outward reach. The book ends by advocating the establishment of Christian neighborhoods settled primarily by women as a way of putting into practice domesticity's expansive potential to Christianize and Americanize immigrants both in Northeastern cities and "all over the West and South, while along the Pacific coast, China and Japan are sending their pagan millions to share our favored soil, climate, and government." No longer a leveling factor among classes within America, domesticity could be extended to those conceived of as foreign both within and beyond American national borders: "Ere long colonies from these prosperous and Christian communities would go forth to shine as 'lights of the world' in all the now darkened nations. Thus the Christian family and Christian neighborhood would become the grand ministry as they were designed to be, in training our whole race for heaven."[17] While Beecher and Stowe emphasize domesticity's service to "darkened nations," the existence of "pagans" as potential converts performs a reciprocal service in the extension of domesticity to single American women. Such Christian neighborhoods would allow unmarried women without children to leave their work in "factories, offices and shops" or their idleness in "refined leisure" to live domestic lives on their own, in some cases by adopting native children. Domesticity's imperial reach posits a way of extending woman's sphere to include not only the heathen but also the unmarried Euro-American woman who can be freed from biological reproduction to rule her own empire of the mother.

If writers about domesticity encouraged the extension of female influence outward to domesticate the foreign, their writings also evoked anxiety about the opposing trajectory that brings foreignness into the home. Analyzing the widespread colonial trope that compares colonized people to children, Ann Stoler and Karen Sánchez-Eppler have both shown how this metaphor can work not only to infantilize the colonized but also to portray white children as young savages in need of civilizing.[18] This metaphor at once extends domesticity outward to the tutelage of heathens while focusing it inward to regulate the threat of foreignness within the boundaries of the home. For Beecher, this internal savagery appears to threaten the physical health of the mother. Throughout the *Treatise*, the vision of the sovereign mother with imperial responsibilities is countered by descriptions of the ailing invalid mother. This contrast can be seen in the titles of the first two chapters, "Peculiar Responsibilities of American Women" and "Difficulties Peculiar to American Women." The latter focuses on the pervasive invalidism that makes American women physically and emotionally unequal to their global responsibilities. In contrast to the ebullient temple building of the first chapter, Beecher ends the second with a quotation from Tocqueville describing a fragile frontier home centered on a lethargic and vulnerable mother whose

> children cluster about her, full of health, turbulence and energy; they are true children of the wilderness; their mother watches them from time to time, with mingled melancholy and joy. To look at their strength, and her languor one might imagine that the life she had given them exhausted her own; and still she regrets not what they cost her. The house, inhabited by these emigrants, has no internal partition or loft. In the one chamber of which it consists, the whole family is gathered for the night. The dwelling itself is a little world; an ark of civilization amid an ocean of foliage. A hundred steps beyond it, the primeval forest spreads its shade and solitude resumes its sway. (24)

The mother's health appears drained not by the external hardships inflicted by the environment but by her intimate tie to her own "children of the wilderness," who violate the border between home and primeval forest. This boundary is partially reinforced by the image of the home as an "ark of civilization" whose internal order should protect its inhabitants from the sea of chaos that surrounds them. Yet the undifferentiated inner space, which lacks "internal partition," replicates rather than defends against the boundlessness of the wilderness. The rest of the treatise, with its detailed attention to the systematic organization of the household, works to "partition" the home in a way that distinguishes it from the external wilderness.[19]

The infirmity of American mothers is a pervasive concern throughout the *Treatise,* yet its physical cause is difficult to locate in Beecher's text. Poor health afflicts middle-class women in Northeastern cities as much as women on the frontier, according to Beecher, and she sees both cases resulting from a geographic and social mobility in which "everything is moving and changing" (16). This movement affects women's health most directly, claims Beecher, by depriving them of reliable domestic servants. With "trained" servants constantly moving up and out, middle-class women must resort to hiring "ignorant" and "poverty-stricken foreigners," with whom they are said in *American Woman's Home* to have a "missionary" relationship (332). Though Beecher does not label these foreigners as the direct cause of illness, their presence disrupts the orderly "system and regularity" of housekeeping, leading American women to be "disheartened, discouraged, and ruined in health" (18). Throughout her *Treatise* Beecher turns the absence of good servants— at first a cause of infirmity—into a remedy; their lack gives middle-class women the opportunity to perform regular domestic labor that will revive their health. By implication, their self-regulated work will also keep "poverty-stricken foreigners" out of their homes. Curiously, then, the mother's ill health stems from the unruly subjects of her domestic empire—children and servants—who bring uncivilized wilderness and undomesticated foreignness into the home. The fear of disease and of the invalidism that characterizes the American woman also serves as a metaphor for anxiety about foreignness within. The mother's domestic empire is at risk of contagion from the very subjects she must domesticate and civilize, her wilderness children and foreign servants, who ultimately infect both the home and the body of the mother.[20]

This reading of Beecher suggests new ways of understanding the intricate means by which domestic discourse generates and relies on images of the foreign. On the one hand, domesticity's "habits of system and order" appear to anchor the home as a stable center in a fluctuating social world with expanding national borders; on the other, domesticity must be spatially and conceptually mobile to travel to the nation's far-flung frontiers. Beecher's use of Tocqueville's ark metaphor suggests both the rootlessness and the self-enclosed mobility necessary for middle-class domesticity to redefine the meaning of habitation to make Euro-Americans feel at home in terrain in which *they* are initially the foreigners. Domesticity inverts this relationship to create a home by rendering prior inhabitants alien and undomesticated and by implicitly nativizing newcomers. The empire of the mother thus shares the logic of the American empire; both follow a double compulsion to conquer and domesticate the foreign, thus incorporating and controlling a threatening foreignness within the borders of the home and the nation.

The imperial scope of domesticity was central to the work of Sarah Josepha Hale throughout her half-century editorship of the influential *Godey's Lady's Book,* as well as to her fiction and history writing. Hale has been viewed by some scholars as advocating a woman's sphere more thoroughly separate from male political concerns than Beecher did.[21] This withdrawal seems confirmed by the refusal of *Godey's* even to mention the Civil War throughout its duration, much less take sides. Yet when Hale conflates the progress of women with the nation's Manifest Destiny in her history writing, other scholars have judged her as inconsistently moving out of woman's sphere into the male political realm.[22] Hale's conception of separate spheres, I will argue, is predicated on the imperial expansion of the nation. Although her writing as editor, essayist, and novelist focused on the interior spaces of the home, with ample advice on housekeeping, clothing, manners, and emotions, she gave equal and related attention to the expansion of female influence through her advocacy of female medical missionaries abroad and the colonization of Africa by former black slaves. Even though Hale seems to avoid the issue of slavery and race relations in her silence about the Civil War, in the 1850s her conception of domesticity takes on a decidedly racial cast, exposing the intimate link between the separateness of gendered spheres and the effort to keep the races apart in separate national spheres.

In 1846, at the beginning of the Mexican War, Hale launched a campaign on the pages of *Godey's Lady's Book* to declare Thanksgiving Day a national holiday, a campaign she avidly pursued until Lincoln made the holiday official in 1863.[23] This effort typified the way in which Hale's map of woman's sphere overlaid national and domestic spaces; *Godey's* published detailed instructions and recipes for preparing the Thanksgiving feast, while it encouraged women readers to agitate for a nationwide holiday as a ritual of national expansion and unification. The power of Thanksgiving Day stemmed from its center in the domestic sphere; Hale imagined millions of families seated around the holiday table at the same time, thereby unifying the vast and shifting space of the national domain through simultaneity in time. This domestic ritual, she wrote in 1852, would unite "our great nation, by its states and families from the St. John to the Rio Grande, from the Atlantic to the Pacific."[24] If the celebration of Thanksgiving unites individual families across regions and brings them together in an imagined collective space, Thanksgiving's continental scope endows each individual family gathering with national meaning. Furthermore, the Thanksgiving story commemorating the founding of New England—which in Hale's version makes no mention of Indians—could create a common history by nationalizing a regional myth of origins and imposing it on the territories most recently wrested from Indians and Mexicans. Hale's campaign to transform Thanksgiving from a regional to a national holiday grew even fiercer with the approach of the Civil War. In 1859 she wrote, "If every state would join in Union Thanksgiving on the 24th of this month, would it not be a renewed pledge of love and loyalty to the Constitution of the United States?"[25] Thanksgiving Day, she hoped, could avert civil war. As a national holiday celebrated primarily in the home, Thanksgiving traverses broad geographic circuits to write a national history of origins, to colonize the western territories, and to unite North and South.

The domestic ritual of Thanksgiving could expand and unify national borders only by also fortifying those borders against foreignness; for Hale, the nation's borders not only defined its geographical limits but also set apart nonwhites within the national domain. In Hale's fiction of the 1850s, Thanksgiving polices the domestic sphere by making black people, both free and enslaved, foreign to the domestic nation and denying them a home within America's expanding borders. In 1852 Hale reissued her novel *Northwood,* which had launched her career in 1827, with a highly publicized chapter about a New Hampshire Thanksgiving dinner showcasing the values of the American republic to a skeptical British visitor. For the 1852 version Hale changed the subtitle from "A Tale of New England" to "Life North and South" to highlight the new material on slavery she had added.[26] Pro-Union yet against abolition, Hale advocated African colonization as the only means of preserving domestic unity by sending all blacks to settle in Africa and Christianize its inhabitants. Colonization in the 1850s had a two-pronged ideology, both to expel blacks to a separate national sphere and to expand U.S. power through the civilizing process; black Christian settlers would thereby become both outcasts from and agents for the American empire.[27]

Hale's 1852 *Northwood* ends with an appeal to use Thanksgiving Day as an occasion to collect money at all American churches "for the purpose of educating and colonizing free people of color and emancipated slaves" (408). This annual collection would contribute to "peaceful emancipation" as "every obstacle to the real freedom of America would be melted before the gushing streams of sympathy and charity" (408). While "sympathy," a sentiment associated with woman's sphere, seems to extend to black slaves, the goal of sympathy in this passage is not to free them but to emancipate white America from their presence. Thanksgiving for Hale thus celebrates national coherence around the domestic sphere while simultaneously rendering blacks within America foreign to the nation.

For Hale, colonization would not simply expel black people from American nationality but would also transform American slavery into a civilizing and domesticating mission. One of her Northern characters explains to the British visitor that "the destiny of America is to instruct the world, which we shall do, with the aid of our Anglo-Saxon brothers over the water. . . . Great Britain has enough to do at home and in the East Indies to last her another century. We have this country and Africa to settle and civilize" (167). When his listener is puzzled by the reference to Africa, he explains, "That is the greatest mission of our Republic, to train here the black man for his duties as a Christian, then free him and send him to Africa, there to plant Free States and organize Christian civilization" (168). The colonization of Africa becomes the goal of slavery by making it part of the civilizing mission of global imperialism. Colonization thus not only banishes blacks from the domestic union but, as the final sentence of *Northwood* proclaims, it proves that "the mission of American slavery is to Christianize Africa" (408).

In 1852 Hale published the novel *Liberia,* which begins where *Northwood* ends, with the settlement of Liberia by freed black slaves.[28] Seen by scholars as a retort to *Uncle Tom's Cabin, Liberia* can also be read as the untold story of Stowe's novel, beginning where she ends, with former black slaves immigrating to Africa.[29] Although the subtitle, "Mr. Peyton's Experiment," places colonization under the aegis of white males, the narrative turns colonization into a project emanating from woman's sphere in at least two directions. In its outward trajectory, the settlement of Liberia appears as an expansion of feminized domestic values. Yet domesticity is not only exported to civilize native Africans; the framing of the novel also makes African colonization necessary to the establishment of domesticity within America as exclusively white. While Hale writes that the purpose of the novel is to "show the advantages Liberia offers to the African," in so doing it construes all black people as foreign to American nationality by asserting that they must remain homeless within the United States. At the same time, Hale paints a picture of American imperialism as the embodiment of the feminine values of domesticity: "What other nation can point to a colony planted from such pure motives of charity; nurtured by the counsels and exertions of its most noble and self-denying statesmen and philanthropists; and sustained, from its feeble commencement up to a period of self-reliance and independence, from pure love of justice and humanity" (iv). In this passage America is figured as a mother raising her baby, Africa, to maturity; the vocabulary of "purity," "charity," "self-denial," and "love" represents colonization as an expansion of the values of woman's separate sphere.

The narrative opens with a threat to American domesticity on two fronts. The last male of a distinguished Virginia family is on his deathbed, helpless to defend his plantation from a rumored slave insurrection; the women of the family, led by his wife, "Virginia," rally with the loyal slaves to defend their home from an insurrection that never occurs. Thus the novel opens with separate spheres gone awry, with the man of the family abed at home and white women and black slaves acting as protectors and soldiers. While the ensuing plot to settle Liberia overtly rewards those slaves for their loyalty by giving them freedom and a homeland, it also serves to reinstate separate spheres and reestablish American domesticity as white.

When the narrative shifts to Africa, colonization has the effect not only of driving black slaves out of American nationhood but also of Americanizing Africa through domesticity. A key figure in the settlement is the slave Keziah, who has nursed the white plantation owners. She is the most responsive to Peyton's proposal for colonization because of her desire both to be free and to Christianize the natives. Her future husband, Polydore, more recently arrived from Africa and thus less "civilized," is afraid to return there because of his memory of native brutality and superstition. This couple represents two faces of enslaved Africans central to the white imagination of colonization: the degenerate heathen represented by the man and the redeemed Christian represented by the woman. Keziah, however, can only become a fully domesticated woman at a geographic remove from American domesticity. When Keziah protects the plantation in Virginia, her maternal impulse is described as that of a wild animal—a "fierce lioness." Only in Africa can she become the domestic center of the new settlement, where she establishes a home that resembles Beecher's Christian neighborhood. Keziah builds a private home with fence and garden, and civilizes her husband while expanding her domestic sphere to adopt native children and open a Christian school.

Keziah's domestication of herself and her surroundings in Africa can be seen as a part of the movement in the novel noted by Susan Ryan, in which the freed black characters are represented as recognizably American only at the safe distance of Africa.[30] Once banished from the domestic sphere of the American nation, they can reproduce themselves for readers as Americans in a foreign terrain. The novel not only narrates the founding of Liberia as a story of colonization, but Hale's storytelling also colonizes Liberia as an imitation of America, replete with images of an open frontier, the *Mayflower,* and the planting of the American flag. A double narrative movement at once contracts American borders to exclude blacks from domestic space and simultaneously expands U.S. borders by re-creating that domestic space in Africa. The novel thus ends with a quotation that compares the Liberian settlers to the Pilgrims and represents them as part of a global expansion of the American nation:

> I do not doubt but that the whole continent of Africa will be regenerated, and I believe the Republic of Liberia will be the great instrument, in the hands of God, in working out this regeneration. The colony of Liberia has succeeded better than the colony of Plymouth did for the same period of time. And yet, in that little company which was wafted across the mighty ocean in the *May Flower,* we see the germs of this already colossal nation, whose feet are in the tropics, while her head reposes upon the snows of Canada. Her right hand she stretches over the Atlantic, feeding the millions of the Old World, and beckoning them to her shores, as a refuge from famine and oppression; and, at the same time, she stretches forth her left hand to the islands of the Pacific, and to the old empires of the East. (303)

African slaves are brought to America to become Christianized and domesticated, but they cannot complete this potential transformation until they return to Africa.

Hale's writing makes race central to woman's sphere not only by excluding non-whites from domestic nationalism but also by seeing the capacity for domesticity as an innate, defining characteristic of the Anglo-Saxon race. Reginald Horsman has shown how by the 1840s the meaning of Anglo-Saxonism in political thought had shifted from a historical understanding of the development of republican institutions to an essentialist definition of a single race that possesses an innate and unique capacity for self-government.[31] His analysis, however, limits this racial formation to the male sphere of politics. Hale's *Woman's Record* (1853), a massive compendium of the history of women from Eve to the present, establishes woman's sphere as central to the racial discourse of Anglo-Saxonism; to her, the empire of the mother spawns the Anglo-Saxon nation and propels its natural inclination toward global power.[32] In her introduction to the fourth part of her volume on the present era, Hale represents America as manifesting the universal progress of women that culminates in the Anglo-Saxon race. To explain the Anglo-Saxon "mastery of the mind over Europe and Asia," she argues that

> if we trace out the causes of this superiority, they would center in the moral influence, which true religion confers on the female sex. . . . There is still a more wonderful example of this uplifting power of the educated female mind. It is only seventy-five years since the Anglo-Saxons in the New World became a nation, then numbering about three million souls. Now this people form the great American republic, with a population of twenty three millions; and the destiny of the world will soon be in their keeping! Religion is free; and the soul which woman always influences where God is worshipped in spirit and truth, is untrammeled by code, or creed, or caste. . . . The result before the world—a miracle of advancement, American mothers train their sons to be men. (564)

Hale here articulates the imperial logic of what has been called "republican motherhood," which ultimately posits the expansion of maternal influence beyond the nation's borders.[33] The Manifest Destiny of the nation unfolds logically from the imperial reach of woman's influence emanating from her separate domestic sphere. Domesticity makes manifest the destiny of the Anglo-Saxon race, while Manifest Destiny becomes in turn the condition for Anglo-Saxon domesticity. For Hale domesticity has two effects on national expansion: It imagines the nation as a home delimited by race and propels the nation outward through the imperial reach of female influence.

Advocating domesticity's expansive mode, *Woman's Record* includes only those nonwhite women whom Hale understood to be contributing to the spread of Christianity to colonized peoples. In the third volume, Hale designates as the most distinguished woman from 1500 to 1830 a white American missionary to Burma, Ann Judson (152). The Fourth Era of *Woman's Record* focuses predominantly on American women as the apex of historical development. In contrast to the aristocratic accomplishments of English women, "in all that contributes to popular education and pure religious sentiment among the masses, the women of America are in advance of all others on the globe. To prove this we need only examine the list of American female missionaries, teachers, editors and authors of works instructive and educational, contained in this 'Record'" (564). While Anglo-Saxon men marched outward to conquer new lands, women had a complementary outward reach from within the domestic sphere.

For Hale, African colonization can be seen as part of the broader global expansion of woman's sphere. In 1853 Hale printed in *Godey's Lady's Book* "An Appeal to the American Christians on Behalf of the Ladies' Medical Missionary Society," in which she argued for the special need for women physicians abroad because they would have unique access to foreign women's bodies and souls.[34] Her argument for the training of female medical missionaries both enlarges the field of white women's agency and feminizes the force of imperial power. She sees female medical missionaries as not only curing disease but also raising the status of women abroad: "All heathen people have a high reverence for medical knowledge. Should they find Christian ladies accomplished in this science, would it not greatly raise the sex in the estimation of those nations, where one of the most serious impediments to moral improvement is the degradation and ignorance to which their females have been for centuries consigned?" (185). Though superior to heathen women in status, American women would accomplish their goal by imagining gender as a common ground, which would give them special access to women abroad. As women they could be more effective imperialists, penetrating those interior feminine colonial spaces, symbolized by the harem, that remain inaccessible to male missionaries:

> Vaccination is difficult of introduction among the people of the east, though suffering dreadfully from the ravages of small-pox. The American mission at Siam writes that thousands of children were, last year, swept away by this disease in the country around them. Female physicians could win their way among these poor children much easier than doctors of the other sex. Surely the ability of American women to learn and practice vaccination will not be questioned, when the more difficult art of inoculation was discovered by the women of Turkey, and introduced into Europe by an English woman! Inoculation is one of the greatest triumphs of remedial skill over a sure loathsome and deadly disease which the annals of Medical Art record. Its discovery belongs to women. I name it here to show that they are gifted with genius for the profession, and only need to be educated to excel in the preventive department.
>
> Let pious, intelligent women be fitly prepared, and what a mission-field for doing good would be opened! In India, China, Turkey, and all over the heathen world, they

would, in their character of physicians, find access to the homes and harems where women dwell, and where the good seed sown would bear an hundredfold, because it would take root in the bosom of the sufferer, and in the heart of childhood. (185)

In this passage the connections among women circulate in many directions, but Hale charts a kind of evolutionary narrative that places American women at the apex of development. Though inoculation was discovered by Turkish women, it can only return to Turkey to save Turkish children through the agency of English women transporting knowledge to Americans, who can then go to Turkey as missionaries and save women who cannot save themselves or their children. While Hale is advocating that unmarried women be trained as missionaries, the needs of heathen women allow female missionaries to conquer their own domestic empire without reproducing biologically. Instead, American women are metaphorically cast as men in a cross-racial union, as they sow seeds in the bosom of heathen women who will bear Christian children. Through the sentiment of female influence, women physicians will transform heathen harems into Christian homes.

My reading of Hale suggests that the concept of female influence so central to domestic discourse and at the heart of the sentimental ethos is underwritten by and abets the imperial expansion of the nation. While the empire of the mother advocated retreat from the world-conquering enterprises of men, this renunciation promised a more thorough kind of world conquest. The empire of the mother shared with the American empire a logical structure and a key contradiction: Both sought to encompass the world outside their borders; yet this same outward movement contributed to and relied on the contraction of the domestic sphere to exclude persons conceived of as racially foreign within those expanding national boundaries.

Understanding the imperial reach of domesticity and its relation to the foreign should help remap the critical terrain on which women's domestic fiction has been constructed. We can chart the broader international and national contexts in which unfold narratives of female development that at first glance seem anchored in local domestic spaces. We can see how such narratives imagine domestic locations in complex negotiation with the foreign. To take a few well-known examples from the 1850s, Susan Warner's *The Wide Wide World* sends its heroine to Scotland, while the world of Maria Cummins's *The Lamplighter* encompasses India, Cuba, the American West, and Brazil. In E.D.E.N. Southworth's *The Hidden Hand,* the resolution of multiple domestic plots in Virginia relies on the participation of the male characters in the Mexican War, while the geographic coordinates of *Uncle Tom's Cabin* extend not only to Africa at the end but also to Haiti and Canada throughout.[35] Such a remapping would involve more than just seeing the geographic settings anew; it would turn inward to the privileged space of the domestic novel—the interiority of the female subject—to find traces of foreignness that must be domesticated or expunged. How does this struggle with foreignness within "woman's sphere" shape the interiority of female subjectivity, the empire of the affections and the heart? While critics such as Gillian Brown, Richard Brodhead, and Nancy Armstrong have taught us how domestic novels represent women as model bourgeois subjects,[36] my remapping would explore how domestic novels produce the racialized national subjectivity of the white middle-class woman in contested international spaces.

Many domestic novels open at physical thresholds, such as windows or doorways, that problematize the relation between interior and exterior; the home and the female self appear fragile and threatened from within and without by foreign forces. These novels then explore the breakdown of the boundaries between internal and external spaces, between the domestic and the foreign, as they struggle to renegotiate and stabilize these domains. This negotiation often takes place not only within the home but also within the heroine. The narrative of female self-discipline that is so central to the domestic novel might be viewed as a kind of civilizing process in which the woman plays the role of both civilizer and savage. Gerty in *The Lamplighter*, for example, like Capitola in *The Hidden Hand*, first appears as an uncivilized street urchin, a heathen unaware of Christianity whose anger is viewed as a "dark infirmity" and whose unruly nature is in need of domesticating. We later learn that she was born in Brazil to the daughter of a ship captain, who was killed by malaria, the "inhospitable southern disease, which takes the stranger for its victim."[37] To become the sovereign mother of her own domestic empire, Gerty must become her own first colonial subject and purge herself of both her origin in a diseased uncivilized terrain and the female anger identified with that "dark" realm. This split between the colonizer and the colonized, seen here within one female character, appears in *Uncle Tom's Cabin* racially externalized onto Eva and Topsy.[38]

My point is that where the domestic novel appears most turned inward to the private sphere of female interiority, we often find subjectivity scripted by narratives of nation and empire. Even at the heart of *The Wide, Wide World*, a novel usually understood as thoroughly closeted in interior space, where the heroine disciplines herself through reading and prayer, her favorite book is the popular biography of George Washington, the father of the nation. Her own journey to live with her Scottish relatives can be seen as a feminized reenactment of the American revolution against the British empire. Similarly, in *The Hidden Hand*, the most inner recess of woman's sphere is conjoined with the male sphere of imperial conquest. While the American men in the novel are invading Mexico, in Virginia, a bandit, significantly named "Black Donald," invades the heroine's chamber and threatens to rape her. To protect the sanctity of her home and her own chastity, Capitola performs a founding national narrative of conquest. She drops the rapist through a trap door in her bedroom into a deep pit dug by the original owner to trick the Indian inhabitants into selling their land. The domestic heroine thus reenacts the originating gesture of imperial appropriation to protect the borders of her domestic empire and the inviolability of the female self.

Feminist criticism of *Uncle Tom's Cabin* has firmly established that the empire of the mother in Stowe's novel extends beyond the home to the national arena of antislavery politics. This expansive movement of female influence, I have been arguing, has an international dimension that helps separate gendered spheres coalesce in the imperial expansion of the nation by redrawing domestic borders against the foreign. In light of my reading of Hale's *Liberia,* we might remap the critical terrain of Stowe's novel to ask how its delineation of domestic space, as both familial and national, relies on and propels the colonization of Africa by the novel's free black characters. Rather than just focusing on their expulsion at the end of the novel, we might locate, in Toni Morrison's terms, the "Africanist presence" throughout the text.[39] Africa appears as both an imperial outpost and a natural embodiment of woman's sphere, a kind of feminized utopia, that is strategically posed as an alternative to Haiti, which hovers as a menacing image of black revolutionary agency. The idea of African colonization does not simply emerge at the end as a racist failure of Stowe's political imagination; rather, colonization underwrites the racial politics of the domestic imagination. The "Africanist presence" throughout *Uncle Tom's Cabin* is intimately bound to the expansionist logic of domesticity itself. In the writing of Stowe and her contemporary proponents of woman's sphere, "Manifest Domesticity" turns an imperial nation into a home by producing and colonizing specters of the foreign that lurk inside and outside its ever shifting borders.

ACKNOWLEDGMENTS

I wish to thank the organizers of the conference "Nineteenth-Century American Women Writers in the Twenty-first Century" (Hartford, Conn., May 1996) for inviting me to present my first formulation of the ideas in this essay. Special thanks to Susan Gillman, Carla Kaplan, Dana D. Nelson, and Priscilla Wald for their helpful and encouraging readings at crucial stages.

NOTES

1 Influential studies of this paradigm by historians and literary critics include Barbara Welter, "The Cult of True Womanhood: 1820–1860," *American Quarterly* 18 (summer 1966): 151–74; Kathryn Kish Sklar, *Catharine Beecher: A Study in American Domesticity* (New Haven, Conn.: Yale University Press, 1973); Nancy Cott, *The Bonds of Womanhood: "Woman's Sphere" in New England, 1780–1835* (New Haven, Conn.: Yale University Press, 1977); Ann Douglas, *The Feminization of American Culture* (New York: Knopf, 1977); Nina Baym, *Woman's Fiction: A Guide to Novels by and about Women in America, 1820–1870* (Ithaca, N.Y.: Cornell University Press, 1978); Mary P. Ryan, *Cradle of the Middle Class: The Family in Oneida County, New York, 1790–1865* (Cambridge: Cambridge University Press, 1981), and *Empire of the Mother: American Writing about Domesticity, 1830–1860* (New York: Institute for Research in History and Haworth Press, 1982); Mary Kelley, *Private Woman, Public Stage: Literary Domesticity in Nineteenth-Century America* (New York: Oxford University Press, 1984); Jane Tompkins, *Sensational Designs: The Cultural Work of American Fiction, 1790–1860* (New York: Oxford University Press, 1985); Gillian Brown, *Domestic Individualism: Imagining Self in Nineteenth-Century America* (Berkeley and Los Angeles: University of California Press, 1990); and the essays in *The Culture of Sentiment: Race, Gender, and Sentimentality in Nineteenth-Century America*, ed. Shirley Samuels (New York: Oxford University Press, 1992). See also the useful review essay by Linda K. Kerber, "Separate Spheres, Female Worlds, Woman's Place: The Rhetoric of Women's History," *Journal of American History* (June 1988): 9–39.

2 On the etymology of the word *domestic* and its relation to colonialism, see Karen Hansen, ed., *African Encounters with Domesticity* (New Brunswick, N.J.: Rutgers University Press, 1992), 2–23; and Anne McClintock, *Imperial Leather: Race, Gender, and Sexuality in the Colonial Conquest* (New York: Routledge, 1995), 31–36. On the uses of domesticity in the colonial context, see Vicente L. Rafael, "Colonial Domesticity: White Women and United States Rule in the Philippines," *American Literature* 67 (Dec. 1995): 639–66.

3 Tompkins, *Sensational Designs*, 143, 144. Despite Tompkins's well-known debate with Ann Douglas, both critics rely on imperial rhetoric. While Tompkins applauds the imperialist impulse of sentimentalism, Douglas derides sentimental writers for a rapacious reach that extends as far as the "colonization of heaven" and the "domestication of death" (240–72).

4 Even recent revisionist studies that situate woman's sphere in relation to racial and class hierarchies often overlook the international context in which these divisions evolve. In the important essays in *Culture of Sentiment*, for example, many of the racialized configurations of domesticity under discussion rely on a foreign or imperial dimension that remains unanalyzed. To take a few examples, Laura Wexler's analysis of Hampton Institute makes no mention of its founding by influential missionaries to Hawaii ("Tender Violence: Literary Eavesdropping, Domestic Fiction, and Educational Reform," 9–38); Karen Halttunen's analysis of a murder trial revolves around the uncertain identity of a white woman's foreign Spanish or Cuban lover ("'Domestic Differences': Competing Narratives of Womanhood in the Murder Trial of Lucretia Chapman," 39–57); Lynn Wardley ties domesticity's obsession with detail to West African fetishism ("Relic, Fetish, Femmage: The Aesthetics of Sentiment in the Work of Stowe," 203–20). Several essays note comparisons of slavery to the oriental harem, including Carolyn Karcher on Lydia Maria Child's antislavery fiction ("Rape, Murder, and Revenge in Slavery's Pleasant Homes: Lydia Maria Child's Antislavery Fiction and the Limits of Genre," 58–72) and Joy Kasson's analysis of Hirams's *The Greek Slave* ("Narratives of the Female Body: *The Greek Slave*," 172–90). The only essay to treat the imperial dimensions of domesticity is Lora Romero's "Vanishing Americans: Gender, Empire, and New Historicism" (115–27).

5 Thomas R. Hietala, *Manifest Design: Anxious Aggrandizement in Late Jacksonian America* (Ithaca, N.Y.: Cornell University Press, 1985).

6 *Cherokee Nation v. the State of Georgia*, in *Major Problems in American Foreign Policy: Documents and Essays*, ed. Thomas G. Paterson, 2 vols. (Lexington, Mass.: Heath, 1989), 1:202.

7 Quoted in Walter La Feber, *The American Age: United States Foreign Policy at Home and Abroad* (New York: Norton, 1989), 112.

8 Quoted in George B. Forgie, *Patricide in the House Divided: A Psychological Interpretation of Lincoln and His Age* (New York: Norton, 1979), 107–8.

9 On popular fiction of the Mexican War, see Robert W. Johannsen, *To the Halls of the Montezumas: The Mexican War in the American Imagination* (New York: Oxford University Press, 1984), 175–204.

10 Sarah Josepha Hale, "Editor's Table," *Godey's Lady's Book,* January 1852, 88.

11 Quoted in Ryan, *Empire of the Mother,* 112.

12 From "The Social Condition of Woman," *North American Review,* April 1836, 513; quoted in Annette Kolodny, *The Land before Her: Fantasy and Experience of the American Frontiers, 1630–1860* (Chapel Hill: University of North Carolina Press, 1984), 166.

13 Catharine Beecher, *A Treatise on Domestic Economy* (Boston: Marsh, Capen, Lyon, and Webb, 1841), 144. Subsequent references to this work are cited parenthetically in the text.

14 Ryan, *Empire of the Mother,* 97–114.

15 Kathryn Kish Sklar is one of the few scholars to consider Beecher's domestic ideology in relation to nation building. She analyzes the *Treatise* as appealing to gender as a common national denominator, and as using domesticity as a means to promote national unity to counterbalance mobility and conflicts based on class and region. Sklar fails to see, however, that this vision of gender as a tool for national unity is predicated on the nation's imperial role *(Catharine Beecher)*. Jenine Abboushi Dallal analyzes the imperial dimensions of Beecher's domestic ideology by contrasting it with the domestic rhetoric of Melville's imperial adventure narratives in "The Beauty of Imperialism: Emerson, Melville, Flaubert, and Al-Shidyac" (Ph.D. diss., Harvard University, 1996), chap. 2.

16 John L. O'Sullivan, "The Great Nation of Futurity," in *Major Problems in American Foreign Policy,* ed. Thomas G. Paterson, 1: 241.

17 Catharine Beecher and Harriet Beecher Stowe, *The American Woman's Home* (Hartford, Conn.: J. B. Ford, 1869), 458–59.

18 Karen Sánchez-Eppler, "Raising Empires like Children: Race, Nation, and Religious Education," *American Literary History* 8 (fall 1996): 399–425; Ann Stoler, *Race and the Education of Desire: Foucault's "History of Sexuality" and the Colonial Order of Things* (Durham, N.C.: Duke University Press, 1995), 137–64.

19 Although the cleanliness and orderliness of the home promise to make American women healthier, Beecher also blames a lack of outdoor exercise for American women's frailty, suggesting that the problematic space outside the home—the foreign—can both cause and cure those "difficulties peculiar to American women."

20 This generalized anxiety about contamination of the domestic sphere by children may stem from the circulation of stories by missionaries who expressed fear of their children being raised by native servants or too closely identifying with native culture. Such stories circulated both in popular mission tracts and in middle-class women's magazines, such as *Godey's* and *Mother's Magazine;* see, for example, Stoler, *Race and the Education of Desire;* and Patricia Grimshaw, *Paths of Duty: American Missionary Wives in Nineteenth-Century Hawaii* (Honolulu: University of Hawaii Press, 1989), 154–78. The licentiousness of men was also seen as a threat to women's health within the home. For example, in "Life on the Rio Grande" (*Godey's Lady's Book,* April 1847), a piece celebrating the opening of public schools in Galveston, Texas, Sarah Josepha Hale quotes a military officer who warns that "liberty is ever degenerating into license, and man is prone to abandon his sentiments and follow his passions. It is woman's high mission, her prerogative and duty, to counsel, to sustain—as to control him" (177). On the borderlands, women have the role of civilizing savagery in their own homes, where men's passions appear as the foreign force to be colonized.

    In general, domesticity is seen as an ideology that develops in middle-class urban centers (and, as Sklar shows, in contrast to European values) and is then exported to the frontier and empire, where it meets challenges and must adapt. It remains to be studied how domestic discourse might develop out of the confrontation with foreign cultures in what has been called the "contact zone" of frontier and empire.

21 Sklar, *Catharine Beecher,* 163; Douglas, *Feminization of American Culture,* 51–54.

22 Nina Baym, "Onward Christian Women: Sarah J. Hale's History of the World," *New England Quarterly* 63 (June 1990): 249–70.

23 Sarah J. Hale, "Editor's Table," *Godey's Lady's Book,* January 1847, 53.

24 Sarah J. Hale, *Godey's Lady's Book,* November 1852, 303.

25 Ruth E. Finley, *The Lady of Godey's, Sarah Josepha Hale* (Philadelphia: Lippincott, 1931), 199.

26 Sarah J. Hale, *Northwood; or, Life North and South: Showing the True Character of Both* (New York: H. Long and Brother, 1852). See Hale's 1852 preface, "A Word with the Reader," on revisions of the 1827 edition. Further references to *Northwood* will be cited parenthetically in the text.

27 On the white ideological framework of African colonization, see George Fredrickson, *The Black Image in the White Mind: The Debate on Afro-American Character and Destiny, 1817–1914* (New York: Harper and Row, 1971), 6–22, 110–17; Susan M. Ryan, "Errand into Africa: Colonization and Nation Building in Sarah J. Hale's *Liberia,*" *New England Quarterly* 68 (Dec. 1995): 558–83.

28 Sarah J. Hale, *Liberia; or Mr. Peyton's Experiment* ([1853] Upper Saddle River, N.J.: Gregg Press, 1968).

29 On *Liberia* as a conservative rebuff to Stowe, see Thomas F. Gossett, *"Uncle Tom's Cabin" and American Culture* (Dallas, Tex.: Southern Methodist University Press, 1985), 235–36.

30 Ryan, "Errand into Africa," 572.

31 Reginald Horsman, *Race and Manifest Destiny: The Origins of American Racial Anglo-Saxonism* (Cambridge: Harvard University Press, 1981), 62–81.

32 Sarah J. Hale, *Woman's Record* (New York: Harper and Brothers, 1853).

33 Linda K. Kerber, *Women of the Republic: Intellect and Ideology in Revolutionary America* (Chapel Hill: University of North Carolina Press, 1980).

34 Sarah J. Hale, "An Appeal to the American Christians on Behalf of the Ladies' Medical Missionary Society," *Godey's Lady's Book,* March 1852, 185–88.

35 Susan Warner, *The Wide Wide World* ([1850] New York: Feminist Press, 1987); Maria Susanna Cummins, *The Lamplighter* ([1854] New Brunswick, N.J.: Rutgers University Press, 1988); E.D.E.N. Southworth, *The Hidden Hand; or, Capitola the Madcap* ([1859] New Brunswick, N.J.: Rutgers University Press, 1988); Harriet Beecher Stowe, *Uncle Tom's Cabin* ([1852] New York: Viking Penguin, 1981).

36 Nancy Armstrong, *Desire and Domestic Fiction: A Political History of the Novel* (New York: Oxford University Press, 1987); Brown, *Domestic Individualism;* Richard Brodhead, "Sparing the Rod: Discipline and Fiction in Antebellum America," in *The New American Studies: Essays from "Representations,"* ed. Philip Fisher (Berkeley and Los Angeles: University of California Press, 1991).

37 Cummins, *The Lamplighter,* 63, 321. On the male characters' involvement in imperial enterprises in India in *The Lamplighter,* see Susan Castellanos, "Masculine Sentimentalism and the Project of Nation-Building" (paper presented at the conference "Nineteenth-Century Women Writers in the Twenty-first Century," Hartford, Conn., May 1996).

38 On this split, see Elizabeth Young, "Topsy-Turvy: Civil War and *Uncle Tom's Cabin,*" chap. 1 of *Disarming the Nation: Women's Writing and the American Civil War* (Chicago: University of Chicago Press, 1999).

39 Toni Morrison, *Playing in the Dark: Whiteness and the Literary Imagination* (Cambridge: Harvard University Press, 1992), 6.

32

PAL AHLUWALIA

When Does a Settler Become a Native?

Citizenship and Identity in a Settler Society

Settlers are made by conquest, not just immigration. Settlers are kept by a form of the state that makes a distinction—particularly juridical—between conquerors and conquered, settlers and natives, and makes it the basis of other distinctions that tend to buttress the conquerors and isolate the conquered, politically. However fictitious these distinctions may appear historically, they become real political facts for they are embodied in real political institutions. —Mahmood Mamdani

. . . today we take pride in an identity . . . open to all, whatever their colour, religion or ethnic background. We celebrate our diversity, we recognise it brings us strength and teaches us a patriotism that enriches and unites our nation rather than divides it. —Tony Blair

As Australia embarks upon another new century, it is once again enveloped by the very concerns of identity and national character which were its focus at the turn of the twentieth century. At the time of its founding, Australia as a settler colony inevitably looked towards its imperial master to provide its defining characteristics. Currently, Australians are attempting to come to terms with their post-colonial identity. Central to this task are notions of citizenship and subjectivity. In the lead up to the fiftieth anniversary of Australian citizenship in 1999, there were renewed calls to make citizenship a meaningful and important part of Australian political life. There were recommendations to deny access to certain rights to non-citizens (Fitzgerald, 1988). In addition, there was and remains a growing sense of Australian nationalism which has resulted in the demand for the promulgation of a Republic. The desire to break away from Britain formally, however, is not simply an assertion of Australian nationalism but a crisis of citizenship, culturally and politically, which has arisen from a multicultural society that even its architects had not envisioned. In short, this is a crisis similar to that which Stuart Hall (1992) termed 'a contestation over what it means to be British.' The contestation over what it means to be Australian is a result of the exclusionary practices and minimalist notions of citizenship which have operated in Australia. The exclusion of Aboriginal people, women, people of colour, gay people and recent migrants has rendered a crisis of citizenship which remains entrapped within certain white settler notions of identity in which 'others' can only be constituted as hyphenated Australians.[1] This process is analogous to Salman Rushdie's experience:

> I have constantly been asked whether I am British, or Indian. The formulation 'Indian-born British writer' has been invented to explain me.
>
> But my new book deals with Pakistan. So what now? British-resident-Indo-Pakistani writer? You see the folly of trying to contain writers [people?] inside passports.
>
> (cited in Welsh, 1997: 56)

In the following pages, it is precisely these tensions of citizenship and identity which are explored within the Australian context.

Settlers and Natives

In his widely acclaimed analysis of Africa, Mahmood Mamdani makes an interesting distinction between settlers and natives and asks the question: when does a settler become a native? (Mamdani, 1998). In Africa, the colonial state governed by racism established the distinction between settler and native by demarcating different rights for a minority white settler and majority black 'native' population. On the one hand, it functioned on the rule of law and rights when it came to settlers who were defined as citizens and, on the other hand, it was a state that ruled over subjects who were not entitled to any rights associated with the settler population. It was only at the moment of decolonisation that the boundaries of civil society were extended to create an indigenous civil society. However, Mamdani points out that this was of limited significance because independence merely de-racialised the state without doing the same in civil society (Mamdani, 1996). The post-colonial Australian state, like the African colonial state, remained racialised and civic rights only became universal once the indigenous population was allowed formally the full minimalist rights of citizenship when, in 1967, racial discriminatory clauses were removed from the constitution (Hanks, 1984: 23–24; Chesterman and Galligan, 1997; Peterson and Sanders, 1998).

It is not intended to suggest that the African case be seen as analogous to that of Australia. The distinction between settler and native in the Australian context holds little relevance because, unlike Africa, Australia is unquestionably a continent of settler independence. The category of native is not one that is appropriate to the Aboriginal peoples not only because of its obvious racist connotations but more importantly because of the exclusionary practices of the white settlers who stripped the rights of Aboriginal peoples through the establishment of the category 'aboriginal native.' By deploying this category, the Commonwealth was able to deny them not only the franchise but also any financial benefits that were available to the white settler population. As Chesterman and Galligan point out, 'this exclusionary regime was meticulously enforced to keep Aboriginal people as non-citizens for more than half a century' (1997: 12).

It was this exclusionary category of 'aboriginal native' which was extended through legislation to refer not only to Australia's indigenous population but also to people from Asia, Africa and the Pacific Islands.[2] This category was developed against the backdrop of British imperial culture which referred to indigenous populations in the colonies as 'natives.' Within Australia, the term had an additional different connotation. In 1873, the visiting Anthony Trollope noted that the government officially called the indigenous population 'Aboriginals' whilst the 'word native is almost universally applied to white colonists born in Australia' (cited in Chesterman and Galligan, 1997: 87). The idea that white colonists born in Australia were natives whilst the indigenous population were not was an important one. It was an idea that went to the heart of the manner in which the continent was settled. The myth of *terra nullius* was dependent upon the non-recognition of the local population and the 'indigenisation' of their white conquerors.

Settler colonies were forged out of the very idea of the elimination of the indigenous population. As Patrick Wolfe has noted, 'the colonizers came to stay—invasion is a structure not an event' (1999: 2). In the triumphant-settler independent continent of Australia, the diminished significance of the indigenous population is indicated by the importance of the question of when it is that a settler becomes a native. In a formal sense, the question can be answered by examining citizenship laws and clauses which ascribe citizenship after fulfilling certain criteria such as place of birth or the fulfilment of residency requirements. But these only entail gaining minimal formal civic rights and obligations. What is more important is how you gain the legitimacy of being transformed from a settler to a native. For those who sought to construct a particular Australian identity—through the white Australia policy and assimilationist ideology—the transformation was one that was limited exclusively to those of Anglo-European origin. It is a legacy that continues to be manifested through exclusionary practices whereby the entitlements of certain citizens, including Aboriginal peoples, women and people of colour are denied.[3]

The 'Australian Way of Life'

The transformation of a settler to a native in the Australian context can be discerned in the way in which settlers chose to portray themselves. These self-images initially were cast as a distinct 'Australian-type' which drew inspiration from social Darwinism and race theory of the nineteenth century. Richard White has pointed out that this type was "British, modified only by unique climatic conditions, or, of more interest, a unique racial type that was thought to be developing from a stock which remained, proudly, '98% British'" (1979: 529). By the 1950s, however, notions of the 'Australian type' gave way to the idea of a unique 'Australian way of life.' This change in the post-war period was necessitated by the large influx of European migrants and the need to ensure that they conformed to a particular 'Anglo-Australia.' It was in this context that the government pursued a policy of assimilation for both migrants and Aboriginal people.

Although there was no precise definition of the 'Australian way of life,' it nevertheless was characterised by assimilation and the view that homogeneity was vital for Australia's future success as a society. Migrants, who were expected to conform, were at a loss as to what this way of life entailed. One questioned:

> What is this Way of Life? No one yet tells me what this is! Yet always they tell me I must adopt it! . . . perhaps I begin to behave like you behave in pubs. I drink beer until I am stupid. Or learn to 'put in the boot' and bash the other fellow with a bottle. . . . Is this the way of life I must learn? Thank you. No. I stay a bloody Reffo!
>
> (cited in White, 1979: 536)

It was precisely this lack of definition of the 'Australian way of life' which was vital to maintaining the power and hegemony of the white Anglo-settler population which remained committed to maintaining Australia's connection with Britain.

The settler subject was thus constructed from exclusionary premises which were altered over time to be able to include those of Celtic and European origins. Australia as a continent of settler independence can be seen as a society that was, and remains, Anglo-European in origin. It is in this context that Louis Hartz's notion of fragmented societies is important despite its limitations. From this perspective, Australia can be seen as an Anglo-fragment society whose institutions and practices reflect the colonial heritage which existed at the point of detachment from Britain (Hartz, 1964). It is this legacy which characterises the manner in which English cultural values and the avowed policy of Anglo-conformity defined the Australian nation through exclusionary and racist policies of the nineteenth century which continue to the present. The rationale for such conformity, which came to be embodied in the policy of assimilation, was captured by Mary Willard's (1967) defense of the White Australia policy as a requirement for the preservation of British Australian nationality. It was in this way that the 'white' race and nation became linked inextricably with Australian national identity.

It may well appear that adapting Mamdani's analysis of Africa with settlers as citizens and Aboriginal people and non-whites as subjects holds true for Australia.

So when does a settler become a native? For the white settler class, this occurred when white colonists were locally born. But as the needs of the economy forced migration to the country and as formal citizenship laws were promulgated, other white settlers were able to become natives when they fulfilled certain minimum requirements after which citizenship was granted.

The task of determining who is a citizen is decided through legislation and altered from time to time. In Australia, while the boundaries of citizenship have been extended in order to accommodate waves of migration, it does not mean that citizenship is equal. As Mamdani points out in the epigraph, 'settlers are made by conquest, not just immigration.' It is in this context that we need to problematise the binary between citizen as settler and subject as native in order to understand how to transcend this distinction so that a single conception of post-colonial citizenship can be forged. This is not a process that can be decreed formally by legislation but is one that is tied integrally to the imagination. It is a process that has to recognise that becoming an Australian is not about conquering but about belonging to a political community of equal and consenting citizens. It is against this backdrop that we need to examine the complexities of citizenship and subjectivity.

The Complexities of Citizenship and Subjectivity

One might well begin by questioning what makes or who is a citizen and who is a subject? In Western political thought, subjects are individuals who have consented to a sovereign's rule and who, by according that consent, have certain rights and obligations. It is on the basis of the relationship between the sovereign and the subject that a polity functions. The consent of the subject 'is thought to provide the sovereign with the *right* to govern, the attendant obligations of those subjects are supposed to provide the sovereign with the capacity to do so' (Hindess, 1996: 13; Ahluwalia, 2001). In response to the problematic of who comes after the subject, Etienne Balibar has responded forcefully, the citizen. The citizen, he notes, 'is that "nonsubject" who comes after the subject, and whose constitution and recognition put an end (in principle) to the subjection of the subject' (Balibar, 1991: 38–39).

The claim that citizens succeed subjects is one that Balibar develops by questioning 'who is the subject of the prince? And who is the citizen who comes after the subject?' (40). While a sovereign's power traditionally was based on divine right with the implication that subjects essentially were obeying God, the modern notion is grounded in the idea that all people are born 'free and equal in rights.' This rupture arises as a result of the *Declaration of the Rights of Man and of the Citizen of 1789* which evokes the sovereignty of the revolutionary citizen. This entails the process whereby the citizen becomes a subject, '*the citizen is the subject*, the citizen is always a *supposed subject* (legal subject, psychological subject, transcendental subject)' (45). In this way, the citizen is '*neither* the individual *nor* the collective . . . *neither* an exclusionary being *nor* a private being' (51). For Balibar, citizenship is a kind of freedom which is rooted in 'natural rights.' Such a perspective shifts the debate that arises in questions of nationality and immigration which are based on 'who are citizens' to one which fundamentally asks 'who is *the* citizen.' The modern notion of citizenship is therefore based upon the idea that a community of autonomous persons has consented to being ruled. It is a perception, however, that is considered to be something of a fiction (Hindess, 1996: 156–158).

In her empirical study of citizenship, Pamela Johnston Conover points out that citizen identities are the defining elements which shape the character of communities. Such identities can be socially cohesive. However, when they are found to be lacking, legitimacy itself becomes problematic. She points out that there are three key components to citizenship. The first is membership in a political community signified by some legal notion. Although in the modern world citizenship is embedded strongly in the nation-state, individuals are also members of other political communities and 'thus citizens experience multiple levels of citizenship nested within each other' (Conover, 1995: 134). It is important to recognise that despite the association of nation-states with citizenship, it is at the local level and in the local contexts that people experience being and express themselves as citizens. The second component is a *sense of citizenship*. This sense is based on the 'affective significance that people give their membership in a particular political community' (134). Finally, there is the practice of citizenship, which entails both political participation as well as civic activity.

The pluralist position on citizenship is one that postulates that citizens are 'those in a body politic who share in the allocation of power' (Laswell and Kaplan, 1952: 217). Such a conception entails the most common perception of citizenship—that it allows one to engage in the political sphere. This is epitomised by being permitted to stand for public office or by voting for those who seek public office. Citizenship evokes also feelings of patriotism with strong allegiance to the flag and institutions which are analogous with the nation. Citizenship, as opposed to residency, in contemporary societies means that one is allowed access to state resources as well as being allowed to participate in the political process.

In his lectures on 'governmentality,' Michel Foucault maintained that, despite the different manner in which the term is utilised, there is, nevertheless, continuity between the government of the self, the government of a household as well as the government of a community or state. The importance of Foucault's views lies in his different conception of government. The work of government, for Foucault, is performed by both state and nonstate agencies which are more 'involved in moulding the public and private behaviour—and even the personalities—of individuals than any conception of those individuals as citizens would allow' (Hindess, 1996: 131).

For Foucault, the relationship between ruler and ruled is more complex and nuanced than simply one which operates on the basis of consent. It is as citizen-subjects that individuals are able to be governed. This conception rests on the acknowledgement that there is a great deal of power that lies beyond the state. As Hindess points out:

> Far from being restricted to the actions of the government . . . the government of societies takes place in a variety of state and non-state contexts. The family, for example, can be seen not only as a potential object of government policy, but also as a means of governing the behaviour of its own members.   (134–135)

In short, Foucault's argument rests on a notion of power that is pervasive and one that operates at different levels in order to carry out its function.

Toby Miller has divided citizenship into four moods. First, there is the right to association which was decreed by classical political theory. Second, liberal political theory extended this right by adding the doctrine of the civil right to relative freedom. Third, there exists the social right to a minimum standard of living guaranteed by the welfare state. The final mood is the postmodern guarantee of access to technologies of communication which are central to one's identity and polity. Miller argues that there is a perceptible shift between the modern and the postmodern. In the former, subjects recognised their debt to the great institutions of the state whilst the postmodern

> . . . derives its power from a sense that such institutions need to relearn what sovereignty is about in polymorphous sovereign states and transnational business and social milieux that are diminishingly homogenous in demographic terms and increasingly heteroglossic in their cultural competence.   (Miller, 1993: 25)

Citizenship has become an important trope in which civil society is seen to be a powerful agent of social change. The notion of shared rights which citizenship evokes is one that has been advocated by all modern emancipatory movements. For example, it was one of the central arguments mounted by the nationalist movements which sought decolonisation. As Miller points out, equal access to citizenship has not translated into equal justice 'because of the propensity toward economic anarchy and political oligarchy and because the discourse of justice increasingly presumes a space of autonomy between person, economy, and polity rather than a policy of assurance by the last on behalf of the first, or some other variant' (223).

Citizenship in itself has a tendency to universalise and fails to recognise difference. It is this need to recognise difference which has meant the problematising of citizenship by feminist scholarship (Benhabib, 1996; Young, 1990). It is because the discourse of citizenship has a tendency to homogenise that it allows for a limited questioning which only seeks to evaluate the 'spread of services within a given type of social organization, not to the shape of that society or the means of defining and dividing it' (Miller, 1993: 230).

This demonstrates the complexities of citizenship and the difficulty in dichotomising individuals simply into either citizens or subjects. What is clear is that the distinction between citizen and subject is complex and entails questions of responsibility, participation and entitlement. In short, individuals in all communities are citizen-subjects. In Australia, the manner in which citizenship has been ascribed to the indigenous and non-Anglo-European population in a formal minimalist sense means that they are not citizen-subjects in the same way as their white counter-parts. The notion of citizenship for these people is nothing more than the right to vote and hence remains formal and minimalist. It is with this in mind that we need to consider citizenship and identity within a post-colonial context.

Citizenship and Subjectivity: Post-colonial Reflections

All societies continuously invent and reinvent themselves. Australia is once again trying to come to terms with its identity, particularly in the aftermath of the success of the Maho case in which the highest judicial body overturned the founding myth of *terra nullius* upon which the modern nation had been built. In addition, marginalised groups within Australia increasingly are demanding that they be recognised and granted in reality the full entitlements of citizenship. It is these pressures which illustrate the fragility of settler societies where national identity is not homogenous but rather is constantly invented. This is necessarily so, because settler colonial societies such as Australia, Canada and New Zealand have not ruptured their imperial ties. In these societies, there has been no war of revolution or formal rupturing which can be equivocated with the decolonisation process of other colonised societies. It is for this reason that Patrick Williams and Laura Chrisman argue for the exclusion of these societies from notions of post-colonialism:

> That these were not simply colonies was formally recognised at the time by Britain
> in granting them Dominion status. Economically and politically, their relation to the
> metropolitan centre bore little resemblance to that of the actual colonies. (1994: 4)

While it is clear that the experiences of the settler colonies cannot simply be equated to that of other colonies, the distinction that Williams and Chrisman make between dominion colonies and actual colonies is highly problematic. The experience of Aboriginal peoples, migrants and even the settlers cannot be erased by such distinctions. Rather, it is important to recognise the complexities of the colonial experience in a myriad of locations and to note, as Diana Brydon has suggested, that, 'Postcolonialism is neither a thing nor an essentialized state; rather, it is a complex of processes designed to circumvent imperial and colonial habits of mind' (1995: 11–12).

In the battle over post-colonialism, what is perhaps forgotten is that the very subjects of empire have endured different forms of colonialism and that it is these different forms of power which need to be recovered. For the post-colonial white settler subjects, there is a dual burden—not only do they have to recover their own narratives but they must also recognise that they have blocked the narratives of the indigenous populations which they rendered invisible. It is this double inscription of resistance and authority which constitutes the settler subject. As Alan Lawson has pointed out, the 'settler subject-position is both postimperial and postcolonial; it has colonized and has been colonized: it must speak of and against both its own oppressiveness and its own oppression' (1995: 28). To view the settler subject in this way is important because it illustrates the manner in which these subjects are trapped between the originating world of Europe which they brought with them as well as 'that other First World, that of the First Nations, whose authority the settlers not only effaced and replaced but also desired' (29). It is through an engagement of these two modes—the colonising and the colonised— that we begin to understand the interstitial cultural space in which settler subjects are located.

The questioning of European forms of knowledge with their universalist prescriptions is a task that has been undertaken by post-structuralism. The liberal humanist conception of the unified autonomous subject who had the capacity to determine his or her destiny is one that has been challenged by post-structuralism. The subject now 'is considered meaningless in itself, a mere cocoon, which, once opened, dissolves into a multiplicity of discursive facets. The subject does not speak, but is spoken by, language. The effect of such analysis is often to assign to the subject a position of passivity' (90). However, the notion of the subject is one that is central to postcolonial theory, for it affects the manner in which colonised peoples come to terms with the conditions which entrap them. It is this perception of their conditions of domination which is vital to their being able to develop strategies of resistance. Hence, Martina Michel has pointed out that post-colonial theory effectively has reformulated the postmodern notion of the subject, 'by shifting our attention from the (fractured) Self to processes of subject formation' (1995: 89).

A major contribution of post-colonial theory has been the reconceptualisation of space and identity. As Edward Said (1978) so stridently demonstrates in *Orientalism*, space is a construction to which identities are assigned. It is through this insight that Henry Giroux has advocated the notion of 'border pedagogy.' He points out that

... the category border signals in the metaphorical and literal sense how power is inscribed differently on the body, culture, history, space, land, and psyche. Borders elicit a recognition of those epistemological, political, cultural, and social margins that distinguish between 'us and them,' delineate zones of terror from locations that are safe, and create new cartographies of identity and difference.   (1992: 23)

The very notion of identity remains tied to the nation. As Said points out, we are 'defined by the nation, which in turn derives its authority from a supposedly unbroken tradition' (1993: xxviii). As identity is always relational, identity formation is tied inextricably to a process of othering. It is here that post-colonial theory has proved to be particularly important in highlighting the invention or fictitious nature of a culturally pure or homogenous identity. This is where Giroux's notion of 'border pedagogy' is useful because it 'presupposes an acknowledgement of the shifting borders that both undermine and reterritorialize different configurations of culture, power, and knowledge' (1992: 23).

Benita Parry argues that the effect of the recognition of the fractured self, however, is the fixing of the marginalised other into a position of silence (Parry, 1987). It is the quest to recover this silenced other which gives post-colonial theory its impetus over other post phenomena. Ascribing agency to the subject allows post-colonialism—in contrast to poststructuralism and postmodernism—to insist that the subject has the capacity to act. Michel points out that this in itself does not allow the subject to determine her or his own position because, 'subject positions continue to be seen as constructs; but as agents the subject constantly acts out, reformulates, challenges, and potentially re-locates these constructs/discourses that assign to her or him a place from which to speak' (Michel, 1995: 91).

The ability to resist is one which is central to the work of both Frantz Fanon and Edward Said (Ashcroft and Ahluwalia, 1999). It is the notion of resistance that 'lies at the heart of postcolonial debate' (Michel, 1995: 92). However, the centrality of resistance does not entail a return to a past essentialised identity, for there is no possibility of such a return. Rather, it is the continual reconstitution of identity under different circumstances which becomes important. It is a process which Said captures in his assertion that the dismantlement of binary oppositions challenges 'the fundamentally static notion of identity that has been the core of cultural thought during the era of imperialism' (1993: xxviii).

This is where post-colonial theory is instructive. It suggests that there are other narratives, other histories which have been subsumed and which need to be recovered. Edward Said offers one way in which this process of recovery can proceed. He makes a distinction between the potentate and the traveller in his writing on the role of the intellectual. Said urges intellectuals to adopt the identity of travellers because they 'suspend the claim of customary routine in order to live in new rhythms and rituals.' Indeed, unlike the potentate 'who must guard only one place and defend its frontiers, the traveler crosses over, traverses territory, and abandons fixed positions, all the time' (Said, 1991: 81).

The modern intellectual's role then is to disrupt prevailing norms because 'dominant norms are today so intimately connected . . . to the nation, which is always triumphalist, always in a position of authority, always exacting loyalty and sub-servience' (Said, 1994: 27). Said urges the intellectual to push the boundaries, to reconcile one's own identity with the reality of other identities, other peoples rather than dominating other cultures. He argues that, despite a proliferation of the liberal rhetoric of equality and justice, injustices continue in many parts of the globe.

It is in this context that the distinction between the settler as citizen and subject as native is interesting, for these are tied to space and identity. In Australia, core universal liberal values of equality, citizenship and justice were denied to the 'abo-riginal natives.' The granting of minimalist citizenship does not mean that these dis-tinctions can now 'simply be erased. We are all too familiar with the exclusionary practices which have been utilised in forging a particular Australian identity. Never-theless, by utilising post-colonialism, we are able to recognise that post-colonial sub-jects have the capacity for agency and that their identities are contingent and multiple. Indeed, we can see that the binary between the citizen and the subject is problematic. As James Donald points out, 'the citizen' needs to be seen as a position and not as an identity. When viewed from such a perspective, it is a position which can be 'occupied in the sense of being spoken from, not in the sense of being given a substantial identity' (Donald, 1996: 174). The citizen as an empty space in such a conceptualisation entails that the 'status of citizenship is contingent on an operative symbolic order that needs to be distinguished from any claims to a cultural identity for the citizen' (175). Hence, to become a citizen in Australia, as in other postcolonial locations, is 'therefore to become a subject within this symbolic order' (175).

Conclusion

Mahmood Mamdani's provocative question of when does a settler become a native is one that is problematised by post-colonial theory. It questions the efficacy of delineating fixed categories such as settler and native which were a product of colo-nialism. Recognising colonialism's domination and subjugation of the 'native,' post-colonialism illustrates the capacity for agency and resistance. In Homi Bhabha's formulation, it is hybridity which challenges colonial domination. This leads to a par-ticular kind of post-colonial subjectivity which functions in an 'interstitial passage between fixed identifications [and which] opens up the possibility of a cultural hybridity that entertains difference without an assumed or imposed hierarchy'

(1994: 4). This does not mean that the systems of oppression which exist in relation to Aboriginal peoples and non-whites are irrelevant. Rather, it points to the complexities of post-colonial subjectivity which cannot be captured in the binary citizen and subject. Post-colonialism points to the possibility of re-imagining the nation by creating a crisis of citizenship which arose out of both minimalist and exclusionary practices.

In Australia, a simple binary such as citizen and subject is problematic precisely because of the manner in which settlers, as citizen-subjects, have transformed themselves into natives by virtue of simply being born there. Post-colonial theory brings questions of subjectivity to the foreground, illustrating the complexities of identity formation. Post-colonial subjects have multiple identities which are shaped continually by the practice of everyday life giving them the capacity to resist, to speak and to act as citizen/subjects. The transformation of the settler into the native cannot be legitimated through conquest but fundamentally must be based on consent. It is a process that is embedded firmly within the imagination. It is through this process that generations of migrants have transformed, adopted or added an Australian identity which renders notions of fixed identities, such as settler and native, problematic.

ACKNOWLEDGMENTS

I wish to thank Paul Nursey-Bray for his comments on this paper.

NOTES

1 See Hage (1998: 49–55). It must be stressed, however, that these exclusions have not had the same effect on all these categories of people. For example, to equate the exclusions and oppression of Aboriginal people with that of white women in Australia would be highly problematic.

2 For an excellent analysis of the manner in which the 'Natal Formula' was developed to exclude coloured immigration in the white settler colonies of Australia, Canada, New Zealand and South Africa, see Huttenback (1976).

3 For an example of how the issue of entitlements has affected women, see Johnson (1999).

REFERENCES

Ahluwalia, Pal (2001) *Politics and Post-Colonial Theory: African Inflections* (London, Routledge).

Ashcroft, Bill, and Ahluwalia, Pal (1999) *Edward Said: The Paradox of Identity* (London, Routledge).

Balibar, Etienne (1991) Citizen subject. In *Who Comes after the Subject,* edited by Eduardo Cadava, Peter Connor and Jean-Luc Nancy (London, Routledge).

Benhabib, Seyla (ed.) (1996) *Democracy and Difference* (Princeton, Princeton University Press).

Bhabha, Homi (1994) *The Location of Culture* (London, Routledge).

Brydon, Diana (1995) Introduction: postcoloniality, reading Canada. *Essays on Canadian Writing* 56(Fall): 1–19.

Chesterman, John, and Galligan, Brian (1997) *Citizens without Rights: Aborigines and Australian Citizenship* (Melbourne, Cambridge University Press).

Conover, Pamela Johnston (1995) Citizen identities and conceptions of the self. *The Journal of Political Philosophy* 3(2): 133–165.

Donald, James (1996) The citizen and the man about town. In *Questions of Cultural Identity*, edited by Stuart Hall and Paul du Gay (London, Sage Publications).

Fitzgerald, S. (1988) *Immigration: A Commitment to Australia*, vol. 1 (Canberra, Australian Government Publishing Service).

Foucault, Michel (1982) The subject and power, translated by Leslie Sawyer. *Critical Inquiry* 8(4): 777–795.

Giroux, Henry (1992) *Border Crossings* (London, Routledge).

Hage, Ghassan (1998) *White Nation: Fantasies of White Supremacy in a Multicultural Society* (Annandale, Pluto Press).

Hall, Stuart (1992) New ethnicities. In *'Race,' Culture and Difference*, edited by J. Donald (London, Sage).

Hanks, Peter (1984) Aborigines and government: the developing framework. In *Aborigines and the Law*, edited by Peter Hanks and Bryan Keon-Cohen (Sydney, George Allen and Unwin).

Hartz, Louis (ed.) (1964) *The Founding of New Societies: Studies in the History of the United States, Latin America, South Africa, Canada and Australia* (London, Harcourt Brace).

Hindess, Barry (1996) *Discourses of Power: From Hobbes to Foucault* (Oxford, Blackwell Publishers).

Huttenback, Robert (1976) *Racism and Empire: White Settlers and Colored Immigrants in the British Self-Governing Colonies, 1830–1910* (Ithaca: Cornell University Press).

Johnson, Carol (1999) The fragility of democratic reform: new challenges in Australian women's citizenship. In *Gender and Democratisation: International Perspectives*, edited by Shirin Rai (London, MacMillan).

Laswell, H. D., and Kaplan, A. (1952) *Power and Society: A Framework for Political Inquiry* (London, Routledge and Keegan Paul).

Lawson, Alan (1995) Postcolonial theory and the 'settler' subject. *Essays on Canadian Writing* 56(Fall): 20–36.

Mamdani, Mahmood (1996) *Citizen and Subject: Contemporary Africa and the Legacy of Late Colonialism* (Princeton, Princeton University Press).

Mamdani, Mahmood (1998) When does a settler become a native? The colonial roots of citizenship. *Pretexts* 7(2): 249–258.

Michel, Martina (1995) Positioning the subject: locating postcolonial studies. *Ariel* 26(1): 83–99.

Miller, Toby (1993) *The Well-Tempered Self: Citizenship, Culture, and the Postmodern Subject* (Baltimore, Johns Hopkins University Press).

Parry, Benita (1987) Problems in current theories of colonial discourse. *Oxford Literary Review* 9(1–2): 27–58.

Peterson, Nicholas, and Sanders, Will (eds.) (1998) *Citizenship and Indigenous Australians* (Melbourne, Cambridge University Press).

Said, Edward (1978) *Orientalism* (New York, Pantheon Rooks).

Said, Edward (1991) Identity, authority, and freedom: the potentate and the traveller. *Pretexts: Studies in Writing and Culture* 3(1–2): 67–81.

Said, Edward (1993) *Culture and Imperialism* (London, Chatto & Windus).

Said, Edward (1994) *Representation of the Intellectual* (London, Vintage).

Welsh, Sarah Lawson (1997) (Un)belonging citizens, unmapped territory: black immigration and British identity in the post-1945 period. In *Not on Any Map: Essays on Postcoloniality and Cultural Nationalism,* edited by Stuart Murray (Exeter, University of Exeter Press).

White, Richard (1979) The Australian Way of Life. *Historical Studies* 18(73): 528–545.

Willard, M. (ed.) (1967) *History of the White Australia Policy to 1920* (Melbourne, Melbourne University Press).

Williams, Patrick, and Chrisman, Laura (eds.) (1994) *Colonial Discourse and Post-Colonial Theory: A Reader* (New York, Columbia University Press).

Wolfe, Patrick (1999) *Settler Colonialism and the Transformation of Anthropology* (London, Cassell).

Young, Robert (1990) *White Mythologies: Writing History and the West* (London, Routledge).

33

DAVID CHIONI MOORE

Is the Post- in Postcolonial the Post- in Post-Soviet?

Toward a Global Postcolonial Critique

Except for Australia in the old days and Cayenne, Sakhalin is the only place left where it is possible to study colonization by criminals: all Europe is interested in it, and we pay no attention to it.　　　　—Anton Chekhov, *The Island: A Journey to Sakhalin*, 1895

"You have delved deeply into the Russian mind of the nineteenth century. . . . It was filled with the same disquiet, the same impassioned and ambiguous torment. To be the extreme eastern end of Europe? Not to be the western bridgehead of Asia? The intellectuals could neither answer these questions nor avoid them."
　　　　　　　　　　　　　　—Cheikh Hamidou Kane, *L'aventure ambiguë*, 1961

But it is above all Budapest and Suez which constitute the decisive moments of this confrontation.　　　　　　—Frantz Fanon, *The Wretched of the Earth*, 1961

Marlow comes through to us not only as a witness of truth, but as one holding those advanced and humane views appropriate to the English liberal tradition which required all Englishmen of decency to be deeply shocked by atrocities in Bulgaria or the Congo of King Leopold of the Belgians or wherever.
　　　　　　　　　　　　　　　—Chinua Achebe, "An Image of Africa:
　　　　　　　　　　　　　Racism in Conrad's *Heart of Darkness*," 1975

As many readers may know, the term "postcolonial"—beginning in the 1980s, with massive growth by the middle 1990s—has come to be the principal designator for a range of activities formerly known as the study of Third World, non-Western, world, emergent, or minority literatures. The term "postcolonial" has come into fashion not only because of evident defects in the former vogue labels but also because "postcolonial" accurately describes, to varying degrees, good chunks of the contemporary political, social, cultural, and literary situations in sub-Saharan Africa, South Asia, the Caribbean, the Arab world, and to lesser or different extents Latin America, Australia, Canada, Ireland, and even the United States. According to a rough consensus, the cultures of postcolonial lands are characterized by tensions between the desire for autonomy and a history of dependence, between the desire for autochthony and the fact of hybrid, part-colonial origin, between resistance and complicity, and between imitation (or mimicry) and originality. Postcolonial peoples' passion to escape from their once colonized situations paradoxically gives the ex-colonials disproportionate weight in the recently freed zones. And the danger of retrenchment, or of a neocolonial relation, is ever present.

In the hands of postcolonial and resistance theorists such as Frantz Fanon, Edward W. Said, Ngũgĩ wa Thiong'o, Gayatri Chakravorty Spivak, and Aimé Césaire, postcolonial perspectives have generated powerful analyses of societies and texts. Postcolonial critique has also illuminated parallels between areas heretofore seen as noncomparable, such as Senegal and India, and it has energized fields like Irish culture studies.[1] Postcolonial studies has also become remarkably autocritical: since its inception, numerous important critics have interrogated the discourse itself.[2] Yet these autocritiques, now a genre of their own, have only strengthened the field's hold. These critiques have tackled questions such as the political utility of the category "postcolonial," the near-disappearance of formerly important terms such as "Third World" and more specific terms like "Africa," the often impenetrable vocabulary of postcolonial studies, and specific concerns about its major claims. In the following pages I supplement these debates by examining an enormous geographic, or rather geopolitical, exclusion embodied in the range of situations that have been generally understood, in postcolonial studies, to be postcolonial. After reviewing what counts as postcolonial, I turn to the post-Soviet sphere: the Baltics, Central and Eastern Europe, the Caucasus, and Central Asia. This essay thereby proposes simultaneous critiques of both too narrow postcolonial and too parochial post-Soviet studies; consequently, it is addressed to both audiences at once. It is written from the perspective of a scholar of the black Atlantic, whose post-Soviet views are those of a comparatist.

It is no doubt true that there is, on this planet, not a single square meter of inhabited land that has not been, at one time or another, colonized and then postcolonial. Across Eurasia, Africa, the Americas, and more, peoples have formed and reformed, conquered and been conquered, moved and dissolved. And virtually all groups on this earth, whatever their claims to migrant, exile, conquering, returned, or indigenous status, have come, at some remove or other, from somewhere else. The result of all this movement, much of which has been arguably criminal, is that many cultural situations, past and present, can be said to bear the postcolonial stamp, often in ways only partly corresponding to current notions.

In roughly 1387, for example, the poet Geoffrey Chaucer was faced with an important choice, somewhat similar to the one Ngũgĩ wa Thiong'o faced in 1980 when he wrote, against English-language fashion, his *Devil on the Cross* in Gĩkũyũ. Chaucer lived at a time when England was a relatively poor margin off Europe's northwest shore, and England's elite culture had been heavily Latinized and Frenchified since the Norman Conquest. And so, Chaucer asked, do I write in a foreign, formerly colonial, transnational Romance tongue, thereby guaranteeing international and local-elite readers and participating in a rich, old, but largely external tradition? Or do I write in the vernacular, "my" language, of narrower geographic compass and socially lower, principally oral use? A similar dilemma for Ngũgĩ and Chaucer, but only Ngũgĩ is today called postcolonial, while Chaucer is perceived to stand at the head of a colonizer's literary history. And yet much of Ngũgĩ's critique of colonial English circa 1980 *(Decolonising)* echoes the sense of French and Latin circa 1440 expressed by Chaucer's near contemporary Osbern Bokenham:

> [þ]is corrupcioun of Englysshe men yn þer modre-tounge [. . .] toke grete augmen-
> tatcioun and encrees after þe commyng of William conquerour. [. . . B]y decre and
> ordynaunce [. . .] children in gramer-scolis ageyns þe consuetude and þe custom of
> all oþer nacyons, here owne modre-tonge lafte and forsakyn, lernyd here [. . .]
> Frenssh [. . .] and to maken here Latyns on þe same wyse. [. . . B]y þe same decre
> lordis sonys and all nobyll and worthy mennys children were fyrste set to lyrnyn and
> spoken Frenssh, or þan þey cowde spekyn Ynglyssh, and all wrytyngis [. . .] in cour-
> tis of the lawe [. . .] be doon yn the same [. . .] thus by processe of tyme barbariȝid
> thei in bothyn and spokyn neythyr good Frenssh nor good Englyssh.[3]

Eight decades later, in 1521, when the brigand Hernán Cortés reached what is now Mexico, early in one of the most brutal chapters in all history, he did not arrive in a pristine land of independent peoples. Rather, he stumbled on a political mael-strom in which the Mexic state dominated neighbor peoples. The young Teticpac woman Malintzín, who served Cortés as translator and guide, was a member of one of these subject peoples. Malintzín's hybridizing, other-identifying, certainly not wholly voluntary, and ultimately self-defeating choice to ally herself with Cortés was therefore initially intended as a decolonizing act. The Khoisan, in present-day South Africa, are a third nonstandard example. The current broad narrative of South African history is that, beginning in the seventeenth century, first Dutch and then English colonists usurped lands rightfully belonging to indigenous Africans such as the Zulu and the Xhosa. It was only in the 1990s that this power distribution began to change. And yet for other South Africans, in particular the Khoisan, the Zulu were also late arrivals and so also counted among the colonizers' ranks. Thus in South Africa today one sees, at fleeting moments, an unusual uniting of the Khoisan with the formerly ruling white minority in the interests of reversing perceived Nguni domination.

I raise these examples—none of which is clear-cut, unambiguous, or un-challengeable—to make the following point. When the term "postcolonial" arose it was rightly envisioned, as I have mentioned, as a replacement for terms like "non-Western," "Third World," "minority," and "emergent." The notion "non-Western" was a sham since it lumped four billion people under a single name and privileged the fragment called the West.[4] "Emergent" worked no better, since the cultures and peoples so described had been producing literature for millennia before most Euro-peans stopped wearing bearskins or began to read; even Goethe was aware of that.[5] "Minority" was even worse. And "Third World," though of honorable, even revolu-tionary, birth and still with strong defenders, also seemed to have flaws: the tertiary status; the recent disappearance of the Second World; the presence of Third Worlds within the First; the odd lumping of, say, Singapore with Mali; and more.[6] "Post-colonial" apparently worked better: it lacked the derogations of the former labels, it specified what unified its compass (a former subjugated relation to Western powers), it embodied a historical dimension, and it opened analytic windows onto common features of peoples who had only recently, and to the extent possible, thrown off their European chains. Equally importantly, though less honorably, "postcolonial" still allowed literature departments to hire just one person in this "field," this several-billion-person space, an outcome that would not have happened (the embarrassment would have been too great) had categories like African, Indian, and Caribbean emerged as strongly separate.

Much less expected, however, is the degree to which the notion "postcolonial" has exceeded its initial scope. Postcolonial theory, as I have observed, was initially a critique of Western power. And yet the West has hardly monopolized colonial activi-ty. For one thing the West has often colonized itself, as when England's subjects col-onized what is now Canada, Australia, New Zealand, and the United States and then fought to free themselves of England. Ireland's long history of English subjugation is equally well known. Thus, the contemporary literatures of Ireland, Australia, Canada, New Zealand, and more reluctantly the United States have been admitted into postcoloniality.[7] But still these additional cases fit, since the colonial hegemon is still England, the familiar villain in places such as Africa and India.

It is more troubling, however, when the postcolonial model reaches even further, if never unproblematically, as in the case of Chaucerian England, the sixteenth-century Mixtec state, the contemporary Khoisan, or, for that matter, Norway and Finland, which emerged from Swedish and Russian thrall only early in the 1900s.[8] In what follows, therefore, I turn to a postcolonial designation for another zone: the post-Soviet sphere—the Baltic states, Central and Eastern Europe (including former Soviet republics and independent "East Bloc" states), the Caucasus, and Central Asia. In my view, at least two features of this giant sphere are significant for cur-rently constituted postcolonial studies: first, how extraordinarily postcolonial the societies of the former Soviet regions are, and, second, how extraordinarily little attention is paid to this fact, at least in these terms.

To suggest a richer understanding of what I mean by post-Soviet postcoloniality, I will describe an area whose postcoloniality is clear—sub-Saharan Africa. A historically rich and important set of cultures, of great diversity and sometimes little unity, sub-Saharan Africa before the arrival of Europeans has a long history of independence, though at times internal strife there is great. Then, an external colonization or imperial control begins at the borders and extends into the center. Indigenous governments are replaced with puppet control or outright rule. African education is revamped to privilege the colonizer's language, and histories and curricula are rewritten from the imperium's perspective. Autochthonous religious traditions are suppressed in the colonial zone, idols are destroyed, and alternative religions and nonreligious ideologies are promoted. The colonized areas of Africa become economic fiefs. Little or no "natural" trade is allowed between the colonies and economies external to the colonizer's network. Economic production is undertaken on a command basis and is geared to the dominant power's interests rather than to local needs. Local currencies, if they exist, are only convertible to the metropolitan specie. Agriculture becomes mass monoculture, and environmental degradation follows. In the human realm, African dissident voices are heard most clearly only in exile, though accession to exile is difficult. Oppositional energies are therefore channeled through forms including mimicry, satire, parody, and jokes. But a characteristic feature of society is cultural stagnation.

And then independence comes, across Africa, all at once. Yet though resistance has been continuous throughout the colonial period, as periods and places of intense struggle have alternated with quieter times and times of great repression, in ways the newfound freedom is less won than handed over. External forces, world forces, or forces internal to the colonizing powers seem responsible for the sudden change. There is no moment of full satisfaction, as when Cornwallis surrendered to Washington at Yorktown in 1781 or when Vietnam defeated France in 1954 and the United States in 1974. Not surprisingly, the newly independent African states are often underprepared for self-rule. Once rich domestic polities have withered, and nationals with government experience are tainted by colonial complicity. Thus, in places the former opposition rapidly assumes control, though it seems at times that they still are better at opposing than at leading. New governments, anxious to expel the colonizer's demons, swing the ideological pendulum, seeking alliance with the former imperium's opponent.

Attempts are then made in Africa to apply wholesale the principles—economic, social, and otherwise—of this great ideological alternative, at times without regard for the applicability of those principles or for their tragic dislocations. In some places lawlessness, graft, corruption, and a continuation of colonial-era ways take hold, fol-

lowed by a human drain, particularly of intellectuals and the economically productive. In other places dictators emerge, often drawing on their training in the colonial
regime. Thus, after an initial euphoria disillusion sets in, resulting from what Neil
Lazarus has called Africa's "preliminary overestimation of emancipatory potential"
(50). Now neither the collapsed imperium, nor the outside alternative, nor the local
elite is seen to have the answers. At times these tensions are expressed in ethnic
terms, since map lines, ethnic categorizations, and the newfound states themselves
are often fabrications of the former powers. Settler colonies uncomfortably remain in
some places, while in others large imported populations stay. These "map distortions," combined with more or less authentic differences, economic hardship, and
radical uncertainty, can result in tragic interethnic tensions.

Postcolonial Africa, I suggest, is like this. But is it only Africa, South Asia, the
Caribbean, and "such places" that are like this? For does not the description of postcoloniality offered here reasonably as well apply to the giant crescent from Estonia
to Kazakhstan, which also includes (it is worth mentioning all twenty-seven nations)
Latvia, Lithuania, Poland, the former East Germany, the Czech Republic, Slovakia,
Hungary, Slovenia, Croatia, Bosnia-Herzegovina, the remaining Yugoslavia, Macedonia, Albania, Romania, Bulgaria, Belarus, Moldova, Ukraine, Georgia, Azerbaijan,
Armenia, Turkmenistan, Uzbekistan, Tajikistan, and Kyrgyzstan? These nations,
some young and some quite old, were unquestionably subject to often brutal Russian
domination (styled as Soviet from the 1920s on) for anywhere from forty to two
hundred years. From this long list I have left out only Afghanistan, whose Anglo- and
Russocoloniality was never complete, and Chechnya, whose grim coloniality is hardly
"post." Africanist close readers of the prior paragraphs will note exceptions in Africa
to the postcolonial characteristics I have listed. And scholars of Eastern and Central
Europe, the Caucasus, and Central Asia might note ways in which these paragraphs
apply imperfectly to specific states there. The post-Soviet world, like the postcolonial
world, is enormously diverse. But review the three preceding paragraphs, only now
with Central and Eastern Europe, the Caucasus, and Central Asia in mind: it should
be clear that the term "postcolonial," and everything that goes with it—language,
economy, politics, resistance, liberation and its hangover—might reasonably be
applied to the formerly Russo- and Soviet-controlled regions post-1989 and -1991,
just as it has been applied to South Asia post-1947 or Africa post-1958. East is
South.

In view of these postcolonial-post-Soviet parallels, two silences are striking. The
first is the silence of postcolonial studies today on the subject of the former Soviet
sphere. And the second, mirrored silence is the failure of scholars specializing in the
formerly Soviet-controlled lands to think of their regions in the useful if by no means
perfect postcolonial terms developed by scholars of, say, Indonesia and Gabon. South
does not speak East, and East not South. In detailing these twin silences, let me turn

first to postcolonial critique. In notable synoptic articles on postcolonial studies and in recent major classroom-use anthologies such as those by Patrick Williams and Laura Chrisman and by Bill Ashcroft and his coeditors, the broadest range of nations is generally mentioned, both colonial and colonized, except for those of the former Soviet sphere. Ella Shohat's fine 1992 article "Notes on the 'Post-Colonial' "—today a classic postcolonial-studies reference—is an excellent case in point. One reason Shohat's essay is so widely cited is that it is apparently exhaustive: it tackles an enormous range of the issues surrounding *postcolonial,* including the term's origins, implied temporality, supplanting of prior designations, political effects, specificity, potential overgenerality, relation with neocoloniality, and more.

The geopolitical range of Shohat's essay is also large, but in a way it is also strange. I apologize in advance for reproducing here every geographic and cultural designator in her essay, but I ask the reader imaginatively to take a colored pencil and cross-hatch on a map all the places mentioned. What will be blank once you finish?

Shohat's article refers specifically to Algeria, Angola, Australia, Brazil, Britain, Canada, Egypt, Germany, Grenada, Italy, Jamaica, Lebanon, Libya, Mozambique, New Zealand, Nigeria, Panama, the Philippines, Senegal, and South Africa, and it mentions with particular frequency France, India, Iraq, and the United States. Adding complexity to those invocations, her article also speaks of (these citations are verbatim) Israel/Palestine, India/Pakistan, Iraq/Kuwait, Kuwait-Iraq, the Gulf states, Anglo-America, Euro-Israel, Europe, North America, the Americas, European Empires, Africa, Asia, central America, the Middle East, Southern Africa, Latin America, Central and South America and the Caribbean, and Puerto Rico. The essay often uses "Third World" and "First World," partly as descriptive terms and partly to interrogate them. Shohat also offers designators for peoples and identities, including (and this list is again complete and verbatim) Aboriginal Australians, the Jindy-worobak in Australia, white Australians, the Algerian, the Algerian in France, Algerians, the *Pied Noir,* the Arab-Jew, Middle Eastern Jews, the [Amazonian] Kayapo, the Zuni in Mexico/U.S., indigenous peoples of the Americas and Afro-diasporic communities, Afro-Brazilians, Afro-Cubans, Anglo-Dutch Europeans, Egyptians, Fourth World peoples, Indians, Malians, New Worlders, Nigerians, Pakistanis, South African Blacks, Sri Lankans, Tunisians, and Turks. The article refers to identities that are African, African American, Anglo-American, Arab, Brazilian, Cuban, Latin American, Mexican, Middle Eastern, Native American, Nicaraguan, Palestinian, and Senegalese. It also mentions the Gulf War, New World Order, Intifada, International Monetary Fund, Anglo-American informational media, Monroe Doctrine, Carter Doctrine, U.S. Independence Day, [United States] Ethnic Studies, Camp David, [the Brazilian] Tropicalist [movement], rap music, pre-Nasser imperialism, [United States–Mexican] Trade Liberalization Treaty, First World multinational corporations,

Third World nation-states, [Christopher] Columbus, and New York Harbor. Finally, Shohat quotes the suggestion that "the post-colonial" might arguably include "African countries, Australia, Bangladesh, Canada, Caribbean countries, India, Malaysia, Malta, New Zealand, Pakistan, Singapore, South Pacific Island countries, and Sri Lanka" (100).[9]

The great blank space on the map I have asked my reader to create is, of course, the former Soviet sphere and China, which Shohat relegates to two passing mentions of the "Second World"—mentions that, despite their brevity, are worth assessing. On the essay's second page she notes, entirely in reference to the eclipse of the term "Third World," the "collapse of the Soviet Communist model [and] the crisis of existing socialism" (100). The penultimate page again situates the massive Soviet sphere and China solely in relation to perceived desires of traditionally constituted Third World peoples: "The collapse of Second World socialism, it should be pointed out, has not altered neo-colonial policies, and on some levels, has generated increased anxiety among such Third World communities as the Palestinians and South African Blacks concerning their struggle for independence without a Second World counterbalance" (111). What is remarkable or, rather, remarkably ordinary here is the way in which a scholar enormously concerned with the fate of colonized and recently decolonized peoples across the planet should treat events that were widely perceived, at least in the twenty-seven nations from Lithuania to Uzbekistan, as a *de*colonization, instead as a distant, indeed abstract (see Shohat's term "model"), *non*colonial event, and as a loss, since it increased the anxieties of, for example, Palestinians and Black South Africans. I should underscore that I do not mean to "pick on" Shohat's essay, which I admire. Rather, I mean only to identify an absence in currently constituted postcolonial discourse—a world system with no theory of its former Second World—which I could demonstrate in dozens of similarly apparently comprehensive essays.

In Eastern and Central European, Caucasian, and Central Asian studies, a diametric lack of engagement with postcoloniality obtains. There has been, to be sure, a growing Western scholarship on nineteenth-century Russian literary orientalism. Drawing on the colonial discourse analysis inaugurated by Said's *Orientalism,* this work focuses on the texts, from Pushkin's 1822 "Prisoner of the Caucasus" to Tolstoy's 1904 *Haji Murat,* that thematize the Russo-Caucasian colonial encounter.[10] However, when one chats with intellectuals in Vilnius or Bishkek or when one reads essays on any of the *current* literatures of the formerly Soviet-dominated sphere, it is difficult to find comparisons between Algeria and Ukraine, Hungary and the Philippines, or Kazakhstan and Cameroon.[11] At times the media today treat the Caucasus, Central Asia, and the former Yugoslavia in Third World terms, but these treatments tend more to awful "Asiatic" tropes than to serious considerations of postcoloniality.[12]

It is difficult to theorize a silence—that is, this lack of dialogue between current postcolonial critique and scholarship on Central and Eastern Europe, the Caucasus, and Central Asia. On the postcolonial side, a historical indebtedness to three-worlds theory is one cause of silence. In three-worlds theory, Western Europe and North America constitute the First, the socialist economies the Second, and all that remains—largely the world's economically weakest

states—by default becomes the Third. An enormous and honorable political commitment to the Third World has been central to much in three-worlds theorizing, the ancestor of postcolonial critique. One aspect of that commitment has been the belief, not without reason, that the First World largely caused the Third World's ills, and an allied belief that the Second's socialism was the best alternative. When most of the Second World collapsed in 1989 and 1991, the collapse resulted in the deflected silence apparent in Shohat, and it still remains difficult, evidently, for three-worlds-raised postcolonial theorists to recognize within the Second World its postcolonial dynamic. In addition, many postcolonialist scholars, in the United States and elsewhere, have been Marxist or strongly left and therefore have been reluctant to make the Soviet Union a French- or British-style villain.

The reluctance, in contrast, of most scholars of the post-Soviet sphere to make a mirrored move—to recognize that their situations might profitably be analyzed with postcolonialist tools initially developed for, say, Tanganyika—may be laid to different reasons. Here I mention two. One obtains for those post-Soviets with claims as "European": all those peoples north and west of the fractured, fissured, "racially" and religiously inflected line that places Azeris, Chechens, Ossetians, Kabardians, Abkhazians, Tatars, "and the like" (in short, "Asiatics") on one side and all Georgians, Armenians, and, broadly, Slavs (or "Europeans") on the other. Because of this discursive line between the "East" and "West," the post-Soviet region's European peoples may be convinced that something radically, even "racially," differentiates them from the postcolonial Filipinos and Ghanaians who might otherwise claim to share their situation.[13]

Across the entire zone, however, on both sides of the post-Soviet region's "European-Asian" split, a second factor blocks postcolonial critique: that factor is, indeed, the region's postcoloniality. As many colonization theorists have argued, one result of extended subjugation is compensatory behavior by the subject peoples. One manifestation of this behavior is an exaggerated desire for authentic sources, generally a mythic set of heroic, purer ancestors who once controlled a greater zone than the people now possess. Another such expression, termed mimicry, occurs when subjugated peoples come to crave the dominating cultural form, which was long simultaneously exalted and withheld. In India a worst case might be the perfectly anglicized Anglo-Indian subject, whose accent, manners, and literary and sporting interests caricature those of some English gentleman who does not exist.

This postcolonial compensatory tug plays out differently in post-Soviet space, since postcolonial desire from Riga to Almaty fixates not on the fallen master Russia but on the glittering Euramerican MTV-and-Coca-Cola beast that broke it. Central and Eastern Europeans type this desire as a return to Westernness that once was theirs. Any traveler to the region quickly learns that what for forty years was called the "East Bloc" is rather "Central Europe."[14] One hears that Prague lies west of Vienna and that the Hungarians stopped the Turk, and one witnesses an increasingly odd competition to be at Europe's "geographic center"—the claimants ranging from Skopje, Macedonia, to a stone plinth twenty miles east of Vilnius, in Lithuania. These assertions of Western affiliation are, of course, not without reason, but one who makes them also doth protest too much. In short, I am arguing that it is, in circular fashion, a postcolonial desire, a headlong westward sprint from colonial Russia's ghost or grasp, that prevents most scholars of the post-Soviet sphere from contemplating "southern" postcoloniality. From all these factors comes the double silence.

In the remainder of this essay I have two aims. First, I investigate the differences between Russo-Soviet and Anglo-Franco forms of (post)colonial relations, since in pressing parallels one must also interrogate their limits. Second, I address the possibility that this paper—which leaves no corner of the planet outside the postcolonial compass—inflates postcoloniality into a category so large as to lose all analytic bite.

First, then, some Russo-Soviet and Anglo-Franco differentiation. Standard accounts of Western colonization suggest a three-part taxonomy. The first colonization type is what one might call the "classic": that of, for example, the British in Kenya and India or the French in Senegal and Vietnam. Here a long-distance but nonetheless strong political, economic, military, and cultural control is exercised over people taken as inferior or, in Said's terms, "Orientalized." A second colonization type is that found in, for example, the United States, Australia, and South Africa, in which the colonizers settle, turning the indigenous populations into "Fourth World" subjects. A third "standard" type of colonization is what one might call dynastic, in which a power conquers neighbor peoples. Ottoman and Hapsburg empires spring to mind, but one must also recall the more successful empires—such as France *inside* its once diverse hexagon—that resulted in the disappearance of the subject peoples as such. Both Ernest Renan and Benedict Anderson have characterized this as a dynamic of memory and forgetting,[15] a process Daniel Defoe memorably described in his 1701 *The True-Born Englishman,* a fragment of which I reprint here:

> The Western Angles all the rest subdu'd;
>
> A bloody Nation, barbarous and rude:
>
> Who by the Tenure of the Sword possest

One part of *Britain,* and subdu'd the rest.

And as great things denominate the small,

The Conqu'ring Part gave Title to the Whole.

The *Scot, Pict, Britain, Roman, Dane* submit,

And with the *English-Saxon* all unite:

And these the Mixture have so close pursu'd,

The very Name and Memory's subdu'd:

No *Roman* now, no *Britain* does remain;

Wales strove to separate, but strove in vain:

The silent Nations undistinguish'd fall,

And *Englishman's* the common Name for all.

Fate jumbl'd them together, God knows how;

What e'er they were, they're *True-Born English* now.

(15)

Now, Russo-Soviet colonial activity fits imperfectly with this three-part taxon-omy. Certainly the notion of dynastic reach can be applied to many Russian moves, though Russia's dynastic language is suffused with rhetorics of sibling unity, as with Ukraine and Belarus, and with rhetorics of to-and-fro, as with historical Polish con-trol and German invasion of Russian-speaking lands. For the Baltic states as well, historically swapped among larger Germanic, Scandinavian, and Slavic neighbors, the notion of a pristine anterior autochthony is mainly a nineteenth-century Herder-ian invention. Second, settler control over native peoples is also found in the Russo-Soviet experience, described most recently for the Eurasian north in Yuri Slezkine's *Arctic Mirrors.* The inhabitants of Kazakhstan and Latvia today, nearly half of whom are ethnic Russian, are another case in point,[16] and the million Koreans now in Cen-tral Asia bear comparison with East Indians in Africa. Third and finally, the "classic" colonial control over distant orientalized populations (again, as with the British in India or the French in Vietnam) is found in nineteenth-century Russian expansions to the Caucasus and Central Asia. Here, however, the case of Russia deviates in two respects from standard Western models: in the lack of ocean between Russia and what it colonized, and in the way that Russia has long been typed (and has typed itself) as neither East nor West.

The first of these two deviations is captured early in Said's *Culture and Imperi-alism,* a book devoted largely to colonial texts from France and Britain. In explaining why he does not tackle Russia, Said writes that "Russia, however, acquired its impe-rial territories almost exclusively by adjacence. Unlike Britain or France, which jumped thousands of miles beyond their own borders to other continents, Russia moved to swallow whatever land or peoples stood next to its borders, which in the process kept moving farther and farther east and south" (10). What is puzzling about this explanation is not only how it seemingly "excuses" brutality by adjacence but also how it grants odd primacy to water. For when one considers the easy Marseille-Algiers sail or the generally pleasant London-Cairo voyage, one is puzzled that the infinitely rougher path from Moscow to Tashkent—which until the opening of the colonial Central Asian railroads in the nineteenth century took months to travel and traversed one thousand miles of freezing-broiling steppe and desert—is granted an "adjacence." Indeed, a lack of adjacent ice-free ocean was exactly Russia's problem, and much of its expansion—toward the Baltics, the Crimea, the Persian Gulf, and finally the Pacific—was a frank attempt to get some.

This widespread adjacence myth is likely influenced by Russia's purported Eurasian character—a notion (expressed at various times by Russians and non-Russians) that has long typed Russia as neither European nor "Asiatic" but as somehow in between, and particularly as more primitive than (Western) Europe.[17] Whatever the truth of this odd, unprovable idea, which rests on hypostasized continental essences, that notion causes analysis of Russian colonization once again to deviate from Western models. It is true that the nineteenth-century Russian southward push to Central Asia mirrored British forays north from India. Indeed, these movements were in explicit competition. One need only scan the curious finger of Afghanistan's northeastern Wakhan valley, ten miles across at its narrowest and two hundred miles long, to see how the imperial enterprises intertwined. In the nineteenth century, as the Russians and British rushed to map the interceding high Pamirs—a process well described in Rudyard Kipling's *Kim,* though *Kim* is generally read solely as a document of British colonization—the fear was that the colonizers' spheres might touch. Thus, in 1893 the slim, separating Wakhan strip, extending all the way to China—a sheer colonial fantasy of the Russo-British mind—was inscribed on maps as belonging to Afghanistan's emir and remains there to this day.

And yet, despite this clear connection, the Russian venture south to Central Asia was not identical to that of Britain overseas in India. Whereas the British mimicked no one but themselves, the Russians were mimicking the French and British, to whom, again, they had long felt culturally inferior. In the later nineteenth century, colonial expansion was the price of admission into Europe's club, and this was Russia's ticket. Recall this essay's first epigraph, from Chekhov: "Except for Australia in the old days and Cayenne [in French Guiana], Sakhalin is the only place left where it is possible to study colonization by criminals: all Europe is interested in it, and we pay no attention to it" (xix). Chekhov made this observation in a 9 March 1890 letter, written six weeks before he began his ethnographic expedition to Sakhalin, an island off Eurasia's Pacific coast. Note that Chekhov not only offers Europe as the colonizing standard but also suggests that "we" Russians do not belong to Europe.

Still, even beyond this colonial adventure on a Western model, the Russian colonial experience embodies yet one other difference from that of France and Britain: a rhetoric of revenge or, indeed, return. Only several centuries before, Muscovy was a Mongol vassal state, and Central Asia's khans held European slaves into the nineteenth century. For those who would characterize Russians as different from the peoples to their south and east, the nineteenth-century Central Asian colonizations thus become revenge. But for those others who held that Russia was already partly "Asiatic," from Russian Eurasianists and Scythianists to Western European Russo-orientalists, Russia's Central Asian conquest constituted a *return*. Here is George Curzon, British viceroy in India from 1899 to 1905, sketcher of the 1919 Polono-Soviet frontier, and self-described authority on Eurasia, in his 1899 book *Russia in Central Asia:*

> [Russia's] conquest of Central Asia is a conquest of Orientals by Orientals, of cognate character by cognate character. It is the fusing of strong with weaker metal, but it is not the expulsion of an impure by a purer element. Civilised Europe has not marched forth to vanquish barbarian Asia. This is no nineteenth-century crusade of manners or morals, but barbarian Asia, after a sojourn in civilised Europe, returns upon its former footsteps to reclaim its kith and kin.   (372)

The complexity of this situation, full of inflammatory typings but by no means a projection of the British only, is perhaps best illustrated by a passage from Mikhail Lermontov's 1840 novel *A Hero of Our Time,* which is set in the Caucasus in the 1830s and concerns Russian military officers sent to secure a colonizer's peace. Though much of the novel offers a society tale along classic European lines, and the pacification of the "Caucasian tribes" is intended merely as a backdrop, one must be alert, as Chinua Achebe informs us ("Image" 12), to read such tales from the perspective of those cast as savage, even incidental, decoration. At one point the angry antihero Pechorin, off in the forest, jumps out from behind a bush to surprise the mounted party of the delicate Princess Mary:

> *"Mon dieu, un circassien!"* ["My God, a Circassian!"] cried the princess in horror.
> To reassure her completely, I made a slight bow and replied in French:
> *"Ne craignez rien, madame. Je ne suis pas plus dangereux que votre cavalier."*
> ["Fear nothing, madam. I am no more dangerous than your mounted escort."]
>   (114; my trans. of French)

Several items are of interest here, items that complicate a monodirectionally orientalist interpretation of this famous text. First, and classically, the Asiatic Circassian—as with Conrad's Congolese—is typed as horrifying; but then Pechorin adopts Circassian identity as a sort of antibourgeois, antiestablishment, perhaps super-Russian romantic wild mask; and finally both Pechorin and Princess Mary use, as was normal for elites in Russia, a Western language to discuss it. Importantly, and consistent with long-term Russian literary practice, in the Russian-language text the

French is rendered in the *Latin* alphabet—a courtesy wholly normal in the culturally subaltern Russian context but one that no Western literature returns even for directly borrowed terms like перестройка.[18] Russia's relations with its colonial possessions east and south and its cultural relations with the West are, then, quite complex.

When Russia moves its colonial enterprise to the West, the situation sharply changes, and I speak here principally of the post–World War II Soviet expansion to the independent Baltics and into nations such as Poland, Hungary, Czechoslovakia, Romania, and Bulgaria. By most classic measures—lack of sovereign power, restrictions on travel, military occupation, lack of convertible specie, a domestic economy ruled by the dominating state, and forced education in the colonizer's tongue—Central Europe's nations were indeed under Russo-Soviet control from roughly 1948 to 1989 or 1991. It is, of course, possible to see these cases as "dynastic," since Russia had often come and gone there, especially in Poland and the Baltics, just as Poles, Lithuanians, and others had invaded Russia. But in ways dynastic colonization is unavailable as a category by 1948: the nineteenth-century ideologies of organic ethnonationhood and national rebirth had culminated, immediately after World War I, in the end of intra-European empires and the establishment of new sovereign and generally ethnically focused states like Finland, Estonia, Lithuania, Latvia, Hungary, Czecho-Slovakia, and a reconstituted Poland. Thus, at least psychologically, the European dynastic era was no more. It is perhaps for this reason that the Lithuanian Forest Brothers fought a guerrilla war against the KGB as late as 1956, their last holdout, like some Japanese soldier in the tropic jungles, emerging only twenty-three years ago.

Thus, if dynastic colonization is out of bounds, it might be profitable, I would argue, to consider the Baltic and Central European states as a distinct fourth case I call "reverse-cultural colonization." Once again, the standard Western story about colonization is that it is always accompanied by orientalization,[19] in which the colonized are seen as passive, ahistorical, feminine, or barbaric. However, in Russian–Central European colonization this relation is reversed, because for several centuries at least Russia has, again, been saddled with the fear or at times belief that it was culturally inferior to the West. *Mittel*-European capitals such as Budapest, Berlin, and Prague were therefore seen in Russia, at least by some, as prizes rather than as burdens needing civilizing from their occupiers. In return, the Central Europeans often saw the colonizing Russo-Soviets as Asiatics. In the closing days of World War II, for example, it frustrated Stalin that while German troops on western fronts surrendered relatively readily to American and British armies, those in the East fought desperately to avoid Soviet capture. The Soviets would exploit this fear in later years when they stationed Central Asian troops in Central Europe during troubled moments in the Warsaw Pact.

It is useful here to recall that Joseph Conrad, the deepest chronicler of the West's colonial forays, was born a Pole in Russian-ruled Ukraine in 1857, a date his father called "the eighty-fifth year of Muscovite oppression" (Najder 11). Though Conrad scholarship has thoroughly investigated his Polish and his Western lives, only rarely do these investigations meet. *Heart of Darkness* (1899), Conrad's best-known tale of the colonial encounter, seems focused on the supposed incomprehensibility of the Congo, but the most unreadable text mentioned in the story is a book marked up in Russian, or "in cipher!" in the narrator's words (66). In Conrad's Swiss- and Russian-set *Under Western Eyes* (1911), the narrator, a specialist in languages, is an Englishman, or rather someone "described as an Englishman" (192), who reveals that though he acquired Russian as a boy he feels "profoundly my European remoteness" when faced with Russia (198). Using language strikingly similar to that he uses for the Congo, Conrad in this tale terms Russia "incomprehensible to the experience of Western Europe" and burdened by "the confused immensity of [its] Eastern borders" (322), victim of "the slavery of a Tartar conquest" (164) and producer of "the gigantic shadow of Russian life deepening [. . .] like the darkness of an advancing night" (210). It is reasonable to suggest, then, a relation between Conrad's masterly, vexed narration of Western colonial encounters and his upbringing in and lifelong identification with the Russocolonized Poland of his birth.

These questions of the shifting, gradated eastern-western European border, especially as regards post-Soviet postcoloniality, are enormously complex. Recently they have been addressed historiographically by Larry Wolff (*Inventing* and "Voltaire's Public") and Milica Bakić-Hayden. They have been asked specifically for the Balkans in two superb Said-inflected studies, by Maria Todorova and by Vesna Goldsworthy, and in two explicitly postcolonialist dissertations, by Nikola Petković and by Dubravka Juraga. All these works highlight the degree to which Eastern Europe and especially the Balkans—inheritors of centuries of colonizing waves from all directions, often more Ottoman and Hapsburg than Russo-Soviet—have returned to their former status as the West's original Third World, its nearest quasi-oriental space. The great Nigerian writer Chinua Achebe, because of his colonial education, is well aware of this. As noted in the last epigraph to this paper, drawn from Achebe's famous essay on Conrad's *Heart of Darkness*, in Achebe's view the nineteenth-century English mind judged Bulgaria the psychological equivalent of "the Congo of King Leopold of the Belgians," to which Achebe adds a genericizing "or wherever."[20] Separately, intellectuals such as Michael Ignatieff, Ryszard Kapuściński, and Timothy Garton Ash have provided comparative though not expressly postcolonial perspectives on this subject. Much more remains unwritten.

––––––––––

I conclude with a brief account of some of this essay's omissions, and with an answer to the question, Whither postcolonial theory when it covers the entire globe? The largest omission in this paper results from my thin consideration of the Soviet experience from 1917 to 1991 and my too easy yoking of it in my repeated "Russo-Soviet." By all accounts, the Soviet Union attempted something very different from the Russian imperium it succeeded: instead of declaring itself an empire, it proposed a multilayered "voluntary" union of republics. Though according to the strictest Marxist-Leninist approach, national identities would eventually dissolve into *homo Sovieticus*, Lenin and his Commissar of Nationalities, Joseph Stalin, developed an approach, "nationalist in form, socialist in content," that offered an alternative to the then current imperial, colonial, caste-based, universalist, and melting-pot ideologies. Thus, in judging if the Soviets were colonizers, one must consider numerous dimensions. Those who would characterize the Soviet experiment as noncolonial can point, inter alia, to the Soviet Union's wish to liberate its toiling masses; its dismantling of many ethnic-Russian privileges in its east and south; its support of many Union languages; its development of factories, hospitals, and schools; its liberation of women from the harem and the veil; its support of Third World anticolonial struggles, seen as intimately connected with the Soviet experiment, from 1923 to 1991; and the fact that some minority of the Soviet sphere's non-Russians wished the Bolshevik regime.

Those who would argue that the Soviets were simply differently configured colonists could point, again inter alia, to the mass and arbitrary relocation of entire non-Russian peoples; the ironic Soviet national fixing of countless formerly less defined identities and the related tortured intertwining of the Uzbek-Kyrgyz-Tajik border to guarantee an ethnic strife; the genocidal settling of the Kazakh nomad millions from 1929 to 1934; the forced monoculture across Central Asia and the consequent ecological disaster of the Aral Sea; the Soviet reconquest of the once independent Baltic states in 1941; the invariable Russian ethnicity of the number-two man in each republic; the inevitable direction of Russia's Third World policy from its Moscow center; and tanks in 1956 and 1968 in Budapest and Prague. Complicating either argument is that the Soviet Union and its predecessor Russian empire were often as lethal to their Russians as to non-Russians, and that the USSR radically devalued specifically Russian identity for several decades. Is the net result of all these items—each subject to a complex bibliography[21]—some version of "colonial," and are its consequences "post"? From an Uzbek, Lithuanian, or Hungarian perspective one would have to answer yes.

As for the risked inflation of the category "postcolonial"—a category already so crazily diverse, ranging from accounting to the Middle Ages, nautical archaeology to the Bible,[22] that one wonders how anyone could unify it even before a Soviet inclusion—I recognize that when terms expand their scope they risk losing analytic force. There is little sense in claiming terms like "colored," for example, if all the world has color. Or perhaps not. In closing, then, I would like to defend an inflation of the postcolonial to include the enormous post-Soviet sphere. Primarily I do so because Russia and then the Soviet Union exercised powerful colonial control over much of the earth for from fifty to two hundred years, much of that control has now ended, and its ending has had manifest effects on the literatures and cultures of the postcolonial-post-Soviet nations, including Russia. Of course, as I have noted, the specific modalities of Russo-Soviet control, as well as their post-Soviet reverberations, have differed from the standard Anglo-Franco cases. But then again, to privilege the Anglo-Franco cases as the colonizing standard and to call the Russo-Soviet experiences deviations, as I have done so far, is wrongly to perpetuate the already superannuated centrality of the Western or Anglo-Franco world. It is time, I think, to break with that tradition.

As for universalizing the postcolonial condition, I close by supporting such a move. Recall the imaginative map I asked readers to draw in response to Ella Shohat's geography. Shohat's signifiers drew a map of the First and Third Worlds, to which I added the Soviet portion of the Second. One might now add China, for China has been buffeted by the Mongols, Manchus, Japanese, and British, and today it imperially-colonially controls Tibet and the giant Turkic Muslim Xinjiang Uighur region.[23] But even after these regions are cross-hatched, certain smaller zones remain unmarked. However, these zones, by their rarity at least, stand not outside but *in relation to* a global (post)coloniality. I speak here, for example, of created buffer states like Nepal, the aforementioned Afghanistan, Iran, and once colonizing Turkey, whose historic freedoms from Western and Russo-Soviet control were due, in part, to occidento-Russian calculation. And now that I have added these, the reader may rightly wonder what still has gone unmentioned. Japan, for one. Long isolated by a conscious choice, Japan ironically avoided the global hegemony of nineteenth-century European power with a westernizing program: a French-style army, a British navy, Dutch civic engineering, a German-model government, and United States–style public education. Japan in the twentieth century saw struggles with the Russians and its own deplorable colonial forays, followed by a total United States military occupation. Does this nation, rarely included in discussions of the postcolonial, stand outside (post)colonial dynamics? And what, theoretically, can one make of Fiji, Western Sahara, Mauritius, Kurdistan, or Cuba?

The African American tradition also includes a substantial discourse on coloniality. Participants from W.E.B. Du Bois to Malcolm X have debated whether African Americans, like other colored peoples around the globe, could be termed colonial. Indeed, the African American engagement here includes a 1930s interchange with Soviet Central Asia.[24] One of the earliest important texts in postcolonial theory, Albert Memmi's 1957 *Portrait du colonisé,* had its English version dedicated "to the American Negro / also colonized." And more recently, the colonial-Trinidadian-born and ordinarily centrist Arnold Rampersad, in a review of the notion of the universal in African American poetry, reflects powerfully and at length on the poetic influence of the "colonial relationship such as that existing between blacks and whites in the United States" (2). Beyond "endocolonial" situations like these,[25] one has also seen the argument that, for example, even nineteenth-century German national identity, in the absence of major colonial engagements, depended heavily on Germans' imaginative participation in the imperial conquests of their English, Dutch, French, and Spanish neighbors.[26]

The colonial encounters of the past two hundred years—from Dakar to Calcutta, Samarkand to Jamaica, Skopje to Tallinn, or Vladivostok to Seattle by the long route[27]—were so global and widespread, in unstandardizable diversity, that every human being and every literature on the planet today stands in relation to them: as neo-, endo- and ex-, as post- and non-. This observation, as this essay has suggested, should recast the views of postcolonial and post-Soviet scholars alike: not so much to help them judge whether place X "is postcolonial or not"—this is not an essay in ontology—but rather to cause them to ask if postcolonial hermeneutics might add richness to studies of place or literature X or Y or Z. In sum, the colonial relation at the turn of the millennium, whatever it may be, is thus not theoretically inflated to a point of weakness, nor is it the property of a certain class or space of peoples, but rather it becomes as fundamental to world identities as other "universal" categories, such as race, and class, and caste, and age, and gender.

ACKNOWLEDGMENTS

Early sparks for this essay were afforded by a Macalester International Faculty Development Seminar in Budapest in July 1995. Fractional versions were given at Crossroads in Cultural Studies in Tampere, Finland, and the Open Society Forum in Vilnius, Lithuania, in July 1996; an African Literature Association meeting in March 1997; the Institute for Oriental Studies of Tashkent State University and the Samarkand State Institute of Foreign Languages, both in Uzbekistan, in October 1998; and the series Race in Europe at the Minda de Gunzburg Center for European Studies at Harvard University, in April 1999. My great thanks go to the organizers and participants in all these venues. I owe further debts to numerous Macalester and national colleagues and Macalester students and to Nicole Palasz and Jennifer Evans. Much of my research was supported by International Research Exchange Board (IREX) and Wallace Foundation grants for travel to the former Soviet Union and by an American Council of Learned Societies/Social Science Research Council International Postdoctoral Fellowship for 1998–99. The title of this paper marks the broader influence of Anthony Appiah.

NOTES

1 See, e.g., Kiberd (*Inventing;* "White Skins") and Waters on Ireland. Though a postcolonial perspective on Ireland is seen as recent, it is not; cf. Hechter.

2 Landmarks include Parry, Hutcheon, Prakash ("Who's Afraid" and "Writing"), McClintock, Shohat, Huggan, Dirlik, Ray and Schwarz, and Ghosh. After 1998 the autocritical debate becomes too large to track. Here I leave apart the related controversies surrounding Ahmad (see esp. his "Jameson's Rhetoric" and *In Theory*), which don't focus on the postcolonial.

3 Qtd. in Burnley 172. Ironically, Bokenham here adapts Ranulph Higden's c. 1327 Latin *Poly-chronicon*. For discussion, see Burnley 133–36.

4 For "the West," see Lewis and Wigen, chs. 2 and 3.

5 In the 31 January 1827 conversation in which Goethe famously first pronounces "Welt-literatur," he discusses a Chinese novel he has just read. His amanuensis Eckermann asks whether it is one of the best. "Not at all," Goethe answers, "the Chinese have thousands of them and already had them at a time when our forefathers still lived in the forests" (228n7).

6 For a characteristic discussion of "Third World" and "Third World literature," see Ahmad, *In Theory*, chs. 1 and 8.

7 For Canadian literature as postcolonial, see Hutcheon and the response by Brydon. For white Australians, New Zealanders, Canadians, and South Africans as postcolonial, see Slemon. Slemon appropriates the term "second world" for these settlers, whom he sees as neither First nor Third. He ignores the more common definition of "Second World"—a sign of the Soviet-sphere absence from the postcolonialist academy. For United States nineteenth-century literature as postcolonial, see Buell; the reluctance I refer to is shown by the limited influence of Buell's article. Subsequent work on United States postcoloniality comes in Stratton; Sharpe; Hulme; and—evidence that the reluctance is now receding—three books from the last three years: Watts; King; and Singh and Schmidt. See also Krupat, who notes that contemporary Native American writers live "in a postcolonial world" but write "from within a colonial context" (54). The strength of settler studies within postcolonial studies partly stems from the Australians Ashcroft, Griffiths, and Tiffin, who wrote the first monograph in the field *(Empire)* and produced one of its first classroom-use anthologies *(Reader)*.

8 After the death of Håkon VI in 1380, Norway was ruled by Denmark and then Sweden for five centuries. In 1905 the king of newly independent Norway took the name Håkon VII on accession. Finland operated as a Swedish duchy for centuries before being transferred to Russia in 1809, and it gained independence in the turmoil of the Russian Revolution in 1917.

9 Shohat expresses reservations about this claim, which is quoted from Ashcroft, Griffiths, and Tiffin *(Empire* 2).

10 See, e.g., Austin; Scotto; Layton; and Brower and Lazzerini.

11 Rare exceptions include Pavlyshyn ("Ukrainian Literature" and "Post-colonial Features"); Tottossy; Yekelchyk; and Lyons.

12 For clear examples, see Kaplan *(Balkan Ghosts* and *Ends)*.

13 An exception is the immediate popularity in Poland of Ryszard Kapuściński's *Cesarz* (1978), which chronicled the downfall of the emperor of Ethiopia and was widely read allegorically for its applicability to local Polish conditions. Notably, *Cesarz* was quickly translated into Spanish but only later into English.

14 Early considerations of this rebirth are found in Schöpflin and Wood.

15 Renan (cf. Anderson, ch. 11) famously observed that a nation must forget the historical brutalities that produced its present unity (11).

16 Postcolonial Mikhail Baryshnikov, born in Riga (the capital of Latvia) in 1948 of Russian parents—his father was a senior military officer sent there after reannexation—is a notable product of this population. In his sole return (1997) to the former USSR since his 1974 defection, Baryshnikov visited only Riga and not Moscow or Saint Petersburg. Baryshnikov had felt himself "a guest always" in Russia, yet he termed his parents "occupiers" in Riga. "The minute I stepped again on Latvian land," he said during his visit, "I realized this was never my home" (Acocella 44).

17 Russian intellectual and literary movements, including Eurasianism (Riasonovsky; Trubetzkoy, "Legacy" and "Pan-Eurasian Nationalism") and Sycthianism (Zamyatin), have promoted this view.

18 That is, *perestroika*. My deferral of the Latin script aims to underscore that point.

19 Or Africanization, Latinization, or other classic forms of Western "othering" and self-construction. See Trouillot in general and Trubetzkoy, "Europe."

20 "Image" 10. The context comes from my telephone interview with Achebe. On the Bulgarian horrors, see Gladstone; Butler-Johnstone; Shannon.

21 Among many recent studies in this shifting landscape, see Motyl; Suny; Lazzerini; Mesbahi; Slezkine ("USSR"); Brubaker; and Khalid.

22 See, respectively, Chua; Cohen; McGhee; and Sugirtharajah.

23 See Adas. For direct considerations of China and postcoloniality that are highly derivative of standard theorists and shamefully say zero about Tibet or Xinjiang Uighur, see Ning; Ning and Xie; M. Xie; and S. Xie. For historically broad Third World support of Tibet, see *Report*. Here I note that all major powers test-detonate their nuclear weapons exclusively in their post- or endocolonies, including China (Lop Nor, in Xinjiang Uighur), the USSR (Kazakhstan; Novaya Zemlya, in the Arctic), the United States (Nevada; the South Pacific; Amchitka Island, in the Aleutians), France (Algeria in 1960; the South Pacific), and Britain (Western Australia in 1952–56). The joint 1980s antinuclear Kazakh-Shoshone Nevada-Semipalatinsk Movement exemplifies truly global endocolonial resistance.

24 See, e.g., Bunche's early "Marxism and the 'Negro Question' " or Hughes's Moscow-published 1934 *A Negro Looks at Soviet Central Asia,* which embraces Soviet Central Asian peoples as liberated versions of their also southern, "colored," cotton-growing American brethren. Cf. Moore. For Afro-diasporic intersections with Soviet-colonial questions, see Blakely; Von Eschen; Padmore; and C.L.R. James on Hungary in 1956 (Lee, Chalieu, and Johnson).

25 The writings of the Ogoni Nigerian Saro-Wiwa are considered landmarks in endocolonial resistance literature.

26 See Zantop for an account of German "imaginary" colonialism. I recognize, of course, that Germany held colonies in Africa from 1884 to 1918, a fraction the size of colonies held worldwide by England, France, the Netherlands, Spain, Portugal, or Russia.

27 For the trip from Vladivostok to San Francisco by the short route, see the Kyrgyz writer Chingiz Aitmatov's 1980 *The Day Lasts More Than a Hundred Years*—a novel that, despite its galactic scope, can be read against Western-colonial railway novels such as Ousmane Sembène's *Les bouts de bois de Dieu.*

WORKS CITED

Achebe, Chinua. "An Image of Africa: Racism in Conrad's Heart of Darkness." 1975. *Hopes and Impediments: Selected Essays*. New York Anchor-Doubleday, 1988. 1–20.

———. Telephone interview. 8 Nov. 1997.

Acocella, Joan. "The Soloist." *New Yorker* 19 Jan. 1998: 44–56.

Adas, Michael. "Imperialism and Colonialism in Comparative Perspective." *International History Review* 20 (1998): 371–88.

Ahmad, Aijaz. *In Theory: Nations, Classes, Literatures*. New York: Routledge, 1992.

———. "Jameson's Rhetoric of Otherness and the 'National Allegory.' " *Social Text* 17 (1987): 3–25.

Aitmatov, Chingiz. *The Day Lasts More Than a Hundred Years*. 1980. Trans. John French. Fwd. Katerina Clark. Bloomington: Indiana UP, 1988.

Anderson, Benedict. *Imagined Communities: Reflections on the Origin and Spread of Nationalism*. Rev. ed. London: Verso, 1991.

Appiah, Kwame Anthony. "Is the Post- in Postmodernism the Post- in Postcolonial?" *Critical Inquiry* 17 (1991): 336–57.

Ashcroft, Bill, Gareth Griffiths, and Helen Tiffin. *The Empire Writes Back: Theory and Practice in Post-colonial Literatures*. New Accents. Ed. Terence Hawkes. London: Routledge, 1989.

———, eds. *The Post-colonial Studies Reader*. London: Routledge, 1995.

Austin, Paul M. "The Exotic Prisoner in Russian Romanticism." *Russian Literature* 16–18 (1984): 217–29.

Bakić-Hayden, Milica. "Nesting Orientalisms: The Case of Former Yugoslavia." *Slavic Review* 54 (1995): 917–31.

Blakely, Allison. *Russia and the Negro: Blacks in Russian History and Thought*. Washington: Howard UP, 1986.

Brower, Daniel R., and Edward J. Lazzerini, eds. *Russia's Orient: Imperial Borderlands and Peoples, 1700–1917*. Bloomington: Indiana UP, 1997.

Brubaker, Rogers. "Nationhood and the National Question in the Soviet Union and Post-Soviet Eurasia: An Institutionalist Account." *Citizenship and National Identity: From Colonialism to Globalism*. Ed. T. K. Oommen. New Delhi: Sage, 1997. 85–119.

Brydon, Diana. "The White Inuit Speaks: Contamination as Literary Strategy." *Past the Last Post: Theorizing Post-colonialism and Post-modernism*. Ed. Ian Adam and Helen Tiffin. Calgary: U of Calgary P, 1990. 191–203.

Buell, Lawrence. "American Literary Emergence as a Postcolonial Phenomenon." *American Literary History* 4 (1992): 411–42.

Bunche, Ralph J. "Marxism and the 'Negro Question.'" 1929. *Selected Speeches and Writings*. Ed. and introd. Charles P. Henry. Ann Arbor: U of Michigan P, 1995.

Burnley, David. *The History of the English Language: A Source Book*. London: Longman, 1992.

Butler-Johnstone, H[enry] A[lexander]. *Bulgarian Horrors, and the Question of the East*. London: Ridgway, 1876.

Chekhov, Anton. *The Island: A Journey to Sakhalin*. 1895. Trans. Luba Terpak and Michael Terpak. New York: Washington Square, 1967.

Chua, Wai Fong. "Postcoloniality, Accounting and Accounting Research." Working paper, School of Accounting, U of New South Wales. 1995.

Cohen, Jeffrey Jerome, ed. *The Postcolonial Middle Ages*. The New Middle Ages. New York: St. Martin's, 2000.

Conrad, Joseph. *Heart of Darkness*. 1899. London: Penguin, 1995.

———. *Under Western Eyes*. 1911. London: Penguin, 1985.

Curzon, George N. *Russia in Central Asia in 1889, and the Anglo-Russian Question*. London: Longmans, Green, 1889.

Defoe, Daniel. *The True-Born Englishman: A Satyr*. London (Black-Fryars): H. Hills, 1708.

Dirlik, Arif. "The Postcolonial Aura: Third World Criticism in the Age of Global Capitalism." *Critical Inquiry* 20 (1994): 328–56.

Fanon, Frantz. *The Wretched of the Earth*. 1961. Trans. Constance Farrington. Introd. Jean-Paul Sartre. New York: Grove, 1968.

Ghosh, Bishnupriya. "The Postcolonial Bazaar: Thoughts on Teaching the Market in Postcolonial Objects." *Postmodern Culture* 9.1 (1998). 18 Dec. 2000 <http://muse.jhu.edu/journals/postmodern_culture/v009/ 9.1 ghosh.html>.

Gladstone, W[illiam] E[wart]. *Bulgarian Horrors and the Question of the East*. London: John Murray, 1876.

Goethe, Johann Wolfgang von. "Some Passages Pertaining to the Concept of World Literature." *Comparative Literature: The Early Years—An Anthology of Essays*. Ed. Hans-Joachim Schulz and Phillip H. Rhein. U of North Carolina Studies in Compar. Lit. 55. Chapel Hill: U of North Carolina P, 1973. 1–11, 227–28.

Goldsworthy, Vesna. *Inventing Ruritania: The Imperialism of the Imagination*. New Haven: Yale UP, 1998.

Hechter, Michael. *Internal Colonialism: The Celtic Fringe in British National Development, 1536–1966*. Berkeley: U of California P, 1975.

Huggan, Graham. "Postcolonialism and Its Discontents." *Transition* 62 (1993): 130–35.

Hughes, Langston. *A Negro Looks at Soviet Central Asia*. Moscow: Co-operative Publishing Soc. of Foreign Workers in the USSR, 1934.

Hulme, Peter. "Including America." *Ariel* 26.1 (1995): 117–23.

Hutcheon, Linda. " 'Circling the Downspout of Empire': Post-colonialism and Postmodernism." *Ariel* 20.4 (1989): 149–75.

Juraga, Dubravka. "Literature, History, and Postcolonial Cultural Identity in Africa and the Balkans: The Search for a Usable Past in Farah, Ngũgĩ, Krleza, and Andric." Diss. U of Arkansas, 1996.

Kane, Cheikh Hamidou. *L'aventure ambiguë*. Paris: Julliard, 1961.

Kaplan, Robert D. *Balkan Ghosts: A Journey through History*. New York: St. Martin's, 1993.

———. *The Ends of the Earth: From Togo to Turkmenistan, from Iran to Cambodia: A Journey to the Frontiers of Anarchy*. New York: Knopf, 1997.

Kapuściński, Ryszard. *Cesarz*. Warszawa: Czytelnik, 1978.

———. *El Emperador: La historia del extrañísimo señor de Ethiopía*. Historia inmediata. Trans. María Dembowska. México: Siglo Veintiuno, 1980.

———. *The Emperor: Downfall of an Autocrat*. Trans. William R. Brand and Katarzyna Mroczkowska-Brand. San Diego: Harcourt, 1983.

Khalid, Adeeb. *The Politics of Muslim Cultural Reform: Jadidism in Central Asia*. Berkeley: U of California P, 1998.

Kiberd, Declan. *Inventing Ireland*. Cambridge: Harvard UP 1996.

———. "White Skins, Black Masks? Celtism and Negritude." *Éire-Ireland* 31.1–2 (1997): 163–75.

King, C. Richard, ed. *Postcolonial America*. Urbana: U of Illinois P, 2000.

Kipling, Rudyard. *Kim*. 1901. Ed. and introd. Edward Said. London: Penguin, 1987.

Krupat, Arnold. "Postcolonialism, Ideology, and Native American Literature." *The Turn to the Native: Studies in Criticism and Culture*. Lincoln: U of Nebraska P, 1996. 30–55.

Layton, Susan. *Russian Literature and Empire: Conquest of the Caucasus from Pushkin to Tolstoy*. Cambridge: Cambridge UP, 1994.

Lazarus, Neil. "Great Expectations and After: The Politics of Postcolonialism in African Fiction." *Social Text* 13–14 (1986): 49–63.

Lazzerini, Edward J. "Defining the Orient: A Nineteenth-Century Russo-Tatar Polemic over Identity and Cultural Representation." *Muslim Communities Reemerge: Historical Perspectives on Nationality, Politics, and Opposition in the Former Soviet Union and Yugoslavia*. Ed. Andreas Kappler et al. Durham: Duke UP, 1994. 33–45.

Lee, Grace C., Pierre Chalieu, and J. R. Johnson [C.L.R. James]. *Facing Reality*. Detroit: Correspondence, 1958.

Lermontov, Mikhail Y. *A Hero of Our Time*. 1840. Trans. Paul Foote. London: Penguin, 1966.

Lewis, Martin, and Kären Wigen. *The Myth of Continents: A Critique of Metageography*. Berkeley: U of California P, 1997.

Lyons, Shawn Thomas. "Uzbek Historical Fiction and Russian Colonialism, 1918–1936." Diss. U of Wisconsin, Madison, 1999.

McClintock, Anne. "The Angel of Progress: Pitfalls of the Term 'Post-colonialism.' " *Social Text* 10.2–3 (31–32) (1992): 84–98.

McGhee, Fred Lee. "Toward a Postcolonial Nautical Archaeology." MA thesis. U of Texas, Austin, 1997.

Memmi, Albert. *The Colonizer and the Colonized*. 1957. Trans. Howard Greenfield. New York: Orion, 1965.

———. *Portrait du colonisé, précédé du Portrait du colonisateur*. Paris: Buchet, 1957.

Mesbahi, Mohiaddin, ed. *Russia and the Third World in the Post-Soviet Era*. Gainesville: U of Florida P, 1994.

Moore, David Chioni. "Local Color, Global 'Color': Langston Hughes, the Black Atlantic, and Soviet Central Asia, 1932." *Research in African Literatures* 27.4 (1996): 49–70.

Motyl, Alexander J., ed. *Thinking Theoretically about Soviet Nationalities: History and Comparison in the Study of the USSR*. New York: Columbia UP, 1992.

Najder, Zdzislaw. *Joseph Conrad: A Chronicle*. Cambridge: Cambridge UP, 1984.

Ngũgĩ wa Thiong'o. *Decolonising the Mind: The Politics of Language in African Literature*. London: Heinemann, 1986.

———. *Devil on the Cross*. 1980. Trans. Ngũgĩ. Oxford: Heinemann, 1982.

Ning, Wang. "Postcolonial Theory and the 'Decolonization' of Chinese Culture." *Ariel* 28.4 (1997): 33–47.

Ning, Wang, and Shaobo Xie, eds. "China and Postcolonialism: A Special Section." Introd. Ning and Xie. *Ariel* 28.4 (1997): 7–72.

Padmore, George, in collaboration with Dorothy Pizer. *How Russia Transformed Her Colonial Empire: A Challenge to the Imperialist Powers*. London: Dobson, 1946.

Parry, Benita. "Problems in Current Theories of Colonial Discourse." *Oxford Literary Review* 9.1–2 (1987): 27–58.

Pavlyshyn, Marko. "Post-colonial Features in Contemporary Ukranian Culture." *Australian Slavonic and East European Studies* 6.2 (1992): 41–55.

———. "Ukrainian Literature and the Erotics of Postcolonialism: Some Modest Propositions." *Harvard Ukrainian Studies* 17 (1993): 110–26.

Petković, Nikola. "The 'Post' in Postcolonial and Postmodern: The Case of Central Europe." Diss. U of Texas, Austin, 1996.

Prakash, Gyan. "Who's Afraid of Postcoloniality?" *Social Text* 14.4 (1996): 187–203.

———. "Writing Post-orientalist Histories of the Third World: Perspectives from Indian Historiography." *Comparative Studies in Society and History* 32 (1990): 383–408.

Rampersad, Arnold. "The Universal and the Particular in Afro-American Poetry." *CLA Journal* 25.1 (1981): 1–17.

Ray, Sangeeta, and Henry Schwarz. "Postcolonial Discourse: The Raw and the Cooked." *Ariel* 26.1 (1995): 147–66.

Renan, Ernest. "What Is a Nation?" 1882. *Nation and Narration*. Ed. Homi K. Bhabha. Trans. Martin Thom. New York: Routledge, 1990. 8–22.

Report of the Afro-Asian Convention on Tibet and against Colonialism in Asia and Africa. New Delhi: Afro-Asian Council, 1960.

Riasonovsky, Nicholas V. "The Emergence of Eurasianism." *California Slavic Studies* 4 (1967): 39–72.

Said, Edward W. *Culture and Imperialism*. New York: Knopf, 1993.

———. *Orientalism*. New York: Pantheon, 1978.

Schöpflin, George, and Nancy Wood, eds. *In Search of Central Europe*. Cambridge, Eng.: Polity, 1989.

Scotto, Peter. "Prisoners of the Caucasus: Ideologies of Imperialism in Lermontov's 'Bela.'" *PMLA* 107 (1992): 246–60.

Sembène, Ousmane. *Les bouts de bois de Dieu*. Paris: Le Livre Contemporain, 1960.

Shannon, R. T. *Gladstone and the Bulgarian Agitation 1876*. 2nd ed. Hassocks: Harvester; Hamden: Archon, 1975.

Sharpe, Jenny. "Is the United States Postcolonial? Transnationalism, Immigration, and Race." *Diaspora* 4.2 (1995): 181–99.

Shohat, Ella. "Notes on the 'Post-Colonial.'" *Social Text* 10.2–3 (31–32) (1992): 99–413.

Singh, Amrijit, and Peter Schmidt, eds. *Postcolonial Theory and the United States: Race, Ethnicity, and Literature*. Jackson: U of Mississippi P, 2000.

Slemon, Stephen. "Unsettling the Empire: Resistance Theory for the Second World." *World Literature Written in English* 30.2 (1990): 30–41.

Slezkine, Yuri. *Arctic Mirrors: Russia and the Small Peoples of the North*. Ithaca: Cornell UP, 1994.

———. "The USSR as a Communal Apartment; or, How a Socialist State Promoted Ethnic Particularism." *Slavic Review* 53 (1994): 414–52.

Stratton, Jon. "The Beast of the Apocalypse: The Postcolonial Experience of the United States." *New Formations* (1993): 35–63.

Sugirtharajah, R. S., ed. *The Postcolonial Bible*. The Bible and Postcolonialism. Sheffield: Sheffield Acad., 1998.

Suny, Ronald Grigor. *The Revenge of the Past: Nationalism, Revolution, and the Collapse of the Soviet Union*. Stanford: Stanford UP, 1993.

Todorova, Maria. *Imagining the Balkans*. New York: Oxford UP, 1997.

Tottossy, Beatrice. "Hungarian Postmodernity and Postcoloniality: The Epistemology of a Literature." Trans. Aristide Melchiouna. *Canadian Review of Comparative Literature / Revue canadienne de littérature comparée* 22 (1995): 881–91.

Trouillot, Michel-Rolph. "Anthropology and the Savage Slot: The Poetics and Politics of Otherness." *Recapturing Anthropology: Working in the Present*. Ed. Richard G. Fox. Santa Fe: School of Amer. Research P, 1991. 17–44.

Trubetzkoy, N. S. "Europe and Mankind." 1920. Trans. Kenneth Brostrom. Trubetzkoy, *"Legacy,"* 1–64.

———. *"The Legacy of Genghis Khan," and Other Essays on Russia's Identity*. Ed. Anatoly Liberman. Ann Arbor: Michigan Slavic, 1991.

———. "The Legacy of Genghis Khan: A Perspective on Russian History Not from the West but from the East." 1925. Trans. Kenneth Brostrom. Trubetzkoy, *"Legacy,"* 161–231.

———. "Pan-Eurasian Nationalism." 1927. Trans. Kenneth Brostrom. Trubetzkoy, *"Legacy,"* 233–44.

Von Eschen, Penny M. *Race against Empire: Black Americans and Anticolonialism, 1937–1957*. Ithaca: Cornell UP, 1997.

Waters, John Paul, ed. *Ireland and Irish Cultural Studies*. Introd. Waters. Special issue of *South Atlantic Quarterly* 95.1 (1996): 1–278.

Watts, Edward. *Writing and Postcolonialism in the Early Republic*. Charlottesville: UP of Virginia, 1998.

Williams, Patrick, and Laura Chrisman, eds. *Colonial Discourse and Post-colonial Theory: A Reader*. New York: Columbia UP, 1994.

Wolff, Larry. *Inventing Eastern Europe: The Map of Civilization in the Mind of the Enlightenment*. Stanford: Stanford UP, 1994.

———. "Voltaire's Public and the Idea of Eastern Europe: Toward a Literary Sociology of a Continental Division." *Slavic Review* 54 (1995): 932–42.

Xie, Ming. "The Postmodern as the Postcolonial: Recognizing Chinese Modernity." *Ariel* 28.4 (1997): 11–32.

Xie, Shaobo. "Rethinking the Problem of Postcolonialism." *New Literary History* 28 (1997): 6–19.

Yekelchyk, Serhy. "The Location of Nation: Postcolonial Perspectives on Ukrainian Historical Debates." *Australian Slavonic and East European Studies* 11.1–2 (1997): 161–84.

Zamyatin, Yevgeny. "Scythians." 1918. *A Soviet Heretic: Essays by Yevgeny Zamyatin*. Ed. and trans. Mirra Ginsburg. Chicago: U of Chicago P, 1970. 21–33.

Zantop, Susanne. *Colonial Fantasies: Conquest, Family, and Nation in Precolonial Germany, 1770–1870*. Durham: Duke UP, 1997.

IX

Globalization and Postcoloniality

A modern teleology of globalization almost invariably marks its beginnings in the post-Columbian era of European colonization and the subsequent spread of global capital enabled by the formation of a world market. But some accounts of globalization tend to resist the binary power structure of the center-periphery model or the hierarchical three-worlds paradigm of uneven development. Nor do they necessarily admit unilateral Euro-American dominance, despite the obvious disparities between the North and the South (yet one more schematic model to add to the list). Others tend to argue for contemporary globalization as a different avatar, albeit more complex and differentiated, of the colonial imperative. The four writers in part IX all critically examine the relationship between globalization and postcolonial discourse, but they range across a spectrum of positions.

Stuart Hall's essay stresses the synergy between diasporic and global patterns centuries after the momentous voyage of Columbus and the expansion of Europe into other parts of the world. Hall's emphasis on multiple identities, on "meanings that are positional and relational," on the limitations of the national model, on "vernacular modernities" is based on fluid interpretations of culture and identity which resist statist and static models. His buoyant examples of "diaspora aesthetic," of the border-defying crossings of cultural flows across the Atlantic world and the migrations of black populations, insist on reconfiguring the inside-outside perspectives of national or even regional locations. "The fate of Caribbean people living in the UK, the US or Canada is no more 'external' to Caribbean history than the Empire was 'external' to the so-called domestic history of Britain, though that is indeed how contemporary historiography constructs them," says Hall. The mutually constitutive zones of influence suggest that the marginal elements, specifically Caribbean peoples and cultures, matter significantly both in the production of a supposedly authentic anterior "Africa" in the Caribbean and in the self-construction of an apparently impermeable European "mother country."

Traditionally located as a mere periphery of Africa, Asia, and Europe, and as an afterthought to the Americas, the Caribbean emerges as a formative space, not a forgotten frontier. The influence of poststructuralist thinking is clear in Hall's supplementary interpretation of the margin and in a statement such as this: "everywhere, hybridity, *differance*." This is precisely the kind of language that Arif Dirlik finds objectionable in cultural theory and postcolonial discourse.

Although Dirlik's attack on postcolonial scholarship is multipronged and includes Indian, Chinese, and U.S. intellectuals, his primary charge about the cooptation of all three groups in the First World begins where Hall ends. Hall's conclusion, citing C.L.R. James, the Marxist intellectual and metropolitan figure par excellence, pays tribute to the "unique insight" of Caribbean people who have lived in the West but are never considered to be fully part of it. Dirlik, however, does not share the sanguine perspective of the illuminations provided by Third World intellectuals who, through the forces of history, find themselves in First World locations. Instead, this change in originary location is what contributes to the mystifying "postcolonial aura," and this particular arrival portends a foreboding blindness to, not appreciation for, the salutary lessons of Marxism.

What Dirlik views as the sloppiness of globalization discourse, its rejection of deterministic structural models, and its foundational or master narratives such as center-periphery, nationalism, and Marxist economism ultimately colludes, he believes, with the continuing inequalities of global capital. Not only does European hegemony get reinforced, but the privileged postcolonial intellectuals in First World academies displace the historical populations in the Third World whose voices are rarely heard and whose agendas rarely matter here. Who and what is identified as postcolonial is not always carefully calculated, says Dirlik. Consequently, he believes, the structural inequalities of different postcolonial populations are obscured by the very small coterie of academics who control postcolonial narratives and who claim a victimized status while gaining professional privilege and cultural capital. According to Dirlik, the intellectual brain drain from Third to First World was itself a specific effect of global capitalism, although its "beneficiaries" obfuscate their class privileges by opportunistically appropriating subaltern or marginal positions. Postcolonial intellectuals, doomed by their very inception in the belly of European capital and now flourishing in the American academy, are therefore fundamentally conservative.

Rey Chow anticipates some of Dirlik's powerful critiques against the "lures of diaspora" but does so without flattening power structures on a vertical scale. Thus, while in Dirlik's formulation, the peoples of the Third World generally appear as less powerful and more genuinely the victims of First World capital than residents of the First World, Chow suggests that the differential power structures do not always correspond to where one lives or even to middle-class identity. Nor is the Third World only inhabited by those subjects who are invariably patronized by the First World or those who inevitably suffer the consequences of its control over capital. Chow exposes, like Dirlik, the hypocrisies of claiming minority status on the part of those occupying relatively privileged positions, but she goes on to reveal that exploiting minority discourse is not the exclusive practice of middle-class, postcolonial intellectuals in the First World. In China, the ostensible pursuit of the "proletarian nation" and the latter's use of minority discourse show a different trajectory of power. Thus, Chow notes that modern Chinese literature, "in its investment in suffering, in social oppression, and in the victimization and silencing of the unprivileged, . . . partakes of the many issues of 'minority discourse' that surface with urgency in the field of cultural studies/cultural criticism in North America today." Ironically, the silenced figure of the subaltern becomes written about obsessively in claiming proletarian identity for a national and literary history.

Chow also argues for a reconsideration of the material effects of the discursive. The discursive, in complaints about its appearance in postcolonial theory, is accused of substituting for or eliding the material. But in Chow's analysis, the discursive can also *produce* material effects. "Instead of causing the reality to disappear, naming is the way to make a certain reality 'proper,' that is to make it real." Although Chow's claim that "language is the absolutely essential means of access to power" may sound too categorical to critics of the discursive politics of postcolonial theory, she points out that connections between language, literature, and power are not as farfetched as those who single-mindedly focus on material structures claim (see Said, chapter 7). "Chinese communism was the dream of materializing that theory [of social change leading to the disappearance of class] by officializing a concept of language and literature in which the minorities, the oppressed, and the exploited are to be vindicated." If Chow is suspicious of romanticizing the minorities, it is because she maps different nodes of minority relationships in which groups operate dynamically. Using the figure of the Chinese woman as an example of internal inequalities within social groups, Chow argues that class difference is only one component of minority status. Rejecting generalized categories of difference and victimization as applied to all non-Western cultures in the aftermath of colonialism, Chow insists that Chinese intellectuals must "fight the crippling effects of Western imperialism and Chinese paternalism at once."

Simon Gikandi is equally interested in heterogeneous discourses and notes that the relationship between globalization and postcoloniality is "perpetually caught between two competing narratives, one of celebration, the other of crisis." He shares with Dirlik the critique of runaway notions of "cultural hybridity," reciprocal exchanges, and antinationalism, which sociologists like Stuart Hall have borrowed, according to Gikandi, from postcolonial vocabularies embedded in the literary imagination rather than in structural accounts. What these vocabularies do not sufficiently take into account, says Gikandi, are the radical disparities in subsistence and survival, which brutally compel the continuing formation of the black diaspora in the Western world.

The dead bodies of Guinean boys in the cargo hold of a plane are the poignant specters of a differently experienced but equally tragic history from that of slaves in the holds of ships in an earlier crossing. Both are forced migrations that must soberly weigh down fanciful images of cultural flows. Along the lines of Chow's analysis, though, Gikandi does not entirely dismiss the productive potential of postcolonial contributions or the historical force of their analyses. Nor does he situate himself as external to the scholarly community he critiques in the First World. He recognizes, for instance, that while declarations of the end of the nation state as a useful unit are premature, a series of failures in various African postcolonies, including their vaunted socialist revolutions, have encouraged the current trend of demonizing the nation state.

But Gikandi is also critical of "the way [the experience of globalization] is represented in postcolonial theory," particularly when it rejects the realities of structural models for the more enabling myths of the literary imagination. He reminds us that knowledge about postcolonial nations, once emerging from the Third World areas of brutal lived experiences, has now shifted, as Dirlik and Chow also point out, to the "émigré native informants" in the comfortable First World academy who may not be in touch with harsh material conditions. Gikandi's critique of the literary perspective of postcolonial theory, unlike Chow's analysis, suggests that it is possible to separate the literary from material considerations. And yet the material is never too far from the literary. If Dirlik believes that capital is responsible for the postcolonial genesis of intellectual migration, Gikandi points in another direction to "one of the most powerful instruments of producing elites in both Britain and its (post)colonies": the study of English. Macaulay's directive on English language education in India (see chapter 9) and similar policies in other colonies impels another diaspora whose arrival in the First World, according to Dirlik, signals the beginning of postcolonial theory. Unlike the aborted migration of the two Guinean boys, this is the migration largely of the elites both at the point of origin and later into prestigious institutions of the First World academies. Dirlik perceives the postcolonial as one more consequence of the triumphant spread of capital; Gikandi wonders if in this instance, at least, the global is only one more element in the triumphant expansion of English nationalism.

34

STUART HALL

Thinking the Diaspora

Home-Thoughts from Abroad

The occasion for this lecture was the fiftieth anniversary of the founding of the University of the West Indies (UWI). Nineteen forty-eight was also, as it happens, the year of the arrival at Tilbury Docks in the UK of the SS *Empire Windrush,* the troopship, with its cargo of West Indian volunteers, returning from home-leave in the Caribbean, together with a small company of civilian migrants. This event signified the start of postwar Caribbean migration to Britain and stands symbolically as the birth date of the Afro-Caribbean postwar black diaspora. Its anniversary in 1998 was celebrated as symbolizing "the irresistible rise of multi-racial Britain."[1]

Migration has been a constant motif of the Caribbean story. But the *Windrush* initiated a new phase of diaspora formation whose legacy is the black Caribbean settlements in the UK. The purpose here is not to offer a historical account of the evolution of this diaspora—though its troubled history deserves to be better known in the Caribbean, even, one (dare one suggest) more systematically studied. The fate of Caribbean people living in the UK, the US or Canada is no more 'external' to Caribbean history than the Empire was 'external' to the so-called domestic history of Britain, though that is indeed how contemporary historiography constructs them. At all events, the question of diaspora is posed here primarily because of the light that it throws on the complexities, not simply of building, but of imagining Caribbean nationhood and identity, in an era of intensifying globalization.

Nations, Benedict Anderson suggests, are not only sovereign political entities but "imagined communities."[2] Thirty years after independence, how are Caribbean nations imagined? This question is central, not only to their peoples but to the arts and culture they produce, where some 'imagined subject' is always in play. Where do their boundaries begin and end, when regionally each is culturally and historically so closely related to its neighbours, and so many live thousands of miles from 'home'? How do we imagine their relation to 'home,' the nature of their 'belongingness'? And how are we to think of national identity and 'belongingness' in the Caribbean in the light of this diaspora experience?

The black settlements in Britain are not totally separated from their roots in the Caribbean. Mary Chamberlain's *Narratives of Exile and Return,* with its life histories of Barbadian migrants to the UK, emphasizes how strong the links remain.[3] As is common to most transnational communities, the extended family—as network and site of memory—is the critical conduit between the two locations. Barbadians, she suggests, have kept alive in exile a strong sense of what 'home' is like and tried to maintain a Barbadian 'cultural identity.' This picture is confirmed by research amongst Caribbean migrants in general in the UK that suggests that, amongst the so-called ethnic minorities in Britain, what we might call 'associational identification' with the cultures of origin remains strong, even into the second and third generation, though the places of origin are no longer the only source of identification.[4] The strength of the umbilical tie is also reflected in the growing numbers of retired Caribbean returnees. Chamberlain's judgement is that "A determination to construct autonomous Barbadian identities in Britain . . . if current trends continue, is likely to be enhanced rather than diminished by time."[5]

However, it would be wrong to see these trends as singular or unambiguous. In the diaspora situation, identities become multiple. Alongside an associative connection with a particular island 'home' there are other centripetal forces: there is the West-Indianness that they share with other West Indian migrants. (George Lamming once remarked that his [and, incidentally, my] generation became 'West Indian,' not in the Caribbean but in London!) There are the similarities with other so-called ethnic minority populations, emergent 'black British' identities, the identification with the localities of settlement, also the symbolic re-identifications with 'African' and more recently with 'African-American' cultures—all jostling for place alongside, say, their 'Barbadianness.'

Mary Chamberlain's interviewees also speak eloquently of how difficult many returnees find reconnecting with the societies of their birth. Many miss the cosmopolitan rhythms of life to which they have become acclimatized. Many feel that 'home' has changed beyond all recognition. In turn, they are seen as having had the natural and spontaneous chains of connection disturbed by their diasporic experiences. They are happy to be home. But history has somehow irrevocably intervened.

This is the familiar, deeply modern, sense of dis-location, which—it increasingly appears—we do not have to travel far to experience. Perhaps we are all, in modern times—after the Fall, so to speak—what the philosopher, Heidegger, called 'Unheimlich'—literally, 'not-at-home.' As Iain Chambers eloquently expresses it:

> We can never go home, return to the primal scene, to the forgotten moment of our
> beginnings and 'authenticity,' for there is always something else between. We can-

not return to a bygone unity, for we can only know the past, memory, the unconscious through its effects, that is when it is brought into language and from there embark on an (interminable) analysis. In front of the 'forest of signs' (Baudelaire) we find ourselves always at the crossroads, holding our stories and memories ('secularized reliques,' as Benjamin, the collector, describes them) while scanning the constellation full of tension that lies before us, seeking the language, the style, that will dominate movement and give it form. Perhaps it is more a question of seeking to be at home here, in the only time and context we have. . .[6]

What light, then, does the diaspora experience throw on issues of cultural identity in the Caribbean? Since this is a conceptual and epistemological, as well as an empirical, question, what does the diaspora experience do to our models of cultural identity? How are we to conceptualize or imagine identity, difference and belongingness, after diaspora? Since 'cultural identity' carries so many overtones of essential unity, primordial oneness, indivisibility and sameness, how are we to 'think' identities inscribed within relations of power and constructed across difference, and disjuncture?

Essentially, it is assumed that cultural identity is fixed by birth, part of nature, imprinted through kinship and lineage in the genes, constitutive of our innermost selves. It is impermeable to something as 'worldly,' secular and superficial as temporarily moving one's place of residence. Poverty, underdevelopment, the lack of opportunities—the legacies of Empire everywhere—may force people to migrate, bringing about the scattering—the dispersal. But each dissemination carries with it the promise of the redemptive return.

This powerful interpretation of the concept of 'diaspora' is the one most familiar to Caribbean people. It has become part of our newly constructed collective sense of self and deeply written in as the subtext in nationalist histories. It is modelled on the modern history of the Jewish people (from whom the term 'diaspora' was first derived), whose fate in the Holocaust—one of the few world-historical events comparable in barbarity to that of modern slavery—is well known. More significant, however, for the Caribbean is the Old Testament version of the story. There we find the analogue, critical to our history, of 'the chosen people,' taken away by violence into slavery in 'Egypt'; their 'suffering' at the hands of 'Babylon'; the leadership of Moses, followed by the Great Exodus—"movement of Jah People"—out of bondage and the return to the Promised Land. This is ur-source of that great New World narrative of freedom, hope and redemption which is repeated again and again throughout slavery—the Exodus and the 'Freedom Ride.' It has provided every black New World liberatory discourse with its governing metaphor. Many believe this Old Testament narrative to be much more powerful for the popular imaginary of New World black people than the so-called Christmas story. (Indeed, in the very week in which this lecture was first delivered at the UWI Cave Hill campus, the *Barbados Advocate*—looking forward to independence celebrations—attached the honorific titles of 'Moses' and 'Aaron' to the 'founding fathers' of Barbadian independence, Errol Barrow and Cameron Tudor!)

In this metaphor, history—which is open to freedom because it is contingent—is represented as teleological and redemptive: circling back to the restoration of its originary moment, healing all rupture, repairing every violent breach through this return. This hope has become, for Caribbean people, condensed into a sort of foundational myth. It is, by any standards, a great vision. Its power—even in the modern world—to move mountains can never be underestimated.

It is, of course, a closed conception of 'tribe,' diaspora and homeland. To have a cultural identity in this sense is to be primordially in touch with an unchanging essential core, which is timeless, binding future and present to past in an unbroken line. This umbilical cord is what we call 'tradition,' the test of which is its truth to its origins, its self-presence to itself, its 'authenticity.' It is, of course, a myth—with all the real power that our governing myths carry to shape our imaginaries, influence our actions, give meaning to our lives and make sense of our history.

Foundational myths are, by definition, transhistorical: not only outside history, but fundamentally a-historical. They are anachronistic and have the structure of a double inscription. Their redemptive power lies in the future, which is yet to come. But they work by ascribing what they predict will happen to their description of what has already happened, of what it was like in the beginning. History, however, like Time's arrow, is, if not linear, then successive. The narrative structure of myths is cyclical. But within history, their meaning is often transformed. It is, after all, precisely this exclusive conception of 'homeland' that led the Serbs to refuse to share their territory—as they have done for centuries—with their Muslim neighbours in Bosnia and justified ethnic cleansing in Kosovo. It is a version of this conception of the Jewish diaspora, and its prophesied 'return' to Israel, that is the source of Israel's quarrel with its Middle Eastern neighbours, for which the Palestinian people have paid so dearly and, paradoxically, by expulsion from what is also, after all, their homeland.

Here, then, is the paradox. Now, our troubles begin. A people cannot live without hope. But there is a problem when we take our metaphors too literally. Questions of cultural identity in diasporas cannot be 'thought' in this way.[7] They have proved so troubling and perplexing for Caribbean people precisely because, with us, identity is irredeemably a historical question. Our societies are composed, not of one, but of many peoples. Their origins are not singular but diverse. Those to whom the land originally belonged have long since, largely, perished—decimated by hard labour and disease. The land cannot be 'sacred' because it was 'violated'—not empty but emptied. Everyone who is here originally belonged somewhere else. Far from being continuous with our pasts, our relation to that history is marked by the most horrendous, violent, abrupt, ruptural breaks. Instead of the slowly evolving pact of civil association so central to the liberal discourse of Western modernity, our 'civil association' was inaugurated by an act of imperial will. What we now call the Caribbean was reborn in and through violence. The pathway to our modernity is marked out by conquest, expropriation, genocide, slavery, the plantation system and the long tutelage of colonial dependency. No wonder in van der Straet's famous engraving of Europe encountering America (c. 1600), Amerigo Vespucci is the commanding male figure, surrounded by the insignia of power, science, knowledge and religion: and 'America' is, as often, allegorized as a woman, naked, in a hammock, surrounded by the emblems of an—as yet unviolated—exotic landscape.[8]

Our peoples have their roots in—or, more accurately, can trace their 'routes' from—the four corners of the globe, from Europe, Africa, Asia, forced together in the fourth corner is the 'primal scene' of the New World. Their 'routes' are anything but 'pure.' The great majorities are 'African' in descent—but, as Shakespeare would have said, "north-by-northwest." We know this term 'Africa' is, in any event, a modern construction, referring to a variety of peoples, tribes, cultures and languages whose principal common point of origin lay in the confluence of the slave trade. In the Caribbean, 'Africa' has since been joined by the East Indians and the Chinese: indenture enters alongside slavery. The distinctiveness of our culture is manifestly the outcome of the most complex interweaving and fusion in the furnace of colonial society, of different African, Asian and European cultural elements.

This hybrid outcome can no longer be easily disaggregated into its original 'authentic' elements. The fear that, somehow, this makes Caribbean culture nothing but a simulacrum or cheap imitation of the cultures of the colonizers need not detain us, for this is so obviously not the case. But the cultural logic at work here is manifestly a 'creolizing' or transcultural one, as Mary Louise Pratt uses the term, following in the tradition of some of the best cultural theoretical writing of the region.[9] Through transculturation "subordinated or marginal groups select and invent from materials transmitted to them by a dominant metropolitan culture." It is a process of the 'contact zone,' a term that invokes "the spatial and temporal co-presence of subjects previously separated by geographic and historical disjunctures . . . whose trajectories now intersect." This perspective is dialogic since it is as interested in how the colonized produce the colonizer as the other way around: the "co-presence, interaction, interlocking of understandings and practices, often [in the Caribbean case, we must say always] within radically asymmetrical relations of power."[10] It is the disjunctive logic that colonization and Western modernity introduced into the world, and its entry into history constituted the world after 1492 as a profoundly unequal but 'global' enterprise and made Caribbean people what David Scott has recently described as "conscripts of modernity."[11]

In the early 1990s, I made a television series, called *Redemption Song,* for BBC2 about the different cultural tributaries within Caribbean culture.[12] In the visits I made in connection with the series, what amazed me was the presence of the same basic trace elements (similarity), together with the ways these had been uniquely combined into different configurations in each place (difference). I felt 'Africa' closest to the surface in Haiti and Jamaica. And yet, the way the African gods had been synthesized with Christian saints in the complex universe of Haitian vodoun is a particular mix only to be found in the Caribbean and Latin America—though there are analogues wherever comparable syncretisms emerged in the wake of colonization. The style of Haitian painting often described as 'primitive' is in fact the most complex rendering—in visionary terms—of this religious 'double-consciousness.' The distinguished Haitian painter whom we filmed—Andre Pierre—said a prayer to both Christian and vodoun gods before he commenced work. Like the Jamaican painter Brother Everald Brown, Pierre saw painting as essentially a visionary and 'spiritual' task. He sang us the 'story' of his canvas—white-robed, tie-headed black 'saints' and travellers crossing The River—as he painted.

I felt close to France in both Haiti and Martinique, but to different Frances: in Haiti, the 'France' of the Old Empire, which the Haitian Revolution (the explosive fusion of African slave resistance and French Republican traditions in the demand for liberty under Toussaint L'Ouverture) brought to its knees; in Martinique, the 'France' of the New Empire—of Republicanism, Gaullism, Parisian 'chic' crossed by the transgressions of black 'style' and the complex affiliations to 'Frenchness' of Fanon and Césaire. In Barbados, as expected, I felt closer to England, and its understated social discipline—as one once did, occasionally, but feels no longer in Jamaica. Nevertheless, the distinctive habits, customs and social etiquette of Barbados are so clearly a translation, through African slavery, of that small-scale, intimate plantation culture that refigured the Barbadian landscape. In Trinidad, above all, the complex traditions of 'the East' in 'the West'—of Indian Carnival Queens, roti stalls on the savannah and Diwali candles glittering in the San Fernando darkness, and the distinctively Spanish Catholic rhythm of sin-contrition-and-absolution (Shrove Tuesday's masque followed by Ash Wednesday mass) that is so close to the Trinidadian character. Everywhere, hybridity, *differance.*

The closed conception of diaspora rests on a binary conception of difference. It is founded on the construction of an exclusionary frontier and depends on the construction of an 'Other' and a fixed opposition between inside and outside. But the syncretized configurations of Caribbean cultural identity require Derrida's notion of *differance*—differences that do not work through binaries, veiled boundaries that do not finally separate but double up as *places de passage,* and meanings that are positional and relational, always on the slide along a spectrum without end or beginning. Difference, we know, is essential to meaning, and meaning is critical for culture. But in a profoundly counter-intuitive move, modern linguistics after Saussure insists that meaning cannot be finally fixed. There is always the inevitable 'slippage' of meaning in the open semiosis of a culture, as that which seems fixed continues to be dialogically reappropriated. The fantasy of a final meaning remains haunted by 'lack' or 'excess,' but is never graspable in the plenitude of its presence to itself. As Bakhtin and Volosinov argued,

> The social multiaccentuality of the ideological sign is a very crucial aspect . . . it is thanks to this intersecting of accents that a sign maintains its vitality and dynamism and the capacity for further development. A sign which has been withdrawn from the pressures of the social struggle .. . inevitably loses its force, degenerating into allegory and becoming the object not of a live social intelligibility but of philological Comprehension.[13]

In this conception, the binary poles of 'sense' and 'nonsense' are constantly undermined by the more open-ended and fluid process of 'making sense in translation.'

This cultural 'logic' has been described by Kobena Mercer as a "diasporic aesthetic."

> Across a whole range of cultural forms there is a powerful syncretic dynamic which critically appropriates elements from the master-codes of the dominant cultures and creolizes them, disarticulating given signs and re-articulating their symbolic meaning otherwise. The subversive force of this hybridizing tendency is most apparent at the level of language itself [including visual language] where creoles, patois and Black English decentre, destabilize and carnivalize the linguistic domination of 'English'—the nation-language of master-discourse—through strategic inflections, reaccentuations and other performative moves in semantic, syntactic and lexical codes.[14]

Caribbean culture is essentially driven by a diasporic aesthetic. In anthropological terms, its cultures are irretrievably 'impure.' This impurity, so often constructed as burden and loss, is itself a necessary condition of their modernity. As the novelist Salman Rushdie once observed, "hybridity, impurity, intermingling, the transformation that comes of new and unexpected combinations of human beings, cultures, ideas, politics, movies, songs" is "how newness enters the world."[15] This is not to suggest that the different elements in a syncretic formation stand in a relation of equality to one another. They are always differently inscribed by relations of power—above all the relations of dependency and subordination sustained by colonialism itself. The independence and postcolonial moments, in which these imperial histories remain actively reworked, are therefore necessarily moments of cultural struggle, of revision and re-appropriation. However, this reconfiguration cannot be represented as a 'going back to where we were before' since, as Chambers reminds us, "there is always something else between."[16] This "something else between" is what makes the Caribbean itself, pre-eminently, the case of a modern diaspora.

The relationship between Caribbean cultures and their diasporas cannot therefore be adequately conceptualized in terms of origin to copy, primary source to pale reflection. It has to be understood as one diaspora to another. Here, the national frame is not very helpful. Nation states impose rigid frontiers within which cultures are expected to flourish. That was the primary relationship between sovereign national polities and their 'imagined communities' in the era of European nation-state dominance. It was also the frame adopted by the nationalist and nation-building politics after independence. The question is whether it still provides a useful framework for understanding cultural exchanges between the black diasporas.

Globalization, of course, is not a new phenomenon. Its history is coterminous with the era of European exploration, conquest and the formation of the capitalist world market. The earlier phases of this so-called global history were held together by the tension between these conflicting poles—the heterogeneity of the global market and the centripetal force of the nation state—constituting between them one of the fundamental rhythms of early capitalist world systems.[17] The Caribbean was one of its key scenarios, across which the stabilization of the European nation-state system was fought through and accomplished in a series of imperial settlements. The apogee of imperialism at the end of the nineteenth century, two world wars and the national independence and decolonizing movements of the twentieth century marked the zenith, and the terminal point, of this phase.

It is now rapidly drawing to a close. Global developments above and below the level of the nation state have undermined the nation's reach and scope of manoeuvre, and with that the scale and comprehensiveness—the panoptic assumptions—of its 'imaginary.' In any event, cultures have always refused to be so perfectly corralled within the national boundaries. They transgress political limits. Caribbean culture, in particular, has not been well served by the national frame. The imposition of national frontiers within the imperial system fragmented the region into separate and estranged national and linguistic entities from which it has never recovered. The alternative frame of "The Black Atlantic," proposed by Paul Gilroy, is a powerful counter-narrative to the discursive insertion of the Caribbean into European national stories, bringing to the surface the lateral exchanges and 'family resemblances' across the region as a whole which a nationalist history obscures.[18]

The new, post-1970s phase of globalization is, of course, still deeply rooted in the structured disparities of wealth and power. But its forms, however uneven, are more 'global' in their operation, planetary in perspective, with transnational corporate interests, the deregulation of world markets and the global flow of capital, technologies and communication systems transcending and side-lining the old nation-state framework. This new 'transnational' phase of the system has its cultural 'centre' everywhere and nowhere. It is becoming 'decentred.' This does not mean that it lacks power, or indeed that nation states have no role in it. But that role has been in many respects subordinated to larger global systemic operations. The rise of supranational formations, such as the European Union, is testimony to the ongoing erosion of national sovereignty. The undoubted hegemonic position of the USA in this system is related, not to its nation-state status but to its global and neo-imperial role and ambitions.

It is therefore important to see this diasporic perspective on culture as subversive of traditional nation-oriented cultural models. Like other globalizing processes cultural globalization is de-territorializing in its effects. Its space-time condensations, driven by new technologies, loosen the tie between culture and 'place.' Glaring disjunctures of time and space are abruptly convened, without obliterating their differential rhythms and times. Cultures, of course, have their 'locations.' But it is no longer easy to say where they originate. What we can chart is more akin to a process of repetition-with-difference, or reciprocity-without-beginning. In this perspective, black British identities are not just a pale reflection of a 'true' Caribbeanness of origin, which is destined to be progressively weakened. They are the outcome of their own relatively autonomous formation. However, the logic that governs them involves the same processes of transplantation, syncretization and diaspora-ization that once produced Caribbean identities, only now operating in a different space and time frame, a different chronotope—in the time of *differance*.

Thus dancehall music and subculture in Britain was, of course, inspired by and takes much of its style and attitude from the dancehall music and subculture of Jamaica. But it now has its own variant black British forms, and its own indigenous locations. The recent 'dancehall' film *Babymother* is 'authentically' located in the mixed-race inner-city zone of Harlesden, in the streets and clubs, the recording studios and live venues, the street life and danger-zones of North London.[19] The three ragga girls, its heroines, shop for their exotic outfits in another suburb of London, Southall, which is familiarly known as Little India.

These *differances* are not without real effects. Unlike the classic representations of dancehall elsewhere, this film charts the struggles of three girls to become ragga dancehall DJs—thereby bringing the vexed issue of sexual politics in Jamaican popular culture dead centre to the narrative, where other versions are still hiding it away behind a cultural nationalist screen. Isaac Julien's documentary film *The Darker Side of Black* has three locations—Kingston, New York and London. Perhaps it is this relative 'freedom of place' that enables him to confront the deep homophobia common to the different variants of gangsta rap without collapsing into the degraded language of 'the innate violence of the black posses' that now disfigures British Sunday journalism.

Dancehall is now an indigenized diasporic musical form—one of several black musics winning the hearts and souls of some white London 'wannabe' kids (that is, 'wannabe black'!), who speak a mean mixture of Trench Town patois, New York hip-hop and estuary English and for whom 'black style' simply is the symbolic equivalent of modern street credibility. (Of course, they are not the only garden-variety of British youth. There are also the skin-heads, swastika-tattooed denizens of abandoned white suburbs such as Eltham, who also practise their violent manoeuvres 'globally' at international football matches, five of whom stabbed the black teenager Stephen Lawrence to death at a South London bus stop, simply because he dared to change buses in their 'territory.')[20] What is now known as jungle music in London is another 'original' crossover (there have been many since British versions of ska, black soul, two-tone and 'roots' reggae) between Jamaican dub, Atlantic Avenue hip-hop and gangsta rap and white techno (as *bangra* and tabla-and-bass are crossover musics between rap, techno and the Indian classical tradition).

In the vernacular cosmopolitan exchanges that allow 'Third' and 'First' World popular musical traditions to fertilize one another, and which have constructed a symbolic space where so-called advanced electronic technology meets the so-called primitive rhythms—where Harlesden becomes Trench Town—there is no traceable origin left, except along a circuitous and discontinuous chain of connections. The proliferation and dissemination of new hybrid and syncretic musical forms can no longer be captured in the centre/periphery model or based simply on some nostalgic and exoticized notion of the recovery of ancient rhythms. It is the story of the production of culture, of new and thoroughly modern diaspora musics—of course, drawing on the materials and forms of many fragmented musical traditions.

Their modernity needs, above all, to be emphasized. In 1998, the Institute for the International Visual Arts and the Whitechapel Gallery organized the first major retrospective of the work of a major Caribbean visual artist, Aubrey Williams (1926–90). Williams was born and worked for many years as an agricultural officer in Guyana. He subsequently lived and painted, at different stages of his career, in England, Guyana, Jamaica and the USA. His paintings embrace a variety of twentieth century styles, from the figurative and the iconographic to abstraction. His major work demonstrates a wide variety of formal influences and inspirational sources— Guyanese myths, artefacts and landscapes, pre-Columbian and Mayan motifs, wildlife, birds and animal figures, Mexican muralism, the symphonies of Shostakovitch, and the abstract-expressionist forms characteristic of postwar British and European modernism. His paintings defy characterization, as simply either Caribbean or British. These vibrant, explosively colourful canvases, with their cosmic shapes and the indistinct traces of forms and figures faintly but suggestively embedded in the abstract surfaces, clearly belong to, but have never been officially recognized as part of, the essential story of 'British modernism.' No doubt his flirtation with European music and abstraction, in some minds, qualified his credentials as a 'Caribbean' painter. Yet, it is the two impulses working together, his translation position between two worlds, several aesthetics, many languages, that establish him as an outstanding, original and formidably modern artist.

In the catalogue produced for the Williams retrospective, the art critic Guy Brett comments:

> Of course, the subtlety of the matter—the complexity of the history that has yet to be written—is that Aubrey Williams' work would have to be considered in three different contexts: that of Guyana, that of the Guyanese and West Indian diaspora in Britain, and that of British society. These contexts would have to be considered to a degree separately, and in their complicated interrelationships, affected by the realities of power. And all would have to be adjusted in relation to Williams' own desire to be simply a modern, contemporary artist, the equal of any other. At one moment he could say, 'I haven't wasted a lot of energy on this roots business . . . I've paid attention to a hundred different things . . . why must I isolate one philosophy?'; at another, 'the crux of the matter inherent in my work since I was a boy has been the human predicament, specifically with regard to the Guyanese situation.'[21]

What, then, about all those efforts to reconstruct Caribbean identities by going back to their originary sources? Were these struggles of cultural recovery useless? Far from it. The reworking of Africa in the Caribbean weave has been the most powerful and subversive element in our cultural politics in the twentieth century. And its capacity to disrupt the post-independence nationalist 'settlement' is certainly not over. But this is not primarily because we are connected to our African past and heritage by an unbreakable chain across which some singular African culture has flowed unchanged down the generations, but because of how we have gone about producing 'Africa' again, within the Caribbean narrative. At every juncture—think of Garveyism, Hibbert, Rastafarianism, the new urban popular culture—it has been a matter of interpreting 'Africa,' rereading 'Africa,' of what 'Africa' could mean to us now, after diaspora.

Anthropologically, this question has often been approached in terms of 'survivals.' The signs and traces of that presence are, of course, everywhere. 'Africa' lives, not only in the retention of African words and syntactic structures in language or rhythmic patterns in music but in the way African speech forms have permanently disrupted, inflected and subverted the way Caribbean people speak, the way they appropriated 'English,' the master tongue. It 'lives' in the way every Caribbean Christian congregation, familiar with every line of the Moody and Sankey hymnal, nonetheless drag and elongate the pace of "Onward Christian Soldiers" back down to a more grounded body-rhythm and vocal register. Africa is alive and well in the diaspora. But it is neither the Africa of those territories, now obscured by the post-colonial map maker, from which slaves were snatched for transportation nor the Africa of today, which is at least four or five different 'continents' rolled into one, its forms of subsistence destroyed, its peoples structurally adjusted into a devastating modern poverty.[22] The 'Africa' that is alive and well in this part of the world is what Africa has become in the New World, in the violent vortex of colonial syncretism, reforged in the furnace of the colonial cook-pot.

Equally significant, then, is the way this 'Africa' provides resources for survival today, alternative histories to those imposed by colonial rule and the raw materials for reworking in new and distinctive cultural patterns and forms. In this perspective, 'survivals' in their original form are massively outweighed by the process of cultural translation. As Sarat Maharaj reminds us

> Translation, as Derrida puts it, is quite unlike buying, selling, swapping—however much it has been conventionally pictured in those terms. It is not a matter of shipping over juicy chunks of meaning from one side of the language barrier to the other—as with fast-food packs at an over-the-counter take away outfit. Meaning is not a readymade, portable thing that can be 'carried over' the divide. The translator is obliged to construct meaning in the source language and then to figure and fashion it a second time round in the materials of the language into which he or she is rendering it. The translator's loyalties are thus divided and split. He or she has to be faithful to the syntax, feel and structure of the source language and faithful to those of the language of translation. . . . We face a double writing, what might be described as a 'perfidious fidelity.' . . . We are drawn into Derrida's 'Babel effect.'[23]

In fact, every significant social movement and every creative development of the arts in the Caribbean in this century has begun with or included this translation-moment of the re-encounter with Afro-Caribbean traditions. The reason is not that Africa is a fixed anthropological point of reference—the hyphenated reference already marks the diasporizing process at work, the way 'Africa' was appropriated into and transformed by the plantation systems of the New World. The reason is that 'Africa' is the signifier, the metaphor, for that dimension of our society and history that has been massively suppressed, systematically dishonoured and endlessly disavowed, and that, despite all that has happened, remains so. This dimension is what Frantz Fanon called "the fact of blackness."[24] Race remains, in spite of everything, the guilty secret, the hidden code, the unspeakable trauma, in the Caribbean. It is 'Africa' that has made it 'speakable,' as a social and cultural condition of our existence.

In the Caribbean cultural formation, white, European, Western, colonizing traces were always positioned as the ascendant element, the voiced aspect: the black, 'African,' enslaved and colonized traces, of which there were many, were always unvoiced, subterranean, and subversive, governed by a different 'logic,' always positioned through subordination or marginalization. Identities formed within the matrix of colonial meanings were constructed so as to foreclose and disavow engagement with the real histories of our society or its cultural 'routes.' The huge efforts made, over many years, not only by academic scholars but by cultural practitioners themselves, to piece together these fragmentary, often illegal, 'routes to the present' and to reconstruct their unspoken genealogies, are the necessary historical groundwork required to make sense of the interpretive matrix and self-images of our culture and to make the invisible visible. That is, the 'work' of translation that the African signifier performs, and the work of 'perfidious fidelity' that Caribbean artists in this post-nationalist moment are required to undertake.

The struggles to rediscover the African 'routes' within the complex configurations of Caribbean culture, and to speak through that prism the ruptures of transportation, slavery, colonization, exploitation and racialization, produced the only successful 'revolution' in the anglophone Caribbean in this century—the so-called cultural revolution of the 1960s—and the making of the black Caribbean subject. In Jamaica, for example, its traces are still to be found in a thousand unexamined places—in religious congregations of all sorts, formal and irregular; in the marginalized voices of popular street preachers and prophets, many of them declared insane; in folk stories and oral narrative forms; in ceremonial occasions and rites of passage; in the new language, music and rhythm of urban popular culture as well as in political and intellectual traditions—in Garveyism, Ethiopianism, revivalism and Rastafarianism. The latter, as we know, looked back to that mythic space 'Ethiopia,' where black kings ruled for a thousand years, the site of a Christian congregation hundreds of years before the Christianization of western Europe. But, as a social movement, it was actually born, as we know, in that fateful but unlocatable 'place' closer to home where Garvey's return met Revd Hibbert's preaching and Bedward's delusive fantasies, leading to the retreat to and the forced dispersal from Pinnacle. It was destined for that wider politicized space where it could speak for those—if the phrase is forgiven—'dispossessed by independence'!

Like all these movements, Rastafarianism represented itself as a 'return.' But what it 'returned' us to was ourselves. In doing so, it produced 'Africa again'—in the diaspora. Rastafarianism drew on many 'lost sources' from the past. But its relevance was grounded in the extraordinarily contemporary practice of reading the Bible through its subversive tradition, through its unorthodoxies, its apocrypha: by reading against the grain, upside-down, turning the text against itself. The 'Babylon' of which it spoke, where its people were still 'suffering,' was not in Egypt but in Kingston—and later, as the name was syntagmatically extended to include the Metropolitan Police, in Brixton, Handsworth, Moss Side and Notting Hill. Rastafarianism played a critical role in the modern movement that made Jamaica and other

Caribbean societies, for the first time, and irrecoverably, 'black.' In a further translation, this strange doctrine and discourse 'saved' the young black souls of second-generation Caribbean migrants in British cities in the 1960s and 1970s, and gave them pride and self-understanding. In Frantz Fanon's terms, it decolonized minds.

At the same time, it is worth recalling the awkward fact that the 'naturalization' of the descriptive term 'black' for the whole of the Caribbean, or the equivalent, 'Afro-Caribbean' for all West Indian migrants abroad, performs its own kind of silencing in our new transnational world. The young Trinidadian artist Steve Ouditt has lived and worked in the USA, England and what he describes as the 'Sucrotopia' of Trinidad. He describes himself as "a post-independence American/English educated Christian Indian Trinidadian West Indian Creole male artist," whose work—in written and installation form—"navigates the difficult terrain between the visual and the verbal." He addresses this issue head-on in one of his recent pieces for his online diary "Enigma of Survival."

> Afro-Caribbean is the blanket term for any Caribbean in England. For real. It is as real as when many well-educated people here say to me, 'You are from the Caribbean, how come, you are not even black, you look Asian.' . . . I do believe that the term 'Afro-Caribbean' is a British naming and perhaps it is supposed to represent the image of the majority of West Indian migrants who came here in the postwar period. And it is used to mark and remember in their past the politics and horrors of slavery, the European classification of Africans as ultrainferior. The fragmentation and loss of 'culture' but with desires to negotiate a new 'Afroness' in this diasporic site. . . . In this specificity I can deal with 'Afro-Caribbean' . . . but not when it is used as the privileged index of horror to settle and centre all other subaltern Caribbean historiographies under an Afrophilia of the Caribbean here in Britain. . . . Trinidad has had a history of indentureship of Indians in labour camp apartheid for as long as it has had 'organized' slavery. . . .[25]

What these examples suggest is that culture is not just a voyage of rediscovery, a return journey. It is not an 'archeology.' Culture is a production. It has its raw materials, its resources, its 'work-of-production.' It depends on a knowledge of tradition as "the changing same" and an effective set of genealogies.[26] But what this 'detour through its pasts' does is to enable us, through culture, to produce ourselves anew, as new kinds of subjects. It is therefore not a question of what our traditions make of us so much as what we make of our traditions. Paradoxically, our cultural identities, in any finished form, lie ahead of us. We are always in the process of cultural formation. Culture is not a matter of ontology, of being, but of becoming.

In its present, hectic and accentuated forms, globalization is busily disentangling and subverting further its own inherited essentializing and homogenizing cultural models, undoing the limits and, in the process, unravelling the darkness of the West's own 'Enlightenment.' Identities thought of as settled and stable are coming to grief on the rocks of a proliferating differentiation. Across the globe, the processes of so-called free and forced migrations are changing the composition, diversifying the cultures and pluralizing the cultural identities of the older dominant nation states, the old imperial powers, and, indeed, of the globe itself.[27] The unregulated flows of peoples and cultures is as broad and as unstoppable as the sponsored flows of capital and technology. The former inaugurate a new process of 'minoritization' within the old metropolitan societies whose cultural homogeneity has long been silently assumed. But these 'minorities' are not effectively ghettoized; they do not long remain enclave settlements. They engage the dominant culture along a very broad front. They belong, in fact, to a transnational movement, and their connections are multiple and lateral. They mark the end of a 'modernity' defined exclusively in Western terms.

In fact, there are two, opposed processes at work in contemporary forms of globalization, which is itself a fundamentally contradictory process. There are the dominant forces of cultural homogenization, by which, because of its ascendancy in the cultural marketplace and its domination of capital, technological and cultural 'flows,' Western culture, more specifically, American culture, threatens to overwhelm all comers, imposing a homogenizing cultural sameness—what has been called the 'McDonald-ization' or 'Nike-ization' of everything. Its effects are to be seen across the world, including the popular life of the Caribbean. But right alongside that are processes that are slowly and subtly decentring Western models, leading to a dissemination of cultural difference across the globe.

These 'other' tendencies do not (yet) have the power, frontally, to confront and repel the former head-on. But they do have the capacity, everywhere, to subvert and 'translate,' to negotiate and indigenize the global cultural onslaught on weaker cultures. And since the new global consumer markets depend precisely on their becoming 'localized' to be effective, there is certain leverage in what may appear at first to be merely 'local.' These days, the 'merely' local and the global are locked together; not because the latter is the local working-through of essentially global effects, but because each is the condition of existence of the other. Once 'modernity' was transmitted from a single centre. Today, it has no such centre. 'Modernities' are everywhere; but they have taken on a vernacular accentuation. The fate and fortunes of the simplest and poorest farmer in the most remote corner of the world depend on the unregulated shifts of the global market—and, for that reason, he or she is now an essential element part of every global calculation. Politicians know the poor will not be cut out of, or defined out of, this 'modernity.' They are not prepared to be immured forever in an immutable 'tradition.' They are determined to construct their own kinds of 'vernacular modernities,' and these are the signifiers of a new kind of transnational, even postnational, transcultural consciousness.

This 'narrative' has no guaranteed happy ending. Many in the old nation states, who are deeply attached to the purer forms of national self-understanding, are literally driven crazy by their erosion. They feel their whole universe threatened by change, and coming down about their ears. 'Cultural difference' of a rigid, ethnicized and unnegotiable kind has taken the place of sexual miscegenation as the primal postcolonial fantasy. A racially driven 'fundamentalism' has surfaced in all these Western European and North American societies, a new kind of defensive and racialized nationalism. Prejudice, injustice, discrimination and violence towards 'the Other,' based on this hypostasized 'cultural difference,' has come to take its place—what Sarat Maharaj has called a sort of "spook look-alike of apartheid"—alongside the older racisms, founded on skin-colour and physiological difference—giving rise in response to a 'politics of recognition,' alongside the struggles against racism and for social justice.

These developments may at first seem remote from the concerns of new emerging nations and cultures of the 'periphery.' But as we suggested, the old centre-periphery, nation-nationalist-culture model is exactly what is breaking down. Emerging cultures that feel threatened by the forces of globalization, diversity and hybridization, or that have failed in the project of modernization, may feel tempted to close down around their nationalist inscriptions and construct defensive walls. The alternative is not to cling to closed, unitary, homogenous models of 'cultural belonging' but to embrace the wider processes—the play of similarity and difference—that are transforming culture worldwide. This is the path of 'diaspora,' which is the pathway of a modern people and a modern culture. This may look, at first, just like—but is really very different from—the old 'internationalism' of European modernism. Jean Fisher has argued that, until recently,

> Internationalism has always referred exclusively to a European-European diasporan axis of political, military and economic affiliations. . . . This entrenched and dominant axis creates, in Mosquera's words, 'zones of silence' elsewhere, making it difficult for lateral communications and other affiliations to take place. Araeen and Oguibe remind us that the present initiative [to define a new internationalism in the arts and culture] is only the most recent in a history of such attempts at cross-cultural dialogue which have been erased from 'established narrations of cultural practice in Britain [and which failed] to overwhelm the deep-seated and firm structures which we interrogate' (Oguibe).[28]

What we have in mind here is something quite different—that 'other' kind of modernity that led C.L.R. James to remark of Caribbean people, "Those people who are in western civilization, who have grown up in it, but made to feel and themselves feeling they are outside it, have a unique insight into their society."[29]

ACKNOWLEDGMENTS

This lecture was first given as part of the celebrations of the fiftieth anniversary of the founding of the University of the West Indies (UWI) held at the Cave Hill campus, Barbados, in November 1998. It appears here in a revised form with the permission of the UWI.

NOTES

1 This is the subtitle of the volume *Windrush,* by Mike Phillips and Trevor Phillips (London: HarperCollins, 1998), that accompanied the BBC TV series.

2 Benedict Anderson, *Imagined Communities* (London: Verso, 1991).

3 Mary Chamberlain, *Narratives of Exile and Return* (Houndsmill: Macmillan, 1998).

4 See T. Modood, R. Berthoud, et al., *Ethnic Minorities in Britain* (London: Policy Studies Institute, 1997).

5 Chamberlain, *Narratives,* p. 132.

6 Iain Chambers, *Border Dialogues: Journeys in Post-Modernity* (London: Routledge, 1990), p. 104.

7 See Stuart Hall, "Cultural Identity and Diaspora," in *Identity: Community, Culture, Difference,* ed. Jonathan Rutherford (London: Lawrence and Wishart, 1990); and S. Hall and P. duGay, eds., *Questions of Cultural Identity* (London: Sage, 1997), pp. 222–37.

8 See Stuart Hall, "The West and the Rest: Discourse and Power," in *Formations of Modernity* (Cambridge: Polity Press and The Open University, 1994), pp. 274–320.

9 Mary Louise Pratt, *Imperial Eyes: Travel Writing and Transculturation* (London: Routledge, 1992). See, *inter alia,* Fernando Ortiz, *Cuban Counterpoint: Tobacco and Sugar* (New York: A. A. Knopf, 1947); Edouard Glissant, *Le discours antillais* (Paris: Editions du Seuil, 1981); Edward Kamau Brathwaite, *The Development of Creole Society in Jamaica, 1770–1820* (Oxford: Oxford University Press, 1971).

10 Pratt, *Imperial Eyes,* pp. 6–7.

11 David Scott, "Conscripts of Modernity" (unpublished paper).

12 *Redemption Song.* Seven programmes made with Barraclough and Carey for BBC2 and transmitted 1989–90.

13 M. Bakhtin and V. N. Volosinov, *Marxism and the Philosophy of Language* (New York and London: Seminar Press, 1973).

14 Kobena Mercer, "Diaspora Culture and the Dialogic Imagination," in *Welcome to the Jungle: New Positions in Black Cultural Studies* (London: Roudedge, 1994), pp. 63–64.

15 Salman Rushdie, *Imaginary Homelands* (London: Granta Books, 1990), p. 394.

16 Chambers, *Border Dialogues,* p. 104.

17 Immanuel Wallerstein, "The National and the Universal," in *Culture, Globalization and the World System,* ed. A. King (London: Macmillan, 1991), pp. 91–106.

18 Paul Gilroy, *The Black Atlantic* (London: Verso, 1993).

19 *Babymother* was released in London, the USA and Jamaica in 1998. It was directed by Julian Henriques, the son of a distinguished Jamaican anthropologist who lives in London and produced by his wife and partner, Parminder Vir, who is from the Punjab. They met, needless to say, from these two poles of Empire, in London.

20 The official inquiry, chaired by Sir William Macpherson, into the death of Stephen Lawrence, convened after five years only as a result of the heroic efforts of his parents, Doreen and

Neville Lawrence, and a small group of black supporters, was a public event and a cause célèbre in 1998, and a turning point in British race relations. It resulted in the judge finding the Metropolitan Police guilty of "institutional racism." See Sir William Macpherson of Cluny, *The Stephen Lawrence Inquiry Report,* Cmnd. 4262-1 (1999).

21 Guy Brett, "A Tragic Excitement," in *Aubrey Williams* (London: Institute for the International Visual Arts and Whitechapel Gallery, 1998), p. 24.

22 See David Scott, "That Event, This Memory: Notes on the Anthropology of African Diasporas in the New World," *Diaspora* 1, no. 3 (1991): 261–84.

23 Sarat Maharaj, "Perfidious Fidelity," in *Global Visions: Towards a New Internationalism in the Visual Arts,* ed. Jean Fisher (London: Institute of the International Visual Arts, 1994), p. 31. The reference is to Jacques Derrida, "Des Tours des Babel," in *Difference in Translation* (Ithaca: Cornell University Press, 1985).

24 The title of one of the most important chapters in Frantz Fanon, *Black Skin, White Masks* (London: Pluto Press, 1986).

25 Steve Ouditt, "Enigma of Survival," in *Annotations 4: Creole-in-Site,* ed. Gilane Tanadros (London: Institute of the International Visual Arts, 1998), pp. 8–9.

26 For "tradition as the changing same," see Gilroy, *The Black Atlantic.*

27 See, for example, Arjun Appadurai, *Modernity at Large* (Minneapolis: University of Minnesota Press, 1996).

28 Jean Fisher, "Editor's Note," in *Global Visions: Towards a New Internationalism in the Visual Arts,* ed. J. Fisher (London: Institute for the International Visual Arts, 1994), p. xii.

29 C.L.R. James, "Africans and Afro-Caribbeans: A Personal View," *Ten* 8, no. 16.

35

ARIF DIRLIK

The Postcolonial Aura

Third World Criticism in the Age of Global Capitalism

"When exactly . . . does the 'post-colonial' begin?" queries Ella Shohat in a recent discussion of the subject.[1] Misreading the question deliberately, I will supply here an answer that is only partially facetious: When Third World intellectuals have arrived in First World academe.

My goal in the discussion below is twofold: to review the term *postcolonial*, and the various intellectual and cultural positions associated with it, in the context of contemporary transformations in global relationships, and to examine the reconsiderations of problems of domination and hegemony as well as of received critical practices that these transformations require. *Postcolonial* is the most recent entrant to achieve prominent visibility in the ranks of those "post" marked words (seminal among them, *postmodernism*) that serve as signposts in(to) contemporary cultural criticism. Unlike other "post" marked words, *postcolonial* claims as its special provenance the terrain that in an earlier day used to go by the name of Third World. It is intended, therefore, to achieve an authentic globalization of cultural discourses by the extension globally of the intellectual concerns and orientations originating at the central sites of Euro-American cultural criticism and by the introduction into the latter of voices and subjectivities from the margins of earlier political and ideological colonialism that now demand a hearing at those very sites at the center. The goal, indeed, is no less than to abolish all distinctions between center and periphery as well as all other "binarisms" that are allegedly a legacy of colonial(ist) ways of thinking and to reveal societies globally in their complex heterogeneity and contingency. Although intellectuals who hail from one part of that terrain, India, have played a conspicuously prominent role in its formulation and dissemination, the appeals of postcoloniality seem to cut across national, regional, and even political boundaries, which on the surface at least seems to substantiate its claims to globalism.

My answer to Shohat's question is only partially facetious because the popularity that the term *postcolonial* has achieved in the last few years has less to do with its rigorousness as a concept or with the new vistas it has opened up for critical inquiry than it does with the increased visibility of academic intellectuals of Third World origin as pacesetters in cultural criticism. I want to suggest that most of the critical themes that postcolonial criticism claims as its fountainhead predated the appearance, or at least the popular currency, of *postcolonial*. Whether there was a postcolonial consciousness (before it was so termed) that might have played a part in the production of those themes is a question to which I will return below. As far as it is possible to tell from the literature, however, it was only from the mid-1980s that the label *postcolonial* was attached to those themes with increasing frequency, and that in conjunction with the use of the label to describe academic intellectuals of Third World origin. From this time, these so-called postcolonial intellectuals seemed to acquire an academic respectability that they did not have before.[2] A description of a diffuse group of intellectuals and their concerns and orientations was to turn by the end of the decade into a description of a global condition, in which sense it has acquired the status of a new orthodoxy both in cultural criticism and in academic programs. Shohat's question above refers to this global condition; yet, given the ambiguity imbedded in the term *postcolonial*, it seems justifiable to redirect her question to the emergence of postcolonial intellectuals in order to put the horse back in front of the cart. This redirection is also intended to underline the First World origins (and situation) of the term.

My answer is also facetious, however, because merely pointing to the ascendant role that intellectuals of Third World origin have played in propagating *postcolonial* as a critical orientation within First World academia begs the question as to why they and their intellectual concerns and orientations have been accorded the respectability that they have. The themes that are now claimed for postcolonial criticism, both in what they repudiate of the past and in what they affirm for the present, I suggest, resonate with concerns and orientations that have their origins in a new world situation that has also become part of consciousness globally over the last decade. I am referring here to that world situation created by transformations within the capitalist world economy, by the emergence of what has been described variously as global capitalism, flexible production, late capitalism, and so on, terms that have disorganized earlier conceptualizations of global relations, especially relations comprehended earlier by such binaries as colonizer/colonized, First World/Third World, and the "West and the Rest," in all of which the nation-state was taken for granted as the global unit of political organization. It is no reflection on the abilities of postcolonial critics to suggest that they and the critical orientations that they represent have acquired a respectability dependent on the conceptual needs of the social, political, and cultural problems thrown up by this new world situation. It is, however, a reflection on the ideology of postcolonialism that, with rare exceptions (see *PCC*),[3] post-colonial critics have been silent on the relationship of the idea of postcolonialism to its context in contemporary capitalism; indeed, they have suppressed the necessity of considering such a possible relationship by repudiating a foundational role to cap-italism in history.

To consider this relationship is my primary goal in the discussion below. I argue, first, that there is a parallel between the ascendancy in cultural criticism of the idea of postcoloniality and an emergent consciousness of global capitalism in the 1980s and, second, that the appeals of the critical themes in postcolonial criticism have much to do with their resonance with the conceptual needs presented by transfor-mations in global relationships caused by changes within the capitalist world econ-omy. This also explains, I think, why a concept that is intended to achieve a radical revision in our comprehension of the world should appear to be complicitous in "the consecration of hegemony," as Shohat has put it ("NP," p. 110). If postcolonial as con-cept has not necessarily served as a fountainhead for the criticism of an earlier ide-ology of global relationships, it has nevertheless helped concentrate under one term what previously had been diffused among many. At the same time, however, post-colonial criticism has been silent about its own status as a possible ideological effect of a new world situation after colonialism. Postcolonial as a description of intellec-tuals of Third World origin needs to be distinguished, I suggest below, from post-colonial as a description of this world situation. In this latter usage, the term mystifies both politically and methodologically a situation that represents not the abolition but the reconfiguration of earlier forms of domination. The complicity of postcolonial in hegemony lies in postcolonialism's diversion of attention from con-temporary problems of social, political, and cultural domination, and in its obfusca-tion of its own relationship to what is but a condition of its emergence, that is, to a global capitalism that, however fragmented in appearance, serves as the structuring principle of global relations.

Postcolonial Intellectuals and Postcolonial Criticism

The term *postcolonial* in its various usages carries a multiplicity of meanings that need to be distinguished for analytical purposes. Three uses of the term seem to me to be especially prominent (and significant): (a) as a literal description of conditions in formerly colonial societies, in which case the term has concrete referents, as in postcolonial societies or postcolonial intellectuals; (b) as a description of a global condition after the period of colonialism, in which case the usage is somewhat more abstract and less concrete in reference, comparable in its vagueness to the earlier term *Third World,* for which it is intended as a substitute; and (c) as a description of a discourse on the above-named conditions that is informed by the epistemological and psychic orientations that are products of those conditions.

Even at its most concrete, the significance of *postcolonial* is not transparent, because each of its meanings is overdetermined by the others. Postcolonial intellectuals are clearly the producers of a postcolonial discourse, but who exactly are the postcolonial intellectuals? Here the contrast between *postcolonial* and its predecessor term, *Third World*, may be revealing. The term *Third World*, postcolonial critics insist, was quite vague in encompassing within one uniform category vastly heterogeneous historical circumstances and in locking in fixed positions, structurally if not geographically, societies and populations that shifted with changing global relationships. Although this objection is quite valid, the fixing of societal locations, misleadingly or not, permitted the identification of say, Third World intellectuals with the concreteness of places of origin. *Postcolonial* does not permit such identification. I wondered above whether there might have been a postcolonial consciousness, by which I mean the consciousness that postcolonial intellectuals claim as a hallmark of their intellectual endeavors, even before it was so labeled. Probably there was, although it was invisible because subsumed under the category Third World. Now that postcoloniality has been released from the fixity of Third World location, the identity of the postcolonial is no longer structural but discursive. Postcolonial in this perspective represents an attempt to regroup intellectuals of uncertain location under the banner of postcolonial discourse. Intellectuals in the flesh may produce the themes that constitute postcolonial discourse, but it is participation in the discourse that defines them as postcolonial intellectuals. Hence it is important to delineate the discourse so as to identify postcolonial intellectuals themselves.

Gyan Prakash frames concisely a question that, I think, provides the point of departure for postcolonial discourse: How does the Third World write "its own history"?[4] Like other postcolonial critics, such as Gayatri Chakravorty Spivak, he finds the answer to his question in the model of historical writing provided by the work on Indian history of the Subaltern Studies group (see "PH" p. 399), which also provides, although it does not exhaust, the major themes in postcolonial discourse.[5]

These themes are enunciated cogently in a recent essay by Prakash, which, to my knowledge, offers the most condensed exposition of postcolonialism currently available. Prakash's introduction to his essay is worth quoting at some length:

> One of the distinct effects of the recent emergence of postcolonial criticism has been to force a radical re-thinking and re-formulation of forms of knowledge and social identities authored and authorized by colonialism and western domination. For this reason, it has also created a ferment in the field of knowledge. This is not to say that colonialism and its legacies remained unquestioned until recently: nationalism and

marxism come immediately to mind as powerful challenges to colonialism. But both of these operated with master-narratives that put Europe at its center. Thus, when nationalism, reversing Orientalist thought, attributed agency and history to the subjected nation, it also staked a claim to the order of Reason and Progress instituted by colonialism; and when marxists pilloried colonialism, their criticism was framed by a universalist mode-of-production narrative. Recent postcolonial criticism, on the other hand, seeks to undo the Eurocentrism produced by the institution of the west's trajectory, its appropriation of the other as History. It does so, however, with the acute realization that postcoloniality is not born and nurtured in a panoptic distance from history. The postcolonial exists as an aftermath, as an after—after being worked over by colonialism. Criticism formed in this process of the enunciation of discourses of domination occupies a space that is neither inside nor outside the history of western domination but in a tangential relation to it. This is what Homi Bhabha calls an in-between, hybrid position of practice and negotiation, or what Gayatri Chakravorty Spivak terms catachresis; "reversing, displacing, and seizing the apparatus of value-coding."[6]

To elaborate on these themes, postcolonial criticism repudiates all master narratives, and since the most powerful current master narratives are the products of a post-Enlightenment European constitution of history and therefore Eurocentric, postcolonial criticism takes the critique of Eurocentrism as its central task. Foremost among these master narratives to be repudiated is the narrative of modernization, in both its bourgeois and its Marxist incarnations. Bourgeois modernization, or "developmentalism," represents the renovation and redeployment of "colonial modernity . . . as economic development" ("PH," p. 393). Marxism, while it rejects bourgeois modernization, nevertheless perpetuates the teleological assumptions of the latter by framing inquiry in a narrative of modes of production in which postcolonial history appears as a transition (or an aborted transition) to capitalism (see "PH," p. 395).[7] The repudiation of the narrative of modes of production, I should add, does not mean the repudiation of Marxism; postcolonial criticism acknowledges a strong Marxist inspiration (see "PC," pp. 14–15 and *PCC*).[8] Needless to say, Orientalism's constitution of the colony as Europe's Other, that is, as an essence without history, must be repudiated. But so must nationalism and its procedures of representation that, while challenging Orientalism, have perpetuated the essentialism of Orientalism by affirming a national essence in history (see "PH," pp. 390–91). If it is necessary to repudiate master narratives, it also is necessary to resist all spatial homogenization and temporal teleology. This requires the repudiation of foundational historical writing. According to Prakash, a foundational view is one that assumes "that history is ultimately founded in and representable through some identity—individual, class, or structure—which resists further decomposition into heterogeneity

("PH," p. 397). The most significant conclusion to follow from the repudiation of foundational historiography is the rejection of capitalism as a foundational category on the grounds that "we cannot thematize Indian history in terms of the development of capitalism and simultaneously contest capitalism's homogenization of the contemporary world" ("PC," p. 13). (Obviously, given the logic of the argument, any Third World country could be substituted here for India.) Postfoundational history, in its repudiation of essence and structure and simultaneous affirmation of heterogeneity, also repudiates any fixing of the Third World subject and, therefore of the Third World as a category:

> The rejection of those modes of thinking which configure the third world in such irreducible essences as religiosity, underdevelopment, poverty, nationhood, [and] non-Westernness . . . unsettle[s] the calm presence that the essentialist categories—east and west, first world and third world—inhabit in our thought. This disruption makes it possible to treat the third world as a variety of shifting positions which have been discursively articulated in history. Viewed in this manner, the Orientalist, nationalist, Marxist, and other historiographies become visible as discursive attempts to constitute their objects of knowledge, that is, the third world. As a result, rather than appearing as a fixed and essential object, the third world emerges as a series of historical positions, including those that enunciate essentialisms.
>
> ["PH," p. 384]

It is noteworthy here that with the repudiation of capitalism and structure as foundational categories there is no mention of a capitalist structuring of the world, however heterogeneous and discrepant the histories within it, as a constituting moment of history. Finally, postfoundational history approaches "third-world identities as relational rather than essential" ("PH," p. 399). Postfoundational history (which is also postcolonial history) shifts attention from national origin to subject-position. The consequence is the following:

> The formation of third-world positions suggests engagement rather than insularity. It is difficult to overlook the fact that all of the third-world voices identified in this essay, speak within and to discourses familiar to the "West" instead of originating from some autonomous essence, which does not warrant the conclusion that the third-world historiography has always been enslaved, but that the careful maintenance and policing of East–West boundaries has never succeeded in stopping the flows across and against boundaries and that the self–other opposition has never quite been able to order all differences into binary opposites. The third world, far from being confined to its assigned space, has penetrated the inner sanctum of the first world in the process of being 'third-worlded'—arousing, inciting, and affiliating with the subordinated others in the first world. It has reached across bound-

aries and barriers to connect with the minority voices in the first world: socialists,

radicals, feminists, minorities.   ["PH," p. 403]

This statement is representative of postcolonialism's stance on contemporary global relations (and of its claims to transcending earlier conceptualizations of the world. So, attention needs to be shifted from national origin to subject-position; hence a politics of location takes precedence over politics informed by fixed categories (in this case the nation, though obviously other categories such as Third World and class are also implied). Also, although First and Third World positions may not be interchangeable, they are nevertheless quite fluid, which implies a need to qualify if not to repudiate binary oppositions in the articulation of their relationship. Hence local interactions take priority over global structures in the shaping of these relationships, which implies that they are better comprehended historically in their heterogeneity than structurally in their fixity. These conclusions follow from the hybridness or "in-betweenness" of the postcolonial subject that is not to be contained within fixed categories or binary oppositions. Since postcolonial criticism has focused on the postcolonial subject to the exclusion of an account of the world outside of the subject, the global condition implied by postcoloniality appears at best as a projection onto the world of postcolonial subjectivity and epistemology—a discursive constitution of the world, in other words, in accordance with the constitution of the postcolonial subject, much as it had been constituted earlier by the epistemologies that are the object of postcolonial criticism.

If postcolonial criticism as discourse is any guide to identifying postcolonial intellectuals, the literal sense of *postcolonial* is its least significant aspect, if it is not altogether misleading. Viewed in terms of the themes that I have outlined above, postcolonial, on the one hand, is broadly inclusive; as intellectual concerns these themes are by no means the monopoly of postcolonial criticism, and one does not have to be post*colonial* in any strict sense of the term to share in them, for which the most eloquent evidence is that they were already central to cultural discussions before they were so labeled. Crucial premises of postcolonial criticism, such as the repudiation of post-Enlightenment metanarratives, were enunciated first in post-structuralist thinking and the various postmodernisms that it has informed.[9] Taking the term literally as post*colonial,* some practitioners of postcolonial criticism describe former settler colonies—such as the United States and Australia—as postcolonial, regardless of their status as First World societies and colonizers themselves of their indigenous populations.[10] (Though to be fair, the latter could also be said of many Third World societies.) At the same time, the themes of postcolonial criticism have been prominent in the cultural discourses of Third World societies that were never, strictly speaking, colonies, or that conducted successful revolutions against Euro-American domination, or, like China, both. Nor are there clear temporal boundaries to the use of the term because the themes it encompasses are as old as the history of colonialism. To use the example of China again, such themes as the status of native history vis-à-vis Euro-American conceptualizations of history, national identity and its contested nature, national historical trajectory in the context of global modernization, and even questions of subjectivity created by a sense of in-betweenness are as old as the history of the Chinese encounter with the Euro-American West.[11] One might go so far as to suggest that, if a crisis in historical consciousness, with all its implications for national and individual identity, is a basic theme of postcoloniality, then the First World itself is postcolonial. To the extent that the Euro-American self-image was shaped by the experience of colonizing the world (since the constitution of the Other is at once also the constitution of the Self), the end of colonialism presents the colonizer as much as the colonized with a problem of identity. The crisis created by the commemoration of the 500th anniversary of Columbus's adventure comes to mind immediately.

On the other hand, the term *postcolonial,* understood in terms of its discursive thematics, excludes from its scope most of those who inhabit or hail from post*colonial* societies. It does not account for the attractions of modernization and nationalism to vast numbers in Third World populations, let alone to those marginalized by national incorporation in the global economy. Prakash seems to acknowledge this when he observes that "outside the first world, in India itself, the power of western discourses operates through its authorization and deployment by the nation-state—the ideologies of modernization and instrumentalist science are so deeply sedimented in the national body politic that they neither manifest themselves nor function exclusively as forms of imperial power" ("PC," p. 10). It excludes the many ethnic groups in post*colonial* societies (among others) that, obviously unaware of their hybridity, go on massacring one another. It also excludes radical postcolonials. Intellectuals in India have asked Gayatri Spivak to explain "questions that arise out of the way you perceive yourself ('The post-colonial diasporic Indian who seeks to decolonize the mind'), and the way you constitute us (for convenience, 'native' intellectuals)," to which Spivak's answer is: "your description of how I constitute you does not seem quite correct. I thought I constituted you, equally with the diasporic Indian, as the post-colonial intellectual!" The interrogators are not quite convinced: "Perhaps the relationship of distance and proximity between you and us is that what we write and teach has political and other actual consequences for us that are in a sense different from the consequences, or lack of consequences, or you." They express doubts in another sense as well: "What are the theories or explanations, the narratives of affiliation and disaffiliation that you bring to the politically contaminated and ambivalent function of the non-resident Indian (NRI) who comes back to India, however temporarily, upon the wings of progress?" (*PCC,* pp. 67–68). As phrased by Prakash, it is not clear that even the work of the *Subaltern Studies* collective, which serves as the inspiration of so much of the thematics of postcoloniality, may be included under postcolonial. I have no wish to impose an unwarranted uniformity on *Subaltern Studies* writers, but it seems that their more radical ideas, chief among them the idea of class, are somewhat watered down in the course of their representation in the enunciation of postcolonial criticism.[12] It is also misleading in my opinion to classify as postcolonial critics intellectuals as widely different politically as Edward Said, Aijaz Ahmad, Homi Bhabha, Gyan Prakash, Gayatri Spivak, and Lata Mani. In a literal sense, they may all share in postcoloniality and some of its themes. Said's situation as a Palestinian intellectual does not permit him to cross the borders of Israel with the ease that his in-betweenness might suggest (which also raises the question for postcolonial critics of what borders are at issue). Ahmad, vehemently critical of the Three Worlds concept, nevertheless grounds his critique within the operations of capital, which is quite different from Prakash's denial of a foundational status to capitalism.[13] Spivak and Mani, though quite cognizant of the different roles in different contexts that in-betweenness imposes upon them, nevertheless ground their politics firmly in feminism (and, in the case of Spivak, Marxism).[14]

Finally, Kwame Anthony Appiah, examining the notion of postcoloniality in Africa, points to another pitfall in the literal use of post*colonial,* this time a temporal one. Appiah shares in the understanding of postcolonial as postmodernization, post–Third World, and postnationalist and points out that while the first generation of African writers after the end of colonialism were nationalists, the second generation has rejected nationalism.[15] In a recent discussion (a response to the controversy provoked by his criticism of postcolonial sub-Saharan Africa), Achille Mbembe suggests why this should be the case when he states that "the younger generation of Africans have no direct or immediate experience" of colonization, whatever role it may have played as a foundational event in African history.[16] Postcolonial, in other words, is applicable not to all of the post*colonial* period but only to that period after colonialism when, among other things, a forgetting of its effects has begun to set in.

What then may be the value of a term that includes so much beyond and excludes so much of its own postulated premise, the colonial? What it leaves us with is what I have already hinted at: postcolonial, rather that a description of anything, is a discourse that seeks to constitute the world in the self-image of intellectuals who view themselves (or have come to view themselves) as postcolonial intellectuals. That is, to recall my initial statement concerning Third World intellectuals who have arrived in First World academe, postcolonial discourse is an expression not so much of agony over identity, as it often appears, but of newfound power. Two further questions need to be addressed before I elaborate further on this proposition: one concerns the role intellectuals from India have played in the enunciation of postcolonial discourse; the other concerns the language of this discourse.

Spivak comments (in passing) in an interview that, "in India, people who can think of the three-worlds explanation are totally pissed off by not being recognized as the centre of the non-aligned nations, rather than a 'Third-World' country" (*PCC*, p. 91). Indian intellectuals (and others in India) are not the only ones "pissed off" at being categorized as just another Third World people; such can be found in any Third World country (my country of origin, Turkey, and the country I study, China, come to mind immediately), which speaks to the sorry state of Third World consciousness, if there is one. It is also impossible to say whether or not Indian intellectuals' anger at such categorization has anything to do with the themes that appear in postcolonial discourse, particularly with the repudiation of Third World as a category. Nevertheless, intellectuals from India, as I noted above, have been prominent in identifying themselves as postcolonial intellectuals as well as in enunciating postcolonial criticism. There is nothing wrong with this, of course, except a certain confusion has been introduced into the discourse. Specific problems in Indian historiography and general problems of a global condition described as postcolonial get confused with the projection globally of subjectivities that are (on the basis of the disagreements among Indian intellectuals to which I alluded above) representative of very few intellectuals in India. Most of the generalizations that appear in the discourse of postcolonial intellectuals from India may appear novel in the historiography of India but are not discoveries from broader perspectives. It is no reflection on the historical writing of *Subaltern Studies* historians that their qualifications of class in Indian history, their views on the nation as contested category, and their injunction that the history of capitalism be understood in terms of the fracturing consequences of local and national resistance to it as well as its triumphant, homogenizing effects, however well taken, do not represent earth-shattering conceptual innovations; as Said notes in his foreword to *Selected Subaltern Studies,* these approaches represent the application in Indian historiography of trends in historical writing that were quite widespread by the 1970s, under the impact of social historians such as E. P. Thompson, Eric Hobsbawm, and a whole host of others.[17] All this indicates is that historians of India were participants in the transformations in historical thinking in all areas, transformations in which Third World sensibilities were just one among a number of events that also included post-structuralism, new ways of thinking about Marxism, and the entry into history of feminism. To be sure, I think it very important that Third World sensibilities be brought into play repeatedly in order to counteract the tendency toward cultural imperialism of First World thinkers and historians who apply concepts of First World derivation globally without giving a second thought to the social differences that must qualify those concepts historically and contextually, but this is no reason to inflate a postcolonial sensibility, especially one that is itself bound by national and local experiences, indefinitely. And yet such a tendency (for which *Subaltern Studies* writers may themselves not be responsible at all) is plainly visible in the exposition of postcoloniality by someone like Prakash, who, writing of Indian historiography in one sentence, projects his observations globally in the very next one.

These observations are not intended to single out postcolonial intellectuals from India, which would be misleading not only about Indian intellectuals in general but also about postcolonial intellectuals in general. The appeals of postcoloniality are not restricted to intellectuals of any one national origin, and the problems to which I pointed above are problems of a general nature, born out of a contradiction between an insistence on heterogeneity, difference, and historicity and a tendency to generalize from the local to the global while denying that there are global forces at work that may condition the local in the first place. What my observations point to is a new assertiveness on the part of Third World intellectuals that makes this procedure possible. Another example may be found among Chinese intellectuals, in the so-called Confucian revival in recent years. These writers obviously do not describe themselves as postcolonial, for their point of departure is the newfound power of Chinese societies within global capitalism that, if anything, shows in their efforts to suppress memories of an earlier day when China, too, suffered from Euro-American hegemony (though not colonialism). In their case the effort takes the form of articulating to the values of capitalism a Confucianism that in an earlier day was deemed to be inconsistent with capitalist modernization. Hence Confucianism has been rendered into a prime mover of capitalist development and has also found quite a sympathetic ear among First World ideologues who now look to a Confucian ethic to relieve the crisis of capitalism.[18] Although Confucianism in its urge to become part of a hegemonic ideology of capitalism differs from postcoloniality, it nevertheless shares with postcoloniality the counterhegemonic self-assertiveness of a group of formerly Third World intellectuals. And it may not be a coincidence that Chinese intellectuals in First World academia have played a major part in the enunciation of this Confucian revival, although it is by no means restricted to them.

The second question that needs to be considered concerns the language of postcolonial discourse, which is the language of First World post-structuralism, as postcolonial critics themselves readily concede, although they do not dwell too long on its implications. Prakash indicates this problem in his statement that "all of the third-world voices identified in 'Writing Post-Orientalist Histories' speak within and to discourses familiar to the 'West,'" but he goes on to conceal its implications in his conclusion that this discursive fluency proves only that the "maintenance and policing of East–West boundaries has never succeeded in stopping the flows across and against boundaries," as if the flows in the two directions have been equal in their potency ("PH," p. 403). More important, Prakash's obfuscation enables us to place temporally a postcoloniality that otherwise may stretch across the entire history of colonialism. Here, once again, a comparison with China may be instructive, this time over the issue of Marxism. Postcolonial critics insist that they are Marxists, but Marxists who reject the "nineteenth-century heritage" of Marxism with its universalistic pretensions that ignored historical differences ("PC," p. 15). Chinese Marxist revolutionaries in the 1930s faced and addressed the problem of articulating Marxism to Chinese conditions (and vice versa). Their answer was that Marxism must be translated into a Chinese vernacular not just in a national but, more importantly, in a local sense: the language of the peasantry. The result was what is commonly called the Sinification of Marxism, embodied in so-called Mao Zedong Thought.[19] The approach of postcolonial critics to a similar problem is not to translate Marxism into a national (which is rejected) or local (which is affirmed) vernacular but to rephrase it in the language of poststructuralism, in which Marxism is deconstructed, decentered, and so on. In other words, a critique that starts off with a repudiation of the universalistic pretensions of Marxist language ends up not with its dispersion into local vernaculars but with a return to another First World language with universalistic epistemological pretensions. It enables us, at least, to locate postcolonial criticism in the contemporary First World.

This is not a particularly telling point. Postcolonial critics recognize that the "critical gaze" their studies "direct at the archeology of knowledge enshrined in the west arises from the fact that most of them are being written in the first-world academy" ("PC," p. 10). In drawing attention to the language of postcolonial discourse, I seek, however, to deconstruct postcolonial intellectuals' professions of hybridity and in-betweenness. The hybridity to which postcolonial criticism refers is uniformly between the post*colonial* and the First World, never, to my knowledge, between one post*colonial* intellectual and another. But hybridity and in-betweenness are not very revealing concepts in the former case either. Whereas postcolonial criticism quite validly points to the overdetermination of concepts and subjectivities (and I am quite sure that postcolonial subjectivity is overdetermined, while less sure that it is more so than any other), it conveniently ignores the part location in ideological and institutional structures plays in the resolution of contradictions presented by hybridity— and the consequences of location in generating vast differences in power.[20] If the language of postcolonial discourse is any guide to its ideological direction, in this case the contradictions presented by hybridity would seem to be given direction by the location of postcolonial intellectuals in the academic institutions of the First World. However much postcolonial intellectuals may insist on hybridity and the transposability of locations, not all positions are equal in power, as Spivak's interrogators in India seem to recognize in their reference to the "wings of progress" that brought her to India. To insist on hybridity against one's own language, it seems to me, is to disguise not only ideological location but also the differences of power that go with different locations. Postcolonial intellectuals in their First World institutional location are ensconced in positions of power not only vis-à-vis the "native" intellectuals back at home but also vis-à-vis their First World neighbors here. My neighbors in Farmville, Virginia, are no match in power for the highly paid, highly prestigious postcolonial intellectuals at Columbia, Princeton, or Duke; some of them might even be willing to swap positions and take the anguish that comes with hybridity so long as it brings with it the power and the prestige it seems to command.

"Postcoloniality," Appiah writes, "has become a condition of pessimism,"[21] and there is much to be pessimistic about the world situation of which postcoloniality is an expression. This is not the message of postcolonialism, however, as it acquires respectability and gains admission in United States academic institutions. Whereas this discourse shares in the same themes as postcolonial discourses everywhere, it rearranges these themes into a celebration of the end of colonialism, as if the only tasks left for the present were to abolish its ideological and cultural legacy. Although this approach may sound convincing, by fixing its gaze on the past it in fact avoids confronting the present. The current global condition appears in the discourse only as a projection of the subjectivities and epistemologies of First World intellectuals of Third World origin; the discourse constitutes the world in the self-image of these intellectuals, which makes it an expression not of powerlessness but of newfound power. Postcolonial intellectuals have arrived in the First World academy not only because they have broken new intellectual ground (although they have rephrased older themes) but also because intellectual orientations that earlier were regarded as marginal or subversive have acquired a new respectability. Postcoloniality, it has been noted, has found favor even among academic conservatives who prefer it to a less tractable vocabulary that insists on keeping in the foreground contemporary problems of political division and oppression.[22]

Postcoloniality already has been the subject of some telling criticism. Critics have noted that, in spite of its insistence on historicity and difference, postcoloniality mimics in its deployment the "ahistorical and universalizing" tendencies in colonialist thinking ("NP," p. 99). "If the theory promises a decentering of history in hybridity, syncreticism, multidimensional time, and so forth," Anne McClintock writes, "the *singularity* of the term effects a re-centering of global history around the single rubric of European time. Colonialism returns at the moment of its disappearance."[23] In a world situation in which severe inequalities persist in older colonial forms or in their neocolonial reconfigurations, moreover, "the unified temporality of 'postcoloniality' risks reproducing the colonial discourse of an allochronic other, living in another time, still lagging behind us, the genuine postcolonials" ("NP," p. 104). The spatial homogenization that accompanies a "unified temporality" not only fails to discriminate between vastly different social and political situations but also, to the extent that it "fails to discriminate between the diverse modalities of hybridity," may end up in "the consecration of hegemony" ("NP," p. 110). Failing to make such discriminations and lacking a sense of totality, postcoloniality, as Rosalind O'Hanlon and

David Washbrook observe, also ends up mimicking methodologically the colonialist epistemology that it sets out to repudiate:

> The solutions it offers—methodological individualism, the depoliticising insulation of social from material domains, a view of social relations that is in practice extremely voluntaristic, the refusal of any kind of programmatic politics—do not seem to us radical, subversive, or emancipatory. They are on the contrary conservative and implicitly authoritarian, as they were indeed when recommended more overtly in the heyday of Britain's own imperial power.[24]

Postcolonialism's repudiation of structure and totality in the name of history ironically ends up not in an affirmation of historicity but in a self-referential, universalizing historicism that reintroduces through the back door an unexamined totality; it projects globally what are but local experiences. The problem here may be the problem of all historicism without a sense of structure. Without a web of translocal relationships, it is impossible to determine what is different, heterogeneous, and local. In his critique of "essentializing" procedures (of India, of the Third World), Prakash offers as a substitute an understanding of these categories in terms of "relationships" but does not elaborate on what these relationships might be. The critique of an essentialist fixing of the Third World is not novel; Carl E. Pletsch's eloquent critique of three worlds theory (without the aid of postcoloniality), published a decade ago, enunciated clearly the problem of ideological essentializing in modernization theory.[25] Nor is Prakash's conceptual "innovation"—relationships—truly new. Pletsch himself pointed to global relationships as part of the conceptual underpinnings of modernization theory as well as to their importance in understanding problems of development, and an understanding of modern global history in terms of relationships, needless to say, is the crucial thesis of world-system analysis.

The difference between world-system analysis and Prakash's postfoundational understanding of relationships is Prakash's rejection of foundational categories, chief among them, capitalism. What O'Hanlon and Washbrook say on this issue is worth quoting at some length:

> What [Prakash's] position leaves quite obscure is what status exactly this category of "capitalist modernity" occupies for him. If our strategy should be to "refuse" it in favour of marginal histories, of multiple and heterogeneous identities, this suggests that capitalist modernity is nothing more than a potentially disposable fiction, held in place simply by our acceptance of its cognitive categories and values. Indeed, Prakash is particularly disparaging of Marxist and social historians' concern with capitalism as a "system" of political economy and coercive instrumentalities. Yet in other moments Prakash tells us that history's proper task is to challenge precisely this "homogenization of the world by contemporary capitalism." If this is so, and

there is indeed a graspable logic to the way in which modern capitalism has spread itself globally, how are we to go about the central task of comprehending this logic in the terms that Prakash suggests? ["AO," p. 147]

Prakash's answer to his critics simply evades the issues raised in this passage (while coming close to granting a central role to capitalism) because to recognize them would make his postfoundational history untenable (see "PC," pp. 13–14). Fernando Coronil outlines the political consequences of the postcolonialist repudiation of metanarratives in his observation that such opposition "produces disjointed mininarratives which reinforce dominant worldviews; reacting against determinisms, it presents free-floating events; refusing to fix identity in structural categories, it essentializes identity through difference; resisting the location of power in structures or institutions, it diffuses it throughout society and ultimately dissolves it."[26] It also relieves "self-defined minority or subaltern critics," O'Hanlon and Washbrook note, of the necessity of "doing what they constantly demand of others, which is to historicise the conditions of their own emergence as authoritative voices—conditions which could hardly be described without reference of some kind to material and class relations" ("AO," pp. 165–66).

Finally, the postcolonial repudiation of the Third World is intimately linked with the repudiation of capitalism's structuring of the modern world. Once again, essentialism serves as a straw man, diverting attention from radical conceptualizations of the Third World that are not essentialist but relational, as in world-system approaches. Rather than fixing it ahistorically, as Prakash would have it, the world-system approach comprehends the Third World as a structural position within a capitalist world order, a position that changes with changing structural relationships. To be sure, world-system analysis, like one based on modernization, locates the Third World discursively, but, as I have argued above, so does postcolonialist analysis. The question then becomes how well competing discourses account for historical changes in global relationships and the oppositional practices to which they point. I will say more on the former below. As for oppositional practices, postcoloniality by its very logic permits little beyond local struggles and, since it makes no reference to structure or totality, directionless ones at that. For all its contradictions, Shohat writes, "'Third World' usefully evokes structural commonalities of struggles. The invocation of the 'Third World' implies a belief that the shared history of neocolonialism and internal racism form sufficient common ground for alliances among . . . diverse peoples. If one does not believe or envision such commonalities, then indeed the term 'Third World' should be discarded" ("NP," p. 111).

The denial of capitalism's foundational status also reveals a culturalism in the postcolonialist argument that has important ideological consequences. This involves the issue of Eurocentrism. Without capitalism as the foundation for European power and the motive force of its globalization, Eurocentrism would have been just another ethnocentrism (comparable to any other ethnocentrism from the Chinese and the Indian to the most trivial tribal solipsism). An exclusive focus on Eurocentrism as a cultural or ideological problem that blurs the power relationships that dynamized it and endowed it with hegemonic persuasiveness fails to explain why, in contrast to regional or local ethnocentrisms, this particular ethnocentrism was able to define modern global history and itself as the universal aspiration and end of that history. By throwing the cover of culture over material relationships, as if the one had little to do with the other, such a focus diverts criticism of capitalism to the criticism of Eurocentric ideology, which not only helps postcolonialism disguise its own ideological limitation but also, ironically, provides an alibi for inequality, exploitation, and oppression in their modern guises under capitalist relationships. The postcolonialist argument projects upon the past the same mystification of the relationship between power and culture that is characteristic of the ideology of global capitalism of which it is a product.

These criticisms, however vehement on occasion, do not necessarily indicate that postcolonialism's critics deny it all value; indeed, critics such as Coronil, McClintock, and Shohat explicitly acknowledge some value to the issues raised by postcolonialism and postcolonial intellectuals. There is no denying that postcolonialism expresses not only a crisis in the ideology of linear progress but also a crisis in the modes of comprehending the world associated with such concepts as Third World and nation-state. Nor is it to be denied that as the global situation has become blurred with the disappearance of socialist states, with the emergence of important differences economically and politically among so-called Third World societies, and with the diasporic motions of populations across national and regional boundaries, fragmentation of the global into the local has emerged into the foreground of historical and political consciousness. Crossing national, cultural, class, gender, and ethnic boundaries, moreover, with its promise of a genuine cosmopolitanism, is appealing in its own right.

Within the institutional site of the First World academy, fragmentation of earlier metanarratives appears benign (except to hidebound conservatives) for its promise of more democratic, multicultural, and cosmopolitan epistemologies. In the world outside the academy, however, it shows in murderous ethnic conflict, continued inequalities among societies, classes and genders, and the absence of oppositional possibilities that, always lacking in coherence, are rendered even more impotent than earlier by the fetishization of difference, fragmentation, and so on.

The confounding of ideological metanarratives with actualities of power renders the predicament more serious. To mistake fragmentation in one realm with fragmentation in the other ignores the possibility that ideological fragmentation may represent not the dissolution of power but its further concentration. It is necessary, to account for this possibility, to retain a sense of structure and totality in the confrontation of fragmentation and locality, the alternative to which may be complicity in the consolidation of hegemony in the very process of questioning it. Although postcoloniality represents an effort to adjust to a changing global situation, it appears for that very reason as an exemplary illustration of this predicament. Critics have hinted at its possible relationship to a new situation in the capitalist transformation of the world. Without examining this relationship at length, I would like to look at this relationship more closely.

Global Capitalism and the Condition of Postcoloniality

David Harvey and Fredric Jameson, among others, perceive a relationship between postmodernism and a new phase in the development of capitalism that has been described variously as late capitalism, flexible production or accumulation, disorganized capitalism, and global capitalism.[27] As a child of postmodernism, postcolonialism too is expressive of the logic of this phase of capitalism, but on Third World terrain.

Fundamental to the structure of the new global capitalism (the term I prefer) is what Folker Fröbel and others have described as "a new international division of labor," that is, the transnationalization of production where, through subcontracting, the process of production (of even the same commodity) is globalized.[28] The international division of labor in production may not be entirely novel, but new technologies have increased spatial extension as well as speed of production to an unprecedented level. These same technologies have endowed capital and production with novel mobility; seeking maximum advantage for capital against labor as well as freedom from social and political interference, production seems to be constantly changing its location—hence flexible production. For, these reasons, analysts perceive in global capitalism a qualitative difference from past, similar practices—indeed, a new phase of capitalism.

Also important to this new phase is the decentering of capitalism nationally. In other words, it is increasingly difficult to point to any nation or region as the center of global capitalism. More than one analyst (in a position of power) has found an analogue to the emerging organization of production in the northern European Hanseatic League of the early modern period (that is, the period before the emergence of nation-states); in other words, a network of urban formations, without a clearly definable center, whose links to one another are far stronger than their relationships to their immediate hinterlands.[29]

The medium linking the contemporary global capitalist network together is the transnational corporation, which has taken over from national markets as the locus of economic activity not as a passive medium for the transmission of capital, commodities, and production but as a determinant of that transmission and its direction. Whereas the analogy with the Hanseatic League suggests decentralization, production under global capitalism is in fact heavily concentrated in the corporation. With power lodged in transnational corporations, which by definition transcend nations in their organization and loyalties, the power of the nation-state to regulate the economy internally is constricted, while global regulation (and defense) of the economic order emerges as a major task. This is manifested not only in the proliferation of global organizations but also in efforts to organize extranational regional organizations to give coherence to the functioning of the economy.[30]

The transnationalization of production is the source at once of unprecedented global unity and of unprecedented fragmentation in the history of capitalism. The homogenization of the globe economically, socially, and culturally is such that Marx's predictions finally seem to be on the point of vindication. At the same time, however, there is a parallel process of fragmentation at work; globally, in the disappearance of a center to capitalism, locally, in the fragmentation of the production process into subnational regions and localities. As supranational regional organizations such as the European Economic Community, the Pacific Basin Economic Community, and the North American Free Trade Zone (to mention some that have been realized or are the objects of intense organizational activity) manifest this fragmentation at the global level, localities within a single nation competing with one another to place themselves in the pathways of transnational capital represent it at the most basic local level. Nations themselves, it is arguable, historically represented attempts to contain fragmentation, but under attack from the outside (transnational organization) and the inside (subnational economic regions and localities), it is not quite clear how this new fragmentation is to be contained.[31]

Yet perhaps the most important consequence of the transnationalizalion of capital is that, for the first time in the history of capitalism, the capitalist mode of production, divorced from its historically specific origins in Europe, appears as an authentically global abstraction. The narrative of capitalism is no longer a narrative of the history of Europe; non-European capitalist societies now make their own claims on the history of capitalism. Corresponding to economic fragmentation, in other words, is cultural fragmentation, or, to put it in its positive guise, multiculturalism. The most dramatic instance of this new cultural situation may be the effort over the last decade to reconcile capitalism with the so-called Confucian values of East Asian societies, which is a reversal of a long-standing conviction (in Europe and East Asia) that Confucianism was historically an obstacle to capitalism. I think it is arguable that the end of Eurocentrism is an illusion because capitalist culture as it has taken shape has Eurocentrism built into the very structure of its narrative, which may explain why, even as Europe and the United States lose their domination of the capitalist world economy, European and American cultural values retain their domination. It is noteworthy that what makes something like the East Asian Confucian revival plausible is not its offer of alternative values to those of Euro-American origin but its articulation of native culture into a capitalist narrative. Having said this, it is important to reiterate nevertheless that the question of world culture has become much more complex than in earlier phases of capitalism.

The fragmentation of space and its consequences for Eurocentrism also imply a fragmentation of the temporality of capitalism; the challenge to Eurocentrism, in other words, means that it is possible to conceive of the future in ways other than those of Euro-American political and social models. Here, once again, it is difficult to distinguish reality from illusion, but the complexity is undeniable.

Finally, the transnationalization of production calls into question earlier divisions of the world into First, Second, and Third Worlds. The Second World, the world of socialism, is for all practical purposes of the past. But the new global configuration also calls into question the distinctions between the First and Third Worlds. Parts of the earlier Third World are today on the pathways of transnational capital and belong in the "developed" sector of the world economy. Likewise, parts of the First World marginalized in the new global economy are hardly distinguishable in way of life from what used to be viewed as the Third World. It may not be fortuitous that the North-South distinction has gradually taken over from the earlier division of the globe into three worlds, unless we remember that the references of North and South are not merely to concrete geographic locations but are also metaphorical. North connotes the pathways of transnational capital, and South, the marginalized populations of the world, regardless of their location—which is where postcoloniality comes in.

Ideologues of global capital have described this condition as "global regionalism" or "global localism," adding quickly, however, that global localism is 80 percent global and only 20 percent local.[32] They have also appropriated for capital the radical ecological slogan, "Think global, act local."[33]

The situation created by global capitalism helps explain certain phenomena that have become apparent over the last two or three decades, but especially since the eighties: global motions of peoples (and, therefore, cultures), the weakening of boundaries (among societies, as well as among social categories), the replications in societies internally of inequalities and discrepancies once associated with colonial differences, simultaneous homogenization and fragmentation within and across societies, the interpenetration of the global and the local, and the disorganization of a world conceived in terms of three worlds or nation-states. Some of these phenomena have also contributed to an appearance of equalization of differences within and across societies, as well as of democratization within and among societies. What is ironic is that the managers of this world situation themselves concede that they (or their organizations) now have the power to appropriate the local for the global, to admit different cultures into the realm of capital (only to break them down and re-make them in accordance with the requirements of production and consumption), and even to reconstitute subjectivities across national boundaries to create produc-ers and consumers more responsive to the operations of capital. Those who do not respond, or the "basket cases" that are not essential to those operations—four-fifths of the global population by the managers' count—need not be colonized; they are simply marginalized. What the new flexible production has made possible is that it is no longer necessary to utilize explicit coercion against labor at home or in colonies abroad. Those peoples or places that are not responsive to the needs (or demands) of capital, or are too far gone to respond "efficiently," simply find themselves out of its pathways. And it is easier even than in the heyday of colonialism or moderniza-tion theory to say convincingly: It is their own fault.

If I may now return to Shohat's question with which I began this essay—"When exactly . . . does the 'post-colonial' begin?"—and give it a less facetious answer con-sistent with her intention, the answer is, with the emergence of global capitalism, not in the sense of an exact coincidence in time but in the sense that the one is a condi-tion for the other. There is little that is remarkable about this conclusion, which is but an extension to postcolonialism of the relationship that Harvey and Jameson have established between postmodernism and developments within capitalism. If post-colonialism is a progeny of postmodernism, then these developments within capital-ism are also directly or indirectly pertinent to understanding postcolonialism. Postcolonial critics readily concede the debt they owe to postmodernist and post-structuralist thinking; indeed, their most original contribution would seem to lie in their rephrasing of older problems in the study of the Third World in the language of poststructuralism. What is truly remarkable, therefore, is that a consideration of the relationship between postcolonialism and global capitalism should be absent from the writings of postcolonial intellectuals, an absence all the more remarkable because this relationship, which pertains not only to cultural and epistemological but also to social and political formations, is arguably less abstract and more direct than any relationship between global capitalism and postmodernism.

Postcoloniality represents a response to a genuine need, the need to overcome a crisis of understanding produced by the inability of old categories to account for the world. The metanarrative of progress that underlies two centuries of thinking is in deep crisis. Not only have we lost faith in progress but also progress has had actual disintegrative effects. More important, over the last decade in particular our sense of a clear progression of time and events has been jumbled. During, these years, con-servatism has become revolutionary (the Reagan revolution); revolutionaries have turned first into conservatives and then into reactionaries (as in formerly socialist countries such as the Soviet Union and China); religious millenarianisms long thought to be castaways from Enlightenment have made a comeback into politics, sometimes, as in the United States, allied to high-tech revolutions; and fascism has been reborn out of the ashes of Communist regimes. The crisis of progress has brought in its wake a crisis of modernization, more in its Marxist than in its bourgeois guise, and called into question the structure of the globe as conceived by modernizationalists and radicals alike in the decades after World War II, that is, as three worlds. Whether they be fixed geographically or structurally, in bourgeois or in Marxist social theory, the three worlds are indeed no longer tenable. The globe has become as jumbled up spatially as the ideology of progress has temporally. Third Worlds have appeared in the First World and First Worlds in the Third. New diasporas have relocated the Self there and the Other here, and consequently borders and boundaries have been confounded. And the flow of culture has been at once homogenizing and heterogenizing; some groups share in a common global culture regardless of location even as they are alienated from the culture of their hinterlands, while others are driven back into cultural legacies long thought to be residual to take refuge in cultural havens that are as far apart from one another as they were at the origins of modernity—even though they may be watching the same TV shows.

Politically speaking, the Second and Third Worlds have been the major casualties of this crisis. The Second World, the world of socialist states, is already, to put it bluntly, history. What has happened to the Third World (the immediate subject of postcoloniality) may be less apparent but no less significant. We may note here that the two major crises of the early nineties that are global in implication are the crises occasioned by Iraq's invasion of Kuwait and the current situation in Somalia. In the Gulf crisis, a Third World country appeared as the imperialist culprit against a socially and politically reactionary but economically powerful neighbor and had to be driven back by the combined armies of the First, Second, and Third Worlds, led by an imperial power now turned into a paradigm of righteousness. The "invasion"—I borrow the word from a TV report—of Somalia, if anything, is more revealing. If in the case of the Gulf crisis one Third World country had to be saved from another, in Somalia we have a Third World country that has to be saved from itself. The Third World, viewed by radicals only two decades ago as a hope for the future, now has to be saved from itself. The crisis could not get much deeper.

Postcoloniality addresses this situation of crisis that eludes understanding in terms of older conceptualizations,[34] which may explain why it created immediate ferment in intellectual circles. But this still begs the question, why now?—and why has it taken the intellectual direction it has? After all, there is more than one conceptual way out of a crisis, and we must inquire why this particular way has acquired immediate popularity—in First World institutions. To put it bluntly, postcoloniality is designed to *avoid* making sense of the current crisis and, in the process, to cover up the origins of postcolonial intellectuals in a global capitalism of which they are not so much victims as beneficiaries.

Postcoloniality resonates with the problems thrown up by global capitalism. As the crisis of the Third World has become inescapably apparent during the decade of the eighties, so have the effects of global capitalism. As the Reagan (and Thatcher) revolution was not so much a revolution heralding a new beginning as a revolution aimed at reorganizing the globe politically so as to give free reign to a global capitalism that strained against the harness of political restrictions. The overthrow of socialist states was one part of the program. Another was taming the Third World, if necessary by invasion, preferably by encirclement with economic sanctions or with Patriot missiles. But these are at best tactics of last resort. By far the best option is control from the inside through the creation of classes amenable to incorporation into or alliance with global capital.

I use the word *control* here advisedly; under conditions of global capitalism, control is not to be imposed, it has to be negotiated. Transnational capital is no longer just Euro-American, and neither is modernity. The complicated social and cultural composition of transnational capitalism makes it difficult to sustain a simple equation between capitalist modernity and Eurocentric (and patriarchal) cultural values and political forms. Others who have achieved success within the capitalist world system demand a voice for their values within the culture of transnational capital; the East Asian Confucian revival to which I referred above is exemplary of the phenomenon. Eurocentrism, as the very condition for the emergence of these alternative voices, retains its cultural hegemony; but it is more evident than ever before that, for this hegemony to be sustained, its boundaries must be rendered more porous in order to absorb alternative cultural possibilities that might otherwise serve as sources of destructive oppositions. (The mutual bashing between Japan and the United States in recent years, which revives racist and Orientalist vocabulary, attests to the dangers of conflict within the very ranks of transnational capital.) And who knows, in the end, what values are most functional to the needs of a changing capital? Commentator after commentator has remarked in recent years that the communitarian values of Confucianism may be more suitable to a contemporary managerial capitalism than the individualistic values of the entrepreneurial capitalism of an earlier day. What is clear is that global capitalism is (and must be) much more fluid culturally than a Eurocentric capitalism.

This is also the condition of postcoloniality and the cultural moves associated with it. Knuckleheaded conservatives, anxious to explain away cultural problems by substituting worries about the machinations of subversives for systemic analysis, attribute the cultural problems that became apparent in the eighties (most recently, multiculturalism) to the invasion of academic institutions and politics in general by Marxists, feminists, ethnics, and so on. What they ignore is the possible relationship between the Reagan economic revolution and these cultural developments. That is, in their very globalism, the cultural requirements of transnational corporations can no longer afford the cultural parochialism of an earlier day. Focusing on liberal arts institutions, some conservative intellectuals overlook how much headway multiculturalism has made with business school administrators and the managers of transnational corporations, who are eager all of a sudden to learn the secrets of East Asian economic success in "oriental" philosophies, who cannibalize cultures all over the world in order to better market their commodities, and who have suddenly become aware of a need to internationalize academic institutions (which often takes the form not of promoting scholarship in a conventional sense but of "importing" and "exporting" students and faculty). While in an earlier day it might have been Marxist and feminist radicals, with the aid of a few ethnics, who spearheaded multiculturalism, by now the initiative has passed into the hands of "enlightened" administrators and trustees who are quite aware of the "manpower" needs of the new economic situation. No longer so much a conflict between conservatives and radicals (although that dimension, too, is obviously there), the conflict shapes up now as a conflict between an older elite, comprised in part of a small business interest now threatened by domestic and foreign competition, and the elite vanguard of international business. Among the foremost and earliest of United States advocates of transnationalism and multiculturalism is the *Harvard Business Review*.

The Reaganites may have been misled by the visions, which have not materialized, of Dinesh D'Souza and his imitators. Their failure to grasp the social and political consequences of economic victory for the transnationalism that they engineered became apparent during the recent elections when, against the calls from right-wingers for a return to such traditional American values as Eurocentrism, patriarchalism, and racism, George Bush often looked befuddled, possibly because he grasped much better than men like Pat Buchanan the dilemmas presented by the victory of transnationalism over all its competitors in the Second and Third Worlds. The result has been the victory of high-tech yuppies, who are much better attuned to the new world situation and to the difficulties it presents. It is no coincidence that Robert Reich, frequent contributor to the *Harvard Business Review,* keen analyst of developments within the capitalist world economy, and an advocate of the borderless economy, is a close confidant of President Clinton.

This is, I think, also the context for the emergence of postcoloniality and for its rapid success in academic institutions as a substitute for earlier conceptualizations of the world. Postcoloniality, in the particular direction it has taken as a discourse, also resonates with the problems of the contemporary world. It addresses issues that may have been present all along in global studies but are now rephrased to attune to issues in global capitalism: Eurocentrism and its relationship to capitalism; the kind of modernity that is relevant to a postmodern, postsocialist, post–Third World situation; the place of the nation in development; the relationship between the local and the global; the place of borders and boundaries in a world where capital, production, and peoples are in constant motion; the status of structures in a world that more than ever seems to be without recognizable structure; interpenetrations and reversals between the different worlds; borderlands subjectivities and episte-mologies (hybridity); homogeneity versus heterogeneity; and so forth.

Postcoloniality, however, is also appealing because it disguises the power rela-tions that shape a seemingly shapeless world and contributes to a conceptualization of that world that both consolidates and subverts possibilities of resistance. Post-colonial critics have engaged in valid criticism of past forms of ideological hegemony but have had little to say about its contemporary figurations. Indeed, in their simul-taneous repudiation of structure and affirmation of the local in problems of oppres-sion and liberation, they have mystified the ways in which totalizing structures persist in the midst of apparent disintegration and fluidity. They have rendered into problems of subjectivity and epistemology concrete and material problems of the everyday world. While capital in its motions continues to structure the world, refus-ing it foundational status renders impossible the cognitive mapping that must be the point of departure for any practice of resistance and leaves such mapping as there is in the domain of those who manage the capitalist world economy.[35] Indeed, in the projection of the current state of conceptual disorganization upon the colonial past, postcolonial critics have also deprived colonialism of any but local logic, so that the historical legacy of colonialism (in Iraq, or Somalia, or, for that matter, any Third World society) appears irrelevant to the present. Thus the burden of persistent prob-lems is shifted onto the victims themselves.

"Postcoloniality," Appiah writes, "is the condition of what we might ungenerously call a *comprador* intelligentsia."[36] I think this is missing the point because the world situation that justified the term *comprador* no longer exists. I would suggest instead that postcoloniality is the condition of the intelligentsia of global capitalism. The question, then, is not whether this global intelligentsia can (or should) return to national loyalties but whether, in recognition of its own class-position in global cap-italism, it can generate a thoroughgoing criticism of its own ideology and formulate practices of resistance against the system of which it is a product.

ACKNOWLEDGMENTS

My being (more or less) one of the Third World intellectuals in First World academe does not privi-lege the criticism of postcolonial intellectuals that I offer below, but it does call for some comment. It is not clear to me how important the views I discuss (or the intellectuals who promote them) are in their impact on contemporary intellectual life. *Postcolonial* has been entering the lexicon of aca-demic programs in recent years, and over the last two years there have been a number of confer-ences and symposia inspired by related vocabulary (postcolonialism, "after Orientalism," and so on), as well as special issues devoted to the subject in periodicals such as *Social Text* and *Public Culture*. But given the small number of intellectuals directly concerned with postcoloniality and the diffuseness in their use of the concept, it might make more sense to study the reception of the term *postcolonial*. Such a study is particularly important, I argue below, because the ideas associated with postcoloniality are significant and widespread as concerns, even if they predate the term *postcolonial* itself. It is not the importance of these ideas that I question, in other words, but their appropriation for postcoloniality. Otherwise, there is a Third World sensibility and mode of perception that has become increasingly visible in cultural discussions over the last decade. I myself share in the concerns (and even some of the viewpoints) of postcolonial intellectuals, though from a somewhat different perspective than those who describe themselves as such. For a recent example of this kind of work, see my "Post-socialism/Flexible Production: Marxism in Contemporary Radicalism," *Polygraph,* no. 6/7 (1993): 133–69.

While relieving them of any complicity in my views, I would like to thank Harry Harootunian, Masao Miyoshi, Roxann Prazniak, Rob Wilson, and Zhang Xudong for their comments and assistance with sources.

NOTES

1 Ella Shohat, "Notes on the 'Post-Colonial,'" *Social Text,* no. 31/32 (1992): 103; hereafter abbreviated "NP."

2 In 1985, Gayatri Spivak insisted in an interview that she did not belong to the "top level of the United States academy" because she taught in the South and the Southwest whereas the "cultural elite in the United States inhabit the Northeastern seaboard or the West coast" (Gayatri Chakravorty Spivak, *The Post-Colonial Critic: Interviews, Strategies, Dialogues,* ed. Sarah Harasym [New York, 1990], p. 114); hereafter abbreviated *PCC.* Since then Spivak has moved to Columbia University.

3 See also Arjun Appadurai, "Global Ethnoscapes: Notes and Queries for a Transnational Anthropology," in *Recapturing Anthropology: Working in the Present,* ed. Richard C. Fox (Santa Fe, N. Mex., 1991), pp. 191–210. Aijaz Ahmad, whom I do not include among the postcolonial critics here, does an excellent job of relating the problems of postcoloniality to contemporary capitalism, if only in passing and somewhat differently from the way I do below. See Aijaz Ahmad, "Jameson's Rhetoric of Otherness and the 'National Allegory.'" *Social Text,* no. 17 (Fall 1987): 3–25 and *In Theory: Classes, Nations, Literatures* (London, 1992).

4 Gyan Prakash, "Writing Post-Orientalist Histories of the Third World: Perspectives from Indian Historiography," *Comparative Studies in Society and History* 32 (Apr. 1990): 383; hereafter abbreviated "PH."

5 See Spivak, "Subaltern Studies: Deconstructing Historiography," in *Selected Subaltern Studies,* ed. Ranajit Guha and Spivak (New York, 1988), pp. 3–32.

6 Prakash, "Postcolonial Criticism and Indian Historiography," *Social Text,* no. 31/32 (1992): 8; hereafter abbreviated "PC." I use Prakash's discussions of postcoloniality as my point of departure here because he has made the most systematic attempts at accounting for the concept and also because his discussions bring to the fore the implications of the concept for historical understanding. As this statement reveals, Prakash himself draws heavily on the characteristics of postcolonial consciousness delineated by others, especially Homi K. Bhabha, who has been responsible for the prominence in discussions of postcoloniality of the vocabulary of hybridity and so on. Bhabha's work, however, is responsible for more than the vocabulary of postcolonialism, as he has proven himself to be something of a master of political mystification and theoretical obfuscation, of a reduction of social and political problems to psychological ones, and of the substitution of post-structuralist linguistic manipulation for historical and social explanation—all of which show up in much postcolonial writing, but rarely with the same virtuosity (and incomprehensibleness) that he brings to it. For some of his more influential writings, see Homi K. Bhabha, "Of Mimicry and Man: The Ambivalence of Colonial

Discourse," *October,* no. 28 (Spring 1984): 125–33; "The Commitment to Theory," in *Questions of Third World Cinema,* ed. Jim Pines and Paul Willemen (London, 1989), pp. 111–32; "The Other Question: Difference, Discrimination and the Discourse of Colonialism," in *Literature, Politics and Theory,* ed. Francis Barker et al. (London, 1986), pp. 148–72; and "Introduction: Narrating the Nation" and "DissemiNation: Time, Narrative, and the Margins of the Modern Nation," in *Nation and Narration,* ed. Bhabha (London, 1990), pp. 1–7, 291–322. Bhabha is exemplary of the Third World intellectual who has been completely reworked by the language of First World cultural criticism.

7 See also Dipesh Chakrabarty, "Postcoloniality and the Artifice of History: Who Speaks for 'Indian' Pasts?" *Representations,* no. 37 (Winter 1992): 4.

8 As the term *subaltern* would indicate, Antonio Gramsci's inspiration is readily visible in the works of *Subaltern Studies* historians.

9 Indeed, Lyotard has defined *postmodern* as "incredulity toward metanarratives" (Jean-François Lyotard, *The Postmodern Condition: A Report on Knowledge,* trans. Geoff Bennington and Brian Massumi [Minneapolis, 1984], p. xxiv).

10 See *The Empire Writes Back: Theory and Practice in Post-Colonial Literatures,* ed. Bill Ashcroft, Gareth Griffiths, and Helen Tiffin (London, 1989), p. 2.

11 For discussions of similar problems in Chinese historiography, see Joseph R. Levenson, *Confucian China and Its Modern Fate: A Trilogy* (Berkeley, 1968); Rey Chow, *Woman and Chinese Modernity: The Politics of Reading between West and East* (Minneapolis, 1991); Arif Dirlik, *Revolution and History: The Origins of Marxist Historiography in China, 1919–1937* (Berkeley, 1978); and Dirlik, "Marxism and Chinese History: The Globalization of Marxist Historical Discourse and the Problem of Hegemony in Marxism," *Journal of Third World Studies* 4 (Spring 1987): 151–64.

12 This is at any rate a question that needs to be clarified. It seems to me that Prakash's denial of foundational status to class goes beyond what is but a *historicization* of class in the work of *Subaltern Studies* historians similiar to that found in, say, E. P. Thompson's *The Making of the English Working Class* (London, 1963). For a note on the question of class, see Chakrabarty, "Invitation to a Dialogue,' *Subaltern Studies: Writings on South Asian History and Society,* ed. Ranajit Guha, 5 vols. (Oxford, 1982–87), 4:364–76. The procedure of generalization may also play a part in the deradicalization of *Subaltern Studies* ideas by removing them from their specific historiographical context where they *do* play an innovative, radical role. For instance, the qualification of the role of colonialism in Indian history is intended by these historians to bring to the fore the mystifications of the past in nationalist histories and hence is a radical act. Made into a general principle of postcolonialism, this qualification downplays the role of colonialism in history. For an acknowledgment of doubt concerning the success of *Subaltern Studies* historiography, see Chakrabarty, "Postcoloniality and the Artifice of History."

13 Note not just the ideas but the tone in the following statement by Ahmad: "But one could start with a radically different premise, namely the proposition that we live not in three worlds but in one; that this world includes the experience of colonialism and imperialism on both sides of Jameson's global divide . . . ; that societies in formations of backward capitalism are as much constituted by the division of classes as are societies in the advanced capitalist countries; that socialism is not restricted to something called the second world but is simply the name of a resistance that saturates the globe today, as capitalism itself does; that the different parts of the capitalist system are to be known not in terms of binary opposition but as a contradictory unity, with differences, yes, but also with profound overlaps" [Ahmed, "Jameson's Rhetoric of Otherness and the 'National Allegory,'" p. 9].

14 See Spivak, "Can the Subaltern Speak?" in *Marxism and the Interpretation of Culture,* ed. Cary Nelson and Lawrence Grossberg (Urbana, Ill., 1988), pp. 271–313, and Lata Mani, "Multiple Mediations: Feminist Scholarship in the Age of Multinational Reception," in *Travelling Theories: Travelling Theorists,* ed. James Clifford and Vivek Dhareshwar (Santa Cruz, Calif., 1989), pp. 1–23.

15 See Kwame Anthony Appiah, "Is the Post- in Postmodernism the Post- in Postcolonial?" *Critical Inquiry* 17 (Winter 1991): 353.

16 Achille Mbembe, "Prosaics of Servitude and Authoritarian Civilities," trans. Janet Roitman, *Public Culture* 5 (Fall 1992): 137.

17 See Edward W. Said, foreword, in *Selected Subaltern Studies,* pp. v–x.

18 For a sampling of essays, see *Confucianism and Modernization: A Symposium,* ed. Joseph P. L. Jiang (Taipei, 1987). Scholars such as Tu Wei-ming and Yu Ying-shih have played a major part in efforts to revive Confucianism, while the quasi-fascist regime of Singapore (especially under Lee Kuan Yew) also has been a major promoter of the idea.

19 For a discussion of this problem in detail, see Dirlik, "Mao Zedong and 'Chinese Marxism,'" *Encyclopedia of Asian Philosophy* (forthcoming).

20 Althusser recognized this problem with specific reference to Mao Zedong Thought. See Louis Althusser, "Contradiction and Overdetermination," *For Marx,* trans. Ben Brewster (New York, 1970), pp. 87–128. For the molding of ideology, see his "Ideology and Ideological State Apparatuses," *Lenin and Philosophy and Other Essays,* trans. Brewster (New York, 1971). pp. 127–86. Mani gives a good (personal) account of the contextual formation of ideology in Mani, "Multiple Mediations." The risk in contextual ideological formation, of course, is that a problem may be transformed into a celebration—or game playing. This is evident in Spivak's "playfulness" throughout *The Post-Colonial Critic* as well as in, say, James Clifford's approach to the question of ethnography and culture. For a brief example of the latter see, among his many works, Clifford, "Notes on Theory and Travel," *Travelling Theory, Travelling Theorists,* pp. 177–88. My objection here is not to the importance of immediate context in the formation of ideology (and the variability and transposability of roles that it implies) but to the way such emphasis on the local mystifies the larger contexts that differentiate power relations and that suggest more stable and directed positions. No matter how much the ethnographer may strive to change places with the native, in the end the ethnographer returns to the First World academy and the native back to the wilds. This is the problem with postcoloniality and is evident in the tendency of so much postcolonial criticism to start off with a sociology of power relationships only to take refuge in aesthetic phraseology.

21 Appiah, "Is the Post- in Postmodernism the Post- in Postcolonial?" p. 3.

22 See the example Shohat gives of her experiences at CUNY ("NP," p. 99).

23 Anne McClintock, "The Angel of Progress: Pitfalls of the Term 'Post-Colonialism,'" *Social Text,* no. 31/32 (1992): 86.

24 Rosalind O'Hanlon and David Washbrook, "After Orientalism: Culture, Criticism, and Politics in the Third World," *Comparative Studies in Society and History 34* (Jan. 1992): 166; hereafter abbreviated "AO."

25 See Carl E. Pletsch, "The Three Worlds, or the Division of Social Scientific Labor, circa 1950–1975," *Comparative Studies in Society and History* 23 (Oct. 1981): 565–90.

26 See Fernando Coronil, "Can Postcoloniality Be Decolonized? Imperial Banality and Postcolonial Power," *Public Culture* 5 (Fall 1992): 99–100.

27 See David Harvey, *The Condition of Postmodernity: An Enquiry into the Origins of Cultural Change* (Oxford, 1989), and Fredric Jameson, "Postmodernism, or the Cultural Logic of Late Capitalism," *New Left Review* 146 (July/Aug. 1984): 53–92.

28 Folker Fröbel, Jürgen Heinrichs, and Otto Kreye, *The New International Division of Labour: Structural Unemployment in Industrialised Countries and Industrialisation in Developing Countries,* trans. Pete Burgess (Cambridge, 1980). "Disorganized capitalism" comes from Claus Offe, *Disorganized Capitalism: Contemporary Transformations of Work and Politics,* ed. John Keane (Cambridge, Mass., 1985), while global capitalism is the term used by Robert J. S. Ross and Kent C. Trachte, *Global Capitalism: The New Leviathan* (Albany, N.Y., 1990). Other noteworthy books on the subject are Leslie Sklair, *Sociology of the Global System* (Baltimore, 1991), which spells out the implications of global capitalism for the Third World, and, especially in light of what I say below of the new presidency of the United States. Robert B. Reich, *The Work of Nations: Preparing Ourselves for Twenty-First Century Capitalism* (New York, 1991). Reich's book incorporates his contributions to the *Harvard Business Review* that have such suggestive titles (in the present context) as "Who is US?" and "Who is Them?" For "subcontracting," see Gary Gereffi, "Global Sourcing and Regional Divisions of Labor in the Pacific Rim," *What Is in a Rim? Critical Perspectives on the Pacific Region Idea* (forthcoming).

29 See Riccardo Petrella, "World City-States of the Future," *New Perspectives Quarterly* 24 (Fall 1991): 59–64. See also William E. Schmidt, "A New Hanseatic League? In a Post–Cold War Era, Scandinavia Rethinks Itself," *New York Times,* 23 Feb. 1992, p. E3.

30 See Kenichi Ohmae, "Beyond Friction to Fact: The Borderless Economy," *New Perspectives Quarterly* 23 (Spring 1990): 21. See also Masao Miyoshi, "A Borderless World? From Colonialism to Transnationalism and the Decline of the Nation-State," *Critical Inquiry* 19 (Summer 1993): 726–51.

31 This phenomenon is addressed in most of the works cited above in footnote 28.

32 See Ohmae, "Beyond Friction to Fact." See also James Gardner, "Global Regionalism," *New Perspectives Quarterly* 25 (Winter 1992): 58–59.

33 William Taylor, "The Logic of Global Business: An Interview with ABB's Percy Barnevik," *Harvard Business Review* 69 (Mar.–Apr. 1991): 91.

34 See Mbembe, "The Banality of Power and the Aesthetics of Vulgarity in the Postcolony," trans. Roitman, *Public Culture* 4 (Spring 1992): 1–30; previously published as "Provisional Notes on the Postcolony," *Africa* 62, no. 1 (1992): 3–37. See also the discussion provoked by this essay in *Public Culture* 5 (Fall 1992): 47–145.

35 See Jameson, "Cognitive Mapping," in *Marxism and the Interpretation of Culture,* pp. 347–57. Jameson has been a forceful advocate of the necessity of retaining a sense of totality and structure in a socialist politics. His own totalization of the global structure has come under severe criticism. See Ahmad, "Jameson's Rhetoric of Otherness." I should stress here that it is not necessary to agree with his particular mode of totalization to recognize the validity of his argument.

36 Appiah, "Is the Post- in Postmodernism the Post- in Postcolonial?" p. 348.

REY CHOW

Against the Lures of Diaspora

Minority Discourse, Chinese Women, and Intellectual Hegemony

Modern Chinese Literature as "Minority Discourse"

The questions I would like to address in this chapter can be stated very simply: Why is it so difficult to bring up the topic of women in the field of Chinese studies? What can the critical spotlight received by "Chinese women" tell us about the discursive politics in play? These questions are not only questions about women and Chinese studies. They have to do with the problematic of the postcolonial discursive space in which many "third world" intellectuals who choose to live in the "first world" function. Within that space, these intellectuals are not only "natives" but spokespersons for "natives" in the "third world." Currently, the prosperity of that space is closely tied up with the vast changes taking place in Western academic institutions, notably in North America, where many intellectuals "of color" are serving as providers of knowledge about their nations and cultures. The way these intellectuals function is therefore inseparable from their status as cultural workers/brokers in diaspora, which may be a result of graduate studies, research, visiting or permanent appointments, immigration, and, in some cases, exile or political asylum. In this chapter I want to use the increasing interest in "women" in the field of Chinese studies as a way to focus the problems of the "third world" intellectual in diaspora. The implications of these problems go far beyond narrow institutional designators such as "women's studies" and "area studies" in which the study of "third world women" is most commonly lodged.

Superficial developments in the humanities across the U.S. indicate the opposite of the first of my opening questions. Following the legitimation of feminist interests in the West, receptivity to women's issues in other parts of the world seems unprecedentedly great at present. In the Asian field, it is not difficult to find research projects, dissertations, books, and conferences devoted to women. For the first time in Asian history, perhaps, we can identify a visible group of scholars, largely women, whose work centers on women. And yet the spotlight on "women" in our field seems also to make the shape and sound of the enemy more pronounced than ever.

I use "enemy" to refer not to an individual but to the attitude that "women" is still not a legitimate scholarly concern. Depending on the occasion, this enemy uses a number of different but related tactics. The first tactic may be described as habitual myopia: "You don't exist because I don't see you." The second is conscience-clearing genitalism:[1] "Women? Well, of course! . . . But I am not a woman myself, so I will keep my mouth shut." The third is scholarly dismissal: "Yes, women's issues are interesting, but they are separate and the feminist approach is too narrow to merit serious study." The fourth is strategic ghettoization: since "women" are all talking about the same thing over and over again, give them a place in every conference all in one corner, let them have their say, and let's get on with our business. These tactics of the enemy—and it is important for us to think of the enemy in terms of a dominant symbolic rather than in terms of individuals, that is, a corpus of attitudes, expressions, discourses, and the *value* espoused in them—are not limited to the China field. They are descriptive of the problems characteristic of the study of non-hegemonic subjects in general.

Leaving aside the issue of women for the time being, I would like to argue that the notion of modern Chinese literature as we know it today depends, implicitly, on the notion of a "minority discourse" in the postcolonial era. As two critics define it, "minority discourse is, in the first instance, the product of damage, of damage more or less systematically inflicted on cultures produced as minorities by the dominant culture."[2] Modern Chinese literature is, in this respect, not different from other postcolonial national literatures; its problems are symptomatic of the histories of non-Western cultures' struggles for cultural as well as national autonomy in the aftermath of Western imperialism. Because postcolonial literatures are linked to the hegemonic discourse of the West as such, they are, in spite of the typical nativist argument for their continuity with the indigenous traditions,[3] always effectively viewed as a kind of minority discourse whose existence has been victimized and whose articulation has been suppressed.

While the "world" significance of modern Chinese literature derives from its status as minority discourse, it is precisely this minority status that makes it so difficult for modern Chinese literature to be legitimized as "world" literature, while other *national* literatures, notably English, French, and Russian, have had much wider claims to an international modernity in spite of their historical and geographical specificity. In spite—and because—of the current clamor for "minority discourses," there is no lack of voices supporting the opposite viewpoint. The debates in the U.S. on the issue of canonicity, for instance, are driven by the urge to perpetuate what has been established as the "universals" of "cultural literacy." In fact, the more fre-quently "minor" voices are heard, the greater is the need expressed by the likes of Allan Bloom and E. D. Hirsch, Jr. for maintaining a canon, so that a Western notion of humanity can remain as the norm.[4] We understand from the Gulf War that it is by resorting to the rhetoric of preserving universals—love, knowledge, justice, tradi-tion, civilization, and so forth, argued both in George Bush's "new world order" and Saddam Hussein's pan-Arabism—that political power sustains its ideological hold on the populace. The rhetoric of universals, in other words, is what ensures the ghetto-ized existence of the other, be it in the form of a different culture, religion, race, or sex. As all of us know, the battle against the ideology embedded in the rhetoric of universals is also one faced by those working on "women" in the China field.

The proposal I want to make, however, is that, for the investigators of "Chinese women," this battle *cannot* simply be fought by a recourse to "minority discourse," or to Chinese women as the suppressed and victimized other. I will explain by dis-cussing the precarious relation between "minority discourse" and "women" in the China field, with special emphasis on the difficult and challenging role of Chinese women intellectuals today.

Consider one of the primary tasks faced by Chinese intellectuals in the twentieth century—that of establishing, in the throes of imperialism, a national literature. If the desire to establish a national literature is a desire for a kind of universal jus-tice—a justice in the eyes of which Chinese literature and culture would become legitimate internationally rather than simply "Chinese"—how is this desire pursued? While there are many efforts to demonstrate modern Chinese literature's continuity with past literary achievements, what distinguishes modern Chinese writings is an investment in suffering, an investment that aims at exposing social injustice. This investment in—or cathexis to—suffering runs through Chinese cultural production from the beginning of the twentieth century to the present—from the upsurge of interest in romantic love in popular Mandarin Duck and Butterfly stories of the 1910s, to the pro-science and pro-democracy attempts at national self-strengthen-ing in May Fourth writings, to the focuses on class struggle in the literature of the 1930s and 1940s, to the official Communist practice of "speaking bitterness" *(suku),* by which peasants were encouraged by cadres of the liberation forces to voice their sufferings at mass meetings in the 1950s and 1960s, and to the outcries of pain and betrayal in the "literature of the wounded" *(shanghen wenxue)* of the post-Cultural Revolution period. In other words, the attempt to establish a *national* literature in the postcolonial era requires a critical edge other than the belief in a magnificent past. For twentieth-century Chinese intellectuals, this critical edge has been *class consciousness.* In orthodox Marxist terms, "class" is that contradiction between the surplus of capital on the one hand and labor on the other. The surplus of capital leads to a situation in which those who do the least work enjoy the most privilege, while those who work continue to have the products of their labor taken or "alienated" from them. The category of "class" thus supplies a means of analyzing social injustice in economic terms, as the unequal distribution of wealth between the rich and the poor.[5] In the Chinese context, in which intellectual work was formerly part of the hegemony of the state, "class consciousness" is inseparable from *cultural* revolution, a revolution that seeks to overthrow not only the economic but specifically the ideological dominance of the ruling classes. Thus even in the crudest usage by the Chinese Communists, "alienated labor" carries ideological as well as economic implications.

The historian Arif Dirlik refers to the use of class for nation-building as the practice of the "proletarian nation." Commenting on a passage from *The Crisis of the Arab Intellectual* by Abdallah Laroui (who derived much of his historicism from Joseph Levenson's work on China), Dirlik writes:

> [The new China is] the "proletarian" nation of revolutionary intellectuals (Li Dazhao, Sun Yat-sen, Mao Zedong come to mind immediately). If it does not bring the proletariat (or the oppressed classes) into the forefront of history, it at least makes them into a central component of the national struggle—as a referent against which the fate of ideas and values must be judged.[6]

We cannot understand modern Chinese literature without understanding the ways in which nationhood and class are intertwined in literary discourse. The use of "class consciousness" as a way to build a national culture is one of the most important signs of Chinese literature's modernity, a modernity that is, as May Fourth and subsequent writings show, self-consciously revolutionary. If modern Chinese literature emerges as an "other," a "minor" literature in the global scene, it also emerges by putting the spotlight on its oppressed classes, among which women occupy one but not the only place.

In its investment in suffering, in social oppression, and in the victimization and silencing of the unprivileged, modern Chinese literature partakes of the many issues of "minority discourse" that surface with urgency in the field of cultural studies/cultural criticism in North America today. Central to such issues is the question "can the subaltern speak?" as we find it in Gayatri Spivak's essay of the same title.[7] In this regard, the history of modern Chinese literature can be seen as a paradigm for contemporary cultural studies, simply because the most "written" figure in this history is none other than the subaltern, whose "speech" has been coming to us through fiction, poetry, political debates, historical writings, journalistic representations, as well as radio plays, films, operas, and regional cultural practices. In a fashion paralleling the theorizations of "minority discourse" that emphasize the production of postcolonial subjects whose speeches and/or writings disrupt the hegemonic discourse of the imperialist, modern Chinese literature specializes, one might argue, in producing figures of minority whose overall effect has been an ongoing protest against the cultural violence they experience at physical, familial, institutional, and national levels. At the same time, the conscious representation of the "minor" as such also leads to a situation in which it is locked in opposition to the "hegemonic" in a permanent bind. The "minor" cannot rid itself of its "minority" status because it is that status that gives it its only legitimacy;[8] support for the "minor," however sincere, always becomes support for the center. In Communist China, one could go as far as saying that "class consciousness," as it becomes an ideological weapon of the state, offers a "critical edge" only insofar as it permanently regenerates the reality of social injustice rather than its dissolution.

How is this so? Let me explain by relating "class consciousness" to the conceptualization of social change *through language*. Among Marxist critics working in the West, the advocacy of "class consciousness" is often closely related to a specific theory of language. For instance, speaking of the "subaltern," Gayatri Spivak says:

> The subaltern is all that is not elite, but the trouble with those kinds of names is that if you have any kind of political interest you name it in the hope that the name will disappear. That's what class consciousness is in the interest of the class disappearing. What politically we want to see is that the name would not be possible.[9]

The theory of language offered here is that the act of articulating something moves and changes it, and therefore may cause it to disappear. In China, however, the relation between language and reality has been very differently conceived because of the lingering force of Confucius's concept of *zhengming*—the rectification of names. The Confucian attitude toward language is expressed in a well-known passage in *Lunyü (The Analects):*

> If names be not correct, language is not in accordance with the truth of things. If language be not in accordance with the truth of things, affairs cannot be carried on to success. . . .
>
> Therefore a superior man considers it necessary that the names he uses may be spoken *appropriately,* and also that what he speaks may be carried out *appropriately.* What the superior man requires is just that in his words there may be nothing incorrect.[10]

For Confucius as for the majority of Chinese people, naming is the opposite of what Spivak suggests. Instead of causing the reality to disappear, naming is the way to make a certain reality "proper," that is, to make it real. That is why it is so important to have the right name and the right language.

To use the words of Slavoj Žižek, we may say that Confucius understood "the radical contingency of naming, the fact that naming itself retroactively constitutes its reference." It is "the name itself, the signifier, which supports the identity of the object."[11] "In other words," Žižek writes, "the only possible definition of an object in its identity is that this is the object which is always designated by the same signifier —tied to the same signifier. It is the signifier which constitutes the kernel of the object's 'identity.'"[12] Strictly speaking, there is nothing false or misleading about Confucius's theory of language. As a process, *zhengming* demonstrates the practical politics involved in any claim to visibility and existence—namely, that such a claim must be at the same time a claim to/in language. Hence, even though—in fact, precisely because—it is *no more than a claim*, language is the absolutely essential means of access to power. In their struggles to be seen and heard, minority groups all prove the truth of Confucius's theory: Before "dismantling" and "decentering" power in the way taught by deconstructionists, they argue, they must first "have" power and be named, that is, recognized, so.

The act of naming, then, is not intrinsically essentialist or hierarchical. It is the social relationships in which names are inserted that may lead to essentialist, hierarchical, and thus detrimental consequences.[13] Historically, the problem with Confucius's teaching was that it was used to address civil servants in their service to the state. A very astute understanding of language was thus instrumentalized in organizing political hierarchy and consolidating centralized state power, with all the reactionary implications that followed. *Zhengming* became a weapon that ensured the immovability of an already established political hegemony and in that sense a paradigmatic case, in Derrida's terms, of *logocentric* governance.

By extension, we understand why, in their mobilization of "class consciousness," the Chinese Communists have actually been following the Confucian model of language as it is inherited in Chinese politics in spite of their overt "ideological" contempt for the Master. The raising of "class consciousness" as official "reeducational" policy during the two decades following 1949 did not so much lead to the disappearance of class as it did to a reification/rectification of the name "class" as the absolute reality to which every citizen had to submit in order to clear their "conscience." Hence, in pursuit of the ideal of the "proletarian nation," strengthening national culture became equal to hounding down the class enemy, even though "class enemy" was *simply a name*. In a discussion of the contemporary Chinese political situation by way of Jacques Lacan's notion of *jouissance*, Kwai-cheung Lo writes:

> The "class enemy" in the Chinese Cultural Revolution is, in a sense, a fetish structuring the jouissance. The whole country is summoned to ferret out the class enemy, to uncover the hidden counterrevolutionaries. The class enemy is everywhere, in every nook and corner of our social life, but it is also nowhere, invisible and arcane. It is clear that the class enemy is jouissance, which is an impossibility but can produce traumatic effects. It is also the *objet petit a*, a pure void which keeps symbolic order working and sets the Cultural Revolution in motion. The paradoxical charac-

ter of the class enemy is that it always returns to the same place, exerts effects on the reality of the subject, and it is itself a nothing, a negativity. Thus, in the end, when we have looked in every corner to ferret out the class enemy, we then have to uncover the enemy in our heart. The Cultural Revolution turns out to be a Stalinist trial. Everyone must examine their whole life, their entire past, down to the smallest detail, to search for the hidden fault and, finally, confess themselves as sinners. . . .

When the people are asked to confess, to "open their hearts to" [*jiaoxin*] the party, and they look deep into their hearts, what they find is not a subject who is unable to express the signified, but a void, a lack which has to be filled out by the object, the sin, the incarnation of impossible enjoyment, jouissance. . . .[14]

In their obsession with the name "class enemy," the "rectification" of which led to the madness of the Cultural Revolution, the Chinese Communists thus proved themselves to be loyal disciples of Confucius's teaching about state control.

Perhaps the greatest and most useful lesson modern Chinese culture has to offer the world is the pitfall of building a nation—"the People's Republic of China"—on a theory of social change—"class consciousness"—in the illusion that the hope offered by that theory—the disappearance of class itself—can actually materialize in human society. Chinese communism was the dream of materializing that theory by officializing a concept of language and literature in which the minorities, the oppressed, and the exploited are to be vindicated. But when the force of "class consciousness" is elevated to official ideology rather than kept strictly as an analytical instrument (as it was in the texts of Marx), it also becomes mechanical and indistinguishable from other ideological strongholds of governmental power.[15] To date, the mainland government is still trying to keep this rhetoric of "class consciousness" alive after its latest abuse of the peaceful seekers of democratic reforms. When a government that was originally founded on the ideal of social justice dwindles to the level of open injustice and continual deception of its people, as the Chinese government does today, we must seek strategies that are alternative to a continual investment in minority, in suffering, and in victimization.

Masculinist Positions in the China Field: Women to the West, Fathers to Chinese Women

The clarified relation between "nation" and "class" in twentieth-century China allows one to ask: How do women intervene? How can we articulate women's *difference* without having that difference turned into a cultural ghettoization of women while the enemy remains intact? How can women "speak"?

Current trends in contemporary cultural studies, while being always supportive of categories of difference, also tend to reinscribe those categories in the form of fixed identities. As in *zhengming*, categories such as "race," "class," and "gender" were originally named in order to point out what has been left out of mainstream categorizations and thus what still remains to be named, seen, and heard. "Names" of "difference" as such are meant as ways for the marginalized to have some access to the center. And yet, one feels that these categories of difference are often used in such a way as to stabilize, rather than challenge, a preestablished method of examining "cultural diversity," whereby "difference" becomes a sheer matter of adding new names in an ever-expanding pluralistic horizon. If categories such as "race," "class," and "gender" are to remain useful means of critical intervention, they must not be lined up with one another in a predictable refrain and attached to all investigations alike as packaging. Instead, as terms of intervention, they must be used to analyze, decode, and criticize one another, so that, for instance, "gender" is not only "gender" but what has been muted in orthodox discussions of class, while "class" is often what notions such as "woman" or even "sexual difference" tend to downplay in order to forge a gendered politics. How do we conceive of gender within class and distinguish class within gender? How is it that scholars, including Asianists, seem more ready to accept "gender" when it is spoken of *generally* across the disciplines, while to bring it up in the interpretation of specific texts within a particular field such as Chinese studies, one still runs the risk of being considered unscholarly and non-objective?

A valid point made by Dirlik is that in order to destroy culturalist hegemony, it is not enough to concentrate on unequal relations between nations (such as those between the "first" and the "third" worlds). What is of similar importance is an investigation of the unequal relations *within* societies. In the context of China, the narrative of "class" as a way to address the unequal relations within society has proved itself inadequate because of its official abuse, an abuse which takes the form of an armed appropriation—a turning into property and propriety—of a particular language, the language of the oppressed or what we have been calling "minority discourse." That is to say, if the past forty years of Chinese political history has been a failed revolution, it is in part because the revolution has been a secret cohabitation between Confucius and the Communists, between *zhengming* and a theory of language in which "naming" is, ideally, the first step to changing social reality. In this cohabitation, Confucius, saturated with practices of bureaucratic hierarchy, remains on top.

After June 4, 1989, it is unlikely that the Chinese intellectuals who have begun careers in the West will "return" to China. In their diaspora, Chinese intellectuals will emerge as a group whose distinction from the "objects" they use for their research will be more and more pronounced. Geographic, linguistic, and political differences are going to turn internationalized Chinese women intellectuals, for instance, into a privileged class vis-à-vis the women in China. As we continue to use Chinese women's writings and lives as the "raw material" for our research in the West, the relationship between us as intellectuals overseas and them "at home" will increasingly take on the coloration of a kind of "master discourse/native informant" relationship. The inequality of this relationship should now be emphasized as that inequality *within* a social group that Dirlik mentions. While intellectuals are rewarded for their work in the West, voices of the oppressed continue to be unheard and intellectual work continues to be persecuted in China. There is very little we can do overseas to change the political situation "back there." The attention bestowed upon Chinese events by the world media is arbitrary. In early 1991, for instance, as global attention was directed toward the Gulf War, the Chinese government's trial and sentencing of the June 4 protesters went largely unnoticed. Whether we like it or not, our position with regard to China is one of waiting and hoping.

As "minority discourse" becomes a hot topic in cultural studies in the West, some overseas Chinese intellectuals are now choosing to speak and write from a "minor" position. While enjoying the privilege of living in the West, they cling, in their discourse, to the status of the neglected "other." While this espousal of minority status may not be stated as such, it is most often detected in discourses which moralistically criticize "the West" in the name of "real" "Chinese" difference or otherness. Depending on the political interest of the person, "Chinese difference" (by which is usually meant Chinese identity) may take the form of a reactionary confirmation of traditional, humanistic attitudes toward "culture" and "knowledge," or it may assume a liberalist guise by reading Chinese culture in terms of the Bakhtinian "dialogic" and "carnivalesque." In some cases, while being fashionably skeptical of "Western theory," these intellectuals nonetheless revere Fredric Jameson's ethnocentric notion that all "third world" texts are necessarily to be read as "national allegories"[16] and proceed to read Chinese culture accordingly. However, to "nationalize" "third world" cultural productions "allegorically" this way is also to "other" them uniformly with a logic of production that originates in the West. What is being forgotten here is how "first world" production comprises not only the production of tangible goods but also intangible value. The latter, as I will argue in the following pages, is exported as ideological exploitation, which plays a far more crucial role in structuring the lives of peoples in the non-West. Without a discussion of "value" as such, the notion that all "third world" peoples are necessarily engaged in national struggles and that all "third world" texts are "national allegories" is quite preposterous.[17] In Jameson's model, "third world" intellectuals are, regardless of their class and gender, made to speak uniformly as minors and women to the West. Following Jameson, many contemporary Chinese intellectuals' desire to play the role of the other confirms what Nancy Armstrong, writing about the historicization of sexuality in the British novel, says: "the modern individual was first and foremost a woman."[18]

Vis-à-vis the "insiders" of the China field, on the other hand, these intellectuals' strategy is decidedly different. There, faced with new types of research and new interests such as women's issues, their attitude becomes, once again, patriarchal and mainstream; women's issues do not interest them the way *their own minority* in relation to "the West" does. Faced with women, their attitude resembles that of right-wingers in the American academy. They defend tradition, sinocentrism, and heritage, and denounce feminist scholarship as unscholarly. It is as if, dealing with the "insiders," they no longer remember the political significance of the "minority discourse" which they speak only when it is opportune for them to do so. They are minors and women when faced with "foreigners"; they are fathers when faced with "insiders," especially women.

To return, then, to the question of why it is so difficult to bring up the topic of women in the field of Chinese studies. It is difficult not because women's issues are insignificant—there has been interest in "woman" and "the new woman" in Chinese writings since before the 1910s. Quite to the contrary, it is because "woman," like the "minor," offers such an indispensable position in *discourse,* traditional and modern, that feminists have difficulty claiming "her." One question that traditionalists in the field often ask feminists is: "But there is no lack of femininity in classical Chinese literature! Why are you saying that the feminine has been suppressed?" A look at Chinese literary history would suggest that these traditionalists are, literally, right: *Chinese literary history has been a history of men who want to become women.* In the past, male authors adopted women's voices and wrote in "feminine" styles; in the modern period, male authors are fascinated by women as a new kind of literary as well as social "content." We may therefore argue that it is in the sense of men preempting women's place as the minor (vis-à-vis both tradition and the West) and claiming that place for themselves that "the Chinese woman," to use Mao Zedong's words to André Malraux, "doesn't yet exist."[19] Chinese women are, in terms of the structure of discourse, a kind of minor of the minor, the other to the woman that is Chinese man.

Throughout the twentieth century, it is the continual creation of alternative *official minor positions* that continually puts off a direct attack on the subjugation of women. To defend the "Chinese culture," pairs of oppositions are always set up: tradition and modernity, China and the West, China and Japan, the Communists and the Nationalists, the feudal landlords and the people, the rich and the poor, and so forth. The place of a minor discourse—as that which must struggle to speak—is therefore always already filled as long as there is always a new political target to fight against. The common view that women's issues always seem to be subsumed under the "larger" historical issues of the nation, the people, and so forth is therefore true but also a reversal of what happens in the process of discourse construction. For in order for us to construct a "large" historical issue, a position of the victim/minor must always already be present. In terms of language, this means that for a (new) signifier to emerge as a positive presence, there must always be a lack/negative supporting it. The producer of the new signifier, however, always occupies (or "identifies with") the space of the lack/negative (since it is empty) in order to articulate. This goes to show why, for instance, among all the "Chinese people," it is the peasants, the ones who are most illiterate, most removed from the intellectuals, and therefore most "lacking" in terms of the dominant symbolic, who most compel progressive Chinese intellectuals' fantasy.[20] Chinese women, on the other hand, are always said to be as powerful as Chinese men: We keep hearing that they "hold up half the sky." If minority discourse is, like all discourse, not simply a fight for the content of oppression it is ostensibly about but also a fight for the ownership—the propriety, the property—of speaking (that is, for *zhengming*), then Chinese women are precluded from that ownership because it has always been assumed by others in the name of the people, the oppressed classes, and the nation.

Precisely because the truly minor is the voiceless, it can be seized upon and spoken for. As Spivak says, "if the subaltern can speak . . . the subaltern is not a subaltern any more."[21] The Chinese Communist government serves a good example of an agency speaking for "minorities" in order to mobilize an entire nation. As such, its governance is in accordance with a notion of marginality "which implicitly valorizes the center."[22] For intellectuals working on "women" in the China field, therefore, the first critical task is to break alliance with this kind of official sponsorship of "minority discourse." Instead, they need to use their work on Chinese women to deconstruct the paternalistic social consequences resulting from a hegemonic practice of *zhengming* itself.

The Dissolute Woman and the Female Saint

In a recent interview with the press in Hong Kong, the Taiwanese feminist Xü Xiaodan, well known for her use of nudity in political campaigns, described her ambition in the following way: "I will enter Congress in the image of a dissolute woman; I will love the people with the soul of a female saint."[23] What is remarkable about Xü Xiaodan's statements is the introduction of a feminist practice that refuses conformity with the Chinese "elite." The meaning of the term "elite" varies from society to society,[24] and I use it here to designate those among the Chinese who have had the privilege of being highly educated and whose views of female sexuality remain in accordance with the Confucian and neo-Confucian notions of female chastity. The point, however, is not for Chinese intellectuals to exclude/excuse themselves from the "elite" but rather to break up the traditional alliance between education and Confucian standards of female sexuality.

While being well educated herself, Xü Xiaodan challenges the traditional morality that demands Chinese women to be chaste, self-sacrificing, and thus virtuous. Her politics is different from the sentimental sponsorship of "the oppressed" that we often encounter in "minority discourse." For if traditional morality organizes female sexuality by upholding the female saint and condemning the dissolute woman, Xü Xiaodan does not simply criticize that morality by speaking up as the "minor"—the dissolute woman—only. Instead she shows that it is by straddling the positive and the negative, the clear distinction between which is absolutely essential for traditional morality's functioning, that she speaks and acts as a feminist. Instead of speaking from the position of "minority," then, she offers a model which by its very impure nature defies the epistemic violence underlying the perpetual dependence of the "minor" on the center. Women's sexuality, hitherto strictly organized according to the difference between the female saint and the dissolute woman, returns to a freedom which is not an arbitrary freedom to act as one wishes but rather a freedom *from* the mutual reinforcement between education and morality, which are welded together by stratifying female sexuality.

Where the notion of "class" allows us the negative capacity to criticize "privilege" but never identify with it, the notion of gender can operate both from and against privilege, allowing us the possibility of both identification and opposition. This means that we can, as we must, attack social injustice without losing sight of the fact that even as "women" speaking for other "women" within the same gender, for instance, we speak from a privileged position. While an orthodox "class consciousness" would have us repress the self-reflexive knowledge of the speaking intellectual's social position as such (since to reflect on one's own privileged voice would be to destroy the illusion that one is speaking purely for universal justice), gender, insofar as it shows the organization of female sexuality in ways that are related but not restricted to class, makes it easier (though not necessary) to reflect on the difference between the speaking subject and the spoken object. This is because that difference (between the privileged and unprivileged) has not been prescribed as the definitive object of attack as it is in "class consciousness." Paradoxically, therefore, it is because "class consciousness" has chosen "social injustice" as its target and its content that it cannot reflect on the form of its own possibly privileged, unjust utterances. Self-reflection of this kind leads only to paralysis, as we see in many examples of May Fourth literature.

Lu Xun's literary texts, I think, best illustrate this point. The question that his stories often imply is: How can intellectuals pretend to be speaking for the oppressed classes since, precisely, we have a voice while they don't? Don't speaking and writing already mark our social privilege and permanently separate us from them? If it is true that "our" speech takes its "raw materials" from the suffering of the oppressed, it is also true that it takes its capital from the scholarly tradition, from the machineries of literacy and education, which are affordable only to a privileged few.

On the other hand, because its target and content is the inequality between the sexes, an issue which is not limited to a narrow definition of class difference (in which having privilege equals "bad" and not having privilege equals "good"), "gender" has room for enabling reflection on the inequality inherent in the construction of discourse, i.e., the difference that separates those who speak and those who are spoken of/for. Precisely because its content is not necessarily economic (in the narrow sense described above), the discourse of gender can know its own economic privilege. Knowing its own form as such does not, unlike in the case of a practice of "class consciousness" that must remain blind to itself, annul its project.

In the field of China studies, gender and women's issues are likely to emerge as the predominant critical paradigm in the years to come. This will be so *not only* because of Chinese women's traditionally "minor" status. Rather, it will be because, even while they may choose, from time to time, to forsake the claims of their "femininity," *intellectual* Chinese women who speak of "Chinese women" will, I hope, not forget their own social position. While they do not lose sight of the oppression of women, these intellectuals should admit rather than repress the inequality inherent in discourse and the difference between them and their "objects." They should articulate women's issues both as "dissolute women" and as "female saints," but never as either one only. If the relative freedom in intellectual work that the Chinese living in the liberal West enjoy is a privilege, Chinese intellectuals must use this privilege as truthfully and as tactically as they can—not merely to speak as exotic minors, but to fight the crippling effects of Western imperialism and Chinese paternalism at once.

Postscript: The Lures of Diaspora

At the two conferences where the bulk of this chapter was presented,[25] there were questions as to whether what I am doing is not a kind of essentialist "identity politics" in which, once again, the "authenticity" of a particular group is privileged. These questions demand a detailed response.

If we describe the postcolonial space in Hegelian terms, we can say that it is a space in which the object (women, minorities, other peoples) encounters its Notion (criterion for testing object), or in which the "being-in-itself" encounters the "being-for-an-other." In this encounter, "consciousness" undergoes a transformation, so that it is no longer only consciousness of the object but also consciousness of itself, of its own knowledge. What consciousness previously took to be the object in-itself, Hegel writes, is not an *in-itself* but an *in-itself* (an object) for *consciousness*. Hence "consciousness" has, in truth, *two* objects—object and knowledge of object—which do not mutually correspond but which are related in a movement Hegel calls experience:

> Since consciousness thus finds that its knowledge does not correspond to its object, the object itself does not stand the test; in other words, the criterion for testing is altered when that for which it was to have been the criterion fails to pass the test; and the testing is not only a testing of what we know, but also a testing of the criterion of what knowing is.
>
> . . . *Inasmuch as the new true object issues from it,* this *dialectical* movement which consciousness exercises on itself and which affects both its knowledge and its object, is precisely what is called *experience* [*Erfahrung*].[26]

Supplementing Hegel, we may say that this *dialectics of experience* finds one of its most compelling personifications in the "third world" intellectual in diaspora. While their cultures once existed for Western historians and anthropologists as objects of inquiry within well-defined geographical domains, the growing presence of these intellectuals in "first world" intellectual circles fundamentally disrupts the production of knowledge—what Edward Said calls Orientalism—that has hitherto proceeded by hiding the agenda of the inquirers and naturalizing the "objects" as givens. To paraphrase Hegel, "first world" inquirers must now cope with the fact that their "objects" no longer correspond to their "consciousness." "Third world" intellectuals, on their part, acquire and affirm their own "consciousness" only to find, continually, that it is a "consciousness" laden with the history of their objecthood. This history confronts them all the more acutely once they live in the "first world," where they discover that, regardless of personal circumstances, they are beheld as "the other."

The explosive nature of this dialectics of experience deals the death blow to older forms of protest that were bound to native territorial and cultural propriety. *For "third world" intellectuals especially,* this means that the recourse to alterity—the other culture, nation, sex, or body in another historical time and geographical space—no longer suffices as a means of intervention simply because alterity as such is still the old pure "object" (the being-in-itself) that has not been dialectically grasped. Such recourse to alterity is repeatedly trapped within the lures of a "self"-image—a nativism—that is, precisely, imperialism's other.

In naming "Chinese women intellectuals," thus, my intention is not to establish them as a more authentic group of investigators whose claim to "women" in the Chinese field would exclude that of other investigators. Naming here is, first and foremost, a way to avoid repeating the well-worn discursive paradigm of Orientalism, in which the peoples of the non-West are taken factographically as "objects" without consciousness while the historical privileges of speaking subjects—in particular the privilege of "having" consciousness—remain unarticulated.

Second, naming is also a way of *not giving in* to the charms of an alterity in which so many of the West's "others" are now called upon to speak. Naming is not so much an act of consolidating power as it is an act of making explicit the historical predicament of investigating "China" and "Chinese women," especially as it pertains to those who are ethnically Chinese and/or sexually women.

Third, it follows that naming the investigators amid the current "multicultural" interest in "women" in non-Western fields is also a means of accentuating the otherwise *muted* fact of intellectual women's privilege as intellectuals and thus (particularly in the Chinese context) as members of the elite. While this privilege is, at this point, hardly acknowledged in the masculinist explorations of modernity, nationhood, and literature, because masculinist explorations are themselves preoccupied with their own minority and womanhood vis-à-vis the West, it is peremptory that women investigators, especially Chinese women investigators investigating the history of Chinese women's social subordination, handle the mode of their speech—which historically straddles the elite and the subaltern—with deliberate care. In naming them as such, therefore, my point is to place on them the burden of a kind of critical awareness that has yet to be articulated in their field. The weight of each of the terms under which they work—Chinese, women, intellectual—means that their alliances with other discursive groups, as well as their self-reflection on their own positions, must always be astute. Both practices, allying with others and reflecting on oneself, are by necessity more demanding than a blanket dismissal of names and identities as "essentialist."[27] Such a dismissal is often the result of an ahistorical espousal of "difference" and "femininity" as is found in some influential theories which, by equating the feminine with the negative and the unrepresentable, dismiss all processes of identification as positivistic. (A good case in point is the work of Julia Kristeva, which is popular with many feminist critics despite Kristeva's unwillingness to name "woman"[28] and to name herself "feminist.") The question on which to insist, however, is not "to name or not to name" but: What is to be gained or lost in naming what and whom, and by whom?

What I am arguing can also be stated in a different way: What are we doing talking about modern Chinese literature and Chinese women in the North American academy in the 1990s? As such activities of speaking and writing are tied less to the oppressed women in Chinese communities "back home" than to our own intellectual careers in the West, we need to unmask ourselves through a scrupulous declaration of self-interest. Such declaration does not clean our hands, but it prevents the continuance of a tendency, rather strong among "third world" intellectuals in diaspora as well as researchers of non-Western cultures in "first world" nations, to sentimentalize precisely those day-to-day realities from which they are distanced.

The diasporic postcolonial space is, as I already indicate, neither the space of the native intellectual protesting against the intrusive presence of foreign imperialists in the indigenous territory nor the space of the postcolonial critic working against the lasting effects of cultural domination in the home country (now an independent "nation") after the phase of territorial imperialism. In the case of China, it is necessary to remember that "Chinese" territory, with the exceptions of Taiwan from 1895 to 1945, Hong Kong from 1842 to 1997, and Macau (occupied by the Portuguese since the mid-sixteenth century) from 1887 to 1997, was never completely "colonized" over a long period by any one foreign power, even though the cultural effects of imperialism are as strong as in other formerly colonized countries in Asia, Africa, and Latin America. One could perhaps say that such cultural effects of foreign dominance are, in fact, *stronger:* they are most explicit, paradoxically, when one sees how the mainland Chinese can hold on to the illusion—born of modern Western imperialism but itself no less imperialistic—of a "native land," a *zuguo,* that was never entirely captured and that therefore remains glorious to this day.

The space of "third world" intellectuals in diaspora is a space that is removed from the "ground" of earlier struggles that were still tied to the "native land." Physical alienation, however, can mean precisely the intensification and aestheticization of the values of "minority" positions that had developed in the earlier struggles and that have now, in "third world" intellectuals' actual circumstances in the West, become defunct. The unself-reflexive sponsorship of "third world" culture, including "third world" women's culture, becomes a mask that conceals the hegemony of these intellectuals over those who are stuck at home.

For "third world" intellectuals, the lures of diaspora consist in this masked hegemony. As in the case of what I call masculinist positions in the China field, their resort to "minority discourse," including the discourse of class and gender struggles, veils their own fatherhood over the "ethnics" at home even while it continues to legitimize them as "ethnics" and "minorities" in the West. In their hands, minority discourse and class struggle, especially when they take the name of another nation, another culture, another sex, or another body, turn into signifiers whose major function is that of discursive exchange for the intellectuals' self-profit. Like "the people," "real people," "the populace," "the peasants," "the poor," "the homeless," and all such names, these signifiers *work* insofar as they gesture toward another place (the lack in discourse-construction) that is "authentic" but that cannot be admitted into the circuit of exchange.

What happens eventually is that this "third world" that is produced, circulated, and purchased by "third world" intellectuals in the cosmopolitan diasporic space will be exported "back home" in the form of values—intangible goods—in such a way as to obstruct the development of the native industry. To be sure, one can perhaps no longer even speak of a "native industry" as such in the multinational corporate

postmodernity, but it remains for these intellectuals to face up to their truthful relation to those "objects of study" behind which they can easily hide—as voyeurs, as
"fellow victims," and as self-appointed custodians.

Hence the necessity to read and write against the lures of diaspora: Any attempt
to deal with "women" or the "oppressed classes" in the "third world" that does not
at the same time come to terms with the historical conditions of its own articulation
is bound to repeat the exploitativeness that used to and still characterizes most
"exchanges" between "West" and "East." Such attempts will also be expediently
assimilated within the plenitude of the hegemonic establishment, with all the
rewards that that entails. No one can do without some such rewards. What one can
do without is the illusion that, through privileged speech, one is helping to save the
wretched of the earth.[29]

NOTES

1 "Genitalism," per Gayatri Spivak, is the attitude that "depending on what kind of genitals you
 have, you can or cannot speak in certain situations." "Questions of Multi-culturalism," *The
 Post-Colonial Critic: Interviews, Strategies, Dialogues,* ed. Sarah Harasym (London: Routledge, 1990), p. 62.

2 Abdul R. JanMohamed and David Lloyd, "Introduction: Minority Discourse—What Is to Be
 Done?" *Cultural Critique,* no. 7 (Fall 1987): 7.

3 Nativism is not necessarily an attitude held by "natives." Scholars who study a particular culture can espouse nativism as a way to fence off disciplinary territories, and this often happens
 in non-Western fields such as Asian studies. For an extended argument on this point, see the
 next chapter.

4 I have in mind Allan Bloom, *The Closing of the American Mind* (New York: Simon & Schuster,
 1987), and E. D. Hirsch, Jr., *Cultural Literacy* (Boston: Houghton Mifflin, 1987).

5 In his study of the history of Chinese communism, Arif Dirlik shows that, beginning in the earliest period of their acquaintance with the ideas of Marx, the Chinese Communists have tended
 to be most fascinated with what is arguably Marx's most problematic area—his economism.
 See Dirlik, *The Origins of Chinese Communism* (Oxford: Oxford University Press, 1989), especially chapters 2 through 6.

6 Arif Dirlik, "Culturalism as Hegemonic Ideology and Liberating Practice," *Cultural Critique,* no.
 6 (Spring 1987): 37.

7 Gayatri Spivak, "Can the Subaltern Speak?" in Cary Nelson and Lawrence Grossberg, eds.,
 Marxism and the Interpretation of Culture (Urbana: University of Illinois Press, 1988), pp.
 271–313.

8 For an argument of this predicament characterizing minority discourse, see Abdul R. Jan-
 Mohamed, *Manichean Aesthetics: The Politics of Literature in Colonial Africa* (Amherst: University of Massachusetts Press, 1983).

9 Gayatri Spivak, "The New Historicism: Political Commitment and the Postmodern Critic," *The
 Post-Colonial Critic,* p. 158.

10 *Confucian Analects,* Chapter III, 5, 7; *The Four Books: The Great Learning, The Doctrine of
 the Mean, Confucian Analects, and The Works of Mencius,* with English translation and notes
 by James Legge (Taipei: Culture Book Co., 1973), p. 298; emphases in the translation.

11 Slavoj Žižek, *The Sublime Object of Ideology* (London: Verso, 1989), p. 95.

12 Žižek, *Sublime Object*, p. 98.

13 As I am writing this in April 1991, a controversy over the ethics of naming rape victims has just broken out across the U.S. media. The immediate cause is the naming by several news institutions (the *Globe*, NBC, and the *New York Times*) of the female victim in an alleged case of rape by a member of the Kennedy family. The pros and cons of whether the victim should be named touch on individual rights to privacy, media consumer needs, the dissemination of news for financial profit, abuses suffered by rape victims at legal proceedings, and more, all of which have to do with social relationships rather than with the pure act of naming itself.

14 Kwai-cheung Lo, "The Real in Lacan: Some Reflections on 'Chinese Symptoms,'" *Polygraph*, no. 4 (1990–91): 86–87.

15 "With great trepidation I would say that Marxism in fact is a critical philosophy. Its transformation into a substantive philosophy, a utopian philosophy that can be adequately represented by revolution and social reform has been in fact a centrist mistake." Spivak, "The *Intervention* Interview," *The Post-Colonial Critic*, p. 131.

16 Fredric Jameson, "Third-World Literature in the Era of Multinational Capital," *Social Text*, no. 15 (Fall 1986): 69.

17 See Spivak's discussion of this point in "The New Historicism," pp. 161–62.

18 Nancy Armstrong, *Desire and Domestic Fiction: A Political History of the Novel* (Oxford: Oxford University Press, 1987), p. 8.

19 Quoted in Juliet Mitchell, *Psychoanalysis and Feminism* (New York: Vintage Books, 1975), p. 416.

20 Kwai-cheung Lo, "The Real in Lacan," p. 89.

21 Spivak, "The New Historicism," p. 158.

22 Spivak, "The New Historicism," p. 156.

23 *Xin Bao/Overseas Chinese Economic Journal* (the U.S. edition of the *Hong Kong Economic Journal*), January 1991.

24 Writing about colonial India, Ranajit Guha uses the term "elite" to describe the dominant social groups, made up of "mainly British officials of the colonial state and foreign industrialists, merchants, financiers, planters, landlords and missionaries," on the one hand, and of powerful indigenous elements at the "all-India" and the "regional and local" levels, on the other. See "On Some Aspects of the Historiography of Colonial India," *Subaltern Studies I: Writings on South Asian History and Society*, ed. Ranajit Guha (Delhi: Oxford University Press, 1986), p. 8. Spivak, while defining the "subaltern" as "all that is not elite" ("The New Historicism," p. 158), points also to the "gendered subaltern" as being paradigmatic of the subaltern subject ("Practical Politics of the Open End," *The Post-Colonial Critic*, p. 103). Because education traditionally plays such an important role in determining class difference in Chinese society, I think the relation between the "elite" and the "subaltern" in China needs to be formulated *primarily* in terms of the way education and gender work together.

25 The conference "Sexuality and Gender in Twentieth-Century Chinese Literature and Society" at the University of Iowa, March 1991, and the panel "Gender, Class, and Twentieth-Century Chinese Fiction" at the annual meeting of the Association for Asian Studies, New Orleans, April 1991.

26 *Hegel's* Phenomenology of Spirit, trans. A. V. Miller, with analysis of the text and foreword by J. N. Findlay (New York: Oxford University Press, 1977), pp. 54–55; emphases in the original.

27 The extensiveness of the philosophical, political, and feminist arguments about "essentialism" is such that I can merely point to it here. Two recent publications readers can consult are Diana Fuss, *Essentially Speaking* (New York: Routledge, 1989), and *differences* 1.2 (Summer 1989), a special issue on essentialism.

28 "In 'woman' I see something that cannot be represented, something that is not said, something above and beyond nomenclatures and ideologies." Kristeva, "Woman Can Never Be Defined," trans. Marilyn A. August, in Elaine Marks and Isabelle de Courtivron, eds., *New French Feminisms* (New York: Schocken Books, 1981), p. 137.

29 I want to acknowledge those who have contributed to the final version of this chapter. I have benefited from comments made by Wendy Larson and Lydia Liu at the conferences at Iowa and in New Orleans. Continual discussions with Kwai-cheung Lo, Tonglin Lu, and Ming-bao Yue about this chapter and other related issues give me the support of a strong critical community. Most of all, I am indebted to Yu-shih Chen for a forceful and enabling critique, which made me restate my concerns with a clarity that had been previously missing.

37

SIMON GIKANDI

Globalization and the Claims of Postcoloniality

Globalization and *postcoloniality* are perhaps two of the most important terms in social and cultural theory today. Since the 1980s, they have functioned as two of the dominant paradigms for explaining the transformation of political and economic relationships in a world that seems to become increasingly interdependent with the passing of time, with boundaries that once defined national cultures becoming fuzzy. The debates on globalization and postcolonialism are now so universal in character, and the literature on these topics is so extensive, that they are difficult to summarize or categorize. And to the extent that it dominates most debates on the nature of society and economy in the social sciences, globalization must be considered one of the constitutive elements of disciplines such as anthropology and sociology. Similarly, it is difficult to conceive an area of literary studies, from medievalism to postmodernism, that is not affected by debates on postcolonial theory and postcoloniality. While diverse writers on globalization and postcolonialism might have differing interpretations of the exact meaning of these categories, or their long-term effect on the institutions of knowledge production in the modern world, they have at least two important things in common: they are concerned with explaining forms of social and cultural organization whose ambition is to transcend the boundaries of the nation-state, and they seek to provide new vistas for understanding cultural flows that can no longer be explained by a homogenous Eurocentric narrative of development and social change. For scholars trying to understand cultural and social production in the new millennium, globalization is attractive both because of its implicit universalism and its ability to reconcile local and global interests. Furthermore, globalization is appealing to social analysts because of what is perceived as its conjunctive and disjunctive form and function. In the first regard, as Jan Nederveen Pieterse has noted, globalization brings the universal and the local together in a moment of conceptual renewal and "momentum of newness."[1] In the second instance, what Arjun Appadurai calls global *mediascapes* and *ideoscapes* have become the site of tension between "cultural homogenization and cultural heterogenization."[2] In both cases, the language that enables conjuncture or disjuncture—hybridity and cultural transition, for example—comes directly from the grammar book of postcolonial theory. In this sense, one could argue that what makes current theories of globalization different from earlier ones, let's say those associated with modernization in the 1950s and 1960s, is their strategic deployment of postcolonial theory.

Besides their shared cultural grammar, however, the relationship between globalization and postcoloniality is not clear; neither are their respective meanings or implications. Is postcoloniality a consequence of the globalization of culture? Do the key terms in both categories describe a general state of cultural transformation in a world where the authority of the nation-state has collapsed, or are they codes for explaining a set of amorphous images and a conflicting set of social conditions? The discourse of globalization is surrounded by a rhetoric of newness, but what exactly are the new vistas that these terms provide analysts of societies and cultures that have acquired a transnational character? Is globalization a real or virtual phenomenon? Where do we locate postcoloniality—in the spaces between and across cultures and traditions or in national states, which, in spite of a certain crisis of legitimacy, still continue to demand affiliation from their citizens and subjects? These questions are made even more urgent by the realization that while we live in a world defined by cultural and economic flows across formally entrenched national boundaries, the world continues to be divided, in stark terms, between its "developed" and "underdeveloped" sectors. It is precisely because of the starkness of this division that the discourse of globalization seems to be perpetually caught between two competing narratives, one of celebration, the other of crisis.

From one perspective, globalization appears to be a sign of the coming into being of a cultural world order that questions the imperial cartography that has defined global relations since the early modern period. Globalization constitutes, in this regard, what Appadurai calls "a complex overlapping, disjunctive order that cannot any longer be understood in terms of existing center-periphery models."[3] And for those who might argue that globalization is simply the Westernization or Americanization of the world, Appadurai makes a crucial distinction between older forms of modernity, whose goal was the rationalization of the world in Weberian terms, to the symbolic economy of a new global culture based on reciprocal rather than nonlinear relationships:

The master narrative of the Enlightenment (and its many variants in Britain, France, and the United States) was constructed with a certain internal logic and presupposed a certain relationship between reading, representation, and the public sphere. . . . But the diaspora of these terms and images across the world, especially since the nineteenth century, has loosened the internal coherence that held them together in a Euro-American master narrative and provided instead a loosely structured synopticon of politics, in which different nation-states, as part of their evolution, have organized their political cultures around different keywords.[4]

Clearly, globalization appeals to advocates of hybridity as diverse as Homi Bhabha and Pieterse because it seems to harmonize the universal and the particular and, in the process, it seems to open up to a multiplicity of cultural relationships unheard of in the age of empire: for Bhabha, the globalization of social spaces reflects a state of "unsatisfaction" that, nevertheless, enables the articulation and enunciation of "a global or transnational imaginary and its 'cosmopolitan subjectivities'"; for Pieterse, it is through hybridity that globalization works against "homogenization, standardization, cultural imperialism, westernization, Americanization."[5]

Nevertheless, this optimistic and celebratory view of globalization, which is particularly pronounced in postcolonial studies because it uses the lexicon that postcolonial theory makes available to us, is constantly haunted by another form of globalization, one defined by a sense of crisis within the postcolony itself. Unsure how to respond to the failure of the nationalist mandate, which promised modernization outside the tutelage of colonialism, citizens of the postcolony are more likely to seek their global identity by invoking the very logic of Enlightenment that postcolonial theory was supposed to deconstruct. For me, there is no better representation of this *other* desire for globalization within the logic of Enlightenment than the following letter left behind by two Guinean boys whose dead bodies were found in the cargo hold of a plane in Brussels in August 1998:

> Excellencies, gentlemen, and responsible citizens of Europe:
>
> It is our great honor and privilege to write to you about our trip and the suffering of the children and youth in Africa. We offer you our most affectionate and respectful salutations. In return, be our support and our help.
>
> We beseech you on behalf of your love for your continent, your people, your families, and above all your children, whom you cherish more than life itself. And for the love of God, who has granted you all the experience, wealth, and power to ably construct and organize your continent. We call upon your graciousness and solidarity to help us in Africa. Our problems are many: war, sickness, hunger, lack of education. We beseech you to excuse us for daring to write this letter to you, important people whom we truly respect. It is to you, and to you only, that we can plead our case.
>
> And if you find that we have sacrificed our lives, it is because we suffer too much in Africa. We need your help in our struggle against poverty and war.
>
> Be mindful of us in Africa. There is no one else for us to turn to.[6]

Although the Guinean boys may now appear to be signs of those others who have been left out of the global dream of prosperity, there is no disputing the fact that the globalization that they had in mind when they became stowaways on the European plane was different from that espoused by postcolonial theorists. The boys were seeking neither cultural hybridity nor ontological difference. Their quest was for a modern life in the European sense of the world; their risky journey from Africa was an attempt to escape both poverty and alterity; it was predicated on the belief that their salvation could only come from that Europe which, only two generations earlier, black nationalists such as Jomo Kenyatta and Aimé Césaire had declared to be the major threat to the prosperity and well-being of Africa.[7]

Now, my primary interest in this discussion is not to adjudicate between the celebratory narrative of globalization and the more dystopic version represented in the letter by the Guinean boys; it is not even my intention to rationalize the actions of Africans who die seeking the dream of a European identity in very colonial and Eurocentric terms. On the contrary, I am interested in using these contrasting views of globalization to foreground at least three closely related problems, which, I believe, call into question many of the claims motivating the theoretical literature on globalization and its relations to postcoloniality.

The first problem arises from the realization that when social scientists try to differentiate older forms of globalization (located solidly within the discourse of colonialism and modernization) from the new forms structured by hybridity and difference, they often tend to fall back on key words borrowed from postcolonial theory. Although some of these key words—the most prominent are *hybridity* and *difference*—have been popular in literary studies since the 1970s, they have been shunned by empirical social scientists who decry the lack of the conceptual foundations that might make them useful analytical categories.[8] At the same time, however, social scientists eager to turn globalization into the site of what Pieterse calls "conceptual renewal" have found the language of postcolonial theory indispensable to their project.[9] In the first part of my discussion, I will argue that part of the attraction of postcolonial theory to questions of globalization lies precisely in its claim that culture, as a social and conceptual category, has escaped "the bounded nation-state society" and has thus become the common property of the world.[10] This point is made powerfully by Bhabha when he asserts that the postcolonial perspective represents a critical departure from "the traditions of sociology of underdevelopment and dependency theory"; as a mode of analysis, postcolonial theory disavows any nationalist or nativist pedagogy that sets up the relations of third world and first world in a binary structure of opposition, recognizing that the social boundaries between first and third worlds are far more complex.[11]

The second problem concerns the rather optimistic claim that the institutions of cultural production provide irrefutable evidence of new global relations. It is important here to note that when advocates of the new global order, most prominently Appadurai and Bhabha, talk about globalization, they conceive it almost exclusively in cultural terms; but it is premature to argue that the images and narratives that denote the new global culture are connected to a global structure or that they are disconnected from earlier or older forms of identity. In other words, there is no reason to suppose that the global flow in images has a homological connection to transformations in social or cultural relationships. My interest here, then, is on the disjuncture between the emergence of global images and the global stories of global subjects, like the two Guinean boys, who are not concerned with ideas or images, but are focused on the material experiences of everyday life and survival. Global images have a certain salience for students of culture, especially postmodern culture, but this does not mean that they are a substitute for material experiences. In regard to cultural images, my argument is that we cannot stop at the site of their contemplation; rather, as Mike Featherstone has noted, we "need to inquire into the grounds, the various generative processes, involving the formation of cultural images and traditions."[12]

The last problem I want to take up in this essay concerns the premature privileging of literary texts—and the institutions that teach them—as the exemplars of globalization. No doubt, the most powerful signs of the new process of globalization come from literary texts and other works of art. For critics looking for the sign of hybridity, heterogeneity, and newness in the new world order, there cannot be a better place to go than Salman Rushdie's *Satanic Verses* or Gabriel García Márquez's *El cieno años de soledad*. Such works are now considered world texts because, as Franco Moretti has argued, they have a frame of reference that is "no longer the nation-state, but a broader entity—a continent, or the world-system as a whole."[13] Surprisingly, however, no reading of these seminal texts is complete without an engagement with the nation-state, its history, its foundational mythologies, and its quotidian experiences. To the extent that they seek to deconstruct the foundational narrative of the nation, these are world texts; yet they cannot do without the framework of the nation. What needs to be underscored here, then, is the persistence of the nation-state in the very literary works that were supposed to gesture toward a transcendental global culture. I will conclude my discussion by arguing that one of the great ironies of the discourse of globalization is that although English literature has become the most obvious sign of transnationalism, it is continuously haunted by its historical—and disciplinary—location in a particular national *ethos* and *ethnos*. What are we going to do with those older categories—nation, culture, and English— which function as the absent structure that shapes and yet haunts global culture and the idea of literature itself?

My contention that postcolonial theory has been the major source of a new grammar for rethinking the global begs a foundational question: Why did culture in general and literature in particular become central terms in the discourse of globalization in the 1980s? There are two obvious explanations for the cultural turn in global studies. The first one is that sometime in the 1980s, cultural and literary theorists became convinced that the debates on globalization that had dominated disciplines such as sociology and anthropology for most of the twentieth century had become hopelessly imprisoned in the classical narrative of modernity, or Wallersteinian world-system theory. These scholars began to elaborate a cultural and literary project whose goal was to show that the real signs of how globalization was being lived, experienced, and interpreted were to be found primarily in the literary and cultural field. It was in literary culture, postcolonial theorists argued, that a new narrative of globalization, one that would take us beyond modernity and colonialism, could be identified and experienced.[14] Thus, if the new theories of globalization that emerged in the 1980s seemed to privilege culture rather than political economy, it was because they were premised on the notion that it was through cultural practices that the difference and hybridity that undermined the Eurocentric narrative of modernity was most evident. An implicit assumption in these debates was that the forms of globalization that had taken place after the postmodernization of society had generated forces and practices that the traditional sociological narrative of globalization could not account for; faced with "the diversity, variety and richness of popular and local discourses" that resisted "play-back systemicity and order," social science had been unable to develop conceptual terms for spatialized symbolic hierarchies.[15]

Given the emphasis placed on culture in the 1980s, sociological theories of globalization predicated on modernization—and hence political economy—were brought face to face with an intractable paradox: on one hand, there was a renewed intellectual interest in sociology's key concern with culture and social formation on both a local and global scale; on the other hand, however, the discipline's explanatory systems no longer seemed to have the efficacy that had made them, at the height of theories of modernization in the 1960s, influential codes for explaining cultural relations across boundaries and large time scales. In these circumstances, as Mike Featherstone has argued in his introduction to *Global Culture,* the challenge of sociology has been "to both theorize and work out modes of systematic investigation which can clarify these globalizing processes and distinctive forms of social life which render problematic what has long been regarded as the basic subject matter for sociology: society, conceived almost exclusively as the bounded nation-state."[16] The implicit assumption here is that a new theory of globalization will have to be conceived beyond the nation-state and the traditional claims of sociology. It is in this context, therefore, that literary culture comes to occupy an important role in the rethinking of globalization outside its traditional home in the nation-state. Even longstanding sociologists of globalization and modernity, such as Zygmunt Bauman, seem increasingly to speak the language of postmodern or postcolonial globalization in which the claims of culture seem to be at odds with traditional theories of modernity and modernization—theories of culture rooted in literary and artistic images rather than social processes.[17]

The second explanation for the cultural turn in global studies can be connected to the emergence of postmodern theories that called into question some of the dominant grand narratives of globalization. Let us recall here that before the emergence of postmodernism as a conceptual mode of explaining the nature of global culture, theories of globalization were constructed around the concept of modernization, a powerful and homogenizing category that appealed as much to colonial systems as it did to nationalist movements in the so-called third world. With the emergence of postmodern theories of cultural formation, however, certain key categories in theories of modernization were called into question. These categories included the efficacy of homogenizing notions such as modernization, the authority of the nation-state as the central institution in the management of social relationships, and the idea of culture as the embodiment of symbolic hierarchies such as patriotism and citizenship. Against the totality implicit in colonial and nationalist theories of globalization, postmodern critics sought to show, after Jean-François Lyotard, that "eclecticism [was] the degree zero of contemporary general culture."[18]

Calling attention to the existence of a variety of decentered narratives and the challenge to the nation-states by transnational movements that were creating new sites of identity—diasporas, for example—outside the boundaries of the state itself, postcolonial theory saw itself as responding to new cultural forms that could not be contained by world-system theories. In one sense, this turn to the literary in global studies was premised on the belief that in order to displace globalization from its national and disciplinary boundaries, it was important to call into question its key terms, mainly the notion of structuralization that dominated world-system theory, the Eurocentric chronology that had enabled its periodization, and the universalism on which its schemes of identity were based. For Homi Bhabha, Stuart Hall, and Arjun Appadurai, who have been some of the most influential figures in this displacement of the idea of globalization, the new mode of global cultural and social relations is defined by its transgression of the boundaries established by the nation-state, the structures of dominant economic and social formations, and what they conceive to be a Eurocentric sense of time. The key assumption in what one may call the cultural version of globalization is that in the old global order, the nation was the reality and category that enabled the socialization of subjects, and hence the structuralization of cultures; now, in transnationality, the nation has become an absent structure. The nation is still an apparatus of enormous symbolic power, but it is also the mechanism that produces what Bhabha calls "a continual slippage of categories, like sexuality, class affiliation, territorial paranoia, or 'cultural difference.'"[19]

The relationship between theories of globalization and the apparatus of the nation, which informs and troubles the postcolonial perspective on the character of global culture, needs to be emphasized for two reasons: First, to dispel the notion that these new theories reject the identity of the nation as "the particular time and place and practice" that generates cultures.[20] On the contrary, it is in the process of displacing the key terms in the grammar of nationalism that we are forced to recognize what Bhabha calls "the measure of the liminality of cultural modernity."[21] It is in this sense that the nation becomes both the form that structures modern identities and the sign of their displacement and alienation. Second, recognition of the ambivalent role nationalism plays in the construction of culture, and the insistence that culture can actually flow between national boundaries, undermines one of the key terms in the narrative of modernity—the assumption that cultures are, by their nature, national in character. Some sociologists such as Roland Robertson insist that globalization is "intimately related to modernity and modernization"; but prominent postcolonial literary scholars seem eager to rethink modernity displaced from its European roots, dislocated to what Hall calls "the dispersed global periphery."[22]

I am trying to suggest that, whatever reservations we may have about postcolonial theory, we need to recognize that the postcolonial perspective on globalization has been the most salient attempt to question older forms of globalization based on the centrality of the nation and theories of modernization. My claim is that a postcolonial theory of globalization involves a rethinking of the temporality of colonial and national modernity. A key argument in the works of postcolonial scholars such as Appadurai, Bhabha, and Hall is that it is in the process of understanding cultural margins and marking social difference that Eurocentric time and its symbolic economies are dispersed and undone. One of the central ironies of "the politics of global flows" in the areas of cultural production, claims Appadurai, is that it plays havoc "with the hegemony of Eurochronology."[23] In addition, postcolonial theories of globalization insist that this displacement of European time—and modernity in general—takes place in the arena of art, culture or, more appropriately, the imaginary.

In order to clarify the above argument, it is important to note that the discourse of neocolonialism, which emerged in most third world countries in the first few decades after decolonization, was not synonymous with what has come to be known as postcolonial theory. The discourse of neocolonialism, which was prominent in the former European colonies in Africa and Asia in the early decades of independence (the 1950s and 1960s), did not try, as postcolonialism was to try to do much later, to set "metropolitan accounts askew."[24] On the contrary, this version of postcolonial theory was premised on the belief that decolonization had failed in one of its crucial mandates—the fulfillment of the dream of modernity and modernization without the tutelage of colonialism. If *globalization* did not appear to be an important term in the discourse of neocolonialism (or its prominent theories of cultural imperialism and underdevelopment) it was because it was seen as a threat to the national interest. Indeed, the major critique of the failed national mandate, contained most vividly in Frantz Fanon's "The Pitfalls of National Consciousness," was premised on the belief that the new ruling class had become an agent of global interests.[25] For most of the 1950s and 1960s *globalization* was without doubt a pejorative term in the discourse of development in many of the newly decolonized countries in Asia, Africa, and the Caribbean.

But by the 1980s two important developments had taken place to change the terms of this debate. In Africa, institutions of modernization premised on self-reliance and the national interest, such as the *Ujamaa* (self-help) project in Tanzania, had all but collapsed; for politicians and intellectuals on the continent, radical and conservative alike, all viable models of "development" demanded some engagement with the forces of globalization either in the form of global capital or multilateral aid organizations such as the International Monetary Fund (IMF) and the World Bank. At about the same time in Asia, new hybrid modernities, this time premised on a mixture of local cultures and global interests, had emerged to challenge the Western narrative of development. Thus, while Africa entered the global narrative out of the despair we detect in the letter by the boys from Guinea, Asian countries, especially Japan and Korea, became leaders in a new narrative of global capital. And yet, although the African and Asian entry into globalization now appears to many analysts to tell two divergent stories—one of failure, the other of success—they have at least one thing in common: they call attention to the shift of the locus of social and economic relations from the national to the global scene. More particularly, they call attention to the collapse of the narrative of decolonization itself.

What do I mean by this? Consider the fact that from the late nineteenth century to the 1960s decolonization in most of the "Third World" had been defined as the restoration of the nation to its imagined precolomal autonomy and the securing of its identity from exogamous forces. In the discourse of decolonization, as Fanon argued, the demand for a national culture—"and the affirmation of such a culture"—represented a "special battlefield" against colonialism. But the value of culture was instrumental: its primary function was to legitimize the national project.[26] By the 1980s, however, even die-hard nationalists were finding it hard to argue that the nation-state was the guarantor of economic freedom or cultural affirmation. Few intellectuals were willing to make the claim that the value of culture was to defend the polity from its presumed enemies; on the contrary, especially among the postcolonial elite, culture was being rescued from the institutions of the state or being turned against the state itself. In Africa, for example, cultural nationalism, in the hands of the political class, had become a form of mystification; by the same token, the nation-state, once deemed to be the defender of postcolonial subjects, was now conceived as the major threat to the well-being of its citizens.[27] And with the increasing movements of people across boundaries and continents, older models of explaining global cultural relationships such as the three-worlds system or the center-periphery paradigm were no longer referring to realities outside themselves; they had become empty signifiers of experiences that did not match the transnational diasporas. By the 1980s such models, and the ecumenies they presupposed, were seen increasingly as extraneous in relation to their objects of analysis. What had transcended nationalism and older models of explaining social relationships was a new global existence, in which, as Bauman has argued, "modern existence forces its culture in opposition to itself."[28]

The point here is that the global culture linked with postmodernism (the subject of postcolonial theory) has brought us to a point where the traditional association between national spaces and cultural practices cannot be sustained: there no longer seems to be a clear relationship between cultural practices and localities. One is as likely to come across Santeria worship in Miami as in Havana. One can watch and enjoy reruns of *Dallas* in Dallas and in the highlands of Kenya. In these circumstances, it doesn't seem to make sense to argue that there is a homological relationship between nations and cultures. Where culture seems to supersede nation, or to be at odds with its claims, then the postcolonial solution sketched above is appealing because, by making culture the primary term in the relationship between "life" and its "images," it is much easier to have a handle on a world in which social realities and cultural representations seemed to be out of joint. This is how postcolonial theories of globalization come to valorize the image and the imaginary:

> The image, the imagined, the imaginary—these are all terms that direct us to something critical and new in global cultural process: *the imagination as a social practice*. No longer mere fantasy (opium for the masses whose real work is elsewhere), no longer simple escape (from a world defined principally by more concrete purposes and structures), no longer elite pastime (thus not relevant to the lives of ordinary people), and no longer mere contemplation irrelevant for new forms of desire and subjectivity, the imagination has become an organized field of social practices, a form of work (in the sense of both labor and culturally organized practice) and a form of negotiation between sites of agency (individuals) and globally defined fields of possibility. This unleashing of the imagination links the play of pastiche (in some settings) to the terror and coercion of states and their competitors. The imagination is now central to all forms of agency, is itself a social fact, and is the key component of the new global order.[29]

But the letter from the Guinean boys provides us with another, more problematic narrative of globalization, one driven by impossible dreams and mediated by not simply the new media, but also older narratives about civilization and development. And it is the existence of this other narrative of death and decay, unwittingly tied to Enlightenment and rationality and tormented by the brutal realities of poverty, that seems to suggest that contrary to the optimistic view expressed by Appadurai and others, globalization might, after all, be a discourse of failure and atrophy. In short, there seems to be a powerful disjuncture between the global narratives and images that attract postcolonial critics and another set of narratives and images which do not exactly fit into a theoretical apparatus that seems bent on difference and hybridity. Postcolonial literature is not, of course, deaf to the disjuncture between its performance of a global culture and the persistence of this other, darker, older narrative of poverty, of failed nationalism, of death, that will simply not go away. Postcolonial theorists may have sought to forget the nation in order to become global, but the nation has not forgotten them. One of the most disturbing aspects of the *Satanic Verses,* for example, is the way it seems to call its upbeat rhetoric of globalization into question by privileging a moment of closure associated with forces—*nation* and *patria*—that the novel had ostensibly set out to undo in its search for newness. Why does a "world" text, one committed to blasphemy and transgression, resort to a romantic closure that affirms the very site of identity that it had set out to undo? In order to answer this question we need to rethink modes of reading and analysis that are focused so much on the familiar tropes of postcolonial theory—globalization, transgression, and hybridity—that they fail to take notice of unfamiliar, but equally powerful, local scenes of being and belonging.

In "Reading the *Satanic Verses,*" Spivak makes two points that are central to the critique of postcolonial theories of globalization that I want to develop in the second part of my discussion: first, she notes that "the *Satanic Verses,* in spite of all its plurality, has a rather aggressive theme: the postcolonial divided between two identities: migrant and national."[30] Second, she notes that "because the migrant as paradigm is a dominant theme in theorizations of postcoloniality, it is easy to overlook Rushdie's resolute effort to represent contemporary India."[31] In my discussion, I have suggested that postcolonial theories of globalization have been influential in the mapping of global culture because they have appeared to be focused on tropes that speak powerfully to the experience of migration. The downside to this focus on migrancy and its images, however, is that the national has tended to be negated, although it is indeed one of the enabling conditions of the trope of migration in the first place. I agree with Spivak that Rushdie's resolute effort to represent contemporary India is overlooked in readings of his novel. But the issue I want to pursue here is not why the national and the local is overlooked in postcolonial theories of global culture and its literature, but the larger questions that are elided in the process. Let me frame the problem this way: since stories about dead Africans in cargo holds of European planes cannot be read as stories of hybridity, diaspora, or métissage, they demand a rethinking of the tropes that have dominated the discourse of postcolonial theory in relation to both global culture and nationalism.

A useful starting point for the kind of rethinking I have in mind here is to simply recognize that although almost all theories of globalization are premised on the assumed marginalization of the nation-state in the domain of culture and the imaginary, there is scant evidence that the same processes are at work in the politics of everyday life, where the rhetoric of globalization is constantly undermined by the resurgence of older forms of nationalism, patriotism, and fundamentalism. We are so accustomed to hearing stories about the triumph of liberal democracy in the world that we often forget that for the majority of people in the ex-colonies the most attractive moments are led by forces that wave the banner of cultural or religious fundamentalism. My argument is that although they seem to have been exorcized from the postcolonial scene of interpretation, such older categories of identity as religion and nationalism, even the protonationalism that has given us recent scenes of horror such as the 1994 genocide in Rwanda, continue to haunt and to shape the idea of culture and literature even in the spaces in between nations and traditions. And it is precisely because the old time (of "tribe," of the protonation, and of *Heimat*) coexists with the new time (of globalization, of newness, of the unhomely) that we have to rethink the politics of global time itself.

Some background is necessary here. The politics of a postcolonial theory of globalization are premised on a temporal disjuncture—the disruption of the temporality of the modern nation by the transnational. Like the geographers of postmodernism, advocates of a postcolonial globalism seem fairly united in their claim that the global flow in culture, and our retrospective reading of modernity from the vantage point of decolonization, disrupts the chronology of Eurocentrism, which was undoubtedly one of the enabling conditions of the modern world system.[32] In the new (ir)rationalization of the world, the process of time does not flow from a European or North American center to a Latin American, Asian, or African periphery; rather, culture flows in both directions. In the world system of images, to use Appadurai's example, the United States is no longer "the puppeteer of a world system of images, but is only one node of a complex transnational construction of imaginary landscape."[33] Originally conceived as the preserve of a specific landscape (the nation), time now moves horizontally across shifting spheres of social life, breaking up the linear, homogenizing, and universalizing narrative of colonialism and modernity.

Unlike their postmodern counterparts, however, postcolonial theories of globalization do not reject the grand narrative of time entirely; rather, what one may call, for lack of a better word, postcolonial temporality, exists in an uneasy, dialectical relation with the politics of modern time and historicism. The new narrative of globalization cannot—does not—reject the temporality of modernity, because modern time is a significant part of its prehistory. Indeed, the postcolonial condition is embedded, through colonialism and nationalism, in the politics of modernity. At the same time, however, the new time of postcoloniality cannot be imprisoned in the politics of modern time and the teleology of modernization for as the *post* in the term suggests, postcolonialism is a condition that must be contained both within and beyond the causality of colonial modernity. As a consequence, Bhabha argues, the postcolonial passage through modernity produces a form of repetition, "the past as projective": "The time-lag of postcolonial modernity moves *forward,* erasing that compliant past tethered to the myth of progress, ordered in the binarism of its cultural logic: past/present, inside/outside."[34]

Nevertheless, this postcolonial attempt to process global culture through the economy of modern time runs against a number of problems. The most obvious problem is that the category of time is itself indistinguishable from the hegemony of European modernity. For whether we consider temporality to be just a descriptive category (an account of epochal change), or a self-conscious engagement with periodization (in which forms of literature are accounted for in terms of specific time periods), modernity is, in Peter Osborne's succinct phrasing, a culture of time and temporalization.[35] And if modernity is the "totalizing temporalization of history," then time is its most important defining category.[36] The truth is, we cannot speak of a new global culture without at the same time accounting for the forms of time consciousness associated with its genesis in modernity, a modern temporality that cannot be conceived outside colonial governmentality. Is the new time embedded in postcoloniality different from the time consciousness of colonialism, what has come to be known as Eurocentric time?[37] And what are the terms—and narratives—that differentiate the temporality of this new global culture from its colonial antecedents? The Guinean boys haunt my discussion because they seem to have confused the difference between the failed temporality of modernity and the time lag of postcolonial time; they were, Bhabha notwithstanding, still tethered to the myth of progress. I think we need to keep their misunderstanding in mind since it might be closer to the social epistemology of many ex-colonial subjects than the more familiar discourse of globalization in postcoloniality.

There is another issue at stake in these discussions of modern temporality: If the narrative of modernity and modernization was predicated on the rationalization of the world, to use Max Weber's famous formulation, how can we articulate a narrative of globalization in which distinctly modern subjects negotiate the line between what Bhabha calls "the teleology of progress" and "the 'timeless' discourse of irrationality?"[38] As we can see here, the key terms in the discourse of modernity—*progress* and *reason* or *(ir)rationality*—have an uncanny way of making their presence felt in theories of postcolonial globalism. The presence of such terms as *progress, time,* and *reason,* in the discourse that was intended to deconstruct them is, nevertheless, predictable rather than surprising, for if we were to present the global identity of postcolonial subjects as simply an opposition between the teleology of progress and an atemporal irrationality, we would inevitably reinforce the narrative of modern hegemony, the one in which the epistemology of Western reason is pitted against the timeless, irrational world of the savage or the primitive.[39] It is in order to avoid this trap that the process of globalization comes to be narrated as simultaneously modern (reasonable, universal, totalized) and differentiated (driven by its own set of rationalities). And yet, as the following example from Bhabha's essay on nation and narration illustrates, drawing the line between modern identity and postcolonial difference can be a complicated affair:

> It is indeed only in the disjunctive time of the nation's modernity—as a knowledge caught between political rationality and its impasse, between the shreds and patches of cultural signification and the certain ties of a nationalist pedagogy—that questions of nation as narration come to be posed. How do we plot the narrative of the nation that must mediate between the teleology of progress tipping over into the timeless discourse of irrationality? How do we understand that homogeneity of modernity—the people—which if pushed too far, may assume something resembling the archaic body of the despotic or totalitarian mass? In the midst of progress and modernity, the language of ambivalence reveals a politics 'without duration,' as Althusser once provocatively wrote: 'Space without places, time without duration.' To write the story of the nation demands that we articulate that archaic ambivalence that informs the time of modernity.[40]

Bhabha maps out the politics of the nation by simultaneously invoking the traditional, symbolic language of the imagined community (in modernity) and by dislocating its narratives of doubling and the interstitial. One of his most powerful claims is that it is in the differentiated time of writing, in the "ambivalent and chiasmic intersection of time and place" and the dialectic of the pedagogical and the performative represented by novels such as the *Satanic Verses,* that a time inside and outside the nation, for and against the epistemology of modernity, can be inscribed; the interstitial represents the condition of possibility of a postnational identity, one which envisages "a certain affective and ethical identification with globality."[41]

Is it possible, however, that we are eager to embrace globalization and its images or fictions because of its amorphous character? This question comes from two directions. From the perspective of the boys from Guinea, who are represented in this discussion as representatives of hundreds of other migrants who die every day trying to get "there" to be "like you," the identification with globality is not ethical but material; they do not seek to occupy the interstitial spaces between nations and cultures, but to leave what they consider to be a failed polity for a successful one. From the perspective of an influential group of social scientists, the problem here is not so much the experience of globalization but the way it is represented in postcolonial theory. There are two main complaints here: the first one is that the more the key-words in postcolonial theories of globalization, most prominently hybridity, become ubiquitous, the more they become diffuse and meaningless.[42] The other complaint is that the emphasis on culture in postcolonial theory hinders the recognition of the global experience as a structural experience (produced out of the complex interaction of politics, economics, the social, and the like). As long as globalization is conceived as a cultural rather than a structural experience, it functions as what Roland Robertson has called "a site of social theoretical interests, interpretative indulgence, or the display of world-ideological preferences"; considered as an aggregate of local experiences in displacement rather than a structure patterned by causal relationships, the culture of globalization cannot account for "the global-human condition."[43] Still, there is no guarantee that a rigorous analysis of social structures will give us any more insights into the immigrants who die in European cargo planes or the sweatshops of New York or Los Angeles, for as Fredric Jameson's acute observation of the chasm between realities and representations has revealed, there is always the possibility that "the sense people have of themselves and their own moment of history may ultimately have nothing whatsoever to do with its reality."[44] Is it possible that the citizens of the new diasporic spheres live through experiences that are "wildly at odds from their own inner experiences and their interior daily life"?[45]

Ultimately, what is at issue here is not that certain forms of globalization are more compelling than others but that many of the codes we use to explain the global phenomenon can be anterior to the people who live through the transnational experience. Like the legendary subalterns of colonial culture, the majority of the postcolonial subjects who live through the experience of globalization cannot speak. And when they speak, they sometimes speak a language that is alien to their liberal sympathizers or the postcolonial émigré elite. Quite often, close encounters with the new migrants in the West challenge liberal sentiments at the core: What do we do when we discover that the subaltern element in the new diasporas, instead of adopting the cosmopolitanism beloved of the postcolonial elite, continues to demand the most fundamentalist forms of cultural identification? What are we to say when Muslims demand Sharia Law in Bradford or when Somali migrants in Seattle (or North Africans in Paris) insist that "circumcising" their daughters is crucial to their identity?

I use these extreme—but quite real—examples to call attention to two significant shortcomings in both the cultural and structural explanations of globalization I mentioned earlier: one of the central shortcomings in these theories is that in their desire to secure the newness of theories of globalization, to posit them as postmodern and postcolonial as it were, many critics and analysts of the phenomenon no longer seem interested in the "Third World" itself as a source of the cultural energies—and the tragedies—that have brought the new migrants to the West. In insisting on the newness of the global, either as a set of structural patterns determined by the narrative of capital, or as a set of images mediated by the new media, analysts tend to forget that what we are calling the new global culture represents less the transformation of the meaning of the imaginary in the modern world than a reorganization of what Mary Douglas calls "the stock of knowledge" that helps us mediate or explain social experiences.[46]

In addition, it is easily assumed that globalization is primarily a mode of transformation of cultural or structural relations in the West itself. And yet, global culture is a result of the transformations in both "First" and "Third Worlds," and especially a transformation of the institutions of knowledge production, and even the enunciative situations, in both zones. Simply put, what has happened in the aftermath of the crisis of decolonization and the collapse of modern institutions of knowledge production in much of the so-called Third World is that the arena in which the meaning of cultural practices is determined has shifted, as has the speech community in which, to cite Douglas, claims and counterclaims about the meaning of texts are made.[47] The rise of the new globalism, like the denotative shift from "Third World" to "Postcolonial," reflects a significant shift in the speech community in which claims about colonialism and nationalism are introduced and discussed.

This point can be better understood if we recall that for most of the 1960s and 1970s, knowledge about postcolonial nations was mediated primarily by intellectuals and writers based in "Third World" countries. The most significant works by what were then known as "Third World" intellectuals such as Ashis Nandy in psychology, Walter Rodney in history, Rex Nettleford in culture, and Andre Gunder Frank in political economy, were published and primarily read in their nations and regions and within the "underdeveloped" world. Although the works of these intellectuals—Rodney's *How Europe Underdeveloped Africa* is a striking example—were cult texts in the "Third World," they were not initially considered scholarly enough to enter the institutions of Western knowledge. Against this background, I want to suggest that the discourse of postcolonialism and postcolonial theories of globalization emerged in the 1980s when the centers of knowledge production about the "Third World" shifted from the periphery to the center, when many leading "Third World" intellectuals became transformed, for political and economic reasons, into émigré native informants. Once the "Third World" speech communities had changed, once the primary audience for cultural discourse was based outside the national state, which could not now be considered to be the legitimizing force for knowledge production, the global had to be reinvented as a substitute for nationalism. It was during the same period that minority communities in the metropolitan centers were adopted as supplements, or even field sites, for the vanishing "Third World."

The last point I want to take up in this essay concerns the privileging of literary texts—the disciplines that teach them—as the exemplars of globalization. For if my discussion so far seems to be caught between the claims of social scientists and literary critics, it is because the two "guilds" of scholarship have been locked in a surreptitious struggle to map out and redefine globalization. As Appadurai notes, "Social scientists look on with bewilderment as their colleagues in English and comparative literature talk (and fight) about matters that, until as recently as fifteen years ago, would have seemed about as relevant to English departments as, say, quantum mechanics."[48] If the fear of social scientists in the wake of poststructuralism was that they were condemned to wait forever outside the philosophy department, their current concern, according to Jean and John Comaroff, is that they are waiting still: "But now we sit, the philosopher at our side, begging an audience with the literary critic."[49] How did the literary critic become the custodian of a postglobal culture in the academy?

Social scientists who complain about the hegemony of the literary in cultural studies forget that it was their rejection of empiricism and historicism that created the condition for the valorization of the literary object in the first place. Once social scientists had defined the new global culture as one built around images, the imagined, and the imaginary, they had in effect invited the rule of the literary. Literary scholars, previously marginalized in debates on globalization, development, and modernization because their preoccupations had ostensibly nothing to do with concrete historical or political experiences, could now claim that they were better suited—and trained—to talk about images than social scientists were. Powerful literary traditions—in English and French, for example—were now positioned to claim that, under the guise of Anglophone literature or Francophonie, their projects had always been global. At the bare bottom, postcolonial theory is the assertion of the centrality of the literary in the diagnosis and representation of the social terrain that we have been discussing under the sign of globalization.

But the claim that English literary studies, to use the example I am most familiar with, were global because they originated in the colonial periphery or were an important part of a linguistic commonwealth calls attention to the paradoxical relation between the discipline and its national and colonial origins. From its beginnings in India, Africa, or Scotland, English has been a discipline that has been defined and shadowed by a double paradox, a paradox that has to be located in the history of the English language and the incorporation of English literature itself into the national curriculum. Consider this: of all the European language literary traditions, English literature is the most global; and yet, wherever it has traveled English has been defined in exclusively national, some might say chauvinistic, terms. This is the first paradox. The second paradox is that in the United States and, more recently, in Britain, English departments have come to be perceived as the custodians of globalization in the university; in real terms, however, these institutions tend to consider English literatures other than British and American as secondary to what they consider to be their main task—the teaching of the literature of England (and, some-times, that of the United States, considered to be an extension of Englishness across the Atlantic). At the same time, however, we cannot underestimate the role of English as the discipline in which many of the major questions regarding globalization, the ones discussed in the first two parts of my essay, are formulated. The turn to culture in global studies, which I discussed earlier, can clearly be attributed to post-colonial scholars such as Edward Said, Bhabha, and Spivak, whose work is located in English. Stuart Hall may appear to be an exception here since his most important work has been in sociology departments, but still, all his education at Oxford and Cambridge was in English; indeed, his turn to sociology has often been explained as an attempt to escape the parochial Englishness that defined the discipline in the period after World War II.

But the rhetoric of globalization inherent in English studies, especially in the aftermath of postcolonial theory, conceals a history and practice that has strongly resisted the expansion of the discipline beyond the boundaries of England. Even when practitioners of English are committed to expanding its horizons, they increasingly seem unable to break out of the organization of the discipline in terms of a set of texts and periods that assume the centrality of England in the business of doing English. One does not need to provide statistics to show that the common periodization of English studies into epochs such as Medieval, Renaissance, Augustan, or Victorian only makes sense if the organization of the discipline is pegged to a certain national history of England. The predominance of this national structure is sometimes easy to ignore, either because certain writers, mostly from minority communities in the metropolitan centers, have been allowed into the canon of Englishness, or because certain spaces have been created for what Spivak has aptly described as the postcolonial ghetto, which is cited as evidence of the new global English studies.[50] Having one's own ghetto might not be a bad thing after centuries of exclusion, but still we need to keep on recalling that time not so long ago when English departments were considered to be the showcases of national culture and European civilization. It was not until the 1960s that major English departments in the United States began to allow Jews, women, and blacks into their faculty. At the University of Michigan, my own institution, it took the rev-olution of the 1960s for people whose first language was not English to be allowed to study for a Ph.D. in the discipline. In 1973, when Wole Soyinka, the distin-guished African writer, proposed to offer a course in African Literature at Cam-bridge University, he was directed to the Department of Social Anthropology because, in his words, the English department, or some influential people in it, "did not believe in any such mythical beast as 'African literature.' "[51] Before we laud English departments for championing globalization, we need to account for this resistance to the Englishness of the other. We need, in particular, to pose the question of why the national paradigm continues to shape literary studies in the age of globalization.

English studies may have started elsewhere, in Africa, in India, on the Celtic fringe, but as numerous studies have shown, once the discipline became established at the center of the university, and as it began to be celebrated as a field that was central to the life of the modern national subject, its institution of exegesis was wrapped up in some of the most essentialist forms of the national imagination.[52] This accounts for the ironic fact that when English spread across the global sphere, it did not travel as a theoretical category that could be transposed and transmuted, but as a social phenomena whose claims would only be translated from one tradition to another in nationalist terms. Thus, when a group of African intellectuals called for the abolition of the English department at the University of Nairobi in 1968, to cite one famous example, their onslaught was directed not at the institution of English itself or how the discipline was taught, but at its inability to be anchored in local traditions and its valorization of alienation rather than local identity. Debates about literature in Africa throughout the 1960s and 1970s were not about the rethinking of the idea of the literary, but attempts to show that African literature in English could make the same exclusive claims that F. R. Leavis had made for English literature in England.[53] Now, the Leavises may not have had a direct effect on the transformation of English in the United States, but the Anglo-Saxonism they had inherited from Mathew Arnold was at the very heart of the organization of literary studies in North America from the Yale of the New Critics to the Agrarianism of the *Sewanee Review*. It is not, hence, an exaggeration to say that the Leavises' influence went beyond the centers where their disciples reigned (the British provincial universities and the colonies) and that it shadowed—and continues to shadow—the study of English literature caught between nationalism and globalization.

I believe this was the important point Terry Eagleton was making in his misunderstood decision to preface *Literary Theory: An Introduction* with a discussion of the relationship between literary theory and the rise of English.[54] What Eagleton was trying to show, I think, was that what was now called literary theory, conceived as a self-conscious critique of institutions of representation and interpretation, was built on an unquestioned view of what English or literature were supposed to be and the role they were expected to play in the politics of nationalism. Eagleton understood, as did most historians of English literature in Britain and its former empire, that the very idea of English studies was premised on a close relationship between the nationalization of literary institutions and what we may consider to be their naturalizing powers. And there is no better example of this relationship than the rhetoric of Englishness in the writings of F. R. Leavis. It was Leavis who, following the example of Mathew Arnold and T. S. Eliot, sought to create an exclusive space for literature as an agent of moral meaning and restitution, a force of humane values against the "Benthamite" climate of industrial culture and modern civilization. It was Leavis who wanted to make English literature the center of English life and culture.[55]

But my concern here is not Leavis's moral economy; rather, I am more interested in how he associated the study of English literature with a particular set of institutions and practices, such as the university and culture, which became, paradoxically, influential in the postcolonial world because of their ability to invoke the national and the universal (or global) in the same discourse. The consequence of this legacy is a startling ambiguity: English literature is simultaneously one of the most universal cultural phenomena, a pantheon that can be traced all the way from the outer Hebrides of Scotland to Suva in Fiji, but English is also one of the most parochial disciplines, constantly associated with very provincial geographies and concerns. I am interested in how Leavis enabled this paradox and why it continues to plague the discipline today.

One important way of coming to terms with this ambiguity is to recall Perry Anderson's important observation that Leavis's critical oeuvre "rested on a metaphysics which he could never expound or defend," and that his obsession with the notion of the nation as an "organic community" reflected his inability to understand literary or cultural difference.[56] From a colonial and postcolonial perspective, however, the enigma of Leavis was precisely that he was able to produce a mode of discourse that was so parochial in its concern with Englishness as a specific British product and still able to exert a lasting influence in colonial and postcolonial worlds where one might have expected all things English to be under nationalist challenge.[57] It is my contention that Leavis's appeal in the colonial world, his global aura as it were, depended both on his aphilosophical method (which enabled him to represent the institutions of literature and exegesis as natural and commonsensical) and his refusal to make literary or cultural difference central to his concerns. By talking about English literature as the product of a natural process inherent in the character of the English nation and people, Leavis was clearly an advocate of the mentality of an insular England; but by ignoring difference altogether, he created a grammar, which turned it into a free-floating cultural object. In other words, he made it possible for his postcolonial successors to substitute for England the new nation that had emerged from decolonization—Kenya, Nigeria, Jamaica, or India. True, Leavis would make the central claim that the writers who represented the "Great Tradition" of English literature were products of the genius of Englishness—the language, the nation, and the culture—but he was also insistent that the morality of action in the works of great writers could be read as a reflection of a generalized moral condition.[58]

Leavis did not have much interest in the transnational, but he was not indifferent to the universality of Englishness; he tended to differentiate the self and the other primarily by language rather than by nation. As far as he was concerned, foreign-born English writers (Henry James and Joseph Conrad, for example) were major custodians of Englishness because of their mastery of the language and the set of moral values ostensibly inherent in it. Mastery of the English language, which was considered integral to a certain moral vision, was what made a writer part of the organic community that was the nation. In effect, Leavis had the uncanny ability to naturalize difference and to make it part of the pantheon of Englishness, and it is my contention that in the process of reading English texts according to the Leavisite grammar, colonial readers were being asked to leave their differences behind and join the common community of Englishness, denoted by literature against the logic of colonial governmentality. At many colonial universities, for example, English was the most popular discipline among undergraduates not simply because of the cultural capital associated with the literary, but because of the psychological security it provided colonial subjects who, in reading the best that had been written and taught, could escape the brutality of everyday life. Colonial readers were later to complain that English literature represented the most manifest sign of their alienation in the imperial world, but as students of the discipline in colonial universities that were branches of major British universities, these readers were steeped in the rituals and practices of Englishness.[59]

In retrospect, the discipline of English literature at the colonial university was an important precursor to the theories of globalization discussed in the first two parts of my essay. Significantly, in Leavis's schema, the universality of the university was intimately connected to what used to be known as literary criticism, for in order to represent the value and meaning of English literature as self-evident, and its attendant moral questions as de facto (as the only questions to consider), Leavis assumed that the values of English literature were "there," uniform, inherent in our modes of being and unaffected by local circumstances or histories. The implicit claim here was that even students in colonial universities, such as Makerere and Ibadan in Africa, could be trained to read culture and morality in literary texts the same way that these tropes were read at University College, London, the "mother" institution. In Leavis's discourse on the university, then, English literature was connected, through the institution of criticism, to the idea of a national community; but it was also through criticism, the act of making interpretative and moral judgments, that the mission of English became universal. Leavis's pronouncements on the university thus brought the national and the universal together in unexpected ways: "The real university is the center of consciousness and human responsibility for the civilized world; it is a creation center of civilization—for the living heritage on which meaning and humane intelligence depend can't, in our time, be maintained without a concentrated creativity somewhere."[60]

Here, as elsewhere, Leavis took it for granted that values or notions such as consciousness, civilization, and human responsibility were embedded in the character of the English nation and that English literature was a mark of its civilizational drive and achievement. At the same time, however, Leavis's discourse had left itself open to universalism: terms such as *the real university, center of consciousness,* and even *civilization* had such a broad meaning that they could easily enter the language of postcolonial nationalism and provide the key terms in the grammar of cultural decolonization. Although Leavis had anchored his terms in an implicit national context, he had generalized them so much that they had become free-floating signifiers. The *real university* could be a university anywhere in the colonial world. More significantly, the idea of the university was simultaneously connected to local and universal concerns. As Bill Readings notes in *The University in Ruins,* while the university might be posited as the safeguard of the state or national cultural interest, it is also mandated to perform an idealistic mission beyond its quotidian function: "The University . . . is not simply an instrument of state policy; rather, the University must embody thought as action, as striving for an ideal."[61]

But how is Leavis's idea of a university education, one rooted in English studies, connected to the emergence of the postcolonial theories of globalization that opened my discussion? In two powerful ways: first, the university—and the study of English that was privileged within it—was one of the most powerful instruments of producing elites in both Britain and its (post)colonies. One of the little known sociological facts about the origins of postcolonial literature and theory is that the study of English literature was crucial in establishing relationships between elites functioning at different spheres of social life and in a variety of postcolonial sectors. What do Homi Bhabha and Arjun Appadurai have in common? They share a common English education at the elite Elphinstone College in Bombay.[62] Bhabha, Rushdie, and Zadie Smith read English at Oxford or Cambridge. We can assume that the texts Spivak was reading at the University of Calcutta were not very different from the ones Wole Soyinka was reading at University College, Ibadan. These relationships can be extended to the domain of politics itself: Bhabha and Thabo Mbeki, the South African president, may not appear to have much in common apart from their colonial backgrounds, but they both read English at Sussex, Mbeki as an undergraduate, Bhabha as a graduate student. Ben Mpaka, the president of Tanzania, read English at Makerere University College in the same years as Ngũgĩ wa Thiong'o, the radical Kenyan novelist, and Susie Tharu (née Oomen), the distinguished Indian feminist literary critic.[63] Unwittingly, the university in Britain and its colonies had created the structure in which postcoloniality would come to be produced both as an experience and a discourse; and in all these cases the (post)colonial university was committed to the Leavis project in one form or another.[64] In these circumstances, what makes Indian worlds accessible to Africans and Britons, and vice versa, more than any real encounters in the cities of the "First" or "Third" Worlds, are the texts of Englishness and the experiences embodied in them.

The second point can be made by recalling the main point I made in the first two parts of this essay—that the new theories and forms of globalization are differentiated from the older sociological ones by the centrality accorded to culture in the analysis of global experiences. It is my contention that the unprecedented valorization of culture in general, and literary culture in particular, in postcolonial theories of globalization, is indebted to the Leavises' project. Like Arnold before him, Leavis established the idea that culture provided a bulwark against materialism in general and industrialization in particular, and that literature was at the heart of what we understood culture to be; where material changes led to ruptures within the presumed organic community of the nation, the poetic tradition represented the "continuity of cultural consciousness."[65]

And yet the argument that culture is the symptom of a new global order has to contend with a difficult question embedded in the Leavis project: How could culture, an idea so powerfully embedded in national traditions, be transformed into a transnational category? This question points to another troublesome part of the Leavis legacy: the predication of the act of criticism itself on a consensual community rooted in the organic body of the nation. Let us recall that Leavis was quite consistent in his claim that critical judgments were not predicated on the critic's ability to establish some measure of distance from his or her object of analysis, but to affirm the consensual community that bound texts, cultural traditions, and readers. For Leavis, a proper critical judgment depended on an interrogative—"This is so, isn't it?"—that was impossible without the concurrence of critics and their interlocutors, both involved in what he called "a collaborative exchange, a collective and creative interplay of judgments."[66] Leavis took it for granted that the writer, the reader, and the critic belonged to what Perry Anderson has aptly called "a shared, stable system of beliefs and values."[67]

The important point to underscore, though, is that for Leavis, criticism was not critique: it did not question the norms underlying English literature or the culture of Englishness; it was not concerned with any substantive history, or social epistemology; instead, the task of criticism was to establish a shared body of implicit and unquestionable values as the imperative for literary studies. For this reason, criticism did not have, nor did it need, a theory. On the contrary, it was a creative process that sought to "establish the poem as something standing in a common world between those discussing, and thus to satisfy our habitual assumption that it does so stand."[68] Leavis was willing to concede that a poem existed for us as private experience, but he was also adamant that its overall meaning depended on its public presence, that the work of art created, or rather was, a moral space "in which minds can meet, and our business is to establish the poem and meet in it."[69] But who were we? What made this economy of reading habitual? What was the character of the minds that met in the poem? Leavis took it for granted that the writer, the work, and the critic shared a common Englishness.

We now scoff at this idea of a consensual Englishness. We call attention to the global nature of English literature and even the multiculturalism of England itself. We counter the xenophobia of the last Thatcherites by pointing to the landscape of English writing as a sign of the globalization of English literature; we point out that English language literature, in Britain itself, is likely to be dominated by Anglo-Indian, Anglo-Japanese, Anglo-Chinese, Afro-Scottish, and Afro-Nigerian artists as much as by writers from the proverbial home counties and the Celtic periphery. And yet, the more one listens to this invocation of the new English literature as one of the most powerful signs of global culture, one wonders whether globality has become a supplement, or even alibi, for prior categories of national culture such as Englishness. Is the global culture of professional émigrés the same as that of those who cross national boundaries in dangerous circumstances? What, indeed, is the consensual community shared by these two groups? The questions need to be addressed if postcolonial theories of globalization are to be something more than a passing fad.

NOTES

1. Jan Nederveen Pieterse, "Hybrid Modernities: Mélange Modernities in Asia," *Sociological Analysis* 1.3 (1998): 75.

2. Arjun Appadurai, *Modernity at Large: Cultural Dimensions of Globalization* (Minneapolis, 1996), 32.

3. Ibid.

4. Ibid., 36.

5. Homi Bhabha, *The Location of Culture* (New York and London, 1994), 204; Pieterse, "Hybrid Modernities," 76.

6. For an English translation of the original letter, written in French, see *Harper's Magazine*, no. 1794 (November 1999), 22. My thanks to James Ferguson for drawing this letter to my attention.

7. See Jomo Kenyatta, *Facing Mount Kenya* (New York, [1938] 1962), 305–6; Aimé Césaire, *Discourse on Colonialism* (New York, 1955), 24–25.

8. See, for example, Roland Robertson, "Mapping the Global Condition: Globalization as the Central Concept," in *Global Culture: Nationalism, Globalization, and Modernity,* ed. Mike Featherstone (London, 1990), 15–30.

9. Pieterse, "Hybrid Modernities," 75.

10. Mike Featherstone, "Global Culture: An Introduction," in Featherstone, *Global Culture,* 2.

11. Homi Bhabha, "Conference Presentation," in *Critical Fictions: The Politics of Imaginative Writing,* ed. Philomena Mariani (Seattle, 1991), 63.

12. Featherstone, "Global Culture," 2.

13. Franco Moretti, *Modern Epic: The World System from Goethe to García Márquez* (London, 1996), 50.

14 For these claims see Appadurai, *Modernity at Large*, 36; Bhabha, *The Location of Culture* (New York and London, 1994), 171–73; and Stuart Hall, "When Was 'the Post-colonial'? Thinking at the Limit," in *The Post-colonial Question: Common Skies, Divided Horizons*, ed. Iain Chambers and Lidia Curti (London and New York, 1996), 242–60.

15 Featherstone, "Global Culture," 2.

16 Ibid., 2.

17 Zygmunt Bauman, "Modernity and Ambivalence," in Featherstone, *Global Culture*, 143–70; and *Globalization: The Human Consequences* (Cambridge, UK, 1998).

18 Jean-François Lyotard, *The Postmodern Condition: A Report on Knowledge*, trans. Geoff Bennington and Brian Massumi (Minneapolis, 1984), 76.

19 Bhabha, *The Location of Culture*, 140.

20 See Featherstone, "Global Culture," 11.

21 Bhabha, *The Location of Culture*, 140.

22 Robertson, "Mapping the Global Condition," 20; Hall, "When Was 'the Post-colonial'?" 250.

23 Appadurai, *Modernity at Large*, 30.

24 Gayatri Chakravorty Spivak, "Reading *The Satanic Verses*," in *Outside in the Teaching Machine* (New York, 1993), 217.

25 Frantz Fanon, "The Pitfalls of National Consciousness," in *The Wretched of the Earth* (New York, 1968), 148–205

26 Fanon, "On National Culture," in *The Wretched of the Earth*, 208–11.

27 For this story, see Achille Mbembe, "The Banality of Power and the Aesthetics of Vulgarity," *Public Culture* 4.2 (1992):1–30.

28 Bauman, "Modernity and Ambivalence," 166–67. Bauman does make the important point that this opposition between existence and culture actually stabilizes modernity, giving it its "uncanny and unprecedented dynamism" (167).

29 Appadurai, *Modernity at Large*, 31.

30 Spivak, "Reading The Satanic Verses," 219.

31 Ibid., 221.

32 See, for example, David Harvey, *The Condition of Postmodernity: An Enquiry into the Origins of Cultural Change* (Oxford, 1989).

33 Appadurai, *Modernity at Large*, 30.

34 Bhabha, *The Location of Culture*, 253.

35 See Peter Osborne, *The Politics of Time: Modernity and Avant-Garde* (London, 1995).

36 Osborne, *The Politics of Time*, x. For other influential accounts of the relation between modernity and temporality, see Jürgen Habermas, *The Philosophical Discourse of Modernity: Twelve Lectures*, trans. Frederick G. Lawrence (Cambridge, MA, 1990), and Reinhart Koselleck, *Futures Past: On the Semantics of Historical Time*, trans. Keith Tribe (Cambridge, MA, 1985).

37 This question, of course, raises the more vexed problem of the identity of modernity itself—is it a Western or global idea? My position is closer to that of Osborne: "Modernity is a Western Idea. Whether it can any longer be thought of as an exclusively Western concept . . . is doubtful." See Osborne, *The Politics of Time*, 16.

38 Bhabha, *The Location of Culture*, 141.

39 For the relation between primitivism, irrationality, and timelessness, see Lucien Lévy-Bruhl's *Primitive Mentality*, trans. Lilian A. Clare (London, 1923).

40 Bhabha, *The Location of Culture*, 142.

41 Homi Bhabha, "Unpacking My Library . . . Again," in Chambers and Curti, *The Postcolonial Question*, 199–241; quotation is on 201.

42 Pieterse, "Hybrid Modernities," 77.

43 Robertson, "Mapping the Global Condition," 16, 17.

44 See Fredric Jameson, *Postmodernism, or The Cultural Logic of Late Capitalism* (Durham, 1991), 281.

45 Ibid., 282.

46 Mary Douglas, "Forgotten Knowledge," in *Shifting Contexts: Transformations in Anthropological Knowledge,* ed. Marilyn Strathern (London and New York, 1995), 13–29; quotation is on 13.

47 Ibid., 13.

48 Appadurai, *Modernity at Large,* 51.

49 Jean and John Comaroff, *Of Revelation and Revolution: Christianity, Colonialism, and Consciousness in South Africa* (Chicago, 1991), 14.

50 Gayatri Chakravorty Spivak, *A Critique of Postcolonial Reason: Toward a History of the Vanishing Present* (Cambridge, MA, 2000), 1.

51 See Wole Soyinka, *Myth, Literature, and the African World* (Cambridge, UK, 1976), vii.

52 The literature on the invention of English is now too numerous to cite here, but the following texts are central to this debate: Franklin E. Court, *Institutionalizing English Literature: The Culture and Politics of Literary Study* (Stanford, 1989); Chris Baldick, *The Social Mission of English Criticism* (Oxford, 1983); Anthony Easthorpe, *Englishness and National Culture* (London and New York, 1999); Brian Doyle, *English and Englishness* (London, 1989). I have discussed the role of the colonial periphery in the shaping of Englishness in *Maps of Englishness* (New York, 1996); for the study of the emergence of English literature in the colonial periphery, see Gauri Viswanathan, *Masks of Conquest* (New York, 1989); and in *The Scottish Invention of English Literature,* ed. Robert Crawford (Cambridge, 1998).

53 See "On the Abolition of the English Department," in Ngũgĩ wa Thiong'o, *Homecoming: Essays on African and Caribbean Literature, Culture and Politics* (Westport, CT, 1972), 145–50. I have discussed the context for this debate in *Ngũgĩ wa Thiong'o* (Cambridge, UK, 2000), but see also Carol Sicherman, "Ngũgĩ's Colonial Education: 'The Subversion . . . of the African Mind,'" *African Studies Review* 38 (December 1995): 35–46.

54 See Terry Eagleton, *Literary Theory: An Introduction* (Minneapolis, 1983).

55 The Leavises are some of the major actors in the histories of English literature cited above (note 34), but for more specific studies of their theory of literature and national legitimation see Francis Mulhern, "English Reading," in *Nation and Narration,* ed. Homi K. Bhabha (London and New York, 1990), 250–64; and Perry Anderson, *English Questions* (London, 1992).

56 See Anderson, *English Questions,* 98.

57 The fact that Leavis's students and disciples ran the major centers of literary studies in the British colonial world should be taken as axiomatic, but for specific histories of English studies at two major African universities, Makerere and Ibadan, see Sicherman, "Ngũgĩ's Colonial Education," and Robert M. Wren, *Those Magical Years: The Making of Nigerian Literature at Ibadan: 1948–1966* (Washington, DC, 1991).

58 See F. R. Leavis, *The Great Tradition* (New York, 1973), 1–27.

59 My evidence here is drawn from universities in Africa and the Caribbean, most of them set up in the 1940s, but the situation may have been different in the older universities in Africa (Fourah Bay College, for example) and India. See the testimony collected by Wren in *Those Magical Years.*

60 F. R. Leavis, *English Literature in Our Time and the University* (London, 1969), 3.

61 Bill Readings, *The University in Ruins* (Cambridge, MA, 1996), 69.

62 Appadurai discusses his Anglophone education in *Modernity at Large,* 2; Bhabha discusses his Elphinstone College education in "The Postcolonial Critic," an interview with David Bennett and Terry Collits, in *Literary India: Comparative Studies in Aesthetics, Colonialism, and Culture,* ed. Patrick Colm Hogan and Lalita Pandit (Albany, NY, 1995), 245.

63 Mpaka and Ngũgĩ are part of a group at Makerere University college who contributed to *Origin East Africa,* a pioneering anthology edited by David Cook (London, 1965); Tharu (Oomen) was in the original cast of Ngũgĩ's play, *The Black Hermit* (London, 1968), produced at the Uganda National Theater, Kampala, to commemorate the country's independence in 1962.

64 It is important here to reiterate the point that the study of English in the new universities established in the colonies after 1945 were dominated by Leavisites in "exile" from Oxbridge. More significantly, it is important to reflect on how key terms in Leavis's work were taken up by his left-wing interlocutors such as Raymond Williams and Simon Hoggart whose grammar, in turn, was to make its way into the postcolonial criticism of Stuart Hall. For the centrality of the idea of the organic community in Williams's work, see *The Country and the City* (New York, 1973). For the influence of Williams on "postcolonialism," see the essays collected in *Raymond Williams: Critical Perspectives,* ed. Terry Eagleton (Cambridge, UK, 1989).

65 Leavis, *English Literature in Our Time,* 43.

66 Ibid., 47.

67 Anderson, *English Questions,* 98.

68 Leavis, *English Literature in Our Time,* 48.

69 Ibid., 48.

Alternative Arrangements
for *Postcolonialisms*

The materials in this volume may be grouped in several different ways depending on the interests of the students and instructors. We provide below some suggestive groupings that may be of pedagogical interest.

AFRICA AND ITS DIASPORA

Leila Ahmed, "The Discourse of the Veil"

Jean Bernabé, Patrick Chamoiseau, and Raphaël Confiant, "In Praise of Creoleness"

Aimé Césaire, From *Discourse on Colonialism*

Timothy S. Chin, "'Bullers' and 'Battymen': Contesting Homophobia in Black Popular Culture and Contemporary Caribbean Literature"

Chinweizu, Onwuchekwa Jemie, and Ihechukwu Madubuike, "The African Novel and Its Critics (1950–1975)"

Carolyn Cooper, "Writing Oral History: Sistern Theatre Collective's *Lionheart Gal*"

Alexander Crummell, "The English Language in Liberia"

Frantz Fanon, "On National Culture"

Simon Gikandi, "Globalization and the Claims of Postcoloniality"

Paul Gilroy, "The Tyrannies of Unanimism"

Stuart Hall, "Thinking the Diaspora: Home-Thoughts from Abroad"

Frederick Lugard, "The Value of British Rule in the Tropics to British Democracy and the Native Races"

Oyèrónké Oyěwùmí, "Colonizing Bodies and Minds: Gender and Colonialism"

Léopold Sédar Senghor, "Negritude: A Humanism of the Twentieth Century"

Ngũgĩ wa Thiong'o, "The Language of African Literature"

Timothy S. Chin, "'Bullers' and 'Battymen'"

Chinweizu, Onwuchekwa Jemie, and Ihechukwu Madubuike, "The African Novel and Its Critics"

Carolyn Cooper, "Writing Oral History: Sistern Theatre Collective's *Lionheart Gal*"

Arif Dirlik, "The Postcolonial Aura: Third World Criticism in the Age of Global Capitalism"

Simon Gikandi, "Globalization and the Claims of Postcoloniality"

Linda Tuhiwai Smith, "Imperialism, History, Writing, and Theory"

Gayatri Chakravorty Spivak, "Three Women's Texts and a Critique of Imperialism"

Ngũgĩ wa Thiong'o, "The Language of African Literature"

COLONIAL EDUCATION

Homi Bhabha, "Of Mimicry and Man: The Ambivalence of Colonial Discourse"

Carolyn Cooper, "Writing Oral History: Sistern Theatre Collective's *Lionheart Gal*"

Alexander Crummell, "The English Language in Liberia"

Frantz Fanon, "On National Culture"

Thomas Babington Macaulay, "Minute on Indian Education, February 2, 1835"

Jana Sequoya, "How (!) Is an Indian?: A Contest of Stories"

Ngũgĩ wa Thiong'o, "The Language of African Literature"

COLONIAL SUBJECTIVITIES

Leila Ahmed, "The Discourse of the Veil"

Jean Bernabé, Patrick Chamoiseau, and Raphaël Confiant, "In Praise of Creoleness"

Homi Bhabha, "Of Mimicry and Man: The Ambivalence of Colonial Discourse"

Carolyn Cooper, "Writing Oral History: Sistern Theatre Collective's *Lionheart Gal*"

Alexander Crummell, "The English Language in Liberia"

Frantz Fanon, "On National Culture"

Paul Gilroy, "The Tyrannies of Unanimism"

David Lloyd, "Outside History: Irish New Histories and the 'Subalternity Effect'"

Roberto Fernández Retamar, "Caliban: Notes towards a Discussion of Culture in Our America"

Léopold Sédar Senghor, "Negritude: A Humanism of the Twentieth Century"

Octave Mannoni, "The Threat of Abandonment"

Oyèrónkẹ́ Oyěwùmí, Colonizing Bodies and Minds: Gender and Colonialism"

Léopold Sédar Senghor, "Negritude: A Humanism of the Twentieth Century"

Ngũgĩ wa Thiong'o, "The Language of African Literature"

RESISTANCE

John Beverley, "Our Rigoberta?: *I, Rigoberta Menchú,* Cultural Authority, and the Problem of Subaltern Agency"

Aimé Césaire, From *Discourse on Colonialism*

Chinweizu, Onwuchekwa Jemie, and Ihechukwu Madubuike, "The African Novel and Its Critics (1950–1975)"

Carolyn Cooper, "Writing Oral History: Sistern Theatre Collective's *Lionheart Gal*"

Frantz Fanon, "On National Culture"

Ranajit Guha, "On Some Aspects of the Historiography of Colonial India"

David Lloyd, "Outside History: Irish New Histories and the 'Subalternity Effect'"

Roberto Fernández Retamar, "Caliban: Notes towards a Discussion of Culture in Our America"

Léopold Sédar Senghor, "Negritude: A Humanism of the Twentieth Century"

Linda Tuhiwai Smith, "Imperialism, History, Writing, and Theory"

Ngũgĩ wa Thiong'o, "The Language of African Literature"

WOMEN

Leila Ahmed, "The Discourse of the Veil"

John Beverley, "Our Rigoberta?: *I, Rigoberta Menchú,* Cultural Authority, and the Problem of Subaltern Agency"

Rey Chow, "Against the Lures of Diaspora: Minority Discourse, Chinese Women, and Intellectual Hegemony"

Carolyn Cooper, "Writing Oral History: Sistern Theatre Collective's *Lionheart Gal*"

Amy Kaplan, "Manifest Domesticity"

Oyèrónkẹ́ Oyěwùmí, "Colonizing Bodies and Minds: Gender and Colonialism"

Gayatri Chakravorty Spivak, "Three Women's Texts and a Critique of Imperialism"

Listed here are the sources of all the texts included in the anthology. In the case of material not in the public domain, the editors gratefully acknowledge permission to reprint as indicated below.

I. IDEOLOGIES OF IMPERIALISM

1 Christopher Columbus, "The Letter of Christopher Columbus on the Discovery of America." Printed by Order of the Lenox Library, 1892, 1–13.

2 Edmund Burke, "Speech in the Impeachment of Warren Hastings." From *The Works of the Right Honourable Edmund Burke,* vol. 9, 348–366. London: Jon C. Nimmo Publishers, 1899.

3 Frederick Lugard, "The Value of British Rule in the Tropics to British Democracy and the Native Races." From *The Dual Mandate in British Tropical Africa,* 606–619. London: W. Blackwood and Sons, 1922.

II. THE CRITIQUE OF COLONIAL DISCOURSE

4 Valentin Y. Mudimbe, "*Romanus Pontifex* (1454) and the Expansion of Europe." From *The Idea of Africa,* 30–37. Bloomington: Indiana University Press, 1994. Reprinted with permission of Indiana University Press.

5 Aimé Césaire, excerpt from *Discourse on Colonialism,* 9–12, 20–25. Trans. Joan Pinkham. New York: Monthly Review Press, 1972. Reprinted with permission of the Monthly Review Foundation.

6 Roberto Fernández Retamar, excerpt from "Caliban: Notes towards a Discussion of Culture in Our America." *Massachusetts Review* 15 (1/2) (Winter/Spring 1974): 11–18. Reprinted with permission of *The Massachusetts Review.*

7 Edward W. Said, "Introduction" to *Orientalism,* 1–28. New York: Pantheon, 1978. Reprinted with permission of Pantheon Books, a division of Random House, Inc.

8 Linda Tuhiwai Smith, "Imperialism, History, Writing, and Theory." From *Decolonizing Methodologies: Research and Indigenous Peoples,* 19–41. London: Zed Press, 1999. Reprinted with permission of Zed Press.

III. THE POLITICS OF LANGUAGE AND LITERARY STUDIES

9 Thomas Babington Macaulay, "Minute on Indian Education, February 2, 1835." From *Selected Writings,* ed. John Clive and Thomas Pinney, 237–251. Chicago: University of Chicago Press, 1972.

10 Alexander Crummell, "The English Language in Liberia." From *The English Language in Liberia,* 6–15, 30–32. New York: Bunce and Co. Printers, 1861.

11 Ngũgĩ wa Thiong'o, "The Language of African Literature." From *Decolonising the Mind: The Politics of Language in African Literature,* 4–33. London: James Currey, 1986. Reprinted with permission of the author.

12 Carolyn Cooper, "Writing Oral History: Sistren Theatre Collective's *Lionheart Gal.*" From *Noises in the Blood: Orality, Gender, and the "Vulgar" Body of Jamaican Popular Culture,* 87–95. Durham: Duke University Press, 1995. All rights reserved. Reprinted with permission of Duke University Press.

IV. NATIONALISMS AND NATIVISMS

13 Léopold Sédar Senghor, "Negritude: A Humanism of the Twentieth Century." In *The Africa Reader: Independent Africa,* ed. Wilfred Cartey and Martin Kilson, 179–180, 184–192. New York: Random House, 1970.

14 Chinweizu, Onwuchekwa Jemie, and Ihechukwu Madubuike, "The African Novel and Its Critics (1950–1975)." Excerpt from *Toward the Decolonization of African Literature,* 7–16. Washington, DC: Howard University Press, 1983.

15 Frantz Fanon, "On National Culture." From *The Wretched of the Earth,* 206–225, 232–248. Trans. Constance Farrington. New York: Grove Press, 1963. Reprinted with permission of Grove/Atlantic, Inc. and by permission of HarperCollins Publishers.

16 Paul Gilroy, "The Tyrannies of Unanimism." From *Against Race: Imagining Political Culture beyond the Color Line,* 207–237. Cambridge, MA: Harvard University Press, 2000. Reprinted with permission of the author.

V. HYBRID IDENTITIES

17 Octave Mannoni, "The Threat of Abandonment." From *Prospero and Caliban: The Psychology of Colonization,* 73–77. Trans. Pamela Powesland. New York: Praeger, 1956.

18 Derek Walcott, "The Caribbean: Culture or Mimicry?" *Journal of Interamerican Studies and World Affairs* 16 (1) (February 1974): 3–13. Reprinted with permission of the University of Miami.

19 Homi Bhabha, "Of Mimicry and Man: The Ambivalence of Colonial Discourse." *October* 28 (1984): 125–133. Reprinted with permission of the author.

20 Jean Bernabé, Patrick Chamoiseau, and Raphaël Confiant, "In Praise of Creoleness." *Callaloo* 13 (1990): 886–894, 902–909. Trans. Mohamed B. Taleb Khyar. Copyright Charles H. Rowell. Reprinted with permission of The Johns Hopkins University Press.

21 Jana Sequoya, "How (!) Is an Indian?: A Contest of Stories." In *New Voices in Native American Literary Criticism,* ed. Arnold Krupat, 453–473. Washington, DC: Smithsonian Institution Press, 1993. Reprinted with permission of the Smithsonian Press.

VI. GENDER AND SEXUALITIES

22 Leila Ahmed, "The Discourse of the Veil." From *Women and Gender in Islam: Historical Roots of a Modern Debate,* 144–168. New Haven: Yale University Press, 1992. Reprinted with permission of Yale University Press.

23 Oyèrónké Oyěwùmí, "Colonizing Bodies and Minds: Gender and Colonialism." From *The Invention of Women: Making an African Sense of Western Gender Discourses,* 121–128, 142–156. Minneapolis: University of Minnesota Press, 1997. Reprinted with permission of the University of Minnesota Press.

24 Gayatri Chakravorty Spivak, "Three Women's Texts and a Critique of Imperialism." In *"Race," Writing, and Difference,* ed. Henry Louis Gates, Jr., 262–280. Chicago: University of Chicago Press, 1985. Reprinted with permission of the author.

25 Timothy S. Chin, " 'Bullers' and 'Battymen': Contesting Homophobia in Black Popular Culture and Contemporary Caribbean Literature." *Callaloo* 20 (1) (1997): 127–141. Copyright Charles H. Rowell. Reprinted with permission of The Johns Hopkins University Press.

VII. READING THE SUBALTERN

26 Ranajit Guha, "Preface" and "On Some Aspects of the Historiography of Colonial India." In *Subaltern Studies* 1, 1–8. Delhi: Oxford University Press, 1982. Reprinted with permission of Oxford University Press India, New Delhi.

27 David Lloyd, "Outside History: Irish New Histories and the 'Subalternity Effect.' " In *Subaltern Studies* 9, 261–280. Delhi: Oxford University Press, 1996. Reprinted with permission of Oxford University Press India, New Delhi.

28 John Beverley, "Our Rigoberta? *I, Rigoberta Menchú,* Cultural Authority, and the Problem of Subaltern Agency." From *Subalternity and Representation: Arguments in Cultural Theory,* 65–84. Durham, NC: Duke University Press, 1999. All rights reserved. Reprinted with permission of Duke University Press.

29 Nicholas Thomas, "The Primitivist and the Postcolonial." From *Colonialism's Culture: Anthropology, Travel, and Government,* 170–192. Princeton, NJ: Princeton University Press, 1994. Reprinted with permission of Princeton University Press.

VIII. COMPARATIVE (POST)COLONIALISMS

30 U.S. Congress, "Public Law 103-150." Calendar no. 185, 103rd Congress, 1st session, October 27, 1993.

31 Amy Kaplan, "Manifest Domesticity." In *No More Separate Spheres!,* ed. Cathy Davidson and Jessamyn Hatcher, 183–207. Durham, NC: Duke University Press, 2002. All rights reserved. Reprinted with permission of Duke University Press.

32 Pal Ahluwalia, "When Does a Settler Become a Native?: Citizenship and Identity in a Settler Society." *Pretexts: Literary and Cultural Studies* 10 (1) (2001): 63–73. Reprinted with permission from the Taylor and Francis Group.

33 David Chioni Moore, "Is the Post- in Postcolonial the Post- in Post-Soviet? Toward a Global Postcolonial Critique." *PMLA* 116 (1) (January 2001): 111–128. Reprinted with permission of the Modern Language Association of America.

IX. GLOBALIZATION AND POSTCOLONIALITY

34 Stuart Hall, "Thinking the Diaspora: Home-Thoughts from Abroad." *Small Axe* 6 (September 1999): 1–18. Reprinted with permission of Indiana University Press.

35 Arif Dirlik, "The Postcolonial Aura: Third World Criticism in the Age of Global Capitalism." *Critical Inquiry* 20 (Winter 1994): 328–356. Reprinted with permission of the University of Chicago Press.

36 Rey Chow, "Against the Lures of Diaspora: Minority Discourse, Chinese Women, and Intellectual Hegemony." In *Writing Diaspora: Tactics of Intervention in Contemporary Cultural*

Studies, 99–119. Bloomington: Indiana University Press, 1993. Reprinted with permission of Indiana University Press.

37 Simon Gikandi, "Globalization and the Claims of Postcoloniality." *South Atlantic Quarterly* 100:3 (Summer 2001): 627–658. All rights reserved. Reprinted with permission of Duke University Press.

Index